■ DISCLAIMERS

This report is the work of the authors. The views expressed in it do not necessarily reflect those of the Geneva Academy of International Humanitarian Law and Human Rights (the Geneva Academy) or Oxford University Press (OUP). The qualification of any situation of armed violence as an armed conflict under international law should not be read such as to trigger war clauses in insurance contracts and does not in any way affect the need for due diligence by any natural or legal person in their work in any of the situations referred to. Furthermore, facts, matters, or opinions contained in the report are provided by the Geneva Academy and OUP without assuming responsibility to any user of the report who may rely on its contents in whole or in part.

The designation of armed non-state actors, states, or territories does not imply any judgement by the Geneva Academy or OUP regarding the legal status of such actors, states, or territories, or their authorities and institutions, or the delimitation of their boundaries, or the status of any states or territories that border them.

The War Report 2012

The War Report 2012

Edited by

Stuart Casey-Maslen

Académie de droit international humanitaire
et de droits humains à Genève
Geneva Academy of International Humanitarian
Law and Human Rights | Geneva
Academy

The Academy, a joint centre of

THE GRADUATE INSTITUTE GENEVA

INSTITUT DE HAUTES
ÉTUDES INTERNATIONALES
ET DU DÉVELOPPEMENT
GRADUATE INSTITUTE
OF INTERNATIONAL AND
DEVELOPMENT STUDIES

UNIVERSITÉ
DE GENÈVE
FACULTÉ DE DROIT

OXFORD
UNIVERSITY PRESS

Great Clarendon Street, Oxford, OX2 6DP,
United Kingdom

Oxford University Press is a department of the University of Oxford.
It furthers the University's objective of excellence in research, scholarship,
and education by publishing worldwide. Oxford is a registered trade mark of
Oxford University Press in the UK and in certain other countries.

Published in the United States of America by Oxford University Press
198 Madison Avenue, New York, NY 10016, United States of America

British Library Cataloguing in Publication Data

Data available

Library of Congress Control Number: 2013949380

ISBN 978-0-19-968908-8

Printed and bound in Great Britain by
Clays Ltd, St Ives plc

▦ EDITOR'S PREFACE

'So long as there are men there will be wars.' So, famously, claimed Albert Einstein. Based on the prevalence of armed conflicts in 2012 it is hard to contest this assertion.[1] For there is scant evidence that humankind has grown tired of bloodshed in combat whether within or across national borders, despite aggressive war between nations having been 'abolished'—in theory at least—by the 1945 Charter of the United Nations (UN).

What is true, though, is that war *sensu stricto*—i.e. armed conflict between nation states—has become relatively uncommon in the modern era, despite the far greater number of such states that exist compared with a century ago. In addition, the significance of a declaration of war[2] has dimmed, and along with it the frequency with which such declarations occur, especially since the end of the 1939–45 War.[3] While rare, however, such formal declarations of war are still made on occasion. At the end of March 2013, for example, the Democratic People's Republic of Korea (DPRK) appeared formally to declare war on the Republic of Korea, its southern neighbour on the peninsula:

From this moment, the north–south relations will be put at the state of war and all the issues arousing between the north and the south will be dealt with according to the wartime regulations.

The state of neither peace nor war has ended on the Korean Peninsula.

Now that the revolutionary armed forces of the DPRK have entered into an actual military action, the inter-Korean relations have naturally entered the state of war. Accordingly, the DPRK will immediately punish any slightest provocation hurting its dignity and sovereignty with resolute and merciless physical actions without any prior notice.[4]

Reduced incidences of declarations of war can also be seen in the evolution over time in treaty texts governing *jus in bello* ('the law applicable in times of war'). Article 2 common

---

[1] Today, war has a broader figurative meaning in ordinary parlance of 'a sustained campaign against an undesirable situation or activity' in addition to its traditional sense of 'a state of armed conflict between different countries or different groups within a country': *Oxford English Dictionary online*, definition of 'war', <http://oxforddictionaries.com/definition/english/war?q=war>.

[2] A declaration of war is a formal declaration by a government that a state of war exists between that nation and another.

[3] More than 70 years have passed since December 1941 when, in the space of a week, the United States of America (USA) and the United Kingdom (UK) each declared war on Japan, and Japan in turn declared war on both the USA and the British Empire, while the USA declared war on Germany and Italy in response to those states' own declarations of belligerency.

[4] See e.g. Max Fisher, 'Here's North Korea's official declaration of "war"', *Washington Post*, posted on 30 March 2013, <http://www.washingtonpost.com/blogs/worldviews/wp/2013/03/30/heres-north-koreas-official-declaration-of-war/>.

to the 1949 Geneva Conventions, which delineates the scope of application of each of the four conventions,[5] provides that 'the present Convention shall apply to all cases of declared war or of any other armed conflict which may arise between two or more of the High Contracting Parties, even if the state of war is not recognized by one of them'. Geneva Convention IV was formally entitled the 'Geneva Convention relative to the Protection of Civilian Persons in Time of *War*'.[6] By 1977, however, the two Additional Protocols[7] to the four 1949 Geneva Conventions generally referred only to the broader and more generic term 'armed conflict'.[8]

Accordingly, this work identifies, describes, and discusses all situations of armed violence in 2012 that amounted to armed conflicts in accordance with the definitions recognized under international humanitarian law (IHL) and international criminal law (ICL).[9] The purpose of the *War Report* is to collect information and data in the public domain and provide legal analysis through a particular legal framework. It is assumed that the *War Report* will be of interest to a varied readership, including academics, charities operating in this field, and others.

The existence of an armed conflict is important because it has far-reaching implications. IHL governing the conduct of hostilities, which is markedly less restrictive in its prohibitions on the use of lethal force than is the international law of law enforcement,[10]

---

[5] The Geneva Convention for the Amelioration of the Condition of the Wounded and Sick in Armed Forces in the Field; the Geneva Convention for the Amelioration of the Condition of Wounded, Sick and Shipwrecked Members of Armed Forces at Sea; the Geneva Convention relative to the Treatment of Prisoners of War; and the Geneva Convention relative to the Protection of Civilian Persons in Time of War, all adopted on 12 August 1949.

[6] Emphasis added.

[7] Protocol Additional to the Geneva Conventions of 12 August 1949, and relating to the Protection of Victims of International Armed Conflicts, adopted in Geneva on 8 June 1977 (the 1977 Additional Protocol I); and Protocol Additional to the Geneva Conventions of 12 August 1949, and relating to the Protection of Victims of Non-International Armed Conflicts, similarly adopted in Geneva on 8 June 1977 (the 1977 Additional Protocol II).

[8] Although the term 'prisoner of war' persists and is unlikely to be replaced anytime soon by 'prisoner of armed conflict'.

[9] According to Antonio Cassese, ICL is 'a body of international rules designed both to proscribe certain categories of conduct (war crimes, crimes against humanity, genocide, torture, aggression, terrorism) and to make those persons who engage in such conduct criminally liable': Antonio Cassese, *International Criminal Law*, 2nd edn, Oxford University Press, Oxford, 2008, p. 3. Cryer states that the 'better view' is that individual acts of torture or terrorism that do not fall within the definitions of war crimes, crimes against humanity, genocide, and aggression are not directly criminalized by international law: Robert Cryer, 'International criminal law' in D. Moeckli, S. Shah, and S. Sivakumaran (eds), *International Human Rights Law*, Oxford University Press, Oxford, 2010, p. 541.

[10] The international law of law enforcement only allows the intentional use of lethal force where strictly unavoidable to protect life and where the threat to life is 'imminent'. This body of international law is composed of three main elements:

- IHRL, especially rights to life, liberty, and security, to peaceful protest (an umbrella right composed of a number of independent rights), and to freedom from torture and other forms of cruel, inhuman, or degrading treatment or punishment;

applies *only* in a situation of armed conflict. Notably, IHL does not prohibit the intentional use of lethal force against a member of the armed forces or a civilian 'participating directly in hostilities' (for the duration of such participation, *see the 'Summary rules' sections in Part I*). Moreover, war crimes may only be committed in connection with an armed conflict.

No supranational body, not even the UN Security Council, is authoritative in its determination or implication that a particular situation of armed violence constitutes an armed conflict; a situation threatening international peace and security is not a synonym for an armed conflict (although, unquestionably, the situations may coincide). Moreover, the existence of an armed conflict is an objective test and not a national 'decision'.[11] Consequently, whether a state affirms that a particular situation does, or does not, amount to an armed conflict is relevant information for the purposes of determining the applicable international law, but is certainly not conclusive.

Further, as explained in more detail later, however significant (and tragic) loss of life may be in any state or territory, the qualification of a situation of armed violence as an armed conflict is not simply a numbers game. Indeed, armed violence within a state may claim not only hundreds, but even thousands, of lives—and may constitute crimes against humanity[12] or even genocide[13]—without necessarily crossing the threshold into armed conflict; other factors are also pertinent, especially the extent of clashes between armies, or between armies and organized armed groups (or between themselves). Thus reports detailing 'wars' based on, for example, 25 or 1,000 battlefield deaths annually can be

---

- customary international law, derived from, inter alia, criminal justice standards, especially the 1979 Code of Conduct for Law Enforcement Officials, and the 1990 Basic Principles on the Use of Force and Firearms by Law Enforcement Officials; and
- general principles of law, which reflect core principles of national criminal law across democratic nations.

[11] Thus, Common Art. 2 to the 1949 Geneva Conventions, which includes the phrase 'all cases of declared war or of any other armed conflict which may arise between two or more of the High Contracting Parties, even if the state of war is not recognized by one of them', should be read as meaning even if *neither* state recognizes the armed conflict.

[12] Crimes against humanity are those crimes that 'shock the conscience of humanity'. Under the Statute of the International Criminal Court (ICC Statute), crimes against humanity occur where certain acts are undertaken as part of a widespread or systematic attack against a civilian population of which attack the perpetrator has knowledge. Such acts are murder, extermination, enslavement, forcible transfer of population, imprisonment, torture, rape, sexual slavery, enforced prostitution, forced pregnancy, enforced sterilization, sexual violence, persecution, enforced disappearance, *apartheid*, and other inhumane acts: Art. 7(1)(a)–(k), ICC Statute.

[13] Under Art. 2 of the 1948 Genocide Convention, genocide is any of the following acts committed with intent to destroy, in whole or in part, a national, ethnical, racial, or religious group, as such: (a) killing members of the group; (b) causing serious bodily or mental harm to members of the group; (c) deliberately inflicting on the group conditions of life calculated to bring about its physical destruction in whole or in part; (d) imposing measures intended to prevent births within the group; or (e) forcibly transferring children of the group to another group.

valuable for political science purposes, but such categorizations should not be taken to have significance under international law.[14]

In fact, two categories of armed conflict—and only two—exist under international humanitarian law: international armed conflict and armed conflict of a non-international character. Any armed conflict that is not international in character is, by definition, of a non-international character. Other typologies sometimes referred to in literature, such as 'transnational' or 'internationalized' armed conflicts, have no basis in international law and, I would argue, serve more to confuse than to clarify. It is, though, possible that the same national territory may be the subject of several armed conflicts ongoing in parallel; although such fragmentation of conflicts is not universally accepted, it nonetheless reflects far better the reality of armed violence and the contrasting nature of the parties that engage in it. A number of the situations discussed in Parts I and II are evidence of this assertion.

These days, the overwhelming majority of armed conflicts are of a non-international character. And while it is true that the treaty-based provisions of international humanitarian law governing international armed conflict are far more extensive than those governing armed conflicts of a non-international character, customary law has served to narrow the practical differences very substantially. As a consequence, the primary distinction in the regulation of the two categories of conflict is that recognition of the prisoner-of-war status of combatants is only required by applicable international law in an international armed conflict.

Part I of this work lists and summarizes the armed conflicts that occurred in 2012 on the basis of explicit criteria that, I believe, best reflect extant international law, certain controversies and imprecision notwithstanding. Determinations that are, or are likely to be, disputed are openly acknowledged. Casualties and displacement provoked by the armed conflicts are also detailed (and sourced), accompanied by requisite caveats as to the accuracy and representativeness of the figures provided.[15] Where alternative figures cannot reasonably be reconciled, both are given.

Part II details the situations of armed conflict around the world, drawing on the work of the Rule of Law in Armed Conflicts (RULAC) project conducted since 2009 under Geneva Academy auspices.[16] The situation profiles outline in each case the qualification of the conflict, its history, the applicable rules,[17] the main parties to the conflict, the

---

[14] See e.g. Anthony Cullen, 'The threshold of non-international armed conflict', *SSRN*, 2008, p. 131, <http://papers.ssrn.com/sol3/papers.cfm?abstract_id=2222757>.

[15] The casualty data research and analysis was conducted by two international experts, Megan Burke and Loren Persi Vicentic.

[16] <http://www.geneva-academy.ch/RULAC/>. Marina Mattirolo conducted significant additional research for the armed conflict profiles.

[17] Adherence by states to selected IHL and human rights treaties is included in each profile. This is not to deny or exclude the application of other treaties.

principal means and methods of warfare they used in 2012, resulting casualties and displacement, and any war crimes investigations, prosecutions, and convictions that either took place during the year or which pertained to acts committed during 2012.

Part III comprises five sections containing a total of 13 chapters, each of which addresses a thematic issue with particular relevance to 2012. The five sections cover the following issues:

- means of warfare;
- methods of warfare;
- detention;
- armed non-state actors and international norms; and
- judicial enforcement of international criminal and humanitarian law.

Maya Brehm opens Part III of this year's *War Report* with consideration of the use of explosive weapons in populated areas in 2012 in, particularly, Afghanistan, Iraq, and Syria, and calls for enhanced normative protection against the humanitarian consequences of such use. This is followed in Chapter 2 by my assessment of the legality under international law of unmanned aerial vehicle (drone) strikes—arguably the future of warfare—in Pakistan in 2012. In Chapter 3, Mireille Widmer discusses the UN Programme of Action on Small Arms and Light Weapons, and the case of Libya/Mali. She calls for measures to improve the implementation of the existing normative framework, but also suggests that new hard law may be needed.

In Chapter 4, Kate Halff's description and analysis of the displacement of civilians globally by armed conflicts and armed violence in 2012, as one might expect, Syria heads the list with more than 15 per cent of the total population already displaced internally or into neighbouring countries. In Chapter 5, Alice Priddy recounts the horrendous toll of sexual violence in conflicts over the course of the year, looking at, among others, the situation in the east of the Democratic Republic of Congo (DRC), as well as that in Syria. She demonstrates how rape as a method of warfare is more than just a slogan; it remains a reality of many conflicts. In Chapter 6, the claim by the North Atlantic Treaty Organization (NATO)'s International Security Assistance Force in Afghanistan that it would 'defeat the Taliban through education' is the backdrop to a broader assessment by Gilles Giacca and Takhmina Karimova of education as a 'battleground' in armed conflicts. In Chapter 7, Nicole Urban relates how, despite prevailing norms, journalists were targeted in conflicts in 2012 as never before.

In Chapter 8, Silvia Suteu scrutinizes the continued maintenance of Guantánamo Bay detention camp within Guantánamo Bay Naval Base, Cuba, as a detainment and interrogation facility of the US military (despite a pledge by US President Obama in

January 2009 to close it within a year).[18] The facility was established in January 2002 by the Bush administration to hold detainees who it had determined were enemies in the so-called 'Global War on Terror'. As of November 2012, more than ten years after its establishment, there were 166 detainees in the facility, according to a US government report.[19] In mid-April 2013, pitched battles took place between inmates and guards, and, as of writing, several detainees had already been on hunger strike for many weeks.[20]

In Chapter 9, Marina Mattirolo reviews the applicability of international norms to armed non-state actors in armed conflicts in 2012, with particular reference to the DRC, Libya, Mali, and Syria. There is now general understanding and acceptance that *jus in bello* includes not only IHL, but also international human rights law (IHRL). The direct application of IHRL to armed non-state actors remains controversial, though is increasingly accepted amid the ongoing debates on the issue.

In Chapter 10, Sharon Weill and Irit Ballas describe Israeli jurisprudence on addressing allegations of torture and the significant obstacles to accountability that the judicial system has generally endorsed. In Chapter 11, Manuel Ventura assesses the implications of South African case law on ICL regarding alleged crimes against humanity committed in Madagascar and Zimbabwe. Although not related to a situation of armed conflict, the resulting jurisprudence may have important consequences for international crimes potentially falling under the jurisdiction of the International Criminal Court (ICC). In Chapter 12, Damien Scalia reviews relevant jurisprudence in the two ad hoc international criminal tribunals in 2012, with particular consideration of the highly contested decision of the Appeals Chamber of the International Criminal Tribunal for the former Yugoslavia (ICTY) in the *Gotovina* case. Finally, in Chapter 13, Manuel Ventura assesses two controversies under international law from the ICC's first ever judgment, in 2012, in the *Lubanga* case.

---

[18] See e.g. Mark Mazzetti and William Glaberson, 'Obama issues directive to shut down Guantánamo', *New York Times*, 21 January 2009, <http://www.nytimes.com/2009/01/22/us/politics/22gitmo.html?ref=guantanamobaynavalbasecuba&_r=0>.

[19] US Government Audit Office (GAO), 'Guantánamo Bay detainees, facilities and factors for consideration if detainees were brought to the United States', *GAO Highlights*, Washington, DC, November 2012, p. 1.

[20] See e.g. Greg Botelho and Barbara Starr, 'Detainees, U.S. guards clash at Guantánamo Bay', *CNN online*, 15 April 2013, <http://edition.cnn.com/2013/04/13/world/americas/guantanamo-inmate-guard-clashes>.

CONTENTS

LIST OF ABBREVIATIONS

ACHPR	African Charter on Human and Peoples' Rights
ACommHPR	African Commission on Human and Peoples' Rights
ACHR	American Convention on Human Rights
ANSA	armed non-state actor
AOAV	Action on Armed Violence
APMBC	Anti-Personnel Mine Ban Convention
AQIM	al-Qaeda in the Islamic Maghreb
BBIED	body-borne improvised explosive device
CAR	Central African Republic
CAT	Convention against Torture and Other Forms of Cruel, Inhuman or Degrading Treatment or Punishment
CCW	Convention on Certain Conventional Weapons
CEDAW	Convention/Committee on the Elimination of All Forms of Discrimination against Women
CESR	Committee on Economic, Social, and Cultural Rights
CIA	Central Intelligence Agency
CCM	Convention on Cluster Munitions
CPA	Comprehensive Peace Agreement
CPJ	Committee to Protect Journalists
CRC	Convention/Committee on the Rights of the Child
DPRK	Democratic People's Republic of Korea
DRC	Democratic Republic of Congo
ECHR	European Convention on Human Rights
ECJ	European Court of Justice
ECOWAS	Economic Community of West African States
ECtHR	European Court of Human Rights
ERW	explosive remnants of war
ESC rights	economic, social, and cultural rights
EU	European Union
FARDC	Forces Armées de la République Démocratique du Congo
FATA	Federally Administered Tribal Areas

FCO	Foreign and Commonwealth Office
FSA	Free Syrian Army
FYROM	former Yugoslav Republic of Macedonia
GAO	US Government Audit Office
GBV	gender-based violence
GCPEA	Global Coalition to Protect Education from Attack
GSS	General Security Services (Israel)
HCJ	High Court of Justice (Israel)
HRW	Human Rights Watch
IAC	international armed conflict
IACPPT	Inter-American Convention to Prevent and Punish Torture and Inhuman or Degrading Treatment
IACHR	Inter-American Convention on Human Rights
IACommHR	Inter-American Commission on Human Rights
IACtHR	Inter-American Court of Human Rights
ICC	International Criminal Court
ICC Statute	Rome Statute of the International Criminal Court
ICCPR	International Covenant on Civil and Political Rights
ICG	International Crisis Group
ICJ	International Court of Justice
ICL	international criminal law
ICRC	International Committee of the Red Cross
ICTs	International Criminal Tribunals
ICTR	International Criminal Tribunal for Rwanda
ICTY	International Criminal Tribunal for the former Yugoslavia
IDMC	Internal Displacement Monitoring Centre
IDP	internally displaced person
IED	improvised explosive device
IFJ	International Federation of Journalists
IHL	international humanitarian law
IHRL	international human rights law
INSI	International News Safety Institute
IPI	International Press Institute
ISA	Israel Security Agency
ISAF	International Security Assistance Force

JCE	joint criminal enterprise
MANPADS	man-portable air defence systems
MOJWA	Movement for Oneness and Jihad in West Africa
MNLA	Mouvement national pour la libération de l'Azawad
MRM	Monitoring and Reporting Mechanism
MSF	Médecins sans Frontières (Doctors without Borders)
NATO	North Atlantic Treaty Organization
NIAC	non-international armed conflict
NPA	National Prosecuting Authority of South Africa
NSAG	non-state armed group
OCHA	UN Office for the Coordination of Humanitarian Affairs
OHCHR	Office of the UN High Commissioner for Human Rights
OPT	Occupied Palestinian Territories
OSCE	Organization for Security and Co-operation in Europe
OTP	Office of the Prosecutor
PEC	Press Emblem Campaign
PNC	Police Nationale Congolaise
POW	prisoner of war
PTSD	post-traumatic stress disorder
RSF	Reporters sans Frontières (Reporters without Borders)
RULAC	rule of law in armed conflicts
SALC	Southern Africa Litigation Centre
SCSL	Special Court for Sierra Leone
SRSG-CIAC	Special Representative of the UN Secretary-General on Children and Armed Conflict
UAE	United Arab Emirates
UAV	unmanned aerial vehicle (or drone)
UK	United Kingdom
UN	United Nations
UNAMA	UN Assistance Mission in Afghanistan
UNESCO	UN Educational, Scientific and Cultural Organization
UNHCR	Office of the UN High Commissioner for Refugees
UNHRC	UN Human Rights Council
UNMAS	UN Mine Action Service

UNODC	UN Office on Drugs and Crime
UNRWA	UN Relief and Works Agency
UNSMIL	UN Support Mission in Libya
USA	United States of America
WHO	World Health Organization

TABLE OF CASES

European Court of Human Rights (ECtHR)

Inter-American Court of Human Rights (IACtHR)

International Court of Justice (ICJ)

CONTENTIOUS CASES

ADVISORY OPINIONS

International Criminal Court (ICC)

International Criminal Tribunal for the former Yugoslavia (ICTY)

International Criminal Tribunal for Rwanda (ICTR)

Permanent Court of Arbitration (PCA)

National courts

TABLE OF TREATIES

Peace agreements and negotiations

Soft law instruments

▓ UNITED NATIONS RESOLUTIONS

Part I

Armed Conflicts in 2012 and their Impacts

Armed conflicts in 2012 and their impacts

Summary

In 2012, at least 37 armed conflicts occurred on the territory of 24 states and territories in: Afghanistan; Azerbaijan; the Central African Republic; Colombia; Cyprus; the Democratic Republic of Congo (DRC); Eritrea; Ethiopia; Georgia; Lebanon; Mali; Mexico; Moldova; Myanmar; Palestine/Gaza; the Philippines; Somalia; South Sudan; Sudan; Syria; Thailand; Turkey; Western Sahara; and Yemen.[1] Of the 38 conflicts, only one was an active international armed conflict (IAC), narrowly defined: that between South Sudan and Sudan.[2] In addition, however, belligerent occupations continued of parts of nine states and territories (Azerbaijan, Cyprus, Eritrea, Georgia, Lebanon,

---

[1] In addition to this list, the following states were also concerned by these armed conflicts in 2012: Albania; Armenia; Australia; Austria; Azerbaijan; Bahrain; Belgium; Bosnia and Herzegovina; Bulgaria; Canada; Croatia; Czech Republic; Denmark; El Salvador; Estonia; Finland; France; the former Yugoslav Republic of Macedonia; Georgia; Germany; Greece; Hungary; Iceland; Ireland; Israel; Italy; Jordan; Republic of Korea; Latvia; Lithuania; Luxembourg; Malaysia; Mongolia; Montenegro; the Netherlands; New Zealand; Norway; Poland; Portugal; Romania; the Russian Federation; Singapore; Slovakia; Slovenia; Spain; Sweden; Tonga; Turkey; Ukraine; United Arab Emirates; the United Kingdom (UK); and the United States of America (USA). Of this list; all states apart from Israel and the Russian Federation were engaged in an armed conflict with the Quetta Shura Taliban in Afghanistan by virtue of their contribution of troops to the North Atlantic Treaty Organization (NATO) International Security Assistance Force (ISAF).

[2] Arguably (but controversially), a second occurred between Pakistan and the USA by virtue of the unmanned aerial vehicle (UAV, or drone) strikes by the USA on Pakistani territory. These strikes were conducted in violation of Pakistan's sovereignty according to the Pakistani government and Pakistan's parliament; and could therefore be considered as acts falling within the scope of an IAC between the two states. This is notwithstanding any complicity in drone strikes that may exist within elements of the Pakistani state, such as its intelligence services. On 5 June 2012, for instance, US Chargé d'affaires Richard Hoagland was summoned to the Pakistani Ministry of Foreign Affairs, which conveyed the government's serious concern about drone strikes in the tribal regions. According to a statement released by the Ministry: 'He was informed that the drone strikes were unlawful, against international law and a violation of Pakistan's sovereignty. Parliament had emphatically stated that they were unacceptable. Drone strikes represented a clear red-line for Pakistan.' See e.g. 'Drone campaign: Pakistan summons US envoy, lodges protest', *Tribune*, 6 June 2012, <http://tribune.com.pk/story/389354/drone-campaign-pakistan-summons-us-envoy-lodges-protest/>. The fact that neither state publicly acknowledges that such an IAC exists is not determinative. See further Ch. 2 of Part III.

Moldova, Palestine, Syria, and Western Sahara). These occupations are governed by the law of military occupation that also forms part of the law of IAC.[3]

Non-international armed conflicts (NIACs) took place in 15 states and territories: Afghanistan, Central African Republic, Colombia, the DRC, Mali, Mexico, Myanmar, the Philippines, Somalia, Sudan, Syria, Thailand, Turkey, and Yemen, as well as Gaza.

The criteria used to make these determinations are detailed below, and where these criteria and/or the resulting determinations are likely to be disputed, this is openly acknowledged.[4] Based on research and analysis of available sources (all of which are clearly cited and some of which are seemingly contradictory), at least 95,000 men, women, and children were killed or injured by acts committed in these conflicts. This is an extremely conservative figure, and is certainly much lower than the true figure.

Added to such shocking statistics, during 2012 some 6.5 million people were newly displaced, whether by armed conflicts or by armed violence, almost twice the figure for the previous year. Worldwide, at the end of 2012 the total number of people internally displaced by 'armed conflict, generalized violence, and human rights violations' was estimated to be 28.8 million, an increase of 2.4 million on the same period in 2011 and the highest figure ever recorded by the Internal Displacement Monitoring Centre (IDMC).[5]

Of course, figures only tell part of any tale, and the risk of depersonalization through statistics is one against which we must remain vigilant. Every death, every injury, every act of torture, every person who goes missing amid conflict is not only an individual tragedy, but also a familial heartbreak and a social blight. The physical, psychological, economic, and societal scars of armed conflict do not easily heal, and too often the method of ending one armed conflict or action in its immediate aftermath sows the seeds of future warfare. As Ambrose Bierce, the nineteenth-century US journalist, wrote: 'Peace, in international affairs, is a period of cheating between two periods of fighting.'

But we must not succumb to pessimism, or worse, to cynicism. There is, in fact, nothing inevitable about the brutal excesses of armed conflict; it is only our collective decisions and actions—as well as our inaction—that make it so. Hence, in documenting armed conflicts and their impacts in 2012, we do not resign ourselves to the 'inevitable', but call rather for concrete and specific action to help facilitate the avoidable.

---

[3] The Elements of Crimes established under the International Criminal Court (ICC) provide that 'the term "international armed conflict" includes military occupation': ICC, 'Elements of crimes', UN doc. PCNICC/2000/1/Add.2 (2000), n. 34. See e.g. Anthony Cullen, 'The threshold of non-international armed conflict', *SSRN*, 2008, p. 132, <http://papers.ssrn.com/sol3/papers.cfm?abstract_id=2222757>.

[4] Controversially, the list of NIACs does not include situations of armed violence in India, Iraq, Niger, or Nigeria, all of which suffered significant casualties in 2012. The reason is the lack of direct combat between army and armed groups, or between armed groups, that we argue is integral to an NIAC, distinguishing it from state oppression and/or terrorist attacks by armed groups.

[5] See further Ch. 4 in Part III. The IDMC has reported annually on displacement since 2001. See <http://www.internal-displacement.org/>.

International law has a critical role to play in this regard. In 1952, Sir Hersch Lauterpacht affirmed in the *British Yearbook of International Law* that 'if international law is the vanishing point of law, the law of war is at the vanishing point of international law'. But as Michael Schmitt has noted:

With respect, history has proven Lauterpacht wrong. Extensive codification has occurred during the six decades since he offered his critique…Albeit somewhat hesitantly, a standing International Criminal Court is now prosecuting war criminals, and both the US and Israeli Supreme Courts have relied upon the law of war to rebuff controversial policies pursued by their governments…It is not hyperbole to say that the law of war is experiencing a 21st century renaissance. Indeed, today even the appellation 'law of war' is out of fashion, replaced by the gentler designation, 'international humanitarian law.'…[T]he law of war is designed to balance military necessity against humanitarian considerations, a notion first articulated in the St. Petersburg Declaration nearly a century and a half ago. In 21st century conflict, at least that experienced thus far, we may be witnessing an emergent, and promising, confluence of the two—where humanitarian considerations can enhance military operations, rather than limit them.[6]

What is an armed conflict?

As noted in the Preface, in accordance with international humanitarian law (IHL) and international criminal law (ICL) there are two categories of armed conflict: IACs and NIACs.[7] A valuable and widely cited general definition of the two categories was advanced by the Appeals Chamber of the International Criminal Tribunal for the former Yugoslavia (ICTY) in a 1995 decision in the *Tadić* case:

[A]n armed conflict exists whenever there is a resort to armed force between States or protracted armed violence between governmental authorities and organized armed groups or between such groups within a State.[8]

---

[6] Michael N. Schmitt, 'The vanishing law of war', *Harvard International Review*, 6 July 2009, <http://hir.harvard.edu/frontiers-of-conflict/the-vanishing-law-of-war>.

[7] See Arts 2 and 3 common to the four 1949 Geneva Conventions.

[8] ICTY, *Prosecutor v. Dusko Tadić (aka 'DULE')*, Decision on the Defence Motion for Interlocutory Appeal on Jurisdiction (Appeals Chamber) (Case No. IT-94-1), 2 October 1995, §70, <http://www.icty.org/x/cases/tadic/acdec/en/51002.htm>. See generally also International Committee of the Red Cross (ICRC), 'How is the term "armed conflict" defined in international humanitarian law?', ICRC Opinion Paper, March 2008, <http://www.icrc.org/eng/assets/files/other/opinion-paper-armed-conflict.pdf>; Sylvain Vité, 'Typology of armed conflicts in international humanitarian law: legal concepts and actual situations', *International Review of the Red Cross*, 91(873) (March 2009), pp. 69–94, <http://www.icrc.org/eng/assets/files/other/irrc-873-vite.pdf>.

Thus, in the view of the ICTY, an IAC exists whenever there is a resort to armed force between states, while an NIAC exists when there is protracted armed violence between governmental authorities and organized armed groups, or between such groups within a state. This needs a little unpicking as clearly the level of violence needed to trigger an IAC differs from—i.e. is significantly lower than—that which is necessary to constitute an NIAC. This issue is discussed below.

Furthermore, and even though this understanding is not universally accepted, it is not a case of 'either–or' in any given situation. Thus everal different armed conflicts, comprising one or both categories, may be ongoing at the same time and in parallel in any one state. Such fragmentation is evidenced in a number of recent armed conflicts. For example, in 2011, an IAC pitted a number of NATO member states against the state of Libya under the Gaddafi regime alongside a separate NIAC between that regime and an organized armed opposition. In 2012, there were, for example, at least two distinct NIACs in Syria, pitting Syrian armed forces (and supporting Shabbiha militia) against the Free Syrian Army and, separately, against Jabhat al-Nusra. In addition, as Israel continues, without Syrian consent, to occupy the Golan Heights, recognized as part of Syrian territory,[9] this amounts to a military occupation governed by the rules applicable to an IAC (*see section 'Criteria for the existence of an international armed conflict'*).

In any event, however, the existence of an armed conflict of either category is generally limited to the areas where the parties to the conflict are conducting hostilities against each other.[10]

CRITERIA FOR THE EXISTENCE OF AN INTERNATIONAL ARMED CONFLICT

The formulation of the ICTY with respect to the definition of an IAC is arguably too narrow in its insistence that the armed force be 'between' two or more states. It is

---

[9] Israel seized the Golan Heights from Syria in the closing stages of the 1967 'Six-Day War'. Most of the Syrian Arab inhabitants fled the area during the conflict. An armistice line was established and the region came under Israeli military control. Syria tried to retake the Golan Heights during the 1973 Middle East War. Despite inflicting heavy losses on Israeli forces, the surprise assault was thwarted. Both states signed an armistice in 1974 and a UN observer force has been in place on the cease-fire line ever since. See 'Golan Heights profile', *BBC*, 30 August 2011, <http://www.bbc.co.uk/news/world-middle-east-14724842>.

[10] There may, however, be war crimes committed by members of parties to the conflict in other areas that are controlled by a party. Consonant with the view of the ICTY, when an armed conflict is in progress, IHL generally applies throughout the territory of the state or states concerned. A number of rules apply throughout the territory of a state engaged in an armed conflict. (See e.g. 1949 Geneva Convention IV, Arts 35–46. See also Robert Kolb and Richard Hyde, *An Introduction to the International Law of Armed Conflicts*, Hart, Oxford, 2008, pp. 94–6.)

undoubtedly true that, as Dietrich Schindler observed: '...the existence of an armed conflict within the meaning of Article 2 common to the Geneva Conventions can always be assumed when parts of the armed forces of two States clash with each other...Any kind of use of arms between two States brings the Conventions into effect.'[11] But, consistent with *jus ad bellum* (the law governing the inter-state use of force), an IAC also exists whenever one state uses any form of armed force *against* another state, irrespective of whether the latter state fights back.[12] This includes the situation in which one state invades another and occupies it, even if there is no armed resistance.[13] Of course, where one state uses armed force on the territory of another state with the latter state's consent, the two states are not engaged in an IAC. This is the case with respect to NATO's military involvement in Afghanistan, for instance.

There may also be an IAC when one state supports an armed non-state actor (ANSA) operating in another state when that support is so significant that the foreign state is deemed to have 'overall control' over the actions of the ANSA.[14] More controversially, an IAC may also exist where there is an armed conflict 'in which peoples are fighting against colonial domination and alien occupation and against racist regimes in the exercise of their right of self-determination'.[15] The threshold for such a conflict is not settled, but is probably the same as for an IAC—that is to say, much lower than it is for an NIAC.

---

[11] Dietrich Schindler, 'The different types of armed conflicts according to the Geneva Conventions and Protocols', *Recueil des cours, Hague Academy of International law (RCADI)*, 163 (1979), p. 131.

[12] Thus, as Hans-Peter Gasser explains, 'any use of armed force by one State against the territory of another, triggers the applicability of the Geneva Conventions between the two States...It is also of no concern whether or not the party attacked resists': Hans-Peter Gasser, 'International humanitarian law: an introduction' in H. Haug (ed.), *Humanity for All: The International Red Cross and Red Crescent Movement*, Paul Haupt, Bern, 1993, pp. 510–11. In contrast, however, as suggested by the International Court of Justice (ICJ) in the *Nicaragua* case, small-scale 'frontier incidents' (e.g. where one soldier fires across an international border) arguably do not constitute an IAC: ICJ, *Case Concerning Military and Paramilitary Activities in and against Nicaragua (Nicaragua v. United States of America)*, Judgment (Merits), 27 June 1986, §195), <http://www.icj-cij.org/docket/files/70/6503.pdf>. See also Christine Gray, *International Law and the Use of Force*, 3rd edn, Oxford University Press, Oxford, 2008, pp. 177–83.

[13] 'The Convention shall also apply to all cases of partial or total occupation of the territory of a High Contracting Party, even if the said occupation meets with no armed resistance': Art. 2 common to the four 1949 Geneva Conventions.

[14] See e.g. ICTY, *Prosecutor v. Tadić*, Judgment (Appeals Chamber) (Case No. IT-94-1-A), 15 July 1999, §§84 and 115 *et seq.*; ICTY, *Prosecutor v. Blaskić*, Judgment (Trial Chamber) (Case No. IT-95-14-T), 3 March 2000, §§149–50. See similarly the views of the Trial Chamber of the ICC in its judgment in the 2012 *Lubanga* case: ICC, *Prosecutor v. Thomas Lubanga Dyilo*, Judgment (Trial Chamber) (Case No. ICC-01/04-01/06), 14 March 2012, §541. The Trial Chamber expressly approved the *Tadić* dicta on this issue.

[15] See Art. 1(4), 1977 Additional Protocol I. The USA and a number of other states opposed this provision vociferously when it was adopted. It has never been applied in practice.

SUMMARY RULES APPLICABLE IN AN INTERNATIONAL ARMED CONFLICT

The basic principles and rules of IHL applicable to the conduct of hostilities in an IAC are set out in the 1907 Hague Regulations and the 1949 Geneva Conventions and their 1977 Additional Protocols, and represent customary law applicable to all. The basis of IHL is the rule of distinction. This rule obliges 'parties to a conflict' (in other words, the warring parties, e.g. South Sudan and Sudan in 2012) to target only military objectives and not the civilian population, or individual civilians or civilian objects (e.g. homes, hospitals, and schools).[16] Deliberately targeting civilians is a serious violation of IHL, as too is failing to distinguish in military operations between civilians and combatants, and both are war crimes under customary international law.[17]

Although it is understood that it is not always possible to avoid civilian casualties in the conduct of hostilities, international law also requires that parties to a conflict take all feasible precautions in any attack to minimize civilian deaths and injuries. In addition, according to the rule of proportionality, attacks that may be expected to cause deaths or injuries among the civilian population, or damage to civilian objects, which would be 'excessive' compared to the expected 'concrete and direct' military advantage must be cancelled. In providing assistance to the civilian population, women and children are to be granted preferential treatment.

Children must not be recruited into armed forces or armed groups, or allowed to take part in hostilities. Recruiting children under 15 years of age is a war crime. The use of inherently indiscriminate weapons, or weapons 'of a nature to cause superfluous injury or unnecessary suffering', is prohibited. In addition, among many other provisions, parties to an international conflict must respect and protect combatants who are *hors de combat*, because of sickness, wounds, detention, or any other cause. Captured combatants (primarily, members of armed forces) are to be accorded the status of prisoner of war, with the associated rights and obligations.[18]

During a belligerent occupation of foreign territory, the applicable law is set out in the 1907 Hague Regulations (Articles 42–56), the 1949 Geneva Convention IV, the 1977 Additional Protocol I, and customary international law. The underpinning of the law of military occupation is that it is a temporary situation, which lasts until a political agreement is reached. During this period, the occupant does not enjoy sovereign rights over the territories it occupies and local law that was applicable prior to the occupation remains in force. At the same time, the occupying power is responsible for administering the local

---

[16] Civilian objects are any buildings or areas that are not lawful military objectives.

[17] Civilians only lose their 'general protection' against hostilities if, and for such time as, they participate directly in hostilities.

[18] These are set out, in particular, in 1949 Geneva Convention III.

life of the population under its control, maintaining it as it was prior to the occupation as closely as possible, and for providing security (Article 43 of the Hague Regulations). In addition, international human rights law (IHRL) is binding on the occupying state extraterritorially with regard to the territories it occupies.[19]

CRITERIA FOR THE EXISTENCE OF A NON-INTERNATIONAL ARMED CONFLICT

In accordance with the definition in the *Tadić* case, an NIAC is a situation of regular and intense armed violence[20] between the security forces of a state, especially the army, and one or more organized non-governmental armed groups. An NIAC will also occur in a situation of intense armed violence between two or more organized armed groups within a state. Situations of 'internal disturbances and tensions', including 'riots, isolated and sporadic acts of violence', and other acts of a similar nature, are explicitly said *not* to amount to armed conflicts.[21] An NIAC will also occur where there is intense armed violence between two or more organized armed groups across an international border.

There are thus three cumulative requirements for an NIAC, according to the *Tadić* definition: first, there must be 'protracted armed violence'; secondly, violence must be conducted by government forces and at least one *organized* non-governmental armed group (or between such groups within a state or across a state's borders); and, thirdly, the violence must be take place *between* the armed forces and at least one organized armed group, or between such groups. These elements are now discussed in turn.

The requirement of 'protracted armed violence' means that a certain threshold of armed violence has been reached.[22] According to the ICTY:

[19] Derogations from certain human rights in accordance with the 1966 International Covenant on Civil and Political Rights may only occur in 'time of public emergency which threatens the life of the nation and the existence of which is officially proclaimed'. Any derogation must be only 'to the extent strictly required by the exigencies of the situation, provided that such measures are not inconsistent with their other obligations under international law and do not involve discrimination solely on the ground of race, colour, sex, language, religion or social origin'.

[20] In the trial judgment in *Tadić* and other cases, the ICTY confirmed that the specific meaning it gave to 'protracted' when qualifying armed violence was an insistence on the intensity of conflict (even though the word's meaning in ordinary parlance is one of long duration, not high intensity): ICTY, *Prosecutor v. Dusko Tadić*, Opinion and Judgment, 7 May 1997, §562; see also ICTY, *Prosecutor v. Ramush Haradinaj, Idriz Balaj, and Lahi Brahimaj*, Judgment (Trial Chamber) (Case No. IT-04-84-T), 3 April 2008, §§40 *et seq.*; ICTY, *Prosecutor v. Slobodan Milosevic*, Decision on Motion for Judgment of Acquittal (Case No. IT-02-54-T), 16 June 2004, §17.

[21] Art. 1(2), 1977 Additional Protocol II.

[22] As the ICRC has noted, 'the violence must reach a certain level of intensity': ICRC, 'International humanitarian law and the challenges of contemporary armed conflicts', Report for the 31st International

In an armed conflict of an internal or mixed character, these closely related criteria are used solely for the purpose, as a minimum, of distinguishing an armed conflict from banditry, unorganized and short-lived insurrections, or terrorist activities, which are not subject to international humanitarian law.[23]

Organized armed groups are those that have a command-and-control structure, typically possess and use a variety of weapons, and control a significant logistical capacity that gives them the capability to conduct regular military operations. When engaged in regular and intense armed confrontations with armed forces or other organized armed groups, such groups are 'party' to an NIAC. These groups are sometimes called rebels, insurgents, terrorists, criminal gangs, or anti-government elements by states; such designations have no consequence for the determination of their status under international law with respect to an armed conflict. It is, however, not necessary that an armed group have a particular political or religious agenda for it to be party to an NIAC; arguably, therefore, an organized armed group whose aim is purely lucrative, such as a drug gang or an organized crime network, can be a party to an armed conflict.

The third criterion is potentially the most controversial. Inherent in the notion of the words 'conflict' and 'between' is, I would argue, the requirement that there be actual combat. In its judgment in the *Haradinaj* case, the ICTY stated that indicative factors for an armed conflict include 'the number, duration and intensity of individual confrontations'.[24] In the *Limaj* case, the ICTY Trial Chamber, in finding that an armed conflict existed in Kosovo before the end of May 1998 between the Kosovo Liberation Army and the Serb forces, stated that:

[B]y the end of May 1998 KLA units were constantly engaged in armed clashes with substantial Serbian forces in areas from the Kosovo–Albanian border in the west, to near Prishtina/Pristina in the east, to Prizren/Prizren and the Kosovo–Macedonian border in the south and the municipality of Mitrovice/Kosovka Mitrovica in the north . . . The ability of the KLA to engage in such varied operations is a further indicator of its level of organisation.[25]

Thus, it is postulated that an armed group that constructs and emplaces (or delivers to a target) improvised explosive devices (IEDs), landmines, vehicle-borne IEDs (VBIEDs), or body-borne IEDs (BBIEDs), but which does not engage in direct 'hostilities' with the armed forces of a state, is *not* engaged in an NIAC. Such situations appear to fall more accurately within the notion expressed by the ICTY in the *Tadić* case and cited above of

Conference of the Red Cross and Red Crescent, Geneva, Switzerland, 28 November–1 December 2011, October 2011, p. 8.

[23] ICTY, *Prosecutor v. Dusko Tadić (aka 'DULE')*, Opinion and Judgment (Trial Chamber) (Case No. IT-94-1-T), 7 May 1997, §562, <http://www.icty.org/x/cases/tadic/tjug/en/tad-tsj70507JT2-e.pdf>.

[24] ICTY, *Prosecutor v. Haradinaj*, Judgment (Trial Chamber) (Case No. IT-04-84-T), 3 April 2008, §49.

[25] ICTY, *Prosecutor v. Fatmir Limaj, Haradin Bala, and Isak Musliu*, Judgment (Trial Chamber) (Case No. IT-03-66-T), 30 November 2005, §172, footnote omitted.

'terrorist activities, which are not subject to international humanitarian law'.[26] As Sandesh Sivakumaran notes, upon ratification of the 1977 Additional Protocol I, the UK entered a declaration whereby 'the term "armed conflict" of itself and in its context denotes a situation of a kind which is not constituted by the commission of ordinary crimes including acts of terrorism whether concerted or in isolation'.[27]

THE DURATION OF AN ARMED CONFLICT

The precise duration of an armed conflict is a difficult issue. The ICTY in the *Tadić* case suggested that IHL applies 'from the initiation of . . . armed conflicts and extends beyond the cessation of hostilities until a general conclusion of peace is reached; or, in the case of internal conflicts, a peaceful settlement is achieved'.[28] While certain IHL obligations will clearly extend beyond the active cessation of hostilities, the notion that the IHL rules governing the conduct of hostilities pertain to acts committed after the point at which active hostilities have effectively ceased is too expansive. Nonetheless, there will often be a fluctuation in the regularity and extent of armed violence during a situation of armed conflict without that oscillation amounting to the active cessation of hostilities.

THE GEOGRAPHICAL SCOPE OF AN ARMED CONFLICT

Common Article 3 to the 1949 Geneva Conventions refers to an NIAC 'occurring in the territory of one of the High Contracting Parties'. This can be taken to mean that an armed conflict is limited to the territory of a single state or that the provisions only apply to a situation in which the territory on which an armed conflict is ongoing is governed by the authority of a state party. If it is the latter, given that, as of 1 September 2013, all United Nations (UN) member states were party to the Geneva Conventions, there is very little territory that would not be covered by the treaty provisions. Further, under customary law, there is arguably no such strict geographical limitation.

---

[26] These situations are governed by the international law of law enforcement, including, in particular, IHRL.

[27] Declaration of 28 January 1998, <http://www.icrc.org/ihl.nsf/NORM/0A9E03F0F2EE757CC1256402003 FB6D2?OpenDocument>, cited in Sandesh Sivakumaran, *The Law of Non-International Armed Conflict*, Oxford University Press, Oxford, 2012, p. 233. Sivakumaran refers to the 'understanding' of the UK as a 'reservation', but it is more accurately termed a 'declaration' because it does not seek to modify the terms of the Protocol with respect to the UK, but rather to set out the UK's understanding of the term. See also e.g. ICTY, *Prosecutor v. Milošević*, Decision on Motion for Judgment of Acquittal (Rule 98*bis* Decision) (Trial Chamber) (Case No. IT-02-54-T), 16 June 2004, §26.

[28] ICTY, *Prosecutor v. Dusko Tadić (aka 'DULE')*, Decision on the Defence Motion for Interlocutory Appeal on Jurisdiction (Appeals Chamber) (Case No. IT-94-1), 2 October 1995, §70.

So, for example, if, as is argued later, armed conflict between Turkey and the Kurdish Worker's Party (PKK) takes place outside Turkey on the territory of the Iraqi Kurdistan region of northern Iraq, as well as on Turkish territory, this constitutes a single armed conflict, not two distinct NIACs.

This position does not, though, mean that a globalized NIAC exists as a matter of international law. Although the USA accepts that it has little to no support for its stance, it continues to argue that it is engaged in a global armed conflict with 'the Taliban, al-Qaeda, and associated forces'.[29] No such conflict exists, for two reasons: first, there is no longer active combat between US forces and al-Qaeda forces in Afghanistan such as to constitute protracted armed violence and therefore an armed conflict (nor has there been for close to a decade); and, secondly, while an NIAC can certainly cross international borders, it is not possible under existing international law for an NIAC to be simply global.[30] Armed conflict must 'have a territorial base whether a single territory, a core territory plus overspill onto different territory, or multiple territories; a global non-international armed conflict does not exist, at least, as a matter of law'.[31]

SUMMARY RULES APPLICABLE IN A NON-INTERNATIONAL ARMED CONFLICT

IHL is applicable to all parties to the conflict, whether state or non-state armed groups. This always includes Common Article 3 to the 1949 Geneva Conventions (by virtue of their universal application under customary international law) and all other provisions of IHL applicable to an NIAC, as well as, in certain circumstances, the 1977 Additional Protocol II.[32] States engaged in an NIAC are also bound by

[29] According to John Brennan, Assistant to the US President for Homeland Security and Counterterrorism, for example, 'As a matter of international law, the United States is in an armed conflict with al-Qa'ida, the Taliban, and associated forces, in response to the 9/11 attacks:' 'The ethics and efficacy of the President's counterterrorism strategy', Remarks of John O. Brennan, Woodrow Wilson International Center for Scholars, Washington, DC, 30 April 2012, <http://www.lawfareblog.com/2012/04/brennanspeech/>.

[30] As John Bellinger acknowledges: 'We are about the only country in the world that thinks we are in an armed conflict with *al-Qaida*. We really need to get on top of this and explain to our allies why it is legal and why it is permissible under international law.' Cited in Dan Roberts, 'US drone strikes being used as alternative to Guantánamo, lawyer says', *The Guardian*, 2 May 2013, <http://www.guardian.co.uk/world/2013/may/02/us-drone-strikes-guantanamo>.

[31] S. Sivakumaran, *The Law of Non-International Armed Conflict*, p. 234.

[32] The scope of application of 1977 Additional Protocol II is set out in Art. 1. In its commentary on the article, the ICRC notes that the Protocol 'only applies to conflicts of a certain degree of intensity and does not have exactly the same field of application as common Article 3, which applies in all situations of non-international armed conflict': *ICRC Commentary on the 1977 Additional Protocols to the Geneva Conventions of 1949*, p. 1348. Certain criteria are required for the application of 1977 Additional Protocol II, namely: a confrontation between the armed forces of the government and opposing 'dissident' armed forces; that the dissident armed forces are under a responsible command; and that they control a part of the territory so as to enable them to 'carry out sustained and concerted military operations' and to implement the Protocol.

both applicable treaty[33] and customary human rights law. In areas in which hostilities are being actively conducted, IHL is widely regarded as the *lex specialis* of *jus in bello*, while outside such areas, human rights law is arguably the corresponding *lex specialis* for the lawful use of force.

There is also increasing acceptance that non-state armed groups are also bound by at least peremptory norms of IHRL (e.g. the prohibitions on summary and arbitrary executions, torture, and enforced disappearances).[34] They may also be bound by other human rights obligations where they control territory. Thus, the UN Assistance Mission in Afghanistan (UNAMA) stated in February 2012 that:

While non-State actors in Afghanistan, including non-State armed groups, cannot formally become parties to international human rights treaties, international human rights law increasingly recognizes that where non-State actors, such as the Taliban, exercise de facto control over territory, they are bound by international human rights obligations.[35]

Accordingly, based on the applicable law, during the conduct of hostilities it is prohibited to attack any civilian taking no direct part in hostilities, or any fighter who has laid down his arms or who is *hors de combat* because of sickness, wounds, detention, or any other cause. Children must not be recruited into armed forces or armed groups, or allowed to take part in hostilities. It is prohibited to attack any civilian objects. Civilian objects are any buildings or areas that are not lawful military objectives. Indiscriminate attacks, namely attacks that do not distinguish between military objectives and civilians and/or civilian objects, are prohibited. The use of inherently indiscriminate weapons, or weapons 'of a nature to cause superfluous injury or unnecessary suffering', is prohibited. Violating any of these rules may constitute a war crime.

Attacks against lawful military objectives (military personnel or equipment) are prohibited if they may be expected to cause 'excessive' harm to either civilians or civilian objects, or a combination of both, in relation to the concrete and direct military

---

[33] Derogations from other human rights in accordance with the 1966 International Covenant on Civil and Political Rights may only occur in 'time of public emergency which threatens the life of the nation and the existence of which is officially proclaimed'. Any derogation must be only 'to the extent strictly required by the exigencies of the situation, provided that such measures are not inconsistent with their other obligations under international law and do not involve discrimination solely on the ground of race, colour, sex, language, religion or social origin'.

[34] See e.g. 'Report of the Independent International Commission of Inquiry on the Syrian Arab Republic', UN doc. A/HRC/19/69, 22 February 2012, §106: 'In this regard, the commission notes that, at a minimum, human rights obligations constituting peremptory international law (*ius cogens*) bind States, individuals and non-State collective entities, including armed groups. Acts violating *ius cogens*—for instance, torture or enforced disappearances—can never be justified.'

[35] See e.g. UN Assistance Mission in Afghanistan (UNAMA), *Afghanistan: Annual Report 2011, Protection of Civilians in Armed Conflict*, Kabul, February 2012, p. iv. See also in this regard Annyssa Bellal, Gilles Giacca, and Stuart Casey-Maslen, 'International law and armed non-state actors in Afghanistan', *International Review of the Red Cross*, 93(881) (2011), pp. 47–79.

advantage anticipated. All feasible precautions must be taken to avoid, and in any event to minimize, incidental loss of civilian life, injury to civilians, and damage to civilian objects.

Enforced disappearances are prohibited. Hostages shall not be taken. Arbitrary deprivation of liberty is prohibited. Anyone detained by a party to an armed conflict must be treated humanely and in accordance with their sex, age, and religious beliefs. Murder, torture, rape, bodily injury, or other cruel, humiliating, or degrading treatment are all prohibited. Summary or arbitrary executions are prohibited. No one may be convicted or sentenced, except pursuant to a fair trial affording all essential judicial guarantees. This includes a defendant's right to know the charges against him/her, to understand the court proceedings, to have the opportunity to conduct a genuine defence, and to be able to appeal against both conviction and sentence. Everyone charged with a criminal offence shall be presumed innocent until proved guilty according to law.

Which armed conflicts occurred in 2012?

The following tables summarize the IACs and NIACs that took place in 2012.

International armed conflicts in 2012

Active conflicts	Military occupations
South Sudan *v.* Sudan	Azerbaijan, partially occupied by Armenia Cyprus, partially occupied by Turkey Eritrea, partially occupied by Ethiopia Georgia, partially occupied by the Russian Federation Lebanon, partially occupied by Israel Moldova, partially occupied by the Russian Federation Palestine, partially occupied by Israel Syria, partially occupied by Israel Western Sahara, partially occupied by Morocco

Non-international armed conflicts in 2012

Situation	Parties to the conflicts
Afghanistan	Afghan armed forces and ISAF *v.* Quetta Shura Taliban Afghan armed forces and ISAF *v.* Haqqani Network Afghan armed forces and ISAF *v.* Hezb-e-Islami
Central African Republic	Central African Republic armed forces *v.* Séléka Central African Republic armed forces and Ugandan People's Defence Forces *v.* Lord's Resistance Army
Colombia	Colombian armed forces *v.* Revolutionary Armed Forces of Colombia (FARC-EP) Colombian armed forces *v.* National Liberation Army (ELN)

DRC	DRC armed forces and MONUSCO *v.* M23
	DRC armed forces *v.* Lord's Resistance Army
	DRC armed forces *v.* Forces Démocratiques de Libération du Rwanda (FDLR)
	DRC armed forces *v.* Allied Democratic Forces/National Army for the Liberation of Uganda (ADF-NALU)
Mali	National Movement for the Liberation of Azawad (MNLA) *v.* al-Qaeda in the Islamic Maghreb (AQIM), Ansar Dine, and the Movement for Oneness and Jihad in West Africa (MOJWA)
Mexico	Mexican army and police *v.* Sinaloa Cartel
	Mexican army and police *v.* Las Zetas gang
	Sinaloa Cartel and Gulf Cartel *v.* Las Zetas gang
Myanmar	Tatmadaw *v.* Kachin Independence Army
Philippines	Philippines armed forces *v.* New People's Army
Somalia	Federal Republic of Somalia armed forces, and AMISOM, and Ethiopia, and USA *v.* al-Shabaab
Sudan	Sudanese armed forces *v.* SPLM/A-North
	Sudanese armed forces *v.* JEM
	Sudanese armed forces *v.* SLA
Syria	Syrian armed forces and Shabbiha *v.* Free Syrian Army
	Syrian armed forces and Shabbiha *v.* al-Nusra
Thailand	Thai armed forces *v.* Barisan Revolusi Nasional independence movement, PULO, and other armed groups
Turkey	Turkish armed forces *v.* Kurdish Worker's Party (PKK)
Yemen	Yemeni armed forces and USA *v.* al-Qaeda in the Arabian Peninsula (conflict ended)
	Yemeni armed forces *v.* al-Houthi
Gaza	Israeli Defense Forces *v.* Hamas and Islamic Jihad

Casualties in armed conflicts in 2012

The *War Report: 2012* presents statistics based on available data on casualties and displaced populations as a result of armed conflict in 2012.[36] Casualties are defined as those people who have been killed or injured during, or directly related to, armed conflict, and include both civilians and combatants/fighters.

Each country report provides detailed information on the sources of the data used, which vary across countries. Casualty data has been collected from all open source material that could be identified. Data sources include:

- the UN and its agencies, including the UN Office for the Coordination of Humanitarian Affairs (OCHA), the Office of the UN High Commissioner for Human Rights (OHCHR), the Special Procedures of the UN Human Rights Council (UNHRC), reports of the UN

---

[36] As noted above, data-gathering and analysis for the *War Report: 2012* was conducted by Megan Burke and Loren Persi Vicentic.

Secretary-General to the UN Security Council, offices of peacekeeping and assistance missions, such as UNAMA and others;

- other international organizations, such as the World Health Organization (WHO) and the ICRC;
- government reporting on casualties in other countries, such as the US Department of State's human rights reports;
- governments of states experiencing conflict, including their police or military, such as in the Philippines;
- international non-governmental organizations (NGOs), such as Amnesty International, Action on Armed Violence (AOAV), Human Rights Watch (HRW), Médecins sans Frontières (MSF), and the International Crisis Group (ICG), among others;
- national NGOs such as the Jammu and Kashmir Coalition of Civil Society and the Azerbaijan Campaign to Ban Landmines;
- media sources, including the media reports[37] compiled by organizations and individuals;
- academics; and
- other sources that compile or analyse reporting, including the Iraq Body Count, the Bureau of Investigative Journalism, and the South Asia Terrorism Portal.

This list is not exhaustive, but demonstrates the types and range of sources reviewed.

In cases in which more than one source of casualty data was identified for a situation in 2012, we have endeavoured to present all relevant datasets, although these present differing casualty totals in many cases. Whenever possible, we have provided some indication of those that reported the most verified, disaggregated, or otherwise usable data.

We have sought to present data that has been disaggregated by the number of people killed versus injured, the number of civilians versus combatants/fighters, the armed force or group responsible for the casualty, and by age and sex, all within the calendar year from 1 January to 31 December 2012. Yet, for 2012, such detailed disaggregation for conflict-related casualties was rarely available.

Many data sources are focused only on civilian casualties and strive to exclude fighter casualties, for example most UN sources. Some other sources present only people killed, for example, and do not differentiate between civilians and combatants. Data on casualties among non-state armed actors was very limited.

---

[37] Media reports do not always provide sufficient detail to determine whether or not a casualty is directly related to armed conflict or another type of violence. We have erred on the side of excluding casualties for which the direct cause is not clear. For compilations of media data, we have used those that collect conflict-related casualties. In some cases, the criteria are broader than ours and data may include casualties from other types of violence. We have noted this in the country report when relevant.

Information on people injured was much more difficult to identify than on people killed. Some organizations that provide humanitarian relief, such as the ICRC or Médecins sans Frontières, register and count injured people who are treated for conflict-related injuries in some contexts, but not in every part of the country or in each country where they work. There is always the possibility of overlap between sources of data on the wounded who received help, since the same person may receive treatment in more than one location.

Little data was available, disaggregated by age and gender, on the numbers of women and children killed and injured in conflict. It is hoped that initiatives such as the UN Monitoring and Reporting Mechanism (MRM) on grave children's rights violations in situations of armed conflict will improve the availability of data on the impact of conflict on children in the future.

The *War Report: 2012* has defined conflict-related casualties[38] as those casualties that have occurred as the direct result of a violent action carried out by participants in a context of armed conflict. This includes the use of weapons such as gunshot wounds, artillery fire, aerial bombing, and drone strikes, as well as physical beatings. It includes both casualties due to landmines and improvised explosive devices (IEDs) used during an existing armed conflict and casualties of landmines and other explosive remnants that have been left behind in the context of armed conflict.

We have not specifically included statistics on the many victims of the indirect effects of conflict, such as those who become ill or die due to the increased levels of disease that often occur in the context of armed violence or because they are unable to access medical care to treat non-conflict-related medical issues due to violence and insecurity. It is, however, possible that indirect victims are sometimes included in the sources used without being identified as such.

In some cases, we have included data from sources that define their casualty data collection more broadly, but that have significant overlap with our case definition. In such cases, we have noted this in the report and have not included these casualty figures in national totals. For example, in Colombia, statistics collected by the Colombian National Human Rights Observatory on 'Violations to the Right to Life and Integrity' have been referred to as conflict-related casualties in some contexts, but in fact include other types of violent homicide. In another example, the Action on Armed Violence dataset includes all casualties from 'explosive-related violence'; while many of these

---

[38] Conflict-related casualties are referred to by different names in different contexts. Victims of armed violence in Mexico are recorded as 'organized crime executions' in the media and by the Trans-border Institute. The ICRC in South Sudan collected data on individuals 'wounded in armed violence', while Médecins sans Frontières in the same country referred to these incidents as 'violence-related injuries'.

casualties may have occurred during armed conflict, it also includes casualties from criminal acts and accidents related to the handling of explosives.

In addition to distinguishing between casualties of civilians and combatants/fighters, wherever possible, we have noted the casualties of particular civilian subgroups that may be especially targeted during armed conflicts. These subgroups include: journalists who have been determined to have been killed or injured due to their work; human rights defenders; humanitarian aid workers who, under IHL, should be warranted special protection in the context of armed conflict; others who have a specific role, such as government officials and tribal leaders; and religious leaders.

It was not possible to include all relevant information. A number of casualties and victims of conflict were reported in the text, but not included in the total numbers of casualties. For example, except in the case of the DRC,[39] victims of sexual violence were not included in totalling persons injured, generally because the data on sexual violence lacked sufficient detail or because it has not been clear if these figures might overlap with casualty data from other sources.[40] Prisoners, detainees, and victims of kidnapping, arbitrary arrest, and arbitrary detention were not included in casualty totals unless they were recorded as killed or injured in the primary casualty source used. We have also not included victims of psychological trauma, such as post-traumatic stress disorder (PTSD) or mental torture, because of the lack of available data, but this in no way reflects a judgement on the status of these victims.

How many people were displaced by armed conflicts in 2012?

The primary source of data on displaced populations used in the *War Report* is the IDMC's 2012 Global Overview report, published in April 2013. We have also compared this to other sources in many cases to ensure that details relevant to conflict-related displacement are highlighted. When the IDMC has reported that the size of the displaced population is unknown, the researchers endeavoured to include figures cited by other reliable sources.

As set out in more detail in Chapter 4, the IDMC has calculated that some 6.5 million people were newly displaced during 2012 by armed conflict, generalized violence, and human rights violations. As of the end of the year, an estimated 28.8 million people were

---

[39] In the DRC, victims of sexual violence have been included in casualty totals due to the availability of detailed and disaggregated data, documented by the UN, including on numbers of adult and child victims.

[40] However, it must be recognized that victims of sexual violence are often injured both physically and psychologically.

displaced internally around the world, the highest figure the IDMC has ever recorded.[41] The increase was the result of large-scale population movements in a number of countries in Africa and the Middle East. The conflicts in Syria and the DRC were responsible for around half of the new displacements, with 2.4 million and 1 million, respectively, while an estimated 500,000 people fled their homes in both India and Sudan.

Libya and Yemen were worst affected in 2011, but in 2012 Syria was the regional hotspot, with a fivefold increase in the number of internally displaced persons (IDPs). By the end of the year, Syria was the world's largest and fastest evolving crisis in terms of new displacement. The country now has more than 3 million IDPs, of whom more than 80 per cent were newly displaced in 2012.

---

[41] This chapter is based on IDMC, *People Displaced by Conflict and Violence, Global Overview 2012*, IDMC, Geneva, April 2013.

Part II

Situations of Armed Conflict in 2012

Situations of armed conflict in 2012

Armed conflict between South Sudan and Sudan in 2012

KEY CONFLICT STATISTICS FOR 2012

Deaths from aerial bombing:	48	(Sources: Reeves; US Department of State)
Injuries from aerial bombing:	86	(Sources: Reeves; US Department of State)
Female civilian injured (Abyei):	1	(Source: UN Secretary-General)
SPLA military deaths:	19–1,200	(Source: Media reports)
SAF military deaths:	15–240	(Source: Media reports)

CLASSIFICATION OF THE CONFLICT

South Sudan[1] and Sudan actively fought an international armed conflict (IAC) in 2012, at least until the signature of an agreement on 27 September 2012.

SUMMARY OF APPLICABLE INTERNATIONAL LAW

Both parties to the conflict were bound by customary and conventional international humanitarian law (IHL) and human rights law, including: the customary IHL rules of distinction, proportionality, and precautions in attacks; the obligation not to recruit and use children as soldiers; and the duty to respect and protect fundamental human rights. This includes the duty to respect the rights to life and to freedom from torture or other forms of cruel, inhuman, or degrading treatment or punishment.

Sudan adhered to the four 1949 Geneva Conventions on 23 September 1957 and to 1977 Additional Protocol I on 7 March 2006. Sudan ratified the 1997 Anti-Personnel Mine Ban Convention (APMBC) on 13 October 2003, becoming a state party on 1 April 2003.

---

[1] On 9 July 2011, South Sudan became a state following its independence from Sudan. It was admitted as a UN member state on 14 July 2011.

South Sudan adhered to the four 1949 Geneva Conventions on 25 March 2013—that is, after the conflict had ostensibly ended. It is not yet party to the 1977 Additional Protocol I. South Sudan deposited an instrument of succession to the APMBC effective on 11 November 2011, becoming a party from that date. Neither state is party to the 2008 Convention on Cluster Munitions (CCM).

HISTORY OF THE CONFLICT

Two particular towns were the focus of armed conflict between South Sudan and Sudan in 2012: Heglig and Abyei, both located in South Kordofan state.

Conflict over Heglig

Heglig is a contested town on the border between Sudan and South Sudan. In April 2012, South Sudan accused the Sudanese army of invading Heglig with artillery supported by combat aircraft, although it claimed to have repelled the attack. Two weeks later, Sudan confirmed that its troops were fighting South Sudanese armed forces in Heglig.[2] Reports from a civilian hospital in Bentiu suggest that, in March–April 2012, air strikes caused the death of 20 civilians and injured a further 79.[3] On 27 September 2012, both parties to the conflict signed a Cooperation Agreement largely focused on the border dispute. Notably, the two states agreed to the establishment of a demilitarized zone along the frontier.[4]

Abyei conflict

The 2005 Comprehensive Peace Agreement (CPA) ended the decades-long conflict between the Sudanese Armed Forces (SAF) and the Sudan People's Liberation Movement/Army (SPLM/A). The CPA included the Abyei Protocol, which planned to replace Abyei district (as it was called when it was a part of South Kordofan state, Sudan) with a new jurisdiction with special administrative status.[5]

Problems with the implementation of the CPA intensified in May 2008, when fighting broke out between northern and southern forces in the disputed oil-rich town of Abyei. To reduce tensions, President al-Bashir and Southern Sudan leader Salva Kiir agreed to

---

[2] 'New war, old enemies: conflict dynamics in South Kordofan', Human Security Baseline Assessment (HSBA) for Sudan and South Sudan Working Paper, Small Arms Survey, March 2013, p. 46.

[3] 'New war, old enemies', p. 46.

[4] 'New war, old enemies', p. 57.

[5] See e.g. Enough Project, 'Enough 101: what is the Abyei area and why is it disputed?', Report, *Relief Web*, 16 January 2013, <http://reliefweb.int/report/sudan/enough-101-what-abyei-area-and-why-it-disputed>.

seek international arbitration to resolve the dispute over Abyei.[6] The Permanent Court of Arbitration rendered a decision on 22 July 2009.[7] Nevertheless, the two parties continued to disagree over the border region, and subsequently a referendum for the residents of Abyei to decide whether to join the south or north was again delayed indefinitely.[8]

On 21 May 2011, the SAF reportedly seized control of Abyei with a force of some 5,000 soldiers after three days of clashes with Southern Sudan forces.[9] The northern advance included shelling, aerial bombardment, and the deployment of tanks. The South Sudanese government declared this an 'act of war', and the United Nations (UN) sent an envoy to Khartoum to intervene.[10] Initial reports suggested that more than 20,000 people fled the area.[11] A few days later South Sudan affirmed having withdrawn its forces from Abyei and a deal on demilitarization was agreed on 20 June 2011.[12] On 27 June 2011, UN Security Council Resolution 1990 authorized the deployment of a UN Interim Security Force for Abyei consisting of Ethiopian troops, which arrived a week after South Sudan formally declared its independence.[13]

Occasional hostilities over the control of the border continued despite the signature of the Cooperation Agreement on 27 September 2012 between the two states.[14] This Agreement reaffirms the commitment of the two states to renounce war, and to implement all security agreements and arrangements reached in previous negotiations.[15] On 8 March 2013, the two states signed a further agreement in which they committed to

---

[6] International Crisis Group (ICG), 'Abyei conflict threatens to escalate into full-scale war', 30 May 2008, <http://www.crisisgroup.org/en/regions/africa/horn-of-africa/sudan/op-eds/mozersky-abyei-conflict-threatens-to-escalate-into-full-scale-war.aspx>.

[7] Permanent Court of Arbitration, *The Government of Sudan/The Sudan People's Liberation Movement/Army* (Abyei Arbitration), 22 July 2009, <http://www.pca-cpa.org/showpage.asp?pag_id=1306>.

[8] Abyei was due to remain under a special administrative status until a final status referendum was conducted. The Abyei Area Referendum was scheduled to occur simultaneously with the southern Sudan Referendum in January 2011, but this did not happen.

[9] 'Sudan: Abyei seizure by North "act of war", says South', *BBC*, 22 May 2011.

[10] 'Sudan: Abyei seizure by North "act of war", says South'.

[11] 'Sudan: Abyei seizure by North "act of war", says South'; see also 'North Sudan seizes disputed Abyei, thousands flee', *Reuters*, 22 May 2011.

[12] See e.g. Joshua Craze, 'Conflict dynamics in Abyei—small arms survey—Sudan', June 2011, <http://www.smallarmssurveysudan.org/fileadmin/docs/working-papers/HSBA-WP-26-Conflict-Dynamics-in-Abyei.pdf>.

[13] Human Security Baseline Assessment for Sudan and South Sudan (HSBA), 'The crisis in Abyei', updated 1 March 2013, <http://www.smallarmssurveysudan.org/fileadmin/docs/facts-figures/abyei/HSBA-Crisis-in-Abyei-March-2013.pdf> and see UN Security Council Resolution 1990, 27 June 2011.

[14] Cooperation Agreement between the Republic of the Sudan and the Republic of South Sudan, Addis Ababa, 27 September 2012. See e.g. Jeffrey Gettleman, 'Sudan and South Sudan sign accord, but several issues are unresolved', *New York Times*, 27 September 2012, <http://www.nytimes.com/2012/09/28/world/africa/sudan-and-south-sudan-sign-cooperation-deal.html?_r=0>.

[15] HSBA, 'The crisis in Abyei', Small Arms Survey, updated 10 March 2013, <http://www.smallarmssurveysudan.org/facts-figures/abyei.html>.

implementing the September 2012 Cooperation Agreement. While the Agreement has led to demilitarization of the border area, it has not led to further progress in negotiations over Abyei.[16]

PARTIES TO THE CONFLICT

Sudanese Armed Forces

The SAF are the armed forces of the Republic of Sudan. They number, according to 2011 International Institute for Strategic Studies estimates, some 109,300. They comprise land forces, a navy, an air force, and the Popular Defence Force.[17]

Sudan People's Liberation Movement/Army (SPLM/A)

The SPLA was formed in 1983 with declared aims of establishing a secular, democratic Sudan.[18] The SPLM/A, as the politico-military movement came to be identified, defined itself as a national movement rather than a strictly southern independence movement.[19] In 2005, the SPLM/A signed the CPA with the government of Sudan, ending the conflict between north and south Sudan.[20]

In 2011, SPLM/A leaders announced that the group would split along a north–south divide if the results of the referendum voted in favour of southern independence from Sudan. Since South Sudan's independence on 9 July 2011, the northern splinter group have seen the SPLM/A intensify its fight with the stated aim of changing the government in Khartoum. In 2012, SPLM—Northern Sector (SPLM-N/SPLA-N) joined forces with three Darfur rebel groups, the Justice and Equality Movement (JEM), the SLM/A—Abdul Wahid al-Nur (SLM-AW/SLA-AW), and the SLM/A—Minni Minnawi (SLM-MM/SLA-MM), forming a new group, the Sudan Revolutionary Front (SRF). The SRF's declared purpose is the toppling of Sudanese President al-Bashir.[21]

---

[16] HSBA, 'The crisis in Abyei'.

[17] See e.g. US Central Intelligence Agency (CIA), 'Africa: Sudan', *The World Factbook*, <http://www.cia.gov/library/publications/the-world-factbook/geos/su.html>.

[18] See e.g. Sudan People's Liberation Army (SPLA)/Sudan People's Liberation Movement (SPLM), *Global Security.org*, 7 November 2011, <http://www.globalsecurity.org/military/world/para/spla.htm>.

[19] See e.g. Sudan Tribune, 'Sudan People's Liberation Army (SPLA)', <http://www.sudantribune.com/spip.php?mot183>.

[20] US Institute of Peace, Peace Agreements: Sudan, as of March 2005.

[21] James Copnall, 'Sudan's Darfur region dabbles with peace', *BBC*, 2 March 2012, <http://www.bbc.co.uk/news/world-africa-17225356>.

UN Interim Security Force for Abyei

The UN Interim Security Force for Abyei (UNISFA) was set up by the UN Security Council under Resolution 1990 of 27 June 2011 as a response to the violence in the Abyei region and with a mandate under Chapter VII of the UN Charter to use force in certain circumstances. The UN force's mandate is to monitor the flashpoint border between the north and the south, and it is authorized to use force to protect civilians and humanitarian workers in Abyei.[22]

CASUALTIES

There is no complete data available on casualties associated with the international conflict between Sudan and South Sudan. Most casualties, both civilian and military, are believed to have occurred during cross-border fighting and aerial bombing in March and April, and between October and December 2012, particularly near the oil-producing area of Heglig, in South Kordofan and close to the border with South Sudan, and in Bentiu, in Unity State within South Sudan.[23]

Media reports, based on information provided either by the South Sudan or Sudanese governments, reported the deaths of anywhere from 19 up to 1,200 deaths of SPLA troops (South Sudanese forces), and between 15 and 240 Sudanese troops during ground battles in Heglig.[24] According to the SPLA commander, a three-day battle on 10–12 December just outside the capital of South Kordofan state killed 89 SAF soldiers and 3 SPLA troops, with 17 SPLA troops injured.[25]

The 'Reeves dataset'[26] identified 48 people killed and 86 injured as a result of SAF bombing between January and 5 June in disputed territories, and in the South Sudan

---

[22] UNISFA, 'Demilitarizing and monitoring peace in the disputed Abyei Area', 11 April 2013, <http://www.un.org/en/peacekeeping/missions/unisfa/>.

[23] Human Rights Watch (HRW), 'Annual report 2013: country summary Sudan', January 2013, p. 2.

[24] 'Over 1,000 S. Sudanese killed at Heglig: commande', *Hindustan Times*, 23 April 2012, <http://www.hindustantimes.com/world-news/Africa/Over-1-000-S-Sudanese-killed-at-Heglig-commander/Article1-844869.aspx>; 'Sudan and the South "open new front" in border clash', *BBC*, 18 April 2012, <http://www.bbc.co.uk/news/world-africa-17753991>.

[25] These casualties are not included in totals above because there were only reports found from the South Sudanese military perspective and no means independently to verify totals: 'The battle of Daldoka', *Nuba Reports*, 28 March 2013, <http://www.nubareports.org/reports/battle-daldoka>.

[26] Eric Reeves, a professor based at Smith College, Northampton, Massachusetts, has spent 14 years as a Sudan researcher and analyst. His dataset collects all public information from UN, non-governmental organization (NGO), government, and media sources on aerial bombings perpetuated by the SAF in Sudanese, South Sudanese, and disputed territories.

states of Unity and Upper Nile. Casualties included both military personnel and civilians, and included one girl, who was killed, and three children, who were injured.[27]

A woman was injured from aerial bombing in the disputed area of Abyei, representing the only casualty identified in 2012 in the area under control of the UNISFA.[28]

WAR CRIMES ALLEGATIONS, INVESTIGATIONS, AND PROSECUTIONS

Neither Sudan nor South Sudan is a party to the 1998 Rome Statute of the International Criminal Court (the ICC Statute). The UN Security Council referred the situation in Darfur since 1 July 2002 in Resolution 1593 (2005). As of 1 September 2013, there had been no referral of the situation of armed conflict between the two states to the Office of the Prosecutor.

---

[27] Eric Reeves, 'Aerial military attacks on civilians and humanitarians in Sudan and South Sudan, 1999–2012', 5 June 2012, <http://www.sudanbombing.org>.

[28] UN Security Council, 'Report of the Secretary-General on the situation in Abyei', UN Doc. S/2012/358, 24 May 2012.

Military occupation of Azerbaijan by Armenia in 2012

KEY CONFLICT STATISTICS FOR 2012

Civilian deaths:	2	(Source: Media reports)
Civilian injured:	1	(Source: Media reports)
Military deaths:	12 (8 Azeri)	(Source: Media reports)
Military injured:	17 (9 Azeri)	(Source: Media reports)
Civilians displaced:	600,000	(Source: IDMC)

CLASSIFICATION OF THE CONFLICT

Armenia and Azerbaijan were engaged in an international armed conflict (IAC) in 2012 by virtue of Armenia's continued military occupation of Azerbaijani territory.

SUMMARY OF APPLICABLE INTERNATIONAL LAW

Both parties to the conflict were bound by customary and conventional international humanitarian law (IHL) and human rights law, including: the customary IHL rules of distinction, proportionality, and precautions in attacks; the obligation not to recruit and use children as soldiers; and the duty to respect and protect fundamental human rights. This includes the duty to respect the rights to life and to freedom from torture or other forms of cruel, inhuman, or degrading treatment or punishment.

The law of military occupation is set out in the 1907 Hague Regulations (Articles 42–56), the 1949 Geneva Convention IV, the 1977 Additional Protocol I, and customary international law. Both states are party to the four 1949 Geneva Conventions, but only Armenia has adhered to the 1977 Additional Protocol I, having ratified in June 1983.

The underpinning of the law of military occupation is that it is a temporary situation, which lasts until a political agreement is reached. During this period, the occupying power does not enjoy sovereign rights over the territories it occupies and local law that was applicable prior to the occupation remains in force. At the same time, the occupying power is responsible for administering the local life of the population under its control, maintaining it as it was prior to the occupation as closely as possible, and for providing security (Article 43 of the Hague Regulations).

In addition, international human rights law (IHRL) is binding on Armenia extra-territorially in the territories it occupies.[1]

Neither state has adhered to the 1997 Anti-Personnel Mine Ban Convention (APMBC) or the 2008 Convention on Cluster Munitions (CCM).

HISTORY OF THE CONFLICT

The re-emergence of violence in the late 1980s between ethnic Armenians and Azeris over the long-disputed region of Nagorno-Karabakh erupted into armed conflict in February 1992 between forces from Armenia and Azerbaijan, as well as Nagorno-Karabakh. The armed conflict led to occupation of more than one-seventh of the territory of Azerbaijan, more than 20,000 casualties, massive refugee flows from both sides, and expulsion of ethnic Armenians from Azerbaijan and ethnic Azeris from Armenia.[2]

A cease-fire between the parties to the conflict was signed on 12 May 1994. Since February 1992, attempts to settle the conflict have been made under the framework of the Minsk Process led by the Presidents of the Organization for Security and Co-operation in Europe (OSCE) Minsk Group's Co-Chair countries, namely France, the Russian Federation, and the United States of America (USA).

The Minsk Process negotiations resulted in a proposal of Basic Principles put forward in November 2007 in Madrid. The Principles were intended to serve as a basis for a comprehensive settlement between Armenia and Azerbaijan, and call, inter alia, for the return of the territories surrounding Nagorno-Karabakh to Azerbaijani control and an interim status for Nagorno-Karabakh, providing guarantees for security and self-governance, as well as international security guarantees that would include a peacekeeping operation.

Talks held in May 2009 in Prague and the commitment made by governments of both states in November 2008 in Moscow are evidence of progress in finding a political settlement to the conflict. But, despite the 15-year-long cease-fire, which is constantly monitored by the OSCE, and continued negotiations for a peaceful settlement of the

---

[1] See e.g. International Court of Justice, *Wall* Advisory Opinion, 2004, §106. As ruled by the European Court of Human Rights (ECtHR), the obligation to secure in occupied territories the rights and freedoms set out in the 1950 European Convention on Human Rights (ECHR) derives from its effective control over occupied territory, whether it is exercised by the occupying state directly, through its armed forces, or through a subordinate local administration. See ECtHR, *Cyprus v. Turkey*, Judgment (App. No. 25781/94), 10 May 2001, §77.

[2] See e.g. 'Nagorno-Karabakh profile', *BBC*, 30 May 2012, <http://www.bbc.co.uk/news/world-europe-18270325>; 'Armenia: Timeline', *BBC*, 27 February 2013, <http://www.bbc.co.uk/news/world-europe-17405415>; 'Azerbaijan profile', *BBC*, 20 March 2012, <http://www.bbc.co.uk/news/world-europe-17047328>.

conflict, the Nagorno-Karabakh situation remains unsolved,[3] with regular violations of the cease-fire involving armed incidents along the line of contact between Armenia and Azerbaijan.[4]

In March 2012, Lawrence Sheets, an International Crisis Group (ICG) expert on the conflict, declared that:

Maintaining the status quo is not an option. The opposing forces will either reach compromises—and thus peace—probably only through increased international pressure. If not, another round of more intense violence will erupt, raising the danger of dragging in the regional heavyweights... World leaders need to think about that threat, and the refugee flows, disrupted energy supplies and destruction and death such renewed warfare could cause.[5]

PARTIES TO THE CONFLICT

The parties to the conflict are the Armenia and Azerbaijan. According to Sheets: '[D]espite the "cease-fire," skirmishes along the front lines cause dozens of deaths and injuries each year. The opposing trenches have moved so close—less than 40 yards in some places—that soldiers on both sides sometimes hurl rocks at each other. Only six international monitors occasionally visit, there are no investigation mechanisms and snipers terrorize civilians living in the area.'[6]

In June 2012, among a number of incidents, Azerbaijan accused Armenia of violating its border and shooting dead five of its soldiers, a day after three Armenians were said to have been killed in the same area. The Armenian Ministry of Defence said its forces had reacted to an attempted crossing by Azeri troops.[7]

CASUALTIES

On 4 June 2012, Armenia accused Azerbaijani forces of killing three Armenian soldiers and injuring six others on the militarized border between the two countries. The Defence

---

[3] See e.g. 'Joint statement by the Presidents of the United States, the Russian Federation and France on Nagorno-Karabakh', Los Cabos, Mexico, 19 June 2012, <http://www.osce.org/mg/91393>; Council of Europe Parliamentary Assembly Resolution 1416 (2005), 'The conflict over the Nagorno-Karabakh region dealt with by the OSCE Minsk Conference', Text adopted by the Assembly on 25 January 2005, <http://assembly.coe.int/Main.asp?link=/Documents/AdoptedText/ta05/ERES1416.htm>.

[4] See e.g. Lawrence Sheets, 'A "frozen conflict" that could boil over', *International Herald Tribune*, 8 March 2012, <http://www.crisisgroup.org/en/regions/europe/south-caucasus/azerbaijan/Op-ed/sheets-a-frozen-conflict-that-could-boil-over.aspx>.

[5] Sheets, 'A "frozen conflict" that could boil over'.

[6] Sheets, 'A "frozen conflict" that could boil over'.

[7] 'Armenian forces kill five Azerbaijani troops on border', *BBC*, 5 June 2012, <http://www.bbc.co.uk/news/world-europe-18328690>.

Ministry of Azerbaijan reportedly denied that its forces shot the Armenians. On 5 June, Azerbaijan accused Armenian forces of killing five Azerbaijani soldiers.[8] On 6 June, one Karabakh soldier was reported killed and two injured by Azerbaijani soldiers who 'attempted to penetrate Karabakh Army positions'.[9]

A total of 15 casualties (five people killed and ten injured) from mines and explosive remnants of war (ERW) were identified during the year. An Azerbaijani soldier died after a mine exploded in the conflict zone between Armenia and Azerbaijan.[10] The Azerbaijan Campaign to Ban Landmines reported that, to end of June 2012, two Azerbaijani soldiers were killed and five injured, and one civilian was killed and another one injured.[11] Another civilian was killed by a landmine in October.[12] Azeri military mine casualties continued, with one killed and another four injured in November and December.[13] Most of these incidents were reported to have occurred in the border areas of the conflict.

DISPLACED

According to the Internal Displacement Monitoring Centre (IDMC), up to 600,000 people remained internally displaced in Azerbaijan as of end 2012. They were displaced

[8] 'Military clashes between Armenia and Azerbaijan threaten stability in region', 13 June 2012, <http://www.jamestown.org/programs/edm/single/?tx_ttnews[tt_news]=39489&cHash=a3c4f8101fdee19184ab04d3 1d07e33e>; 'Three killed in Armenia-Azerbaijan border clash', *Hurriyet*, 4 June 2012, <http://www.hurriyetdailynews.com/three-killed-in-armenia-azerbaijan-border-clash.aspx?pageID=238&nid=22338>; 'Deadly clashes along Azeri-Armenia border', 5 June 2012, <http://www.aljazeera.com/news/europe/2012/06/20126511213101530.html>; 'Armenian forces kill five Azerbaijani troops on border', *BBC*, 5 June 2012, <http://www.bbc.co.uk/news/world-europe-18328690>.

[9] 'Azeris attack Karabakh border', *RIA Novosti*, 6 June 2010, <http://en.rian.ru/world/20120606/173881374.html>.

[10] 'Azerbaijani–Armenian border clash not to plunge Nagorno-Karabakh into war', *Today's Zaman*, 10 June 2012, <http://www.todayszaman.com/news-283047-azerbaijani-armenian-border-clash-not-to-plunge-nagorno-karabakh-into-war.html>.

[11] 'Mine and UXOs victims registered in Azerbaijan in 2012', 9 July 2012, <http://dmot.info/index.php?option=com_content&view=article&id=807:mine-and-uxos-victims-registered-in-azerbaijan-in-2012-&catid=1:demining&Itemid=3>.

[12] 'Azerbaijan's Interior Ministry issues statement on Terter resident hit by landmine', 27 October 2012, <http://en.apa.az/news/181439>.

[13] 'One more soldier of Azerbaijani army hits landmine', *News.az*, 28 November 2012, <http://www.news.az/articles/society/72741>; 'Azerbaijani soldier hits landmine', *News.az*, 19 November 2012, <http://www.news.az/articles/society/72205>; 'Two Azerbaijani soldiers hit landmine', 21 November 2012, <http://en.apa.az/news_two_azerbaijani_soldiers_hit_landmine___182943.html>; 'Azerbaijani soldier hits landmine', 14 November 2012, <http://en.apa.az/news/182505>; 'Land mine injures Azerbaijani officer on border with Armenia-controlled region', *Radio Free Europe*, 4 December 2012, <http://legalpronews.findlaw.com/article/0eNF4lA8rCgpB>.

between 1988 and 1994 during the armed conflict between Azerbaijan and Armenia over the territory of Nagorno-Karabakh.[14]

WAR CRIMES ALLEGATIONS, INVESTIGATIONS, AND PROSECUTIONS

Neither state is party to the 1998 Rome Statute of the International Criminal Court (the ICC Statute). Armenia has signed, but not ratified, the ICC Statute.

---

[14] IDMC, 'Global overview 2012', April 2013, p. 45.

Military occupation of Cyprus by Turkey in 2012

CLASSIFICATION OF THE CONFLICT

Turkey and Cyprus were engaged in an international armed conflict (IAC) in 2012 by virtue of Turkish forces' continued military occupation of territory in the north of the Republic of Cyprus.

SUMMARY OF APPLICABLE INTERNATIONAL LAW

Both parties to the conflict were bound by customary and conventional international humanitarian law (IHL) and human rights law, including: the customary IHL rules of distinction, proportionality, and precautions in attacks; the obligation not to recruit and use children as soldiers; and the duty to respect and protect fundamental human rights. This includes the duty to respect the rights to life and to freedom from torture or other forms of cruel, inhuman, or degrading treatment or punishment.

The law of military occupation is set out in the 1907 Hague Regulations (Articles 42–56), the 1949 Geneva Convention IV, the 1977 Additional Protocol I, and customary international law. Both states are party to the four 1949 Geneva Conventions, but only Cyprus has adhered to the 1977 Additional Protocol I.

The underpinning of the law of military occupation is that it is a temporary situation, which lasts until a political agreement is reached. During this period, the occupying power does not enjoy sovereign rights over the territories it occupies and local law that was applicable prior to the occupation remains in force. At the same time, the occupying power is responsible for administering the local life of the population under its control, maintaining it as it was prior to the occupation as closely as possible, and for providing security (Article 43 of the Hague Regulations).

In addition, international human rights law (IHRL) is binding on Turkey extraterritorially in the territories it occupies.[1] As ruled by the European Court of Human Rights (ECtHR), the obligation to secure in occupied territories the rights and freedoms set out in the 1950 European Convention on Human Rights (ECHR) derives from Turkey's effective control over occupied territory, whether it is exercised by the occupying state directly, through its armed forces, or through a subordinate local administration. The ECtHR has ruled that Turkey exercises effective control over the north by virtue of its maintaining many thousands of its troops there.[2]

---

[1] See e.g. International Court of Justice (ICJ), *Wall* Advisory Opinion, 2004, §106.

[2] See ECtHR, *Cyprus v. Turkey*, Judgment (App. No. 25781/94), 10 May 2001, §77; ECtHR, *Loizidou v. Turkey*, Judgment (Merits) (App. No. 15318/89), 18 December 1996, §§52, 54, and 56.

Both Cyprus and Turkey have adhered to the 1997 Anti-Personnel Mine Ban Convention (APMBC). In 2012, Cyprus was granted a three-year extension to its July 2013 mine-clearance deadline under the Convention on the basis that it was not in a position to clear mines in the north of the island that was occupied.[3] Neither state has adhered to the 2008 Convention on Cluster Munitions (CCM), although Cyprus is a signatory.

HISTORY OF THE CONFLICT[4]

Cyprus has been divided since 1974, when Turkey invaded the north in response to a military coup on the island backed by the Greek government in Athens. Cyprus was effectively partitioned, with the northern third inhabited by Turkish Cypriots and the southern two-thirds by Greek Cypriots. A 'Green Line' with a buffer zone, dividing the two parts from Morphou through Nicosia to Famagusta, is patrolled by United Nations (UN) troops.

UN Security Council Resolution 353 of 20 July 1974 requested the withdrawal without delay from the Republic of Cyprus of foreign military personnel. UN General Assembly Resolution 37/253 of 16 May 1983 declared that 'part of the territory of the Republic of Cyprus is still occupied by foreign forces'.

In 1983, the Turkish-held area declared itself the Turkish Republic of Northern Cyprus. Turkey recognizes only the Turkish Cypriot authorities and is believed still today to maintain more than 10,000 troops in the north of the island. No other government has recognized the north as a state.

As European Union (EU) entry for the Republic of Cyprus approached, a UN reunification plan was put to both communities in twin referenda in April 2004. The plan was endorsed by Turkish Cypriots (although not by their then-leader Rauf Denktash), but it was overwhelmingly rejected by Greek Cypriots. Because both sides had to approve the proposals, the island remained divided as it joined the EU in May 2004.

More than two years later, hopes of progress were rekindled at UN-sponsored talks between Cypriot President Tassos Papadopolous and Turkish Cypriot leader Mehmet Ali Talat. The two agreed on a series of confidence-building measures and contacts between the communities. Hopes were given further impetus by the election of Demetris Christophas as President in February 2008. Christophas immediately began talks with Mehmet Ali Talat on reuniting the country as a federal state.

---

[3] See e.g. Convention on the Prohibition of the Use, Stockpiling, Production and Transfer of Anti-Personnel Mines and on their Destruction, Twelfth Meeting of the States Parties, Final Report, <http://www.apminebanconvention.org/fileadmin/pdf/mbc/MSP/12MSP/12MSP-FinalReport-Dec2012.pdf>.

[4] Unless otherwise stated, this section is based on 'Timeline: Cyprus', BBC, 13 December 2011, <http://news.bbc.co.uk/2/hi/europe/country_profiles/1021835.stm>.

In April 2008, the two sides reopened a major crossing in the divided Cypriot capital of Nicosia.[5] In September 2008, Greek and Turkish Cypriot leaders launched intensive negotiations aimed at ending the division of the island. In January 2010, President Christofias and Turkish Cypriot leader Mehmet Ali Talat resumed talks on reunification in a downbeat mood, and no progress was made. In April, Dervis Eroglu, who favours independence, won the Turkish north's leadership contest, beating the pro-unity incumbent. The following month, reunification talks resumed.[6]

In early March 2012, Turkey's European Affairs Minister Egemen Bağış told a Turkish Cypriot newspaper that Turkey would consider annexing northern Cyprus, which is technically EU territory, if talks between Greek and Turkish Cypriots fail to reach a deal on reunification of the island.[7]

On 24 February 2013, Democratic Rally (DISI) leader Nicos Anastasiades won the Republic of Cyprus presidential elections, leading to hopes that this might give a boost to reunification talks, because he supported a looser federation model favoured by many Turkish Cypriots. On 7 April 2013, however, Turkish Foreign Minister Ahmet Davutoğlu criticized the Greek Cypriots for not restarting reunification talks. A spokesman for the Republic of Cyprus government said that the current conditions were not good.[8]

PARTIES TO THE CONFLICT

The parties to the conflict are Cyprus and Turkey.

The UN Peacekeeping Force in Cyprus (UNFICYP) is a UN peacekeeping force established under UN Security Council Resolution 186 to prevent a recurrence of fighting following intercommunal violence between the Greek Cypriots and Turkish Cypriots, to contribute to the maintenance and restoration of law and order, and to facilitate a return to normal conditions. On 30 November 2012, 80 UNFICYP peacekeepers confronted Turkish soldiers in the buffer zone over the construction of fence on the Turkish side; Turkish forces later agreed to take it down.[9]

---

[5] 'Symbolic Cyprus crossing reopens', *BBC*, 3 April 2008, <http://news.bbc.co.uk/2/hi/europe/7327866.stm>.

[6] 'Timeline: Cyprus', *BBC*.

[7] 'Turkey says it could annex northern Cyprus', *Euractiv.com*, 5 March 2012 (updated 25 June 2012), <http://www.euractiv.com/enlargement/turkey-annex-northern-cyprus-news-511280>.

[8] International Crisis Group (ICG), 'Cyprus', Crisis Watch Database, 1 May 2013, <http://www.crisisgroup.org/en/publication-type/crisiswatch/crisiswatch-database.aspx?CountryIDs=%7bE05C4D66-8127-4572-A43D-BD84BE10E453%7d&StartDate=20120101&EndDate=20130505>.

[9] ICG, 'Cyprus', Crisis Watch Database, 30 December 2012.

CASUALTIES

No casualties were identified in 2012 as a result of the Turkish occupation in Cyprus.

DISPLACED

According to the Internal Displacement Monitoring Centre (IDMC), 210,144 people in Cyprus were displaced to areas under the control of the Cypriot government as of the end of 2012. This figure includes all those displaced since 1974, including 90,000 children born in displacement.[10]

WAR CRIMES ALLEGATIONS, INVESTIGATIONS, AND PROSECUTIONS

Cyprus ratified the 1998 Rome Statute of the International Criminal Court (the ICC Statute) in March 2002. Turkey is neither a party nor a signatory to the ICC Statute. In accordance with the ICC Statute, the Court may exercise jurisdiction over war crimes alleged to have been committed by Cypriot nationals or on its territory. No allegations of war crimes are known to have been made against either Cypriot or Turkish military personnel regarding any acts concerning the occupation in 2012.

[10] IDMC, 'Global overview 2012', April 2013, p. 44.

Military occupation of Eritrea by Ethiopia in 2012

KEY CONFLICT STATISTICS FOR 2012

Civilian deaths:	5 (in Ethiopia)	(Source: UN)
Civilians injured:	2 (in Ethiopia)	(Source: UN)
Civilians displaced:	Undetermined in Ethiopia	
	Up to 10,000 in Eritrea	(Source: IDMC)

CLASSIFICATION OF THE CONFLICT

Eritrea and Ethiopia were engaged in an international armed conflict (IAC) in 2012 by virtue of Ethiopia's continued military occupation of Eritrean territory.

SUMMARY OF APPLICABLE INTERNATIONAL LAW

Both parties to the conflict were bound by customary and conventional international humanitarian law (IHL) and human rights law, including: the customary IHL rules of distinction, proportionality, and precautions in attacks; the obligation not to recruit and use children as soldiers; and the duty to respect and protect fundamental human rights. This includes the duty to respect the rights to life and to freedom from torture or other forms of cruel, inhuman, or degrading treatment or punishment.

The law of military occupation is set out in the 1907 Hague Regulations (Articles 42–56), the 1949 Geneva Convention IV, the 1977 Additional Protocol I, and customary international law. Both states are party to the four 1949 Geneva Conventions, but only Ethiopia has adhered to the 1977 Additional Protocol I, having ratified in April 1994.

The underpinning of the law of military occupation is that it is a temporary situation, which lasts until a political agreement is reached. During this period, the occupying power does not enjoy sovereign rights over the territories it occupies and local law that was applicable prior to the occupation remains in force. At the same time, the occupying power is responsible for administering the local life of the population under its control, maintaining it as it was prior to the occupation as closely as possible, and for providing security (Article 43 of the Hague Regulations).

In addition, international human rights law (IHRL) is binding on Ethiopia extraterritorially in the territories it occupies within Eritrea.[1]

---

[1] See e.g. International Court of Justice (ICJ), *Wall* Advisory Opinion, 2004, §106; ICJ, *Armed Activities on the Territory of the Congo* (*Democratic Republic of the Congo v. Uganda*), Judgment, 19 December 2005.

Both states are party to the 1997 Anti-Personnel Mine Ban Convention (APMBC), but neither state has adhered to the 2008 Convention on Cluster Munitions (CCM).

HISTORY OF THE CONFLICT[2]

Formerly an Italian colony, Eritrea was occupied by the British in 1941. In 1952, the United Nations (UN) resolved to establish it as an autonomous entity federated with Ethiopia as a compromise between Ethiopian claims of sovereignty and Eritrean aspirations for independence. However, ten years later the Ethiopian emperor, Haile Selassie, decided to annex it completely, thus triggering a 32-year armed struggle. An alliance of the Eritrean People's Liberation Front (EPLF) and a coalition of Ethiopian resistance movements defeated the forces of Haile Selassie's communist successor, Mengistu Haile Mariam.

In 1993, in a referendum supported by Ethiopia, Eritreans voted almost unanimously for independence. Ethiopia was left landlocked. In 1998, border disputes around the town of Badme erupted into open hostilities. The conflict ended with a peace deal in June 2000, but not before leaving both sides with tens of thousands of military deaths. A security zone, patrolled by UN forces until the middle of 2008, separated the two nations.

Eritrea accuses Ethiopia of refusing to withdraw from the village of Badme, where the 1998 war began, despite an Eritrea–Ethiopia Boundary Commission[3] ruling in 2002 that Badme belonged to Eritrea. Eritrea has repeatedly called on the international community to enforce the Commission's ruling, while Ethiopia has insisted that further border talks are needed.[4]

Renewed clashes were reported at the Eritrean–Ethiopian border in March 2012, sparking increased international concern over a potential reignition of the conflict. On 15 March 2012, Ethiopian forces launched a military assault on positions inside Eritrea, claiming that the latter was training 'subversive groups' to carry out attacks inside Ethiopia. The raid was believed to be the first attack by Ethiopian troops inside Eritrean territory since the end of the war in 2000 and targeted three camps where rebels

---

[2] Unless otherwise stated, this section is based on 'Eritrea profile', *BBC*, 21 January 2013, <http://www.bbc.co.uk/news/world-africa-13349078>.

[3] The Permanent Court of Arbitration (PCA) served as registry for the Commission, which was established pursuant to an Agreement of 12 December 2000 between the government of the State of Eritrea and the government of the Federal Democratic Republic of Ethiopia, with a mandate 'to delimit and demarcate the colonial treaty border based on pertinent colonial treaties (1900, 1902, and 1908) and applicable international law'. The work of the Commission can be accessed at <http://www.pca-cpa.org/showpage.asp?pag_id=1150>.

[4] See e.g. Martin Plaut, 'Are Ethiopia and Eritrea heading back to war?', *BBC*, 21 March 2012, <http://www.bbc.co.uk/news/world-africa-17433871>.

belonging to a faction of the Afar Revolutionary Democratic Unity Front (ARDUF) were allegedly trained. The Ethiopian government spokesperson warned that similar actions might be carried out again: 'As long as Eritrea remains a launching pad for attacks against Ethiopia, similar measures will continue to be taken.'[5] On 16 March 2012, Eritrea announced that it would not retaliate, seeking instead to use the 'appropriate diplomatic channels' to resolve the issue and denying that it was harbouring rebels.[6] Further clashes were reported in May 2012,[7] but no details were confirmed.

PARTIES TO THE CONFLICT

The parties to the conflict are Eritrea and Ethiopia. Details of weaponry used in the incursion(s) in 2012 are not known.

CASUALTIES

In January 2012, members of the ARDUF killed five European tourists in eastern Ethiopia and injured two others. According to the UN Monitoring Group on Somalia and Eritrea, ARDUF fighters were hosted and trained in Eritrea as recently as December 2011, and some of those responsible for the killings had been based at a training camp in Eritrea.[8] ARDUF claimed to have killed 16 Ethiopian soldiers in the raid, a claim that was not confirmed by any other source.[9]

In March 2012, Ethiopian forces attacked several militants based on Eritrean territory.[10] No casualty figures were available from the attacks; however, the Irish government reported that a number of people were killed in the attacks.[11]

There were reports of other attacks in Ethiopia where the assailants were not identified; in March, a bus was attacked in the Gambella region, killing 12 people and injuring

---

[5] 'Eritrea "will not fight Ethiopia"', *BBC*, 16 March 2012, <http://www.bbc.co.uk/news/world-africa-17397091>.

[6] 'Eritrea "will not fight Ethiopia"', *BBC*.

[7] See e.g. International Crisis Group, 'Eritrea: scenarios for future transition', Africa Report No. 200, 28 March 2013, p. 3.

[8] 'Letter dated 11 July 2012 from the Chair of the Security Council Committee pursuant to resolutions 751 (1992) and 1907 (2009) concerning Somalia and Eritrea addressed to the President of the Security Council', UN Security Council, UN doc. S/2012/545, 13 July 2012, p. 5.

[9] 'Letter dated 11 July 2012 from the Chair of the Security Council Committee', p. 12.

[10] Jeffrey Gettleman, 'Ethiopia hits at bases run by militants in Eritrea', *New York Times*, 15 March 2012, <http://www.nytimes.com/2012/03/16/world/africa/ethiopian-troops-enter-eritrea.html?_r=0>.

[11] Irish Department of Foreign Affairs and Trade, 'Travel advice by country: Ethiopia', 21 February 2013, <http://www.dfa.ie/home/index.aspx?id=8564>.

eight;[12] and in May, tourists travelling in the Omo Valley region were attacked and one of the travellers was injured.[13]

DISPLACED

As of end 2012, the number of displaced persons in Ethiopia was unknown. Conflict-related displacement in the country was caused by localized violence in the regions of Gambella and Benishangul-Gumuz, and by protracted violent conflict in the Oromiya and Somali regions. According to the Internal Displacement Monitoring Centre (IDMC), there were believed to be up to 10,000 displaced persons in Eritrea, all from previous years.[14]

WAR CRIMES ALLEGATIONS, INVESTIGATIONS, AND PROSECUTIONS

Neither state is party to the 1998 Rome Statute of the International Criminal Court (the ICC Statute). Eritrea has signed, but not ratified, the ICC Statute. The ICC may not exercise jurisdiction over war crimes alleged to have been committed by its nationals on its territory unless the situation is referred to the Court by the UN Security Council. No allegations of war crimes are known to have been made against either Eritrean or Ethiopian military personnel regarding any acts concerning the occupation in 2012.

[12] 'Ethiopia—19 shot dead in bus attack', *News24*, 13 March 2012, <http://www.news24.com/Africa/News/Ethiopia-19-shot-dead-in-bus-attack-20120313>.

[13] Irish Department of Foreign Affairs and Trade, 'Travel advice by country: Ethiopia', 21 February 2013. These casualties have not been included in the casualty statistics above, since the relation to armed conflict is not clear.

[14] IDMC, 'Global overview 2012', April 2013, pp. 18 and 24.

Military occupation of Georgia by Russia in 2012

KEY CONFLICT STATISTICS FOR 2012

Civilian deaths:	1	(Source: US Department of State)
Georgian military deaths:	0	
Georgian military injured:	0	
Russian military deaths:	0	
Russian military injured:	0	
Civilians displaced:	280,000	(Source: IDMC)

CLASSIFICATION OF THE CONFLICT

Georgia and the Russian Federation were engaged in an international armed conflict (IAC) in 2012 by virtue of Russia's continued military occupation of Georgian territory. The law of military occupation continues to apply in any areas in Georgia in which the Russian forces exercise authority (see Article 42, 1907 Hague Regulations). This is believed to include Abkhazia, as well as South Ossetia. Several thousand Russian troops are stationed in both break-away entities.

SUMMARY OF APPLICABLE INTERNATIONAL LAW

Both parties to the conflict were bound by customary and conventional international humanitarian law (IHL) and human rights law, including: the customary IHL rules of distinction, proportionality, and precautions in attacks; the obligation not to recruit and use children as soldiers; and the duty to respect and protect fundamental human rights. This includes the duty to respect the rights to life and to freedom from torture or other forms of cruel, inhuman, or degrading treatment or punishment.

The law of military occupation is set out in the 1907 Hague Regulations (Articles 42–56), the 1949 Geneva Convention IV, the 1977 Additional Protocol I, and customary international law. Both states are party to the four 1949 Geneva Conventions and to the 1977 Additional Protocol I, Georgia having adhered to the Protocol in September 1993 and Russia having adhered to it in September 1989.

The underpinning of the law of military occupation is that it is a temporary situation, which lasts until a political agreement is reached. During this period, the occupying power does not enjoy sovereign rights over the territories it occupies and local law that was applicable prior to the occupation remains in force. At the same time, the occupying power is responsible for administering the local life of the population under its control, maintaining it as it was prior to the occupation as closely as possible, and for providing security (Article 43 of the Hague Regulations).

In addition, international human rights law (IHRL) is binding on Russia extraterritorially in territory it occupies within Georgia.[1] In December 2011, the European Court of Human Rights (ECtHR) declared admissible a case brought by Georgia against Russia, arising out of the 2008 armed conflict between Georgia and Russia.[2] In the words of the Court:

> The applicant Government submitted that, in the course of indiscriminate and disproportionate attacks by Russian forces and/or by the separatist forces under their control, hundreds of civilians were injured, killed, detained or went missing, thousands of civilians had their property and homes destroyed and over 300,000 people were forced to leave Abkhazia and South Ossetia.

As of writing, the Court had not yet adjudicated on the merits of the case.

Neither state is party to the 1997 Anti-Personnel Mine Ban Convention (APMBC) or the 2008 Convention on Cluster Munitions (CCM).

HISTORY OF THE CONFLICT[3]

In 1991–92, South Ossetian and Abkhazian armed groups fought to break away from Georgia. Both regions have close ties with Moscow. On 14 May 1994, the parties signed in Moscow the Agreement on a Cease-fire and Separation of Forces, agreeing to the deployment of a peacekeeping force from the Commonwealth of Independent States (CIS) composed mainly of Russian troops. The Georgian parliament has demanded that the Russian peacekeepers in both regions be replaced by an international force.

Over the years, sporadic clashes have continued and the achievement of a comprehensive political settlement, including a settlement on the future political status of Abkhazia and South Ossetia and the return of refugees and displaced persons, remained impossible. On 7 August 2008, hostilities broke out between Georgia and South Ossetia, which led to a major Russian military intervention.

---

[1] See e.g. International Court of Justice (ICJ), *Wall* Advisory Opinion, 2004, §106. As ruled by the European Court of Human Rights (ECtHR), the obligation to secure in occupied territories the rights and freedoms set out in the 1950 European Convention on Human Rights (ECHR) derives from its effective control over occupied territory, whether it is exercised by the occupying state directly, through its armed forces, or through a subordinate local administration. See ECtHR, *Cyprus v. Turkey*, Judgment (App. No. 25781/94), 10 May 2001, §77.

[2] ECtHR, *Georgia v. Russia, No. 2*, Decision on Admissibility (App. No. 38263/08), 19 December 2011.

[3] This section is based on 'Georgia profile', *BBC*, 2 October 2012, <http://www.bbc.co.uk/news/world-europe-17301647>.

On 8 August 2008, after heavy fighting between Georgian and South Ossetian forces, Russian troops entered South Ossetia, claiming the need to protect Russian citizens and supporting the separatist movement (a considerable number of South Ossetians hold Russian nationality). The intervention involved Russian troops moving beyond South Ossetian boundaries and launching strikes near the Georgian capital. On 9 August 2008, the Georgian parliament approved a presidential decree declaring a 'state of war'.[4]

On 12 August 2008, a cease-fire, 'the six-point plan', was negotiated by the European Union (EU). However, it was not fully respected and did not achieve a complete withdrawal of Russian forces, which continued to occupy parts of Georgia. According to the International Crisis Group (ICG), as of mid-2011, Moscow was maintaining 7,000 to 9,000 combat, security, and border forces in those two territories, and was building and refurbishing permanent military bases there, in violation of the cease-fire.[5] South Ossetia remains dependent on Russian aid, both monetary and military.

In the aftermath of the 2008 conflict, South Ossetia and Abkhazia declared independence from Georgia, which was recognized only by Russia and a few other countries. This recognition was strongly condemned by the EU, the United States of America (USA), and the Organization for Security and Co-operation in Europe (OSCE). The North Atlantic Treaty Organization (NATO) continues to support Georgia's territorial integrity and sovereignty within its internationally recognized borders, and to call on Russia to reverse its decision to recognize the independence of the two break-away regions. Moreover, NATO does not recognize elections that took place in South Ossetia in 2009 and Abkhazia in 2011.

The 16-year-old United Nations Observer Mission in Georgia (UNOMIG), entrusted with overseeing the cease-fire accord between the government and Abkhaz separatists in the country's north-western region, terminated its mandate, effective of 30 June 2009, following Russia's Security Council veto of the extension of the Mission's presence. The mandate of the OSCE Mission to Georgia active in the region since 1992 likewise expired on 30 June 2009 as a result of failure of the OSCE's 56 participating states to reach consensus on extending the Mission's mandate.

In October 2011, Russian President Dmitry Medvedev ratified agreements concluded the previous year with Abkhazia and South Ossetia, under which Moscow would set up military bases in the break-away republics. The treaties allow Russia to operate military bases in Abkhazia and South Ossetia for an initial term of 49 years, with possible extensions for an additional 15 years.[6]

---

[4] See generally the report of the Independent International Fact-Finding Mission on the Conflict in Georgia (IIFFMCG—CEIIG), mandated by the Council of the European Union, <http://www.ceiig.ch/Report.html>.

[5] ICG, 'Georgia–Russia: learn to live like neighbours', Europe Briefing No. 658, August 2011, Overview, <http://www.crisisgroup.org/en/regions/europe/south-caucasus/georgia/B065-georgia-russia-learn-to-live-like-neighbours.aspx>.

[6] 'Medvedev ratifies Abkhazia, S. Ossetia military base deployment', *RIA Novosti*, Moscow, 6 October 2011, <http://en.rian.ru/military_news/20111006/167440872.html>.

In September 2012, two senior South Ossetian politicians accused Georgia of engaging in a new military build-up that they feared presaged an attack on their break-away region. The European Union Monitoring Mission (EUMM) released a statement a few days later saying it 'has not observed any evidence to support those claims'. At the same time, the EUMM said it had registered, and conveyed to the Russian authorities its concern about, a concentration of Russian forces along the 'administrative boundary line' separating South Ossetia from the rest of Georgia.[7] On 21 September, Georgia's Ministry of Foreign Affairs issued a statement expressing concern at the deployment 'in recent weeks' of Russian troops and armour along the administrative boundary line. It called on international organizations and Georgia's foreign partners to convey to the Russian leadership that such an 'aggressive posture' is unacceptable.

PARTIES TO THE CONFLICT

The parties to the conflict are Georgia and the Russian Federation, as well as Abkhaz and South Ossetian military forces.

CASUALTIES

The US Department of State reported that although a cease-fire remained in effect in South Ossetia in 2012, violent incidents occurred. No details of conflict casualties were reported. However, a landmine in the South Ossetia reportedly killed a local man in November.[8]

DISPLACED

Most internally displaced persons (IDPs) in Georgia were displaced as a result of conflict in Abkhazia and South Ossetia in the early 1990s, or by renewed conflict over South Ossetia between Georgia and the Russian Federation in 2008. According to the Internal Displacement Monitoring Centre (IDMC), there were reported to be up to 280,000 IDPs in Georgia as of end 2012 and another estimated 10,000 IDPs in South Ossetia from conflict periods.[9]

---

[7] Liz Fuller, 'Georgia, South Ossetia both claim preparations for new hostilities', Caucasus Report, *Radio Free Europe*, 21 September 2012, <http://www.rferl.org/content/georgia-south-ossetia-trade-accusations-of-preparing-for-war/24716583.html>.

[8] US Department of State, 'Country reports on human rights practices 2012: Georgia', 19 April 2013.

[9] IDMC, 'Global overview 2012', April 2013, p. 46.

WAR CRIMES ALLEGATIONS, INVESTIGATIONS, AND PROSECUTIONS

Georgia is party to the 1998 Rome Statute of the International Criminal Court (the ICC Statute), having adhered in September 2003. Russia has signed, but not ratified, the ICC Statute. In accordance with the ICC Statute, the Court may exercise jurisdiction over war crimes alleged to have been committed by Georgian nationals or on its territory. No allegations of war crimes are known to have been made against either Georgian or Russian military personnel regarding any acts concerning the military occupation in 2012.

Military occupation of Lebanon by Israel in 2012

KEY CONFLICT STATISTICS FOR 2012

Total reported killed: 0
Total reported injured: 0
Civilians displaced: Unknown

CLASSIFICATION OF THE CONFLICT

Israel and Lebanon were engaged in an international armed conflict (IAC) in 2012 by virtue of Israel's continued military occupation of Lebanese territory, namely the Shebaa Farms area.

SUMMARY OF APPLICABLE INTERNATIONAL LAW

Both parties to the conflict were bound by customary and conventional international humanitarian law (IHL) and human rights law, including: the customary IHL rules of distinction, proportionality, and precautions in attacks; the obligation not to recruit and use children as soldiers; and the duty to respect and protect fundamental human rights. This includes the duty to respect the rights to life and to freedom from torture or other forms of cruel, inhuman, or degrading treatment or punishment.

The law of military occupation is set out in the 1907 Hague Regulations (Articles 42–56), the 1949 Geneva Convention IV, the 1977 Additional Protocol I, and customary international law. Both states are party to the four 1949 Geneva Conventions, but only Lebanon is party to the 1977 Additional Protocol I, having acceded in July 1997.

The underpinning of the law of military occupation is that it is a temporary situation, which lasts until a political agreement is reached. During this period, the occupying power does not enjoy sovereign rights over the territories it occupies and local law that was applicable prior to the occupation remains in force. At the same time, the occupying power is responsible for administering the local life of the population under its control, maintaining it as it was prior to the occupation as closely as possible, and for providing security (Article 43 of the Hague Regulations).

Lebanon is bound domestically by customary and conventional international human rights law (IHRL). In addition, IHRL is binding on Israel extraterritorially in territory it occupies within Lebanon.[1]

Neither state is party to the 1997 Anti-Personnel Mine Ban Convention (APMBC) or the 2008 Convention on Cluster Munitions (CCM).

HISTORY OF THE CONFLICT

Shebaa Farms is a roughly 8-square-mile area of disputed land in southern Lebanon[2] that has been occupied by Israel since the 1967 Arab–Israeli war.[3] In addition to its military strategic value,[4] the area is said to be important because of the water it provides.[5] In 2001, the Arab League declared that:

The leaders affirm their support for Lebanon for the complete liberation of its territory from Israeli occupation up to the internationally recognized boundaries, including the Shab'a farmlands.[6]

In 2005, the Secretary-General of the United Nations (UN) reported to the UN Security Council as follows:

The United Nations has made abundantly clear that no violations of the Blue Line are acceptable. The continually asserted position of the Government of Lebanon that the Blue Line is not valid in the Shab'a farms area is not compatible with Security Council resolutions. The Council has recognized the Blue Line as valid for purposes of confirming Israel's withdrawal pursuant to resolution 425 (1978). The Government of Lebanon should heed the Council's repeated calls for the parties to respect the Blue Line in its entirety.[7]

---

[1] See e.g. International Court of Justice (ICJ), *Wall* Advisory Opinion, 2004, §106; ICJ, *Armed Activities on the Territory of the Congo* (*Democratic Republic of the Congo v. Uganda*), Judgment, 19 December 2005.

[2] It has also sometimes been asserted that the area falls within Syrian territory.

[3] For an academic review of the history of the area, see e.g. Asher Kaufman, 'Understanding the Shebaa Farms dispute: roots of the anomaly and prospects for resolution', *Palestine-Israel Journal of Politics, Economics and Culture*, 11(1) (2004), <http://www.pij.org/details.php?id=9>.

[4] See e.g. Yaniv Berman (Media Line), 'Shebaa Farms—nub of conflict', *Ynetnews.com*, 8 October 2006, <http://www.ynetnews.com/articles/0,7340,L-3289532,00.html>.

[5] 'Analysis: Shebaa Farms key to Levant hydro-diplomacy', *IRIN*, Beirut, 10 September 2009, <http://www.irinnews.org/Report/86092/Analysis-Shebaa-Farms-key-to-Levant-hydro-diplomacy>.

[6] Final communiqué of the Thirteenth Arab Summit Conference, Amman, Hashemite Kingdom of Jordan, 27 and 28 March 2001, §20, in 'Letter dated 6 April 2001 from the Permanent Representative of Jordan to the United Nations addressed to the Secretary-General', UN doc. A/55/892 and S/2001/342, 10 April 2001, <http://web.archive.org/web/20070828174552/http://domino.un.org/unispal.NSF/2ee9468747556b2d85256cf60060d2a6/07cd1234c61b141585256a42004e8df2!OpenDocument>.

[7] 'Report of the Secretary-General on the United Nations Interim Force in Lebanon (for the period from 21 July 2004 to 20 January 2005)', UN doc. S/2005/36, 20 January 2005, §28.

PARTIES TO THE CONFLICT

The parties to the conflict are Israel and Lebanon, as well as, potentially, Hezbollah.

CASUALTIES

No casualties were identified in the occupied Shebaa Farms area in 2012.

DISPLACED

No figures were available for displacement from the occupied Shebaa Farms area for 2012.

WAR CRIMES ALLEGATIONS, INVESTIGATIONS, AND PROSECUTIONS

Neither Israel nor Lebanon is a state party to the 1998 Rome Statute of the International Criminal Court (the ICC Statute). Neither has signed the ICC Statute. No allegations of war crimes are known to have been made against either Israeli or Lebanese military personnel regarding any acts concerning the Shebaa Farms area in 2012.

Military occupation of Moldova by Russia in 2012

KEY CONFLICT STATISTICS FOR 2012

Civilian deaths: 1   (Source: Media reports)
Civilians displaced: Unknown

CLASSIFICATION OF THE CONFLICT

Moldova and the Russian Federation were engaged in an international armed conflict (IAC) in 2012 by virtue of Russia's continued military occupation of Moldovan territory, namely Transdniestria.

SUMMARY OF APPLICABLE INTERNATIONAL LAW

Both parties to the conflict were bound by customary and conventional international humanitarian law (IHL) and human rights law, including: the customary IHL rules of distinction, proportionality, and precautions in attacks; the obligation not to recruit and use children as soldiers; and the duty to respect and protect fundamental human rights. This includes the duty to respect the rights to life and to freedom from torture or other forms of cruel, inhuman, or degrading treatment or punishment.

The law of military occupation is set out in the 1907 Hague Regulations (Articles 42–56), the 1949 Geneva Convention IV, the 1977 Additional Protocol I, and customary international law. Both states are party to the four 1949 Geneva Conventions and to the 1977 Additional Protocol I, Moldova having adhered in May 1993 and Russia having adhered in September 1989.

The underpinning of the law of military occupation is that it is a temporary situation, which lasts until a political agreement is reached. During this period, the occupying power does not enjoy sovereign rights over the territories it occupies and local law that was applicable prior to the occupation remains in force. At the same time, the occupying power is responsible for administering the local life of the population under its control, maintaining it as it was prior to the occupation as closely as possible, and for providing security (Article 43 of the Hague Regulations).

The law of military occupation continues to apply in any areas in Moldova in which the Russian forces exercise authority (see Article 42, 1907 Hague Regulations). Some

2,500 Russian troops are believed to be stationed in the break-away entity of Transdniestria.[1]

In addition, international human rights law (IHRL) is binding on Russia extraterritorially in territory it occupies within Moldova.[2]

Moldova is party to the 1997 Anti-Personnel Mine Ban Convention (APMBC) and to the 2008 Convention on Cluster Munitions (CCM), but Russia is party to neither instrument.

HISTORY OF THE CONFLICT

The Republic of Moldova (Moldova) gained independence in 1991, in the aftermath of the collapse of the Soviet Union. The region east of the Dniester (also known as Transdniester, or Transnistria) had enjoyed formal autonomy within Ukraine prior to 1940, but was subsequently combined with the region between the rivers Dniester and Prut, formerly known as Bessarabia, to form the Moldovan Soviet Socialist Republic.[3]

Before Moldova's declaration of independence, Transdniestria, a strip of land between the river Dniester and the border with Ukraine, unilaterally declared its own independence. The move came after alarm over increasing Moldovan nationalism, a possible reunification with Romania, and a 1989 language law proclaiming Moldovan as the official language. A 'Transdniestrian Moldovan Republic' (TMR), or 'Pridnestrovskaya Moldavskaya Respublica' in Russian, was proclaimed in Tiraspol on 2 September 1990. This led to localized combat, in which several hundred people were killed and thousands more displaced.

---

[1] Alexander Tanas, 'Moldova blocks Russian plan to expand presence in rebel enclave', *Reuters*, Chisinau, 17 November 2012, <http://www.reuters.com/article/2012/11/17/moldova-russia-idUSL5E8MH0LT20121117>.

[2] See e.g. International Court of Justice (ICJ), *Wall* Advisory Opinion, 2004, §106. As ruled by the European Court of Human Rights (ECtHR), the obligation to secure in occupied territories the rights and freedoms set out in the 1950 European Convention on Human Rights (ECHR) derives from its effective control over occupied territory, whether it is exercised by the occupying state directly, through its armed forces, or through a subordinate local administration. See ECtHR, *Cyprus v. Turkey*, Judgment (App. No. 25781/94), 10 May 2001, §77.

[3] This section is based on 'Moldova profile', *BBC*, 14 February 2013, <http://www.bbc.co.uk/news/world-europe-17601580>; 'Transdniestrian conflict: Origins and main issues', based on the Background Paper 'The Transdniestrian conflict in Moldova: origins and main issues', Vienna, 10 June 1994, CSCE Conflict Prevention Centre; Ceslav Ciobanu, 'NATO/EU enlargement: Moldova and the "frozen and forgotten" conflicts in post-Soviet states', US Institute of Peace, Washington DC, 22 July 2004; International Crisis Group (ICG), 'Moldova: regional tensions over Transdniestria', Europe Report No. 157, Chisinau, 2004; see also European Parliament resolution on human rights violations in Transnistria and the need for European Union (EU) support for the settlement of the frozen conflict in the Republic of Moldova, Resolution No. B6-0292/2007, 10 July 2007.

The TMR is said to have organized paramilitary 'workers' detachments', on the basis of which a fully armed and professional 'Republican Guard' was created in 1991. On 2 September 1991, Transdniestrian authorities voted to join the Soviet Union. On 28 March 1992, a state of emergency was introduced in Moldova. Fighting continued, however, with the summer of 1992 seeing a peak in armed clashes and victims, particularly in a battle over the city of Tighina/Bendery. Human Rights Watch (HRW) alleged that the Russian 14th Army, stationed on the left bank of the Dniester, directly or indirectly assisted the secessionists.[4]

After peacekeeping within the Commission on Security and Cooperation in Europe (CSCE) or the Commonwealth of Independent States (CIS) frameworks was ruled out, a Moldovan–Russian initiative, signed in Moscow on 21 July 1992, found more success. The agreement called for an immediate cease-fire and the establishment of a demilitarized zone, 10 km to the left and right of the Dniester river. A tripartite Joint Control Commission was to be set up, comprising representatives of Moldova, Russia, and the TMR. Russian peacekeepers were brought in, alongside Moldovan and Transdniestrian ones, to stabilize the region and have remained in place ever since. In 2007, a US proposal for their replacement with an international peacekeeping contingent was rejected by Tiraspol authorities.

While Transdniestria enjoys de facto autonomy, the Republic of Moldova and the international community do not recognize its independence. A September 2006 Transdniestrian referendum, reasserting independence and the wish for adhesion to Russia, went similarly unrecognized. It is frequently referred to as a 'frozen conflict'.

In 2004, the ECtHR concluded that Transdniestria, which was 'set up in 1991–92 with the support of the Russian Federation, vested with organs of power and its own administration, remains under the effective authority, or at the very least under the decisive influence, of the Russian Federation, and in any event that it survives by virtue of the military, economic, financial and political support given to it by the Russian Federation'.[5]

The Moldovan Ministry of Foreign Affairs lodged a formal protest with the Russian ambassador, demanding that Moscow agree to transform the Transdniestria peacekeeping mission into a civil one with an international mandate, after a Russian peacekeeping soldier shot dead a Moldovan man at a checkpoint in the separatist region on 1 January 2012. On 12 January, Moldovan, Transdniestrian, and Russian representatives met to discuss tensions at checkpoints.[6]

---

[4] HRW, 'War or peace? Human rights and Russian military involvement in the "near abroad"', 5(22) (December 1993), <http://www.hrw.org/legacy/reports/1993/russia/>.

[5] ECtHR, *Ilascu and ors v. Moldova and Russia*, Judgment (App. No. 48787/99), 8 July 2004, §392.

[6] ICG, 'Moldova', Crisis Watch Database, 1 February 2012, <http://www.crisisgroup.org/en/publication-type/crisiswatch/crisiswatch-database.aspx?CountryIDs=%7b8DA7B2AE-B336-425A-8A7D-6679D17D511A%7d&StartDate=20120101&EndDate=20130505>.

During 2012, hopes rose for a negotiated settlement to the situation in Transdniestria. On 27 September, the EU lifted a travel ban on the former political leadership of the Transdniestrian region in recognition of progress in negotiations to settle the conflict.[7] In February 2013, talks on Transdniestria took place in Lviv, with representatives from Russia, Ukraine, the United States of America (USA), the EU, and the Organization for Security and Co-operation in Europe (OSCE), as well as Moldova and Transdniestria; the OSCE urged all sides to maintain momentum in negotiations set to continue in May 2013.[8]

PARTIES TO THE CONFLICT

The parties to the conflict are Moldova and the Russian Federation, as well as Transnistrian military forces.

CASUALTIES

On 1 January 2012, Russian peacekeepers shot and killed a teenager as he drove through a checkpoint in Transdniestria.[9]

DISPLACED

The number of displaced persons in Moldova in 2012 was not reported. Previous estimates were 100,000 internally displaced persons (IDPs) or refugees due to the conflict of the 1990s.[10]

---

[7] EU Council, 'Council lifts sanctions to recognize progress in Transnistria negotiations', *Consilium*, 27 September 2012, <http://www.consilium.europa.eu/uedocs/cms_Data/docs/pressdata/EN/foraff/132616.pdf>.

[8] ICG, 'Moldova', Crisis Watch Database, 1 March 2013, <http://www.crisisgroup.org/en/publication-type/crisiswatch/crisiswatch-database.aspx?CountryIDs=%7b8DA7B2AE-B336-425A-8A7D-6679D17D511A%7d&StartDate=20120101&EndDate=20130505>.

[9] 'OSCE is concerned about the tragic incident from Transnistria', *Moldova.org*, 6 January 2012, <http://politicom.moldova.org/news/osce-is-concerned-about-the-tragic-incident-from-transnistria-227604-eng.html>; Ellen Barry, 'Shooting at checkpoint raises tensions in a disputed region claimed by Moldova', *New York Times*, 3 January 2012, <http://www.nytimes.com/2012/01/04/world/europe/shooting-raises-tensions-between-moldova-and-russia.html?_r=1&>.

[10] Marius Vahl and Michael Emerson, 'Moldova and the Transnistrian conflict', in *Europeanization and Conflict Resolution: Case Studies from the Divided Periphery*, Academia Press, Gent, 2004.

WAR CRIMES ALLEGATIONS, INVESTIGATIONS, AND PROSECUTIONS

Moldova is party to the 1998 Rome Statute of the International Criminal Court (the ICC Statute), having adhered in October 2010. Russia has signed, but not ratified, the ICC Statute. In accordance with the ICC Statute, the Court may exercise jurisdiction over war crimes alleged to have been committed by Moldovan nationals or on its territory, including Transdniestria. No allegations of war crimes are known to have been made against Moldovan, Russian, or Transdniestrian military personnel regarding any acts concerning Transdniestria in 2012.

Military occupation of Palestine by Israel in 2012

KEY CONFLICT STATISTICS FOR 2012

Deaths in Palestine (including those participating in hostilities):	266	(Source: OCHA)
Deaths of Palestinian militants/ civilians participating in hostilities:	142	(Source: B'Tselem/OCHA)
Injured in Palestine:	397	(Source: OCHA)
Israeli deaths:	9	(Source: US Department of State)
Israeli injured:	307	(Source: US Department of State)
Civilians displaced:	144,500	(Source: IDMC, 'Global overview', 2012)

CLASSIFICATION OF THE CONFLICT

Israel and Palestine were engaged in an international armed conflict (IAC) in 2012 by virtue of Israel's continued military occupation of Palestinian territory, namely Gaza, East Jerusalem, and parts of the West Bank. Palestine was accorded the status of non-member observer state in the United Nations (UN) by the UN General Assembly on 29 November 2012.[1]

SUMMARY OF APPLICABLE INTERNATIONAL LAW

Both parties to the conflict were bound by customary and conventional international humanitarian law (IHL) and human rights law, including: the customary IHL rules of distinction, proportionality, and precautions in attacks; the obligation not to recruit and use children as soldiers; and the duty to respect and protect fundamental human rights. This includes the duty to respect the rights to life and to freedom from torture or other forms of cruel, inhuman, or degrading treatment or punishment.

The law of military occupation is set out in the 1907 Hague Regulations (Articles 42–56), the 1949 Geneva Convention IV, the 1977 Additional Protocol I, and customary international law. Only Israel is party to the four 1949 Geneva Conventions and neither state is party to the 1977 Additional Protocol I.

The underpinning of the law of military occupation is that it is a temporary situation, which lasts until a political agreement is reached. During this period, the occupying

---

[1] Resolution 67/19 was adopted by 138 votes to 9, with 41 abstentions.

power does not enjoy sovereign rights over the territories it occupies and local law that was applicable prior to the occupation remains in force. At the same time, the occupying power is responsible for administering the local life of the population under its control, maintaining it as it was prior to the occupation as closely as possible, and for providing security (Article 43 of the Hague Regulations).

In addition, international human rights law (IHRL) is binding on Israel extraterritorially in territory within Palestine it occupies.[2]

Neither state is party to the 1997 Anti-Personnel Mine Ban Convention (APMBC) or the 2008 Convention on Cluster Munitions (CCM).

HISTORY OF THE CONFLICT[3]

The Palestinian population of around 10 or 11 million people is divided between historic Palestine and a diaspora, mainly in neighbouring Arab countries. Efforts to create a Palestinian state on the West Bank of the River Jordan and Gaza on the Mediterranean coast have been frustrated by the continuing conflict with Israel and disputes over the status of diaspora Palestinians.

The war that followed Israel's declaration of independence in 1948 saw the former British mandate of Palestine partitioned between Israel, Trans-Jordan, and Egypt. Hundreds of thousands of Palestinians fled or were forced out of their native land during the war, in what they call the *Nakba* ('Catastrophe'). The demand of these refugees and their descendants to return to their former homes remains one of the most fiercely debated aspects of the dispute with Israel.

The Palestinian national movement gradually regrouped in the West Bank and Gaza, run respectively by Jordan and Egypt, and in refugee camps in neighbouring Arab states. The Palestine Liberation Organization (PLO) emerged as its leading umbrella group shortly before the Six-Day War of 1967, during which Israel captured the West Bank, Gaza, and East Jerusalem.

The PLO under Yasser Arafat gradually won international recognition as the representative of the Palestinian people, culminating in the Oslo Accords with Israel in 1993. The Accords established a Palestinian National Authority (PNA—also referred to as the Palestinian Authority, or PA) as an interim body to run parts of Gaza and the West Bank (but not East Jerusalem) pending an agreed solution to the conflict.

The PNA functions as an agency of the PLO, which represents Palestinians at international bodies. It is led by a directly elected president, who appoints a prime

---

[2] See e.g. International Court of Justice (ICJ), *Wall* Advisory Opinion, 2004, §106.

[3] Unless otherwise stated, this section is based on 'Palestinian territories profile', *BBC*, 28 February 2013, <http://www.bbc.co.uk/news/world-middle-east-14630174>.

minister and government, which must have the support of the elected Legislative Council. Its civilian and security writ runs in urban areas (Area A) under the Oslo Accords, with civilian, but not security, control over rural areas (Area B).

The Israeli occupation of the West Bank—with its continuing settlement building and military checkpoints—and Palestinian attacks have slowed progress towards a final agreement and led many on both sides to dispute the worth of the Accords. Israel retains full control over by-pass roads, settlements and the Jordan Valley, and makes incursions into urban areas against armed groups.

In 2005, Israel completed the withdrawal of all its troops and settlers from the Gaza Strip, but it retains control of the airspace, seafront, and access—including deliveries of food and other goods—apart from the crossing with Egypt. The Islamist Hamas movement, which runs Gaza, explicitly rejects the Oslo Accords and its charter calls for Israel's 'nullification'.

PARTIES TO THE CONFLICT

The parties to the IAC are Israel and Palestine. A separate non-international armed conflict (NIAC) broke out in Gaza in mid-November 2012. This NIAC is discussed later in Part II.

CASUALTIES

The UN Office for the Coordination of Humanitarian Affairs (OCHA) recorded 266 Palestinian deaths in 2012 (including 43 children) by the Israeli Defense Forces (IDF) in 'direct conflict'. Most of the deaths occurred in Gaza, with nine in the West Bank.[4] Another 391 Palestinians (including 49 children) and 6 foreigners were recorded as injured by the IDF in 'direct conflict', including 18 in Gaza and 379 in the West Bank. These OCHA figures include casualties during the period of the conflict related to Operation Pillar of Defense in Gaza in November 2012.[5] The US Department of State noted that, as of the end of October 2012, Israeli security forces had killed at least 68 Palestinians in Gaza and a further 7 in the West Bank.[6] In the West Bank, including East

---

[4] Direct conflict includes military operations, targeted killings, search and arrest, demonstrations, and border incidents.

[5] OCHA, 'Protection of civilians: casualties database', <http://www.ochaopt.org/poc.aspx>.

[6] US Department of State, 'Country reports on human rights practices 2012: Israel and the Occupied Territories—the Occupied Territories', 19 April 2013.

Jerusalem, Israeli settlers injured 151 Palestinians as of 27 November 2012, according to Human Rights Watch (HRW).[7]

Through the end of October, B'Tselem, an Israeli non-governmental organization (NGO), recorded 68 Palestinians who allegedly participated in the hostilities and were killed by Israeli security forces (four were said to be children, some of whom were bystanders).[8] The OCHA recorded 74 Palestinian militant deaths in the November conflict.[9]

In Gaza, Hamas's armed wing was reported to have extrajudicially executed seven men for allegedly collaborating with Israel in November. The internal security agency and Hamas police were alleged to have tortured or ill-treated 121 people as of 31 October. In the West Bank, 142 complaints of torture and ill-treatment by West Bank PA security services were reported as of 31 October; allegedly tens of people were tortured on suspicion of either support for Hamas or attacks against the PA.[10]

According to data compiled by the Israel Security Agency (ISA), nine people in Israel were killed and 307 injured by Palestinian rockets and mortar shell attacks during 2012.[11]

DISPLACEMENT

As of end 2012, some 144,500 people were believed to be in protracted displacement across Palestinian territory, some of them since 1967.[12]

WAR CRIMES ALLEGATIONS, INVESTIGATIONS, AND PROSECUTIONS

Neither Israel nor Palestine is a state party to the 1998 Rome Statute of the International Criminal Court (the ICC Statute). Neither has signed the ICC Statute.

---

[7] HRW, 'World report 2013: Israel–Palestine', <http://www.hrw.org/world-report/2013/country-chapters/israel-palestine>. The OCHA recorded 51 Palestinian injured by Israeli settlers in the West Bank: OCHA, 'Protection of civilians: casualties database', <http://www.ochaopt.org/poc.aspx>.

[8] B'Tselem—The Israeli Information Center for Human Rights in the Occupied Territories, <http://www.btselem.org/statistics/fatalities/after-cast-lead/by-date-of-event/gaza/palestinians-who-took-part-in-the-hostilities-and-were-killed-by-israeli-security-forces>. As of 1 May, B'Tselem data for civilians killed who had not taken part in hostilities was updated through September 2012 (77).

[9] Data from OCHA, 24 April 2013. Earlier accounts reported 103 or 101 civilian Palestinian casualties.

[10] Reporting of the Independent Commission for Human Rights (ICHR), a Palestinian human rights body, cited in HRW, 'World Report 2013: Israel–Palestine', <http://www.hrw.org/world-report/2013/country-chapters/israel-palestine>.

[11] US Department of State, 'Country reports on human rights practices 2012: Israel and the Occupied Territories', 19 April 2013.

[12] Internal Displacement Monitoring Centre (IDMC), 'Global overview 2012', April 2013, p. 58.

In addition to any allegations of arbitrary killings or torture, the transfer of populations into or from Palestine is generally considered to be a violation of international law. According to the report of the independent international fact-finding mission to investigate the implications of the Israeli settlements on the civil, political, economic, social, and cultural rights of the Palestinian people throughout the Occupied Palestinian Territory, including East Jerusalem:

A situation of military occupation prevails in the Occupied Palestinian Territory . . . Article 49 of the Fourth Geneva Convention . . . prohibits the occupying Power from transferring parts of its own civilian population into the territory that it occupies. This prohibition has attained the status of customary international law. The mission notes that the Israeli settlements in the Occupied Palestinian Territory, including East Jerusalem, violate this provision and are, thus, illegal under international law.[13] . . . The transfer of Israeli citizens into the Occupied Palestinian Territory, prohibited under international humanitarian law and international criminal law, is a central feature of the practices and policies of Israel.[14]

The mission considered that, with regard to the settlements, Israel is committing 'serious breaches of its obligations under the right to self-determination and certain obligations' under IHL, 'including the obligation not to transfer its population into the Occupied Palestinian Territory'.[15] It noted that the 1998 ICC Statute:

. . . establishes the jurisdiction of the International Criminal Court over the deportation or transfer, directly or indirectly, by the occupying Power of parts of its own population into the territory it occupies, or the deportation or transfer of all or parts of the population of the occupied territory within or outside that territory. Ratification of the Statute by Palestine may lead to accountability for gross violations of human rights law and serious violations of international humanitarian law and justice for victims.[16]

In January 2009, the Palestinian Minister of Justice sent a document to the ICC recognizing the jurisdiction of the Court. This declaration has not yet been accepted.

---

[13] See e.g. ICJ *Wall* Advisory Opinion of 9 July 2004, §120; UN Security Council Resolution 471 (1980); General Assembly Resolutions 3092 (XXVIII), 47/172 and 66/225; Commission on Human Rights Resolution 2000/8; Human Rights Council Resolutions 13/7 and 16/31; Council of the European Union, Conclusions on the Middle East Peace Process, 3166th Foreign Affairs Council Meeting, 14 May 2012.

[14] 'Report of the independent international fact-finding mission to investigate the implications of the Israeli settlements on the civil, political, economic, social and cultural rights of the Palestinian people throughout the Occupied Palestinian Territory, including East Jerusalem', Human Rights Council, UN doc. A/HRC/22/63, 7 February 2013, §§13, 16, and 38.

[15] 'Report of the independent international fact-finding mission', §104.

[16] 'Report of the independent international fact-finding mission', §104.

Military occupation of Syria by Israel in 2012

KEY CONFLICT STATISTICS FOR 2012

Military deaths:	2	(Source: UN)
Military injured:	2	(Source: UN)
Civilians displaced:	450,000 in Syria	(Source: IDMC)

CLASSIFICATION OF THE CONFLICT

Israel and Syria were engaged in an international armed conflict (IAC) in 2012 by virtue of Israel's continued military occupation of Syrian territory, namely the Golan Heights.

SUMMARY OF APPLICABLE INTERNATIONAL LAW

Both parties to the conflict were bound by customary and conventional international humanitarian law (IHL) and human rights law, including: the customary IHL rules of distinction, proportionality, and precautions in attacks; the obligation not to recruit and use children as soldiers; and the duty to respect and protect fundamental human rights. This includes the duty to respect the rights to life and to freedom from torture or other forms of cruel, inhuman, or degrading treatment or punishment.

The law of military occupation is set out in the 1907 Hague Regulations (Articles 42–56), the 1949 Geneva Convention IV, the 1977 Additional Protocol I, and customary international law. Both states are party to the four 1949 Geneva Conventions, but only Syria is party to the 1977 Additional Protocol I, having acceded in November 1993.

The underpinning of the law of military occupation is that it is a temporary situation, which lasts until a political agreement is reached. During this period, the occupying power does not enjoy sovereign rights over the territories it occupies and local law that was applicable prior to the occupation remains in force. At the same time, the occupying power is responsible for administering the local life of the population under its control, maintaining it as it was prior to the occupation as closely as possible, and for providing security (Article 43 of the Hague Regulations).

In addition, international human rights law (IHRL) is binding on Israel extraterritorially in territory it occupies within Syria.[1]

---

[1] See e.g. International Court of Justice (ICJ), *Wall* Advisory Opinion, 2004, §106.

Neither state is party to the 1997 Anti-Personnel Mine Ban Convention (APMBC) or the 2008 Convention on Cluster Munitions (CCM).

HISTORY OF THE CONFLICT[2]

Syria remains in conflict with Israel, which occupies part of the Golan Heights it seized in 1967 in the closing stages of the Six-Day War. Most of the Syrian Arab inhabitants fled the area during the conflict. An armistice line was established and the region came under Israeli military control. Almost immediately Israel began to settle the Golan. Today, there are believed to be 20,000 Israeli settlers and 20,000 Syrians, mostly Druze.

Syria tried to retake the Golan Heights during the 1973 Middle East war. Despite inflicting heavy losses on Israeli forces, the surprise assault was thwarted. Both countries signed an armistice in 1974 and a United Nations Disengagement Observer Force (UNDOF) has been in place on the cease-fire line since 1974. Israel unilaterally annexed the Golan Heights in 1981. The move was not recognized internationally. Lebanon claims the Shebaa Farms area.

Overlooking northern Israel and southern Syria, the Heights give Israel an excellent vantage point for monitoring Syrian movements. The topography provides a natural buffer against any military thrust from Syria. The area is also a key source of water for an arid region. Rainwater from the Golan's catchment feeds into the Jordan River. The area provides a third of Israel's water supply. The land is fertile, with the volcanic soil being used to cultivate vineyards and orchards, and to raise cattle.

Syria wants to secure the return of the Golan Heights as part of any peace deal. During peace talks brokered by the United States of America (USA) in 1999–2000, Israeli Prime Minister Ehud Barak had offered to return most of the Golan to Syria. But the main sticking point during the 1999 talks is also likely to bedevil any future discussions: Syria wants a full Israeli withdrawal to the pre-1967 border. This would give Damascus control of the eastern shore of the Sea of Galilee—Israel's main source of fresh water. Israel wishes to retain control of Galilee and says the border is located a few hundred metres to the east of the shore.

PARTIES TO THE CONFLICT

The parties to the conflict are Israel and Syria.

---

[2] Unless otherwise stated, this section is based on 'Golan Heights profile', *BBC*, 30 August 2011, <http://www.bbc.co.uk/news/world-middle-east-14724842>.

CASUALTIES

On 18 November, Syrian authorities reported that two Syrian soldiers were killed and two others injured by Israeli Defense Forces (IDF) firing across the cease-fire line. The UNDOF confirmed that the IDF had fired missiles across the cease-fire line in the direction of Bir Ajam in the Syrian-controlled part of the Golan Heights. However, due to the security situation, UNDOF was not able to confirm any casualties in the direction of fire.[3]

DISPLACEMENT

In 2012, there were still more than 450,000 internally displaced persons in Syria as a result of the Israeli occupation of the Golan Heights in 1967.[4]

WAR CRIMES ALLEGATIONS, INVESTIGATIONS, AND PROSECUTIONS

Neither Israel nor Syria is a state party to the 1998 Rome Statute of the International Criminal Court (the ICC Statute). Syria is a signatory state to the ICC Statute. No allegations of war crimes are known to have been made against either Israeli or Syrian military personnel regarding any acts concerning the Golan Heights in 2012.

---

[3] 'Report of the Secretary-General on the United Nations Disengagement Observer Force for the period from 1 July to 31 December 2012', UN doc. S/2012/897, 27 November 2012.

[4] Internal Displacement Monitoring Centre (IDMC), 'Global overview 2012', April 2013, p. 59.

Military occupation of Western Sahara by Morocco in 2012

KEY CONFLICT STATISTICS FOR 2012

Total deaths:	3 (Apr. 2012–Apr. 2013)	(Source: UN Secretary-General)
Total injured:	39 (Apr. 2012–Apr. 2013)	(Sources: UN Secretary-General; SAVHRV)
Civilians displaced:	165,000	(Source: UNHCR)

CLASSIFICATION OF THE CONFLICT

Morocco and the Sahrawi Arab Democratic Republic were engaged in an international armed conflict (IAC) in 2012 by virtue of Morocco's continued military occupation of foreign territory, namely Western Sahara. Western Sahara is not universally recognized as a state, although the Sahrawi Arab Democratic Republic has been a member of the African Union since 1984.

SUMMARY OF APPLICABLE INTERNATIONAL LAW

Both parties to the conflict were bound by customary and conventional international humanitarian law (IHL) and human rights law, including: the customary IHL rules of distinction, proportionality, and precautions in attacks; the obligation not to recruit and use children as soldiers; and the duty to respect and protect fundamental human rights. This includes the duty to respect the rights to life and to freedom from torture or other forms of cruel, inhuman, or degrading treatment or punishment.

The law of military occupation is set out in the 1907 Hague Regulations (Articles 42–56), the 1949 Geneva Convention IV, the 1977 Additional Protocol I, and customary international law. Morocco is party to the four 1949 Geneva Conventions and adhered to the 1977 Additional Protocol I in June 2011. The Sahrawi Arab Democratic Republic is party to neither instrument.

The underpinning of the law of military occupation is that it is a temporary situation, which lasts until a political agreement is reached. During this period, the occupying power does not enjoy sovereign rights over the territories it occupies and local law that was applicable prior to the occupation remains in force. At the same time, the occupying power is responsible for administering the local life of the population under its control, maintaining it as it was prior to the occupation as closely as possible, and for providing security (Article 43 of the Hague Regulations).

In addition, international human rights law (IHRL) is binding on Morocco extra-territorially in territory it occupies within Western Sahara.[1]

Neither Morocco nor the Sahrawi Arab Democratic Republic is party to the 1997 Anti-Personnel Mine Ban Convention (APMBC) or the 2008 Convention on Cluster Munitions (CCM).

HISTORY OF THE CONFLICT[2]

The status of the Western Sahara remains unresolved. Morocco annexed the territory in 1975, and a guerrilla war with Algerian-backed pro-independence forces ended in 1991. United Nations (UN) efforts have failed to break the political deadlock. Polisario (Popular Front for the Liberation of Saguia el-Hamra and Río de Oro) was set up on 10 May 1973 and established itself as the sole representative of the Saharan people. Some 100,000 refugees still live in Polisario's camps in Algeria. In February 1976, Polisario declared the establishment of the Sahrawi Arab Democratic Republic. The current President of the Republic, Mohamed Abdelaziz, was elected Secretary-General of Polisario in August 1976.

In October 1975, the ICJ rejected territorial claims by Morocco and Mauritania.[3] The Court recognized the Saharawis' right to self-determination and Spain agreed to organize a referendum. But, in November 1975, Moroccan King Hassan II ordered a 'Green March' of more than 300,000 Moroccans into the territory. Spain backed down and negotiated a settlement with Morocco and Mauritania, known as the Madrid Agreement. Signed on 14 November 1975, the deal partitioned the region. Morocco acquired two-thirds in the north and Mauritania the remaining third. Spain agreed to end colonial rule.

In August 1978, one month after a coup, a new Mauritanian government signed a peace deal with Polisario and renounced all territorial claims. Morocco moved to occupy areas allocated to Mauritania. Algeria in turn allowed refugees to settle in its southern town of Tindouf, where Polisario still has its main base.

In April 1991, the UN established MINURSO, the UN Mission for a Referendum in Western Sahara. Its mandate was to implement a peace plan outlined in a 1990 Security Council resolution. In September 1991, a UN-brokered cease-fire was declared. The peace plan provided for a transition period, leading to a referendum in January 1992.

---

[1] See e.g. International Court of Justice (ICJ), *Wall* Advisory Opinion, 2004, §106.

[2] Unless otherwise stated, this section is based on 'Western Sahara profile', *BBC*, 18 April 2013, <http://www.bbc.co.uk/news/world-africa-14115273>.

[3] ICJ, *Western Sahara*, Advisory Opinion, 16 October 1975, <http://www.icj-cij.org/docket/files/61/6195.pdf>.

Western Saharans would choose between independence and integration with Morocco. While the cease-fire held, the mission was never fully deployed, nor was the transition period ever completed. A key sticking point was an 'identification process' to decide who was eligible to vote. Identification was to be based on a census carried out by Spain in 1973. Polisario wanted to rule out Moroccans who settled in Western Sahara after the Green March.

In a new bid to break the deadlock, UN Envoy James Baker submitted a Framework Agreement, known as the 'Third Way', in June 2001. It provided for autonomy for Saharawis under Moroccan sovereignty, a referendum after a four-year transition period, and voting rights for Moroccan settlers resident in Western Sahara for over a year. This formula was rejected by Polisario and Algeria. Then, in July 2003, the UN adopted a compromise resolution proposing that Western Sahara become a semi-autonomous region of Morocco for a transition period of up to five years. A referendum would then take place on independence, semi-autonomy, or integration with Morocco.

Polisario signalled its readiness to accept, but Morocco rejected the plan, citing security concerns. Envoy James Baker resigned in June 2004 and the UN process remains deadlocked. Talks resumed between Morocco and the Polisario Front in March 2008 in New York, with Mauritania and Algeria also attending. They made no progress. In November 2010, several people were killed in violent clashes between Moroccan security forces and protesters near the capital Laayoune, shortly before UN-mediated talks on the future of the territory were due to open in New York.

On 22 April 2013, a senior official from the Polisario Front warned that failure by the UN to let peacekeepers monitor human rights in Western Sahara could push the region toward armed conflict.[4] A few days later, the UN Security Council adopted Resolution 2099 in which it extended the mandate of MINURSO until 30 April 2014.[5]

PARTIES TO THE CONFLICT

The parties to the conflict are Morocco and the Polisario armed forces.

CASUALTIES

The overall number of casualties in Western Sahara in 2012 was not monitored or reported. The UN Security Council resolution of 2012, which renewed the mandate of

[4] John Irish, 'U.N. failure boosts Western Sahara conflict risk: Polisario', *Reuters*, Paris, 22 April 2013, <http://www.reuters.com/article/2013/04/22/us-france-westernsahara-idUSBRE93L13D20130422>.
[5] UN Security Council Resolution 2099, 25 April 2013, §1.

MINURSO, did not enlarge that mandate to include human rights monitoring.[6] MINURSO did, however, have a mandate to monitor casualties of landmines and explosive remnants of war (ERW). Between April 2012 and April 2013, 33 people were injured and three were killed by landmines and ERW. Two people were injured in the Polisario-controlled territory of Western Sahara, east of the Berm.[7] All other casualties occurred west of the Berm, in Moroccan-controlled territory.[8]

According to the US State Department, 'In contrast with 2011, there were no reports that the [Moroccan] Government or its agents committed arbitrary or unlawful killings' in Western Sahara in 2012.[9] According to the Saharan Association of Victims of Human Rights Violations (SAVHRV), seven Saharawi students were injured by Moroccan forces on 1 October 2012 during a protest in the city of Essmara.[10] Three humanitarian aid workers who were kidnapped from the refugee camps south of Tindouf in October 2011 by the Movement for Oneness and Jihad in West Africa (MOJWA) were released in July 2012.[11]

Although the numbers of such casualties were not reported, the UN Special Rapporteur on torture, following a visit to Western Sahara in September 2012, concluded that there was a pattern of excessive use of force during demonstrations, including kidnapping and abandonment in the desert, and of torture and ill-treatment by police officers and security personnel of alleged or known supporters of the independence of Western Sahara, both outside and inside detention centres.[12]

---

[6] Human Rights Watch (HRW) reported that MINURSO is one of the only peacekeeping operations created since 1990 that has no human rights monitoring component: HRW, 'Annual report 2013: Morocco/Western Sahara', <http://www.hrw.org/world-report/2013/country-chapters/morocco/western-sahara>.

[7] For geographical details of the Berm, see e.g. 'Moroccan wall: the Berm of Western Sahara', *Basement Geographer*, 7 February 2011, <http://basementgeographer.com/moroccan-wall-the-berm-of-western-sahara/>.

[8] Mine/ERW casualty figures for the 2012 calendar year were not available as of 1 May 2013: 'Report of the Secretary-General on the situation concerning Western Sahara', UN Security Council, UN doc. S/2013/220, 8 April 2013, p. 10.

[9] US Department of State, 'Country reports on human rights practices 2012: Morocco', 19 April 2013; 'Country reports on human rights practices 2012: Western Sahara', 19 April 2013. There was one report that a government security official committed an unlawful killing in 2011: US Department of State, 'Country reports on human rights practices 2011: Western Sahara', 24 May 2012.

[10] SAVHRV, 'Violencia contra parados y diplomados saharauis en paro en Smara/Sahara Occidental', ('Violence against Saharawi students during demonstration in Essmara, Western Sahara'), 3 October 2012, <http://asvdh.net/6963>.

[11] 'Report of the Secretary-General on the situation concerning Western Sahara', UN Security Council, UN doc. S/2013/220, 8 April 2013, p. 11.

[12] 'Report of the Secretary-General on the situation concerning Western Sahara', p. 17.

DISPLACEMENT

The total number of Saharawis displaced by the Moroccan occupation of Western Sahara is unknown.[13] The government of Algeria estimated that 165,000 Sahrawis were living in refugee camps on Algerian territory in 2012.[14]

WAR CRIMES ALLEGATIONS, INVESTIGATIONS, AND PROSECUTIONS

Neither Morocco nor the Sahrawi Arab Democratic Republic is a state party to the 1998 Rome Statute of the International Criminal Court (the ICC Statute). Morocco has signed the ICC Statute.

---

[13] Internal Displacement Monitoring Centre (IDMC), 'Global overview 2012', April 2013, p. 55.

[14] United Nations High Commissioner for Refugees (UNHCR), 'Global appeal 2013 update: populations of concern to UNHCR', Data as of January 2012, <http://www.unhcr.org/50a9f81b27.html>.

Armed conflict in Afghanistan in 2012

KEY CONFLICT STATISTICS FOR 2012

Civilian deaths:	2,754	(Source: UNAMA)
Civilian injured:	4,805	(Source: UNAMA)
Civilian female deaths:	301 (includes girls)	(Source: UNAMA)
Civilian female injured:	563 (includes girls)	(Source: UNAMA)
Civilian child deaths:	488	(Source: UNAMA)
Civilian child injured:	814	(Source: UNAMA)
Afghan military deaths:	3,400+ soldiers and police	(Source: Brookings)
Afghan military injured:	327 (incomplete, Jan.–Jun.)	(Source: US Congressional Research Service)
ISAF military deaths:	402	(Source: iCasualties.org)
US military female deaths:	8	(Source: US Military)
US military injured:	2,447 (Jan.–Sep.)	(Source: iCasualties.org)
Civilians displaced:	492,000+	(Source: IDMC)

CLASSIFICATION OF THE CONFLICTS

Afghanistan is involved in an armed conflict of a non-international character (NIAC) in which the armed forces of the government of Afghanistan and a coalition of states operating under the umbrella of the North Atlantic Treaty Organization (NATO)-led International Security Assistance Force (ISAF)[1] are fighting against the 'Quetta Shura' Taliban.[2]

There are also arguably separate NIACs against other non-state armed groups, particularly the Haqqani Network[3] and Hezb-e-Islami, although the *War Report* is not

---

[1] United Nations Mission in Afghanistan (UNAMA), 'Afghanistan, mid-year report 2012, protection of civilians in armed conflict', Kabul, July 2012, p. ii.

[2] The term 'Quetta Shura' is a composite taken from the name of the town in Pakistan to which Mullah Omar relocated in 2001 and the Supreme Shura that governed Afghanistan in the early 1990s. See e.g. Jeffrey Dressler and Carl Forsberg, 'The Quetta Shura Taliban in Southern Afghanistan', Backgrounder, Institute for the Study of War, September 2009, p. 1, <http://www.understandingwar.org/report/quetta-shura-taliban-southern-afghanistan>.

[3] The extent to which the Haqqani Network is a separate armed group from the Taliban is a matter of dispute. In September 2012, the US Secretary of State, Hillary Clinton, declared that the USA had listed the Haqqani Network to be a foreign terrorist organization: 'U.S. designates Haqqani Network a terrorist group', *Reuters*, 8 September 2012, <http://www.reuters.com/article/2012/09/08/us-usa-security-haqqani-idUSBRE88606I20120908>. The Taliban subsequently issued a statement that there is no separate entity or network in Afghanistan by the name of Haqqani, claiming that Jalaluddin Haqqani, the head of the Haqqani Network, was a member of the Quetta Shura, the Taliban's leadership council. See e.g. Bill Roggio, 'Taliban call Haqqani Network a "conjured entity"', *The Long War Journal*, 9 September

certain that direct combat between each of these groups and the Afghan government forces and/or ISAF is of sufficient frequency and intensity to amount to an NIAC. The position of the UNAMA is, however, that:

[T]he armed conflict in Afghanistan is a non-international armed conflict between the Government of Afghanistan and its armed forces supported by international military forces... and non-State armed groups... including the Taliban, Haqqani Network, Hezb-e-Islami and others... [4]

SUMMARY OF APPLICABLE INTERNATIONAL LAW

All parties to the conflict are bound by, inter alia: Common Article 3 to the 1949 Geneva Conventions; the customary international humanitarian law (IHL) rules of distinction, proportionality, and precautions in attacks; the obligation not to recruit and use children as soldiers; and the duty to respect, at a minimum, fundamental human rights. This includes the duty to respect the rights to life and to freedom from torture or other forms of cruel, inhuman, or degrading treatment or punishment.[5]

Afghanistan acceded to the 1997 Anti-Personnel Mine Ban Convention (APMBC) on 11 September 2002, becoming a state party on 1 March 2003, and to the 2008 Convention on Cluster Munitions (CCM) on 8 September 2011, becoming a state party on 1 March 2012. Most of the members of ISAF, apart from the United States of America (USA), are also party to the APMBC and several are party to the CCM.

In addition, all states parties to the 1977 Additional Protocol II operating militarily in Afghanistan—not merely Afghanistan itself—are bound by that instrument in the NIAC

2012,   <http://www.longwarjournal.org/archives/2012/09/taliban_call_haqqani.php#ixzz2RwasSJN5>. Dressler argues, however, that the Haqqanis 'do not fully follow the guidance of the Quetta Shura Taliban, because they maintain a separate power base and leadership structure': Jeffrey A. Dressler, 'The Haqqani Network: a strategic threat', Afghanistan Report No. 9, Institute for the Study of War, March 2012, p. 8, <http://www.understandingwar.org/sites/default/files/Haqqani_StrategicThreatweb_29MAR_0.pdf>.

[4] UNAMA, 'Afghanistan, mid-year report 2012, protection of civilians in armed conflict', Kabul, July 2012, p. ii.

[5] According to UNAMA:

While non-State actors in Afghanistan, including non-State armed groups, cannot formally become parties to international human rights treaties, international human rights law increasingly recognizes that where non-State actors, such as the Taliban, exercise *de facto* control over territory, they are bound by international human rights obligations.

UNAMA, 'Afghanistan, annual report 2011, protection of civilians in armed conflict', Kabul, February 2012, p. iv, citing United Nations (UN) Secretary-General, 'Report of the Secretary-General's panel of experts on accountability in Sri Lanka', 31 March 2011, para. 188, and 'Report of the International Commission of Inquiry to investigate all alleged violations of international human rights law in the Libyan Arab Jamahiriya', UN doc. A/HRC/17/44, 1 June 2011. See similarly UNAMA, 'Afghanistan, mid-year report 2012, protection of civilians in armed conflict', Kabul, July 2012, p. iii.

with the Quetta Shura Taliban,[6] as are the Quetta Shura Taliban themselves. Afghanistan is bound as a state party to the two 1966 Covenants (on civil and political rights, and on economic, social and cultural rights, while other states parties to the two 1966 Covenants operating militarily in Afghanistan are bound extraterritorially.[7]

HISTORY OF THE CONFLICT[8]

Afghanistan has been engulfed in almost perpetual conflict since the Soviet invasion in 1979. The ongoing NIAC has now been raging for more than ten years.

Emerging as a force in the 1990s, the Taliban—originally a group of Islamic scholars drawn from the largest ethnic group in Afghanistan, the Pashtuns—had control of about 90 per cent of the country until late 2001, although the Taliban were recognized as the legitimate government of 'the Islamic Emirate of Afghanistan' by only three states (Pakistan, Saudi Arabia, and the United Arab Emirates). Following the attacks by al-Qaeda on the USA on 11 September 2001, which were masterminded by Osama Bin

---

[6] Afghanistan ratified the 1977 Additional Protocol II in 2009. In addition to binding Afghanistan, the Protocol is also arguably applicable to each ISAF member state that has adhered to the Protocol and which is a party to the conflict with the Taliban. This is because the 1977 Additional Protocol II applies to 'all armed conflicts' that are not covered by Art. 1 of the 1977 Additional Protocol I and which take place 'in the territory of' a state party 'between its armed forces and dissident armed forces or other organized armed groups which, under responsible command, exercise such control over a part of its territory as to enable them to carry out sustained and concerted military operations and to implement this Protocol'. This applies the provisions of the Protocol to the relevant armed conflict as a whole, not merely to the armed forces of the state on whose territory the conflict is ongoing, as well as the dissident armed forces or other organized armed groups fighting against those government armed forces. The USA is not a state party to the Protocol. Of course, the provisions of the Protocol that are reflected in customary law are binding on all states.

[7] The USA has previously contested the application of the 1966 International Covenant on Civil and Political Rights extraterritorially, based on its reading of Art. 2(1) of the Covenant as requiring both domestic presence of any given person within US territory *and* US jurisdiction over that person. In December 2011, however, in its fourth periodic report to the Human Rights Committee, the USA stated that:

The United States is mindful that in General Comment 31 (2004) the Committee presented the view that 'States Parties are required by article 2, paragraph 1, to respect and to ensure the Covenant rights to all persons who may be within their territory and to all persons subject to their jurisdiction. This means that a State party must respect and ensure the rights laid down in the Covenant to anyone within the power or effective control of that State Party, even if not situated within the territory of the State Party.' The United States is also aware of the jurisprudence of the International Court of Justice ('ICJ'), which has found the ICCPR 'applicable in respect of acts done by a State in the exercise of its jurisdiction outside its own territory,' as well as positions taken by other States Parties.

'Fourth Periodic Report of the United States of America to the United Nations Committee on Human Rights Concerning the International Covenant on Civil and Political Rights', 30 December 2011, §506, <http://www.state.gov/j/drl/rls/179781.htm>.

[8] Unless otherwise stated, this section is based on 'Afghanistan country profile', *BBC*, Updated 12 September 2012, <http://www.bbc.co.uk/news/world-south-asia-12011352>.

Laden from Afghanistan, the Taliban refused US demands that they hand over Bin Laden. This led to the USA initiating an aerial bombing campaign in October 2001, enabling opposition groups to drive the Taliban from power. But since the fall of the regime in 2001, Taliban and other *Mujahedeen* fighters have regrouped into a number of different armed groups (*see section 'Major non-state armed groups'*). The Taliban are conducting a widespread insurgency, particularly in the south and east of the country, while the Afghan government has struggled to extend its effective authority beyond the capital.[9]

The conflict has seen continued use of Coalition airpower, including armed drone strikes, against suspected Taliban and other fighters not only in Afghanistan, but also in neighbouring Pakistan. Taliban and other armed groups have made widespread use of improvised explosive devices (IEDs), which have inflicted a heavy toll on foreign Coalition troops (some 40 per cent of all hostile fatalities in 2012), but an even heavier toll among the civilian population. UNAMA's report for 2012 stated as follows:

Indiscriminate and unlawful use of improvised explosive devices (IEDs) by Anti-Government Elements [UNAMA's term for non-state armed groups] remained the biggest killers of civilians in 2012 and accounts for the majority of civilian casualties.[10]

Civilian casualties resulting from targeted killings by non-state armed groups increased by 53 per cent in the first six months of 2012 compared to the same period in 2011: 'Between 1 January and 30 June 2012, UNAMA documented the death of 255 civilians and wounding of 101 others in 237 separate incidents of targeted killings or attempts, compared with 190 civilian deaths and 43 injuries during the same period in 2011.'[11] UNAMA noted that non-state armed groups have continued to target community leaders, governmental authorities, and civilians that they suspect of supporting the government or military forces.[12]

UNAMA noted that, in late 2011, ISAF Commander General John R. Allen had issued two public tactical directives that concerned civilian casualties (30 November) and the conduct of night search operations (1 December), and that since then there has been a reduction in civilian casualties in all tactics used by government and allied forces. 'This is particularly evident in search operations which remain a core tactic used by military

---

[9] See e.g. International Crisis Group (ICG), 'Afghanistan: the long, hard road to the 2014 transition', Asia Report No. 236, 8 October 2012, p. 16, <http://www.crisisgroup.org/en/regions/asia/south-asia/afghanistan .aspx>.

[10] UNAMA, 'Afghanistan, report 2012, protection of civilians in armed conflict', Kabul, February 2013, pp. 17–18.

[11] UNAMA, 'Afghanistan, mid-year report 2012, protection of civilians in armed conflict', Kabul, July 2012, p. 3.

[12] UNAMA, 'Afghanistan, mid-year report 2012, protection of civilians in armed conflict'; UNAMA, 'Afghanistan, report 2012, protection of civilians in armed conflict', Kabul, February 2013, p. 24.

forces yet the numbers of civilian casualties from such operations continue to decrease.'[13]

Also in 2012, the eleventh year of the conflict, NATO backed plans to hand over combat duties to Afghan forces by mid-2013. Some 130,000 NATO-led combat troops are scheduled to leave Afghanistan by December 2014. Meanwhile, tentative steps towards a negotiated peace agreement were made in early 2012, when the Taliban announced plans to open an office in Qatar for talks with US officials. In October 2012, however, the ICG cautioned that: 'Plagued by factionalism and corruption, Afghanistan is far from ready to assume responsibility for security when U.S. and NATO forces withdraw in 2014.'[14]

PARTIES TO THE CONFLICT

Afghan forces

As of March 2013, the strength of the Afghan National Army (ANA) was reported to stand at 175,000, while the Afghan National Police (ANP) numbered 107,000.[15] The totals were significantly below Coalition projections, while the attrition rate was extremely high, with more than 5,000 soldiers quitting every month. In addition, three of every ten new soldiers recruited into the ANA are lost because they are sacked, captured, or killed in action, threatening the force's long-term effectiveness.[16] According to *The Independent* newspaper, the ANP was considered by the United Kingdom (UK) Foreign and Commonwealth Office (FCO) to be 'endemically corrupt' and riven with problems, including nepotism and drug abuse.[17] A confidential FCO report obtained by the British newspaper on the performance of the Afghan Uniform Police (AUP), the nation's major law enforcement body, observed in October: 'Unless radical change is introduced to improve the actual and perceived integrity and legitimacy of officers within the AUP, then the organisation will continue to provide an ineffective and tainted service to citizens . . . for decades to come.'[18]

---

[13] UNAMA, 'Afghanistan, mid-year report 2012, protection of civilians in armed conflict', Kabul, July 2012, p. 36.

[14] ICG, 'Afghanistan: the long, hard road to the 2014 transition', Executive Summary.

[15] Brian Brady and Jonathan Owen, 'Nato alarm over Afghan army crisis: loss of recruits threatens security as handover looms', *The Independent*, 31 March 2013, <http://www.independent.co.uk/news/world/asia/nato-alarm-over-afghan-army-crisis-loss-of-recruits-threatens-security-as-handover-looms-8555238.html>.

[16] Brady and Owen, 'Nato alarm over Afghan army crisis'.

[17] Brian Brady, 'Taliban preys on Afghanistan's corrupt police force', *The Independent*, 23 December 2012, <http://www.independent.co.uk/news/world/asia/taliban-preys-on-afghanistans-corrupt-police-force-8430111.html>.

[18] Brady, 'Taliban preys on Afghanistan's corrupt police force'.

ISAF

As of December 2012, some 102,000 NATO troops from 50 contributing nations were serving in ISAF in Afghanistan.[19] Of these, the bulk—about 68,000—was composed of US troops. ISAF was created following the Bonn Conference in December 2001. On 11 August 2003, NATO assumed leadership of the ISAF operation, ending the six-month national rotations. The Alliance became responsible for the command, coordination, and planning of the force, including the provision of a force commander and headquarters on the ground in Afghanistan. ISAF's mandate was initially limited to providing security in and around Kabul. In October 2003, the UN extended ISAF's mandate to cover the whole of Afghanistan (UN Security Council Resolution 1510), paving the way for an expansion of the mission across the country. In 2012, the eleventh year of the conflict, NATO backed plans to hand over combat duties to Afghan forces by mid-2013. Some 130,000 NATO-led combat troops will leave Afghanistan by December 2014.

The Taliban

The largest non-state armed group fighting against the Afghan regime, the Taliban in Afghanistan (Quetta Shura Taliban) are still believed to be led by Mullah Omar, a village clergyman who lost his right eye fighting Soviet forces in the 1980s. The Taliban are thought by some to be only about 20,000 strong. But it has become increasingly clear to NATO that it cannot defeat the insurgents, and many areas of the country are under their de facto control. Indeed, a shadow Taliban administration is in place in many areas that is sometimes considered more responsive and certainly less corrupt than official structures.[20]

The Haqqani Network

A former anti-Soviet group in the 1980s and led by one of the most prominent families in Afghanistan's Khost, the Haqqani Network commands far fewer fighters than the

---

[19] ISAF, 'International Security Assistance Force (ISAF): key facts and figures', 3 December 2012, <http://www.nato.int/isaf/docu/epub/pdf/placemat.pdf>. The 50 states included Albania, Armenia, Australia, Austria, Azerbaijan, Bahrain, Belgium, Bosnia and Herzegovina, Bulgaria, Canada, Croatia, Czech Republic, Denmark, El Salvador, Estonia, Finland, Georgia, Germany, Greece, Hungary, Iceland, Ireland, Italy, Jordan, Republic of Korea, Latvia, Lithuania, Luxembourg, the former Yugoslav Republic of Macedonia, Malaysia, Mongolia, Montenegro, the Netherlands, Norway, Poland, Portugal, Romania, Singapore, Slovakia, Slovenia, Spain, Tonga, Sweden, Turkey, Ukraine, United Arab Emirates, the UK, and the USA.

[20] Bilal Sarwary, 'Why Taliban are so strong in Afghanistan', *BBC*, 2 February 2012, <http://www.bbc.co.uk/news/world-asia-16851949>.

Taliban, with whom it is believed to be allied, but has been described by US military leaders as 'the most resilient enemy network out there'.[21] The network operates along the border with Pakistan, where the escalating campaign against it, including drone strikes, has been targeting its fighters. Exploratory talks had taken place between the Haqqani Network and the US administration prior to a series of attacks by Haqqani in late 2011,[22] and on 16 April 2012 the organization launched a coordinated set of attacks against Kabul.[23]

Hezb-e-Islami Gulbuddin

Hezb-e-Islami Gulbuddin (HIG) is led by Gulbuddin Hekmatyar, a rebel military commander during the 1980s conflict with the Soviets and one of the key figures in the civil war that followed the Soviet withdrawal. He was Prime Minister of Afghanistan from 1993 to 1994 and again briefly in 1996. HIG is active in eastern Afghanistan.[24] The group claimed responsibility for a suicide attack on a minibus that killed nine people, including foreigners, near Kabul airport in September 2012, claiming it was launched in retaliation for a film in the USA mocking the Prophet Mohammad. According to a Reuters report:

'A woman wearing a suicide vest blew herself up in response to the anti-Islam video,' said Zubair Sediqqi, a spokesman for Hizb-i-Islami, which does not usually carry out such attacks.[25]

CASUALTIES

The total of 7,559 civilian casualties identified in 2012 (killed and injured) reflected a 12 per cent reduction in civilian deaths compared with the previous year (2,754 in 2012, down from 3,131 in 2011) and a very slight increase in the number of injured civilians (4,805 in 2012, compared to 4,706 in 2011).[26] IEDs caused 34 per cent of all recorded

[21] See e.g. Jeffrey A. Dressler, 'The Haqqani Network: from Pakistan to Afghanistan', Institute for the Study of War, October 2010; Dressler, 'The Haqqani Network: a strategic threat'.

[22] 'US met Haqqani Network: Clinton', *Agence France-Presse*, 21 October 2011, <http://www.google.com/hostednews/afp/article/ALeqM5hz4uYNnvG0peGVe_XM9yxU00WcuQ?docId=CNG.e1771690f71c3d2-c94aa0c8833fbddc0.61>.

[23] 'Afghan attacks: Fighting "over" in Kabul', *BBC*, 16 April 2012, <http://www.bbc.co.uk/news/world-asia-17724261>.

[24] See e.g. 'Hizb-i-Islami—Gulbuddin (HIG) (Afghanistan)' in *Jane's World Insurgency and Terrorism*, Jane's Information Group, 1 February 2012.

[25] 'Suicide attack in Afghan capital claimed by Hezb-e-Islami', *Reuters*, 17 September 2012, <http://www.reuters.com/article/2012/09/18/us-afghanistan-blast-hezb-idUSBRE88H06M20120918>.

[26] UNAMA recorded a total of 7,837 civilian casualties for 2011: UNAMA, 'Afghanistan, annual report 2012, protection of civilians in armed conflict', Kabul, February 2013, p. 1.

civilian conflict casualties in 2012; 868 civilians were killed and a further 1,663 injured, marking a 3 per cent increase from 2011.[27] US military casualties decreased by almost one half compared to 2011. IEDs were reported to have killed 104 and injured 1,744 US military personnel in 2012, compared with 196 killed and 3,542 injured in 2011.[28] There was a 108 per cent increase in civilian casualties from targeted killings (1,077 civilian casualties, including 379 injured) as compared with the previous year.[29]

The majority of child casualties (788) were attributed to non-state armed groups, which UNAMA refers to as 'anti-government elements', and 174 child casualties to 'pro-government forces'. The remaining child casualties were not attributed to any party to the conflict; most (160) were casualties of explosive remnants of war (ERW).[30] As in previous years, in 2012 children were the group most vulnerable to harm from ERW, representing 77 per cent of all recorded ERW casualties.[31] UNAMA noted that three children died while carrying out suicide attacks, and five boys who were used as bodyguards and 'dancing boys' were reportedly also sexually abused.[32]

UNAMA documented five incidents of drone strikes, which resulted in 16 civilian deaths and three injuries in 2012, an increase from one such drone incident documented in 2011.[33]

The online database website iCasualties reported 310 US military deaths in 2012.[34] The US military reported 313 deaths, including 76 that were not from hostilities or the classification of which was pending verification.[35] iCasualties reported 92 non-US ISAF deaths in 2012, including 44 UK military deaths.[36] In 2012, at least 221 employees of US private

[27] According to UNAMA, 70 per cent of the IEDs were victim-activated. UNAMA reiterated its position that victim-activated (pressure plate) IEDs are indiscriminate as they cannot distinguish between a civilian and military objective, making their use illegal under international law. See UNAMA, 'Afghanistan, annual report 2012, protection of civilians in armed conflict', p. 14.

[28] 'IED casualties dropped 50 per cent in Afghanistan in 2012', *USA Today*, 18 January 2013, <http://www.usatoday.com/story/news/world/2013/01/18/ied-casualties-down-afghanistan-2012/1839609/>. The report also claims that, in 2012, Afghan troops suffered a 124 per cent increase in the number of IED attacks against them. No casualty data is included for Afghan military.

[29] Of the 1,077 civilian casualties, targeted killings and injuries of government civilian employees increased by 700 per cent.

[30] ERW comprises unexploded ordnance and abandoned explosive ordnance. See Protocol V to the Convention on Certain Conventional Weapons.

[31] UNAMA, 'Afghanistan, annual report 2012, protection of civilians in armed conflict', Kabul, February 2013, p. 55.

[32] UNAMA, 'Afghanistan, annual report 2012, protection of civilians in armed conflict', p. 56. UNAMA's 2012 data on 864 female casualties overlapped with data on 1,302 child casualties.

[33] UNAMA, 'Afghanistan, annual report 2012, protection of civilians in armed conflict', p. 34.

[34] Iraq Coalition Casualty Count (iCasualties.org), <http://icasualties.org/oef/>.

[35] Statistical analysis of data from Defence Casualties Analysis System: Conflict Casualties Operation Enduring Freedom, <http://www.dmdc.osd.mil/dcas/pages/casualties_oef.xhtml>.

[36] Other ISAF fatalities were reported as: Albania, 1; Australia, 7; France, 8; Georgia, 7; Italy, 5; NATO, 2; New Zealand, 6; and Turkey, 12. See iCasualties, <http://icasualties.org/oef/>.

contractors were registered as killed in Afghanistan. This represented a decrease from 386 reported in 2011.[37] The *Private Security Monitor* reported another 4,939 injured contractors.[38] These casualties are not believed to have been included in the above data. Estimated fatalities of 1,200 ANA and 2,200 ANP personnel in 2012 represented a significant increase on a combined total of 1,950 in 2011.[39]

UNAMA did not distinguish between different 'anti-government elements' in casualty reporting.[40] However, a number of incidents attributed specifically to the Haqqani Network and one to Hezb-e-Islami were identified through media reporting in 2012. In April, Haqqani Network attacks on foreign embassies and the Afghan parliament resulted in the death of four civilians and 11 members of the Afghan security forces; at least 35 individuals from non-state armed groups also died.[41] In June, the Haqqani Network carried out a suicide truck bomb and complex attack on a US base near Khost.[42] This resulted in the death of five Afghan civilians and two US troops; 14 insurgents were killed; more than 100 US troops had minor injuries.[43] Another 20 deaths occurred

---

[37] According to publicly available data from the US Department of Labor. The 2012 data was measured as the changes in number of total contractor deaths recorded since 2001: 1,316 in 2012; 1,095 in 2011; and 709 in 2010. See <http://www.dol.gov/owcp/dlhwc/dbaallnation12-31-12.htm>, <http://www.dol.gov/owcp/dlhwc/dbaallnation12-31-11.htm>, and <http://www.dol.gov/owcp/dlhwc/dbaallnation12-31-10.htm>. Also reported by the Brookings Institute: the numbers correspond to new claims during the period; the deaths may have occurred in a prior period. See 'Brookings Afghanistan Index', 28 February 2013, p. 13.

[38] Private Security Monitor, 'Data and statistics', undated, accessed 29 April 2013, <http://psm.du .edu/articles_reports_statistics/data_and_statistics.html>. The Private Security Monitor recorded 168 private security contractor deaths in Afghanistan in 2012 and 386 in 2011.

[39] 'Brookings Afghanistan Index', 28 February 2013, p. 14. Brookings' estimated numbers are based on reports of monthly averages through November.

[40] This term is used by UNAMA to include those groups who identify as 'Taliban', as well as Haqqani Network, Hezb-e-Islami, Islamic Movement of Uzbekistan, Islamic Jihad Union, Lashkari Tayyiba, Jaysh Muhammed, and armed criminal groups.

[41] 'Haqqani Network behind Afghan attacks: U.S. envoy', *Reuters*, 19 April 2012, <http://www.reuters .com/article/2012/04/19/us-afghanistan-haqqani-usa-idUSBRE83I0KT20120419>. Thirty-six of the attackers were killed and 11 others, including civilians and police, according to the Ministry of the Interior: 'Afghans blame Haqqani Network for attacks', *USA Today*, 16 April 2012, <http://usatoday30.usatoday .com/news/world/afghanistan/story/2012-04-16/afghanistan-attacks/54305360/1>.

[42] 'Attack on US base kills 15 in Afghanistan: NATO', *Agence France-Presse*, 1 June 2012, <http://www .google.com/hostednews/afp/article/ALeqM5gB4exChvX65rMIvpy5FeEVueisDg?docId=CNG.09eeab8ceab-1c034a82edb8120872601.7b1>.

[43] 'New details emerge about complex attack on FOB Salerno', *Long War Journal*, 10 June 2012, <http://www.longwarjournal.org/archives/2012/06/new_details_emerge_a.php>. According to this report, 'an RC East spokesman revealed that the attackers were wearing uniforms of both the Afghan National Security Forces and the US army'. See also 'Shocking Taliban propaganda video captures the moments leading up to massive suicide bombing at U.S. base that killed two Americans', *Daily Mail*, 25 July 2012, <http://www.dailymail.co.uk/news/article-2177983/Fort-Salerno-bombing-Taliban-video-shows-blast-killed-John-Kirkland-Vincent-Ellis.html>; 'Attack on US base kills 15 in Afghanistan: NATO', *Agence France-Presse*, 1 June 2012, <http://www.google.com/hostednews/afp/article/ALeqM5gB4exChvX65rMIvpy5FeEVueisDg>.

during a siege at a hotel in Kabul.[44] In September 2012, Hezb-e-Islami carried out a suicide bombing in Kabul resulting in 12 deaths, including nine foreign workers.[45]

In 2012, the UN reported that patterns of sexual violence against women and girls in Afghanistan had changed based on changes in the ongoing conflict. Acts of sexual violence included abduction, assault, rape, and sexual abuse of women and children in communities under the influence or control of anti-government elements, including the Taliban and other warlords. The stigma around the topic of sexual violence prevented victims from reporting crimes. In many instances, children and women who reported being victims of sexual violence were themselves accused of crimes, and publicly stoned or punished. The UN also reported having received reports of boys and men being assaulted or threatened with sexual violence by members of the National Directorate of Security and the ANP while in detention.[46]

DISPLACED

At least 100,400 Afghans were newly displaced by conflict in 2012.[47]

WAR CRIMES ALLEGATIONS, INVESTIGATIONS, AND PROSECUTIONS

Afghanistan has been a state party to the 1998 Rome Statute of the International Criminal Court (the ICC Statute) since February 2003. The ICC has jurisdiction over ICC Statute crimes committed on the territory of Afghanistan or by its nationals since 1 May 2003. The Office of the Prosecutor received 87 communications under Article 15 of the ICC Statute between 1 June 2006 and 30 September 2012. The preliminary examination of the situation was made public in 2007: 'The Office of the Prosecutor has been

---

[44] 'NATO Commander links Haqqani Network to Kabul attack', *Reuters*, 22 June 2012, <http://www .reuters.com/article/2012/06/22/us-afghanistan-hotel-haqqani-idUSBRE85L0MX20120622>.

[45] Casualties reported included eight South Africans and a Kyrgyz national, although these nationalities were not found in any totals for 2012: 'Afghanistan's softer insurgents claim suicide attack. What next?', *Christian Science Monitor*, 19 September 2012, <http://www.csmonitor.com/World/Asia-South-Central/ 2012/0919/Afghanistan-s-softer-insurgents-claim-suicide-attack.-What-next>; <http://muftah.org/afghan-militant-group-hezb-e-islami-says-it-will-field-candidate-in-next-presidential-election/>. See also 'Suicide attack in Afghan capital claimed by Hezb-e-Islami', *Reuters*, 17 September 2012, <http://www .reuters. com/article/2012/09/18/us-afghanistan-blast-hezb-idUSBRE88H06M20120918>:   'Hezb-e-Islami claimed responsibility for a suicide attack on a minibus that killed nine people, including foreigners, near Kabul airport on Tuesday and said it was launched in retaliation for a film mocking the Prophet Mohammad.'

[46] 'Report of the Secretary-General on sexual violence in conflict', UN doc. S/2013/149, advance copy dated 12 March 2013, §§15–19.

[47] Internal Displacement Monitoring Centre (IDMC), 'Global overview 2012', April 2013, p. 65.

examining alleged crimes within the jurisdiction of the Court, including torture; attacks on humanitarian targets and the UN; attacks on protected objects; and recruitment of child soldiers. The Office of the Prosecutor has sent requests for information to the government of Afghanistan and has not yet received an answer.'[48]

In addition, a number of investigations and prosecutions were conducted of international military personnel engaged in the conflict in Afghanistan during 2012. Some of the high-profile cases are summarized below.

In December 2012, the US army announced that an army sergeant accused of murdering 16 civilians in two Afghanistan villages would be court-martialled and could face the death penalty if convicted. The military's General Court-Martial Convening Authority referred charges against Staff Sergeant Robert Bales to a general court-martial after a review of evidence from a pre-trial hearing in November 2012.[49] In April 2013, a judge decided that defence attorneys were required to advise military prosecutors by 29 May if they planned to pursue a mental health defence to the charges. Bales's attorneys had asserted that the accused was suffering from post-traumatic stress disorder (PTSD)[50] and a brain injury even before his deployment to Afghanistan.[51]

Bales, aged 39, faced charges of premeditated murder and other crimes in the pre-dawn shooting and stabbing attack on two villages in southern Afghanistan early on 11 March 2012. Prosecutors asserted that he left his remote base, attacked one village, returned to the base, and then slipped away again to attack another nearby compound. Sixteen people were killed, nine of them children, and six other civilians wounded. Army prosecutors suggested Bales went on the rampage in revenge for a

---

[48] ICC, 'Office of the Prosecutor, communications, referrals and preliminary examinations, Afghanistan', undated, accessed 30 April 2013, <http://www.icc-cpi.int/en_menus/icc/structure%20of%20the%20court/office%20of%20the%20prosecutor/comm%20and%20ref/afghanistan/Pages/afghanistan.aspx>. See Office of the Prosecutor (OTP), 'OTP Report on Preliminary Examination Activities 2012', ICC, 13 November 2012, <http://www.icc-cpi.int/NR/rdonlyres/C433C462-7C4E-4358-8A72-8D99FD00E8CD/285209/OTP2012ReportonPreliminaryExaminations22Nov2012.pdf>.

[49] See e.g. 'Afghanistan massacre case: army to seek death penalty against US soldier', *NBC News*, 19 December 2012, <http://usnews.nbcnews.com/_news/2012/12/19/16021178-afghanistan-massacre-case-army-to-seek-death-penalty-against-us-soldier?lite>.

[50] PTSD can occur after someone goes through a traumatic event such as combat, assault, or disaster: 'PTSD overview', US Department of Veterans Affairs, 25 May 2011. According to one medical expert:

Neurobiological research indicates that PTSD may be associated with stable neurobiological alterations in both the central and autonomic nervous systems. Psychophysiological alterations associated with PTSD include hyper-arousal of the sympathetic nervous system, increased sensitivity and augmentation of the acoustic-startle eye blink reflex, and sleep abnormalities. Neuropharmacologic and neuroendocrine abnormalities have been detected in most brain mechanisms that have evolved for coping, adaptation, and preservation of the species.

Dr Matthew J. Friedman, 'PTSD history and overview', US Department of Veterans Affairs, 31 January 2007, <http://www.ptsd.va.gov/professional/pages/ptsd-overview.asp>.

[51] Johnson, 'U.S. soldier accused of Afghan killings faces deadline for mental defense'.

bomb attack on his unit in which a fellow soldier lost a leg.[52] In early June 2013, Bales pleaded guilty to the charges, saying to the military judge that the act 'was without legal justification'.[53] In August 2013, Bales was convicted and sentences to life imprisonment without possibility of parole.[54]

In September 2012, the US Marine Corps announced that two Marine officers would be court-martialled for allegedly urinating on the bodies of Taliban fighters in Afghanistan and posing for unofficial photos with casualties, The charges against Staff Sergeant Joseph W. Chamblin and Staff Sergeant Edward W. Deptola were in addition to administrative punishments announced in August 2012 for three other, more junior Marines for their role in the events. Staff Sergeant Chamblin pleaded guilty to the charges against him in December 2012 and was sentenced to 30 days' confinement, reduced in rank, fined, and ordered to forfeit part of his pay for six months.[55] The court-martial of Staff Sergeant Edward W. Deptola opened in January 2013.[56] He was demoted one rank as punishment for his conviction. In May 2013, it was announced that a third soldier, Captain James V. Clement, would be tried for dereliction of duty, conduct unbecoming an officer, and failure to stop misconduct by those under his command.[57]

In October 2012, the UK Ministry of Defence announced that seven Royal Marine Commandos had been arrested by Royal Military Police in the UK and were being questioned about the suspected execution of an injured Taliban prisoner in 2011.[58]

In January 2013, UNAMA issued a damning report on torture in facilities run by the Afghan police and the National Directorate for Security between October 2011 and October 2012, saying that more than half of the 635 conflict-related detainees it interviewed had been tortured.[59] Forms of torture included hanging suspects by the wrists from chains for long periods and threatening them with sexual violence. Many of those

---

[52] 'Afghanistan massacre case: army to seek death penalty against US soldier', *NBC News*, 19 December 2012.

[53] See e.g. 'Sgt. Robert Bales describes killing 16 Afghans', *CBS News*, 5 June 2013, <http://www.cbsnews.com/8301-201_162-57587761/sgt-robert-bales-describes-killing-16-afghans/>.

[54] Associated Press, 'Robert Bales sentenced to life in prison for Afghanistan massacre', *The Guardian*, 23 August 2013, <http://www.theguardian.com/world/2013/aug/23/afghanistan-massacre-robert-bales-trial>.

[55] 'Marine officer faces trial over video of snipers urinating on corpses of dead Taliban fighters', *Daily Mail*, 14 May 2013, <http://www.dailymail.co.uk/news/article-2324120/Marine-officer-faces-trial-video-snipers-urinating-corpses-dead-Taliban-fighters.html#ixzz2WjvTL71E>.

[56] 'U.S. Marine faces court martial for urinating on Taliban fighter corpses', *Daily News*, 16 January 2013, <http://www.nydailynews.com/news/national/marine-charged-urinating-dead-taliban-fighters-article-1.1241138#ixzz2IcT72ZSD>.

[57] 'Marine officer faces trial over video of snipers urinating on corpses of dead Taliban fighters', *Daily Mail*, 14 May 2013.

[58] 'Royal Marines arrested in murder inquiry', *BBC*, 25 October 2012, <http://www.bbc.co.uk/news/uk-19918398>.

[59] UNAMA and Office of the UN High Commissioner for Human Rights (OHCHR), 'Treatment of conflict-related detainees in Afghan custody, one year on', Kabul, January 2013, <http://unama.unmissions.org/LinkClick.aspx?fileticket=VsBL0S5b37o%3D&tabid=12254&language=en-US>.

tortured to extract confessions were children under the age of 18. Despite international humanitarian and human rights law unequivocally prohibiting torture,[60] the UN found a persistent lack of accountability for those who engaged in torture, with few investigations and no prosecutions of those responsible:

Where torture occurred, it generally took the form of abusive interrogation techniques in which . . . [Security Forces] officials deliberately inflicted severe pain and suffering on detainees during interrogations aimed mainly at obtaining a confession or information. Such practices amounting to torture are among the most serious human rights violations under international law and are crimes under Afghan law.[61]

The organization said the findings reinforced the urgent need for reforms in the judiciary, prosecution, and law enforcement sectors. Its recommendations included the creation of an independent national preventive mechanism on torture.

In October 2012, ISAF had suspended the transfer of detainees to some Afghan facilities over reports of torture. A spokesman for the President conceded there may be some cases of abuse, but denied that torture was government policy. An Afghan government spokesman, Aimal Faizi, stated that: 'While the Afghan government takes very seriously the allegations made in the UN report, we also question the motivations behind this report and the way it was conducted.'[62] Moreover, Deputy Interior Minister Abdul Rahman Rahman said at a press conference in Kabul: 'The Ministry of Interior dismisses the allegation of mistreatment, systematic torture, beating with pipes or cables, forced confessions, hanging and other types of torture mentioned in the report. We are ready to investigate about all the above allegations together with UNAMA.'[63]

---

[60] According to UNAMA and OHCHR:

The absolute prohibition against torture is a peremptory *jus cogens* norm of customary international law. Several international treaties to which Afghanistan is a party also prohibit torture. These include the *Convention against Torture and Other Cruel, Inhuman or Degrading Treatment or Punishment*, the *International Covenant on Civil and Political Rights* (ICCPR), the *Geneva Conventions of 1949*, the *Rome Statute of the International Criminal Court* and the *Convention on the Rights of the Child* (CRC) article 37(a).

UNAMA and OHCHR, 'Treatment of conflict-related detainees in Afghan custody, one year on', p. 97.

[61] UNAMA and OHCHR, 'Treatment of conflict-related detainees in Afghan custody, one year on', p. 4.

[62] AFP, 'Torture of prisoners persists in Afghanistan: UN—Methods include beatings, electric shocks and hanging suspects by the wrists from chains for long periods', *Gulf News*, 21 January 2013, <http://gulfnews.com/news/world/afghanistan/torture-of-prisoners-persists-in-afghanistan-un-1.1135673>.

[63] Shakeela Ahbrimkhil, 'Afghan officials differ over torture use in prisons', *Tolonews*, 21 January 2013, <http://tolonews.com/en/afghanistan/9155-afghan-officials-differ-over-torture-use-in-prisons>.

Armed conflict in the Central African Republic in 2012

KEY CONFLICT STATISTICS FOR 2012

Military deaths:	20	(Sources: OCHA; Agence France-Presse)
Military injured:	5	(Source: OCHA)
Police deaths:	2	(Source: OCHA)
Civilian deaths:	32	(Sources: OCHA; US Department of State)
Civilian injured:	8	(Sources: OCHA; US Department of State)
Civilians displaced:	132,000 (est.)	(Source: IDMC, 'Global overview', 2012)

CLASSIFICATION OF THE CONFLICTS

Central African Republic (CAR) armed forces were involved in an armed conflict of a non-international character (NIAC) with the Séléka coalition of rebel forces from December 2012. The conflict reached the threshold for applicability of the 1977 Additional Protocol II.

There was a separate lower intensity NIAC during 2012 between the CAR and Ugandan armed forces with the Lord's Resistance Army (LRA).

SUMMARY OF APPLICABLE INTERNATIONAL LAW

All parties to the conflicts are bound by, inter alia: Common Article 3 to the 1949 Geneva Conventions; the customary international humanitarian law (IHL) rules of distinction, proportionality, and precautions in attacks; and the duty to respect, at a minimum, fundamental human rights. This includes the duty to respect the rights to life and to freedom from torture or other forms of cruel, inhuman, or degrading treatment or punishment.

In addition, the CAR is a state party to the 1977 Additional Protocol II, which applies to the NIAC with Séléka, as well as to the two 1966 Covenants (on civil and political rights, and on economic, social, and cultural rights). Uganda is bound extraterritorially by its human rights obligations.[1]

The CAR acceded to the 1997 Anti-Personnel Mine Ban Convention (APMBC) in November 2002, becoming a state party on 1 May 2003, and has signed, but not yet ratified,

---

[1] See e.g. International Court of Justice (ICJ), *Wall* Advisory Opinion, 2004, §106; ICJ, *Armed Activities on the Territory of the Congo (Democratic Republic of the Congo v. Uganda)*, Judgment, 19 December 2005.

the 2008 Convention on Cluster Munitions (CCM). Uganda and South Africa are also states parties to the APMBC and signatories to the CCM.

HISTORY OF THE CONFLICT[2]

The CAR has been unstable since its independence from France in 1960. Illegal weapons proliferate across the country, the legacy of years of unrest that has displaced tens of thousands of people, many across the border into Chad.

Three main rebel groups have been operating in the CAR over the last few decades: the People's Army for the Restoration of Democracy (APRD), which operated in the north and north-west of the country; the Union of Democratic Forces for Unity (UFDR) in the north-east of the country; and the Democratic Front of the Central African People (Front démocratique du peuple centrafricain, or FDPC).[3]

In the south-east of the country, the Central African Republic Armed Forces (FACA), together with the Ugandan People's Defence Force (UPDF), have been fighting members of the Ugandan armed group, the LRA, who have been active in the CAR since February 2008.[4]

Some progress towards stabilizing the country was made between 2008 and 2012. In 2008, the UFDR and APRD signed the Libreville Comprehensive Peace Agreement (CPA) with Bozizé's government committing, inter alia, to actively participate in the disarmament, demobilization, and reintegration (DDR) programme in the north-east of the country.[5] However, the Convention of Patriots for Justice and Peace (CPJP) has remained active, especially in the north of the country where it has been responsible for attacks against the FACA, as well as civilians.[6]

In August 2012, the last historic armed group, the CPJP, signed a peace deal. In November, however, the new Séléka rebel alliance (*see section 'Parties to the conflicts', for a description of the group*) marched south, taking town after town, capturing the capital

---

[2] Unless otherwise stated, this section is based on 'Central African Republic profile', *BBC*, 1 March 2013, <http://www.bbc.co.uk/news/world-africa-13150040>.

[3] 'Report of the Secretary-General on the situation in the Central African Republic and on the activities of the United Nations Integrated Peacebuilding Office in that country', UN doc. S/2011/739, 28 November 2011.

[4] Frank Nyakairu, 'Uganda: Kony crosses into Central African Republic', *The Monitor*, 16 March 2008, <http://allafrica.com/stories/200803160004.html>.

[5] S. Spittaels and F. Hilgert, *Mapping Conflict Motives, Central African Republic*, International Peace Information Service (IPIS), 17 February 2009, p. 9, <http://www.ipisresearch.be/mapping_car.php>.

[6] 'Report of the Secretary-General on the situation in the Central African Republic and on the activities of the United Nations Integrated Peacebuilding Office in that country', UN doc. S/2011/739, 28 November 2011.

in March 2013 and ousting President Francois Bozize. FACA army chiefs pledged allegiance to the country's self-proclaimed president, Michel Djotodia, as the former rebel leader consolidated control four days after his fighters seized the capital.[7]

Gender-based violence was prevalent throughout the country in 2012, particularly in conflict zones. The United Nations (UN) received reports of multiple allegations of sexual violence, including rape of women and girls by various armed groups in areas under non-state actor control.[8]

PARTIES TO THE CONFLICTS

Central African Republic Armed Forces

The FACA are reported to have at most 3,500 men. Ill-equipped, unmotivated, and poorly trained, the FACA are said to have offered relatively little active resistance to Séléka fighters in 2012.[9]

South African National Defence Forces

South Africa has been providing military assistance to the CAR for several years.[10] On 8 January 2013, the South African National Defence Forces (SANDF) deployed 200 additional troops to the CAR.[11] SANDF troops suffered 13 casualties from 1 Parachute Battalion and 27 wounded while defending against the advancing Séléka.[12]

---

[7] Ange Aboa, 'Central African Republic army chiefs pledge allegiance to coup leader', *Reuters*, Bangui, 28 March 2013, <http://www.reuters.com/article/2013/03/28/us-centralafrica-rebels-idUSBRE92R0F420130328>.

[8] These groups included Séléka, several of its member factions, and the FDPC: 'Report of the Secretary-General on sexual violence in conflict', UN Security Council, UN doc. S/2013/149, advance copy dated 12 March 2013, §§20–3.

[9] 'Seleka, Central Africa's motley rebel coalition', *Agence France-Presse*, Bangui, 1 January 2013, <http://www.google.com/hostednews/afp/article/ALeqM5iXnB5C8UnKeG6cE8tkOPhHhcKl9w>.

[10] 'Training and support provided by the South African Army (SANDF) to the Army of the Central African Republic (CAR)', National Assembly, Written Reply Question No. 78, Question Paper No. 1, 10 February 2011, <http://www.webcitation.org/6FSUjNfSd>.

[11] 'South Africa bolsters its troops in the Central African Republic', *IRIN*, Johannesburg, 8 January 2013, <http://www.irinnews.org/Report/97194/South-Africa-bolsters-its-troops-in-the-Central-African-Republic>.

[12] 'South Africa bolsters its troops in the Central African Republic', *IRIN*; Christopher Torchia (Associated Press), 'Hard questions for South Africa over CAR battle', *Boston Globe*, 28 March 2013, <http://www.bostonglobe.com/news/world/2013/03/27/hard-questions-for-south-africa-over-car-battle/xCIdsC9R8cn-TGWopEuEN0H/story.html>; Ange Aboa, 'Central African Republic army chiefs pledge allegiance to coup leader', *Reuters*, Bangui, 28 March 2013.

African Union force

An African Union-authorized, Uganda-led force bringing together soldiers from the CAR, the Democratic Republic of Congo (DRC), South Sudan, and Uganda, was launched at the end of March 2012 with the mission of hunting down LRA leader Joseph Kony.[13]

Séléka

Séléka is a coalition of rebel groups (the word means 'alliance' in the country's language, Sango), most of whom were signatories to the 2008 Libreville CPA with the government. In September 2012, however, dissident factions of the main signatory groups largely from the north of the country, the UFDR, the Wa Kodro Salute Patriotic Convention, and the CPJP, banded together as Séléka.[14] The coalition numbers between 1,000 and 2,000 fighters, according to one expert at the Paris-based National Centre for Scientific Research.[15]

The People's Army for the Restoration of Democracy

The People's Army for the Restoration of Democracy (APRD) was a rebel group operating in the north-west of the country. The APRD was formed in 2006 following the 2003 *coup* that overthrew President Ange-Félix Patassé. It is one of several groups that fought in the 2004–07 CAR Bush War. The group participated in the 2008 Inclusive Peace Dialog, starting its conversion from a military coalition to a political front. In June 2008, along with the UFDR, the APRD signed a CPA in Libreville. In early 2009, it entered a coalition government with Bozizé and other civil and military opposition groups. In May 2012, the armed group officially announced its dissolution.[16]

The Union of Democratic Forces for Unity

The UFDR is an armed group, composed of the mainly Muslim Gula ethnic group, which fought against the government in the CAR Civil War (2004–07). The UFDR was

[13] 'AU to launch 5,000-strong force for Kony hunt on Saturday', *Thomson Reuters Foundation*, 23 March 2012, <http://www.trust.org/item/?map=au-to-launch-5000-strong-force-for-kony-hunt-on-saturday/>.

[14] 'Seleka, Central Africa's motley rebel coalition', *Agence France-Presse*, Bangui, 1 January 2013.

[15] Roland Marchal, a specialist in Central African conflicts, cited in 'Seleka, Central Africa's motley rebel coalition', *Agence France-Presse*.

[16] 'Security Council Press Statement on Central African Republic', UN Security Council, UN doc. SC/10665 AFR/2400, 6 June 2012, <http://www.un.org/News/Press/docs/2012/sc10665.doc.htm>. See also 'Central African Republic: security hopes improve after main rebel groups disband', *IRIN*, 5 June 2012, <http://www .irinnews.org/printreport.aspx?reportid=95586>.

formed in September 2006 and is active in the Arabic-speaking north-eastern prefectures of Vakanga and Haute Kotto. On 13 April 2007, a peace agreement between the government and the UFDR was signed in Birao. The agreement provided for an amnesty for the UFDR, its recognition as a political party, and the eventual integration of its fighters into the army. Subsequently, the UFDR also signed the Libreville's CPA in June 2008.[17] In December 2012, seven months after having officially announced its dissolution,[18] a faction of the UFDR joined the attacks by Séléka.[19]

The Democratic Front of the Central African People (FDPC)

The FDPC is the third rebel movement that, in the past, controlled part of the country, albeit only a very small area. As of 11 November 2008, it seemed that the FDPC had ceased to exist as an active military movement. Before that time, it controlled a stretch of road of about 15 km between the Central African town of Kabo and the Chadian border, near the village of Nabanza where its command post is located. The FDPC was the first of the CAR's rebel groups to sign a cease-fire agreement with the government in December 2006 in Syrte, Libya.[20]

Lord's Resistance Army

Formed in 1992 in an attempt to unify a resistance movement fractured by the marginalization of the Uganda Democratic Christian Army, the LRA promotes a radical form of Christianity that it wanted to make the foundation of a new Ugandan government.[21] The group has entered the DRC, but since 2007 it has been largely operating in the CAR. The LRA is, among other things, accused of having killed and maimed civilians, including children, committed grave acts of sexual violence, abductions, and recruitment of child soldiers, looting of villages, and attacks on aid agencies. 2012 saw the rise of LRA attacks along the DRC–CAR border, with the Office of the UN High Commissioner for Refugees (UNHCR) describing the situation there as 'extremely fragile'.[22] The UN

---

[17] Spittaels and Hilgert, *Mapping Conflict Motives, Central African Republic*, pp. 9–10.

[18] 'Central African Republic: security hopes improve after main rebel groups disband', *IRIN*.

[19] 'CAR: Security Council extends mandate of UN office, calls on parties to abide by ceasefire pact', UN press release, 24 January 2013, <http://www.un.org/apps/news/story.asp?NewsID=43992# .UQee99uDnTo>.

[20] Spittaels and Hilgert, *Mapping Conflict Motives, Central African Republic*.

[21] National Consortium for the Study of Terrorism and Responses to Terrorism (START), 'Terrorist organization profile: Lord's Resistance Army (LRA)', undated, accessed 9 May 2013, <http://www.start.umd.edu/start/data_collections/tops/terrorist_organization_profile.asp?id=3513>.

[22] Emma Batha, 'Attacks by Kony's LRA on the rise in central Africa', *Thomson Reuters Foundation*, 30 March 2012, <http://www.trust.org/item/?map=attacks-by-konys-lra-on-the-rise-in-central-africa/>.

reported 85 abductions by the LRA in 2012.[23] The LRA also kidnapped children and forced them to fight, or to act as sex slaves. In September, at least 55 people were kidnapped during LRA raids; reportedly half were girls. Also in September, an unknown armed group abducted two Chinese road workers.[24]

CASUALTIES

Although government forces and armed groups maintained a cease-fire for much of the year, civilians were killed as a result of continuing internal conflicts, according to the US Department of State.[25] In 2012, 23 deaths in 43 attacks by the LRA were reported by the UN.[26] Other unidentified armed groups killed nine civilians and injured at least eight in three attacks during the year.[27]

In December 2012, during the Séléka advance, 14 Central African soldiers were reported as having been killed in attacks.[28]

DISPLACED

In December 2012, the security situation in CAR deteriorated as the Séléka rebel alliance took control of much of the northern part of the country and advanced towards the

[23] 'Report of the Secretary-General on the situation in the Central African Republic and on the activities of the United Nations Integrated Peacebuilding Office in that country', UN Security Council, UN doc. S/2012/956, 21 December 2012.

[24] US Department of State, 'Country reports on human rights practices 2012: Central African Republic', 19 April 2013.

[25] US Department of State, 'Country reports on human rights practices 2012: Central African Republic', 19 April 2013.

[26] UN Office for the Coordination of Humanitarian Affairs (OCHA), 'LRA regional update: Central African Republic, DR Congo and South Sudan (October–December 2012)'; 'Report of the Secretary-General on the situation in the Central African Republic and on the activities of the United Nations Integrated Peacebuilding Office in that country', UN Security Council, UN doc. S/2012/956, 21 December 2012.

[27] US Department of State, 'Country reports on human rights practices 2012: Central African Republic', 19 April 2013. The LRA also likely killed 13 miners, whose mutilated bodies were found near Bakouma in March. It is not clear from reporting if these are included in the 2012 total of casualties by the LRA.

[28] 'Chad troops enter Central Africa to help fight rebels: military', *Agence France-Presse*, 18 December 2012, <http://reliefweb.int/report/central-african-republic/chad-troops-enter-central-africa-help-fight-rebels-military>. UN Security Council members issued statements on 19 and 27 December (UN docs SC/10867 and SC/10874), as well as a report on the situation on 21 December (UN doc. S/2012/956), but this reporting did not include civilian or military casualties of the Séléka conflict in 2012.

capital Bangui;[29] as a result, an estimated 80,000 people were displaced between December 2012 and early January 2013.[30]

In October 2012, there were estimated to be some 52,000 internally displaced persons (IDPs) in the CAR. Approximately 35,000 IDPs returned to their places of origin during the year. In areas affected by LRA-related violence, there were 21,000 IDPs[31] in addition to some 3,000 Congolese refugees in camps.[32]

WAR CRIMES ALLEGATIONS, INVESTIGATIONS, AND PROSECUTIONS

The CAR adhered to the 1998 Rome Statute of the International Criminal Court (the ICC Statute) in October 2001. In accordance with the ICC Statute, the Court has jurisdiction over ICC Statute crimes committed on the territory of CAR or by its nationals.

On 22 May 2007, the ICC Office of the Prosecutor (OTP) announced the decision to open an investigation in the CAR. The trial of Jean-Pierre Bemba Gombo, the alleged President and Commander-in-Chief of the Mouvement de libération du Congo (MLC), has been ongoing since 22 November 2010. He has been charged with two counts of crimes against humanity and three counts of war crimes.[33]

---

[29] US Department of State, 'Country reports on human rights practices 2012: Central African Republic', 19 April 2013.

[30] IDMC, 'Global overview 2012', April 2013.

[31] IDMC, 'Global overview 2012', pp. 20–1.

[32] OCHA, 'LRA regional update: Central African Republic, DR Congo and South Sudan (October–December 2012)'.

[33] ICC, 'Situation in the Central African Republic, *Prosecutor v. Jean-Pierre Bemba Gombo*', <http://www.icc-cpi.int/EN_Menus/ICC/Situations%20and%20Cases/Situations/Situation%20ICC%200105/Pages/situation%20icc-0105.aspx>.

Armed conflict in Colombia in 2012

KEY CONFLICT STATISTICS FOR 2012

Civilian deaths:	291	(Sources: UNHCHR; Somos Defensores; PAICMA; CHRO)
Civilian injured:	175	(Source: PAICMA)
Child deaths:	13	(Source: PAICMA)
Child injured:	53	(Source: PAICMA)
Military deaths:	33	(Source: PAICMA)
Military injured:	246	(Source: PAICMA)
Civilians displaced:	4.9–5.5 million (31 Dec. 2012)	(Source: IDMC)

CLASSIFICATION OF THE CONFLICTS

Colombian armed forces were involved in armed conflicts of a non-international character (NIACs) with the Revolutionary Armed Forces of Colombia (FARC-EP) and with the National Liberation Army (ELN) in 2012. Both conflicts reached the threshold for applicability of the 1977 Additional Protocol II.

SUMMARY OF APPLICABLE INTERNATIONAL LAW

All parties to the conflicts are bound by, inter alia: Common Article 3 to the 1949 Geneva Conventions and the 1977 Additional Protocol II; the customary international humanitarian law (IHL) rules of distinction, proportionality, and precautions in attacks; the obligation not to recruit and use children as soldiers; and the duty to respect, at a minimum, fundamental human rights. This includes the duty to respect the rights to life and to freedom from torture or other forms of cruel, inhuman, or degrading treatment or punishment. In addition, Colombia is a state party to the two 1966 Covenants (on civil and political rights, and on economic, social, and cultural rights).

Colombia ratified the 1997 Anti-Personnel Mine Ban Convention (APMBC) in September 2000, becoming a state party on 1 March 2001, and has signed, but not ratified, the 2008 Convention on Cluster Munitions (CCM).

HISTORY OF THE CONFLICT[1]

Colombia has endured armed conflict between the government and several left-wing armed groups (notably the FARC-EP and the ELN) for more half a century. An underlying reason for the conflict's continuity is the income generated by the coca leaf traffic.[2] The US government has also been involved in the country through Plan Colombia, an initiative originally intended to support Colombian anti-drug efforts. In that context, Colombian forces receive training and equipment to eliminate smugglers and eradicate coca crops, with US assistance.[3]

The activities of the guerrillas led to the formation of right-wing paramilitary organizations, primarily the United Self-Defence Forces of Colombia (AUC), as a means of protecting landowners, drug lords, and local businessmen from attacks and kidnappings by guerrilla forces. There have been regular accusations of linkages between the paramilitaries and the state in waging war against the guerrillas, although this has been denied by the government. Since their origins, both the guerrillas and the paramilitaries have become increasingly involved in criminal activities (such as kidnapping, extortion, bombings, murder, and hijackings), and have given a new dimension to the problem of narco-trafficking.

Over the years, the government of Colombia has held several peace talks and negotiations with guerrilla groups, with different degrees of success. Recent years have also seen the power of the paramilitaries diminish. Following generous and controversial amnesty legislation,[4] which offered significantly reduced jail terms, by mid-2006 about 95 per cent of the total estimated AUC force was disbanded.[5]

In October 2012, negotiators from the Colombian government and FARC-EP rebels met for their first direct peace talks for a decade in Oslo, Norway. FARC-EP's head negotiator, Ivan Marquez, said that they came 'with an olive branch', but peace did not mean 'arms go quiet'.[6] Colombian President Juan Manuel Santos rejected FARC calls for a cease-fire, saying military operations would continue until a final agreement was

---

[1] Unless otherwise stated, this section is based on 'Colombia profile', *BBC*, 20 November 2012, <http://www.bbc.co.uk/news/world-latin-america-19390026>.

[2] UCDP Conflict Encyclopaedia, 'Colombian conflict backgrounder', December 2011, <http://www.ucdp.uu.se/gpdatabase/gpcountry.php?id=35&regionSelect=5-Southern_Americas#>.

[3] Jeremy McDermott, 'Colombia changes tactics in drugs war', *BBC*, 31 August 2000, <http://news.bbc.co.uk/2/hi/americas/891289.stm>.

[4] Center for Justice and Accountability, 'Colombia: The Justice and Peace Law', August 2005, <http://www.cja.org/article.php?id=863>.

[5] Council on Foreign Relations, 'Colombia's right-wing paramilitaries and splinter groups', 11 January 2008, <http://www.cfr.org/colombia/colombias-right-wing-paramilitaries-splinter-groups/p15239?breadcrumb=%2Fpublication%2Fpublication_list%3Ftype%3Dbackgrounder%26page%3D9>.

[6] 'Colombia and Farc negotiators launch Norway peace talks', *BBC*, 18 October 2012, <http://www.bbc.co.uk/news/world-latin-america-19994289?print=true>.

reached.[7] After the launch of the process, both parties agreed to move the talks to Havana, Cuba, in November 2012. Negotiations were due first to tackle land reform and subsequently other core issues, such as the end of armed conflict, guarantees for the exercise of political opposition and citizen participation, drug trafficking, and the rights of the victims of the conflict.[8]

In January 2013, while the peace talks were ongoing, the FARC ended its unilateral two-month cease-fire by launching a series of attacks in both the northern and south-western parts of the country.[9] Ivan Marquez excluded the possibility of an extension of the truce unless the Colombian government agreed to join it.[10]

PARTIES TO THE CONFLICTS

Colombian armed forces

In March 2012, it was claimed that the effective combat strength of the National Army (Ejército Nacional) was considerably less than that suggested by the total strength figures.[11] Despite having a total of 226,352 members in 2008, well over half of the army, or 128,818 personnel in early 2009, could not legally be used for combat duty because they were serving their obligatory military service.[12]

According to Human Rights Watch (HRW), over the past decade, the Colombian army 'committed an alarming number of extrajudicial killings of civilians. In many cases—commonly referred to as "false positives"—army personnel murdered civilians and reported them as combatants killed in action, apparently in response to pressure to boost body counts'.[13] As of August 2012, the Human Rights Unit of the Attorney General's office 'was investigating 1,727 cases of alleged extrajudicial executions committed by state agents throughout the country involving nearly 3,000 victims. Most cases are attributed to the army and occurred between 2004 and 2008. There has been a

---

[7] 'Colombia's President Santos rejects Farc ceasefire call', *BBC*, 7 September 2012, <http://www.bbc.co.uk/news/world-latin-america-19514814>.

[8] 'Colombia's Farc peace talks resume in Cuba', *BBC*, 5 December 2012, <http://www.bbc.co.uk/news/world-latin-america-20618131>.

[9] 'FARC launch several attacks after ceasefire ends', *Colombia Reports*, 21 January 2013, <http://colombiareports.com/colombia-news/news/27783-farc-launch-several-attacks-after-ceasefire-ends.html>.

[10] 'FARC proponen un alto al fuego bilateral', *Semana*, 20 January 2013, <http://www.semana.com/nacion/articulo/farc-proponen-alto-fuego-bilateral/330251-3>.

[11] GlobalSecurity.org, 'Colombia—Army (Ejercito Nacional)', 4 March 2012, <http://www.globalsecurity.org/military/world/colombia/colombia_army.htm>.

[12] GlobalSecurity.org, 'Colombia—Army (Ejercito Nacional)'.

[13] HRW, 'World report 2013: Colombia', <http://www.hrw.org/world-report/2013/country-chapters/colombia?page=2>.

dramatic reduction in cases of alleged extrajudicial killings attributed to the security forces since 2009; nevertheless, some cases were reported in 2011 and 2012'.[14]

Revolutionary Armed Forces of Colombia (FARC-EP)

The oldest and largest of Colombia's left-wing rebel groups, the FARC-EP, was formed in 1964 with a mission to overthrow the government and install a Marxist regime through armed struggle. The FARC early on gained the support of the Soviet Union, and continued to have strong ties to the Colombian Communist Party until the mid-1980s. When paramilitary forces fought with the group in the 1990s, the FARC began financing its campaign through involvement in and taxation of the illegal drug trade,[15] as well as kidnapping and extortion. In combination with acts of violence against civilians, this led to a loss of support among the civilian population.

In 2008, the FARC was estimated to have between 10,000 and 15,000 fighters. These were organized into fronts characterized by a relatively strong hierarchy and discipline; the FARC secretariat reportedly had a high degree of control over all fronts, with centralized income and direct communication with commanders via radio. Since the death in 2008 of its long-time spiritual and military commander, Pedro Antonio Marín, alias 'Manuel Marulanda', the rebel group has begun moving towards building up its urban networks and increasing its political outreach, after the military defeats suffered during Álvaro Uribe's presidency (2002–10).[16]

In February 2012, the group pledged to renounce kidnapping, although it has not renounced violence.[17] While it has significantly weakened, the FARC remains on US and European lists of terrorist organizations. Since November 2012, the group has been actively engaged in peace negotiations with the Colombian government.

---

[14] HRW, 'World report 2013: Colombia'.

[15] According to a US Department of Justice indictment in 2006, the FARC generates more than 50 per cent of the world's cocaine and more than 60 per cent of the cocaine that enters the United States of America (USA). See US Department of Justice, 'United States charges 50 leaders of narco-terrorist FARC in Colombia with supplying more than half of the world's cocaine', 22 March 2002, <http://searchjustice.usdoj.gov/search?q=cache:mnp5e3rWob0J:www.justice.gov/opa/pr/2006/March/06_crm_163.html+FARC&output=xml_no_dtd&ie=iso-8859-1&client=default_frontend&proxystylesheet=default_frontend&site=default_collection&access=p&oe=windows-1252>.

[16] Main websites consulted: <http://www.cedema.org/>; <http://www.resistencia-colombia.org/>; <http://anncol.info/>; <http://www.abpnoticias.com/>; <http://twitter.com/#!/FARC_COLOMBIA>; <http://anncol1.blogspot.com/>.

[17] Secretariado del Estado Mayor Central de las FARC-EP, 'Comunicado publico sobre retenciones y prisioneros', Montañas de Colombia, 26 February 2012, <http://www.resistencia-colombia.org/index.php?option=com_content&view=article&id=1212:secretariado-del-estado-mayor-central-de-las-farc-ep&catid=22&Itemid=37>.

National Liberation Army (ELN)

Founded in 1964, the Ejército de Liberación Nacional (ELN) is the second-largest leftist rebel group in Colombia after the FARC. The ELN ideology is based on Marxism-Leninism as well as liberation theology, a predominantly Catholic philosophy with a strong emphasis on social awareness and justice. The ELN considered itself a liberation movement, formed with the goal of ousting the ruling government.[18] The group believes that foreign involvement in Colombia's oil industry violates the country's sovereignty and that foreign companies are unfairly exploiting Colombia's natural resources. It was long seen as more politically motivated than the FARC, staying out of the illegal drugs trade on ideological grounds.[19]

The ELN reached the height of its power in the late 1990s, carrying out hundreds of kidnappings and hitting infrastructure such as oil pipelines. The ELN ranks have since declined from around 4,000 to an estimated 1,500, suffering defeats at the hands of the security forces and paramilitaries.[20] However, in October 2009, ELN rebels were able to spring one of their leaders from jail, indicating that they were not a completely spent force. In recent years, ELN units have become involved in the drugs trade, often forming alliances with criminal gangs. The ELN remains on US and European lists of terrorist organizations.[21]

United Self-Defence Forces of Colombia (AUC)

An umbrella organization for right-wing paramilitaries, the AUC is led by Carlos Castaño and in 2008 was said to have more than 10,000 men under arms. It was formed in 1997 by landowners and drug traffickers to respond to rebel kidnappings and extortion.[22] Believed to have links to certain local military commanders, the AUC often recruited its troops among former Colombian army soldiers. Following the AUC's decision to enter into peace talks with the government in 2002, several militant factions separated from the main group and continued their armed campaign against rebels.[23] The AUC signed an

---

[18]   Council on Foreign Relations, 'FARC, ELN: Colombia's left-wing guerrillas', 19 August 2009, <http://www.cfr.org/colombia/farc-eln-colombias-left-wing-guerrillas/p9272>.

[19]   Portal Voces de Colombia: Ejército de Liberacion National, <http://www.eln-voces.com/index.php/en/>.

[20]   Portal Voces de Colombia: Ejército de Liberacion National.

[21]   Globalsecurity.org, 'Ejército de Liberación Nacional (ELN): National Liberation Army', <http://www.globalsecurity.org/military/world/para/eln.htm>.

[22]   Council on Foreign Relations, 'Colombia's right-wing paramilitaries and splinter groups', 11 January 2008, <http://www.cfr.org/colombia/colombias-right-wing-paramilitaries-splinter-groups/p15239?breadcrumb=%2Fpublication%2Fpublication_list%3Ftype%3Dbackgrounder%26page%3D9>.

[23]   Globalsecurity.org, 'United Self-Defense Forces/Group of Colombia (AUC—Autodefensas Unidas de Colombia)', <http://www.globalsecurity.org/military/world/para/auc.htm>.

agreement with the government in 2003 to demobilize its forces, a process that was concluded in 2006 when the government announced that the AUC no longer existed.

CASUALTIES

For 2012, there was no comprehensive source of conflict-related casualties in Colombia. The Colombian National Human Rights Observatory tracked and published homicide statistics that it refers to as 'violations to the right to life and integrity'; it reported 13,602 homicides recorded by the National Institute of Legal Medicine and 15,038 recorded by the Directorate of Criminal Investigation.[24] These figures were also cited by the United Nations (UN) Office for the Coordination of Humanitarian Affairs (OCHA) in regard to the humanitarian situation in Colombia.[25]

In December 2011, a newly formed government unit responsible for the registry of conflict-related victims began operating under the new National Victim's Law (Law 1448 of 2011). As of 1 May 2013, the registry had not made data on registered victims available.[26]

Victim-activated explosives, including anti-personnel mines, improvised explosive devices (IEDs), and explosive remnants of war (ERW), caused a total of 496 casualties in 2012. The Colombian Presidential Program for Mine Action (PAICMA) recorded 279 casualties among members of the armed forces and 217 among civilians. There were 66 child casualties.[27]

Action on Armed Violence (AOAV) identified 317 civilian casualties from 35 incidents of explosive violence in 2012. With available data, it was not possible to determine whether or not these casualties overlap with casualties reported by other sources.[28]

In 2012, at least three employees of American private contractors were registered as killed in Colombia.[29]

[24] Observatorio Derechos Humanos y Derecho Internacional Humanitario (Human Rights and Humanitarian Law Observatory), 'Estadisticas nacionales sobre derechos a la vida y a la integridad' ('National statistics on the right to life and integrity'), <http://www.derechoshumanos.gov.co/Observatorio/Paginas/Observatorio.aspx>.

[25] OCHA, 'Colombia humanitarian situation: synopsis July–December 2012', p. 7.

[26] Unidad para la Atencion y Reparacion Integral de las Victimas (Unit for the Care and Reparation of Victims), <http://www.unidadvictimas.gov.co/index.php>.

[27] Analysis of PAICMA casualty data, 'Situación nacional 1990– Febrero 2013' ('National situation 1990–February 2013'), undated, <http://www.accioncontraminas.gov.co>.

[28] AOAV, 'An explosive situation: monitoring explosive violence in 2012', March 2013, p. 10.

[29] According to publicly available data from the US Department of Labor. The 2012 data was measured as the changes in number of total contractor deaths recorded since 2001: 11 in 2012; and 8 in 2011. See <http://www.dol.gov/owcp/dlhwc/dbaallnation12-31-12.htm> and <http://www.dol.gov/owcp/dlhwc/dbaallnation12-31-11.htm>.

Somos Defensores, a Colombian human rights organization, documented the death of 69 human rights activists in the country during 2012.[30] Amnesty International reported the killing of 40 human rights defenders in 2012 to the Human Rights Council.[31] According to the Colombian National Human Rights Observatory, two mayors, five municipal council members, 20 trade union members, and 76 indigenous persons were killed in 2012.[32] It also documented 66 deaths from 14 massacres occurring between 1 January and 31 July 2012. During the same period, 196 people were kidnapped.[33] The government alleged that armed non-state actors (ANSAs) were responsible for at least 33 kidnapping cases (17 by the FARC and 16 by the ELN) in 2012.[34]

The UN Secretary-General's report on sexual violence in conflict found that sexual violence was a persistent practice within the armed conflict in Colombia in 2012. It did not provide statistics, but reported that armed non-state groups, including the FARC, used sexual violence forcefully to displace populations from lucrative mining or agriculture zones, or in strategic corridors for narco-trafficking. Survivors and women's groups indicated that many victims of sexual violence were children, and that incidents of sexual violence included abductions and subsequent rape, sexual slavery, and forced abortions by armed non-state groups.[35]

DISPLACED

In 2012, Colombia remained the country with the highest number of internally displaced persons (IDPs) in the world, with a total of between 4.9 and 5.5 million by the end of the year and with some 230,000 new displacements occurring during the year. Ethnic minority groups, including indigenous and Afro-Colombian people, made up a significant

---

[30] Somos Defensores, 'El efecto placebo: informe anual 2012 sistema de información sobre agresiones contra defensoras y defensores de derechos humanos en Colombia' ('The placebo effect: 2012 annual report of the monitoring system of aggressions against human rights defenders in Colombia'), Bogota, 15 February 2013, <http://www.somosdefensores.org/attachments/article/412/informe%20somos%20defensores%20español% 20FINAL%202012.pdf>.

[31] 'Written statement submitted by Amnesty International', Human Rights Council, UN doc. A/HRC/22/ NGO/174, 27 February 2013, p. 3.

[32] Data of the Human Rights and Humanitarian Law Observatory, reported in OCHA, 'Colombia Humanitarian Situation: Synopsis July–December 2012', p. 7.

[33] Observatorio Derechos Humanos y Derecho Internacional Humanitario (Human Rights and Humanitarian Law Observatory), 'Estadisticas nacionales sobre derechos a la vida y a la integridad' ('National statistics on the right to life and integrity'), <http://www.derechoshumanos.gov.co/Observatorio/Paginas/ Observatorio.aspx>.

[34] US Department of State, 'Country reports on human rights practices 2012: Colombia', 19 April 2013.

[35] 'Report of the Secretary-General on sexual violence in conflict', UN doc. A/67/792–S/2013/149, 14 March 2013, §24.

proportion of IDPs. A disproportionate number of women and people under the age of 25 have also been displaced.[36]

WAR CRIMES ALLEGATIONS, INVESTIGATIONS, AND PROSECUTIONS

Colombia adhered to the 1998 Rome Statute of the International Criminal Court (the ICC Statute) in August 2002. The ICC has jurisdiction over ICC Statute crimes committed on the territory of Colombia or by its nationals since 1 November 2002, in cases in which national courts are unwilling or unable to prosecute. However, the Court only has jurisdiction over war crimes since 1 November 2009, in accordance with Colombia's declaration pursuant to Article 124 of the ICC Statute.[37]

The OTP has 'determined that there is a reasonable basis to believe' that, from 1 November 2002 to November 2012, 'acts constituting crimes against humanity have been committed by non-State actors, namely the FARC, ELN and paramilitary groups'.[38] 'There is also a reasonable basis to believe' that, from 1 November 2009 to November 2012, 'acts constituting war crimes have been committed by the FARC and the ELN: murder . . . and attacking civilians; torture and cruel treatment . . . and outrages upon personal dignity . . . ; taking of hostages . . . ; rape and other forms of sexual violence . . . ; conscripting, enlisting and using children to participate actively in hostilities'.[39]

The OTP has further noted that because paramilitary armed groups demobilized as of 2006, they are not considered a party to the armed conflict during the period over which the ICC has jurisdiction over war crimes:

Nonetheless, the Office continues to analyse whether so called 'successor paramilitary groups' or 'new illegal armed groups' could qualify as organised armed groups that are parties to the armed conflict or would satisfy the requirements of organisational policy for the purpose of crimes against humanity. The Government of Colombia refers to these groups as criminal bands (bandas criminales or BACRIM), and does not consider them as organized armed groups that are parties to the armed conflict.[40]

With regard to state actors, the OTP stated as follows:

State actors, in particular members of the Colombian army, have also allegedly deliberately killed thousands of civilians to bolster success rates in the context of the internal armed conflict and to obtain monetary profit from the State's funds. Executed civilians were reported as guerrillas killed

---

[36] Internal Displacement Monitoring Centre (IDMC), 'Global overview 2012', April 2013, p. 38.
[37] ICC Office of the Prosecutor (OTP), 'Report on preliminary examination activities 2012', November 2012, §98.
[38] ICC OTP, 'Report on preliminary examination activities 2012', §102.
[39] ICC OTP, 'Report on preliminary examination activities 2012', §103.
[40] ICC OTP, 'Report on preliminary examination activities 2012', §104.

in combat after alterations of the crime scene. Allegedly, these killings, also known as 'falsos positivos' (false positives), started during the 1980s and occurred with greatest frequency from 2004 until 2008. The available information indicates that these killings were carried out by members of the armed forces, at times operating jointly with paramilitaries and civilians, as a part of an attack directed against civilians in different parts of Colombia. Killings were in some cases preceded by arbitrary detentions, torture and other forms of ill-treatment.[41]

The OTP found a 'reasonable basis to believe that the acts described above were committed pursuant to a policy adopted at least at the level of certain brigades within the armed forces, constituting the existence of a State or organizational policy to commit such crimes'. It concluded that murder and enforced disappearance constituting crimes against humanity have been committed by organs of the state.[42] It further found a reasonable basis to believe that, in the period from 1 November 2009 to November 2012, members of state forces committed the following war crimes: murder and attacking civilians; torture and cruel treatment, and outrages upon personal dignity; and rape and other forms of sexual violence.[43]

---

[41] ICC OTP, 'Report on preliminary examination activities 2012', §105.
[42] ICC OTP, 'Report on preliminary examination activities 2012', §106.
[43] ICC OTP, 'Report on preliminary examination activities 2012', §107.

Armed conflict in the Democratic Republic of Congo in 2012

KEY CONFLICT STATISTICS FOR 2012

Total recorded deaths:	183	
Civilian deaths:	41+	(Sources: UN; HRW)
Civilians injured by sexual violence:	764 (280 children)	(Source: UN)
Civilian female deaths:	4+	(Source: UN)
Child deaths:	20	(Sources: UN; Media reports; HRW)
Children injured:	37	(Source: UN)
Military deaths:	2–9	(Sources: UN; Media reports)
NSAG members killed:	9–113	(Source: Media reports)
Peacekeepers injured:	6	(Source: Media reports)
Civilians displaced:	2.7 million (Dec. 2012)	(Source: IDMC)

CLASSIFICATION OF THE CONFLICTS

The Armed Forces of the Democratic Republic of the Congo (FARDC) were involved in an armed conflict of a non-international character (NIAC) with M23. The conflict reached the threshold for applicability of the 1977 Additional Protocol II.

There were also separate NIACs in 2012 with the Lord's Resistance Army (LRA), the Forces Démocratiques de Libération du Rwanda (FDLR), and the Allied Democratic Forces/National Army for the Liberation of Uganda (ADF-NALU).

SUMMARY OF APPLICABLE INTERNATIONAL LAW

All parties to the conflicts are bound by, inter alia: Common Article 3 to the 1949 Geneva Conventions; the customary international humanitarian law (IHL) rules of distinction, proportionality, and precautions in attacks; the obligation not to recruit and use children as soldiers; and the duty to respect, at a minimum, fundamental human rights. This includes the duty to respect the rights to life and to freedom from torture or other forms of cruel, inhuman, or degrading treatment or punishment.

In addition, the Democratic Republic of the Congo (DRC) is a state party to the 1977 Additional Protocol II, which applies to the NIAC with M23, as well as to the two 1966 Covenants (on civil and political rights, and on economic, social and cultural rights). States participating in the United Nations Organization Stabilization

Mission in the Democratic Republic of the Congo (MONUSCO) are bound extraterritorially by their human rights obligations.[1]

The DRC acceded to the 1997 Anti-Personnel Mine Ban Convention (APMBC) in May 2002, becoming a state party on 1 November 2002, and has signed, but not yet ratified, the 2008 Convention on Cluster Munitions (CCM). States participating in MONUSCO who are party to the APMBC and CCM are bound by those instruments. In any event, the United Nations (UN) Secretary-General's Bulletin requires that UN peacekeeping forces engaged as a party in an armed conflict not use anti-personnel mines.[2]

HISTORY OF THE CONFLICT[3]

The DRC is the site of one of the world's worst ongoing humanitarian crises. Mortality studies estimate that up to 1,200 people have died each day from conflict-related causes, mostly disease and malnutrition, but also from ongoing violence. Rebel factions have been fighting the government, fighting each other, attacking civilians, and subjected to infighting. The vast country, the size of Western Europe, is rich in natural resources, a fact that has often been at the heart of conflicts.[4]

The government in Kinshasa does not effectively control large parts of the country and tension remains high in the east, particularly in North and South Kivu provinces, with conflict ongoing in a number of areas. With the help of the UN Mission in the Democratic Republic of Congo (MONUC), the country was able to overcome major logistic and political challenges to hold its first 'free and fair' elections in 40 years in 2006. Joseph Kabila won the elections, but his government faced huge challenges in rebuilding state institutions that were accountable to the Congolese people. Renewed violence in the east and brutal government crackdowns in the west underscored the country's continued fragility.

In January 2008, the 'Acte d'engagement' was signed in Goma between the government, the National Congress for the Defence of the People (NCDP, known in French as CNDP), the Mayi-Mayi, and several other armed groups. However, the agreement did not include Hutu militia still active in the area, causing serious doubt as to whether or

---

[1] See e.g. International Court of Justice (ICJ), *Wall* Advisory Opinion, 2004, §106; ICJ, *Armed Activities on the Territory of the Congo* (*Democratic Republic of the Congo v. Uganda*), Judgment, 19 December 2005.

[2] 'Secretary-General's Bulletin: Observance by United Nations forces of international humanitarian law', New York, UN doc. ST/SGB/1999/13, 6 August 1999.

[3] Unless otherwise stated, this section is based on 'Democratic Republic of Congo profile', *BBC*, 25 March 2013, <http://www.bbc.co.uk/news/world-africa-13283212>.

[4] Human Rights Watch (HRW), 'Democratic Republic of Congo: renewed crisis in North Kivu', October 2007, pp. 3–4, <http://www.hrw.org/reports/2007/10/23/renewed-crisis-north-kivu>.

not it would be successful.[5] Indeed, in October 2008, the situation worsened significantly in the east of the country as fighting and displacement increased in North Kivu, following an advance by the NCDP.[6] Tensions between Rwanda and the DRC also escalated over alleged Rwandan support for the NCDP.

In an attempt to bring the situation under control, the government in January 2009 invited in troops from Rwanda to help set up a joint operation against the Rwandan rebel Hutu militias active in eastern DRC. On 23 March 2009, the NCDP signed a peace treaty with the Congolese government, under which it became a political party, and up to 300 former NCDP soldiers were integrated into the FARDC.[7] In November 2011, despite allegations of irregularities and human rights abuses against the population, elections were held confirming another term for incumbent President Kabila.

In April 2012, conflict broke out again in the Kivu province. A new militia, the M23, appeared on the scene, first demanding the implementation of the 23 March 2009 peace deal, but subsequently taking the provincial capital, Goma, and threatening Kinshasa. The group was formed after former members of the NCDP mutinied against the FARDC to protest against the claimed inability of the government to implement the peace agreement.[8] The group was alleged to have been supported by both Rwanda and Uganda.[9] In late December 2012, the M23 left Goma, agreed to a cease-fire, and started negotiations with the government. In early 2013, negotiations resumed and were ongoing.[10] By April, however, talks between M23 and the government had stalled. On 12 April, M23 rebels warned of reprisals if they were attacked by the 3,069-strong UN intervention force expected to deploy in late April.[11]

On 23 February 2013, a Peace, Security and Cooperation Framework agreement for the DRC and the region[12] was signed in Addis Ababa by the DRC, Angola, Burundi, the Central African Republic (CAR), the Republic of Congo, Rwanda, South Africa, South

---

[5] Radio France Internationale (RFI), *Accord de paix signé à Goma*, 23 January 2008, <http://www.rfi.fr/actufr/articles/097/article_61837.asp>.

[6] 'Goma: application de l'acte d'engagement, des pistes de solution en vue', *Radio Okapi*, 7 February 2008, <http://radiookapi.net/sans-categorie/2008/02/07/goma-application-de-l%E2%80%99acte-d%E2%80%99engagement-des-pistes-de-solution-en-vue/>.

[7] Peace Agreement between the Government and le Congrès National pour la Défense du Peuple (CNDP), 23 March 2009, <http://www.iccwomen.org/publications/Peace_Agreement_between_the_Government_and_the_CNDP.pdf>.

[8] 'DRC: Understanding armed group M23', *IRIN*, 22 June 2012, <http://www.irinnews.org/report/95715/DRC-Understanding-armed-group-M23>.

[9] HRW, 'DR Congo: Rwanda should stop aiding war crimes suspect', 4 June 2012, <http://www.hrw.org/news/2012/06/03/dr-congo-rwanda-should-stop-aiding-war-crimes-suspect-0>.

[10] 'Congo's M23 rebels say peace deal possible by end-February', *Reuters*, 1 February 2013, <http://www.reuters.com/article/2013/02/01/congo-democratic-idUSL5N0B140F20130201>.

[11] International Crisis Group (ICG), 'Crisis watch database: DR Congo', 1 May 2013, <http://www.crisisgroup.org/en/publication-type/crisiswatch/crisiswatch-database.aspx?CountryIDs=%7bC076CDFE-2B2D-4642-8895-5EF27AE4E416%7d&StartDate=20120101&EndDate=20130505>.

[12] Available at <http://www.peaceau.org/uploads/scanned-on-24022013-125543.pdf>.

Sudan, Tanzania, Uganda, and Zambia. States agreed to abstain from interfering in the internal affairs of their neighbours, while the DRC agreed to structural and security sector reform. The UN Secretary-General, the Chairperson of the African Union Commission, the Chairperson of the Southern African Development Community (SADC), and the Chairperson of the International Conference on the Great Lakes Region (ICGLR) also signed the agreement as witnesses.

PARTIES TO THE CONFLICTS

Armed Forces of the Democratic Republic of Congo

There have been long-standing concerns about FARDC compliance with international law, which continued in 2012.[13] In November 2012, according to a report by the UN, violations of human rights law and IHL committed by FARDC soldiers were:

…perpetrated in a systematic manner and with extreme violence, mostly as FARDC units retreated from the front lines and regrouped in and around the town of Minova, Kalehe territory, South Kivu province. In this context, at least 102 women and 33 girls were victims of rape or other acts of sexual violence perpetrated by FARDC soldiers. FARDC soldiers were also responsible for the arbitrary execution of at least two people, violations of the right to physical integrity of at least 24 civilians, cases of forced labour and the widespread looting of villages.[14]

Amnesty International reported that nine soldiers from the Congolese armed forces, including a lieutenant colonel, were convicted of crimes against humanity, notably rape, committed on 1 January in the town of Fizi, South Kivu. They were sentenced to jail in February 2012 'in a rare example of perpetrators being promptly brought to justice'.[15] In 2009, several UN officials were reported by one commentator as acknowledging privately that the army is a major problem, largely due to corruption that results in food and pay meant for soldiers being diverted and a military structure that contains many former warlords.[16] In a 2009 report alleging FARDC abuses, HRW urged the UN to stop supporting government offensives against eastern rebels until the abuses ceased.[17]

---

[13] See e.g. Amnesty International, '10 facts you should know about the crisis in the DRC', 20 March 2013, <http://responsibilitytoprotect.org/index.php/component/content/article/35-r2pcs-topics/4715-amnesty-international-10-facts-you-should-know-about-the-crisis-in-the-drc>.

[14] UN Joint Human Rights Office (UNJHRO), 'UNJHRO report on Human Rights violations by FARDC and M23 in Goma, Sake, and around Minova. 15 November–2 December 2012', May 2013, Summary, <http://www.ohchr.org/Documents/Countries/ZR/UNJHROMay2013_en.pdf>.

[15] Amnesty International, 'Annual report 2012: Democratic Republic of the Congo', <http://www.amnesty.org/en/region/democratic-republic-congo/report-2012>.

[16] Adam Hochschild, 'Rape of the Congo', *New York Review of Books*, 56(13) (13 August 2009).

[17] HRW, 'You will be punished', 13 December 2009, <http://www.hrw.org/en/node/87142/section/4>.

National Congress for the Defence of the People (NCDP) → M23

The National Congress for the Defence of the People (NCDP) is a political armed militia established by Laurent Nkunda in the Kivu region of the DRC in December 2006.[18] In January 2009, the NCDP split and Nkunda was arrested by Rwanda. On 23 March 2009, the NCDP signed a peace treaty with the Congolese government, under which it became a political party. A few hundred former NCDP soldiers, as agreed in the peace deal, were then integrated into the FARDC.[19]

The M23 armed group was formed on 4 April 2012 after close to 300 soldiers, all former members of the NCDP, mutinied against the FARDC, complaining of poor conditions.[20] The new armed group called itself the M23 (March 23 Movement) since soldiers claimed their mutiny was to protest against the Congolese government's failure to fully implement the 23 March 2009 peace agreement, which had integrated them into the Congolese army.[21] In June, the UN High Commissioner for Human Rights, Navi Pillay, identified five of the M23's leaders as 'among the worst perpetrators of human rights violations in the DRC, or in the world'. They include General Bosco Ntaganda, who was sought on two arrest warrants by the International Criminal Court (ICC) for war crimes and crimes against humanity in Ituri district, and Colonel Sultani Makenga, who is implicated in the recruitment of children and several massacres in eastern Congo.[22]

Since then, the M23 rebels have been active in the North Kivu province, fighting government forces in the Rutshuru and Masisi territories. In July 2012, members of this group captured several towns north of Goma, the provincial capital of North Kivu province, and on 11 November they entered Goma itself, taking control of the city and the airport.[23] As a result, more than 200 people have been killed and the number of internally displaced persons has risen to 1.7 million. The rebels agreed to the peace talks in December after the International Conference on the Great Lakes Region pressured them, and by the end of the year the M23 left Goma. In February 2013, the armed group said it expected to sign a peace deal with the government by the end of the month

---

[18] GlobalSecurity.org, 'National Committee for the Defense of the People (CNDP)', August 2012, <http://www.globalsecurity.org/military/world/para/cndp.htm>.

[19] UPCD Conflict Encyclopedia, 'DRC, general non-state conflict information', July 2012, <http://www.ucdp.uu.se/gpdatabase/gpcountry.php?id=38&regionSelect=2-Southern_Africa>.

[20] 'Q&A: DR Congo's M23 rebels', *BBC*, 23 November 2012, <http://www.bbc.co.uk/news/world-africa-20438531>.

[21] 'DRC: Understanding armed group M23', *IRIN*.

[22] 'UN Human Rights chief fears more rapes, killings in Congo by M23', *United Nations Radio*, 19 June 2012, <http://www.unmultimedia.org/radio/english/2012/06/un-human-rights-chief-fears-more-rapes-killings-in-congo-by-m23/>.

[23] Africa Updates, 'DRC Congo: M23 rebels capture Goma City in eastern DRC Congo', 11 November 2012.

ending its ten-month revolt.[24] In May, however, peace talks, which were still ongoing, were broken off, and fighting had erupted again between M23 and the FARDC.[25]

ADF-NALU[26]

The Allied Democratic Forces-National Army for the Liberation of Uganda (Forces démocratiques alliées-Armée nationale de libération de l'Ouganda, or ADF-NALU) is one of the oldest, but least-known armed groups in the east of the DRC and the only one in the area to be considered an Islamist terrorist organization. Although it does not represent the same destabilizing threat as the M23, it has managed to stand its ground against the FARDC since 2010. Created in the DRC in 1995 and located in the mountainous DRC–Uganda border area, this Congolese–Ugandan armed group has shown remarkable resilience attributable to its geostrategic position, its successful integration into the cross-border economy, and corruption in the security forces.

Formed of an alliance of several armed groups supported by external actors (Mobutu Sese Seko's Zaire and Hassan al-Turabi's Sudan), the ADF-NALU initially fought the Ugandan government of Yoweri Museveni. However, despite its Ugandan origins, it never managed to gain a foothold in its own country and instead settled in eastern Congo, particularly in the remote mountainous border areas. There it became integrated into local communities, participated in cross-border trade, and forged relationships with various armed groups in eastern Congo, as well as with both Congolese and Ugandan civilian and military authorities. Given their location in this 'grey zone', the ADF-NALU's lost fighters have been able to survive despite not winning a battle in more than 15 years and having been defeated several times, but never neutralized.

Due to the ADF-NALU's leader, Jamil Mukulu, a Christian convert to Islam, the group has transformed from a purely Congolese–Ugandan problem into one with regional dimensions, as a component of the trend of radical Islamism in East Africa. However, little is known about such purported links between ADF-NALU and radical Islamist organizations in the region.

---

[24] 'Congo's M23 rebels say peace deal possible by end-February', *Reuters*, 1 February 2013.

[25] 'M23 rebels suspend peace talks with Congo over UN mandate', *Press TV*, 2 May 2013, <http://www.presstv.com/detail/2013/05/02/301353/m23-suspends-peace-talks-with-congo/>; Edmund Kagire, 'M23 rebels, DRC forces clash again as UN chief arrives on peace tour visit', *East African*, 25 May 2013, <http://www.theeastafrican.co.ke/news/-/2558/1862726/-/k93yxrz/-/index.html>.

[26] This armed group profile is taken from ICG, 'Eastern Congo: the ADF-NALU's lost rebellion', Africa Briefing No. 93, 19 December 2012, <http://www.crisisgroup.org/en/regions/africa/central-africa/dr-congo/b093-eastern-congo-the-adf-nalus-lost-rebellion.aspx>.

FDLR

As the ICG noted already in 2005, the continued existence in the DRC of 8,000 to 10,000 Hutu rebels with links to the 1994 genocide in their home country, Rwanda, is a key source of regional instability.[27] Although too weak to imperil Rwanda's government, and although many of its members are not themselves *genocidaires*, the FDLR gave Kigali justification for interference in the DRC for many years. In 2012, however, the FDLR, which is based in North Kivu, also attacked people inside Rwanda.[28] A second attack occurred in early December 2012.[29]

Congolese Rally for Democracy

The RCD (Congolese Rally for Democracy), was a rebel group fighting the DRC government in the 1998–2002 conflict. The armed force of the group was called the ANC (Armée Nationale Congolaise, or the Congolese National Army). Since its formation, the RCD has split into several different movements. The most important split occurred in May 1999 after a conflict over control of Kisangani between the movement's alleged main backers Rwanda and Uganda. The two states had opposing views on RCD's approach: whether or not the RCD should have a political approach to back up its military tactics. The main faction of the rebel group was the RCD-Goma, which controlled a significant part of the eastern DRC, including South Kivu, some parts of North Kivu, the provinces Katanga, Maniema, Kasai, and the town of Kisangani.[30]

Mayi-Mayi

The Mayi-Mayi, or Mai-Mai (Congolese Swahili for 'Water Water'), is a loose association of traditional Congolese local defence forces, which primarily fought Rwandan government forces and their Congolese allies. It is opposed to 'Tutsi domination' and the RCD, but is otherwise seemingly without any clear objective and frequently changes allegiances.[31] No homogeneity exists between the various Mayi-Mayi groups.

---

[27] ICG, 'The Congo: solving the FDLR problem once and for all', Africa Briefing No. 25, 12 May 2005, <http://www.crisisgroup.org/en/regions/africa/central-africa/dr-congo/b025-the-congo-solving-the-fdlr-problem-once-and-for-all.aspx>.

[28] AFP, 'Attaque des rebelles du FDLR contre le Rwanda, selon Kigali', *LeMonde.fr*, 27 November 2012, <http://www.lemonde.fr/afrique/article/2012/11/27/attaque-des-rebelles-du-fdlr-contre-le-rwanda-selon-kigali_1796279_3212.html>.

[29] 'Rwanda says FDLR rebels cross from Congo, attack wardens', *Reuters*, Kigali, 2 December 2012, <http://www.reuters.com/article/2012/12/02/us-rwanda-attack-idUSBRE8B10A020121202>.

[30] For further information, see GlobalSecurity.org, 'Rassemblement congolais pour la democratie (RCD)', <http://www.globalsecurity.org/military/world/para/rcd.htm>.

[31] UPCD Conflict Encyclopedia, 'DRC, general non-state conflict information', July 2012, <http://www.ucdp.uu.se/gpdatabase/gpcountry.php?id=38&regionSelect=2-Southern_Africa>.

After participating in the Kivu conflict (2004–09), the Mayi-Mayi groups signed the *Acte d'engagement* (Goma, 23 January 2008) committing themselves to an immediate cease-fire, to disengagement of forces from frontline positions, and to abide by international human rights law (IHRL).[32]

Since the start of the M23 rebellion, the FDLR and other Congolese armed groups, including the Mayi-Mayi, have also increased their military activities, expanding their areas of control and killing hundreds of civilians in other parts of North Kivu and South Kivu, according to the UN and local human rights activists. These militias appear to have taken advantage of rising ethnic tensions and the security vacuum created by the Congolese army's focus on the M23 rebels.[33]

Lord's Resistance Army and other non-state armed groups

Formed in 1992 in an attempt to unify a resistance movement fractured by the marginalization of the Uganda Democratic Christian Army, the LRA promotes a radical form of Christianity that it wanted to make the foundation of a new Ugandan government.[34] It was claimed that the group entered the DRC in 2005, but since 2007 it has also operated in the CAR.

Other armed non-state actors (ANSAs) involved in the conflict include: the Union des Patriotes Congolais (UPC); the Nationalist and Integrationist Front (FNI); the Movement for the Liberation of Congo (MLC); Forces Populaires pour la Démocratie au Congo (FPDC); the Mouvement Révolutionnaires du Congo (or Congo Revolutionary Movement, a newly formed militia alliance located in the province of Ituri); and the People's Redemption Army (PRA). Also, foreign ANSAs active in DRC are: Burundian Forces for the Defence of Democracy (FDD); ex-Rwandan armed forces; Interahamwe fighters (now called the Forces Démocratiques de Libération du Rwanda, FDLR); the West Nile Bank Front (WBNF); the ADF-NALU; the Uganda National Rescue Front II (UNRF II); the Former Ugandan National Army (FUNA); the PRA; and the Rasta Movement (composed of former Hutu militants who fled to the DRC following the Rwandan genocide).

---

[32] GlobalSecurity.org, 'Mayi-Mayi/Mai Mai', June 2012, <http://www.globalsecurity.org/military/world/para/mayi-mayi.htm>.

[33] 'Katanga: les Maï-Maï tuent plus de 65 personnes en l'espace de trois semaines à Mwemena', *Radio Okapi*, 6 February 2013, <http://radiookapi.net/actualite/2013/02/09/katanga-les-mai-mai-tuent-plus-de-65-personnes-en-lespace-de-trois-semaines-mwemena/#more-142939>.

[34] National Consortium for the Study of Terrorism and Responses to Terrorism (START), 'Terrorist organization profile: Lord's Resistance Army (LRA)', undated, accessed 9 May 2013, <http://www.start.umd.edu/start/data_collections/tops/terrorist_organization_profile.asp?id=3513>.

MONUC and MONUSCO

The UN Security Council established the United Nations Organization Mission in the Democratic Republic of the Congo (MONUC)[35] to facilitate the implementation of the 'Lusaka Accord' signed in 1999 by its Resolution 1279 of 30 November 1999.[36] Later, in a series of resolutions, the Council expanded the mandate of MONUC to the supervision of the implementation of the cease-fire agreement and assigned multiple related additional tasks.

Extending the mandate of MONUC for the last time until 30 June 2010, the Security Council, by Resolution 1925 of 28 May 2010 decided that, from 1 July 2010, it would bear the title 'United Nations Organization Stabilization Mission in the Democratic Republic of the Congo (MONUSCO)',[37] in view of the new phase reached in the country. Emphasizing that the protection of civilians must be given priority, the Council authorized MONUSCO to use all necessary means to carry out its protection mandate, including the effective protection of civilians, humanitarian personnel, and human rights defenders under imminent threat of physical violence, as well as the protection of UN personnel, facilities, installations, and equipment. The Mission would also support government efforts to fight impunity and ensure the protection of civilians from violations of international human rights and humanitarian law, including all forms of sexual and gender-based violence. In July 2012, the Security Council extended MONUSCO's mandate until 30 June 2013 and further detailed its mission.[38]

CASUALTIES

There was a lack of definitive information on the numbers of casualties caused by the M23 Movement during 2012. The UN reported that 'hundreds of civilians were killed' in a series of coordinated attacks by Raia Mutomboki militia under the command of M23 from May 2012 to the end of 2012.[39] HRW reported that M23 deliberately killed at least 15 civilians; three died from the wounds of rape by M23 fighters. HRW also

---

[35] For further information, visit the MONUC webpage, <http://www.un.org/en/peacekeeping/missions/monuc/>.

[36] UN Security Council Resolution 1279, 30 November 1999.

[37] For further information, visit the MONUSCO webpage, <http://monusco.unmissions.org/>.

[38] UN Security Council Resolution 2053, 30 June 2012.

[39] 'Sanctions Committee concerning Democratic Republic of Congo adds two individuals, two entities to sanctions list', UN Security Council, UN doc. SC/10876, 31 December 2012, <http://www.un.org/News/Press/docs/2012/sc10876.doc.htm>.

documented 24 summary executions, including of 21 civilians, by M23 fighters in and around Goma between 19 November and 2 December.[40]

MONUSCO documented 41 child casualties as a direct result of violent conflict. Those casualties included four children who had been killed and 37 others who had been injured. The majority occurred during armed clashes between the FARDC and M23 from 19 to 22 November in and around Goma.[41] A FARDC soldier reportedly killed a boy on 25 November.[42]

The FDLR militia was reported to have been involved in at least 71 killings in 2012 (including 19 children and 12 women).[43] In October, the FDLR also seriously wounded six Indian MONUSCO peacekeepers in an attack.[44]

During 2012, the LRA were reported to have killed 22 people and abducted another 131 in 169 attacks.[45]

Media reporting on military and non-state armed actor casualties lacked consistency. A regional governor was reported as claiming that at least 44 M23 fighters were killed in fighting on 15 November.[46] In another account, the regional governor was reported as saying that 113 M23 rebels wearing Rwandan army uniforms were said to have been killed, but a M23 military spokesperson said it had no fatalities and only two wounded, and claimed the killing of nine FARDC troops and the injuring of 100.[47] On 14 December 2012, two FARDC soldiers were killed during armed clashes with the M23.[48]

---

[40] HRW, 'DR Congo: M23 rebels committing war crimes', 11 September 2012, <http://www.hrw.org/news/2012/09/11/dr-congo-m23-rebels-committing-war-crimes>; HRW, 'DR Congo: war crimes by M23', 5 February 2013, <http://www.hrw.org/news/2013/02/05/dr-congo-war-crimes-m23-congolese-army>.

[41] 'Report of the Secretary-General on the United Nations Organization Stabilization Mission in the Democratic Republic of the Congo', UN doc. S/2013/96, 15 February 2013, §14.

[42] HRW, 'DR Congo: war crimes by M23, Congolese Army', 5 February 2013, <http://www.hrw.org/news/2013/02/05/dr-congo-war-crimes-m23-congolese-army>.

[43] 'Sanctions Committee concerning Democratic Republic of Congo adds two individuals, two entities to sanctions list', UN Security Council, UN doc. SC/10876, 31 December 2012, <http://www.un.org/News/Press/docs/2012/sc10876.doc.htm>.

[44] 'Rwanda: FDLR kills five civilians, injures peacekeepers', *Allafrica.com*, 19 October 2012, <http://allafrica.com/stories/201210190035.html>.

[45] UN Office for the Coordination of Humanitarian Affairs (OCHA), 'LRA regional update: Central African Republic, DR Congo and South Sudan (October–December 2012)'.

[46] 'Briefing: DRC's M23 rebellion under pressure', *IRIN*, 16 November 2012, <http://www.irinnews.org/Report/96804/Briefing-DRC-apos-s-M23-rebellion-under-pressure>; see also 'Congo governor: 44 killed in new fighting between M23 rebels and army in eastern region', *Fox News*, 15 November 2012, <http://www.foxnews.com/world/2012/11/15/congo-fighting-resumes-between-m23-rebels-and-army-in-eastern-region/>.

[47] 'M23 rebels reject claims of mass casualties in DR Congo', *RNW*, 16 November 2012, <http://www.rnw.nl/africa/bulletin/m23-rebels-reject-claims-mass-casualties-dr-congo>.

[48] 'Report of the Secretary-General on the United Nations Organization Stabilization Mission in the Democratic Republic of the Congo', UN doc. S/2013/96, 15 February 2013, §55.

SEXUAL VIOLENCE AND RAPE

Between December 2011 and November 2012, the UN documented 764 victims of sexual violence in conflict in DRC, including 280 children. Just over half of all documented cases were attributed to government security forces (390 victims, including 158 children): FARDC (345) and the Police Nationale Congolaise (PNC) (30), and the state intelligence agency Agence Nationale Renseignements (ANR) (15). The remaining 374 cases were attributed to non-state armed groups, including: the FDLR; Mayi-Mayi Lumumba (Mayi-Mayi Simba and Morgan's group); Forces de Résistance Patriotiques de l'Ituri (FRPI); Forces de Défense Congolaises (FDC); M23; Raïa Mutomboki; and others, including the ADF-NALU, the LRA, the Nyatura armed group, and various Mayi-Mayi militias.[49]

Sexual violence cases sometimes included individuals being victimized multiple times and some victims were killed by the attacks. HRW reported the following instances. The FDLR raped six women and a girl in March 2012, then attacked the village again in April and raped three of the women for the second time.[50] Two other women died from the wounds resulting from rape by M23 fighters, and M23 shot and killed a woman who was three months pregnant when she resisted being raped.[51] M23 rebels also raped a 10-year-old girl, who died from the injuries.[52]

DISPLACED

As of December 2012, there were approximately 2.7 million internally displaced persons (IDPs) in the DRC, 1 million more than reported at the end of 2011, due to increased conflict and violence. Many IDPs had found themselves in protracted and multiple displacements.[53] The M23 offensive in November resulted in the displacement of some 140,000 people.[54]

---

[49] 'Report of the Secretary-General on Sexual violence in Conflict', UN doc. S/2013/149, advance copy dated 12 March 2013, para 40.

[50] 'Sanctions Committee concerning Democratic Republic of Congo adds two individuals, two entities to sanctions list', UN Security Council, UN doc. SC/10876, 31 December 2012, <http://www.un.org/News/Press/docs/2012/sc10876.doc.htm>.

[51] HRW, 'DR Congo: M23 rebels committing war crimes', 11 September 2012, <http://www.hrw.org/news/2012/09/11/dr-congo-m23-rebels-committing-war-crimes>.

[52] HRW, 'DR Congo: war crimes by M23', 5 February 2013, Congolese Army, <http://www.hrw.org/news/2013/02/05/dr-congo-war-crimes-m23-congolese-army>.

[53] Internal Displacement Monitoring Centre (IDMC), 'Global overview 2012', April 2013, p. 23.

[54] 'Report of the Secretary-General on the United Nations Organization Stabilization Mission in the Democratic Republic of the Congo', UN doc. S/2013/96, 15 February 2013, §23.

WAR CRIMES ALLEGATIONS, INVESTIGATIONS, AND PROSECUTIONS

The DRC adhered to the 1998 Rome Statute of the International Criminal Court (the ICC Statute) in April 2002, and therefore, in accordance with the ICC Statute, the Court may exercise jurisdiction over war crimes alleged to have been committed by nationals or on its territory.

During 2012, the ICC conducted a number of investigations and prosecutions of ANSAs' members involved in the conflict. The ICC Chief Prosecutor opened in June 2004 the first ICC investigation, after the DRC referred the situation in the country to the Court. Since then, seven arrest warrants have been issued for war crimes and crimes against humanity. Some of the high-profile cases are summarized below.

Prosecutor v. Thomas Lubanga Dyilo

The trial of Thomas Lubanga Dyilo, which opened on 26 January 2009 before Trial Chamber I of the ICC, is the first trial in the history of the Court, and the first international criminal law trial that has seen victims participate fully in the proceedings.

On 14 March 2012, the ICC issued its first verdict in *Prosecutor v. Thomas Lubanga Dyilo*,[55] finding the former leader of the Union of Congolese Patriots guilty, as a co-perpetrator, of the war crimes of conscripting and enlisting children under the age of 15 and using them to participate actively in hostilities. On 10 July 2012, the Court sentenced Mr Lubanga to 14 years' imprisonment.

Prosecutor v. Germain Katanga and Mathieu Ngudjolo Chui

On 25 September 2009, Trial Chamber II of the ICC upheld the admissibility of the war crimes/crimes against humanity case against former Congolese militia leader Germain Katanga, and former head of the FNI and a colonel in the FARDC, Mathieu Ngudjolo Chui.[56] Their trial started on 24 November 2009. On 18 December 2012, the Trial Chamber acquitted Mathieu Ngudjolo Chui of crimes against humanity and war crimes committed during the attack on the village of Bogoro, in Ituri district.[57] The Prosecution decided to appeal the verdict.

---

[55] ICC, Judgment pursuant to Art. 74 of the Statute, 14 March 2012.

[56] ICC, Decision of Trial Chamber II of 12 June 2009 on the Admissibility of the Case *The Prosecutor v. Germain Katanga and Mathieu Ngudjolo Chui* (Case No. ICC-01/04-01/07 OA 8), 25 September 2009.

[57] ICC, *Prosecutor v. Mathieu Ngudjolo Chui*, Judgment (Case No. ICC-01/04-02/12-3), 18 December 2012.

Prosecutor v. Callixte Mbarushimana

Callixte Mbarushimana, the alleged Executive Secretary of the Forces Démocratiques pour la Libération du Rwanda—Forces Combattantes Abacunguzi (FDLR-FCA, FDLR), was arrested by French authorities on 11 October 2010. The confirmation of charges hearing in the case began on 16 September 2011. Mbarushimana was accused of five counts of crimes against humanity and six counts of war crimes committed in the DRC in 2009. In its 'Decision on the confirmation of charges' of 16 December 2011, Pre-Trial Chamber I found that the Prosecution failed to reach the evidentiary threshold set by the ICC Statute. The former accused was released on 23 December 2011.[58]

Other cases

On 14 May 2012, the Office of the Prosecutor announced it was seeking two new arrest warrants in the situation in the DRC. The warrants concern Bosco Ntaganda, for the crimes committed as a top commander of Thomas Lubanga's militia, the UPC/FPLC, and a leader of one of the most active militia in the Kivu provinces, Sylvestre Mudacumura, the Supreme Commander of the FDLR-FOCA.[59] On 18 March 2013, Bosco Ntaganda surrendered to staff at the US embassy in Kigali, ending violent infighting between M23 rebel factions in DRC that had reportedly killed more 150. Ntaganda was transferred to ICC custody on 22 March.[60]

[58] ICC, *Prosecutor v. Callixte Mbarushimana*, Decision on the confirmation of charges (Case No. ICC-01/04-01/10), 16 December 2011.

[59] UN News Center, 'ICC prosecutor pushes for arrest of rebel leaders wanted for DR Congo crimes', 14 May 2012, <http://www.un.org/apps/news/story.asp?NewsID=41992#.UREuntuwVrs>.

[60] ICG, 'Crisis Watch Database: DR Congo', 1 April 2013, <http://www.crisisgroup.org/en/publication-type/crisiswatch/crisiswatch-database.aspx?CountryIDs=%7bC076CDFE-2B2D-4642-8895-5EF27AE4E416%-7d&StartDate=20120101&EndDate=20130505>.

Armed conflict in Gaza in 2012

KEY CONFLICT STATISTICS FOR 2012

Palestinian civilian deaths:	100	(Source: OCHA)
Palestinians injured:	1,269 (est.)	(Sources: UN; IDMC)
Palestinian children deaths:	39	(Source: OCHA)
Israeli civilian deaths:	4	(Source: OHCHR)
Israeli civilians injured:	219	(Source: OCHA)
Palestinian militant deaths:	74	(Source: OCHA)
Israeli military deaths:	2	(Source: OHCHR)
Israeli military injured:	20	(Source: OHCHR)
Civilians displaced:	144,500	(Source: IDMC)

CLASSIFICATION OF THE CONFLICT

Israeli armed forces were involved in an armed conflict of a non-international character (NIAC) with Hamas and Islamic Jihad for eight days in November 2012. This characterization is controversial. Some might characterize the conflict as international.[1]

SUMMARY OF APPLICABLE INTERNATIONAL LAW

All parties to the conflict were bound by, inter alia: Common Article 3 to the 1949 Geneva Conventions; the customary international humanitarian law (IHL) rules of distinction, proportionality, and precautions in attacks; the obligation not to recruit and use children as soldiers; and the duty to respect, at a minimum, fundamental human rights. This includes the duty to respect the rights to life and to freedom from

---

[1] Views differ as to the legal qualification of the conflict between Israel and the Palestinians. One view would be that the entire conflict, including the armed conflict in November 2012 in the Gaza Strip, is an international armed conflict (IAC). According to the late Antonio Cassese, for example, 'An armed conflict which takes place between an Occupying Power and rebel or insurgent groups—whether or not they are terrorist in character—in an occupied territory, amounts to an international armed conflict:' A. Cassese, *International Law*, 2nd edn, Oxford University Press, Oxford, 2005, p. 420. The view of the *War Report* for the purposes of this entry, however, is that the conflict in Gaza in November 2012 was an armed conflict of a non-international character (NIAC) between Israel and Palestinian non-state armed groups. This NIAC took place within the context of a broader military occupation by Israel, which is generally governed by the law of IAC.

torture or other forms of cruel, inhuman, or degrading treatment or punishment. In addition, Israel is bound extraterritorially by its human rights obligations.[2]

Israel has not adhered to either the 1997 Anti-Personnel Mine Ban Convention (APMBC) or the 2008 Convention on Cluster Munitions (CCM).

HISTORY OF THE CONFLICT[3]

In early 2006, Hamas won legislative elections in the Palestinian territories challenging Fatah's leadership of the Palestinian national movement. Tensions over control of Palestinian security forces soon erupted into the 2007 Battle of Gaza, after which Hamas retained control of Gaza while its officials were ousted from government positions in the West Bank. Israel and Egypt then imposed an economic blockade on Gaza, on the grounds that Fatah forces were no longer providing security there.

In June 2008, as part of an Egyptian-brokered cease-fire, Hamas ceased rocket attacks on Israel. After four months of calm, the conflict escalated and Israel launched Operation Cast Lead (27 December 2008–18 January 2009), stating that the three weeks of air and ground assaults were in response to repeated rocket and mortar fire into Israel. After the Gaza War, Hamas continued to govern the Gaza Strip and Israel maintained its economic blockade over the area.[4]

The beginning of 2012 was marked by an increase in violence and tension in the Occupied Palestinian Territories and Israel. Palestinian militants fired rockets into southern Israel, while Israeli military forces responded with strikes in the Gaza Strip. On 14 November 2012, Israel Defense Forces (IDF) launched Operation Pillar of Defense in response to an increase of Hamas rockets following the killing, by the IDF, of Ahmed Jabari, chief of Hamas's Gaza military wing.[5] The aims of the military operation, according to the Israeli government, were to 'halt rocket attacks against civilian targets originating from the Gaza Strip'[6] and 'to disrupt the capabilities of

---

[2] See e.g. International Court of Justice (ICJ), *Wall* Advisory Opinion, 2004, §106; ICJ, *Armed Activities on the Territory of the Congo (Democratic Republic of the Congo v. Uganda)*, Judgment, 19 December 2005.

[3] Unless otherwise stated, this section is based on 'Palestinian territories profile', *BBC*, 28 February 2013, <http://www.bbc.co.uk/news/world-middle-east-14630174>, and Council on Foreign Relations, 'Backgrounder: Hamas', 27 November 2012, <http://www.cfr.org/israel/hamas/p8968>.

[4] 'Palestinian territories profile', *BBC*.

[5] Robert Wright, 'Who started the Israel–Gaza conflict?', *The Atlantic*, 6 November 2012, <http://www.theatlantic.com/international/archive/2012/11/who-started-the-israel-gaza-conflict/265374/>.

[6] Nidal al-Mughrabi (Reuters), 'Hamas leader defiant as Israel eases Gaza curbs', *Chicago Tribune*, 24 November 2012, <http://articles.chicagotribune.com/2012-11-24/news/sns-rt-us-palestinians-israel-hamasbre8ad0wp-20121114_1_gaza-curbs-gaza-fishermen-hamas-leader>.

militant organizations'.[7] According to the Israeli government, the operation began in response to Palestinian groups launching more than 100 rockets at Israel over a 24-hour period,[8] an attack on an Israeli military patrol jeep within Israeli borders by Gaza militants, and a tunnel explosion caused by improvised explosive devices (IEDs) near Israeli soldiers on the Israeli side of the fence.[9] Palestinians blamed the Israeli government for the escalation of violence, accusing the IDF of attacks on Gazan civilians in the days leading up to the operation, and citing the blockade of the Gaza Strip, and occupation of West Bank and East Jerusalem, as the reasons for rocket attacks.[10]

During Operation Pillar of Defense, the IDF struck more than 1,500 sites in the Gaza Strip, including rocket launch-pads, weapon storages, government buildings, and apartment blocks.[11] Gaza officials claimed that 133 Palestinians had been killed in the conflict, of whom 79 were fighters, 53 were civilians, and one was a policeman; they also estimated that 840 Palestinians were wounded.[12] Eight Palestinians were executed by members of the Ezzeddeen al-Qassam Brigades for alleged collaboration with Israel.[13] During the eight-day conflict, Hamas, the al-Qassam Brigades, and Islamic Jihad intensified their rocket attacks on Israeli cities, in an operation code-named Operation Stones of Baked Clay by the al-Qassam Brigades. According to the records, more than 1,456 rockets were launched into Israel, and an additional 142 fell inside Gaza itself.[14] By the end of the operation, six Israelis had been killed and 240 injured.[15] The United Nations (UN) Security Council held an emergency session on the situation, but could not reach a

---

[7] Yaakov Lappin, 'IAF strike kills Hamas military chief Jabari', *Jerusalem Post*, 14 November 2012, <http://www.jpost.com/Defense/Article.aspx?id=291779>.

[8] Yaakov Lappin and Tovah Lazaroff, 'Gaza groups pound Israel with over 100 rockets', *Jerusalem Post*, 12 December 2012, <http://www.jpost.com/Defense/Article.aspx?id=291300>.

[9] Israel Ministry of Foreign Affairs, 'Operation Pillar of Defense—selected statements', 20 November 2012, <http://www.mfa.gov.il/MFA/Government/Speeches+by+Israeli+leaders/2012/Operation_Pillar_of_Defense-Statements.htm>.

[10] 'Israel warns Hamas of "heavy price" for Gaza rockets', *Agence France-Presse*, 11 November 2012, <http://www.google.com/hostednews/afp/article/ALeqM5jRUtS7PreKQztfBnueg5yNep0ROg?docId=CNG.eceda380b55ad442c0c0b524c5263e34.61>.

[11] 'Factbox: Gaza targets bombed by Israel', *Reuters*, 21 November 2012, <http://www.reuters.com/article/2012/11/21/us-palestinians-israel-gaza-idUSBRE8AK0H920121121>.

[12] 'Israeli strikes kill 23 in bloodiest day for Gaza', *News International*, 19 November 2012, <http://www.thenews.com.pk/Todays-News-13-18932-Israeli-strikes-kill-23-in-bloodiest-day-for-Gaza>.

[13] Jodi Rudoren and Fares Akram, 'Mistaken lull, simple errand, death in Gaza', *New York Times*, 16 November 2012, <http://www.nytimes.com/2012/11/17/world/middleeast/in-gaza-tragic-result-for-misplaced-hopes-of-cease-fire.html?hp>.

[14] 'Tel Aviv, 21 November 2012—Secretary-General's remarks to the Security Council', UN Secretary-General's statement, 21 November 2012.

[15] Israel Ministry of Foreign Affairs, 'Israel under fire—November 2012', 22 November 2012, <http://www.mfa.gov.il/MFA/Terrorism-+Obstacle+to+Peace/Hamas+war+against+Israel/Israel_under_fire-November_2012.htm>.

decision.[16] On 21 November, after days of negotiation mediated by Egypt, a cease-fire was announced between Hamas and Israel.[17]

PARTIES TO THE CONFLICT

Israeli Defense Forces

According to its website, the IDF:

... are the State of Israel's military force. The IDF is subordinate to the directions of the democratic civilian authorities and the laws of the state. The goal of the IDF is to protect the existence of the State of Israel and her independence, and to thwart all enemy efforts to disrupt the normal way of life in Israel. IDF soldiers are obligated to fight, to dedicate all their strength and even sacrifice their lives in order to protect the State of Israel, her citizens and residents. IDF soldiers will operate according to the IDF values and orders, while adhering to the laws of the state and norms of human dignity, and honoring the values of the State of Israel as a Jewish and democratic state.[18]

Hamas → Ezzeddeen al-Qassam Brigades

Hamas was formed in late 1987 in the midst of the first Palestinian Intifada. Its roots are in the Palestinian branch of the Muslim Brotherhood.[19] The group's charter calls for establishing an Islamic Palestinian state in place of Israel, and rejects all agreements made between the Palestine Liberation Organization (PLO) and Israel.[20] More recently, Hamas has publicly expressed a willingness to accept a long-term cessation of hostilities if Israel agrees to a Palestinian state based on the 1967 borders with Jerusalem as its capital. Hamas's strength is concentrated in the Gaza Strip and areas of the West Bank.

Hamas has a military wing, the Ezzeddeen al-Qassam Brigades (EQB), which was established in the 1990s and has, since then, conducted many anti-Israeli attacks in Israel and the Palestinian territories. Attacks on civilian targets have included rocket attacks and, from 1993 to 2006, suicide bombings. Military targets included Israeli

---

[16] 'Gaza toll rises as UN calls for end to the bloodshed', *The Telegraph*, 15 November 2012, <http://www.telegraph.co.uk/news/worldnews/middleeast/israel/9679500/Gaza-toll-rises-as-UN-calls-for-end-to-the-bloodshed.html>.

[17] Paul Owen and Tom McCarthy, 'Israel–Gaza: truce talks ongoing in Cairo—as it happened', *The Guardian*, 19 November 2012, <http://www.guardian.co.uk/world/middle-east-live/2012/nov/19/israel-gaza-hamas-rocket-fire-idf-bombing>.

[18] IDF website, 'Doctrine', <http://www.idf.il/1497-en/Dover.aspx>.

[19] National Counterterrorism Center, 'Hamas', 31 December 2012, <http://www.nctc.gov/site/groups/hamas.html>.

[20] Hamas Charter 1988, available at The Jerusalem Fund, <http://www.thejerusalemfund.org/www.thejerusalemfund.org/carryover/documents/charter.html>.

outposts and border crossings, and rival Palestinian militias in the occupied territories. While the group receives some support from foreign countries and movements, it remains independent.[21]

Palestinian Islamic Jihad (PIJ) → al-Quds Brigades

Islamic Jihad was formed by militant Palestinians in the Gaza Strip during the 1970s. The group is committed to the creation of an Islamic state in all of historical Palestine and the destruction of Israel through attacks against Israeli military and civilian targets. The group's central leadership resides in Syria, but PIJ maintains small regional offices in Beirut and Tehran. PIJ receives financial assistance primarily from Iran.[22] PIJ refuses to participate in the Palestinian Authority's political process and rejects all negotiations with Israel. The group's paramilitary wing—the al-Quds Brigades—has conducted numerous attacks, including large-scale suicide bombings.[23] PIJ's most recent suicide bombing was in January 2007 in the southern Israeli city of Eilat, killing three people. Since then the group has conducted numerous rocket attacks against Israeli targets near the Gaza Strip using indigenously produced rockets. The group actively participated in the 2012 eight-day conflict against Israel.

CASUALTIES

Data from the UN Office for the Coordination of Humanitarian Affairs (OCHA) identified a total of 174 Palestinians killed during escalation of conflict in Palestine (Israel *v.* Hamas and Islamic Jihad) on 14–21 November 2012. Of these, 100 were said to be civilian: 94 Palestinian civilians were killed as a result of Israeli military action (including 36 children and 14 women); another six Palestinian civilians, including three children and one woman, were reported killed by Palestinian rockets falling short. Additionally, 74 Palestinian militants were killed as a result of Israeli military action.[24] Hundreds of persons were reportedly injured.[25] An earlier account identified approximately 1,269 Palestinians as having been injured.[26]

---

[21] Ezzedeen al-Qassam Brigades-Information Office, <http://www.qassam.ps/index.html>.

[22] National Consortium for the Study of Terrorism and Responses to Terrorism, 'Palestinian Islamic Jihad (PIJ)', 31 December 2012, <http://www.start.umd.edu/start/data_collections/tops/terrorist_organization_profile.asp?id=82>.

[23] Council on Foreign Relations, 'Palestinian Islamic Jihad', 10 April 2008, <http://www.cfr.org/israel/palestinian-islamic-jihad/p15984>.

[24] Data provided by OCHA on 24 April 2013.

[25] 'Human rights situation in Palestine and other occupied Arab territories: report of the United Nations High Commissioner for Human Rights on the implementation of Human Rights Council resolutions S-9/1 and S-12/1', Human Rights Council, UN doc. A/HRC/22/35/Add.1, 6 March 2013.

[26] 'Tel Aviv, 21 November 2012—Secretary-General's remarks to the [UN] Security Council [as delivered]', <http://www.un.org/sg/statements/index.asp?nid=6452>. During the November conflict,

In the context of the crisis, four Israeli civilians were reportedly killed and 219 Israeli civilians were injured. Two Israeli military were reportedly killed and 20 Israeli military injured.[27]

Attacks by Israeli Defence Forces (IDF) on media offices and journalists in Gaza City were said to have killed two cameramen and injured at least eight journalists.[28]

DISPLACED

The Israeli military offensive in Gaza in November 2012 temporarily displaced 12,000 Palestinians. Most returned soon after the end of hostilities. However, almost 2,500 people whose homes were destroyed during the offensive were still living in displacement at the year's end. The firing of rockets into Israel by Palestinian armed groups during the hostilities caused the temporary displacement of hundreds of Israelis.[29]

WAR CRIMES ALLEGATIONS, INVESTIGATIONS, AND PROSECUTIONS

In December 2012, Human Rights Watch (HRW) reported that Palestinian armed groups launched hundreds of inherently indiscriminate rockets against Israeli population centres in violation of the laws of war.[30] HRW research in Gaza:

---

among casualties, five Palestinian civilians, including three children, were reportedly killed by armed drones: 'Human rights situation in Palestine and other occupied Arab territories: report of the United Nations High Commissioner for Human Rights on the implementation of Human Rights Council resolutions S-9/1 and S-12/1'.

[27] 'Human rights situation in Palestine and other occupied Arab territories: report of the United Nations High Commissioner for Human Rights on the implementation of Human Rights Council resolutions S-9/1 and S-12/1'. According to a news article cited by the UN, the IDF estimated the number of Palestinians killed at 177, including approximately 120 fighters, and the number of injured, including an unspecified number of civilians, at 900. Gaza's Ministry of Health estimated the number of Palestinians killed at 189, and persons injured at 1,526. The Israeli Ministry of Foreign Affairs also reported six Israelis killed 'by rockets and mortars' in 'Behind the headlines: ceasefire ends Operation Pillar of Defense', <http://new.mfa.gov.il/MFA/ForeignPolicy/Issues/Pages/BTH_Ceasefire_Pillar_of_Defense_21-Nov-2012.aspx>.

[28] 'Human rights situation in Palestine and other occupied Arab territories: report of the United Nations High Commissioner for Human Rights on the implementation of Human Rights Council resolutions S-9/1 and S-12/1'.

[29] Internal Displacement Monitoring Centre (IDMC), 'Global overview 2012', April 2013, p. 58.

[30] HRW, 'Gaza: Palestinian rockets unlawfully targeted Israeli civilians, residents describe deaths, destruction from attacks', Jerusalem, 24 December 2012, <http://www.hrw.org/news/2012/12/24/gaza-palestinian-rockets-unlawfully-targeted-israeli-civilians>.

...found that armed groups repeatedly fired rockets from densely populated areas, near homes, businesses, and a hotel, unnecessarily placing civilians in the vicinity at grave risk from Israeli counter-fire.[31]

In February 2012, HRW claimed that at least 18 Israeli airstrikes during the fighting in Gaza in November 2012 were in 'apparent violation of the laws of war', after a detailed investigation into the attacks.[32] These airstrikes reportedly killed at least 43 Palestinian civilians, including 12 children.[33] According to HRW, its field investigations:

...found 14 strikes by aerial drones or other aircraft for which there was no indication of a legitimate military target at the site at the time of the attack. In four other cases, attacks may have targeted Palestinian fighters, but appeared to use indiscriminate means or caused disproportionate harm to civilians.[34]

HRW has declared that it sent detailed information about the cases to the IDF on 14 January 2013, requesting further information. At a meeting on 24 January and in subsequent phone conversations, the military spokesperson's office told the organization that the military chief of staff had ordered a general (*aluf*) to conduct an 'operational debriefing' (*tahkir mivtza'i*) concerning 'dozens' of Israeli attacks during the conflict, including the cases HRW investigated, which would be completed by late February 2013.

---

[31] HRW, 'Gaza: Palestinian rockets unlawfully targeted Israeli civilians, residents describe deaths, destruction from attacks'.

[32] HRW, 'Israel: Gaza airstrikes violated laws of war, Israeli attacks killed civilians, destroyed homes without lawful justification', 12 February 2013, <http://www.hrw.org/news/2013/02/12/israel-gaza-airstrikes-violated-laws-war>.

[33] HRW, 'Israel: Gaza airstrikes violated laws of war, Israeli attacks killed civilians, destroyed homes without lawful justification'.

[34] HRW, 'Israel: Gaza airstrikes violated laws of war, Israeli attacks killed civilians, destroyed homes without lawful justification'.

Armed conflict in Mali in 2012

KEY CONFLICT STATISTICS FOR 2012

Civilian deaths:	32	(Sources: OHCHR; OCHA; AOAV; Amnesty International)
Civilian injured:	72	(Sources: OHCHR; OCHA; AOAV; Amnesty International)
Child deaths:	7	(Sources: OHCHR; OCHA; AOAV; Amnesty International)
Child injured:	26	(Sources: OHCHR; OCHA; AOAV; Amnesty International)
Mali military deaths:	84	(Source: OHCHR)
MNLA military death:	7	(Source: OHCHR)
Military/civilian deaths:	82 (not disagg.)	(Source: US DOS)
Civilians displaced:	227,000 (31 Dec. 2012)	(Source: IDMC)

CLASSIFICATION OF THE CONFLICT

Four Malian armed groups, al-Qaeda in the Islamic Maghreb (AQIM), Ansar Dine, and the Movement for Oneness and Jihad in West Africa (MOJWA) on one side, and the National Movement for the Liberation of Azawad (MNLA) on the other, were involved in an armed conflict of a non-international character (NIAC) in the second half of 2012.

If the armed violence between Malian armed groups and the Malian armed forces in early 2012 did reach the threshold of intensity ('protracted armed violence') to be considered an NIAC, this conflict appears to have effectively ended by April 2012.

2013 update: The intervention of French armed forces and subsequently other African states in early 2013 against jihadist groups, particularly AQIM and the MOJWA, amounted to an NIAC in January–April 2013.

SUMMARY OF APPLICABLE INTERNATIONAL LAW

All parties to the conflict in 2012 were bound by, inter alia: Common Article 3 to the 1949 Geneva Conventions; the customary international humanitarian law (IHL) rules of distinction, proportionality, and precautions in attacks; the obligation not to recruit and use children as soldiers; and the duty to respect, at a minimum, fundamental human rights. This includes the duty to respect the rights to life and to freedom from torture or other forms of cruel, inhuman, or degrading treatment or punishment.

2013 update: Mali adhered to the 1977 Additional Protocol II in February 1989. In 2013, the Protocol was applicable to the NIAC between Mali and AQIM and the MOJWA, as well as to France in its conflict with AQIM and the MOJWA.[1] In addition, Mali has domestic human rights obligations, including as a state party to the two 1966 Covenants (on civil and political rights, and on economic, social and cultural rights), while France, as a state party to the two 1966 Covenants, is bound extraterritorially.[2] All parties must, as a minimum, respect fundamental human rights.

Mali adhered to the 1997 Anti-Personnel Mine Ban Convention (APMBC) in June 1998, becoming a state party on 1 December 1998, and to the 2008 Convention on Cluster Munitions (CCM) in June 2010, becoming a state party on 1 December 2010. France is a state party to both disarmament treaties.

HISTORY OF THE CONFLICT[3]

Since May 2006, Mali has been engaged in low-intensity conflict in the north of the country between the government and a number of ethnic Tuareg non-state armed groups then under the umbrella of the 23 May Democratic Alliance for Change. In July 2008, the government and the group agreed a cease-fire after four days of talks in the Algerian capital, Algiers. Mali, Africa's third-biggest gold producer, had struggled to end the escalating militancy by the Tuareg nomads who took up arms demanding greater rights for their people. The conflict followed similar rebellions in the 1960s and 1990s by the Tuareg.

On 22 March 2012, a military coup in the capital, Bamako, overthrew the elected President Amadou Toumani Toure. The coup came in the aftermath of a series of losses suffered by Malian armed forces in the face of the Tuaregs, who had received new weaponry from Libya. On 6 April 2012, the MNLA, a new umbrella group for Tuareg rebels, proclaimed the independence of the Azawad, a territory in northern Mali.[4]

---

[1] 1977 Additional Protocol II was ratified by Mali in 1989 and by France in 1984. France is bound because the 1977 Additional Protocol II applies to 'all armed conflicts' that are not covered by Art. 1 of 1977 Additional Protocol I and which take place 'in the territory of' a state party 'between its armed forces and dissident armed forces or other organized armed groups which, under responsible command, exercise such control over a part of its territory as to enable them to carry out sustained and concerted military operations and to implement this Protocol'. This applies the provisions of the Protocol to the relevant armed conflict as a whole, not merely to the armed forces of the state on whose territory the conflict is ongoing, as well as the dissident armed forces or other organized armed groups fighting against those government armed forces.

[2] See e.g. International Court of Justice (ICJ), *Wall* Advisory Opinion, 2004, §106; ICJ, *Armed Activities on the Territory of the Congo* (*Democratic Republic of the Congo v. Uganda*), Judgment, 19 December 2005.

[3] Unless otherwise stated, this section is based on 'Mali profile', *BBC*, 9 April 2013, <http://www.bbc.co.uk/news/world-africa-13881370> and <http://www.bbc.co.uk/news/world-africa-13881978>.

[4] The MNLA has its own website: <http://www.mnlamov.net/english.html>.

Among others, the African Union, the European Union (EU), and the United States of America (USA) did not recognize the putative new state.[5]

On 9 April 2012, the United Nations (UN) Security Council reaffirmed 'the need to uphold and respect the sovereignty, unity and territorial integrity of Mali and reject categorically any declarations to the contrary', and demanded 'an immediate cessation of hostilities in the north of Mali by rebel groups'.[6] In May 2012, the Economic Community of West African States (ECOWAS) decided to send a force of 3,000 regional soldiers to Mali in an effort to restore stability even though the military junta opposed the idea.

In May 2012, the MNLA and Islamist militant group Ansar Dine[7] sought to merge, declaring northern Mali to be an Islamic state. Ansar Dine began to impose Islamic law in Timbuktu. AQIM 'endorsed' the deal. But by June, the already strained relationship between Ansar Dine and the MNLA imploded, and following fierce combat with Ansar Dine and the MOJWA, the MNLA was expelled from the main northern cities of Gao, Kidal, and Timbuktu by July 2012. The town of Douentza followed in September, seeing the Islamists come ever closer to government-held territory.[8]

In July 2012, the UN Human Rights Council adopted a resolution condemning:

... the human rights violations and acts of violence committed in northern Mali, in particular by rebels, terrorist groups and other organized transnational crime networks, including the violence perpetrated against women and children, the killings, hostage-takings, pillaging, theft and destruction of religious and cultural sites, as well as the recruitment of child soldiers, and calls for the perpetrators of these acts to be brought to justice.[9]

In contrast, instead of the reference to 'human rights violations', UN Security Council resolutions on the situation in Mali have referred to 'abuses of human rights and violations of international humanitarian law'.[10] Similar references were included by the UN Secretary-General in his report on Mali released in November 2012.[11]

---

[5] 'Briefing: War and peace—Mali repeats the cycle', *IRIN*, 29 March 2012, <http://www.irinnews.org/Report/95186/Briefing-War-and-peace-Mali-repeats-the-cycle>.

[6] UN Security Council Press Statement on Mali, 10 April 2012, <http://www.un.org/News/Press/docs/2012/sc10603.doc.htm>.

[7] Ansar Dine was founded by Tuareg rebel Iyad Ag Ghaly.

[8] 'Rupture entre le MNLA et Ansar Dine au nord du Mali', *RFI*, 20 March 2012, <http://www.rfi.fr/afrique/20120320-nord-mali-rupture-mnla-ancar-dine-touaregs-Iyad Ag Ghali>.

[9] Human Rights Council Resolution 20/17, 17 July 2012, §2.

[10] UN Security Council Resolution 2056 (2012), 5 July 2012, §13, Resolution 2071, 12 October 2012, §14, and Resolution 2085, 20 December 2012, §6. According to Resolution 2085, for instance, the Council:

Condemn[ed] strongly all abuses of human rights in the north of Mali by armed rebels, terrorist and other extremist groups, including those involving violence against civilians, notably women and children, killings, hostage-taking, pillaging, theft, destruction of cultural and religious sites and recruitment of child soldiers, reiterating that some of such acts may amount to crimes under the Rome Statute [ICC Statute] and that their perpetrators must be held accountable and noting that the Transitional authorities of Mali referred the situation in Mali since January 2012 to the International Criminal Court on 13 July 2012.

[11] The Secretary-General refers to 'gross human rights abuses': 'Report of the Secretary-General on the situation in Mali', UN doc. S/2012/894, 29 November 2012, §§21 and 75.

In November 2012, ECOWAS, backed by the UN and African Union, agreed to launch a coordinated military expedition to recapture the north. France, the USA, and the United Kingdom (UK) announced logistical support for the mission, which was to comprise some 3,300 military.

On 11 January 2013, the French military began operations against the Islamists. Forces from other African Union states were deployed shortly after. By 8 February, rebel-held territory had been retaken by the Malian military, with help from the international coalition.[12] In April, France began withdrawal of its troops.

PARTIES TO THE CONFLICT

National Movement for the Liberation of Azawad (MNLA)

The MNLA was formed in 2011, partly by well-armed Tuareg fighters returning from Libya, where they had supported Gaddafi loyalists. The MNLA is one of two rebel groups to have gained ground in the area after Mali's government was ousted in a coup.[13] The government accused the movement of having links to AQIM, although the MNLA firmly denied the claims.

By 30 March 2012, the MNLA, along with Ansar Dine, were in control of virtually all of northern Mali. In April, the MNLA proclaimed independence of the Azawad, adding it would respect existing borders with neighbouring states and adhere to the UN Charter. The statement also called for recognition from the international community, which was subsequently denied.[14] Meanwhile, tensions between the MNLA and Ansar Dine culminated in the Battle of Gao (27 June 2012), in which the MNLA effectively lost control of northern Mali's cities.

The MNLA declared its support for France's military intervention in January 2013 and has, for the time being, given up its demand for independence, saying it will settle, as a first step, for autonomy.[15]

---

[12] 'L'opération militaire française au Mali entre dans une nouvelle phase', *RFI*, 14 January 2013, <http://www.rfi.fr/afrique/20130113-operation-militaire-francaise-mali-nouvelle-phase-serval>.

[13] The President of Mali, Amadou Toumani Toure, was deposed on 22 March 2012 in a coup in the capital, Bamako, by soldiers angry at his handling of the Tuareg rebellion in the north. The mutineers charged he had left the army poorly equipped to fight the Tuareg rebels in the north. See GlobalSecurity.org, 'MNLA', September 2012, <http://www.globalsecurity.org/military/world/war/tuareg-mali-2012.htm>.

[14] MNLA, Déclaration d'indépendance de l'Azawad, 6 April 2012, <http://www.mnlamov.net/component/content/article/169-declaration-dindependance-de-lazawad.html>.

[15] See e.g. 'French battle Mali rebels in Sahara, Tuaregs an issue', *Chicago Tribune*, 6 February 2013, <http://articles.chicagotribune.com/2013-02-06/news/sns-rt-mali-rebels-pix-tvl5n0b63da-20130206_1_adrar-des-ifoghas-mountains-tuaregs-interim-president-dioncounda-traore>.

al-Qaeda in the Islamic Maghreb (AQIM)

AQIM is a Salafi-jihadist militant group operating in North Africa's Sahara and Sahel. The group was created during Algeria's earlier internal armed conflict, and has since become an al-Qaeda affiliate. In recent months, AQIM has expanded its foothold in northern Mali.[16] In early 2013, a French-led military intervention halted the southward advance of Islamist insurgents.

AQIM has been designated as a terrorist organization by both the USA and the EU. AQIM's main objectives include the eradication of Western influence from North Africa by overthrowing 'unbeliever' governments, and installing regimes based on Shari'a law. AQIM's tactics include the use of guerrilla-style raids, assassinations, and suicide bombings of military, government, and civilian targets.[17]

Ansar Dine

Ansar Dine (which means 'defenders of the religion' in Arabic) was created in December 2011. The group is led by its founder Iyad Ag Ghaly, who was a leader of the Tuareg rebellions in the 1990s. Unlike the MNLA, Ansar Dine's goal is to impose Islamic law over the whole country without necessarily challenging the territorial integrity of Mali.[18] Ansar Dine's members were allegedly responsible for the destruction of UN Educational, Scientific and Cultural Organization (UNESCO) world heritage sites in Timbuktu, while the imposition of Shari'a in their controlled areas led thousands to flee.[19] In November 2012, in light of the planned ECOWAS intervention, the group issued a statement rejecting all forms of extremism and terrorism and committing itself in the fight against transnational organized crime.[20] This declaration seemed to mark the will for Ansar Dine to distance itself publicly from AQIM. However, a few months later, the two rebel groups were reported to be operating in close collaboration.[21]

---

[16] GlobalSecurity.org, 'al-Qaeda in the Islamic Maghreb', June 2011, <http://www.globalsecurity.org/military/world/para/gspc.htm>.

[17] Council on Foreign Relations, 'al-Qaeda in the Islamic Maghreb (AQIM)', January 2013, <http://www.cfr.org/north-africa/al-qaeda-islamic-maghreb-aqim/p12717>.

[18] Amnesty International UK, 'Media briefing—Mali unrest 2012–2013', January 2013, p. 5, <http://www.amnesty.org.uk/uploads/documents/doc_22968.pdf>.

[19] 'Strange bedfellows: The MNLA's on-again, off-again marriage with Ansar Dine', 7 June 2012, France 24, <http://www.france24.com/en/20120605-mali-strange-bedfellows-mnla-ansar-dine-al-qaeda-aqim-islamists-tuareg>.

[20] 'Mali: les islamistes d'Ansar Dine assurent refuser le "terrorisme"', *Le Monde*, 6 November 2012, <http://www.lemonde.fr/afrique/article/2012/11/06/les-islamistes-d-ansar-dine-rejettent-le-terrorisme_1786631_3212.html>.

[21] 'Au nord du Mali, Ansar Dine et Aqmi œuvrent main dans la main', *RFI*, 3 January 2013, <http://www.rfi.fr/ameriques/20130103-nord-mali-ansar-dine-aqmi-tombouctou-azawad>.

Mouvement pour le Tawhîd et du Jihad en Afrique de l'Ouest (MOJWA)

The Mouvement pour le Tawhîd et du Jihad en Afrique de l'Ouest (Movement for Oneness and Jihad in West Africa, or MOJWA) is an active terrorist group that emerged from AQIM in mid-2011. In a video announcing its creation on 12 December 2011, the rebel group openly declared its intent to spread jihad and impose Shari'a law in West Africa, namely in Algeria and northern Mali. The MOJWA was among the rebel groups that took control of northern Mali after the military coup on 21 March 2012. On 1 September, the group seized the town of Douentza from a local self-defence militia. The capture of the town, situated in the Mopti region of Mali, was the southern-most point of the occupied territory, a fact that caused great concern in Bamako.[22]

On 5 December 2012, the group was listed as a terrorist organization associated with al-Qaeda by the UN Security Council.[23]

CASUALTIES

Civilian casualties

No comprehensive source of data on civilian casualties in Mali for 2012 was available; however, reporting from various sources sometimes distinguished casualties by age or gender. Between April and 29 July, the Office of the UN High Commissioner for Human Rights (OHCHR) identified seven civilians who were killed due to conflict, including three women and one child. At least two of the deaths were attributed to the Ansar Dine.[24] Action on Armed Violence (AOAV), through media reports, identified the death of a 4-year-old girl and the injury of ten other civilians, all women and children, when a combat helicopter bombed a displaced-persons camp on 22 February 2012.[25] In March to mid-December 2012, 31 incidents were recorded as a result of explosive remnants of war (ERW), resulting in 52 casualties, including 31 children. At least five of these children were killed.[26] Another 16 civilian casualties were identified from stray bullets. Given the

---

[22] Anne Look, 'Islamic militant group in Northern Mali expanding southward', *Voice of America*, 4 September 2012, <http://www.voanews.com/content/islamic_militant_group_in_northern_mali_expanding_southward/1501473.html>.

[23] 'Security Council al-Qaida Sanctions Committee adds one entity to its sanctions list', UN press release, UN doc. SC/18407, 5 December 2012, <http://www.un.org/News/Press/docs//2012/sc10847.doc.htm>.

[24] 'Report of the United Nations High Commissioner for Human Rights on the situation of human rights in Mali', Human Rights Council, UN doc. A/HRC/22/33, 7 January 2013, pp. 9–10.

[25] AOAV, 'Explosive Violence: February 2012', <http://www.aoav.org.uk/uploads/changing_policy/The%20Impact%20of%20Explosive%>; US Department of State, 'Country reports on human rights practices 2012: Mali', 19 April 2013.

[26] UNICEF, 'Two-thirds of victims of left-over munitions in Mali are children', Bamako/Geneva, 5 March 2013, <http://www.unicef.org/infobycountry/media_68078.html>.

fact that access to information was limited, the true numbers of casualties were expected to be higher.[27]

OHCHR reported ten victims of punitive amputation by non-state armed groups, attributed to the application of Shari'a law. The first amputation was carried out by members of MOJWA on 8 August 2012 after a summary trial for stealing cattle.[28] Amnesty International also documented seven cases of punitive amputations; it is not possible to tell from reporting if these are the same cases or others.[29] Amnesty International documented the extrajudicial executions of 16 members of a movement of Muslim preachers, the Dawa, in Diabaly on 8 September 2012.[30]

During 2012, the MOJWA kidnapped seven Algerian diplomats and a French national. Three Algerian hostages were released later in the year, one was executed, and the three other Algerians and the French national remained in MOJWA's control as of the end of the year. On 17 July, MOJWA released three aid workers—two Spaniards and an Italian—who they had kidnapped in October 2011.[31]

By the end of 2012, human rights and humanitarian organizations had reported several hundreds of cases of gender-based violence, including sexual violence.[32] During the year, a total of 211 cases were identified of different forms of sexual violence (rape, sexual slavery, forced marriage, torture and sexual violence in places of detention, gang rapes, abduction, and sexual violence during house-to-house operations or at checkpoints). Systematic and widespread sexual violence was reportedly used to punish, intimidate, and subjugate women and girls by the MNLA, Ansar Dine, and the MOJWA. In rebel-controlled zones, rape was said to have been used as a method of warfare contributing to the mass displacement of the civilian population.[33]

Casualties among the security forces

On 24 January 2012, 153 soldiers of the Mali armed forces were captured and 84 of these were executed, accounting for all confirmed Malian military fatalities in 2012. Fighters

---

[27] UN Office for the Coordination of Humanitarian Affairs (OCHA), 'Mali humanitarian bulletin: Issue 4', 7 January 2013, p. 3.

[28] 'Report of the United Nations High Commissioner for Human Rights on the situation of human rights in Mali', Human Rights Council, UN doc. A/HRC/22/33, 7 January 2013, pp. 9–10.

[29] Amnesty International, 'Mali: Civilians bear the brunt of the conflict', London, September 2012, p. 6.

[30] Amnesty International, 'Mali: Civilians bear the brunt of the conflict', p. 13.

[31] US Department of State, 'Country reports on human rights practices 2012: Mali', 19 April 2013.

[32] OCHA, 'Mali humanitarian bulletin: Issue 4', 7 January 2013, p. 5.

[33] 'Report of the Secretary-General on sexual violence in conflict', UN doc. S/2013/149, 14 March 2013, §§50–7.

carrying out the massacre were identified as belonging to MNLA; Ansar Dine also claimed responsibility for the attack.[34]

The OHCHR reported that nine MNLA militants were captured by Malian soldiers and that seven were executed in retaliation for the MNLA offensive. These casualties were not confirmed by the Malian military.[35] In March 2012, Ansar Dine captured the military garrison town of Aguelhoc in Kidal Region and subsequently executed 82 people, including soldiers and civilians.[36]

DISPLACED

The armed uprising in northern Mali in January 2012, and the conflict and human rights abuses that followed, led to the displacement of at least 227,000 people in Mali by the end of 2012.[37]

WAR CRIMES ALLEGATIONS, INVESTIGATIONS, AND PROSECUTIONS

Mali adhered to the Rome Statute of the International Criminal Court (the ICC Statute) on 16 August 2000, and therefore the ICC may exercise jurisdiction over war crimes alleged to have been committed by Malian nationals or on Malian territory since 1 July 2002, in cases in which national courts are unwilling or unable to prosecute. On 18 July 2012, the Malian government referred 'the situation in Mali since January 2012' to the ICC.[38]

In January 2013, the ICC Office of the Prosecutor (OTP) opened an investigation into alleged crimes committed in Mali, with a focus on the northern part of the country. In its report, the Court concludes that, based in the information available, there is a reasonable basis to believe that war crimes have been committed in the context of an NIAC in Mali since around 17 January 2012.[39] The ICC report also states that 'the information available does not provide a reasonable basis to believe that crimes against humanity under Article 7 have been committed'.[40]

---

[34] 'Report of the United Nations High Commissioner for Human Rights on the situation of human rights in Mali', Human Rights Council, UN doc. A/HRC/22/33, 7 January 2013, p. 9.

[35] 'Report of the United Nations High Commissioner for Human Rights on the situation of human rights in Mali', p. 9.

[36] US Department of State, 'Country reports on human rights practices 2012: Mali', 19 April 2013.

[37] Internal Displacement Monitoring Centre (IDMC), 'Global overview 2012', April 2013, p. 26.

[38] ICC Office of the Prosecutor (OTP), 'Report on preliminary examination activities 2012', November 2012, §165.

[39] ICC OTP, 'Situation in Mali—Article 53(1) report', 16 January 2013, §133.

[40] ICC OTP, 'Situation in Mali—Article 53(1) report', §128.

Both conclusions are questionable in fact and in law. The fighting between Malian armed groups and the Malian armed forces in early 2012 was sporadic, low-scale, and seems to have caused relatively few casualties, despite unconfirmed claims on both sides to have inflicted many combat deaths. In contrast, the systematic nature of physical and sexual abuse inflicted by armed groups on the civilian population after the Malian forces retreated from the north of the country could be considered to amount to widespread or systematic persecution, and therefore to constitute crimes against humanity.

If the armed violence between Malian armed groups and the Malian armed forces in early 2012 did reach the threshold of intensity ('protracted armed violence') to be considered an NIAC, this conflict appears to have effectively ended by April 2012.[41] The OTP reported that the rebellion started with an attack by MNLA on a military base in the town of Menaka in the Gao region on 17 January 2012. Ansar Dine, as well as other armed groups, joined the rebellion, without necessarily coordinating operations between each other. Between 30 March and 2 April 2012, the rebels advanced and took the main cities and military bases of Gao, Kidal, and Timbuktu, forcing the Malian military to withdraw to the southern regions of Mali.[42]

---

[41] ICC OTP, 'Situation in Mali—Article 53(1) report', §§59–63.
[42] ICC OTP, 'Situation in Mali—Article 53(1) report', §§26–8.

Armed conflict in Mexico in 2012

KEY CONFLICT STATISTICS FOR 2012

Civilian male deaths:	8,473 (Jan.–Nov.)	(Source: Trans-border Institute)
Civilian female deaths:	685 (Jan.–Nov.)	(Source: Trans-border Institute)
Police deaths:	392 (Jan.–Nov.)	(Source: Trans-border Institute)
Military deaths:	24 (Jan.–Nov.)	(Source: Trans-border Institute)
Civilians displaced:	160,000 (31 Dec. 2012)	(Source: IDMC, 'Global overview', 2012)

CLASSIFICATION OF THE CONFLICTS

Mexico's security forces were involved in separate armed conflicts of a non-international character (NIACs) with, at least, the Sinaloa Cartel and Las Zetas gang in 2012. The Sinaloa Cartel and Gulf Cartel were also engaged in an NIAC with Las Zetas gang in 2012. That this drug-related violence constitutes an armed conflict is controversial.

SUMMARY OF APPLICABLE INTERNATIONAL LAW

All parties to the conflict in 2012 were bound by, inter alia: Common Article 3 to the 1949 Geneva Conventions; the customary international humanitarian law (IHL) rules of distinction, proportionality, and precautions in attacks; the obligation not to recruit and use children as soldiers; and the duty to respect, at a minimum, fundamental human rights. This includes the duty to respect the rights to life and to freedom from torture or other forms of cruel, inhuman, or degrading treatment or punishment.

In addition, Mexico and its security forces have domestic human rights obligations under customary law and as a state party to the two 1966 Covenants (on civil and political rights, and on economic, social, and cultural rights).

HISTORY OF THE CONFLICT[1]

Violent crime remains a major concern in Mexico, which has one of the highest rates of kidnappings in the world, and where 60,000 people or more are reported to have died

---

[1] Unless otherwise stated, this section is based on 'Mexico profile', *BBC*, 9 April 2013, <http://www.bbc.co.uk/news/world-latin-america-18095241>.

in drug-related violence since December 2006.[2] Since that month, when it launched Operation Michoacan, the Mexican government has been involved in a 'war' against several criminal organizations related to drug trafficking: the drug cartels.[3] The military assault mobilized 6,500 federal troops, leading to an explosion of violence as the drug cartels fought both the army and each other.

This action is regarded as the first major operation against organized crime, and is generally viewed as the starting point of the war between the government and the drug cartels.[4] As time progressed, then-President Calderón escalated the anti-drug campaign, in which some 45,000 troops have been involved in addition to state and federal police forces.

As of 2011, Mexico's military had reportedly captured 11,544 people who were believed to have been involved with the cartels and organized crime.[5] Confronting the cartels directly resulted in public killings and torture from both the cartels and government security forces, perpetuating fear among civilians regarding the 'war on drugs'.[6] As cartel leaders have been removed from their positions, either through arrest or death, power struggles within the cartels have become more intense, resulting in greater violence between the cartels,[7] and splintering the organizations, creating between 60 and 80 new cartels.[8] Fighting between the cartels even continued in prison. On 19 February 2012, in Apodaca, Nuevo Leon, 44 inmates were said to have been killed in a prison riot probably caused by a brawl between the Gulf Cartel and Los Zetas.[9]

On 1 May 2012, armed confrontation between the Mexican military and cartel members in Choix, Sinaloa, left 27 people dead.[10] By May, it was claimed that the fight among drug

---

[2] See e.g. 'Q&A: Mexico's drug-related violence', *BBC*, 24 December 2012, <http://www.bbc.co.uk/news/world-latin-america-10681249>; 'Mexican daily: nearly 60,000 drug war deaths under Calderon', *Fox News Latino*, 1 November 2012, <http://latino.foxnews.com/latino/news/2012/11/01/mexican-daily-nearly-60000-drug-war-deaths-under-calderon/>.

[3] Powerful cartels control the trafficking of drugs from South America to the United States of America (USA), a business that is worth an estimated US$13 billion a year.

[4] Ioan Grillo (Associated Press), 'Mexico cracks down on violence', *Seattle Post-Intelligencer*, 11 December 2006, <http://www.seattlepi.com/national/article/Mexico-cracks-down-on-violence-1222154.php>.

[5] SEDENA Mexican National Defence Department, '4 de Diciembre de 2011—Lomas de Sotelo, D.F.', 4 December 2012, <http://www.sedena.gob.mx/index.php/sala-de-prensa/comunicados-de-prensa/8123-4-de-diciembre-de-2011-lomas-de-sotelo-df>.

[6] Human Rights Watch (HRW), 'Neither rights nor security—killings, torture, and disappearances in Mexico's "war on drugs"', 9 November 2011, <http://www.hrw.org/reports/2011/11/09/neither-rights-nor-security-0>.

[7] 'Q&A: Mexico's drug-related violence', *BBC*, 24 December 2012, <http://www.bbc.co.uk/news/world-latin-america-10681249>.

[8] Lizbeth Diaz, 'Crime crackdown created more drug cartels: top Mexican official', *Reuters*, Mexico City, 19 December 2012, <http://uk.reuters.com/article/2012/12/19/us-mexico-drugs-idUSBRE8BI01E20121219>.

[9] 'Events related to organized crime', *Borderland Beat*, <http://www.borderlandbeat.com/2009/04/events-of-organized-crime.html>.

[10] Events related to organized crime', *Borderland Beat*.

cartels had boiled down largely to a battle between the Zetas and the Sinaloa Cartel, the oldest and largest trafficking network in Mexico. The Zetas once controlled much of north-eastern Mexico, but Sinaloa loyalists steadily moved into the region and allied themselves with the Gulf Cartel, a formerly dominant group that created the Zetas, but has since turned on them.[11]

Another concern in the war on drug trafficking is corruption of certain branches of the military. In May 2012, for instance, an assault in which nearly 50 bodies were found on a local highway on the border with the United States of America (USA) led to the arrests of four high-ranking Mexican military officials. The officials were suspected of being on cartel payrolls and alerting the cartels in advance of military action against them.[12]

For several months in the first half of 2012, Mexico's army moved thousands of troops into territory controlled by the Zetas. At the end of June, the army killed a senior cartel figure during a major shootout, 'although it came at the cost of turning a Mexican city into a warzone'.[13] According to local press reports, the hours-long battle began in the border city of Nuevo Laredo, when forces loyal to the boss of a major Zetas drug-trafficking operation, Gerardo Guerra-Valdez, attacked military personnel moving on the cartel's 'command structure'. When the military fought back, cartel gunmen began blockading key roads stretching from the city's downtown, near the World Trade Bridge connecting Nuevo Laredo to Texas. They were said to be heavily armed with rocket and grenade launchers, as well as assault rifles, and included in their convoy was at least one armoured vehicle.[14]

In July 2012, Enrique Peña Nieto was elected as Mexican President, succeeding Felipe Calderón. A few days after his election, the President issued a declaration affirming his will to continue the 'war on drugs', but announcing his intention to shift strategy to focus on repressing violence against civilians rather than targeting cartel leaders.[15]

In October 2012, Heriberto Lazcano, known as 'El Lazca' and the main leader of the Zetas, was killed by Mexican Marines in a fierce battle involving guns and grenades in Coahuila State in northern Mexico.[16]

---

[11] Tracy Wilkinson, 'Dozens of bodies, many mutilated, dumped in Mexico', *Los Angeles Times*, 13 May 2012, <http://articles.latimes.com/2012/may/13/world/la-fg-mexico-bodies-20120514>.

[12] Wilkinson, 'Dozens of bodies, many mutilated, dumped in Mexico'.

[13] Robert Beckhusen, 'Mexico kills cartel big shot, but drug violence worsens', 3 July 2012, <http://www.wired.com/dangerroom/2012/03/cartel-leader-killed/>.

[14] Beckhusen, 'Mexico kills cartel big shot, but drug violence worsens'.

[15] Nicholas Casey, 'Mexico's new president vows to continue fight against drug gangs', *Wall Street Journal*, 4 July 2012, <http://online.wsj.com/article/SB10001424052702304708604577505411765045648.html>.

[16] Randal C. Archibold, 'Mexico kills a drug kingpin, but the body gets away', *New York Times*, 9 October 2012, <http://www.nytimes.com/2012/10/10/world/americas/mexico-zetas.html?ref=drugtrafficking>.

Mexico's northern border towns are experiencing the worst of the violence. Ciudad Juarez (just across from El Paso in Texas) is the city suffering the most. There are also high levels of violence in Michoacan and Guerrero states. Many other areas do not, however, experience high levels of serious crime. The overall murder rate is lower than that of El Salvador.

PARTIES TO THE CONFLICTS

Mexican security forces

Former President Calderón deployed more than 50,000 troops and federal police against the cartels.[17] Since 2006, more than 3,000 Mexican soldiers and police have been killed by the cartels.[18]

Los Zetas

In 1999, the Gulf Cartel's leader decided to hire a group of former elite military soldiers from both the Airmobile Special Forces Group (GAFE) and the Amphibian Group of Special Forces (GANFE) to work for him. This group became known as Los Zetas and began operating as a private army for the Gulf Cartel. In 2007, the Gulf Cartel leader, Osiel Cardenas Guillen, was arrested and extradited. This gave Los Zetas the chance to start out on its own and to gradually set up its own independent drugs, arms, and human-trafficking networks.[19]

In early 2010, Los Zetas made public its split from the Gulf Cartel and began a bloody war against it over control of north-east Mexico's drug trade routes.[20] This war caused the deaths of thousands of cartel members and, due to alliance structures, also involved other cartels, namely the Sinaloa Cartel, which fought the Zetas in 2010 and 2011.[21] Los Zetas, described by the USA as 'the most technologically advanced, sophisticated and

---

[17] 'Q&A: Mexico's drug-related violence', *BBC*, 24 December 2012, <http://www.bbc.co.uk/news/world-latin-america-10681249>.

[18] The Mexican government's database, which catalogues murders presumed to be linked to organized crime, lists 30,913 execution-style killings, 3,153 killings in what are termed 'confrontations' or shootouts, and 546 deaths classified as 'aggression' or other clashes.

[19] Jorge Chabat, 'Dos carteles dominan la guerra de las drogas en México', *Informador.com.mx*, 7 October 2011, <http://www.informador.com.mx/mexico/2011/327768/6/dos-carteles-dominan-la-guerra-de-las-drogas-en-mexico.htm>.

[20] Aimee Rawlins, 'Mexico's drug war', Council on Foreign Relations, 11 January 2013, <http://www.cfr.org/mexico/mexicos-drug-war/p13689>.

[21] 'Q&A: Mexico's drug-related violence', *BBC*, 24 December 2012, <http://www.bbc.co.uk/news/world-latin-america-10681249>.

dangerous cartel operating in Mexico',[22] is notorious for targeting civilians in large-scale attacks, such as the 2011 San Fernando massacre.[23]

Sinaloa Cartel

The Sinaloa Cartel is a drug-trafficking and organized crime cartel based in the city of Culiacán, Sinaloa, with operations in the Mexican states of Baja California, Durango, Sonora, and Chihuahua. The cartel is also known as the 'Guzmán-Loera Organization', by the name of its leader Joaquín 'El Chapo' Guzmán, Mexico's most-wanted drug trafficker, but also as the 'Pacific Cartel', the 'Federation', and the 'Blood Alliance'. The Sinaloa Cartel has a presence in 17 Mexican states, with important centres in Mexico City, Tepic, Toluca, Zacatecas, Guadalajara, and most of the state of Sinaloa. In March 2003, it began to contest the Gulf Cartel's domination of the coveted south-west Texas corridor following the arrest of Gulf Cartel leader Osiel Cárdenas.[24] The cartel is considered by the US intelligence community to be 'the most powerful drug trafficking organisation in the world'.[25]

The cartel is primarily involved in the smuggling and distribution of Colombian cocaine, Mexican marijuana, methamphetamine, and Mexican and south-east Asian heroin into the USA.[26] As of May 2010, several Mexican and US media outlets claimed that Sinaloa had infiltrated the Mexican federal government and military, and that it had colluded with it to destroy the other cartels.[27] In 2012, the cartel emerged victorious from a bloody battle started in mid-2008 with the Juarez Cartel over control of Ciudad Juarez, which caused up to 12,000 people to die in drug-related violence.[28]

---

[22] Michael Ware, 'Los Zetas called Mexico's most dangerous drug cartel', *CNN*, 6 August 2009, <http://edition.cnn.com/2009/WORLD/americas/08/06/mexico.drug.cartels/index.html>.

[23] In that attack, which took place in April 2011, 193 people were murdered. See 'Localizan 7 nuevas narcofosas en San Fernando, suman 193 víctimas', *International Business Times*, 7 June 2011, <http://mx.ibtimes.com/articles/14057/20110607/fosas-clandestinas-san-fernadno-tamaulipas-narcotrafico-zetas.htm>.

[24] InSightCrime, 'Organized crime in the Americas, Sinaloa Cartel', December 2012, <http://www .cfr.org/mexico/mexicos-drug-war/p13689>.

[25] Alicia A. Caldwell and Mark Stevenson (Associated Press), 'U.S. intelligence says Sinaloa Cartel has won battle for Ciudad Juarez drug routes', *CNS*, 9 April 2010, <http://cnsnews.com/node/63984>.

[26] InSightCrime, 'Organized crime in the Americas, Sinaloa Cartel'.

[27] John Burnett and Marisa Penalosa, 'Mexico's drug war: a rigged fight?', *NPR*, 19 May 2010, <http://www.npr.org/templates/story/story.php?storyId=126890838>.

[28] Uppsala Conflict Data Program Conflict Encyclopedia, 'Mexico, non-state conflict info, *Juarez Cartel—Sinaloa Cartel*', June 2012, <http://www.ucdp.uu.se/gpdatabase/gpcountry.php?id=107&regionSelect=4-Central_Americas>.

Gulf Cartel

The Gulf Cartel (Cartel del Golfo), based in Matamoros, Tamaulipas, has been one of Mexico's two dominant cartels in recent years. The cartel has a decentralized structure and is made up of several subgroups, as well as numerous gangs tied to the organization.[29] The group used to have an armed wing, Los Zetas, which was created by a group of deserters from the Mexican military's Special Forces: it was the first time that a drug cartel controlled such a sophisticated and well-trained armed group.[30] In 2010, Los Zeta and the Gulf Cartel split, and there followed a brutal fight between the two cartels that deeply weakened the power of the Gulf Cartel.[31]

The Gulf Cartel's network is international, and is believed to have dealings with crime groups in Europe, West Africa, Asia, Central America, South America, and the USA. The Cartel not only deals with drug trafficking, but also operates through protection rackets, assassinations, extortions, kidnappings, and other criminal activities.[32]

CASUALTIES

The Trans-border Institute (TBI)[33] compiled data on 9,158 'organized-crime executions' in Mexico from 1 January to 30 November 2012.[34] *Milenio*, a Mexican newspaper, reported 12,390 'organized crime-style homicides' for the full year, through the end of 2012; however, this data was not disaggregated, making it difficult to compare with the TBI dataset.[35] Among the total TBI casualties identified for 11 months of the year, 1,267 (about 14 per cent) showed signs that the victim had been tortured prior to execution and 521 of the casualties were decapitated.[36]

---

[29] InSightCrime, 'Organized crime in the Americas, the Gulf Cartel', December 2012, <http://www .insightcrime.org/groups-mexico/gulf-cartel>.

[30] 'Q&A: Mexico's drug-related violence', *BBC*, 24 December 2012, <http://www.bbc.co.uk/news/world-latin-america-10681249>.

[31] Uppsala Conflict Data Program Conflict Encyclopedia, 'Mexico, non-state conflict info, *The Gulf Cartel*', June 2012, <http://www.ucdp.uu.se/gpdatabase/gpcountry.php?id=107&regionSelect=4-Central_Americas>.

[32] Judith Warner, *U.S. Border Security: A Reference Handbook*, ABC-CLIO, 2010, p. 381.

[33] Founded in 1994, the Trans-Border Institute, based within the University of San Diego, seeks to promote understanding, dialogue, and cooperation across the USA–Mexico border. See 'About TBI', <http://www.sandiego.edu/peacestudies/institutes/tbi/about/>.

[34] TBI compiles data from the Mexican newspaper *Reforma* on drug-related killings as reported at the state level on a weekly basis, as well as the annual totals by state from 2006 to the end of 2012. In December 2012, *Reforma* stopped publishing weekly data totals and state statistics were no longer available (as of 1 May 2013). See Cory Molzahn, Octavio Rodriguez Ferreira, and David A. Shirk, 'Drug violence in Mexico: data and analysis through 2012', TBI, February 2013, p. 29, <http://justiceinmexico.files.wordpress.com/2013/02/130206-dvm-2013-final.pdf>.

[35] Molzahn, Ferreira, and Shirk, 'Drug violence in Mexico: data and analysis through 2012', p. 31.

[36] TBI, Justice in Mexico Project, 'Narcobarometro data set', 30 April 2013, <http://www.sandiego .edu/peacestudies/institutes/tbi/resources/data_portal.php>.

The 9,158 casualties compiled by TBI in 2012 indicate a decrease compared to the 11,631 casualties recorded by TBI for the same period in 2011, from January to November. The number of police and military deaths recorded to November of 2012 (392 police and 24 military personnel) also showed a decrease compared to the 557 police deaths and 45 military deaths reported by TBI for 11 months in 2011.[37]

TBI analysis of available data found that the vast majority of victims were men, with just 9 per cent of the victims identified as female, and that the average age of the victims was 32.[38] Among casualties compiled by TBI, eight mayors or former mayors were killed, as well as ten journalists. One of the ten journalist victims was a woman, at least six reportedly showed signs of torture, and at least five were reported to have been dismembered.[39]

A survey released in 2012 found that women human rights defenders in Mexico were targets of organized-crime-related violence and half of all women human rights defenders surveyed reported suffering violence as a direct consequence of their work. The violence against women human rights defenders presented gender-specific characteristics in nearly all cases. In addition, three-quarters (76 per cent) of the women human rights defenders surveyed identified gender-specific aspects of violence, including sexual violence, in cases of violence against other women whom they supported to seek justice. The government (national, state, and local) and its security forces were responsible for the violence and threats of violence in 55 per cent of all cases.[40]

On 9 January 2013, President Peña Nieto signed a General Victims Law designed to provide assistance and compensation to crime victims, including relatives of those killed in drug-related violence over the previous six years.[41]

DISPLACED

An estimated 160,000 people were displaced in Mexico by the end of 2012 as a result of conflict and violence. The largest cause of new displacement was drug-cartel violence and human rights abuses, in the form of fighting between cartels and government forces, extortions, kidnappings, assassinations, and threats against civilians.[42]

---

[37] TBI, Justice in Mexico Project, 'Narcobarometro data set'

[38] Molzahn, Ferreira, and Shirk, 'Drug violence in Mexico: data and analysis through 2012', p. 29.

[39] Molzahn, Ferreira, and Shirk, 'Drug violence in Mexico: data and analysis through 2012', p. 31.

[40] Nobel Women's Initiative, 'From survivors to defenders: women confronting violence in Mexico, Honduras & Guatemala', 1 June 2012, p. 22, <http://nobelwomensinitiative.org/wp-content/uploads/2012/06/Report_AmericasDelgation-2012.pdf>.

[41] International Crisis Group (ICG), 'Mexico: 1 February 2013', Crisis Watch Database, <http://www.crisisgroup.org/en/publication-type/crisiswatch/crisiswatch-database.aspx?CountryIDs=%7b3EFE234A-BC0A-4A77-95C4-392053CD71D4%7d&StartDate=20120101&EndDate=20130505>.

[42] Internal Displacement Monitoring Centre (IDMC), 'Global overview 2012', April 2013, p. 39.

WAR CRIMES ALLEGATIONS, INVESTIGATIONS, AND PROSECUTIONS

If an armed conflict is indeed occurring, war crimes may have been committed. Mexico became a state party to the 1998 Rome Statute of the International Criminal Court (the ICC Statute) on 1 January 2006. In November 2011, Mexican human rights activists, supported by 23,000 signatures of Mexican citizens, asked the ICC to investigate President Felipe Calderón, senior Mexican government officials, and the country's most-wanted drug trafficker, the Sinaloa Cartel boss Joaquin 'Shorty' Guzmán, accusing them of allowing subordinates to kill, torture, and kidnap civilians.[43]

The following month, however, speaking at the Federal Judicial Institute in Mexico City, the then-Prosecutor of the ICC stated that he would not take up the case, reportedly proclaiming that: 'We don't judge political decisions or political responsibility.'[44] The Mexican foreign ministry heavily criticized the request that the ICC investigate, saying that it 'categorically rejects' the notion that President Calderón's 'security policy might constitute an international crime', arguing that if the government 'had not acted with the forcefulness it has shown . . . many families in different communities in the country would be at the mercy of the criminals'.[45] The President's office subsequently announced that it was considering legal action against those who had made the complaint.[46]

On 21 August 2012, Mexico's Supreme Court's decision by eight to two declared unconstitutional the core provision of a law that had allowed the military to try criminal offences against civilians by military tribunals.[47] The case involved the June 2009 killing of Bonfilio Rubio, an indigenous man, after he was shot by the military while on his bus at a checkpoint near the town of Huamuxtitlan, in southern Mexico. The military's attorney argued that it had jurisdiction over the case since article 57.II(a) of the Military Code read that all crimes committed by soldiers on duty are considered crimes concerning military conduct, rather than crimes against civilians.[48] Nonetheless, a Mexican federal law ensures that 'military courts in no case and for no reason may extend their jurisdiction over people who do not belong to the army'. The Supreme Court affirmed that a military tribunal for military offences against civilians was manifestly unconstitutional. According

---

[43] 'Activists accuse Mexican president of war crimes in drug crackdown', *The Guardian*, 26 November 2011, <http://www.guardian.co.uk/world/2011/nov/26/mexican-president-war-crimes-drug>.

[44] 'ICC won't take up case of Mexico's drug war', *Latin American Herald Tribune*, December 2011, <http://www.laht.com/article.asp?ArticleId=439519&CategoryId=14091>.

[45] 'ICC won't take up case of Mexico's drug war', *Latin American Herald Tribune*, 4 November 2011, <http://www.laht.com/article.asp?ArticleId=439519&CategoryId=14091>.

[46] 'Mexico eyes legal action against ICC case "slander"', *Reuters*, 27 November 2011, <http://www.reuters.com/article/2011/11/28/us-mexico-icc-idUSTRE7AR03720111128>.

[47] Justin Halatyn, 'Mexican Supreme Court upholds civilian control in drug war', *Hemispheric Affairs*, 17 September 2012, <http://www.coha.org/mexican-supreme-court-upholds-civilian-control-in-drug-war/>.

[48] Such crimes include rape, murder, and torture.

to the Mexican legal system, however, four similar judgments are needed to set a binding legal precedent.[49]

The armed forces opened nearly 5,000 investigations into criminal wrongdoing between 2007 and 2012, but only 38 ended in sentencing, according to HRW.[50]

[49] 'Mexico's Supreme Court rejects military trials code', *BBC*, 22 August 2012, <http://www.bbc.co.uk/news/world-latin-america-19343919>. See also 'Mexican daily: nearly 60,000 drug war deaths under Calderon', *Fox News Latino*, 1 November 2012, <http://latino.foxnews.com/latino/news/2012/11/01/mexican-daily-nearly-60000-drug-war-deaths-under-calderon/>.

[50] Gabriel Stargardter, 'Mexico security forces abducted dozens in drug war: rights group', *Reuters*, 21 February 2013, <http://uk.reuters.com/article/2013/02/21/us-mexico-disappeared-idUSBRE91K03Q20130221>.

Armed conflict in Myanmar in 2012

KEY CONFLICT STATISTICS FOR 2012

Myanmar army deaths:	60 (min.)	(Source: Media reports)
Civilians displaced:	450,000 (31 Dec. 2012)	(Source: IDMC)

CLASSIFICATION OF THE CONFLICT

Myanmar's army was involved in an armed conflict of a non-international character (NIAC) with, at least, the Kachin Independence Army (KIA) in 2012. There were sporadic clashes with a number of other non-state armed groups, despite the existence of cease-fires with most of them and a general reduction in armed violence.

SUMMARY OF APPLICABLE INTERNATIONAL LAW

All parties to the conflict in 2012 were bound by, inter alia: Common Article 3 to the 1949 Geneva Conventions; the customary international humanitarian law (IHL) rules of distinction, proportionality, and precautions in attacks; the obligation not to recruit and use children as soldiers; and the duty to respect, at a minimum, fundamental human rights. This includes the duty to respect the rights to life and to freedom from torture or other forms of cruel, inhuman, or degrading treatment or punishment.

HISTORY OF THE CONFLICT[1]

Myanmar, previously known as Burma, has been a one-party, military-governed state since 1962, when a military coup led by General Ne Win abolished the federal system and established the 'Burmese Way to Socialism'. In 1974, a new constitution was voted, transferring power from the armed forces to a People's Assembly headed by military leaders. Following a popular uprising in 1988, the State Law and Order Restoration

---

[1] Unless otherwise stated, this section is based on 'Burma profile', *BBC*, 2 April 2013, <http://www.bbc.co.uk/news/world-asia-pacific-12990563>.

Council (SLORC) was formed, and declared martial law in 1989. The armed conflict involving the government and numerous non-state armed groups, most of which claim to represent the interests of a particular ethnic group, has primarily affected the frontier areas bordering Bangladesh, China, India, and Thailand.[2]

Mass demonstrations began in 2007 (known as the Saffron Revolution) when a small string of protest about living standards gained strength, led by pro-democracy activists and Buddhist monks. The protests were violently repressed by the government. Sanctions from numerous countries and civil unrest were sparked by the demonstrations and gave way to crucial steps toward democracy, including elections in 2010 and 2012. They also led to the release from house arrest of the country's most visible figure, pro-democracy leader and Nobel Laureate Aung San Suu Kyi.[3] The ongoing armed conflicts have led to a protracted humanitarian crisis, with civilians, particularly women and children, facing the brunt of long-standing armed conflicts and their consequences.[4]

In April 2012 elections, Aung San Suu Kyi's party won 43 of 45 seats up for election. Although the small parliamentary victory was expected to have only a tangible effect, it served as a symbolic victory for democracy. However, internal tensions continue, threatening the country's stability. On 28 May 2012, the rape and murder of a Buddhist woman by Muslim men was the trigger that led long-simmering tensions between the Buddhist Rakhine and the Muslim Rohingya communities to flare in Rakhine state in June. Dozens were killed, hundreds of houses were burned, and 75,000 mostly Rohingya were displaced by subsequent intercommunal violence.[5] Widespread violence erupted again on 21 October in new areas of Rakhine state; in this second wave, the attacks appeared to be well coordinated and directed towards Muslims in general and not just Rohingya, which represents a potentially serious escalation.[6]

[2] Council on Foreign Relations, 'Understanding Myanmar', 10 July 2012, <http://www.cfr.org/human-rights/understanding-myanmar/p14385>.

[3] International Crisis Group (ICG), 'Burma/Myanmar: after the crackdown', Asia Report No. 144, 31 January 2008, <http://www.crisisgroup.org/~/media/Files/asia/south-east-asia/burma-myanmar/144_burma_myanmar___after_the_crackdown.ashx>.

[4] 'Burma-Myanmar (1988: first combat deaths)', *Ploughshares*, March 2012, <http://ploughshares.ca/pl_armedconflict/burma-myanmar-1988-first-combat-deaths/>.

[5] Amnesty International, 'Myanmar: abuses against Rohingya erode human rights progress', 19 July 2012, <http://www.amnesty.org/en/news/myanmar-rohingya-abuses-show-human-rights-progress-backtracking-2012-07-19>.

[6] ICG, 'Myanmar: storm clouds on the horizon', Asia Report No. 238, November 2012, <http://www.crisisgroup.org/en/regions/asia/south-east-asia/myanmar/238-myanmar-storm-clouds-on-the-horizon.aspx>.

PARTIES TO THE CONFLICT

Myanmar army

The Myanmar army, officially known as Tatmadaw Kyi, had an estimated strength of some 200,000 to 350,000 in 2010.[7] In 2011, following transition from military junta government to civilian parliamentary government, a military draft was enacted whereby all males between 18 and 35 and all females between 18 and 27 years of age can be called for two years' military service in time of national emergency.

Kachin Independence Army

The KIA is the military arm of the Kachin Independence Organization (KIO), a political group composed of ethnic Kachins in northern Myanmar. The Kachins are a coalition of six tribes whose homeland encompasses territory in Yunnan, China, and north-east India, in addition to Kachin state in Myanmar. Fighting erupted with government armed forces in Kachin state in June 2011 for the first time since an earlier peace deal in 1994. The *New Light of Myanmar* reported 11 clashes in the last week of April 2012, including what it said was an attack on a government border guard base. It said 29 of the 31 dead were Kachin rebels, while government forces suffered two dead and 15 wounded. In May 2012, the Associated Press reported that the group had 8,000 troops.[8]

Fighting between the KIA and the Myanmar military escalated in December 2012.[9] In January–February 2013, Myanmar's army launched an attack that surrounded Laiza, the biggest town controlled by the KIA near the Chinese border, breaking a short-lived government cease-fire. The government and the KIA reached an agreement to disengage and begin political dialogue after Chinese-sponsored talks in the southern Chinese town of Ruili.[10] By June 2013, there were reports of a possible breakthrough in peace talks.[11]

---

[7] Andrew Selth (Griffith Asia Institute), 'Burma's armed forces: does size matter?', *East Asia Forum*, 17 September 2010, <http://www.eastasiaforum.org/2010/09/17/burmas-armed-forces-does-size-matter/>.

[8] Associated Press, 'Burma, State Media: 31 dead in latest Kachin clashes', *The Irrawaddy*, 5 May 2012, <http://www.irrawaddy.org/archives/3691>.

[9] Internal Displacement Monitoring Centre (IDMC), 'Global overview 2012', April 2013, p. 68; see also 'Army steps up air offensive against Kachin rebels', *Democratic Voice of Burma*, 28 December 2012, <http://www.dvb.no/news/army-steps-up-air-offensive-against-kachin-rebels/25425>.

[10] 'Burma profile: Timeline', *BBC*, 2 April 2013, <http://www.bbc.co.uk/news/world-asia-pacific-12992883>.

[11] See e.g. ICG, 'A tentative peace in Myanmar's Kachin conflict', Yangon/Jakarta/Brussels, 12 June 2013, <http://www.crisisgroup.org/en/publication-type/media-releases/2013/asia/myanmar-a-tentative-peace-in-myanmars-kachin-conflict.aspx>.

Major non-state armed groups

The following are the current, most active, ethnic armed groups fighting against the Myanmar regime. They are divided into two categories: those who have signed cease-fire agreements with the government; and those who have not.[12]

Non-cease-fire groups

- Karen National Union (KNU), approximately 5,000 members
- Karen National Liberation Army (KNLA), 2,000–4,000 members
- Karenni National Progressive Party (KNPP), 800–2,000 members
- All Burma Students' Democratic Front (ABSDF), approximately 2,000 members
- Mong Thai Army (MTA), approximately 3,000 members
- Mon National Liberation Army (MNLA), approximately 1,000 members
- Myanmar National Democratic Alliance Army (MNDAA), approximately 1,000 members[13]

Cease-fire groups

- Shan State Army (SSA), which merged with the Shan State National Army (SSNA) in 2005, and has a militia of about 10,000 members[14]
- United Wa State Army (UWSA), approximately 15,000–20,000 members (Before signing a cease-fire agreement, the UWSA fought alongside government troops against the SSA.)
- Kachin Independence Organization (KIO), approximately 8,000 members
- Kachin Independence Army (military wing of KIO)
- New Mon State Party (NMSP)
- New Democratic Army—Kachin (NDA-K)
- Mon National Liberation Army (MNLA), approximately 1,000 members

---

[12] Some of the rebel groups have signed cease-fire agreements, but have since then taken up arms again, following the 2004 government order to hand over their weapons: 'Burma-Myanmar (1988: first combat deaths)', *Ploughshares*, March 2012, <http://ploughshares.ca/pl_armedconflict/burma-myanmar-1988-first-combat-deaths/>.

[13] 'Burma-Myanmar (1988: first combat deaths)', *Ploughshares*, March 2012.

[14] It was reported that, in May 2013, the Myanmar government and the SSA-North reached a high-level four-point agreement in Shan state, following talks between them. The talks between the two sides took place after a series of clashes. The government and the SSA-North had signed an initial five-point peace agreement at central level in Taunggyii in January 2012, which mainly covered a cease-fire. The SSA-South, under the Restoration Council of Shan State (RCSS), had reached an 11-point initial peace pact with the central government in Taunggyii, Shan state, earlier in January 2012. See 'Myanmar gov't, Shan ethnic army reach fresh agreement', *Global Times*, 12 May 2013, <http://www.globaltimes.cn/content/780880.shtml#.UY84FxZBtwE>.

- Myanmar National Democratic Alliance Army (MNDAA), approximately 1,000 members[15]

In May 2013, the government claimed that ten of 11 ethnic armed groups had signed preliminary peace pacts with the government at state or central levels since President U Thein Sein announced a peace offer with ethnic armed groups in August 2011.[16]

CASUALTIES

There was a serious lack of reporting on conflict-related casualties in 2012 in Myanmar, and civilian casualties in particular. By the end of 2012, the government had reached preliminary cease-fire agreements with all major armed ethnic groups except the KIA in Kachin state, where armed conflict continued and escalated in December.[17] In February, one man was killed by Myanmar troops.[18] In September, a girl was reportedly killed in cross-fire between government troops and the KIA in Kachin state.[19] Kachin bloggers also reported casualties intermittently in 2012, including a report of a pregnant woman killed in January; however, several posts did not include numbers of casualties.[20]

In September, five Myanmar army soldiers and one KIA soldier were killed in a battle.[21] KIA bloggers reported that ten Burmese Myanmar army soldiers were killed and another seven injured in fighting with joint KIA and Ta'ang National Liberation Army forces in October.[22] Another media report estimated that some 40 Myanmar army soldiers were killed during fighting in Kachin state in the first half of December.[23]

The government signed cease-fire agreements with the KNU, the Shan State Army, and the New Mon State Party. The January 2012 cease-fire agreement with the KNU resulted

[15] 'Myanmar gov't, Shan ethnic army reach fresh agreement', *Global Times.*

[16] 'Myanmar gov't, Shan ethnic army reach fresh agreement', *Global Times.*

[17] US Department of State, 'Country reports on human rights practices 2012: Burma', 19 April 2013.

[18] Simon Roughneen, 'Distrust and displacement on Kachin frontline', *The Irrawaddy*, 28 February 2012, <http://www.simonroughneen.com/asia/seasia/burma/distrust-and-displacement-on-kachin-frontline-the-irrawaddy/>.

[19] US Department of State, 'Country reports on human rights practices 2012: Burma', 19 April 2013.

[20] See 'Burmese army killed Kachin pregnant woman and unborn baby', *Kachinland News*, 11 January 2012, <http://kachinnews-at.blogspot.com/2012/01/burmese-army-killed-kachin-pregnant.html>.

[21] 'Burmese army escalates its offensive war in Kachin region', *Kachinland News*, 2 October 2012, <http://kachinlandnews.com/?p=22345>.

[22] 'Kachin and Ta-ang army join fight against Burmese government army', *Kachinland News*, 6 October 2012, <http://kachinlandnews.com/?p=22348>.

[23] 'Kachin state fighting escalates as new front opens', *The Irrawaddy*, 14 December 2012, <http://www.irrawaddy.org/archives/21311>. In another account, '[s]cores of Burmese soldiers were injured or killed during fighting on 9–10 December': 'Fighting worsens in Kachin state: dozens reported killed', *The Irrawaddy*, 11 December 2012, <http://www.irrawaddy.org/archives/20960>.

in a significant decrease in fighting in Karen state.[24] In February 2012, the KNLA, the armed wing of the KNU, estimated at least six Myanmar army soldiers and seven others had been injured by landmines in Karen state since the cease-fire talks about one month earlier.[25] There were some other reports of violence and killing in Karen state: for example, in June, two men were beaten by Myanmar army soldiers on the accusation of being spies, with one dying from his wounds.[26] A Ta'ang National Liberation Army member from Northern Shan state was reportedly killed after arrest by the Myanmar army in November.[27]

During the year, there were more than 100 disappearances reported in Kachin state. It was also reported that, on 17 June, a person was taken from an internally displaced person (IDP) camp in Kachin state and beaten for alleged association with the KIO.[28]

The United Nations (UN) Secretary-General has reported that allegations of sexual violence, including rape committed by government forces, remained a concern in Kachin state.[29] The US Department of State reported on human rights groups' accounts of instances of rape of civilians and IDPs by the government and armed ethnic groups in both Shan and Kachin states. In one instance, according to a Kachin women's organization, some ten soldiers beat, stabbed, and raped a woman over a period of three days.[30]

DISPLACED

At least 166,000 people were newly displaced in Myanmar in 2012, with at least 450,000 IDPs throughout the country that year. Fighting between the KIA and the Myanmar military escalated in December 2012; by the end of the year, more than 75,000 people had been internally displaced, with some 40,000 living in areas controlled by the KIO.[31]

WAR CRIMES ALLEGATIONS, INVESTIGATIONS, AND PROSECUTIONS

Myanmar is not a party to the 1998 Rome Statute of the International Criminal Court (the ICC Statute).

---

[24] US Department of State, 'Country reports on human rights practices 2012: Burma', 19 April 2013.
[25] 'Burma army reinforcements run into Karen minefield—six dead', *Karen News*, 12 February 2012, <http://karennews.org/2012/02/burma-army-reinforcements-run-into-karen-minefield-six-dead.html>.
[26] 'Burma army torture leaves one man dead in Pa'an', *Karen News*, 19 November 2012, <http://karennews.org/2012/11/burma-army-torture-leaves-one-man-dead-in-paan.html/>.
[27] 'Ethnic soldier arrested and killed by government troops', *Karen News*, 14 November 2012, <http://karennews.org/2012/11/ethnic-soldier-arrested-and-killed-by-government-troops.html/>.
[28] US Department of State, 'Country reports on human rights practices 2012: Burma', 19 April 2013.
[29] 'Report of the Secretary-General on sexual violence in conflict', UN doc. S/2013/149, 14 March 2013, §58.
[30] US Department of State, 'Country reports on human rights practices 2012: Burma', 19 April 2013.
[31] IDMC, 'Global overview 2012', April 2013, p. 68.

Armed conflict in the Philippines in 2012

KEY CONFLICT STATISTICS FOR 2012

Total deaths:	74	(Sources: Media reports; US Department of State)
Total injured:	244	(Source: COE-DAT)
Civilians killed:	59+	(Sources: Media reports; US Department of State)
Military (AFP) deaths:	103	(Source: Media reports)
Police deaths:	8	(Source: Media reports)
Insurgent deaths:	14 (min.)	(Source: US Department of State)
Civilians displaced:	178,000 (31 Dec. 2012)	(Source: IDMC)

CLASSIFICATION OF THE CONFLICT

Philippine armed forces were involved in an armed conflict of a non-international character (NIAC) with the New People's Army (NPA) in 2012, including on Mindanao. The conflict reached the threshold for applicability of the 1977 Additional Protocol II.

SUMMARY OF APPLICABLE INTERNATIONAL LAW

Both parties to the conflict are bound by, inter alia: Common Article 3 to the 1949 Geneva Conventions and the 1977 Additional Protocol II;[1] the customary international humanitarian law (IHL) rules of distinction, proportionality, and precautions in attacks; the obligation not to recruit and use children as soldiers; and the duty to respect, at a minimum, fundamental human rights. This includes the duty to respect the rights to life and to freedom from torture or other forms of cruel, inhuman, or degrading treatment or punishment.

---

[1] In March 2013, the Philippines adhered to the 1977 Additional Protocol I with the following declaration:

a) The application of Protocol I, particularly Articles 1(4), 4 and 96(3) shall not affect the legal status of the Parties to the conflict, nor the legal status of the concerned territory; as such, no claim of status of belligerency may be invoked therefrom; b) The application of Protocol I may in no case be invoked in internal armed conflicts within sovereign States; c) The terms 'armed conflict' and 'conflict' do not include the commission of ordinary crimes, whether collective or isolated.

Articles 1(4) and 96(3) potentially extend the notion of international armed conflict (IAC) to those in which 'peoples are fighting against colonial domination and alien occupation and against racist régimes in the exercise of their right of self-determination'.

The Philippines adhered to the 1997 Anti-Personnel Mine Ban Convention (APMBC) in February 2000, becoming a state party on 1 August 2000, and has signed, but not yet ratified, the 2008 Convention on Cluster Munitions (CCM). In addition, the Philippines is a state party to the two 1966 Covenants (on civil and political rights, and on economic, social and cultural rights).

HISTORY OF THE CONFLICT[2]

Conflict on Mindanao

Frequent armed clashes between government forces and armed opposition groups occur primarily on the southern island of Mindanao, although a peace accord has been signed with one group, and there is an ongoing cease-fire and peace talks with another.[3]

After the Philippines gained independence in 1946, a massive resettlement programme began that drastically changed the religious make-up of the southern island of Mindanao, which had historically been populated and ruled by Muslims. By 1983, 80 per cent of the population of Mindanao was Christian, a shift that caused deep resentment among the Muslim population. Since 1971, the government of the predominantly Roman Catholic Philippines has faced armed opposition from several Muslim groups. Earlier, opposition came from the Moro National Liberation Front (MNLF), which sought greater autonomy for the island of Mindanao. More recently, it comes from break-away groups the Moro Islamic Liberation Front (MILF) and the fundamentalist Abu Sayyaf Group (ASG), both of which seek Mindanao independence. The government agreed to a framework that led to the establishment of an autonomous region of four Mindanao provinces in 1990.[4] In 1996, the government and the MNLF signed a peace agreement, but other Mindanao Muslim rebels and Christian groups opposed the settlement. In 2009, a cease-fire was signed by the government and the MILF, which was largely held, contributing to a significant reduction of fatalities and violent incidents.

The government and the MILF resumed talks in January 2011. Nearly two years later, in October 2012, the government signed a framework peace plan with the MILF.[5] Under

---

[2] Unless otherwise stated, this section is based on 'Philippines profile', *BBC*, 18 December 2012, <http://www.bbc.co.uk/news/world-asia-15521300>.

[3] International Crisis Group (ICG), 'The Philippines: back to the table, warily, in Mindanao', 14 March 2011, <http://www.crisisgroup.org/en/regions/asia/south-east-asia/philippines/B119-the-philippines-back-to-the-table-warily-in-mindanao.aspx>.

[4] GlobalSecurity.org, 'Moro Islamic Liberation Front', December 2012, <http://www.globalsecurity.org/military/world/para/milf.htm>.

[5] The agreement was signed on 15 October 2012 in Malaysia. See ICG, 'The Philippines: breakthrough in Mindanao', 5 December 2012, <http://www.crisisgroup.org/en/publication-type/media-releases/2012/asia/the-philippines-breakthrough-in-mindanao.aspx>.

this plan, both parties agreed to create a new political entity called Bangsamoro (after the Moro people) to replace the Autonomous Region in Muslim Mindanao (ARMM). The draft framework should give the leaders of Bangsamoro more political and economic powers, and provide for the gradual transfer of law enforcement from the army to the Bangsamoro police in a 'phased and gradual manner'.[6] The agreement also provides for a 'just and equitable share' of the region's copious natural resources, and pledges to address the needs of poverty-stricken communities.[7] In exchange for this, the MILF committed to stop armed movements against the government, which also retains its control over national security and foreign policy.

Conflict with the New People's Army

Since 1969, the Communist Party of the Philippines (CPP) and its military arm, the NPA, have fought the national government for political control and land reform. The NPA's armed struggle against military forces and police and civilian militia units resulted in heavy casualties during the 1980s. In 1992, the government's National Unification Commission established an amnesty that revived peace talks with the rebels. In 1998, a month after newly elected President Joseph Estrada signed a human rights agreement with the communist rebels, the government postponed planned peace talks. In spite of renewed efforts in 1999 and 2001, the peace process made no progress.[8]

The global war on terror has impacted on the conflict as Philippine government forces have received external arms, funding, and training, mostly from the United States of America (USA), in order to defeat the rebel fighters. In February 2004, a peace process was revived, with representatives of the NPA meeting government officials in Oslo. But little progress was made, and peace talks were suspended after rebels blamed the government for their inclusion on the US list of terrorist groups.[9] In 2007, President Gloria Arroyo announced an intensified campaign against the rebels, with the goal of destroying the group by 2010. In 2011, despite formal peace talks between the NPA and government forces, violent clashes continued, especially in the Eastern Visayas, Negros, and parts of Mindanao. Both parties to the conflict continued to be accused of gross human rights violations.[10]

[6] 'Govt, MILF agree to create "Bangsamoro" to replace ARMM', *GMA News*, 7 October 2012, <http://www.gmanetwork.com/news/story/277218/news/nation/govt-milf-agree-to-create-bangsamoro-to-replace-armm>.

[7] 'Philippines and Muslim rebels sign key peace plan', *BBC*, 15 October 2012, <http://www.bbc.co.uk/news/world-asia-19944101>.

[8] 'Guide to the Philippines conflict', *BBC*, 18 December 2009, <http://news.bbc.co.uk/2/hi/asia-pacific/7887521.stm>.

[9] 'Guide to the Philippines conflict', *BBC*.

[10] Human Rights Watch (HRW), 'We told the children not to enter', 31 January 2012, <http://www.hrw.org/news/2012/01/31/we-told-children-not-enter>.

The NPA, the MILF, and Abu Sayyaf Group (ASG) allegedly continued to recruit and use children as soldiers in 2012. The Philippine army at times used schools for military purposes and civil-military operations, despite a Philippine law prohibiting such activities.[11]

PARTIES TO THE CONFLICT

Philippine Armed Forces

The Armed Forces of the Philippines (AFP) is composed of an army, navy, and air force. The AFP is a volunteer force with a total active strength of some 200,000 and more than 178,000 personnel in reserve service.[12]

Moro Islamic Liberation Front (MILF)

The MILF is a Sunni Islamist group located in the southern Philippines. Its main base is the central region of Mindanao Island, and it has a presence on remote southern islands of Basilan, Jolo, Tawi-tawi, and Palawan. The group was formed in 1978 after the split with the MNLF, an Islamist group formed in the 1960s following the Jabidah massacre to achieve greater Bangsamoro autonomy in the southern Philippines. The separation took place after the MNLF signed a deal with the government accepting an autonomy set-up in the south that the MILF refused to accept, deciding instead to continue its insurgency operations.[13]

The armed wing of the MILF is known as the Bangsomoro Islamic Armed Forces (BIAF). From the late 1990s, the MILF allowed al-Qaeda and Jemaah Islamiah, a south-east Asian regional militant network linked to al-Qaeda, to seek shelter and train in its bases. In 2004, however, it severed its links with al-Qaeda to save talks with the government and to avoid being labelled a foreign terrorist group by the USA and other Western states. Nonetheless, the Philippine security officials accuse some MILF members of sheltering dozens of Islamist militants from Indonesia, Malaysia, and Singapore.[14]

Since 1997, peace talks between the government and the MILF have been on and off. Cease-fire agreements have been broken at least three times, with troops launching

---

[11] HRW, 'World report 2013: Philippines', January 2013, <http://www.hrw.org/world-report/2013/country-chapters/philippines>.

[12] Global Firepower, 'Philippines military strength', <http://www.globalfirepower.com/country-military-strength-detail.asp?country_id=Philippines>.

[13] 'Guide to the Philippines conflict', *BBC*, 18 December 2009, <http://news.bbc.co.uk/2/hi/asia-pacific/7887521.stm>.

[14] Council of Foreign Relations, 'Terrorism havens: Philippines', 1 June 2009, <http://www.cfr.org/philippines/terrorism-havens-philippines/p9365>.

offensives in response to deadly bombings and attacks on Christian communities. In December 2009, negotiators from the government and the MILF met again in Kuala Lumpur and reached a cease-fire agreement.[15] A decision was taken to revive an International Monitoring Team (IMT) of cease-fire observers and an ad hoc joint action group, which would try to isolate Muslim militants from criminal groups in rebel-controlled areas. In October 2012, after resuming talks with the government, the MILF signed a framework peace plan. Soon after the conclusion of the negotiations, the MILF launched a far-reaching campaign aiming at explaining the content of the newly signed peace framework agreement to its several hundred thousand members in southern Philippines.[16]

New People's Army (NPA)

The NPA is the military wing of the CPP created on 29 March 1969. While strongest in the northern region, it also has a presence in northern and eastern Mindanao. The CPP and its armed wing are considered the main threat to the country's security.[17] After its creation, the NPA began guerrilla warfare against the regime of President Ferdinand Marcos over political control and land reform. The NPA's methods of warfare consisted of assassinating government officials, ambushing army troops, and killing rural residents who refused to pay 'revolutionary taxes'.[18] The armed group gradually increased its strength through the 1970s and 1980s, growing from about 350 armed members in 1971 to more than 20,000 by the late 1980s. Nowadays, this tendency has inverted: the NPA is largely decreasing after years of losses on the battlefield, with only about 4,200 fighters as of 2012 from a peak of 26,000 in the 1980s.[19] After numerous failed attempts, in June 2012, the National Democratic Front of the Philippines (NDFP), which is the legal arm of the CPP, met in Oslo in an effort to pave the way for the resumption of formal talks between the panels with the aim 'to resolve the armed conflict and attain a just and lasting peace'.[20]

[15] ICG, 'The Philippines: back to the table, warily, in Mindanao', 14 March 2011, <http://www.crisisgroup.org/en/regions/asia/south-east-asia/philippines/B119-the-philippines-back-to-the-table-warily-in-mindanao.aspx>.

[16] 'Philippine insurgent group campaigns to explain peace deal to members', *Xinhua*, 3 November 2012, <http://news.xinhuanet.com/english/world/2012-11/03/c_131948954.htm>.

[17] R. B. Ferrer and R. G. Cabangbang, 'Non-international armed conflicts in the Philippines', *International Law Studies*, 88 (19 July 2012), pp. 263–78, <http://www.usnwc.edu/getattachment/a8f30074-6e7d-44b2-8d01-445698986206/Non-International-Armed-Conflicts-in-the-Philippin.aspx>.

[18] Federation of American Scientists, 'New People's Army (NPA)', 3 May 2004, <http://www.fas.org/irp/world/para/npa.htm>.

[19] Ferrer and Cabangbang, 'Non-international armed conflicts in the Philippines', p. 265.

[20] NDFP, 'GPH and NDFP agree to continue meaningful discussions prior to formal talks', 16 June 2012, <http://www.ndfp.net/joom15/index.php/peace-talks-mainmenu-75/1445-gph-and-ndfp-agree-to-continue-meaningful-discussions-prior-to-formal-talks.html>; 'Communists ready to resume talks with Philippines',

CASUALTIES

There was no accurate figure for conflict-related casualties in the Philippines in 2012.

The AFP claimed that, in 2012, NPA activities resulted in the deaths of 53 civilians. In addition, 81 AFP members and 22 members of the Citizen Armed Force Geographical Unit (CAFGU), which the military controls and supervises, and eight Philippines National Police (PNP) officers died in clashes with the NPA during the year; 374 violent incidents by the NPA were recorded in 2012.[21] The AFP affirmed that it was 'able to successfully neutralize 555 NPA personalities in 2012 of which, 367 voluntarily surrendered to the government'.[22]

According to the US Department of State, ten NPA militants and four ASG militants were killed during the year, and on 7 September, the ASG allegedly killed six civilians in Basilan province.[23]

HRW reported that NPA military action had a regular impact on civilians in 2012: for example, on 1 September, NPA fighters threw a grenade at a military outpost in Davao City, but instead hit and wounded civilians.[24] On 27 July, the NPA was said to have killed two tribal leaders.[25]

The North Atlantic Treaty Organization (NATO)-accredited Centre of Excellence—Defence against Terrorism (COE-DAT), based in Turkey, recorded 133 people killed, 244 injured, and another 11 abducted in terrorism incidents in Philippines in 2012 in 101 attacks.[26]

Action on Armed Violence (AOAV) found 292 civilian casualties of explosive violence in the Philippines in 2012; civilians made up 75 per cent of all casualties from explosive violence.[27]

Inquiry News, 17 June 2012, <http://newsinfo.inquirer.net/214067/communists-ready-to-resume-talks-with-philippines>.

[21] 'NPA kills an innocent civilian every week in 2012', *Agence France-Presse*, 6 February 2013, <http://www.afp.mil.ph/index.php/19-afp-data-articles/latest-news/1107-npa-kills-an-innocent-civilian-every-week-in-2012>.

[22] 'NPA kills an innocent civilian every week in 2012', *Agence France-Presse*.

[23] US Department of State, 'Country reports on human rights practices 2012: the Philippines', 19 April 2013, <http://www.state.gov/j/drl/rls/hrrpt/humanrightsreport/index.htm?year=2012&dlid=204231>.

[24] HRW, 'World report 2013: Philippines', January 2013, <http://www.hrw.org/world-report/2013/country-chapters/philippines>.

[25] US Department of State, 'Country reports on human rights practices 2012: the Philippines', 19 April 2013.

[26] COE-DAT, 'Centre of Excellence Defence Against Terrorism: 2012 annual terrorism report', p. 12.

[27] AOAV, 'An explosive situation: monitoring explosive violence in 2012', April 2013, <http://aoav.files.wordpress.com/2013/06/an-explosive-situation-explosive-violence-in-2012.pdf>. These casualties have not been included in the totals above, since it is not possible to confirm how many casualties were related to armed conflict.

Without providing specific figures, HRW reported that several extrajudicial killings in 2012 were attributed to members of the CAFGU. So-called death squad killings occurred in Davao City, in the southern Philippines, and other cities in 2012.[28]

According to the Committee to Protect Journalists, seven journalists were killed in the Philippines in 2012. At least one journalist was killed in relation to his work, four others were killed under unclear circumstances, and at least two more were attacked by unidentified gunmen.[29] Reporters without Borders identified four journalists killed because of their activities as journalists during 2012.[30]

In July, a Dutch aid worker was killed; it was believed that his death was politically motivated, although not attributed to a particular insurgent group.[31]

DISPLACED

An estimated 178,000 people were newly displaced by conflict and violence during 2012 in Mindanao in the southern Philippines. However, because many displaced persons were not registered, by the end of 2012, only 1,200 people were living in government-recognized camps and relocation sites.[32]

WAR CRIMES ALLEGATIONS, INVESTIGATIONS, AND PROSECUTIONS

The Philippines adhered to the 1998 Rome Statute of the International Criminal Court (the ICC Statute) on 30 August 2011. In accordance with ICC Statute, the Court has jurisdiction over ICC Statute crimes committed on the territory of the Philippines or by its nationals since 1 November 2011.

---

[28] HRW, 'World report 2013: Philippines', January 2013, <http://www.hrw.org/world-report/2013/country-chapters/philippines>.

[29] Committee to Protect Journalists, 'Attacks on the Press 2012: Philippines key developments', <http://www.cpj.org/2013/02/attacks-on-the-press-in-2012-philippines.php>.

[30] Reporters without Borders, '2012: journalists killed', <http://en.rsf.org/press-freedom-barometer-journalists-killed.html?annee=2012>.

[31] 'Aid worker 3rd Dutch to die in Philippines in a week', *Philippine Daily Inquirer*, 3 July 2012, <http://globalnation.inquirer.net/42763/aid-worker-3rd-dutch-to-die-in-philippines-in-a-week#ixzz2STF4MMqN>; Kings Guard Security, 'Dutch aid worker murdered in Philippines', <http://www.kgsec.com/dutch-aid-worker-murdered-in-philippines/>.

[32] Internal Displacement Monitoring Centre (IDMC), 'Global overview 2012', April 2013, p. 71.

Armed conflict in Somalia in 2012

KEY CONFLICT STATISTICS FOR 2012

Total deaths:	Unknown, but at least hundreds	(Sources: WHO; Media reports; AOAV)
Injured:	6,680 (at least, in Mogadishu only)	(Source: WHO)
Child deaths:	100+	(Source: UN)
UN staff death:	1	(Source: UN)
UN staff injured:	1	(Source: UN)
Humanitarian worker deaths:	9	(Source: UN)
Military deaths:	Unknown	(Source: Media)
Civilians displaced:	1.1–1.36 million (31 Dec. 2012)	(Source: IDMC)

CLASSIFICATION OF THE CONFLICT

The Federal Republic of Somalia, supported by Ethiopian forces and an African Union force (AMISOM) composed largely of Burundian, Kenyan, and Ugandan soldiers, was involved in an armed conflict of a non-international character (NIAC) with al-Shabaab. The United States of America (USA) has also sent armed drones into Somalia to target al-Shabaab members and is therefore also arguably a party to the conflict.[1]

In 2012, the conflict reached the threshold for applicability of the 1977 Additional Protocol II, but it did not apply as such, because Somalia is not party to this instrument.

SUMMARY OF APPLICABLE INTERNATIONAL LAW

All parties to the conflict are bound by, inter alia: Common Article 3 to the 1949 Geneva Conventions; the customary international humanitarian law (IHL) rules of distinction, proportionality, and precautions in attacks; the obligation not to recruit and use children as soldiers; and the duty to respect, at a minimum, fundamental human rights. This includes the duty to respect the rights to life and to freedom from torture or other forms of cruel, inhuman, or degrading treatment or punishment.

---

[1] According to the Bureau of Investigative Journalism, 'Little is still known about US drone strikes in Somalia, with only two credibly reported incidents in 2012. One of those killed was a British-Somali militant, Bilal al-Barjawi': Chris Woods, Jack Serle, and Alice K. Ross, 'Emerging from the shadows: US covert drone strikes in 2012', *Bureau of Investigative Journalism*, 3 January 2013, <http://www.thebureauinvestigates.com/2013/01/03/emerging-from-the-shadows-us-covert-drone-strikes-in-2012-2/>.

In addition, Somalia has human rights obligations as a state party to the two 1966 Covenants (on civil and political rights, and on economic, social, and cultural rights). Other states participating in military action against al-Shabaab are bound extraterritorially by their human rights obligations.[2]

Somalia acceded to the 1997 Anti-Personnel Mine Ban Convention (APMBC) in April 2012, becoming a state party on 1 October 2012, and has signed, but not yet ratified, the 2008 Convention on Cluster Munitions (CCM). States participating in the African Union Mission in Somalia (AMISOM) who are party to the APMBC and CCM are bound by those instruments. Although not directly applicable to the situation in Somalia because the United Nations (UN) is not engaged as a party to the armed conflict, the UN Secretary-General's Bulletin requires that UN peacekeeping forces not use anti-personnel mines.[3]

HISTORY OF THE CONFLICT[4]

Somalia has been without an effective central government since President Siad Barre was overthrown in 1991. In 2004, after protracted talks in Kenya, the main warlords and politicians signed a deal to set up a new parliament, which later appointed a president. The fledgling administration, the fourteenth attempt to establish a government since 1991, faced a formidable task in bringing reconciliation to a country divided into clan fiefdoms. Its authority was further compromised in 2006 by the rise of Islamists, who gained control of much of the south, including the capital, after their militias kicked out the warlords who had ruled the roost for 15 years.

With the backing of Ethiopian troops, forces loyal to the interim administration seized control from the Islamists at the end of 2006. Islamist insurgents—including al-Shabaab, which later declared allegiance to al-Qaeda and in 2012 announced that it was merging with it—fought back against the government and Ethiopian forces, regaining control of most of southern Somalia by late 2008.

In May 2012, African Union and Somali government forces captured Afgoye, a town south of Mogadishu, thereby cutting al-Shabaab territory in half. In August, Somalia's first formal parliament in more than 20 years was sworn in at Mogadishu airport, in a heavily secured area of the city. This marked the end of the eight-year 'transitional period'. The same month, pro-government forces captured the port of Merca, 70 km south of Mogadishu, from al-Shabaab. In October, Kismayo, the country's second-largest

---

[2] See e.g. International Court of Justice (ICJ), *Wall* Advisory Opinion, 2004, §106; ICJ, *Armed Activities on the Territory of the Congo (Democratic Republic of the Congo v. Uganda)*, Judgment, 19 December 2005.

[3] 'Secretary-General's Bulletin: Observance by United Nations forces of international humanitarian law', New York, UN doc. ST/SGB/1999/13, 6 August 1999.

[4] Unless otherwise stated, this section is based on 'Somalia profile', *BBC*, 17 April 2013, <http://www.bbc.co.uk/news/world-africa-14094503>.

port and the last major city held by al-Shabaab, fell to African Union and government forces, as did the town of Wanla Weyn 90 km north-west of Mogadishu.[5]

Ethiopia's involvement

Ethiopian troops entered the country in December 2006 to help Somalia's interim government oust the Union of Islamic Courts, which had taken control of much of southern Somalia. Ethiopian troop presence was violently opposed by Somali non-state armed groups.[6] In late 2008, Ethiopia announced it would withdraw all its forces by the end of the year. Theoretically, Ethiopia's presence in Somalia ended in early 2009, when it pulled its troops under an agreement between the transitional Somali government and moderate Islamists.[7]

However, reports persisted of Ethiopia's involvement in Somalia, where it has been fighting al-Shabaab. In March 2012, Ethiopian troops entered Somalia and fighting ensued, with deaths reported on both sides.[8]

Kenyan involvement

In October 2011, hundreds of Kenyan troops entered Somalia, escalating their efforts to fight the al-Shabaab, which it accused of kidnappings and of raiding Kenyan coastal resorts and refugee camps. The group soon threatened reprisals against Kenya and witnesses reported seeing al-Shabaab fighters move toward the areas invaded.[9] By 2012, heavy fighting was being reported between Somali and Kenyan forces and al-Shabaab in the south of Somalia. Kenyan troops were said to have killed dozens of militants.[10] By February 2012, they had captured the Baidoa base from the militants, followed by El Bur base by the end of March 2012.[11] The operation was making significant advances as of April 2012, with the al-Shabaab leadership said to become fractured following its losses.[12]

---

[5] 'Somalia profile: timeline', *BBC*, 17 April 2013, <http://www.bbc.co.uk/news/world-africa-14094632>.

[6] 'Ethiopia in Somalia: one year on', *BBC*, 28 December 2007, <http://news.bbc.co.uk/2/hi/africa/7155868.stm>.

[7] International Crisis Group (ICG), 'Somalia conflict history', September 2008, <http://www.crisisgroup.org/en/publication-type/key-issues/research-resources/conflict-histories/somalia.aspx>.

[8] 'In March 2012, Ethiopian troops had entered Somalia', *Boston.com*, 22 March 2012, <http://www.boston.com/news/world/africa/articles/2012/03/22/somali_ethiopian_troops_seize_town_fighters_flee/>.

[9] Human Rights Watch (HRW), 'Kenya: human rights concerns of operation "Linda Nchi"', 18 November 2011, <http://www.hrw.org/news/2011/11/18/kenya-human-rights-concerns-operation-linda-nchi>.

[10] 'Heavy fighting in Southern Somalia', *Somalia Report*, 1 May 2012, <http://www.somaliareport.com/index.php/post/2456/Heavy_Fighting_in_Southern_Somalia>.

[11] 'al-Shabab forces lose Somali base of El Bur', *BBC*, 26 March 2012, <http://www.bbc.co.uk/news/world-africa-17516440>.

[12] Jamestown Foundation, 'Somalia's neighbors making progress against al-Shabaab despite threats of retaliation', *Terrorism Monitor*, 10(7) (6 April 2012), <http://www.unhcr.org/refworld/country,,,SOM,4f854f9a2,0.html>.

Somaliland and Puntland

Armed violence has occurred sporadically between security forces from Somaliland and Puntland. In an unprecedented sign of cooperation, the two regions, differentiated by Somaliland's striving for independence and Puntland's recognition of Mogadishu as its capital, agreed in 2010 to tackle security threats together.[13] In January 2012, leaders of the northern regions of Sool, Sanaag, and Cayn banded together into a new state called Khaatumo, and declared that they wanted to become an independent region within Somalia.[14] Somaliland troops have clashed with Khaatumo secessionists, with dozens of victims, and the tensions have strained relations with Puntland as well. Thousands have also been displaced by the conflict.[15]

Piracy

In November 2008, Somali pirates were accused of forming an 'unholy high seas alliance' with some of the country's Islamist insurgents.[16] Although it is generally agreed that the pirates are not a party to the armed conflict, it has been alleged that certain insurgents are using pirates to smuggle weapons and supplies, and help provide bases in return.[17]

PARTIES TO THE CONFLICT

The African Union Mission in Somalia (AMISOM)

AMISOM is an active, regional peacekeeping mission operated by the African Union with the approval of the United Nations (UN). It was created by the African Union's Peace and Security Council on 19 January 2007 with an initial six-month mandate paving the way for some 8,000 troops to enter the country, but leaving the origin of those forces unclear.[18] In accordance with the decision of the African Union Peace and Security Council on 19 January 2007, AMISOM's mandate is: to provide support to the

---

[13] Ploughshares Project, 'Somalia (1988—first combat deaths)', March 2012, <http://ploughshares.ca/pl_armedconflict/somalia-1988-first-combat-deaths/>.

[14] 'Somaliland troops and separatists clash, five killed', *Reuters*, 1 April 2012, <http://www.trust.org/alertnet/news/somaliland-troops-and-separatists-clash-five-killed/>.

[15] 'SOMALIA: Fighting displaces thousands in Somaliland', *IRIN Africa*, 9 February 2012, <http://www.irinnews.org/report/94821/somalia-fighting-displaces-thousands-in-somaliland>.

[16] 'Rules frustrate anti-piracy efforts', *BBC*, 9 December 2008, <http://news.bbc.co.uk/2/hi/africa/7735144.stm>.

[17] Thilo Neumann and Tim René Salomon, 'Fishing in troubled waters—Somalia's maritime zones and the case for reinterpretation', *American Society of International Law (ASIL) Insights*, 16(9) (15 March 2012).

[18] AMISOM, 'AMISOM background', March 2007, <http://amisom-au.org/about/amisom-background/>.

transitional federal institutions (TFIs) of Somalia in their efforts towards stabilization of the situation in the country and the furtherance of dialogue and reconciliation; to facilitate the provision of humanitarian assistance; and to create conducive conditions for long-term stabilization, reconstruction, and development in Somalia.[19]

al-Shabaab

al-Shabaab (literally, 'the youth') is a radical Islamist group of young fighters that grew rapidly in influence in Somalia, especially around Mogadishu. Placed on the USA's list of 'foreign terrorist organizations', al-Shabaab began as the militia wing of the Union of Islamic Courts (UIC). The armed group is fighting an insurgency against the UN-backed Transitional Federal Government (TFG), which is based in Somalia's capital, Mogadishu. al-Shabaab has targeted AMISOM peacekeepers for their support of the TFG. The group has also repeatedly threatened the USA and the West, and has demonstrated the capacity to strike beyond Somalia's borders.

In 2009–10, the militant group controlled most of central and southern Somalia south of the autonomous region of Puntland. Since the February 2011 military offensives by AMISOM, Somali government troops, and Somali Sufi militia forces, al-Shabaab has suffered a series of significant territorial and strategic setbacks.[20] In February 2012, the armed group released a joint video with al-Qaeda, announcing that the two groups had merged, causing internal divisions within al-Shabaab's leadership to materialize.[21] In April 2012, after being pushed out of central Somalia, militants moved north into Puntland in a move that the region's president claimed was driven by their desire to strengthen ties with al-Qaeda in the Arabian Peninsula (in Yemen).[22]

Hizbul Islam

Founded in February 2009, Hizbul Islam was an umbrella organization of four groups, led by Islamist cleric Sheikh Hassan Dahir Aweys, which had been previously part of the UIC administration. Also listed on the US list of terrorist organizations, Hizbul Islam carried out attacks on the government alongside al-Shabaab. In December 2010, Hizbul

---

[19] AMISOM, 'Status of Mission Agreement (SOMA)', 6 March 2007, <http://amisom-au.org/status-of-mission-agreement-soma/>.

[20] Council on International Relations, 'Backgrounder al-Shabaab', 5 February 2013, <http://www.cfr.org/somalia/al-shabaab/p18650?breadcrumb=%2Fpublication%2Fpublication_list%3Ftype%3Dbackgrounder%26page%3D4>; see also 'al-Shabab's tactical and media strategies in the wake of its battlefield setbacks', *CTC Sentinel*, 6(3) (March 2013), pp. 12–16.

[21] 'Somalia's al-Shabab join al-Qaeda', *BBC*, 10 February 2012, <http://www.bbc.co.uk/news/world-africa-16979440>.

[22] 'Somalia's al-Shabab Islamists move north into Puntland', *BBC*, 11 April 2012, <http://www.bbc.co.uk/news/world-africa-17674996>.

Islam merged into al-Shabaab, under the name 'al-Shabaab', but, in September 2012, Hizbul Islam's spokesman issued a public statement announcing it was leaving the organization. A political analyst affirmed that the two groups experienced ideological differences: '[F]rom the beginning, al-Shabaab had adopted the al-Qaeda ideology, which knows no geographical borders and sees the whole world as an open space to stage its military operations.'[23] Also Hizbul Islam did not agree with al-Shabaab's union with al-Qaeda.

CASUALTIES

No accurate casualty figures are available for Somalia for 2012.[24]

According to the World Health Organization (WHO), in 2012 there were 6,680 casualties recorded from weapon-related injuries (230 were children under the age of 5); a total of 145 deaths above the age of 5 and 13 deaths below the age of 5 were registered by the WHO. The statistics were collected from four hospitals in Mogadishu.[25] However, it is very difficult to present exact figures, because there is often no reporting and many wounded people never receive hospital treatment.[26]

Action on Armed Violence (AOAV) identified 605 casualties of explosive weapons in Somalia in 2012; 67 per cent were civilians, leaving some 200 military casualties.[27] The UN reported that 157 civilian casualties were caused by improvised explosive devices (IEDs). [28]

Reporters without Borders described 2012 as the 'deadliest year' on record for journalists in Somalia, with at least 18 killed.[29] Journalist deaths were usually due to

---

[23] Those are the words of Abdirahman Mohamud, a political analyst, in an interview with Sabahi: 'Hizbul Islam's split from al-Shabaab further isolates militant group', *Sabahi*, 27 September 2012, <http://sabahionline.com/en_GB/articles/hoa/articles/features/2012/09/27/feature-01>.

[24] UN reporting did not include overall casualty totals and the online news source Somalia Report, which compiled an extensive, but non-comprehensive, estimate of casualties from reports by medics, local residents, and media, stopped updating reporting at the end of 2011.

[25] WHO, 'Somalia emergency weekly health update', 30 December 2012, <http://www.emro.who.int/images/stories/somalia/documents/Somalia_Emergency_Weekly_Health_Update_December_2012.pdf>.

[26] Landinfo—Country of Origin Information Centre, 'Update on security and human rights issues in South-Central Somalia, including in Mogadishu', January 2013, <http://www.refworld.org/docid/511ca6b12.html>.

[27] AOAV, 'An explosive situation: monitoring explosive violence in 2012', April 2013, <http://aoav.files.wordpress.com/2013/06/an-explosive-situation-explosive-violence-in-2012.pdf>.

[28] 'Report of the Secretary-General on Somalia', UN Security Council, UN doc. S/2013/69, 31 January 2013, §37.

[29] Reporters without Borders, 'Journalist gunned down outside Mogadishu home', 22 April 2013, <http://en.rsf.org/somalia-journalist-gunned-down-outside-22-04-2013,44407.html>. Other accounts of journalist fatalities included 15 journalists reported killed in 2012 in HRW, 'World report 2013: Somalia', <http://www.hrw .org/world-report/2013/country-chapters/somalia>, and a total of ten journalists reported killed in 'Report of the Secretary-General on Somalia', UN doc. S/2013/69, 31 January 2013, §37.

targeted killings, not people caught in the cross-fire between the pro-government forces and militias.[30]

Scanning of media reports identified more than 520 deaths of al-Shabaab fighters during 2012. Most were killed by Kenya Defence Forces troops from AMISOM. Far fewer AMISOM casualties were reported and the numbers available in media stories do not seem to provide a reasonable account.[31]

Between only August and the end of December, there were said to be 100 killings (84 boys, 16 girls), 192 people wounded (138 boys, 57 girls), 86 incidents of sexual violence and rape (1 boy, 85 girls), and 528 abductions (489 boys, 39 girls).[32]

Between January and November 2012, more than 1,700 rape cases were registered in Mogadishu and surrounding areas. Almost one-third of the recorded incidents were against children, including both boys and girls.[33]

DISPLACED

The Internal Displacement Monitoring Centre (IDMC) reported that between 1.1 million and 1.36 million people in Somalia were internally displaced as of December 2012. The Office of the UN High Commissioner for Human Rights (OHCHR) and its

---

[30] 'Somali journalist on braving Mogadishu', *BBC*, 5 November 2012, <http://www.bbc.co.uk/news/20170168>.

[31] 'Kenyan troops "kill 60 al-Shabab fighters" in Somalia', *BBC*, 7 January 12, <http://www.bbc.co.uk/news/world-africa-16455039>; 'Somali security forces kill al-Shabaab leader, arrest 16 in Mogadishu raid', *Sabahi*, 23 November 2012, <http://sabahionline.com/en_GB/articles/hoa/articles/newsbriefs/2012/11/23/newsbrief-02>; 'British "al-Qaida member" killed in US drone attack in Somalia', *The Guardian*, 22 January 2012, <http://www.guardian.co.uk/world/2012/jan/22/british-al-qaida-suspect-drone-somalia>; 'KDF kill 200 al shabaab in Miido, Somalia', *Kenya Reporter*, 6 September 2012, <http://karizmwangi.wordpress.com/2012/09/06/kdf-kill-200-al-shabaab-in-miidosomalia/>; 'Six al Shabaab killed by KDF in Aglibax', *The Star*, 10 March 2012, <http://www.the-star.co.ke/news/article-26879/six-al-shabaab-killed-kdf-aglibax>; 'KDF kill 73 al Shabaab militants in Somalia', *Standard Online*, 16 August 2012, <http://www.standardmedia.co.ke/?articleID=2000064191>; 'Kenya: 100 al Shabaab killed in Miido battlefield', *AllAfrica.com*, 11 September 2012, <http://allafrica.com/stories/201209120112.html>; 'Six al-Shabaab killed in ambush', *Daily Nation*, 23 January 2012, <http://www.nation.co.ke/News/Six-Al-Shabaab-killed-in-ambush-/-/1056/1312846/-/k2bcpb/-/index.html>; 'Five "al-Shabaab" suspects and one Kenyan soldier killed in Kismayo', *Hiiraan Online*, 27 October 2012, <http://www.hiiraan.com/news4/2012/Oct/26570/five_al_shabaab_suspects_and_one_kenyan_soldier_killed_in_kismayo.aspx>; 'AMISOM forces capture Miido town, 36 al-Shabaab killed', *Modern Ghana*, 3 September 2012, <http://www.modernghana.com/news/415187/1/amisom-forces-capture-miido-town-36-alshabaab-kill.html>; 'In Somalia, 27 al-Shabab militants killed', *Press TV*, 8 December 2012, <http://www.presstv.com/detail/2012/12/08/276952/in-somalia-27-alshabab-militants-killed>.

[32] 'Report of the Secretary-General on Somalia', UN doc. S/2013/69, 31 January 2013.

[33] 'Report of the Secretary-General on Sexual violence in Conflict', UN doc. S/2013/149, 14 March 2013, §61.

partners estimated that there were around 920,000 internally displaced people (IDPs) in south-central Somalia, 130,000 in Puntland, and 84,000 in Somaliland.[34]

WAR CRIMES ALLEGATIONS, INVESTIGATIONS, AND PROSECUTIONS

Somalia is not a party to the 1998 Rome Statute of the International Criminal Court (the ICC Statute).

Somalia is believed to have executed a number of captured al-Shabaab fighters in 2012 following summary convictions by military courts. It is not known whether the charges were war crimes or insurrection.

---

[34] IDMC, 'Global overview 2012', April 2013, p. 29.

Armed conflict in Sudan in 2012

KEY CONFLICT STATISTICS FOR 2012

Darfur

Total deaths:	1,637+	(Source: US Department of State)
Civilian deaths:	1,315+	(Sources: Reeves; US Department of State)
Civilian injuries:	19	(Source: Reeves)
UNAMID peacekeeper deaths:	9	(Sources: UNAMID; OCHA)
UNAMID peacekeepers injured:	23	(Sources: UNAMID; OCHA)
Civilians displaced:	1.5 million (31 Dec. 2012)	(Source: IDMC)

S. Kordofan/Blue Nile states

Deaths from aerial bombing:	87	(Sources: Reeves; US Department of State)
Injuries from aerial bombing:	158	(Sources: Reeves; US Department of State)
Civilian deaths (other conflict causes):	9	(Sources: US Department of State; UN)
Civilians displaced:	695,000 (31 Dec. 2012)	(Source: IDMC)

CLASSIFICATION OF THE CONFLICTS

Sudanese armed forces were involved in armed conflicts of a non-international character (NIACs) with non-state armed groups in Darfur in 2012, particularly the Sudan Liberation Movement/Army (SLM/A) and the Justice and Equality Movement (JEM). A hybrid African Union/United Nations peacekeeping operation in Darfur (UNAMID) was formally established by United Nations (UN) Security Council Resolution on 31 July 2007.[1]

A separate NIAC was ongoing in Southern Kordofan and Blue Nile states in 2012 between Sudanese armed forces and the Sudan People's Liberation Movement/Army-North (SPLM-North).

SUMMARY OF APPLICABLE INTERNATIONAL LAW

All parties to the conflict are bound by, inter alia: Common Article 3 to the 1949 Geneva Conventions; the customary international humanitarian law (IHL) rules of distinction,

---

[1] UN Security Council Resolution 1769 (2007).

proportionality, and precautions in attacks; the obligation not to recruit and use children as soldiers; and the duty to respect, at a minimum, fundamental human rights. This includes the duty to respect the rights to life and to freedom from torture or other forms of cruel, inhuman, or degrading treatment or punishment.

In addition, Sudan is a state party to the two 1966 Covenants (on civil and political rights, and on economic, social, and cultural rights). Other states participating in UNAMID are bound extraterritorially by their human rights obligations.[2]

Sudan ratified the 1997 Anti-Personnel Mine Ban Convention (APMBC) in October 2003, becoming a state party on 1 March 2013. Although it has not signed the 2008 Convention on Cluster Munitions (CCM), it has denied—implausibly—ever having used cluster munitions.[3] States participating in UNAMID who are party to the APMBC and CCM are bound by those instruments. Although not directly applicable to the situation in Sudan because the UN is not engaged as a party to the armed conflict, the UN Secretary-General's Bulletin requires that UN peacekeeping forces not use anti-personnel mines.[4]

HISTORY OF THE CONFLICTS[5]

Sudan, once the largest and one of the most geographically diverse states in Africa, split into two countries in July 2011 after the south voted for independence following decades of conflict and violence. Continuing conflict in the western region of Darfur has driven many hundreds of thousands of people from their homes and is estimated to have killed tens, if not hundreds, of thousands of people.

The conflict in Darfur

Fighting broke out in early 2003 when non-state armed groups seeking greater autonomy began an insurrection.[6] Pro-government Arab militias were accused of carrying out

---

[2] See e.g. International Court of Justice (ICJ), *Wall* Advisory Opinion, 2004, §106; ICJ, *Armed Activities on the Territory of the Congo* (*Democratic Republic of the Congo v. Uganda*), Judgment, 19 December 2005.

[3] See e.g. Cluster Munition Monitor, 'Sudan: cluster munition ban policy', July 2012, <http://the-monitor .org/index.php/cp/display/region_profiles/theme/2214>. The Monitor cites a representative of Sudan's Permanent Mission to the UN in Geneva who stated, in April 2012, that: 'Sudan is not a producing country and does not own stockpiles, and did not use it before, neither in the far past, nor the near one. So any accusations to my country in this field are groundless. Accusations always come from political activists working against my country, such as the politicized constituencies.'

[4] 'Secretary-General's Bulletin: Observance by United Nations forces of international humanitarian law', New York, 6 August 1999.

[5] Unless otherwise stated, this section is based on 'Sudan profile', *BBC*, 14 March 2013, <http://www.bbc .co.uk/news/world-africa-14094995>.

[6] Darfur Australia Network, 'The situation in Darfur', December 2010, <http://www.darfuraustralia.org/ darfur/background>.

a campaign of ethnic cleansing against non-Arab groups in the region. An African Union peacekeeping force was deployed in the Darfur region, and in 2007 the UN Security Council authorized a 'hybrid' UN/African Union force, UNAMID.[7]

In April 2008, the UN Under-Secretary-General for Humanitarian Affairs, John Holmes, told the UN Security Council that the situation inside Darfur had only worsened in the past 12 months, despite the efforts of the international community. Mr Holmes said as many as 300,000 people were estimated to have died in Darfur since early 2003.[8] This figure included deaths from disease, malnutrition, and reduced life expectancy, as well as from direct combat. In addition to the death toll, more than 2.7 million people had been displaced by the fighting, the vast majority still living within the arid region in the west of the country. Around 260,000 refugees had fled to neighbouring Chad.[9]

A Commission of Inquiry set up by the UN Security Council in 2004 considered allegations that war crimes and crimes against humanity had been committed during the conflict.[10] Subsequently, arrest warrants were issued by the International Criminal Court (ICC) for a number of Sudanese government officials and the head of the so-called Janjaweed.[11] The government refused to extradite the accused to The Hague for trial. Bahr Idriss Abu Garda, a Darfur non-state armed group member, appeared before the ICC on 18 May 2009.[12] On 8 February 2010, Pre-Trial Chamber I refused to confirm the charges against Mr Abu Garda.

The conflict in Darfur has also strained relations between Sudan and Chad, to the west. Both countries have accused each other of cross-border incursions.[13] In early May 2008, one of the armed groups in Darfur launched an assault on the Sudanese capital, Khartoum. The attack by the JEM was repelled, with the government calling for the JEM to be listed as a terrorist group and also blaming Chad for its alleged support for the group. Chad denied the charges and closed its border, claiming Sudan was planning an attack.[14]

---

[7] UNAMID was established on 31 July 2007 by UN Security Council Resolution 1769.

[8] UNMIS, 'Media Monitoring Report', 23 April 2008, <http://unmis.unmissions.org/Portals/UNMIS/2008Docs/patch1/mmr-apr23.pdf>.

[9] UNMIS, 'Media Monitoring Report'.

[10] 'Report of the International Commission of Inquiry on Darfur to the United Nations Secretary-General', 25 January 2005, <http://www.icc-cpi.int/NR/rdonlyres/F87E244D-B27C-4A0A-BE1B-D27CECB5649E/278008/Report_to_UN_on_Darfur.pdf>.

[11] ICC, 'Situation in Darfur, Sudan', 11 April 2013, <http://www.icc-cpi.int/EN_Menus/ICC/Situations and Cases/Situations/Situation ICC 0205/Pages/situation icc-0205.aspx>.

[12] ICC, *Prosecutor v. Bahar Idriss Abu Garda*, 18 May 2009, <http://www.icc-cpi.int/en_menus/icc/situations and cases/situations/situation icc 0205/related cases/icc02050209/Pages/icc02050209.aspx>.

[13] Gérard Prunier, 'Chad: caught in the Darfur crossfire', *Le Monde Diplomatique*, March 2008, <http://mondediplo.com/2008/03/05chad>.

[14] 'Assault heralds change in Sudan', *BBC*, 12 May 2008, <http://news.bbc.co.uk/2/hi/africa/7396404.stm>.

In 2010, the JEM announced it was boycotting peace talks with the government, accusing it of launching new raids. There were reports of peace talks again in 2011 and in 2012;[15] a JEM splinter group announced its interest in signing the Doha Document for Peace.[16] A surge in government-led attacks was reported in late 2010 to early 2011, and the region remained isolated from aid workers and from UNAMID. Despite waning international attention, attacks against civilians continued in Darfur.

Violence persisted in 2012. In early June, the Sudanese Armed Forces (SAF) said that 45 JEM rebels had been killed in east Darfur, while the JEM claimed that it had seized an army compound.[17] In late October, Sudan Liberation Army (SLA) rebels reportedly attacked al-Fashir, North Darfur's state capital and a government stronghold.[18] In November, the JEM stepped up military operations in Darfur, attacking an SAF military convoy, while the SLA-Minni Minawi said on 17 November that it had bombarded al-Fashir.[19] As of December 2012, little progress towards a durable peace had been made and episodes of violence continued to be reported.[20] On 28 December, Darfur Sudan Revolutionary Forces (SRF) troops led by Abdul Wahid al-Nur claimed that they had captured two garrison towns in West Jebel Marra.[21]

Fighting continued in 2013. The Sudanese government signed a peace deal with the JEM splinter faction led by Mohammed Bashar on 6 April; subsequently that month fighting erupted between the JEM and Bashar's splinter faction, reportedly killing JEM-Bashar Commander Saleh Mohammed Jerbo, who had been indicted by ICC for war crimes.[22]

Southern Kordofan and Blue Nile states

In May–June 2011, tensions were rising in Sudan between the ruling National Congress Party (NCP) and remaining forces of the former southern rebel Sudan People's

[15] Human Rights Watch (HRW), 'World report 2012: Sudan', January 2012, <http://www.hrw.org/world-report-2012/world-report-2012-sudan>.

[16] The Doha Document for Peace in Darfur (DDPD) was finalized at the All Darfur Stakeholders Conference in May 2011, in Doha, Qatar. On 14 July, the government of Sudan and the Liberation and Justice Movement signed a protocol committing themselves to the Document, which is now the framework for the comprehensive peace process in Darfur. See e.g. UNAMID, 'Doha Document for Peace in Darfur', <http://unamid.unmissions.org/Default.aspx?tabid=11060&language=en-US>.

[17] International Crisis Group (ICG), 'Crisis Watch Database: Sudan', 1 July 2012, <http://www.crisisgroup.org/en/publication-type/crisiswatch/crisiswatch-database.aspx?CountryIDs=%7b32C9AB67-B387-455B-ACE5-30C7B3800A8B%7d&StartDate=20120101&EndDate=20130505>.

[18] ICG, 'Crisis Watch Database: Sudan', 1 November 2012.

[19] ICG, 'Crisis Watch Database: Sudan', 1 December 2012.

[20] Radio Dabanga (Hilversum), 'Sudan: Ambassador Smith—"Security Situation in Darfur Deteriorated Compared to 2011"', AllAfrica.com, 19 September 2012, <http://allafrica.com/stories/201209200049.html>.

[21] ICG, 'Crisis Watch Database: Sudan', 30 December 2012.

[22] ICG, 'Crisis Watch Database: Sudan', 1 May 2013.

Liberation Movement/Army (SPLM/A) still present in Sudan over political and security arrangements in Southern Kordofan, Sudan's only oil-producing state, and Blue Nile state.[23] In September 2011, fighting spread to neighbouring Blue Nile state, and a few days later Sudanese authorities issued a ban on the SPLM-North, the successor to the SPLM after South Sudan's independence in July 2011, and arrested many of its members.[24] According to HRW, Sudanese forces have carried out indiscriminate aerial bombardment and shelling of populated areas, killing and injuring civilians and causing serious damage to civilian property, including homes, schools, clinics, crops, and livestock.[25]

As of December 2012, Sudanese armed forces maintained control over the capital Kadugli, and other main towns and areas near Dilling, Talodi, Dellami, Rashad, Abbasiya, and Abu Jibeiha. The SPLA–North controlled large areas of the countryside around Kadugli, particularly in El Buram, Um Durein, and Heiban localities, and mountainous areas north-west of Kadugli.[26]

PARTIES TO THE CONFLICTS

The conflict in Darfur

Sudan Liberation Movement/Army (SLM/A). In 2006, the SLM split into two main factions, divided on the issue of the Darfur Peace Agreement. The Sudan Liberation Movement-Minni Minnawi signed the Darfur Peace Agreement in May 2006, but formally withdrew from the peace agreement in February 2011. The SLM (al-Nur) was formed in 2006, led by Abdul Wahid al-Nur. It rejected the Darfur Peace Agreement. It has become known as the SLM-Abdul Wahid, and is a member of the SRF.[27]

Justice and Equality Movement (JEM). The JEM is a rebel group involved in the Darfur conflict of Sudan, led by Khalil Ibrahim. Along with other rebel groups, such as the SLM, it is fighting against the Sudanese government, including the government's proxy militia, the Janjaweed. The JEM is also a member of the Eastern Front, a rebel coalition formerly

---

[23] For further details on the reasons of the tensions, see Office of the UN High Commissioner on Human Rights (UNHCHR), 'Preliminary report on violations of international human rights and humanitarian law in Southern Kordofan from 5 to 30 June 2011', August 2011, pp. 2–3.

[24] HRW, 'Under siege', December 2012, pp. 18–21, <http://www.hrw.org/reports/2012/12/11/under-siege>.

[25] HRW, 'Under siege', December 2012, pp. 3–5.

[26] HRW, 'Under siege', December 2012, pp. 20–1.

[27] See e.g. 'Sudan Liberation Movement/Army—Abdel Wahid (SLM-AW/SLA-AW)', *Sudan Tribune*, September 2011, <http://www.sudantribune.com/spip.php?mot163>.

active in the east of Sudan along the Eritrean border. The JEM embraces an Islamist ideology.[28]

After years of refusing to attend peace talks with Khartoum, the JEM finally signed a goodwill agreement at talks brokered by Qatar at the beginning of 2009. However, it soon fell apart after Sudanese President Omar al-Bashir expelled international development and aid groups from Darfur when the ICC in The Hague issued a warrant for his arrest in connection with international crimes allegedly committed in Darfur.[29] The JEM withdrew its support for the accord until, it said, Khartoum reinstated the aid groups. The JEM signed a truce with Sudan's government in February 2010, and until December 2012, the group has been in and out negotiations to sign the Doha Document for Peace.[30] The JEM has also provided support to rebels in South Kordofan, with its involvement said to have proven decisive in key battles.[31]

UNAMID. UNAMID is a joint African Union/United Nations hybrid operation in Darfur, authorized by Security Council Resolution 1769 (2007). It is not strictly a party to the conflict, although it has as its core mandate the protection of civilians. It is also tasked with contributing to security for humanitarian assistance, monitoring and verifying implementation of agreements, assisting an inclusive political process, contributing to the promotion of human rights and the rule of law, and monitoring and reporting on the situation along the borders with Chad and the Central African Republic (CAR).[32] The mandate is renewed yearly, and the adoption of UN Security Council Resolution 2063 on 31 July 2012 extended the mission for a further 12 months, until 31 July 2013.

The conflict in South Kordofan

Sudan People's Liberation Army/Movement (SPLA/M). The SPLA was formed in 1983, and has since fought against the governments of Nimeiri, Sadiq al-Mahdi, and President Omar Bashir. It is largely, but not exclusively, Christian and its declared aims

---

[28] 'Who are Sudan's Darfur rebels?', *BBC*, 23 February 2010, <http://news.bbc.co.uk/2/hi/africa/7039360.stm>.

[29] Institute for the Study of Violent Groups, 'Justice and Equality Movement', December 2011, <http://vkb.isvg.org/Wiki/Justice_and_Equality_Movement>.

[30] Small Arms Survey, 'Justice and Equality Movement', October 2012, <http://www.smallarmssurveysudan.org/fileadmin/docs/facts-figures/sudan/darfur/armed-groups/opposition/HSBA-Armed-Groups-JEM.pdf>.

[31] Small Arms Survey, Human Security Baseline Assessment (HSBA) for Sudan and South Sudan Working Paper, 'New war, old enemies: conflict dynamics in South Kordofan', March 2013, p. 29, <http://www.smallarmssurveysudan.org/project/project-summary.html>.

[32] UNAMID, 'Protecting civilians, facilitating humanitarian aid and helping political process in Darfur', <http://www.un.org/en/peacekeeping/missions/unamid/>.

are the establishment of a secular, democratic Sudan. Although many southerners preferred independence, it talked primarily of unity within a federal system.[33] The SPLA/M, as the politico-military movement came to be identified, defined itself as a national movement rather than a strictly southern independence movement. Its platform promoted the concept of the 'New Sudan', a secular state that provides social, economic, and political justice for all communities.[34]

In 2005, the SPLA/M signed the Comprehensive Peace Agreement (CPA) with the Sudanese government, ending the civil war between north and south Sudan, and guaranteeing the armed group prominent position in the Sudanese government, as well as the organization of a referendum for independence of South Sudan.[35] In 2011, SPLA/M leaders announced that the group would split along a north–south divide if the results of the referendum returned a vote in favour of independence from Sudan. Since the declaration of independence of South Sudan on 9 July 2011, reports on the northern splinter of the group have seen it intensify its fight with the stated aim of changing the government in Khartoum. In 2012, SPLM-North joined forces with three Darfur rebel groups, the JEM and two Sudan liberation armies, forming a new group: the Sudan Revolutionary Front (SRF). Its declared purpose is to topple Sudanese President al-Bashir and it has already conducted joint operations in South Kordofan.[36]

CASUALTIES

According to the US Department of State, there were 1,637 'violent deaths' in Darfur in 2012. US Department of State reporting does not distinguish between civilian and fighter deaths, nor does it provide precise figures of which group or force was responsible for which deaths. However, the State Department did report that most casualties were a result of aerial bombing by the SAF and of clashes between the SAF and rebel groups, including the umbrella SRF.[37] In one such clash on 25 September, there were reported to be up to 80 civilian casualties.[38] On 17 October, fighting between

---

[33] Global Security.org, 'Sudan People's Liberation Army (SPLA)/Sudan People's Liberation Movement (SPLM)', December 2004, <http://www.globalsecurity.org/military/world/para/spla.htm>.

[34] 'Sudan People's Liberation Army (SPLA)', *Sudan Tribune*, December 2012, <http://www.sudantribune.com/spip.php?mot183>.

[35] United States Institute of Peace, 'Peace agreements: Sudan', March 2005, <http://www.usip.org/publications/peace-agreements-sudan>.

[36] 'Sudan's Darfur region dabbles with peace', *BBC*, 2 March 2012, <http://www.bbc.co.uk/news/world-africa-17225356>.

[37] US Department of State, 'Country reports on human rights practices 2012: Sudan', 19 April 2013.

[38] US Department of State, 'Country reports on human rights practices 2012: Sudan', 19 April 2013; 'Report of the Secretary-General on the African Union-United Nations Hybrid Operation in Darfur', UN Security Council, UN doc. S/2013/22, 10 January 2013, p. 5.

the SLA and the government's Popular Defence Forces (PDF) resulted in the deaths of 14 members of the PDF. In retaliation, on 2 November, members of the PDF were reported to have killed ten civilians and abducted another.[39]

A more detailed though partial dataset of casualties as a result of aerial bombing by the SAF, compiled by Eric Reeves,[40] identified 35 killed and 19 injured as a result of six incidents of bombing in Darfur between 1 January and 5 June 2012. Deaths included ten children and 18 women; another two children and six women were injured.[41]

In seven separate incidents, nine UNAMID peacekeepers were killed and another 23 were injured. UNAMID reporting did not identify the armed groups responsible, describing the incidents as 'ambushes' or 'attacks by armed assailants'.[42]

Between December 2011 and December 2012, 121 cases of sexual violence in Darfur were reported to UNAMID. Cases involving 99 victims (52 children, including nine boys) were documented. Alleged offences included: rapes and gang rapes; abduction for sexual purposes; sexual slavery and injuries/assaults related to sexual violence attacks; and attempted attacks. Of the documented cases, 13 victims were abducted and subjected to sexual abuse.[43]

DISPLACED

The Internal Displacement Monitoring Centre (IDMC) estimated that 2.23 million persons were displaced across Sudan as of the end of 2012, a result of tensions and border clashes with South Sudan, the escalation of conflict in South Kordofan and Blue Nile between government forces and the SPLM-N, and an increase in violence in Darfur. This included 1,498,000 in Darfur and Eastern Sudan and 695,000 in South Kordofan and Blue Nile, although limited humanitarian access in these states made numbers difficult to verify.[44] At least 500,000 were newly displaced during 2012.[45]

---

[39] US Department of State, 'Country reports on human rights practices 2012: Sudan', 19 April 2013.

[40] Eric Reeves, a professor at Smith College, Northampton Massachusetts, has spent 14 years working as a Sudan researcher and analyst. His dataset collects all public information from UN, non-governmental organization (NGO), government, and media sources on aerial bombings by the SAF in Sudanese, South Sudanese, and disputed territories.

[41] Eric Reeves, 'Aerial military attacks on civilians and humanitarians in Sudan and South Sudan, 1999–2012', 5 June 2012, <http://www.sudanbombing.org>.

[42] UNAMID, 'Information kit', updated to end October 2012; Office for the Coordination of Humanitarian Affairs (OCHA), 'Sudan humanitarian update 4th quarter 2012', p. 4.

[43] 'Report of the Secretary-General on sexual violence in Conflict', UN doc. S/2013/149, advance copy dated 12 March 2013, §73.

[44] IDMC, 'Global overview 2012', April 2013, p. 19.

[45] IDMC, 'Global overview 2012', April 2013, p. 31.

WAR CRIMES ALLEGATIONS, INVESTIGATIONS, AND PROSECUTIONS

Sudan is not a party to the 1998 Rome Statute of the International Criminal Court (the ICC Statute). The situation in Darfur since 1 July 2002 was referred to the Court's Office of the Prosecutor (OTP) by UN Security Council Resolution 1593 on 31 March 2005, in accordance with the ICC Statute.[46]

On 1 March 2012, an ICC Pre-Trial Chamber issued a warrant of arrest against Mr Abdel Raheem Muhammad Hussein (Hussein) for 41 counts of crimes against humanity and war crimes allegedly committed in the context of the situation in Darfur. Mr Hussein is currently Minister of National Defence of the Sudanese government and a former Minister of the Interior and former Sudanese President's Special Representative in Darfur.[47] The successful execution of the arrest warrant was still pending as of 1 September 2013.

Three existing arrest warrants, issued since 2007 against the Sudanese President and two senior government officials, have still to be executed. Omar Hassan Ahmad al-Bashir has been President of the Republic of Sudan since 16 October 1993. A first warrant of arrest was issued in March 2009 and a second in July 2010. He is allegedly criminally responsible for five counts of crimes against humanity, two counts of war crimes, and three counts of genocide.[48] Ahmad Muhammad Harun ('Ahmad Harun') is a former Sudanese Minister of State for the Interior and is Minister of State for Humanitarian Affairs of Sudan. A warrant of arrest was issued in April 2007 for his alleged criminal responsibility for 20 counts of crimes against humanity and 22 counts of war crimes. Ali Muhammad Ali Abd-al-Rahman ('Ali Kushayb'), alleged leader of the Militia/Janjaweed, is being sought for his alleged criminal responsibility for 22 counts of crimes against humanity and 28 counts of war crimes. Both warrants were issued in April 2007.[49]

Two members of the JEM are due to stand trial beginning in May 2014, Abdallah Banda Abakaer Nourain and Saleh Mohammed Jerbo Jamus. They are charged with three war crimes under the ICC Statute: violence to life; intentionally directing attacks against personnel, installations, material, units or vehicles involved in a peacekeeping mission; and pillaging.[50]

---

[46] Art. 13(b), ICC Statute.

[47] ICC, 'The ICC issues a warrant of arrest for the Sudanese Minister Abdel Raheem Muhammad Hussein', Press release, 1 March 2012, <http://www.icc-cpi.int/en_menus/icc/situations and cases/situations/situation icc 0205/related cases/icc02050112/press releases/Pages/pr770.aspx>.

[48] ICC, *Prosecutor v. Omar Hassan Ahmad Al Bashir*, Case No. ICC-02/05-01/09.

[49] ICC, *Prosecutor v. Ahmad Muhammad Harun ('Ahmad Harun') and Ali Muhammad Ali Abd-Al-Rahman ('Ali Kushayb')*, Case No. ICC-02/05-01/07, <http://www.icc-cpi.int/en_menus/icc/situations% 20and%20cases/situations/situation%20icc%200205/related%20cases/icc%200205%200107/Pages/darfur_% 20sudan.aspx>.

[50] ICC, *Prosecutor v. Abdallah Banda Abakaer Nourain and Saleh Mohammed Jerbo Jamus*, Case No. ICC-02/05-03/09, <http://cpi.int/en_menus/icc/situations%20and%20cases/situations/situation%20icc% 200205/related%20cases/icc02050309/Pages/icc02050309.aspx>.

Armed conflict in Syria in 2012

KEY CONFLICT STATISTICS FOR 2012

Total deaths:	55,000 (est.)	(Source: OHCHR)
Total deaths:	44,940 (recorded)	(Source: Center for Documentation)
Civilian deaths:	31,000+	(Source: Center for Documentation)
Female deaths:	2,593	(Source: Center for Documentation)
Child deaths:	3,981	(Source: Center for Documentation)
'Regime' deaths:	6,673	(Source: Center for Documentation)
Opposition fighter deaths:	7,312	(Source: Center for Documentation)
Civilians displaced:	3 million (31 Dec. 2012)	(Source: IDMC)

CLASSIFICATION OF THE CONFLICTS

Syrian armed forces and allied militia were involved in separate armed conflicts of a non-international character (NIACs) with the Free Syrian Army (FSA) and with al-Nusra Front in 2012, dating from, at the latest, May. Both conflicts reached the threshold for applicability of the 1977 Additional Protocol II, but Syria is not a party to the Protocol.

In early May 2012, the President of the International Committee of the Red Cross (ICRC) declared that the violence in at least two places had reached the threshold of an NIAC. In June 2012, the United Nations (UN) Under-Secretary-General for Peacekeeping Operations, Hervé Ladsous, stated that the situation in Syria could be called a civil war.[1] The same month, the latest report by the Independent International Commission of Inquiry on Syria was more conservative, stating that the violence in some areas 'bears the characteristics of a non-international armed conflict'.[2] On 17 July 2012, the ICRC reiterated its earlier declaration, adding, in a press release, that:

As the situation has evolved, the ICRC has continued to monitor the conflict in the country. The ICRC concludes that there is currently a non-international (internal) armed conflict occurring in Syria opposing Government Forces and a number of organised armed opposition groups operating in several parts of the country (including, but not limited to, Homs, Idlib and Hama).[3]

---

[1] 'Syria in civil war, U.N. official says', *Reuters*, 12 June 2012, <http://www.reuters.com/article/2012/06/12/us-syria-idUSBRE85B0DZ20120612>.

[2] 'Independent International Commission of Inquiry on the Syrian Arab Republic, Oral Update', UN doc. A/HRC/20/CRP.1, 26 June 2012, §5, <http://www.ohchr.org/Documents/HRBodies/HRCouncil/RegularSession/Session20/COI_OralUpdate_A.HRC.20.CRP.1.pdf>.

[3] ICRC, 'Syria: ICRC and Syrian Arab Red Crescent maintain aid effort amid increased fighting', 17 July 2012, <http://www.icrc.org/eng/resources/documents/update/2012/syria-update-2012-07-17.htm>.

In September 2012, the Human Rights Council extended the mandate of the Commission of Inquiry, requesting it to investigate 'all massacres', including allegations of war crimes and crimes against humanity.[4]

SUMMARY OF APPLICABLE INTERNATIONAL LAW

All parties to the conflicts are bound by, inter alia: Common Article 3 to the 1949 Geneva Conventions; the customary international humanitarian law (IHL) rules of distinction, proportionality, and precautions in attacks; the obligation not to recruit and use children as soldiers; and the duty to respect, at a minimum, fundamental human rights. This includes the duty to respect the rights to life and to freedom from torture or other forms of cruel, inhuman, or degrading treatment or punishment.

In addition, Syria is a state party to the two 1966 Covenants (on civil and political rights, and on economic, social, and cultural rights). Syria is not a state party to the 1997 Anti-Personnel Mine Ban Convention (APMBC) or the 2008 Convention on Cluster Munitions (CCM).

HISTORY OF THE CONFLICT[5]

Anti-government protests erupted in Syria in March 2011, with demonstrators calling for reforms and for the overthrowing of President Assad's regime. Government forces responded violently and, in joint operations with security forces and allied militia known as Shabbiha, engaged in excessive use of force, kidnappings, torture, and other forms or ill-treatment. The UN Independent International Commission of Inquiry, established by the Human Rights Council, in its first report in November 2011, called the abuses carried out by Syrian authorities 'crimes against humanity'.[6] The opposition became progressively organized when the main armed opposition group, the FSA (composed largely of defectors from the Syrian army), and the Syrian National Council announced, in December 2011, that they would coordinate their efforts.[7]

According to the November 2011 report by the Independent International Commission of Inquiry on Syria:

---

[4] Human Rights Council Resolution 21/26, 'Situation of human rights in the Syrian Arab Republic', 17 October 2012.

[5] Unless otherwise stated, this section is based on 'Syria profile', *BBC*, 1 May 2013, <http://www.bbc.co.uk/news/world-middle-east-14703856>.

[6] 'Report of the Independent International Commission of Inquiry on the Syrian Arab Republic', UN doc. A/HRC/S-17/2/Add.1, 23 November 2011, §1, <http://www2.ohchr.org/english/bodies/hrcouncil/specialsession/17/docs/A-HRC-S-17-2-Add1.pdf>.

[7] Derek Henry Flood, 'An overview of Syria's armed revolution', *CTC Sentinel*, 5(4), April 2012.

The Commission is concerned that the armed violence in the Syrian Arab Republic risks rising to the level of an 'internal armed conflict' under international law. Should this occur, international humanitarian law would apply.[8]

In November 2011, despite initially agreeing to a League of Arab States work-plan aiming at ending the violence, the Syrian government failed to cooperate and was suspended from the League, as well as being made the subject of sanctions. The United States of America (USA) and the European Union (EU) had already instituted sanctions against the regime.[9] Following a year of violent clashes and the failure to adopt a Security Council Resolution on the Syrian situation,[10] the UN Secretary-General and the Arab League appointed Kofi Annan as Joint Special Envoy with the mandate to bring a negotiated peace and the halting of hostilities.[11]

By February 2012, the Commission of Inquiry had reported that Syria was 'on the brink' of an NIAC:

International humanitarian law is applicable if the situation can be qualified as an armed conflict, which depends on the intensity of the violence and the level of organization of participating parties. While the commission is gravely concerned that the violence in certain areas may have reached the requisite level of intensity, it was unable to verify that the Free Syrian Army (FSA), local groups identifying themselves as such or other anti-Government armed groups had reached the necessary level of organization.[12]

On 27 March 2012, it was announced that the Syrian government had agreed to a six-point plan put forth by the Special Envoy.[13] The fragile cease-fire entered into effect on 12 April 2012 and UN observers began their monitoring work on 16 April 2012, despite reports of ongoing shellfire from government forces in Homs and other areas.[14]

---

[8] 'Report of the Independent International Commission of Inquiry on the Syrian Arab Republic', Human Rights Council, UN doc. A/HRC/S-17/2/Add.1, 23 November 2011, §97.

[9] Council on Foreign Relations, 'Syria's crisis and the global response', 3 April 2013, <http://www.cfr.org/syria/syrias-crisis-global-response/p28402>.

[10] 'Security Council fails to adopt draft resolution condemning Syria's crackdown on anti-government protesters, owing to veto by Russian federation, China', UN press release, UN doc. SC/10403 4 October 2011, <https://www.un.org/News/Press/docs/2011/sc10403.doc.htm>.

[11] 'Secretary-General, Kofi Annan appointed joint special envoy of United Nations, League of Arab States on Syrian crisis', UN press release, UN doc. SG/SM/14124, 23 February 2012, <http://www.un.org/News/Press/docs/2012/sgsm14124.doc.htm>.

[12] 'Report of the Independent International Commission of Inquiry on the Syrian Arab Republic', Human Rights Council, UN doc. A/HRC/19/69, 22 February 2012, §13, <http://www.ohchr.org/Documents/HRBodies/HRCouncil/RegularSession/Session19/A-HRC-19-69.pdf>.

[13] 'Syrian government accepts UN-Arab League envoy's six-point plan to end crisis', *UN News Centre*, 27 March 2012, <http://www.un.org/apps/news/story.asp?NewsID=41646#.UWqmTqJA3To>.

[14] International Crisis Group (ICG), 'Crisis Watch Database: Syria', 14 April 2013, <http://www.crisisgroup.org/en/publication-type/crisiswatch/crisiswatch-database.aspx?CountryIDs=%7B1341CC4D-F195-4B82-A9B9-0411818FDB03%7D>.

More than 100 civilians, including women and children, were infamously killed in the Houla massacre on 25 May 2012, in an attack strongly condemned by the Human Rights Council and by the Security Council.[15] Reports continued to surface of forces linked to the Syrian government being responsible for abuses including indiscriminate attacks, extrajudicial executions, enforced disappearances, torture, and sexual violence.[16] In June 2012, the UN announced it was suspending its mission in Syria, due to its monitors' inability to conduct patrols, and following reports of them being shot at.[17]

In June 2012, the UN Secretary-General published a report on the situation of human rights in Syria, which stated, inter alia, the following:

Violence and killings, including during armed clashes, continued throughout the country. An increase in the use of explosive devices, inflicting loss of life among civilians, was also reported. Credible reports indicated that Government security and armed forces continued, unabated, to commit serious violations of human rights, including by the shelling of civilian areas and the use of lethal force against demonstrators, arbitrary arrests, torture and summary and extrajudicial execution of activists, defectors and opponents. Furthermore, ongoing violations by armed anti-Government forces continued to be reported, including cases of kidnapping and abduction, and the torture and killing of members of the security and armed forces and pro-Government elements.[18]

On 30 June 2012, the UN-backed Action Group on Syria agreed on the necessary steps for the implementation of the six-point peace plan and for the country to transition toward stability.[19] Meanwhile, members of the Syrian opposition, having previously criticized the UN peace plan, met in Cairo to discuss a political transition plan backed by the UN, Russia, and the USA. President Assad renewed his commitment to the plan in early July 2012.[20] However, fighting continued, with a helicopter and tank attack in opposition-controlled Hama taking 220 civilian lives in mid-July 2012.[21] In late October,

[15] Global Research, 'Syria: The Houla Massacre and the subversion of the peace plan', 7 June 2012, <http://www.globalresearch.ca/syria-the-houla-massacre-and-the-subversion-of-the-peace-plan/31300>.

[16] Human Rights Watch (HRW), 'Torture archipelago: arbitrary arrests, torture, and enforced disappearances in Syria's underground prisons since March 2011', 3 July 2012, <http://www.hrw.org/reports/2012/07/03/torture-archipelago-0>.

[17] 'UN suspends monitoring activities in Syria amid escalating violence', *UN News Centre*, 16 June 2012, <http://www.un.org/apps/news/story.asp?NewsID=42251#.UWqnPqJA3To>.

[18] 'Situation of human rights in the Syrian Arab Republic: implementation of Human Rights Council resolution 19/22: Report of the Secretary-General', Human Rights Council, UN doc. A/HRC/20/37, 22 June 2012, para. 14.

[19] 'Final communiqué of the Action Group for Syria', 30 June 2012, <http://www.unog.ch/80256EDD006B9C2E/(httpNewsByYear_en)/18F70DBC923963B1C1257A2D0060696B?OpenDocument>.

[20] Council on Foreign Relations, 'Syria's crisis and the global response', 3 April 2013, <http://www.cfr.org/syria/syrias-crisis-global-response/p28402>.

[21] 'Hama massacre: more than 200 killed in Tramseh, mostly civilians, opposition says', *Reuters*, 13 July 2012, <http://www.huffingtonpost.com/2012/07/13/hama-massacre-tramseh_n_1670255.html>.

Lakhdar Brahimi[22] arranged for a cease-fire during Eid al-Adha in late October, but it quickly collapsed as both rebels and the Syrian army resumed large-scale operations[23] that were still ongoing at time of writing.

PARTIES TO THE CONFLICTS

Syrian Armed Forces

The current strength of the Syrian army is unknown. In March 2013, the International Institute of Strategic Studies reported that, from a notional strength of 220,000, the army had withered to a core of about 50,000 the regime could rely on, while the Institute for the Study of War in Washington estimated the loyal core at 65,000.[24] It was claimed that, in addition, Iran and Hezbollah had built a 50,000-strong parallel force in Syria to help prolong the life of the Assad regime and to maintain their influence after his fall.[25]

Free Syrian Army

The main armed opposition group during the 2011–12 clashes was the FSA. Its formation was announced on 29 July 2011 in a video released on the Internet by a uniformed group of deserters from the Syrian military who called upon members of the Syrian army to defect and join them.[26] Although most of the FSA's members are Sunni Arabs (Syria's largest community), the organization also includes battalions made up of Kurds, Turkmen, Palestinians, and Druze. In December 2011, the Syrian opposition became more unified, with the FSA agreeing to coordinate its efforts with the non-violence-advocating Syrian National Council.[27] Opposition fighters have been accused by the UN of committing widespread human rights violations.[28]

---

[22] On 17 August 2012, Brahimi was appointed by the UN Secretary-General as the new peace envoy to Syria, following Kofi Annan's resignation.

[23] 'Syria profile', *BBC*, 25 March 2013.

[24] Julian Borger, 'Iran and Hezbollah "have built 50,000-strong force to help Syrian regime"', *The Guardian*, 14 March 2013, <http://www.guardian.co.uk/world/2013/mar/14/iran-hezbollah-force-syrian-regime>.

[25] Borger, 'Iran and Hezbollah "have built 50,000-strong force to help Syrian regime"', citing an Israeli military chief.

[26] 'Free Syrian Army founded by seven officers to fight the Syrian army', *Syria Comment*, 29 July 2011, <http://www.joshualandis.com/blog/free-syrian-army-established-to-fight-the-syrian-army/>.

[27] Institute for the Study of War, 'Syria's armed opposition', Middle East Security Report No. 3, March 2012, p. 9, <http://www.understandingwar.org/sites/default/files/Syrias_Armed_Opposition.pdf>.

[28] 'Report of the Independent International Commission of Inquiry on the Syrian Arab Republic', UN doc. A/HRC/19/69, 22 February 2012, §§105–20.

The FSA operates throughout Syria, both in urban areas and in the countryside. Forces are active in the north-west (Idlib, Aleppo), the central region (Homs, Hama, and Rastan), the coast around Latakia, the south (Daraa and Houran), the east (Dayr al-Zawr, Abu Kamal), and the Damascus area.[29] The largest concentration of these forces appears to be in the central region (Homs, Hama, and surrounding areas). The armed opposition's increased effectiveness in 2012 has fuelled the rebels' growth, but it also forced the Assad regime to increase its use of force.[30] The FSA remains highly fractured both politically and militarily; however, in November 2012, several Syrian resistance factions came together to form an umbrella organization known as the National Coalition of Syrian Revolutionary and Opposition Forces.[31] This new resistance group was soon recognized by several countries such as the UK, France, Turkey, and a number of Gulf Arab states.[32] In December 2012, the FSA went through a major restructuring process, bringing Brigadier-General Selim Idris to replace the army's former senior officer, Colonel Riad al-Assad.[33]

Jabhat al-Nusra[34]

The al-Nusra Front (*al-Nusra* meaning 'support' in Arabic) first announced its existence with a video posted online in January 2012. In the statement, the group said it was behind many of the suicide bombings that have rocked Syria since the uprising began in March 2011. Since its first public appearance, al-Nusra is thought to have led numerous guerrilla attacks against strategic state targets, including the capture of a key airbase in the north. The USA has blacklisted the group as a terrorist organization in response to the bombing campaigns and its status as an Islamist organization with links to al-Qaeda. In rebel-held areas in the northern city of Aleppo, it has taken over distribution of flour to bakeries and set up a Shari'a court to administer Islamic law.

As of May 2013, the FSA was said to be losing fighters and capabilities to Jabhat al-Nusra, which is emerging as the best-equipped, financed, and motivated force fighting

---

[29] 'An overview of Syria's armed revolution', *CTC Sentinel*, 5(4) (April 2012), <http://www.ctc.usma.edu/wp-content/uploads/2012/04/CTCSentinel-Vol5Iss41.pdf>.

[30] Institute for the Study of War, 'Syria's armed opposition', Middle East Security Report No. 3, March 2012, p. 11, <http://www.understandingwar.org/sites/default/files/Syrias_Armed_Opposition.pdf>.

[31] Council on Foreign Relations, 'Syria's crisis and the global response', 3 April 2013, <http://www.cfr.org/syria/syrias-crisis-global-response/p28402>.

[32] Council on Foreign Relations, 'Syria's crisis and the global response', 3 April 2013.

[33] Council on Foreign Relations, 'Syria's crisis and the global response', 3 April 2013.

[34] 'Profile: Syria's al-Nusra Front', *BBC*, 10 April 2013, <http://www.bbc.co.uk/news/world-middle-east-18048033>; Mona Mahmood and Ian Black, 'Free Syrian Army rebels defect to Islamist group Jabhat al-Nusra', *The Guardian*, 8 May 2013, <http://www.guardian.co.uk/world/2013/may/08/free-syrian-army-rebels-defect-islamist-group>.

Bashar al-Assad's regime. al-Nusra is said to have developed a reputation for discipline and honesty.

United Nations Supervision Mission in Syria (UNSMIS)

UNSMIS was established by UN Security Council Resolution 2043 of 21 April 2012, initially for a 90-day period, to monitor a cessation of armed violence in all its forms by all parties and to monitor and support the full implementation of the Joint Special Envoy's six-point plan to end the conflict in Syria.[35] After an initial lull, hostilities in Syria resumed, and on 15 June 2012 UNSMIS had to suspend its activities owing to an intensification of armed violence across the country.[36] On 20 July 2012, the Security Council extended the mission for 30 days and said that any further extension could be possible only 'in the event that the Secretary-General reports and the Security Council confirms the cessation of the use of heavy weapons and a reduction in the level of violence sufficient by all sides' to allow UNSMIS monitors to implement their mandate. As those conditions were not met, the UNSMIS mandate came to an end at midnight on 19 August 2012.[37]

CASUALTIES

Based on its publically stated estimates, the UN count of fatalities in the Syrian conflict is greater than 55,000 for 2012. More than 60,000 deaths were estimated since the beginning of the violence to the end of 2012,[38] less the previous UN estimate of more than 5,000 deaths to the end of 2011.[39] The estimate of 60,000 for the period since March 2011

---

[35] UN Security Council Resolution 2043, 21 April 2012.

[36] UNSMIS, 'Monitoring a cessation of armed violence in all its forms', 14 April 2013, <http://www.un.org/en/peacekeeping/missions/unsmis/>.

[37] UNSMIS, 'Monitoring a cessation of armed violence in all its forms', 14 April 2013.

[38] Office of the UN High Commissioner for Human Rights (OHCHR), 'Data analysis suggests over 60,000 people killed in Syria conflict: Pillay', 2 January 2013, <http://www.ohchr.org/en/NewsEvents/Pages/DisplayNews.aspx?NewsID=12912&LangID=E>.

[39] 'Syria: 5,000 dead in violence, says UN human rights chief', *The Guardian*, 13 December 2011, <http://www.guardian.co.uk/world/2011/dec/12/syria-5000-dead-violence-un>; 'UN raises death toll to 5,000', *The Guardian*, 13 December 2011, <http://www.guardian.co.uk/world/middle-east-live/2011/dec/13/syria-un-raises-death-toll-to-5000-live-updates>. The UN count of 5,000 fatalities was 1,000 higher than an estimate released ten days earlier. It included civilians, army defectors, and those executed for refusing to shoot civilians, but not soldiers or security personnel killed by opposition forces. See also 'Syria death toll hits 5,000 as insurgency spreads', *Reuters*, 13 December 2012, <http://www.reuters.com/article/2011/12/13/us-syria-idUSTRE7B90F520111213>.

was reported to be 'far higher than recent estimates by anti-regime activists'.[40] For example, one of the principal casualty monitoring groups, the oft-quoted Syrian Observatory for Human Rights, documented some 45,048 deaths from the beginning of the conflict to the end of 2012.[41] However, the analysis of seven casualty data sources commissioned by the OHCHR[42] found that 59,648 unique deaths could be identified for the period from March 2011 to November 2012.[43]

The Center for Documentation of Violations in Syria (VDC)[44] recorded 44,940 conflict-related deaths in Syria for calendar year 2012; 30,943 were recorded as civilians and 7,312 as 'non-civilian',[45] including 41 boys killed as 'non-civilians'.[46] VDC data included 2,583 women and 3,973 children: 2,751 boys and 1,222 girls. Most fatalities (31,121) resulted from explosions, shelling, aerial attacks, or shootings.[47] Another 6,995 casualties were caused by single acts, or multiple combinations, of executions, kidnappings, torture, and detention. The deaths of 6,685 Syrian 'regime' forces[48] were also recorded. These included male and female civilians associated with the Syria state; seven of ten women killed were civilians. As an indication of the overall reliability of the data, only 5 per cent of the available data from the VDC was excluded from the OHCHR analysis as 'unidentifiable'.[49]

The Syrian Revolution Martyr Database included information on 41,900 fatalities for calendar year 2012, including 37,197 civilian and 4,703 military casualties: 37,850

---

[40] 'Syria death toll at 60,000, UN Human Rights Office says', *Huffington Post*, 1 February 2013, <http://www.huffingtonpost.com/2013/01/02/syria-death-toll-60000_n_2395826.html>.

[41] 'Casualty count proves inexact science, rights group finds', *Globe and Mail*, 27 March 2013, <hhtp://m.theglobeandmail.com/news/world/casualty-count-proves-inexact-science-rights-group-finds/article10467644/?service=mobile >; 'Syria death toll spirals as Brahimi mission stumbles', *Agence France-Presse*, 26 December 2012, <http://reliefweb.int/report/syrian-arab-republic/syria-death-toll-spirals-brahimi-mission-stumbles>.

[42] These were: the Center for Documentation of Violations in Syria; the Syrian Network for Human Rights (SNHR); the Syrian Revolution General Council (which was combined with the SNHR); the Revolution Martyr Database; the March 15 Group; the Syrian Observatory for Human Rights; and the Syrian government.

[43] Disaggregated data was not included in the report. The analysis used manual classifications and a data mining technique called an 'alternating decision tree' to identify duplicate records from among the seven sources for removal. For a fuller description of the methodology used, see Megan Price, Jeff Klingner, and Patrick Ball, 'Preliminary statistical analysis of documentation of killings in the Syrian Arab Republic', Benetech, 2 January 2013, <http://www.ohchr.org/Documents/Countries/SY/PreliminaryStatAnalysisKillingsInSyria.pdf>.

[44] VDC, <http://www.vdc-sy.info/index.php/en/>.

[45] The non-civilian category contains information on defected recruits and officers, and FSA non-military volunteers.

[46] No 'non-civilian' casualties were recorded among women or girls.

[47] This included 'explosions, shelling, warplane shelling' (16,065) and 'shooting' (15,056).

[48] Including police and civilians. The category also includes Hezbollah forces.

[49] The VDC provided the highest number of identifiable fatality records from any single data source from among data sources included in a major analysis of Syrian casualty data for OCHA in 2012; it also had the largest number of fatalities disaggregated by gender of all sources reviewed for OCHA. See Price, Klingner, and Ball, 'Preliminary statistical analysis of documentation of killings in the Syrian Arab Republic', pp. 3 and 9.

male and 4,050 female.[50] However, the figures seem less reliable overall; some 23 per cent of the total were excluded by the analysis for OHCHR as 'unidentifiable'.[51] The Syrian Revolution Martyr Database registered some fatalities without recording names.[52]

The Committee to Protect Journalists reported 28 journalists killed in Syria in 2012 where the motive was confirmed and another five with the motive for the killing pending confirmation.[53] Reporters without Borders identified 23 journalists killed and 21 imprisoned since March 2011.[54] The VDC was reported to have collected information on 120 doctors, 65 medical aid workers, and 50 nurses killed, and 469 doctors jailed since March 2011.[55] The Syrian American Medical Society reported the killing of 14 doctors, all in the month of July 2012.[56]

No reasonable figures for people injured by conflict in 2012 were available; however, statistics from medical interventions gave some idea of the scope. US humanitarian funding was used to treat 410,000 patients in Syria and to perform more than 25,800 surgical interventions in field hospitals.[57] The ICRC helped evacuate 1,573 Syrian casualties to Lebanese hospitals.[58] From late June 2012, when it set up its first hospital in the north of Syria, to early January 2013, Médecins sans Frontières (MSF) conducted more than 10,000 medical consultations and performed more than 900 surgical interventions. Many patients had injuries related to the violence, including from shootings and explosive weapons.[59]

---

[50] Syrian Revolution Matryr, <http://syrianshuhada.com>.

[51] The Syrian Revolution Martyr Database had the next highest number of identifiable fatality records after the VDC: Price, Klingner, and Ball, 'Preliminary statistical analysis of documentation of killings in the Syrian Arab Republic', pp. 3 and 9.

[52] 'Syria crisis: counting the victims', *BBC*, 29 May 2012, <http://www.bbc.co.uk/news/world-middle-east-18093967>.

[53] Committee to Protect Journalists: Press Freedom Online, 'Syria', <http://www.cpj.org/killed/mideast/syria/>.

[54] In addition, Reporters without Borders included 18 'netizens' imprisoned and 58 'netizens and citizen journalists' killed. See Reporters without Borders, 'Syria', <http://en.rsf.org/syria.html>.

[55] 'In Syria's civil war, doctors find themselves in cross hairs', *New York Times*, 23 March 2013, <http://www.nytimes.com/2013/03/24/world/middleeast/on-both-sides-in-syrian-war-doctors-are-often-the-target.html?pagewanted=all&_r=0>.

[56] Syrian American Medical Society, 'Martyred doctors in Syria', 7 August 2012, <http://sams-usa.net/martyred-doctors-in-syria/>.

[57] US Department of State, 'U.S. response to the Syria humanitarian crisis in 2012', 10 January 2013, <http://www.state.gov/r/pa/prs/ps/2013/01/202705.htm>.

[58] ICRC, 'Lebanon: what the ICRC is doing to help Syrian wounded and refugees', 29 November 2012, <http://www.icrc.org/eng/resources/documents/fact-figures/2012-11-30-lebanon-syrian-refugees.htm>.

[59] MSF, 'MSF treats 44 wounded in bomb and rocket attacks in northwestern Syria', 17 January 2013, <http://www.doctorswithoutborders.org/press/release.cfm?id=6565>; MSF, 'Syria two years on: the failure of international aid so far', March 2013, p. 18, <http://www.doctorswithoutborders.org/publications/article.cfm?id=6669>.

The VDC recorded 3,090 detainees and another 922 people missing in 2012.[60] HRW reported that the government detained tens of thousands of protesters and activists, who were subject to beatings, electric shocks, rape, and other rights abuses.[61] The SNHR reported 4,000 cases of rape and mutilation of women and girls, 700 of whom were prisoners.[62] Between February and June 2012, the Independent International Commission of Inquiry on Syria recorded numerous incidents of sexual violence committed by government soldiers and allied militia (referred to as Shabbiha):

...who allegedly entered homes and raped women and girls in front of male family members, sometimes killing them afterwards, and forced men at gunpoint to rape their wives and daughters.

The UN also expressed concern about allegations of abduction, and rape of women and girls by armed opposition groups, and the presence of foreign fighters, but had been unable to collect information on sexual violence committed by these armed groups.[63]

The UN Commission of Inquiry on Syria also reported instances of rape and sexual assault against men and boys as part of torture or ill-treatment. Two male members of the same family, detained from January to March 2012, described intelligence agents forcing them to rape each other.[64]

DISPLACED

According to the Internal Displacement Monitoring Centre (IDMC), during 2012, some 2.4 million people were newly displaced in Syria. The number increased drastically from just over 150,000 recently internally displaced persons (IDPs) at the beginning of the year. This led to a total of at least 3 million IDPs in Syria by end 2012, including persons previously displaced from Golan Heights in 1967.[65]

---

[60] VDC, <http://www.vdc-sy.info/index.php/en/>.

[61] HRW, 'UN: human rights monitors still needed in Syria', 14 August 2012, <http://www.hrw.org/news/2012/08/14/un-human-rights-monitors-still-needed-syria>.

[62] US Department of State, 'Country reports on human rights practices 2012: Syria', 19 April 2013.

[63] 'Report of the Secretary-General on sexual violence in conflict', UN doc. S/2013/149, advance copy dated 12 March 2013, §§84–8. The Commission concluded that there are reasonable grounds to believe that such acts of sexual violence perpetrated in connection to the armed conflict could amount to war crimes. The Commission also found that the rapes that occurred during the military operations in Homs in February and March 2012 and in al-Haffe in June 2012, as part of a widespread or systematic attack against a civilian population, could be prosecuted as crimes against humanity. See Commission reports of 16 August 2012 (UN doc. A/HRC/21/50) and 5 February 2013 (UN doc. A/HRC/22/59).

[64] 'Report of the Secretary-General on sexual violence in conflict', UN doc. S/2013/149, advance copy dated 12 March 2013, §87.

[65] IDMC, 'Global overview 2012', April 2013, p. 59.

WAR CRIMES ALLEGATIONS, INVESTIGATIONS, AND PROSECUTIONS

Syria is not a party to the 1998 Rome Statute of the International Criminal Court (the ICC Statute).

In August 2012, the Independent Commission of Inquiry reported that the situation of human rights in Syria had 'deteriorated significantly' since 15 February 2012. The Commission found 'reasonable grounds to believe that Government forces and the Shabbiha had committed the crimes against humanity of murder and of torture, war crimes and gross violations of international human rights law and international humanitarian law, including unlawful killing, torture, arbitrary arrest and detention, sexual violence, indiscriminate attack, pillaging and destruction of property'. The Commission also found reasonable grounds to believe 'that war crimes, including murder, extrajudicial execution and torture, had been perpetrated by organized anti-Government armed groups'. The violations and abuses committed by anti-government armed groups did not, however, reach 'the gravity, frequency and scale of those committed by Government forces and the Shabbiha'.[66]

In February 2013, in its fourth report, the Commission stated that the situation of human rights in the Syrian Arab Republic had again continued to deteriorate. It concluded that, since July 2012:

Government forces and affiliated militia committed the crimes against humanity of murder, torture, rape, enforced disappearance and other inhumane acts. War crimes and gross violations of international human rights and humanitarian law—including arbitrary arrest and detention, unlawful attack, attacking protected objects, and pillaging and destruction of property—were also committed.

Anti-Government armed groups have committed war crimes, including murder, torture, hostage-taking and attacking protected objects. They continue to endanger the civilian population by positioning military objectives inside civilian areas. Where armed groups carried out bombings in predominantly civilian areas, it had the effect of spreading terror and amounted to the war crime of attacking civilians. The violations and abuses committed by anti-government armed groups did not, however, reach the intensity and scale of those committed by government forces and affiliated militia. Both government-affiliated militia and anti-government armed groups were found to have violated the Optional Protocol to the Convention on the Rights of the Child on the involvement of children in armed conflict, to which the Syrian Arab Republic is a party. Government-affiliated militia used children under the age of 18 in direct hostilities. Children under the age of 15 actively participated in hostilities as part of anti-government armed groups, conduct that constitutes the war crime of using, conscripting and enlisting children.[67]

---

[66] 'Report of the Independent International Commission of Inquiry on the Syrian Arab Republic', UN doc. A/HRC/21/50, 16 August 2012, Summary.

[67] 'Report of the Independent International Commission of Inquiry on the Syrian Arab Republic', UN doc. A/HRC/22/59, 5 February 2013, Summary.

Armed conflict in Thailand in 2012

KEY CONFLICT STATISTICS FOR 2012

Civilian deaths:	222	(Source: Abuza Incident Database)
Civilian injured:	797	(Source: Abuza Incident Database)
Military deaths:	23	(Source: Abuza Incident Database)
Military injured:	151	(Source: Abuza Incident Database)
Police deaths:	14	(Source: Abuza Incident Database)
Police injured:	38	(Source: Abuza Incident Database)
Paramilitary deaths:	74	(Source: Abuza Incident Database)
Paramilitary injured:	92	(Source: Abuza Incident Database)
Non-state armed group deaths:	28	(Source: Abuza Incident Database)
Civilians displaced:	240,000 (est. 31 Dec. 2012)	(Source: IDMC)

CLASSIFICATION OF THE CONFLICT

Thai armed and security forces were involved in an armed conflict of a non-international character (NIAC) with a number of non-state armed groups in the south of the country in 2012.

SUMMARY OF APPLICABLE INTERNATIONAL LAW

All parties to the conflicts are bound by, inter alia: Common Article 3 to the 1949 Geneva Conventions; the customary international humanitarian law (IHL) rules of distinction, proportionality, and precautions in attacks; the obligation not to recruit and use children as soldiers; and the duty to respect, at a minimum, fundamental human rights. This includes the duty to respect the rights to life and to freedom from torture or other forms of cruel, inhuman, or degrading treatment or punishment. In addition, Thailand is a state party to the two 1966 Covenants (on civil and political rights, and on economic, social and cultural rights).

Thailand adhered to the 1997 Anti-Personnel Mine Ban Convention (APMBC) in November 1998, becoming a state party on 1 May 1999, but has not adhered to the 2008 Convention on Cluster Munitions (CCM). Thailand is not party to the 1977 Additional Protocol II.

HISTORY OF THE CONFLICT[1]

Political turmoil and a decades-old conflict between the security forces and non-state armed groups in the south of Thailand have increased since 2004. The violence is believed to have claimed more than 5,000 deaths in areas where the ethnic Malay population are predominantly Muslim (80 per cent), in contrast with the rest of Thailand, which is essentially Buddhist. Negotiations between government officials and representatives of armed non-state actors (ANSAs), who have been seeking independence for the provinces of Yala, Narathiwat, Pattani, and five districts of Songkhla province—Chana, Na Thawi, Saba Yoi, Sadao, and Thepa—appear to have stalled.[2]

Successive governments, beginning with the one of Thaksin Shinawatra (2001–06), have proved unable to control the insurgency in the deep south. The imposition of martial law since January 2004, as well as an emergency decree enacted in July 2005, has granted more powers to Thai security forces in the region. According to human rights groups, this law enables the central government to ban any types of political gathering, to censor the media, and to detain people without charge.[3]

In April 2009, non-state armed groups were blamed for nine deaths on 27 April, the day before the fifth anniversary of the Krue Sae mosque incident in which non-state armed groups members launched attacks on police checkpoints, culminating in a siege of Krue Se mosque in Pattani. Security forces were reported to have killed 32 people who were holed up in the mosque, sparking widespread condemnation.

Overall, however, in 2007 to 2012, the frequency of violence had been steadily decreasing. Since early 2012, however, the pattern of violence in the south of the country has become more complex and intense. This includes attacks such as the March 2012 blast, which is said to have resulted in several hundred casualties.[4] As a result, one source reported 1,647 casualties in the first ten months of 2012, surpassing the 2011 total of 1,464.[5]

[1] Unless otherwise stated, this section is based on 'Thailand profile', *BBC*, 6 December 2012, <http://www.bbc.co.uk/news/world-asia-15581957>.

[2] Benjamin Zawacki, 'Politically inconvenient, legally correct: a non-international armed conflict in Southern Thailand', *Journal of Conflict and Security Law*, 18 September 2012, pp. 1–29, <http://jcsl.oxfordjournals.org/content/early/2012/09/18/jcsl.krs025.full.pdf+html> (subscription needed).

[3] International Crisis Group (ICG), 'Thailand: the evolving conflict in the south', Asia Report No. 241, 11 December 2012, pp. 2–3, <http://www.crisisgroup.org/~/media/Files/asia/south-east-asia/thailand/241-thailand-the-evolving-conflict-in-the-south.pdf>.

[4] On 31 March 2012, a car bomb exploded in Yala, a busy commercial area, and was followed by a second and a third explosion a few hours later in other crowded commercial districts in the south of the country: Deep South Watch database, 10 April 2013, <http://www.deepsouthwatch.org/node/3803>.

[5] ICG, 'Thailand: the evolving conflict in the south', p. 4.

Attacks continued in 2013, despite attempts at initiating political dialogue. In April, insurgents stepped up attacks in the southern-most provinces following the first meeting of a dialogue process between Bangkok and insurgent representatives on 28 March.[6]

PARTIES TO THE CONFLICT

Thai Armed and Security Forces

Both the army and the police have been engaged in counter-insurgency in the south of the country. It is claimed that the armed forces have struggled to adapt to fighting in a part of the country where many of the soldiers do not understand the Malay dialect spoken by the majority of the people.[7] In addition, one Bangkok-based security consultancy, PSA Asia, has asserted that the Thai state's efforts to reduce the violence has been hampered by a historical rivalry between the police and the military. This 'is an additional impediment to forming a strategic response to growing Islamic insurgent violence in south Thailand', PSA said in an advisory sent to its clients in early 2013.[8]

Major non-state armed groups

A variety of non-state armed groups have reportedly been engaged in violent struggle in the south, which has intensified in the past years. The main ones are described below.

National Revolutionary Front-Coordinate (BRN-C). The National Revolutionary Front (Barisan Revolusi Nasional, or BRN) is an armed group based in northern Malaysia and operating in southern Thailand. The BRN was founded in 1963 as a response to compulsory registration by the central Thai government of traditional Muslim boarding schools following the imposition of a secular curriculum. In the beginning, the BRN's focus was more religious than military, but it also claimed independence and maintained close relationships with the communist groups in the south.[9] The BRN fractured during the 1980s, splitting into three factions: BRN-Ulama, which renounced violence to focus on religious activities; BRN-Congress, which focused almost exclusively on military

---

[6] ICG, 'Crisis Watch Database: Thailand', 1 May 2013, <http://www.crisisgroup.org/en/publication-type/crisiswatch/crisiswatch-database.aspx?CountryIDs=%7b76949589-2EB7-430A-8A44-24A2594012CC%7d&StartDate=20120101&EndDate=20130531>.

[7] James Hookway, 'Muslim insurgents widen Thailand attacks', *Wall Street Journal*, Updated 28 February 2013, <http://online.wsj.com/article/SB10001424127887324906004578289220025564486.html>.

[8] Cited in Hookway, 'Muslim insurgents widen Thailand attacks'.

[9] B. Zawacki, 'Politically inconvenient, legally correct: a non-international armed conflict in Southern Thailand', *Journal of Conflict and Security Law*, 18 September 2012, p. 4.

operations; and BRN-Coordinate, which engaged in both political activities and urban sabotage.[10]

Pattani United Liberation Organization (PULO). Formed in 1968, PULO has promoted the succession of an independent Malay Muslim state across the southern part of Thailand. PULO has identified itself as a 'moderate' separatist group focused on Malay nationalism, as opposed to Islamic or religious principles. While the organization split into two separate factions (old and new PULO) in the 1990s, exiled senior members have now reconciled differences and are alleged to have headquarters based in Malaysia. In the 1990s, PULO started launching large attacks either targeting civilians or using indiscriminate methods of violence, while New PULO focused on low-intensity attacks targeting exclusively military objectives. In 1997, however, PULO and New PULO formed a tactical alliance known as Unity (Bersatu), initiating a campaign targeting governmental authorities.[11]

PULO is seen as more of a political umbrella organization for the myriad armed groups thought to be involved in the insurgency. Today, it operates mainly from exile in Syria and Sweden. In October 2012, the group published a comprehensive List of Core Principles it agreed to respect when fighting, including the prohibition on attacking civilians and the obligation to abide by fundamental IHL principles when launching an attack.[12]

The United Front for the Independence of Pattani (Bersatu). This group was formed in 1989 out of five smaller groups: BRN-Congress; elements of PULO; the then Gerakan Mujahidin Patani (GMP); Barisan Islam Pembebsan Pattani; and the now defunct Islamic Front for the Liberation of Pattani.[13]

Gerakan Mujahadeen Islam Pattani (GMIP). Established in part by Afghan veterans in 1995 to support a separate Islamic state, the GMIP is committed to forming an independent Islamic state. The GMIP is suspected of having links to international militant Islamist organizations.[14]

---

[10] Zawacki, 'Politically inconvenient, legally correct: a non-international armed conflict in Southern Thailand', p. 6.

[11] Zawacki, 'Politically inconvenient, legally correct: a non-international armed conflict in Southern Thailand', p. 5.

[12] PULO, 'List of Core Principles of Pulo's engagement rules', 4 October 2012, <http://www.puloinfo.net/statements.asp?ID=40>.

[13] Council on International Relations, 'The Muslim insurgency in Southern Thailand', 10 September 2008, <http://www.cfr.org/thailand/muslim-insurgency-southern-thailand/p12531?breadcrumb=/region/290/southeast_asia>.

[14] Council on International Relations, 'The Muslim insurgency in Southern Thailand', 10 September 2008.

CASUALTIES

Conflict-related casualty data used for 2012 was collected by Professor Zachary Abuza,[15] based on open source reporting. Professor Abuza believes that the total numbers in his incident database are low, as not every attack is recorded and many people who die from their injuries go unreported in the press.[16] Other sources, such as the non-governmental organization (NGO) Deep South Watch, reported different casualty numbers, counting more than 1,300 people killed and injured in the period January–September 2012, but the data available was incomplete or not adequately disaggregated according to casualty types.[17]

Among civilian casualties recorded in the Abuza Incident Database, 32 village chiefs and deputy village chiefs were killed and eight others injured, seven teachers were killed and nine injured, and two monks were injured. Other recorded civilian casualties, including civil servants, amounted to 183 killed and 778 injured.

Casualties among military personnel and other armed actors included 174 soldiers, 52 police, and 166 paramilitary rangers and village defence volunteers. The 28 non-state armed groups fighters recorded as killed included only those whose bodies were collected by security forces. Often militants carried away their dead and these went unrecorded; in addition, there is no reasonable count of how many militants were injured. In 2012, 67 militants were arrested and another 104 surrendered. It is possible some of those were wounded, while those injured and not arrested tended to be treated by doctors in private.[18]

Action on Armed Violence (AOAV) identified 60 incidents of explosive violence in Thailand, resulting in 769 civilian casualties in 2012. With available data, it was not possible to determine whether or not these casualties overlap with the other casualties reported.[19]

Human Rights Watch (HRW) noted that local human rights groups reported the 'disappearance' of one person in Joh Airong district on 17 January 2012, when armed security personnel forced him into their pick-up truck and drove away.[20]

---

[15] Professor of Political Science and International Relations at Simmons College, Boston. The dataset is referred to as the 'Abuza Incident Database'.

[16] Email from Zachary Abuza, 30 April 2013.

[17] See Deep South Watch, '9 months into the 9th year: amidst the enigmatic violence, the Pa(t)tani peace process still keeps on moving', 23 December 2012, <http://www.deepsouthwatch.org/node/3803; see also ISRA News, <http://www.isranews.org/south-news/scoop/item/18593.html>.

[18] Email from Zachary Abuza, 30 April 2013.

[19] AOAV, 'An explosive situation: monitoring explosive violence in 2012', March 2013, p. 10, <http://aoav.files.wordpress.com/2013/06/an-explosive-situation-explosive-violence-in-2012.pdf>. There were 139 bombings recorded in the Abuza Incident Database for 2012. An additional 33 defused or 'dud' bombs were recorded.

[20] HRW, 'World report 2013: Thailand', <http://www.hrw.org/world-report/2013/country-chapters/thailand>.

DISPLACED

The Internal Monitoring Displacement Centre (IDMC) has estimated that up to 240,000 people may have left their homes in the conflict-affected southern provinces of Thailand since 2004.[21] Some internally displaced persons (IDPs) moved due to the violence directly, while many others moved owing to the impact of violence on economic conditions, education, and social services. The IDMC reported that the absence of a UN presence in the affected provinces has seriously limited its capacity to report on human rights violations or related displacement.[22]

WAR CRIMES ALLEGATIONS, INVESTIGATIONS, AND PROSECUTIONS

Thailand has signed, but not ratified, the 1998 Rome Statute of the International Criminal Court (the ICC Statute).

[21] IDMC, 'Global overview 2012', April 2013, p. 64.
[22] IDMC, 'Global overview 2012', April 2013, p. 73. The IDMC reported that the Thai government had not assessed the extent of displacement, but had provided some assistance to victims of insurgent violence, as well as to their families.

Armed conflict in Turkey in 2012

KEY CONFLICT STATISTICS FOR 2012

Civilian deaths:	17 (to October)	(Source: US Department of State)
Civilian injured:	65 (to October)	(Source: US Department of State)
Military/security deaths:	147 (to October)	(Source: US Department of State)
Military/security deaths:	179	(Source: ICG)
Military/security injured:	813 (to October)	(Source: US Department of State)
Non-states armed actor deaths:	973 (to October)	(Source: US Department of State)
Non-state armed actor deaths:	328	(Source: ICG)
Non-state armed actor injured:	328 (to October)	(Source: US Department of State)
Civilians displaced:	954,000+ (31 Dec. 2012)	(Source: IDMC)

CLASSIFICATION OF THE CONFLICT

Turkish armed and security forces were involved in an armed conflict of a non-international character (NIAC) with the Kurdish Worker's Party (PKK) in the south-east of the country and in the Iraqi Kurdistan region in northern Iraq in 2012. After months of talks, Abdullah Öcalan ordered his fighters to stop attacking Turkey and withdraw from the country from May 2013, effectively ending the insurgency.

SUMMARY OF APPLICABLE INTERNATIONAL LAW

All parties to the conflicts are bound by, inter alia: Common Article 3 to the 1949 Geneva Conventions; the customary international humanitarian law (IHL) rules of distinction, proportionality, and precautions in attacks; the obligation not to recruit and use children as soldiers; and the duty to respect, at a minimum, fundamental human rights. This includes the duty to respect the rights to life and to freedom from torture or other forms of cruel, inhuman, or degrading treatment or punishment. In addition, Turkey is a state party to the two 1966 Covenants (on civil and political rights, and on economic, social, and cultural rights).

Turkey adhered to the 1997 Anti-Personnel Mine Ban Convention (APMBC) in September 2003, becoming a state party on 1 March 2004, but has not adhered to the 2008 Convention on Cluster Munitions (CCM). Turkey is not party to the 1977 Additional Protocol II.

HISTORY OF THE CONFLICT[1]

The Kurdish minority represents 15 per cent of Turkey's 73 million people. Around half of its Kurdish population lives in cities in the western part of the country and the other half live in the impoverished south-east, where they are the ethnic majority.

The Kurdish Workers' Party (PKK), formed in 1978, has been waging a guerrilla war for Kurdish independence in south-eastern Turkey since 1984. In the 1990s, the PKK shifted its goal from an independent Kurdish state to greater autonomy and an improvement of rights for Kurdish people in Turkey, including the right to teach their language in schools. A government campaign to depopulate pro-PKK villages in Turkey created at least 500,000 internally displaced persons (IDPs). Military operations mostly took place in south-eastern Turkey, but since 1992 the Turkish government has also launched periodic air strikes and ground assaults on PKK camps in the northern mountainous area along the border with Iraq.[2]

Between 2009 and 2011, the Turkish government and the PKK met to hold high-level secret talks in Oslo, Norway. The negotiation processes collapsed in June 2011, after a clash between Turkish soldiers and the PKK in which 14 Turkish soldiers were killed.[3] After the talks failed, the intensity of hostilities escalated rapidly, with some of the heaviest fighting seen since the beginning of the conflict.[4]

In 2012, the PKK stepped up and diversified its insurgency in the south-east, taking its campaign to a new level by launching major attacks in urban areas, as well as setting up checkpoints on roads. The campaign was initially successful, but PKK's limited mobility left some of its units more vulnerable to attack by the Turkish security forces and the organization suffered heavy casualties as a result.[5]

In September, a handful of Kurdish nationalist prisoners in Turkish jails started a hunger strike, and by mid-November, they were more than 700. Their demands were: full Kurdish language rights, including allowing its use in courts and as a medium of instruction in schools; an easing of the isolation of Öcalan on the prison island of İmralı; and the establishment of 'democratic autonomy' for predominantly Kurdish areas of Turkey.[6] On 17 November, in a message delivered by his brother, Öcalan called for

---

[1] Unless otherwise stated, this section is based on 'Turkey profile', *BBC*, 25 April 2013, <http://www.bbc.co.uk/news/world-europe-17988453>.

[2] International Crisis Group (ICG), 'Turkey, the PKK and the Kurdish settlement', Europe Report No. 219, 11 September 2012, <http://www.crisisgroup.org/~/media/Files/europe/turkey-cyprus/turkey/219-turkey-the-pkk-and-a-kurdish-settlement.pdf>.

[3] 'Profile: the PKK', *BBC*, 21 March 2013, <http://www.bbc.co.uk/news/world-europe-20971100>.

[4] 'Turkey (2003—first combat deaths for this phase of the conflict)', *Ploughshares*, March 2013, <http://ploughshares.ca/pl_armedconflict/turkey-2003-first-combat-deaths-for-this-phase-of-the-conflict/>.

[5] Gareth H. Jenkins, 'Conflicting narratives, deflating hopes: prospects for the Imrali process', *Turkey Analyst*, 6(5) (13 March 2013), <http://www.silkroadstudies.org/new/inside/turkey/2013/130313A.html>.

[6] Jenkins, 'Conflicting narratives, deflating hopes: prospects for the Imrali process'.

an end to the hunger strike. That same day, the hunger strikers all promptly abandoned their fast, demonstrating Öcalan's continuing influence and iconic status for Kurdish nationalists.[7]

In December 2012, the Turkish State declared its will to start closed negotiations with PKK's leader Öcalan, initiating the so-called 'İmrali Process', aiming, inter alia, at disarming rebels.[8] After months of talks, in March, Abdullah Öcalan ordered his fighters to stop attacking Turkey and withdraw from the country from May 2013, effectively ending the insurgency. In April, the military leader of the PKK, Murat Karayilan, said that PKK fighters would begin to withdraw from Turkey in early May.[9] As of writing, Kurdish rebel fighters had begun leaving south-eastern Turkey for their safe havens in Iraq under a cease-fire, according to Kurdish sources.[10]

Turkey's incursions into Iraq

According to Turkey, about 4,000 PKK fighters are based in the Kurdistan region in northern Iraq. On 17 October 2007, the Turkish parliament voted to authorize military operations against the PKK in northern Iraq for a year. Since that decision, the Turkish military has launched occasional air strikes, and even conducted a ground incursion on 22–29 February 2008. According to a report by CNN, as many as 10,000 Turkish troops were involved in the operation, the first major incursion by Turkey into Iraq since Saddam Hussein was toppled in 2003. Following that operation, the Iraqi government published the following statement: 'The Ministerial Council understands the legitimate interests of Turkey and will not allow its territory to be used for operations that threaten security and stability.'[11] On 10 July 2008, a Joint Political Declaration on border security was concluded in Baghdad between the prime ministers of the two countries.[12]

In March and May 2011, Turkish military forces killed 15 PKK militants crossing the Turkish border into Iraq. One Turkish soldier was also killed. After an increase in PKK attacks, in 2012 Turkey stepped up air operations against suspected PKK rebels in northern Iraq, causing increasing tensions between Ankara and Baghdad. On 11 October 2012, a government motion seeking a one-year extension of the mandate from the

---

[7] Jenkins, 'Conflicting narratives, deflating hopes: prospects for the Imrali process'.

[8] 'Timeline: PKK conflict with Turkey', *Al Jazeera*, 21 March 2013, <http://www.aljazeera.com/news/europe/2013/03/2013320652845642.html>.

[9] 'Turkey profile: Timeline', *BBC*, 25 April 2013, <http://www.bbc.co.uk/news/world-europe-17994865>.

[10] 'Kurdish PKK rebels "begin leaving Turkey" after truce', *BBC*, 8 May 2013, <http://www.bbc.co.uk/news/world-europe-22448118>.

[11] Iraqi Ministry of Foreign Affairs, News archive, 'Ministerial Council condemns Turkish military incursion', 26 February 2008, <http://www.mofa.gov.iq/en/articles/display.aspx?gid=1&id=4325>.

[12] Iraqi Ministry of Foreign Affairs, News archive, 'Iraq and Turkey establish Supreme Council for strategic cooperation between both countries', 12 July 2008, <http://www.mofa.gov.iq/en/articles/display.aspx?gid=1&id=5006>.

Turkish parliament to conduct military operations against the outlawed PKK in northern Iraq was approved.[13]

PARTIES TO THE CONFLICT

Turkish Armed and Security Forces

The Turkish army of some half a million soldiers is said to be the largest in size after the USA within the North Atlantic Treaty Organization (NATO). The Ministry of Defence of Turkey has five divisions: the Air Force; the Navy; the Army; the Gendarmerie; and the Coast Guard.[14]

The Kurdistan Workers' Party (PKK)

The group, which has Marxist-Leninist roots, was formed in 1978 by Abdullah Öcalan and a few co-conspirators. With the aim of creating an independent Kurdish state within Turkey, the PKK launched an armed struggle against the Turkish government in 1984. The group has relied on guerrilla warfare, including kidnappings of foreign tourists, suicide bombings, and attacks on Turkish diplomatic offices in Europe. During the conflict, which reached a peak in the mid-1990s, thousands of villages were destroyed in the largely Kurdish south-east and east of Turkey, and hundreds of thousands of Kurds fled to cities in other parts of the country.[15]

In the 1990s, the organization backed down on its demands for an independent Kurdish state, calling instead for more autonomy for the Kurds.[16] Nonetheless, the armed group remains highly organized and well-financed entity, with several thousand men and women under arms and millions of Kurdish sympathizers in Turkey. The PKK has established bases in Iraq, Iran, and Syria, and deep-rooted support networks in Europe.[17]

The PKK is listed as a terrorist organization by numerous governments, including Turkey, the European Union (EU), and the United States of America (USA).[18] The Iraqi

---

[13] Tim Arango and Duraid Adnan, 'For Iraq, year ends the way it began, with guns drawn', *New York Times*, 3 December 2012, <http://www.nytimes.com/2012/12/04/world/middleeast/iraqs-latest-crisis-is-a-standoff-with-northern-kurds.html?_r=0>.

[14] Yuri Mavashev, 'Turkey's defense power grows at pace to be envied', *Pravda.ru*, 31 January 2012, <http://english.pravda.ru/world/asia/31-01-2012/120376-turkey_defense_power-0/>.

[15] Council on Foreign Relations, 'Inside the Kurdistan Workers Party (PKK)', 19 October 2007, <http://www.cfr.org/turkey/inside-kurdistan-workers-party-pkk/p14576>.

[16] 'Profile: the PKK', *BBC*, 21 March 2013, <http://www.bbc.co.uk/news/world-europe-20971100>.

[17] ICG, 'Turkey, the PKK and the Kurdish settlement', p. 7.

[18] Council on Foreign Relations, 'Inside the Kurdistan Workers Party (PKK)', 19 October 2007.

Kurdish Party has been accused by the Turkish military of supporting the PKK, but it denies the accusations. The PKK suffered a major blow in 1999 when its leader, Abdullah Öcalan, was arrested and jailed for treason.[19]

The Kurdish Freedom Falcons (TAK)

The Kurdistan Freedom Falcons (also known as the Kurdistan Freedom Hawks, or the Kurdish Vengeance Brigade) is a militant group that has committed attacks throughout Turkey, operating in southern Turkey and northern Iraq with a goal of securing Kurdish secession from Turkey. The TAK split off from the PKK when it became dissatisfied with the group's tactics. Most of the group's attacks are directed against tourist areas in Istanbul, Ankara, and southern coastal resort areas.[20] In August 2012, the group claimed responsibility for an attack on a Turkish military bus that killed two Turkish soldiers and injured 12 people.[21]

CASUALTIES

Based on reports from Turkish security forces for the first ten months of 2012,[22] the US Department of State reported that armed clashes with the PKK caused 82 civilian casualties (17 killed, 65 injured) and 960 military casualties (147 killed, 813 injured) among security forces. There were 584 PKK or 'alleged terrorist' casualties (560 killed, 24 injured) and another 71 were captured inside the Turkey in 2012. Most of the clashes between the PKK and security forces occurred in the south-east of Turkey.[23]

In 2012, Turkish military air strikes and ground attacks on areas where the PKK was active in northern Iraq resulted in another 717 PKK casualties or 'persons alleged to be terrorists' (413 killed and 304 injured). According to press reports, an airstrike killed two civilians in the Iraqi province of Sulaymaniyah on 7 November.[24]

The Human Rights Foundation, a Turkish non-governmental organization (NGO), reported that landmines and unexploded ordnance (UXO) killed 14 civilians and injured another 34 in 2012. According to reports by the Gendarmerie, landmines killed three civilians and injured 24, and killed 32 security personnel and injured another 109 in

---

[19] 'Profile: the PKK', *BBC*, 21 March 2013, <http://www.bbc.co.uk/news/world-europe-20971100>.
[20] 'Timeline: Turkey attacks', *BBC*, 27 July 2008, <http://news.bbc.co.uk/2/hi/europe/5292122.stm>.
[21] 'Kurdistan Freedom Falcons TAK group claims responsibility for Turkish army bus attack', *Ekurd.net*, 12 August 2012, <http://www.ekurd.net/mismas/articles/misc2012/8/turkey4094.htm.>
[22] Including the military, Turkish National Police, and Gendarmerie.
[23] US Department of State, 'Country reports on human rights practices 2012: Turkey', 19 April 2013.
[24] US Department of State, 'Country reports on human rights practices 2012: Turkey', 19 April 2013.

2012.[25] Turkey reported that there were 82 casualties (16 killed and 66 injured) of landmines 'laid by *PKK/Kongra Gel*' in 2012.[26] It is not known how many of these casualties are included among the conflict casualty totals for 2012.

The ICG has kept an informal, minimum tally of conflict-related fatalities based on public reports on both sides since the upsurge in violence started afresh in June 2011. According to this count, in 2012, the ICG recorded 524 deaths: 17 civilians; 179 Turkish security forces including military, police, and village guard militia; and 328 PKK members.[27]

DISPLACED

The Internal Displacement Monitoring Centre (IDMC) estimated that at least 954,000 people were displaced internally within Turkey as of end 2012. Counter-insurgency operations against the PKK in Hakkari province displaced several hundred people in August. Violence along Turkey's border with Syria may also have led to further displacements, but no figures were available.[28]

WAR CRIMES ALLEGATIONS, INVESTIGATIONS, AND PROSECUTIONS

Turkey is not party to the 1998 Rome Statute of the International Criminal Court (the ICC Statute).

[25] US Department of State, 'Country reports on human rights practices 2012: Turkey', 19 April 2013.

[26] In Form J of its Art. 7 transparency report under the APMBC for calendar year 2012.

[27] ICG casualty data in email from Didem Akyel Collinsworth, Turkey and Cyprus Analyst for ICG's Turkey/Cyprus Project, 23 April 2013. The ICG data includes casualties reported to have occurred in northern Iraq or directly in the borderline areas of Turkey, and casualties from previously emplaced landmines and UXO. Data is mostly from media sources and numbers vary from source to source; the figures are normally presented as rounded approximations.

[28] IDMC, 'Global overview 2012', April 2013, p. 51.

Armed conflict in Yemen in 2012

KEY CONFLICT STATISTICS FOR 2012

Civilian deaths:	116–34	(Sources: BIJ; Landmine Monitor)
Civilians injured:	133+	(Sources: BIJ; Landmine Monitor)
Yemen military deaths:	233	(Source: BIJ)
Yemen military injuries:	302	(Sources: BIJ; Landmine Monitor)
AQAP deaths:	554–711	(Source: BIJ)
Other deaths:	47 (victim status unknown)	(Source: BIJ)
Other injuries:	208 (victim status unknown)	(Source: BIJ)
Civilians displaced:	385,000–545,000 (31 Dec. 2012)	(Source: IDMC)

CLASSIFICATION OF THE CONFLICTS

Yemeni armed forces were involved in two distinct armed conflicts of a non-international character (NIACs) in 2012, one with the Houthi rebels in the north of Yemen, and the other, until June 2012, with al-Qaeda in the Arabian Peninsula (AQAP). In the latter conflict, Yemeni forces were supported by drone strikes operated by the US Central Intelligence Agency (CIA). Both conflicts reached the threshold for applicability of the 1977 Additional Protocol II.

SUMMARY OF APPLICABLE INTERNATIONAL LAW

All parties to the conflicts are bound by, inter alia: Common Article 3 to the 1949 Geneva Conventions and 1977 Additional Protocol II; the customary international humanitarian law (IHL) rules of distinction, proportionality, and precautions in attacks; the obligation not to recruit and use children as soldiers; and the duty to respect, at a minimum, fundamental human rights. This includes the duty to respect the rights to life and to freedom from torture or other forms of cruel, inhuman, or degrading treatment or punishment. In addition, Yemen is a state party to the two 1966 Covenants (on civil and political rights, and on economic, social, and cultural rights).

Yemen adhered to the 1997 Anti-Personnel Mine Ban Convention (APMBC) in September 1998, becoming a state party on 1 March 1999, but is not a party to the 2008 Convention on Cluster Munitions (CCM).

HISTORY OF THE CONFLICT[1]

The conflict in the Sa'da region

Conflict between Yemeni government forces and Houthi rebels began in 2004. Husain al-Houthi founded the Believing Youth movement in the 1990s, aimed at reviving Zaidi Islam, a branch of Shi'ism found mainly in Yemen, to counter growing fundamentalist Sunni trends in the northern Yemeni governorates where Zaidis dominate. The conflict began as isolated clashes between the Believing Youth movement (Houthis) and the army in Sa'da.[2]

Since the clashes of 2004, there have been periods of sustained fighting, mostly in the countryside, but escalating in June 2008 to the outskirts of Sanaa. In August 2009, the government launched a major offensive against the Houthis in the Sa'da and Amran provinces, backed by air strikes and artillery fire and resulting in some of the fiercest fighting. Dozens were reportedly killed on both sides, including Houthi leaders and civilians.[3] An estimated 200,000 persons were reportedly displaced from their homes in the northern governorates in 2009–10.[4]

Furthermore, the conflict acquired a regional dimension, with the Yemeni authorities accusing Iran of backing the Houthis, while the Houthis accused Saudi Arabia of supporting the Yemeni government. In October 2009, clashes broke out between the Houthis and Saudi security forces along the border of the two countries. On 4 November 2009, Houthis reportedly fought their way across the border into Saudi Arabia and took 'full control' of a mountainous section of the border region of Jabal al-Dukhan.[5]

A cease-fire seemed to have been reached between the Yemeni government and the Houthis in February 2010, although episodes of violence continued to occur sporadically.[6] An estimated 200,000 persons were displaced from their homes in the northern governorates in 2009–10.[7] In 2011–12, the Houthis continued fighting against

[1] Unless otherwise stated, this section is based on 'Yemen profile', *BBC*, 12 September 2012, <http://www.bbc.co.uk/news/world-middle-east-14704852>.

[2] Human Rights Watch (HRW), 'Disappearances and arbitrary arrests in the armed conflict with Huthi rebels in Yemen', 24 October 2008, pp. 10–12, <http://www.hrw.org/en/reports/2008/10/24/disappearances-and-arbitrary-arrests-armed-conflict-huthi-rebels-yemen-0>.

[3] 'A critical war in a fragile country: Yemen's battle with the Shiite al Houthi rebels', *Critical Threats*, 31 August 2009, <http://www.criticalthreats.org/yemen/critical-war-fragile-country-yemens-battle-shiite-al-houthi-rebels>.

[4] Office of the United Nations High Commissioner for Refugees (UNHCR), 'More than 200,000 displaced by the conflict in Yemen', Press release, 12 January 2010, <http://www.unhcr.se/en/media/press-releases/artikel/8e6a57b4a95019884040a369d1ead582/more-than-200000-displaced-by-the-c.html>.

[5] 'Yemen (2004—first combat deaths)', *Ploughshares*, March 2012, <http://ploughshares.ca/pl_armedconflict/yemen-2004-first-combat-deaths/>.

[6] 'Yemeni cease-fire breached', *CNN*, 13 February 2010, <http://edition.cnn.com/2010/WORLD/meast/02/13/yemen.violence/index.html?_s=PM:WORLD>.

[7] UNHCR, 'More than 200,000 displaced by the conflict in Yemen', Press release, 12 January 2010.

tribal militia, gaining control of various towns and villages near the northern Syrian border.[8]

There were continuing reports of US involvement in the Yemeni conflict, which has been accused of covertly aiding the government by using drones and fighter jets against the rebels.[9]

al-Qaeda in the Arabian Peninsula (AQAP) in the south of Yemen

The Yemeni government has admitted the presence of AQAP within its borders in 2009. In January 2010, under international pressure, it declared 'open war' against the group.[10] The United States of America (USA) has used drones in operations against AQAP, which has resulted in high-profile killings, such as that of the Anwar al-Awlaki leader in September 2011. Drone attacks continued into 2012.[11]

According to the Ploughshares project, much of southern Yemen, especially Abyan Province, was captured by AQAP in the first half of 2011, including the city of Jaar in March 2011. By early 2012, as Yemen's military fractured and split amidst widespread popular protests, AQAP seized and held several towns in the southern Yemeni governorates of Abyan and Shabwa.[12] The group is exploiting the political instability of the country to consolidate its power in the southern regions.[13] Following the election of Abd Rabu Mansur Hadi as Yemen's President in February (2012), the USA increased the number of strikes in the country. In May and June 2012, it backed a sustained military offensive launched by Yemeni armed forces against AQAP, forcing the group to abandon the towns it had previously captured.[14]

[8] 'Yemen (2004—first combat deaths)', *Ploughshares*, March 2012, <http://ploughshares.ca/pl_ar medconflict/yemen-2004-first-combat-deaths/>.

[9] Middle East Policy Council, 'Drone warfare in Yemen: fostering Emirates through counterterrorism', 17 September 2012, <http://mepc.org/journal/middle-east-policy-archives/drone-warfare-yemen-fostering-emirates-through-counterterrorism>.

[10] Council on Foreign Relations, 'al-Qaeda in the Arabian Peninsula (AQAP)', 24 May 2012, <http://www.cfr.org/yemen/al-qaeda-arabian-peninsula-aqap/p9369>.

[11] Council on Foreign Relations, 'Obama and the laws of war', 10 May 2012, <http://www.cfr.org/counterterrorism/obama-laws-war/p28209>.

[12] 'Yemen (2004—first combat deaths)', *Ploughshares*, March 2012, <http://ploughshares.ca/pl_ar medconflict/yemen-2004-first-combat-deaths/>.

[13] International Crisis Group (ICG), 'Yemen: enduring conflicts, threatened transition', Middle East Report No. 125, 3 July 2012, <http://www.crisisgroup.org/en/regions/middle-east-north-africa/iraq-iran-gulf/yemen/125-yemen-enduring-conflicts-threatened-transition.aspx>.

[14] 'A profile of AQAP's upper echelon', *CTC Sentinel*, 5(7) (July 2012), pp. 6–8, <http://www.ctc.usma.edu/wp-content/uploads/2012/07/CTCSentinel-Vol5Iss72.pdf>.

PARTIES TO THE CONFLICT

Yemeni Armed Forces

Total Yemeni armed forces are reported by one source to number some 66,000 active personnel.[15] In April 2013, United Nations (UN) Secretary-General Ban Ki-moon welcomed Yemeni President Abdrabuh Mansour Hadi's efforts to restructure the nation's security sector, in particular the armed forces, 'with a view to integrating them under unified, national and professional leadership and command based on the rule of law'.[16]

al-Houthi

al-Houthi is a Zaidi Shia insurgent group operating in Yemen. The group takes its name from Hussein Badreddin al-Houthi, its former commander, who was reportedly killed by Yemeni army forces in September 2004. al-Houthi has asserted that its actions are for the defence of its community from government discrimination, although the Yemeni government has in turn accused it of wishing to destabilize the government and 'stirring anti-American sentiment'. The group has responded to the 'Arab Spring' movement, and since protests began in Yemen in September 2011, the group has aligned itself with the 'revolutionary youth' positions calling for the downfall of the regime and justice for its victims.[17] In 2011–12, the Houthis continued fighting to establish control over specific areas in the northern part of the country. They continue to send mixed signals about whether or not they will be willing to participate in national politics by opening negotiations with the government.

al-Qaeda in the Arabian Peninsula

The militant Islamist group al-Qaeda in the Arabian Peninsula (AQAP) was formed in January 2009 through a union of the Saudi and Yemeni branches of al-Qaeda.[18] The primary objectives of AQAP refer to the principles of militant jihad, seeking to purge Muslim countries of Western influence and to replace secular 'apostate' governments

---

[15] Nationmaster.com, <http://www.nationmaster.com/country/ym-yemen/mil-military>.

[16] 'Yemen: Ban, Security Council welcome efforts to reform armed forces', UN Press release, New York, 12 April 2013, <http://www.un.org/apps/news/story.asp?NewsID=44638#.UZCwtxZBvX4>.

[17] 'Yemen's Huthi movement in the wake of the Arab Spring', *CTC Sentinel*, 5(8) (August 2012), p. 1, <http://www.ctc.usma.edu/posts/yemens-huthi-movement-in-the-wake-of-the-arab-spring>.

[18] Council on Foreign Relations, 'al-Qaeda in the Arabian Peninsula (AQAP)', 24 May 2012, <http://www.cfr.org/yemen/al-qaeda-arabian-peninsula-aqap/p9369>.

with fundamentalist Islamic regimes based on Shari'a law. Associated AQAP objectives include overthrowing the Saudi monarchy and the Yemeni government, assassinating Western nationals and their allies, striking at related interests in the region, such as embassies and energy concerns, and attacking the US homeland.[19] The Yemeni government admitted the presence of al-Qaeda within its borders in 2009. In January 2010, under international pressure, Yemen declared 'open war' on the group and the USA started launching drone attacks against the group.[20] In May 2012, the armed group declared itself responsible for two major attacks, a foiled airliner bomb plot,[21] and a suicide bombing in the capital of Sana'a, resulting in a violent reaction by Yemeni troops backed by the USA.[22]

CASUALTIES

There was no comprehensive source of data on conflict-related casualties in Yemen for 2012. The most detailed casualty data was available through the Bureau of Investigative Journalism (BIJ)'s Yemen 2012 dataset.[23] While focused on casualties as a result of drone strikes, the BIJ data also provides information on other conflict-related casualties. As a result of drone strikes in 2012, BIJ identified civilian deaths in the range of 40–58, including one employee of the International Committee of the Red Cross (ICRC), 481–638 deaths among insurgents, and the death of 23 people of whom the status was unknown.[24] It also identified an estimated 200 people who were injured from drone strikes, including at least 13 children, at least one woman, and a religious leader. *The Long War Journal*, another project to track casualties from drone strikes, identified 35

[19] 'The evolving terrorist threat in Yemen', *CTC Sentinel*, 3(9) (September 2010), pp. 5–6, <http://www.ctc.usma.edu/wp-content/uploads/2010/10/CTCSentinel-Vol3Iss92.pdf>.

[20] 'Yemen (2004—first combat deaths)', *Ploughshares*, March 2012, <http://ploughshares.ca/pl_armedconflict/yemen-2004-first-combat-deaths/>.

[21] Sudarsan Raghavan, Peter Finn, and Greg Mille, 'A foiled airliner bomb plot', *Washington Post*, 9 May 2012, <http://articles.washingtonpost.com/2012-05-09/world/35456649_1_underwear-bomb-bomb-plot-al-qaeda>.

[22] 'Suicide bomber kills 90 in Yemen, al-Qaeda vows more attacks', *Reuters*, 21 May 2012, <http://www.reuters.com/article/2012/05/21/us-yemen-suicidebomb-deathtoll-idUSBRE84K0O720120521>.

[23] The BIJ collects data reported by US and Yemeni government, military, and intelligence officials, and by credible media, academic, and other sources. It provides all available details for each drone strike identified through one or more sources: BIJ, 'Yemen: reported US covert action 2012', 8 May 2012 (regularly updated), <http://www.thebureauinvestigates.com/2012/05/08/yemen-reported-us-covert-action-2012/>.

[24] Because casualty details sometimes differ across sources, the BIJ provides a minimum to maximum range of casualties for each incident. Sums here represent a strike-by-strike analysis of BIJ data to determine a total minimum and maximum for all drone strikes identified during the year.

civilian casualties and 193 casualties among insurgents from 42 US CIA air strikes in Yemen in 2012.[25]

BIJ data includes details of several other conflict-related events including: the death of three people who were executed by Ansar al-Sharia for allegedly having provided intelligence in connection with a 31 January drone strike; the death of 90 Yemeni military personnel following the attack on a military base by Ansar al-Shari'a; the death of another 32 Yemeni military in retaliation for a drone strike on 6 May; and three Ansar al-Shari'a suicide bomb attacks that killed at least 111 Yemeni military personnel, five civilians, at least two insurgents, and injured 300 Yemeni military personnel and at least 20 civilians. Battles in Loder, Abyan, between 11 and 22 April killed 72 insurgents and another 21 fighters for whom no details were reported.[26]

The Landmine and Cluster Munition Monitor reported 191 casualties from landmines and explosive remnants of war (ERW), of whom 189 were civilians, including mine-clearance personnel. Landmines and ERW killed eight children and injured 29.[27]

Action on Armed Violence (AOAV) reported approximately 2,000 casualties from explosive violence, of whom 312 were civilians.[28] However, it was not reported how many casualties were conflict-related and it was not possible to compare details with other sources.

The UN Office for the Coordination of Humanitarian Affairs (OCHA) reported that, during 2012, children in Yemen were subject to a number of grave rights violations, often related to conflict. From 1 January to the end of September, OCHA verified that 164 children (135 boys and 29 girls) had been victims of killing (31), maiming (98), use and recruitment (29), and sexual abuse (six).[29]

Armed groups, including Ansar al-Shari'a, reportedly committed a range of human rights abuses against women and girls, including forced marriages of young girls, sexual slavery, and sexual exploitation. Up to 100 girls in Abyan were forcibly married to leaders or members of armed groups. The UN reported that the girls and their families were reluctant to report the abuses due to fear of reprisals by the groups involved.[30]

HRW, Médecins sans Frontières (MSF), and local non-governmental organizations (NGOs) reported several incidents where government security personnel or insurgents

---

[25] Bill Roggio and Bob Barry, 'Charting the data for US air strikes in Yemen, 2002–2013', *The Long War Journal*, 21 April 2013, <http://www.longwarjournal.org/multimedia/Yemen/code/Yemen-strike.php>.

[26] BIJ, 'Yemen: reported US covert action 2012', 8 May 2012 (regularly updated), <http://www.thebureauinvestigates.com/2012/05/08/yemen-reported-us-covert-action-2012/>.

[27] International Campaign to Ban Landmines (ICBL)–Cluster Mine Coalition (CMC), 'Landmine and Cluster Munition Monitor: country profile Yemen 2013', advance copy made available on 1 May 2013.

[28] AOAV, 'Explosive violence: February 2012', <http://www.aoav.org.uk/uploads/changing_policy/The%20Impact%20of%20Explosive%>.

[29] OCHA, 'Secondary data review March–October 2012: Yemen complex emergency', p. 28.

[30] 'Report of the Secretary-General on sexual violence in conflict', UN doc. S/2013/149, advance copy dated 12 March 2013, §91.

(Houthis in northern Yemen) interrupted the delivery of humanitarian assistance, including by forcibly removing patients from medical facilities at gunpoint. MSF ceased working in Aden in October in response to those activities.[31] An ICRC staff member abducted on 21 April near the town of Hodeida was freed in July.[32]

DISPLACED

According to the Internal Displacement Monitoring Centre (IDMC), the number of displaced persons in Yemen fluctuated throughout the year, with 132,000 new displacements and several thousand returns in both the north and south of the country. At its peak, the total number of displaced persons was 545,000; by the end of the year, there remained 385,000 internally displaced persons (IDPs).[33]

WAR CRIMES ALLEGATIONS, INVESTIGATIONS, AND PROSECUTIONS

Yemen has signed, but not ratified, the 1998 Rome Statute of the International Criminal Court (the ICC Statute).

[31] US Department of State, 'Country reports on human rights practices 2012: Yemen', 19 April 2013.
[32] ICRC, 'Yemen: ICRC confirms that abducted staff member is free', 14 July 2012, <http://www.icrc.org/eng/resources/documents/news-release/2012/yemen-news-2012-07-14.htm>.
[33] IDMC, 'Global overview 2012', April 2013, p. 60.

Part III

Important Themes in Armed Conflicts in 2012

1 The use of explosive weapons in populated areas in 2012

Maya Brehm*

There was black smoke everywhere, and broken glass. The bomb hit the corner of the street, and the shrapnel flew straight into the line [of people waiting in front of the bakery]. Everyone there was either killed or heavily injured. I saw one man on the ground without a leg, another without an arm, then a 16-year-old boy whom I knew...without a head....One of my cousins...lost his arm and leg, and died afterward.

Testimony by 'Qais', Aleppo, August 2012[1]

Introduction

In 2012, as in previous years, 'explosive violence' (the use of explosive weapons) was geographically widespread and its humanitarian impact was devastating. The testimony above illustrates the immense suffering caused to civilians by the use of explosive weapons in Syrian villages and cities in 2012, and continuing into 2013. Images of immense devastation are by now closely associated with the conflict in Syria. Entire neighbourhoods have been levelled to the ground by shelling and bombardment using mortars and artillery shells, rockets, air-dropped bombs, including cluster munitions, and powerful improvised explosive devices (IEDs).

Explosive weapons function mainly through blast and fragment projection (fragmentation) in the area around the point of detonation. The International Committee of the Red Cross (ICRC) observed that the use of explosive weapons in populated areas (for example urban residential neighbourhoods or villages) 'exposes the civilian

---

* Maya Brehm is a researcher at the Geneva Academy.
[1] Qais is a 44-year-old tailor, who worked as a volunteer at Aqyoul bakery in the Bab al-Hadid neighbourhood of Aleppo city. He was wounded in the attack that took place on 21 August 2012, when a helicopter dropped two bombs near the bakery: Human Rights Watch (HRW), 'Death from the skies', 11 April 2013, <http://www.hrw.org/reports/2013/04/11/death-skies>.

population and infrastructure to heightened—and even extreme—risks of incidental or indiscriminate death, injury or destruction'.[2] In 2012, according to data compiled by the British non-governmental organization (NGO) Action on Armed Violence (AOAV), the overwhelming majority (91 per cent) of casualties from the use of explosive weapons in populated areas were civilians.[3]

Recognition has grown over recent years that use of explosive weapons in populated areas constitutes a distinct humanitarian problem. NGOs affiliated with the International Network on Explosive Weapons (INEW),[4] the ICRC, United Nations (UN) bodies, and a growing number of states have identified this form of armed violence as a core challenge to the protection of civilians in armed conflict, and, more specifically, to the protection of children.[5] Efforts are under way to reduce and prevent harm from explosive violence, including through more systematic data collection and analysis of its human costs, and by support for more focused international policy discussions. In this regard, the need for further normative development has been considered.

This chapter starts by presenting data collected in 2012 on the pattern of harm associated with the use of explosive weapons in populated areas around the world. It then assesses the use of explosive weapons in populated areas under existing international law, discussing legal constraints imposed on the use of explosive weapons by weapons treaties and international humanitarian law (IHL) governing the conduct of hostilities. In this connection, the chapter looks at how the use of cluster munitions in populated areas is addressed in the report of the Independent International Commission of Inquiry on Syria, and in the 2012 judgment by the Inter-American Court of Human Rights (IACtHR) in the *Santo Domingo* case (regarding the use of cluster munitions in a village in Colombia). Also examined is the controversial judgment by the Appeals Chamber of the International Criminal Tribunal for the former Yugoslavia (ICTY) in the *Gotovina* case, which deals with artillery shelling of populated areas. The chapter then analyses the use of explosive weapons under international human rights law (IHRL), and concludes with an initial determination of whether international law adequately protects civilians against documented harm from the use of explosive weapons in populated areas.

---

[2] ICRC, 'International humanitarian law and the challenges of contemporary armed conflicts', Doc. 31IC/11/5.1.2, October 2011, p. 41.

[3] Henry Dodd and Robert Perkins, *An Explosive Situation: Monitoring Explosive Violence in 2012*, AOAV, London, March 2013 (*AOAV Monitoring Explosive Violence in 2012*), p. 3. For the purposes of AOAV data collection, 'casualty' means those killed or physically injured by an incident involving the use of an explosive weapon. On the distinction between 'armed actors' and 'civilians', see further below.

[4] For more information about INEW, visit <http://www.inew.org/>.

[5] For compilations of policy statements expressing concern about the use of explosive weapons in populated areas, see <http://explosiveweapons.info/resources/> and <http://www.inew.org/acknowledgements>.

A. **The humanitarian impact of explosive violence**

The use of explosive weapons in populated areas has a devastating humanitarian impact. Incidents of explosive violence generally produce multiple casualties.[6] People in the vicinity of an explosion are at grave risk of suffering mutilating ballistic, blast, as well as burn injuries. The blast can cause the traumatic amputation of limbs, the rupture of internal organs, and blunt trauma. Fragmentation can lead to deep penetration wounds. Victims of explosive violence tend to suffer multiple and severe injuries that they may not survive, or which may result in life-long mental and physical disability.[7]

Explosive violence in populated areas can have indirect and prolonged impacts. Explosive weapons can seriously damage or completely destroy homes, productive assets, and public infrastructure, which can have serious knock-on effects on the well-being and survival of communities. Explosive weapons are a key threat to the provision of health care during armed conflicts.[8] Explosive weapons can also impede delivery of humanitarian aid.[9] A connection between explosive weapon use in populated areas and population displacement has also been demonstrated.[10] Finally, explosive weapons tend to leave behind unexploded ordnance that poses a continued threat of injury and death, constitutes an obstacle to the safe return of displaced populations, and impedes livelihood activities, such as agriculture or grazing.[11]

Explosive weapons kill and injure significant numbers of people who are civilians. Overall, civilians made up 78 per cent of casualties recorded by AOAV in 2012.[12] Of all

---

[6] Richard Moyes, 'Explosive violence: the problem of explosive weapons', *Landmine Action*, August 2009, p. 23. According to data collected by AOAV, on average 16 people were killed or injured in explosive weapon incidents in a populated area in 2012. Certain explosive weapon types are associated with even higher numbers of victims per incident: *AOAV Monitoring Explosive Violence in 2012*, p. 15.

[7] On the medical impacts of explosive weapons, see e.g. Ronald F. Bellamy and Russ Zajtchuk (eds), *Conventional Warfare, Ballistic, Blast, and Burn Injuries*, vol. 5, Textbook of Military Medicine, Series of Combat Casualty Care, Office of the Surgeon General, Department of the Army, United States of America (USA), 1991.

[8] ICRC, *Health Care in Danger: A Sixteen-Country Study*, ICRC, Geneva, 2011.

[9] Christina Wille and Larissa Fast, 'Humanitarian staff security in armed conflict: policy implications resulting from changes in the operating environment for humanitarian agencies', Policy Brief, Insecurity Insight, Switzerland, 2013, p. 6.

[10] Simon Bagshaw, 'Driving displacement: explosive weapons in populated areas', *Forced Migration Review*, 41, December 2012.

[11] For more information, see Geneva International Centre for Humanitarian Demining (GICHD), *A Guide to Mine Action*, 4th edn, Geneva, June 2010. Explosive materials can also have toxic properties: on this issue, see Mohamed Ghalaieny, 'Toxic harm: humanitarian and environmental concerns from military-origin contamination', Discussion paper, The Toxic Remnants of War Project, February 2013.

[12] For the purposes of data collection, AOAV assumes all casualties to be 'civilians' unless otherwise stated. Casualties are recorded as 'armed actors' if they are reported as being members of the military, members of non-state armed groups, or security personnel who are likely to be armed. See *AOAV Monitoring Explosive Violence in 2012*, p. 38. This notion of 'civilians' will most often, but not in all cases, accord with the definition of a civilian protected from attack under IHL or with that of a bystander under

recorded incidents in 2012, 61 per cent took place in what AOAV considered to be a 'populated area'.[13] In these incidents, 91 per cent of casualties were civilians. When explosive weapons were used in other places, civilians made up 32 per cent of casualties. That civilians make up a bigger proportion of victims in populated areas compared to other places is not surprising, given population density, the blast and fragmentation effects of explosive weapons, and their capacity to cause entire buildings to collapse, crushing people within them. Even so, the proportion of civilian casualties in such contexts is staggeringly high, and has risen by 26 per cent, compared to 2011.[14] While some civilian harm results from attacks that target civilians in complete disregard of international law, it is alarming that even among incidents in populated areas in which parties reportedly targeted armed actors or other military objectives, 80 per cent of casualties were still civilian.[15] There is also concern that particularly vulnerable population groups may be disproportionately affected by explosive violence. However, age- and gender-disaggregated data is sketchy.[16]

Although harm from explosive violence occurs in many states and territories, the impact varies widely. In 2012, Afghanistan, Iraq, Nigeria, and Pakistan experienced high levels of explosive violence.[17] The single most affected country by explosive violence was

IHRL. In 2012, AOAV recorded 2,742 explosive violence incidents in which 34,758 people were killed or injured. AOAV makes no claim to capture every casualty from explosive violence. The data is gathered from English-language media sources, and captures only death and injury *directly* resulting from explosive weapon use. This method allows the identification of significant patterns of harm and provides a measure of the scope and scale of the violence, but it under-represents harm from large-scale explosive violence, such as continuous shelling over several days. For more information on the methodology, see *AOAV Monitoring Explosive Violence in 2012*, pp. 38–9.

[13] The notion of 'populated area' used by AOAV is based on the 1980 Protocol III to the Convention on Certain Conventional Weapons (CCW): *AOAV Monitoring Explosive Violence in 2012*, p. 38.

[14] For data on earlier years, see Henry Dodd and Robert Perkins, *Monitoring Explosive Violence: The EVMP Dataset 2011*, AOAV, March 2012; Moyes, 'Explosive violence: the problem of explosive weapons'.

[15] *AOAV Monitoring Explosive Violence in 2012*, p. 15.

[16] Madelyn Hsiao-Rei Hicks et al., 'The weapons that kill civilians: deaths of children and noncombatants in Iraq, 2003–2008', *New England Journal of Medicine*, 360(16) (16 April 2009), pp. 1585–8; Richard Moyes, 'Impact of explosive weapons by gender and age—Iraq 2003–2011', AOAV, June 2012, found women (and children) to be at a particular risk of harm in Iraq. Men make up the majority of victims from certain IEDs in Nepal according to a study by Oleg O. Bilukha et al., 'Fatal and non-fatal injuries due to intentional explosions in Nepal, 2008–2011: analysis of surveillance data', *Conflict and Health*, 7(5) (2013). Hector Guerra, 'The use of hand grenades in Mexico: a problem of explosive violence in populated areas? A media review, 2011–2012', SEHLAC, 2013, reaches a similar finding on victims of grenades in Mexico. On the impact of airstrikes on children in Afghanistan, see United Nations Assistance Mission in Afghanistan (UNAMA), 'Mid-year report on protection of civilians in armed conflict 2012', August 2012, p. 49. On the impact of explosive weapons on children in Syria, see Save the Children, 'Childhood under fire: the impact of two years of conflict in Syria', March 2013.

[17] On a positive note, explosive violence seems to have decreased in Yemen, Somalia, and Libya compared to 2011, and ceased to be recorded in Côte d'Ivoire: *AOAV Monitoring Explosive Violence in 2012*, p. 9.

Syria, with much of the violence taking place in populated areas.[18] For example, in December 2012, shelling in Yarmouk camp, home to around 160,000 Palestinian refugees, resulted in scores of civilian deaths and injuries.[19]

In terms of the impact of different types of explosive weapon, ground-launched explosive weapons tended to be used more frequently in populated areas than did those dropped from the air. As in 2011, mortars were among the most problematic ground-launched explosive weapons, with a staggering 90 per cent of mortar shell casualties overall being civilians.[20] Ground-launched explosive weapons were often used in large numbers and as part of sustained shelling, such as during the offensive by Syrian armed forces on Homs between February and April 2012, one of the most populated cities in Syria. Grenades and various types of IED—often used by non-state actors—have also caused significant harm in 2012 (discussed below). Among air-launched explosive weapons, air-dropped bombs and rockets stood out in 2012 as having caused particularly high percentages of civilian casualties (82 per cent) when used in populated areas.[21] On 18 November 2012, for example, Israeli forces dropped a large bomb on a three-storey home in Gaza city. The Gaza Strip is one of the world's most densely populated areas. This attack killed ten members of the Dalu family household (one man, five women, and four children), as well as a young man and an elderly woman living next door.[22]

NON-STATE ACTOR USE OF EXPLOSIVE WEAPONS

Non-state actors have gained increasing access to a range of explosive weapon types, some of which can be delivered over large distances and have great explosive power. In

---

[18] The Independent International Commission of Inquiry on Syria established by the Human Rights Council noted that 'Most deaths in Bab Amr during the military operation that began in February 2012 were caused by extensive and indiscriminate shelling by government forces of primarily civilian infrastructure and residential areas': 'Report of the Independent International Commission of Inquiry on the situation in the Syrian Arab Republic', Human Rights Council, UN doc. A/HRC/21/50, 16 August 2012, §91.

[19] UN Office for the Coordination of Humanitarian Affairs (OCHA), 'Crisis growing as violence intensifies: one in five Syrians in need of assistance', *Humanitarian Bulletin: Syria*, (15), (11–24 December 2012), p. 1.

[20] *AOAV Monitoring Explosive Violence in 2012*, pp. 23–4. For example, on 27 August 2012, a volley of mortar rounds hit a residential area in Sheikh Mero Baba, Pakistan, killing nine people on the spot and one in the hospital, and destroying several houses: 'Khyber agency: mortar shell death toll reaches 10', *Express Tribune*, 27 August 2012.

[21] *AOAV Monitoring Explosive Violence in 2012*, p. 21.

[22] HRW considers that the attack amounted to a 'clear violation of the laws of war', an assessment shared by other NGOs, but not by the Israeli Military Advocate General. See HRW, 'Israel/Gaza: Israeli airstrike on home unlawful, deadliest strike of Gaza fighting killed 12', 7 December 2012, <http://www.hrw.org/news/2012/12/07/israelgaza-israeli-airstrike-home-unlawful>; Israel, Military Advocate General, 'The examination of alleged misconduct during Operation "Pillar of Defence"—an update', 11 April 2013 [incorrectly dated 'April 11, 2012'], <http://www.law.idf.il/SIP_STORAGE/files/4/1364.pdf>.

2012, AOAV recorded more than 70 non-state armed actors using explosive weapons.[23] In Syria, opposition groups have gained access to rocket-propelled grenades (RPGs), mortars, heavy machine guns, heavy anti-aircraft machine guns, cannons, surface-to-air missiles, anti-tank missiles, howitzers, and multiple-launch rocket systems through defecting government armed forces, captured military bases or ammunition storage areas, and foreign suppliers.[24] In spite of considerable efforts by states to prevent non-state actors from obtaining man-portable air defence systems (MANPADS)—a light explosive weapon seen to pose a particular threat to civil aviation—these weapons are said to have made their way from Libyan stockpiles into northern Mali after the collapse of the Gaddafi regime.[25] In some parts of the world, criminal organizations increasingly resort to the use of explosive weapons, including grenades and shoulder-fired rockets. That such weapons have become part of the arsenals of Mexican drug cartels is well documented. The neighbouring US state, Texas, has identified explosive weapon use by the cartels as one of the greatest threats to public safety in Texas.[26]

Most prominent among explosive weapons used by non-state actors are various types of *improvised* explosive weapon, often subsumed under the term 'improvised explosive devices'.[27] Many IEDs are of relatively 'rudimentary design', but some non-state actors have developed powerful and sophisticated devices. IEDs account for a growing number of military casualties in many contexts and are an important source of civilian harm.[28] According to AOAV, the percentage of IED casualties that were civilians increased in 2012 to 81, compared to 76 in 2011. Car bombs in populated areas had a major humanitarian impact and caused almost half (48 per cent) of all civilian casualties

---

[23] *AOAV Monitoring Explosive Violence in 2012*, p. 18. Those with the highest recorded use of explosive weapons were the Islamic State of Iraq, the (Quetta Shura) Taliban, groups with links to the Free Syrian Army, Tehrik-i-Taliban (Pakistani Taliban), al-Shabaab (Somalia), and Boko Haram (Nigeria).

[24] For more information, see 'Brown Moses Blog' at <http://brown-moses.blogspot.ch/>, and 'Syria's descent: what weapons do the rebels have?', *Channel 4*, 27 March 2013, <http://www.channel4.com/news/syrias-descent-what-weapons-do-the-rebels-have>.

[25] Morgan L. Roach and Jessica Zuckerman, 'MANPADS on the loose: countering weapons proliferation in North Africa and the Sahel', Issue Brief on Arms Control and Non-proliferation, Heritage Foundation, 5 November 2012. See further in this regard Ch. 3 in this book.

[26] Grenades were the most frequently recorded type of ground-launched explosive weapon in 2012: *AOAV Monitoring Explosive Violence in 2012*, p. 24. See also Hector Guerra, 'The use of hand grenades in Mexico: a problem of explosive violence in populated areas'; Texas Department of Public Safety, 'Texas public safety threat overview 2013', February 2013, p. 16.

[27] Note that use of improvised explosive weapons by states has also been reported in 2012. Sudanese and Syrian forces have both dropped so-called 'barrel bombs' on populated areas from the air: *AOAV Monitoring Explosive Violence in 2012*, p. 22; HRW, 'Under siege: indiscriminate bombing and abuses in Sudan's Southern Kordofan and Blue Nile states', 12 December 2012, pp. 35–6, <http://www.hrw.org/reports/2012/12/11/under-siege>.

[28] US Joint IED Defeat Organization (JIEDDO), 'Counter-IED strategic plan 2012–2016', January 2012, p. 3; International Institute for Strategic Studies (IISS), 'IEDs: the home-made bombs that changed modern war', *Strategic Comments*, Edition No. 24, 9 August 2012; see also Christopher J. Chivers, 'Syrian rebels hone bomb skills to even the odds', *New York Times*, 18 July 2012.

from IED use in 2012.[29] IED use was especially intense in Afghanistan, Iraq, and Pakistan.[30] On 14 January 2012, for instance, a bomb targeting Shi'ite pilgrims in Basra (Iraq) killed 53 people and wounded around 137 other people.[31] Other places were also affected: several bombings in Kaduna and other Nigerian towns caused dozens of victims over the course of the year.[32]

In view of its humanitarian impact, non-state actor use of explosive weapons deserves focused attention. However, this should not detract from broader concerns around the use of explosive weapons in populated areas. In situations of armed conflict, the tendency of parties to an armed conflict—states and non-state actors alike—to conduct hostilities in populated areas places civilians at grave and perhaps increasing risk of harm.

B. The use of explosive weapons in populated areas under international humanitarian and weapons law

Antonio Cassese remarked in 1976 that: 'States have adopted two different approaches to the banning of weapons. They have either laid down general principles concerning broad and unspecified categories of weapons, or they have agreed upon restraints on the use of specific weapons.'[33] International law regulating the use of explosive weapons illustrates both of these approaches. A comprehensive treatment of the regulation of explosive weapons under IHL is beyond the scope of this chapter. The following discussion highlights some of the pertinent treaties and applicable customary rules.

WEAPON TREATIES ON SPECIFIC TYPES OF EXPLOSIVE WEAPON

The 1868 St Petersburg Declaration, the first formal agreement banning a particular weapon, outlaws the employment 'in time of war between civilized nations' of 'any projectile of a weight below 400 grammes, which is either explosive or charged with

---

[29] *AOAV Monitoring Explosive Violence in 2012*, p. 26. IED use involving the self-killing of the perpetrator ('suicide attacks') stood out as a particular concern.

[30] According to UNAMA, IEDs are the 'biggest killer of civilians' in Afghanistan: UNAMA, 'Afghanistan annual report 2012—protection of civilians in armed conflict', February 2013, p. 17.

[31] 'Suicide bombing hits Shiite pilgrims at major ritual in Iraq, 53 killed', *Xinhua*, 14 January 2012, <http://news.xinhuanet.com/english/world/2012-01/15/c_131360598.htm>.

[32] 'Nigerian church blasts kill 21 in Kaduna state', *The Guardian*, 17 June 2012, <http://www.guardian.co.uk/world/2012/jun/17/nigeria-church-blasts-kaduna>.

[33] Antonio Cassese, 'Means of warfare: the present and the emerging law', *Revue belge de droit international*, 12(1) (1976), p. 143.

fulminating or inflammable substances'.[34] At the time, the prohibition concerned explosive and incendiary rifle projectiles that were developed in the 1850s mainly to blow up ammunition wagons. A subsequent modification of a Russian projectile of this type resulted in it exploding on contact with soft substances, including human flesh. The much more severe wound that resulted compared to traditional non-explosive rifle bullets gave the impetus for the St Petersburg prohibition, which enshrines the more general rule against the 'employment of weapons, projectiles and material and methods of warfare of a nature to cause superfluous injury or unnecessary suffering'.[35]

Experts involved in the discussions at the time recognized that the technological boundary drawn at 400 grams was tenuous: some suggested the bullet was properly speaking 'a shell', and opponents of the ban questioned whether other explosive weapons were really more humane.[36] By 'fix[ing] the technical limits at which the necessities of war ought to yield to the requirements of humanity' at 400 grams, the drafters of the Declaration implicitly legitimized other explosive weapons. Mortar shells, rockets, and cannon projectiles were not considered 'contrary to the laws of humanity', but became formally part of 'the necessities of war' in spite of their humanitarian impact. It has since proven difficult under IHL to articulate humanitarian concerns relating to the degree of suffering, severity of injury, or likelihood of death resulting from explosive weapon use.[37] Concern about the humanitarian impact of explosive weapons is, thus, mainly formulated in terms of the protection of civilians. IHL rules protecting civilians from harm do not, however, provide an opportunity to link patterns of injury to specific weapon technologies.[38]

Certain agreements in the framework of the 1980 Convention on Certain Conventional Weapons (CCW) focus on the protection of civilians from the effects of explosive weapons.[39] These agreements resulted from expert discussions held in the 1970s with a

---

[34] Declaration Renouncing the Use, in Time of War, of Explosive Projectiles under 400 Grammes Weight, St Petersburg, 29 November–11 December 1868.

[35] This so-called 'SIrUS rule' is a rule of customary IHL, applicable in both international and non-international armed conflicts (IACs and NIACs, respectively): ICRC, Customary IHL Study, Rule 70.

[36] Frits Kalshoven, 'Arms, armaments and international law', *Recueil des Cours de Acadeímie de droit international de La Haye*, 191 (1985), p. 209. See also Antonio Cassese, 'Means of warfare: the present and the emerging law', pp. 149–50: 'The same projectiles were instead allowed if fired by artillery.'

[37] Concerns about the types of injury and degree of suffering caused by explosive weapons were, however, raised in expert discussions in the 1970s and in relation to explosive remnants of war. See ICRC, 'Weapons that may cause unnecessary suffering or have indiscriminate effects', Report on the Work of Experts, 1973, pp. 45–8; Timothy L. H. McCormack et al., 'Parties' responses to the questionnaire: International Humanitarian Law & Explosive Remnants of War', Report to the Group of Governmental Experts of the States Parties to the CCW, March 2006, pp. 24–5.

[38] Under IHL, civilians must not be the object of attack, and must be generally protected against the effects of hostilities. The dominant view is thus that the 'SIrUS' rule only finds application in relation to combatants (and possibly civilians directly participation in hostilities).

[39] Convention on Prohibitions or Restrictions on the Use of Certain Conventional Weapons which May be Deemed to be Excessively Injurious or to Have Indiscriminate Effects, 10 October 1980. Other relevant

view to elaborating prohibitions or restrictions on certain conventional weapons that may cause unnecessary suffering or have indiscriminate effects. In these discussions, 'explosive and penetrating weapons' were identified as one of the principal categories of weapons for consideration. By 1976, however, '[n]o general ban on blast and fragmentation weapons as a class' had been proposed, and experts 'concentrated their attention on specific weapons falling within this category'.[40] The only explicit reflection of a categorical approach to explosive weapons in modern treaty law is found in a provision of the 1980 Protocol III to the CCW, which excludes from the definition of an 'incendiary weapon', and hence from the scope of the Protocol, '[m]unitions designed to combine penetration, blast or fragmentation effects with an additional incendiary effect, such as armour-piercing projectiles, fragmentation shells, explosive bombs and similar combined-effects munitions'.[41]

A categorical approach to explosive weapons is implicit in Protocol V to the CCW, which concerns those weapons that produce explosive remnants of war (ERW). The Protocol places no restrictions on use of weapons, but establishes responsibility on users of explosive weapons to minimize their post-conflict risks and effects.[42] CCW Protocol II and Amended Protocol II impose limited prohibitions and some restrictions on the use of certain landmines, booby-traps, and other devices in order to 'protect the civilian population from unintended exposure to dangerous explosives'.[43] Amended Protocol II, notably, establishes a presumption against the use of booby-traps and other devices, including IEDs, 'in any city, town, village or other area containing a similar concentration of civilians'.[44]

---

instruments on explosive weapons are the Convention (VIII) relative to the Laying of Automatic Submarine Contact Mines, 18 October 1907, and Declaration (XIV) Prohibiting the Discharge of Projectiles and Explosives from Balloons, 18 October 1907.

[40] ICRC, 'Conference of government experts on the use of certain conventional weapons, Report, Second Session', Lugano, 28 January–26 February 1976, p. 17.

[41] Art. 1(1)(ii), Protocol on Prohibitions or Restrictions on the Use of Incendiary Weapons (Protocol III), 10 October 1980.

[42] Art. 5, Protocol on Explosive Remnants of War, 28 November 2003, and Part 3 of the Technical Annex. See also Moyes, 'Explosive violence: the problem of explosive weapons', *Landmine Action*, August 2009, p. 61.

[43] Michael N. Schmitt, 'Military necessity and humanity in international humanitarian law: preserving the delicate balance', *Virginia Journal of International Law*, 50(4) (2010), p. 814.

[44] Arts 2(5) and 7(3), Protocol on Prohibitions or Restrictions on the Use of Mines, Booby-Traps and Other Devices, as amended on 3 May 1996. IEDs designed to be exploded by the presence or proximity of, or contact with, a person or a vehicle are captured by the Protocol's provisions on mines. IEDs may also fall within the Protocol's provisions on booby-traps. Discussions by an open-ended Group of Experts established by the Tenth Annual Conference of the High Contracting Parties (2008) to Amended Protocol II on IEDs has resulted in a 'Compilation of existing guidelines, best practices, and other recommendations aimed at addressing the diversion or illicit use of materials which can be used for IEDs' (<http://www.unog.ch>), to be updated on an ongoing basis. For analysis, see Geneva Academy of International Humanitarian Law and Human Rights (ADH), 'A need for greater restrictions on the use of improvised explosive devices?', 'Food-for-thought' paper, Geneva, 24 April 2012.

Two instruments take matters further and completely ban two types of explosive weapon. The 1997 Anti-Personnel Mine Ban Convention (APMBC) prohibits the use, development, production, acquisition, stockpiling, retention, or transfer of any kind, and under any circumstances, of anti-personnel mines, as defined under the Convention.[45] A similar treaty prohibition was agreed in 2008 on cluster munitions.[46] Both treaties impose obligations to destroy stockpiles and to clear contaminated land within specified time periods. The 2008 CCM also contains ground-breaking provisions for the benefit of victims of cluster munitions.[47] The process bringing about the CCM was informed by evidence of the human cost of cluster-munition use, and oriented toward devising legal standards that effectively prevent such 'unacceptable harm'. This orientation has raised questions about the humanitarian impact of explosive weapons more broadly, especially those with wide-area effects.[48]

RULES GOVERNING THE CONDUCT OF HOSTILITIES

Explosive weapons are not formally recognized as a distinct weapon category under international law, but explosive weapons as a means of warfare and their use as a method of warfare are regulated by the rules of IHL governing the conduct of hostilities.[49] The starting point is that '[i]n any armed conflict, the right of the Parties to the conflict to choose methods or means of warfare is not unlimited', and that, in order to ensure respect for and protect the civilian population and civilian objects, parties to an armed conflict 'shall at all times distinguish between the civilian population and combatants and between civilian objects and military objectives and accordingly shall direct their operations only against military objectives'. Consequently, civilians and civilian objects may not be targeted, and the civilian population and individual civilians enjoy 'general protection ... against dangers arising from military operations'. To give effect to this protection, indiscriminate attacks are prohibited under IHL. The 1977 Additional Protocol I to the 1949 Geneva Conventions defines indiscriminate attacks as:

---

[45] Art. 1, Convention on the Prohibition of the Use, Stockpiling, Production and Transfer of Anti-Personnel Mines and on their Destruction, 18 September 1997.

[46] Art. 1, Convention on Cluster Munitions (CCM), 30 May 2008.

[47] See Bonnie Docherty, 'Breaking new ground: The Convention on Cluster Munitions and the evolution of international humanitarian law', *Human Rights Quarterly*, 31(4) (2009).

[48] John Borrie, *Unacceptable Harm: A History of How the Treaty to Ban Cluster Munitions was Won*, United Nations, Geneva, 2009, p. 335.

[49] On the concept of 'hostilities', see Nils Melzer, *Targeted Killing in International Law*, Oxford University Press, Oxford, 2008, pp. 269–78.

(a) those which are not directed at a specific military objective;

(b) those which employ a method or means of combat which cannot be directed at a specific military objective; or

(c) those which employ a method or means of combat the effects of which cannot be limited as required by this Protocol; and consequently, in each such case, are of a nature to strike military objectives and civilians or civilian objects without distinction.[50]

Also, with a view to protecting the civilian population, parties to an armed conflict must take 'constant care . . . to spare the civilian population, civilians and civilian objects', including by avoiding locating 'military objectives within or near densely populated areas', and by taking 'all feasible precautions in the choice of means and methods of attack with a view to avoiding, and in any event to minimizing, incidental loss of civilian life, injury to civilians and damage to civilian objects'.[51]

EXPLOSIVE WEAPONS WITH WIDE-AREA EFFECTS AND THE PROHIBITION ON INDISCRIMINATE ATTACKS

The use of explosive weapons in close proximity to places where civilians live, work, or congregate raises significant challenges under the above rules. The use, in populated areas, of explosive weapons that affect a wide area with blast and fragmentation has been singled out as a particular concern for the protection of civilians. Such use is associated with consistently high levels of harm to civilians, and calls have been voiced to put an end to this practice, including by the UN Secretary-General. In his 2012 report on the protection of civilians in armed conflict to the Security Council, he urged all parties to conflict 'to refrain from using explosive weapons with a wide-area impact in densely populated areas'.[52]

Wide-area effects can be due to several factors: an individual explosive weapon having a large blast or fragmentation radius; multiple explosive weapons being launched at an area; insufficient precision in the delivery of an explosive weapon; or a combination of

---

[50] Art. 51(4), Protocol Additional to the Geneva Conventions of 12 August 1949, and relating to the Protection of Victims of International Armed Conflicts (Protocol I), 8 June 1977. The prohibition on indiscriminate attacks is a rule of customary international law applicable in both international and non-international armed conflicts. See ICRC, Customary IHL Study, Rules 11 and 12.

[51] Arts 48, 51, and 57, 1977 Additional Protocol I.

[52] 'Report of the Secretary-General on the Protection of Civilians in Armed Conflict', UN doc. S/2012/ 376, 22 May 2012, §75. See also ICRC, 'International humanitarian law and the challenges of contemporary armed conflicts', Doc. 31IC/11/5.1.2, October 2011, pp. 4 and 42. See also 'Report of the Special Representative of the Secretary-General for Children and Armed Conflict', UN doc. A/67/256, 6 August 2012, §69. Statements to this effect were also made by, among others, Austria, Belgium, Germany, Sweden, and the European Union: <http://www.inew.org/acknowledgements>.

these factors.[53] Humanitarian concern around the use of weapons with wide-area effects in populated areas is often expressed in terms of the use of 'heavy weapons' in populated centres.[54] UN Security Council Resolution 2042 (2012) and the annexed Six-Point Proposal of the Joint Special Envoy of the UN and the League of Arab States, for instance, calls on the Syrian government to 'cease all use of heavy weapons in such centres'.[55]

In the absence of a weapon-specific treaty, it is unclear what the prohibition on indiscriminate attacks implies for the use, in populated areas, of explosive weapons with wide-area effects.[56] Doctrine distinguishes between the permissibility of a weapon (means of warfare)—which can be said to be 'per se', 'by nature', or 'inherently' indiscriminate, and hence violates IHL in *all* circumstances—and the permissibility of particular uses made of the weapon (methods of warfare), which may or may not violate IHL, depending on the circumstances. As a matter of customary international law, 'the use of weapons which are by nature indiscriminate is prohibited'.[57] V1 and V2 rockets, Scud missiles, or Katyusha rockets are widely considered to be such indiscriminate weapons, even in the absence of a treaty prohibition, on the grounds that they *cannot be directed* at a specific military objective. Reference is to the rule expressed in Article 51(4)(b) of the 1977 Additional Protocol I.[58] In contrast, the effect of the other prongs of the prohibition on indiscriminate attacks on the legality of other explosive weapons, and their use in a particular setting, remains subject to controversy.[59] Can the effects of an attack by long-range artillery or unguided mortars, of a 500kg air-dropped bomb, of a multiple barrel rocket launcher, or of a cluster-munition strike on targets in a populated

---

[53] Ben Clarke, 'Proportionality in armed conflicts: a principle in need of clarification?', *International Humanitarian Legal Studies*, 3(1) (2012), p. 113. For illustrations, see AOAV, 'Wide of the mark: Syria and the use of explosive weapons with wide area effects', December 2012.

[54] 'Heavy weapons' are not formally reflected in IHRL or IHL instruments, but in connection with arms control, the term evokes the divide between small arms and light weapons (SALW) and major conventional weapons, a distinction oriented toward different-sized calibres and the portability of weapons. The primary issue of humanitarian concern is death and injury to civilians, and damage to civilian objects from the use of heavy *explosive* weapons in populated areas. See Richard Moyes, Maya Brehm, and Thomas Nash, 'Heavy weapons and civilian protection', *Article 36*, August 2012, <http://www.article36.org/wp-content/uploads/2012/08/Heavy-weapons-and-civilian-protection.pdf>.

[55] UN Security Council Resolution 2042 (14 April 2012). A Presidential Statement reiterates this call in similar terms: UN doc. S/PRST/2012/10, 5 April 2012, <http://daccess-dds-ny.un.org/doc/UNDOC/GEN/N12/285/18/PDF/N1228518.pdf?OpenElement>.

[56] The general rules of IHL governing the conduct of hostilities 'do not amount to safe standards of conduct' when it comes to the permissibility of weapon use, with 'distressing' results: Cassese, 'Means of warfare: the present and the emerging law', p. 147.

[57] ICRC, Customary IHL Study, Rule 71. International Court of Justice (ICJ), *Legality of the Threat or Use of Nuclear Weapons*, Advisory Opinion, 8 July 1996, §78.

[58] See, notably, ICRC, Customary IHL Study, Practice Relating to Rule 71.

[59] ICRC, Commentary on the Additional Protocols of 8 June 1977 to the Geneva Conventions of 12 August 1949, 1987 (ICRC Commentary on the 1977 Additional Protocols), §1424: 'Certain other weapons that may have an indiscriminate effect continue to be the object of controversy...These include, for example, certain blast and fragmentation weapons...'

area really be 'limited as required' under IHL? Or are such attacks 'of a nature to strike military objectives and civilians or civilian objects without distinction'?

These questions, it is routinely argued, must be decided on a case-by-case basis, taking into account the particular circumstances of the attack. According to the dominant doctrinal view, no generic determination can be made of the permissibility of a weapon, nor of its use in a set of circumstances (such as, in populated areas), as long as there are conceivable circumstances (however hypothetical) in which the weapon could be used in compliance with IHL. It is submitted that an approach purely based on a case-by-case analysis, and the tendency to consider weapons as indiscriminate only when they cannot be accurately delivered, unduly limits the potential of the prohibition on indiscriminate attacks to protect civilians against the effects of explosive weapons.[60] Participants in a 1973 ICRC expert meeting felt that the fact that weapons are capable of being used indiscriminately is 'a ground for prohibiting *such types of use*' and that 'the *normal or typical use* of the weapons may be one which has indiscriminate effects'.[61] Many of the drafters of Article 51(4)(c) of the 1977 Additional Protocol I were of the view that:

[T]he definition [of the term 'indiscriminate attacks'] was *not* intended to mean that there are means or methods of combat whose use would involve an indiscriminate attack in *all* circumstances. Rather it was intended to take account of the fact that means or methods of combat which can be used perfectly legitimately in some situations could, in other circumstances, have effects that would be contrary to some limitations contained in the Protocol, in which event *their use in those circumstances would involve an indiscriminate attack.*[62]

The ICRC noted in 2011, in respect to explosive weapons, that: 'A circumstance that could make the use of a certain weapon indiscriminate is certainly its use in a densely populated area'.[63]

---

[60] Cassese notes that 'the prohibitory intent of those rules [the general rules banning indiscriminate weapons] has proved scarcely effective' and that the majority's position on this question is 'tantamount to saying that States consider the general principle on indiscriminate weapons to have become valueless': A. Cassese, 'The prohibition of indiscriminate means of warfare' in Antonio Cassese, Paola Gaeta, and Salvatore Zappalà, *The Human Dimension of International Law: Selected Papers of Antonio Cassese*, Oxford University Press, Oxford, 2008, pp. 183–5.

[61] ICRC, 'Weapons that may cause unnecessary suffering or have indiscriminate effects', Report on the Work of Experts, 1973, §27 (emphasis added).

[62] ICRC Commentary on the 1977 Additional Protocols, §1962 (emphasis added). At §1963, the Commentary cites the example of the use of an explosive weapon in a populated area: '[I]f a 10 ton bomb is used to destroy a single building, it is inevitable that the effects will be very extensive and will annihilate or damage neighboring buildings, while a less powerful missile would suffice to destroy the building.'

[63] ICRC, 'International humanitarian law and the challenges of contemporary armed conflicts', Doc. 31IC/11/5.1.2, October 2011, p. 41. Consider also ICRC Commentary on the 1977 Additional Protocols, §§2185 and 2190 in respect of Art. 57, 1977 Additional Protocol I: '[T]he precautions prescribed here will be of greatest importance in urban areas because such areas are most densely populated'; noting also that some of the drafters feared the 'general rule of bombardments of reducing incidental loss to a minimum was insufficient for this particular situation [bombardments on towns and cities behind the lines]'.

The prohibition on area bombardment

A categorical approach to the use of explosive weapons with wide-area effects in populated areas finds some recognition in the prohibition on area bombardment, one of two indicative examples of indiscriminate attacks listed in Article 51(5) of the 1977 Additional Protocol I. 'Area bombardment' is defined as 'an attack by bombardment by any methods or means which treats as a single military objective a number of clearly separated and distinct military objectives located in a city, town, village or other area containing a similar concentration of civilians or civilian objects'.[64] The provision demonstrates that the prohibition on indiscriminate attacks itself evolved with particular reference to explosive weapons. The prohibition is a response to the devastating effects of 'saturation' or 'carpet' bombing of population centres practised during and following the 1939–45 War, but it equally applies to use of ground-launched explosive weapons ('except for direct fire by small arms').[65]

The prohibition reflects concern for the protection of civilians when explosive weapons are used in the context of 'a city, town, village or other area containing a similar concentration of civilians or civilian objects'.[66] 'Populated area', 'densely populated area', and 'concentration of civilians' are well-established, largely equivalent legal notions used in various instruments in relation to the protection of civilians from the effects of hostilities. Importantly, these locations can be of temporary nature. CCW Protocol III, for instance, defines 'concentration of civilians' as 'any concentration of civilians, be it permanent or temporary, such as in inhabited parts of cities, or inhabited towns or villages, or as in camps or columns of refugees or evacuees, or groups of nomads'.[67]

The provision on area bombardment has been said to specify 'in clear and unambiguous terms the circumstances under which a means of combat is illegal for its

---

[64] Art. 51(5)(a), 1977 Additional Protocol I. The term 'area bombardment' is not used in the Protocol, but under customary IHL, the norm is generally referred to as the prohibition on 'area bombardment': ICRC, Customary IHL Study, Rule 13.

[65] ICRC Commentary on the 1977 Additional Protocols, §1968. For a detailed discussion, see Hans Blix, 'Area bombardment: rules and reasons', *British Yearbook of International Law*, 49(1) (1987), pp. 31–69. Note that the rule on area bombardment is also reflected in Art. 3(9) of CCW Amended Protocol II.

[66] For an overview of legal rules specifically addressing 'bombardment', see Avril McDonald and Thomas Bruha, 'Bombardment', *Max Planck Encyclopaedia of Public International Law*, <http://www.mpepil.com>. Some provisions in the ICTY and the ICC Statutes retain the differentiation between 'bombardment' and attacks. It is doubtful, though, that the specific mention of bombardment retains legal significance for the regulation of the conduct of hostilities today. At least since the adoption of the 1977 Additional Protocol I, bombardment has been subsumed under the broader notion of 'attack'. For a discussion, see Maya Brehm, *Protecting Civilians from the Effects of Explosive Weapons: An Analysis of International Legal and Policy Standards*, United Nations, Geneva, 2012, pp. 130–3.

[67] See Art. 4(2), CCW Protocol II; Art. 7(3), CCW Amended Protocol II; Arts 1(2) and 2(2), CCW Protocol III.

indiscriminateness'.[68] Yet grave harm to civilians from the bombing and shelling of cities, towns, and villages testifies to its limits. Although the shelling of an entire residential area of a town is forbidden if clearly separated and distinct military objects within that area or town can be targeted separately, this formulation leaves some degree of latitude in determining when military objectives should be considered to be 'clearly separated and distinct'. Moreover, the determination of whether such separate targeting is feasible is taken with a view to 'the means available' to the attacker, and it is not clear how this assessment is made.[69]

Another challenge relates to the spatial delimitation of military objectives. A military objective itself can be of considerable size. 'Barrage fire', for instance, is 'designed to fill a volume of space or area rather than aimed specifically at a given target', and 'distributed fire' aims at dispersing fire 'to engage most effectively an area target'. This typically involves the use of 'area weapons', such as cluster munitions.[70] It has been noted that 'area weapons have an obvious and uncontrollable tendency towards indiscriminateness'.[71] While cluster munitions are subject to a treaty ban, in part because of their indiscriminate 'area effects',[72] the distribution of explosive force over an area by firing salvos of rockets at it is still a fairly common practice.[73] According to the ICRC Commentary on 1977 Additional Protocol I, area targeting could 'of course . . . only concern limited areas and not vast stretches of territory', applying 'primarily to narrow passages, bridgeheads or strategic points such as hills or mountain passes'. Presumably, this is because even area targeting has to comply with the prohibition on disproportionate attacks.[74]

The prohibition on disproportionate attacks

The second indicative example of an indiscriminate attack given in the 1977 Additional Protocol I concerns a disproportionate attack, defined as 'an attack which may be

---

[68] Cassese, 'The prohibition of indiscriminate means of warfare', p. 186.

[69] ICRC Commentary on the 1977 Additional Protocols, §§1972 and 1975; Blix, 'Area bombardment: rules and reasons', p. 66.

[70] See the definitions provided in NATO, 'NATO glossary of terms and definitions', Doc. AAP-06(2012) (2), 2012, pp. 2-B-1 and 2-D-8. The glossary defines an area target as a 'a target consisting of an area rather than a single point' (p. 2-A-18). Mortars and artillery are generally considered 'area weapons'. See e.g. UN doc. A/HRC/12/48, 25 September 2009, §697.

[71] ICRC, 'Weapons that may cause unnecessary suffering or have indiscriminate effects', 1973, p. 48.

[72] Art. 2(2)(c), CCM. Cluster munitions are also described as 'area weapons' in ICRC, 'Humanitarian, military, technical and legal challenges of cluster munitions', Montreux, Switzerland, 18–20 April 2007, p. 17.

[73] An M270 multiple launch rocket system (MLRS) can fire 12 rockets in less than a minute. Multiple barrel rocket launchers are unsuited for point-targeting, and their use is considered inappropriate in populated areas by some. See e.g. page 4 of 'Lt.-General Applegate's Comments on Expert Witness Reports' in Public Annex I to the Notice of Filing of Public Redacted Version of Prosecution Response to Gotovina's Second Rule 115 Motion, and Request for Change in Status of Corrigendum, 3 August 2012, <http://icr.icty.org/LegalRef/CMSDocStore/Public/English/Notice/NotIndexable/IT-06-90-A/MOT8710R0000360087.pdf>.

[74] ICRC Commentary on the 1977 Additional Protocols, §1955.

expected to cause incidental loss of civilian life, injury to civilians, damage to civilian objects, or a combination thereof, which would be excessive in relation to the concrete and direct military advantage anticipated'.[75] The difficulties, uncertainties, and considerable disagreement surrounding this rule have been discussed extensively in doctrine and jurisprudence.[76] Suffice it to say here that although the presence of civilians and civilian objects, and population density, must play a role in determining the legality of area targeting, the act of balancing involved in a proportionality assessment does not in and of itself prevent extensive (as opposed to excessive) civilian harm.[77]

A related concern is the wide-ranging and potentially long-term negative effects on the civilian population that can result from the use, in populated areas, of explosive weapons with wide-area effects. Explosive weapons have an extraordinary capacity to reduce the built environment to rubble.[78] The protection of homes, bridges, market stalls, electricity generation facilities, water pumping stations, and hospitals is a critical component in the protection of civilians during armed conflict. But the protection under IHL of civilian objects from attack varies, is not absolute, and public services' infrastructure is at particular risk of becoming a legitimate military objective.[79] In the past, these concerns have been articulated in terms of the question to what extent 'reverberating' and 'cumulative' effects should be factored into the proportionality assessment. It remains a matter of dispute which indirect or long-term effects on civilians are 'foreseeable' and should, hence, be 'expected' to cause disproportionate civilian harm.[80] To what extent these debates have supported an interpretation of the proportionality rule that is more protective of civilian objects, and by extension civilians, is unclear.

---

[75] Art. 51(5)(b), 1977 Additional Protocols. Launching a disproportionate attack is prohibited under customary IHL applicable in both IACs and NIACs: ICRC, Customary IHL Study, Rule 14.

[76] For a recent overview, see Clarke, 'Proportionality in armed conflicts: a principle in need of clarification?', pp. 73–123.

[77] The contrary view is expressed in ICRC Commentary on the 1977 Additional Protocols, §1980. This interpretation has been challenged. See e.g. Michael N. Schmitt, 'Precision attack and international humanitarian law', *International Review of the Red Cross*, 87(859) (September 2005), p. 457.

[78] See e.g. 'Syria's civil war leaves its cities, economy and cultural heritage in shambles', *Associated Press*, 9 October 2012, <http://www.foxnews.com/world/2012/10/09/syria-civil-war-leaves-its-cities-economy-and-cultural-heritage-in-shambles/>.

[79] For a discussion, see Brehm, *Protecting Civilians from the Effects of Explosive Weapons*, pp. 125–9; see also Thomas W. Smith, 'The new law of war: legitimizing hi-tech and infrastructural violence', *International Studies Quarterly*, 46 (2002), pp. 355–74.

[80] See ICTY, *Prosecutor v. Kupreškić and ors*, Judgment (Trial Chamber) (Case No. ICTY-95-16-T), 14 January 2000, §526; Final Report to the Prosecutor by the Committee Established to Review the NATO Bombing Campaign against the Federal Republic of Yugoslavia, §52, <http://www.icty.org/sid/10052>; McCormack et al., 'Parties' responses to the questionnaire: International Humanitarian Law & Explosive Remnants of War', pp. 18–21; HRW, 'Responses to the IHL and ERW questionnaire and the McCormack Report', Memorandum to CCW Delegates, March 2006. For a more recent discussion, see Rebecca J. Barber, 'The proportionality equation: balancing military objectives with civilian lives in the armed conflict in Afghanistan', *Journal of Conflict and Security Law*, 15(3) (2010), pp. 480–1.

CLUSTER MUNITIONS

There have been several reports of Syrian armed forces using cluster munitions in 2012 (and continuing into 2013) in populated areas.[81] There is ample evidence that the use of cluster munitions causes unacceptably high levels of civilian harm, both in the short and long terms. Concern about their wide-area effects has been raised for decades,[82] states have on numerous occasions called for an end to their use in concentrations of civilians,[83] several UN special rapporteurs have expressed the view that 'to blanket an area occupied by large numbers of civilians with small and volatile explosives' would have an impact that would 'obviously be indiscriminate',[84] the ICTY Trial Chamber in the *Martić* case described the M-87 Orkan cluster munition as a 'non-guided high dispersion weapon' and as 'an indiscriminate weapon',[85] and more than 80 states consider cluster munitions unacceptable and have formally committed to eliminate these explosive weapons.[86]

In spite of all this, the Commission of Inquiry investigating the use of cluster munitions *in populated urban areas* in Syria found itself unable to report anything more definite by the end of 2012 than that it was assessing '*whether* the use of cluster munitions was indiscriminate'.[87] Although the treaty ban on cluster munitions has not, as yet, crystallized into a customary prohibition applicable to all states, the existence of the CCM and the reasons underlying its adoption should at the very least give rise to the presumption that the use of cluster munitions in populated areas is incompatible with IHL.[88]

---

[81] HRW, 'Syria: mounting casualties from cluster munitions', 16 March 2013, <http://www.hrw.org/news/2013/03/16/syria-mounting-casualties-cluster-munitions>.

[82] See e.g. Eric Prokosch, 'Armes à fragmentation: tendances actuelles', *International Review of the Red Cross*, 57(684) (1975), p. 712.

[83] One example is the 'Declaration on Cluster Munitions' by 25 states at the Third Review Conference of the States Parties to the CCW, UN doc. CCW/CONF.III/WP.18, 20 November 2006.

[84] 'Report of the Special Rapporteur on extrajudicial, summary or arbitrary executions, Philip Alston; the Special Rapporteur on the right of everyone to the enjoyment of the highest attainable standard of physical and mental health, Paul Hunt; the Representative of the Secretary-General on human rights of internally displaced persons, Walter Kälin; and the Special Rapporteur on adequate housing as a component of the right to an adequate standard of living, Miloon Kothari—Mission to Lebanon and Israel (7–14 September 2006)', UN doc. A/HRC/2/7, 2 October 2006, §56.

[85] ICTY, *Prosecutor v. Martić*, Judgment (Trial Chamber) (Case No. ICTY-95-11-T), 12 June 2007, §463.

[86] By end May 2012, the CCM had 83 states parties. A further 28 signatories were bound under international law to refrain from acts that would defeat the object and purpose of the treaty.

[87] 'Independent International Commission of Inquiry on the Syrian Arab Republic established pursuant to United Nations Human Rights Council Resolutions S-17/1, 19/22 and 21/26', Periodic Update, 20 December 2012, §41 (emphasis added.)

[88] Some consider that cluster munitions are 'indiscriminate by their nature', e.g. Darren Vallentgoed, 'The last round? A post-Gotovina reassessment of the legality of using artillery against built-up areas', *Journal of Conflict and Security Law*, 18(1) (2013), p. 41.

The IACtHR also dealt with cluster munitions use in the context of a populated area, in the case of *Santo Domingo Massacre v. Colombia*, decided on 30 November 2012.[89] In December 1998, the Colombian air force had dropped a cluster munition (of the type AN-M1A2) on the centre of the village of Santo Domingo (Colombia) in the course of a 'counter-guerrilla offensive'. The attack killed 17 people and injured 27 others, including many children, and caused the displacement of the village's inhabitants. The Court, interpreting the 1969 American Convention on Human Rights (ACHR) in light of the relevant rules of IHL, addressed the rules of proportionality and of distinction, but its analysis focused on the obligation to take precautionary measures. The Court highlighted a variety of factors about the cluster munition, including the wide impact area of its six submunitions. It called the cluster munition an imprecise weapon ('*una arma imprecisa*') and considered that the use of any air-dropped explosive weapon ('*armamento explosivo*') was dangerous, and therefore needed to be strictly controlled to ensure that damage would be caused *only* to the selected target. The Court found that the instructions given for the weapon's employment were imprecise, especially with respect to the minimum distance of the strike location to the village, and noted that military manuals in use in December 1998 indicated that this type of weapon should not be used in or near a populated area. In view of the weapon's lethality and its limited accuracy ('*capacidad letal y la precisión limitada*') the Court concluded that the use of the cluster munition in or near the village of Santo Domingo violated the attacker's precautionary obligations under IHL, and consequently, amounted to a violation, by Colombia, of the rights to life and to physical, mental, and moral integrity under the ACHR.[90]

ARTILLERY SHELLING OF POPULATED AREAS

Another case decided in November 2012, the ICTY Appeals Chamber judgment in the *Gotovina* case, may have far-reaching ramifications for assessing the permissibility of explosive weapons with wide-area effects in populated areas. Colonel General Ante Gotovina was a Croatian commander in charge of the military offensive ('Operation Storm') launched on 4 August 1995 to retake the Krajina region of Croatia. The ICTY Trial Chamber found Gotovina guilty for joint criminal enterprise with respect to war crimes and crimes against humanity committed by artillery shelling of several towns.[91]

---

[89] IACtHR, *Caso Masacre de Santo Domingo v. Colombia*, Judgment, Series C No. 259, 30 November 2012, §§210–30 (in Spanish).

[90] Arts 4(1) and 5(1), 1969 ACHR.

[91] Unlawful shelling was not charged in the indictment as a separate offence, but allegations of unlawful shelling are implicit in charges of crimes against humanity and violations of the laws and customs of war. Unlawful shelling was the primary basis of Gotovina's conviction by the Trial Chamber. For more information about the case, see Walter B. Huffmann, 'Margin of error: potential pitfalls of the ruling in *The Prosecutor v. Ante Gotovina*', *Military Law Review*, 211 (Spring 2012), pp. 1–56.

The shelling involved long-range, unobserved fire from 130mm tube artillery and 122mm BM-21 multiple barrel rocket launchers. The Trial Chamber noted that multiple barrel rocket launchers 'are generally less accurate than Howitzers or mortars', but that their use 'was not inherently indiscriminate'.[92] But it also found that 'even a small number of artillery projectiles can have great effects on nearby civilians', and evaluated a range of factors to assess the permissibility of the shelling, including the accuracy of artillery, the blast and fragmentation effects of artillery shells, the time of shelling and the likelihood and number of civilians present in the target area, the number and calibre of shells fired, and the distance they were fired from.[93]

Although recognized as having 'the potential to be a great beacon for international law by adding significant definition to the legal paradigm' that governs 'complex targeting decisions involving the use of artillery against ... military objectives in populated areas', the trial judgment was also heavily criticized.[94] One key point of contention was the Trial Chamber's decision—in respect of the low percentage of artillery projectiles for which it could establish impact sites—to treat projectiles that impacted within a distance of 200 metres of an identified artillery target as deliberately fired at that artillery target.[95] The Trial Chamber considered the error margin of 200 metres—the length of two soccer fields—to be a generous margin, to the benefit of the accused. By contrast, projectiles that impacted further away from an identified military target served as an indicator of an unlawful attack on civilians and civilian objects.

The Appeals Chamber judgment focused almost exclusively on this '200-metre standard', treating it as the 'cornerstone and the organising principle' of the Trial Chamber's 'Impact Analysis'. The majority of the Appeals Chamber considered that the Trial Chamber had committed a legal error by failing to give a 'specific basis on which it arrived at a 200 metre margin of error'.[96] Having done away with the 200-metre standard, the majority then found it could not:

... exclude the possibility that all of the impact sites considered in the Trial Judgement were the result of shelling aimed at targets that the Trial Chamber considered to be legitimate. The fact that a relatively large number of shells fell more than 200 metres from fixed artillery targets could be consistent with a much broader range of error.[97]

---

[92] *Prosecutor v. Ante Gotovina and ors*, Judgment (Trial Chamber) (Case No. ICTY-06-90-T), 15 April 2011, §1897.

[93] *Prosecutor v. Ante Gotovina and ors*, Judgment (Trial Chamber), 15 April 2011, §1910.

[94] International Humanitarian Law Clinic, Emory University School of Law, *Operational Law Experts Roundtable on the Gotovina Judgment: Military Operations, Battlefield Reality and the Judgment's Impact on Effective Implementation and Enforcement of International Humanitarian Law*, p. 2, <http://www.antegotovina.com/doc/Gotovina_Meeting_Report.pdf>.

[95] *Prosecutor v. Gotovina and ors*, Judgment (Trial Chamber), §1898.

[96] *Prosecutor v. Ante Gotovina and ors*, Judgment (Appeals Chamber) (Case No. ICTY-06-90-A), 16 November 2012, §64.

[97] *Prosecutor v. Ante Gotovina and ors*, Judgment (Appeals Chamber), 16 November 2012, §65.

Evidence of unlawful attacks was thus considered inconclusive, and the convictions were reversed.

Two strongly worded dissenting opinions were joined to this judgment. Judge Agius expressed concern that the majority had lost sight 'of the essential question in this appeals case, being whether, based on the totality of the evidence, it was reasonable for the Trial Chamber to conclude that the attacks on the Four Towns were unlawful'. In his view, the majority erroneously regarded the 200-metre standard as the critical piece underpinning all of the Trial Chamber's finding, failed to show that the Trial Chamber had committed an error of law, patently failed to articulate any legal standard with which to replace the 200-metre standard, and instead had adopted an 'unacceptably speculative' approach, in effect, raising the acceptable margin of error ad infinitum.[98] Judge Pocar found the majority's approach 'wholly erroneous'. In his view, the Appeals Chamber failed in its mission to clarify the correct legal standard, and, therefore, omitted to assess whether the shelling attacks on the towns were lawful or not. In the words of Judge Pocar, 'the paucity of the legal analysis in the Majority's reasoning opens more questions than it provides legal answers'. The questions Judge Pocar outlines are critical not only to the application of international criminal law, but also, more fundamentally, to the application of core rules on the conduct of hostilities:

> Does the Majority consider that the correct legal standard was a 400-metre standard? A 100-metre standard? A 0-metre standard?...Does the Majority consider that a legal standard can be established on a margin of error of artillery weapons? Does the Majority consider that a trial chamber is entitled in law to establish a presumption of legality to assess the evidence of the shelling attacks and the artillery impacts in order to establish the lawfulness of the attack? Is a trial chamber not limited in its analysis to the strict application of IHL principles?...Does the Majority consider that the Trial Chamber should have applied the principles of customary IHL in its analysis? If so, which exact IHL principles should the Trial Chamber have applied in assessing whether the artillery attack was lawful? Does the Majority consider that the minimum applicable legal standard was to analyse whether the shelling was aimed at targeting military objectives offering a definite military advantage, whether it was done in respect of the principle of proportionality and after all precautionary measures had been taken?[99]

The foregoing discussion about cluster munition strikes and artillery shelling in populated areas suggests that IHL, as applied in practice, does not establish a strong barrier against the use of explosive weapons with wide-area effects in such settings. In light of the great destructive power of explosive weapons and the pattern of civilian harm associated with their use in populated areas, it may therefore be necessary to strengthen

---

[98] Dissenting Opinion of Judge Carmel Agius, *Prosecutor v. Gotovina*, Judgment (Appeals Chamber), 16 November 2012, §§3, 20–1.

[99] Dissenting Opinion of Judge Fausto Pocar, *Prosecutor v. Gotovina*, Judgment (Appeals Chamber), 16 November 2012, §§5, 13–14.

key IHL rules on the conduct of hostilities. In order to better protect civilians, greater constraints on the use of explosive weapons with wide-area effects are needed. Support for such a direction can already be found in legal doctrine and operational policies of states.[100]

C. **The use of explosive weapons under international human rights law**

Due to their blast and fragmentation effects, the use of explosive weapons raises a host of human rights concerns, first and foremost in relation to the right to life. Human rights are inherent to all human beings and it is almost universally accepted today that IHRL applies at all times, including in situations of armed conflict.[101] As is clear from the foregoing discussion, explosive weapons tend to be associated with military action. Nevertheless, concern about the humanitarian impacts of explosive violence extends beyond use of force governed by the rules of IHL, not least because, in practice, the boundary between the conduct of hostilities and use of lethal force for other purposes is often contested.

States do not, as a general rule, use explosive weapons for law enforcement. But explosive weapons risk making increasing inroads into policing, especially in the context of the fight against organized crime and efforts to combat terrorism.[102] Since 2009,

---

[100] Consider restrictions on the use of 'indirect fire' in populated areas, and the designation of restricted or no-fire zones: Rule 27(A), *Rules of Engagement Handbook*, International Institute of Humanitarian Law, San Remo, 2009; 'For the record: Maj. Gen. Nathan Mugisha discusses civilian casualties', *AMISOM News Bulletin*, 30 November 2010; 'Comments by Major General Ashmore' in 'Public Annex III to the Notice of Filing of Public Redacted Version of Prosecution Response to Gotovina's Second Rule 115 Motion, and Request for Change in Status of Corrigendum, 3 August 2012', <http://icr.icty.org/LegalRef/CMSDocStore/Public/English/Notice/NotIndexable/IT-06-90-A/MOT8710R0000360087.pdf>. Consider also increasing restrictions on airstrikes by the NATO International Security Assistance Force (ISAF) in Afghanistan: Eric Schmitt, 'Allies restrict airstrikes on Taliban in civilian homes', *New York Times*, 10 June 2012. See the statement of Turkey in European Commission of Human Rights, *Cagirga v. Turkey*, Decision (App. No. 21895/93), 19 October 1994, discarding the use of 'long-range weapons' in a populated area. See also suggestions for reforming IHL by Peter Rowe, 'Kosovo 1999: The air campaign', *International Review of the Red Cross*, 82(837) (2000), <http://www.icrc.org/eng/resources/documents/misc/57jqct.htm>; Clarke, 'Proportionality in armed conflicts: a principle in need of clarification?', p. 113; Vallentgoed, 'The last round? a post-Gotovina reassessment of the legality of using artillery against built-up areas', p. 39 ('there may well be no place for artillery in cities').

[101] ICJ, *Legal Consequences of the Construction of a Wall in the Occupied Palestinian Territory*, Advisory Opinion, 9 July 2004, §106.

[102] Explosives play a limited role in policing. Usually reserved to special units, they are used for breaching, as decoys, or in flash-bang grenades. Against the background of growing militarization of policing and the increasing use of military forces for law enforcement in some societies, 'military weaponry', including explosive weapons, risks being increasingly used for law enforcement tasks. This trend is furthered by the

several Mexican state police forces have been equipped with explosive (fragmentation) hand grenades to close the so-called 'calibre gap' in the escalating fight against drug cartels, and requests for more such weapons are pending.[103] The year 2012 also saw the continued use of drones to deliver explosive weapons. Some drone strikes were carried out by the US Central Intelligence Agency (CIA), purportedly in action taken against persons suspected of terrorist offences.

Recourse by states to explosive force is also a reaction to increasing use of explosive weapons by non-state armed actors (discussed above). Other non-state actors' access to explosives tends to be strictly limited to specified civilian applications. They are, usually, not allowed to own or use explosive weapons, and the prevention and repression of terrorist 'bombings' is the subject of a number of international treaties. In spite of this, IEDs and other explosive weapons will likely continue to play a prominent role in non-state actor armed violence. Although there is growing recognition that non-state actors can, under certain circumstances, be bound by IHRL,[104] the following discussion focuses on the use of lethal force by states.

THE USE OF EXPLOSIVE WEAPONS FOR PURPOSES OTHER THAN THE CONDUCT OF HOSTILITIES

Use of explosive weapons against or among persons clearly involves a grave risk to human life. Human rights treaties formulate the right to life—generally, a non-derogable right—in terms of protection from 'arbitrary' deprivation of life. Translating subjective human rights into rules of conduct for state officials, the 1979 Code of Conduct for Law Enforcement Officials and the more detailed 1990 Basic Principles on the Use of Force and Firearms by Law Enforcement Officials (BPUFF) set out the circumstances and modalities of the use of force for law enforcement purposes, whether by members of the police or military or other state security forces who carry out law enforcement tasks.[105]

---

development of smaller and lighter explosive weapons (grenades, small mortar rounds), and of cartridge-based explosive projectiles with the significant risk of anti-personnel applications. Such weapons (such as the XM25 Counter-Defilade Target Engagement System, the FRAG-12 explosive shotgun round, or the K11 dual-calibre air-burst weapon) are increasingly used in the military context, where they constitute a challenge to the scope of the customary prohibition on exploding bullets.

[103] Geoffrey Ramsey, 'Mexican state police seek increased firepower', *InSight Crime: Organized Crime in the Americas*, 22 February 2011; H. Guerra, 'The use of hand grenades in Mexico', pp. 4–5.

[104] For a brief introduction, see e.g. Office of the UN High Commissioner for Human Rights (OHCHR), *International Legal Protection of Human Rights in Armed Conflict*, 2011, pp. 23–7.

[105] Code of Conduct for Law Enforcement Officials, adopted by UN General Assembly Resolution 34/169 (17 December 1979); Basic Principles on the Use of Force and Firearms by Law Enforcement Officials, adopted by the Eighth UN Congress on the Prevention of Crime and the Treatment of Offenders,

The BPUFF draw an important technological boundary at the use of 'firearms'. Firearms are considered the ultimate means, and are regulated by 'special provisions'. The BPUFF do not define the term 'firearms', but refer to the 'discharging' of firearms, suggesting the shooting or firing of a projectile or weapon.[106] This would exclude the use of emplaced or hand-thrown (and possibly air-dropped) explosive weapon types from the notion of a 'firearm'. But because there is no universally accepted definition of the term 'firearm' under international law, and because some instruments use the term in a broad sense,[107] the BPUFF's text does not explicitly exclude explosive weapons from the realm of law enforcement, nor does it make clear whether some or all explosive weapons would fall within the purview of its 'special provisions' on firearms. Likewise, the BPUFF's call on states to adopt national rules and regulations that 'prohibit the use of those firearms and ammunition that cause unwarranted injury or present an unwarranted risk' does not provide an explicit barrier against the use of explosive weapons.[108] Even so, explosive weapon use seems at odds with the general orientation of the BPUFF, in all but exceptional circumstances.[109]

Given that the use of explosive weapons against or among persons bears a high risk of causing fatal injury, such use must be considered a use of lethal force.[110] Whenever the use of potentially lethal force is strictly unavoidable, states must still endeavour to 'minimise to the greatest extent possible any risk to . . . life', in the words of the European Court of Human Rights (ECtHR).[111] Since the projection of fragments from a detonation cannot be controlled or aimed, the use of an explosive weapon among a group of persons seems to run counter to the principle that 'shooting indiscriminately into a crowd is not allowed and may only be targeted at the person or persons constituting the threat of death or serious injury'.[112]

---

27 August–7 September 1990. The BPUFF have gained acceptance as a universal standard for the use of force in law enforcement operations: Melzer, *Targeted Killing in International Law*, p. 200.

[106] Principles 9–11, BPUFF.

[107] See e.g. Art. 1(3)(b), Organization of American States, Inter-American Convention against the Illicit Manufacturing of and Trafficking in Firearms, Ammunition, Explosives, and Other Related Materials, 14 November 1997.

[108] Principle 11(c), BPUFF.

[109] Principle 2 states the objective in relation to 'types of weapons and ammunition' to 'increasingly restrain the application of means capable of causing death or injury to persons', and pursuant to Principle 5, whenever the lawful use of force and firearms is unavoidable, law enforcement officials shall 'minimize damage and injury, and respect and preserve human life'.

[110] In ECtHR, *Goncharuk v. Russia*, Judgment (App. No. 58643/00), 4 October 2007, §74, the applicant was wounded by shrapnel in a shelling attack on Grozny. With reference to 'the injuries sustained by her', the Court concluded 'that the *degree and type of force* used' (emphasis added) brought the facts of the case within the ambit of the Convention's provision on the right to life.

[111] ECtHR, *Makaratzis v. Greece*, Judgment (App. No. 50385/99), 20 December 2004, §60.

[112] 'Report of the Special Rapporteur on extrajudicial, summary or arbitrary executions, Christof Heyns', UN doc. A/HRC/17/28, 23 May 2011, §61. Regarding the discharging of 'bursts of automatic fire in a

Considering the high probability that the use of an explosive weapon against a suspected offender will cause severe and likely fatal injury, any use of an explosive weapon against a person constitutes deliberate use of lethal force.[113] Such use of force is presumed illegal unless 'it is required to protect life (making lethal force proportionate) and there is no other means... of preventing that threat to life (making lethal force necessary). The proportionality requirement limits the permissible level of force based on the threat posed by the suspect to others. The necessity requirement imposes an obligation to minimize the level of force used, regardless of the amount that would be proportionate.'[114]

Use of an explosive weapon against or among people thus involves a degree of lethal force, and often a manner of employing lethal force that will in all but the most extraordinary circumstances be more hazardous to human life than absolutely necessary to achieve a legitimate aim. The cases of *Güleç v. Turkey* and *Neira-Allegría and ors v. Peru* illustrate the challenges involved. Although neither case addresses the use of an explosive weapon, arbitrary deprivation of life resulted from fragment projection in the first case, and from blast effects in the second.[115] The case of *Mansuroğlu v. Turkey* before the ECtHR involved the use by police of an explosive weapon, probably a hand grenade, against a suspect. The Court found it 'impossible to understand' in the circumstances of that case how the police could have found it 'absolutely necessary to respond with such force—including bullets and explosive weapons—as to cause numerous extremely serious injuries'.[116]

---

populated area', see ECtHR, *Nachova and ors v. Bulgaria*, Judgment (App. Nos 43577/98; 43579/98), 6 July 2005, §149.

[113] ECtHR, *Finogenov and ors v. Russia*, Judgment, (App. Nos 18299/03; 27311/03), 20 December 2011, §232: 'In the present case, however, the gas used by the Russian security forces, while dangerous, was not supposed to kill, in contrast, for example, to bombs or air missiles.'

[114] 'Report of the Special Rapporteur on extrajudicial, summary or arbitrary executions, Philip Alston', UN doc. A/HRC/14/24/Add.6, 28 May 2010, §§32–3. Principle 9 of the BPUFF reflects this standard. The 'intentional, premeditated and deliberate act of killing' (a 'targeted killing') can, however, never be the sole objective of a law enforcement operation. On this topic, see Melzer, *Targeted Killing in International Law*, 2008.

[115] ECtHR, *Güleç v. Turkey*, Judgment (App. No. 21593/93), 27 July 1998; IACtHR, *Neira-Alegría and ors v. Peru*, Judgment, Series C No. 21, 19 January 1995.

[116] ECtHR, *Information Note on the Court's case-law*, No. 105, February 2008, p. 6. The judgment is in French and the pertinent passage reads in relevant parts: '[I]l n'existe dans le dossier aucun élément concret qui démontre qu'au moment des faits Mazlum Mansuroğlu était armé et qu'il s'est bien servi de son arme contre les policiers... Par conséquent, il n'est pas possible de comprendre comment ces derniers ont pu se retrouver dans la nécessité absolue de riposter par une force de frappe—balles et explosifs—ayant causé tant de blessures extrêmement graves...' See ECtHR, *Mansuroğlu v. Turkey*, Judgment (App. No. 43443/98), 26 February 2008, §§97–8.

'EXCEPTIONAL MEASURES' IN A 'DIFFICULT SITUATION'

In spite of the above, IHRL does not explicitly forbid the use of explosive weapons. On several occasions, the ECtHR recognized that such use, even against and among people, could be permissible. In *Isayeva v. Russia* and *Isayeva and ors v. Russia*, two cases brought by petitioners from Chechnya, the Court considered it conceivable that there may be situations that call for 'exceptional measures' by the state to regain control and to suppress an armed insurgency, which could presumably comprise the deployment of army units equipped with combat weapons, including military aviation and artillery.[117] In other cases relating to Chechnya, the Court was even prepared to accept that 'the Russian authorities had no choice other than to carry out aerial strikes' on a town in order to retake that town. Such use, the Court is aware, 'could entail, as a regrettable but unavoidable consequence, human casualties'.[118]

The ECtHR has been criticized for applying 'the doctrines it has developed on the use of force in law enforcement operations even to large battles involving thousands of insurgents, artillery attacks, and aerial bombardment'.[119] Mindful of interpreting the obligation to protect the right to life in a way that does not impose 'an impossible or disproportionate burden' on the authorities, the Court, in such situations, in effect relaxes the strict IHRL requirements applicable to the use of lethal force. The Court does not in all cases consider the use of explosive weapons (even in large quantities) in populated areas problematic per se,[120] and has even hinted that the use of missiles may be an option for an attack in the vicinity of inhabited settlements.[121] This approach risks giving the impression that the use, in populated areas, of explosive weapons with wide-area effects may conceivably be permissible in 'difficult situations' other than armed conflict, because the legitimate aims pursued in these cases are not limited to the quelling of a 'riot or insurrection', and in any case such situations may occur outside of armed conflict.

Despite rhetoric to the contrary, though, the Court's argumentation in these cases is probably best seen as an attempt at applying IHRL in the light of IHL rules governing the conduct of hostilities.[122] It is widely accepted (although not by the respective

---

[117] ECtHR, *Isayeva v. Russia*, Judgment (App. No. 57950/00), 24 February 2005, §180; ECtHR, *Isayeva, Yusupova and Bazayeva v. Russia*, Judgment (App. Nos 57947/00; 57948/00; 57949/00), 24 February 2005, § 178.

[118] ECtHR, *Kerimova and ors v. Russia*, Judgment (App. Nos 17170/04; 20792/04; 22448/04; 23360/04; 5681/05; 5684/05), 3 May 2011, §§246, 248; ECtHR, *Khamzayev and ors v. Russia*, Judgment (App. No. 1503/02), 3 May 2011, §§178, 180.

[119] William Abresch, 'A human rights law of internal armed conflict: the European Court of Human Rights in Chechnya', *European Journal of International Law*, 16(4) (September 2005), p. 742.

[120] For a discussion, see Maya Brehm, *Protecting Civilians from the Effects of Explosive Weapons*, pp. 112–15.

[121] *Kerimova and ors v. Russia*, Judgment, 3 May 2011, §254; *Khamzayev and ors v. Russia*, Judgment, 3 May 2011, §186.

[122] Melzer, *Targeted Killing in International Law*, pp. 277, 391–2.

governments) that the violence in Chechnya and clashes between the Kurdish Worker's Party (PKK) and Turkey amounted to NIACs,[123] and it has been affirmed elsewhere that IHRL is relevant to the conduct of hostilities.[124] This interpretation reinforces the presumption that use of explosive weapons, especially of air-dropped bombs, missiles, and artillery, in populated areas, is reserved for the conduct of hostilities. It should also be stressed that even in situations in which the ECtHR interpreted the requirement of necessity liberally, it nevertheless found violations of the right to life when explosive weapons with wide-area effects were used in or near towns or villages, not least due to the state's failure 'to minimise, to the greatest extent possible, the risk of a loss of life, both for persons at whom the measures were directed and for civilians'.[125] For example, in *Kerimova and ors v. Russia*, the Court found that the use of 'a high-explosive indiscriminate type of weapon' (high-explosive fragmentation bombs of calibre 250–70 kg) in a populated area is 'impossible to reconcile' with the degree of caution expected from a law enforcement body in a democratic society and 'stands in flagrant contrast' to the aim of protecting lives from unlawful violence.[126]

Concluding remarks

Data presented in the first section of this chapter shows that the use of explosive weapons in populated areas had a devastating humanitarian impact in 2012, as it did in previous

---

[123] See e.g. Abresch, 'A human rights law of internal armed conflict: the European Court of Human Rights in Chechnya', p. 741; Melzer, *Targeted Killing in International Law*, p. 385: 'The Court has repeatedly qualified the confrontation between Turkey and the PKK as a non-international armed conflict, and thus, has implicitly recognized the applicability of the paradigm of hostilities to the armed clashes between the involved parties.'

[124] For example, in 'Human rights situation in Palestine and other occupied Arab territories, Report of the high-level fact-finding mission to Beit Hanoun established under Council resolution S-3/1', UN doc. A/HRC/9/26, 1 September 2008, §12: '[I]nternational human rights law and international humanitarian law, both of which are relevant to the shelling of Beit Hanoun.' See also UN doc. A/HRC/12/48, 25 September 2009, §268.

[125] *Kerimova and ors v. Russia*, Judgment, 3 May 2011, §§246, 248; *Khamzayev and ors v. Russia*, Judgment, 3 May 2011, §248.

[126] *Kerimova and ors v. Russia*, Judgment, 3 May 2011, § 253. Similarly, in ECtHR, *Esmukhambetov and ors v. Russia*, Judgment (App. No. 23445/03), 29 March 2011, §§149–50, the Court considered the 'use of indiscriminate weapons [air-dropped bombs] within a populated area' to be 'manifestly disproportionate' to the achievement of the purpose under Art. 2(2)(a) of the European Convention on Human Rights (ECHR). See also *Isayeva, Yusupova and Bazayeva v. Russia*, Judgment, 24 February 2005, §§195–7, in which the Court found that the military used 'an extremely powerful weapon' (12 S-24 non-guided air-to-ground missiles) and referred to 'the apparent disproportionality in the weapons used'. In *Isayeva v. Russia*, §§190–1, the Court considered the use of 'heavy free-falling high-explosion aviation bombs FAB-250 and FAB-500 with a damage radius exceeding 1,000 metres' and of 'other non-guided heavy combat weapons' in a populated area 'impossible to reconcile with the degree of caution expected from a law-enforcement body in a democratic society'.

years. Given the extraordinary capacity of explosive weapons to damage public infra-structure and private property, explosive violence in populated areas also tends to have far-reaching and long-term indirect impacts on communities. Yet, under IHL, harm from explosive weapons other than exploding bullets is generally considered part of the 'necessities of war'. Today, 'the idea of a weapon that kills or injures by blasting pieces of flesh off the victim is generally not considered problematic, because blasting pieces of flesh off people is seen as common in armed conflict'. In spite of an extensive pattern of death and injury to civilians and damage to buildings associated with the use of explosive weapons (particularly those with wide-area effects) in populated areas, the technology is considered 'normal' in armed conflict, and its use is seen as 'inevitable'.[127]

International treaties ban two types of explosive weapon—anti-personnel landmines and cluster munitions—and the use of certain other explosive weapon types is restricted, but explosive weapons are not formally recognized as a category of weapons whose use in populated areas calls for a differential treatment under IHL. The rules of IHL governing the conduct of hostilities aim to protect civilians against the effects of hostilities. But aside from blanketing entire cities with explosive force in clear violation of the prohib-ition on area bombardment, and apart from the recognition that certain unguided rockets are 'inherently indiscriminate', IHL provides little guidance about what the general rules on the conduct of hostilities imply for the choice of means and methods of warfare in specific situations.

It is perhaps correct to say that 'no court or authoritative treatise has ever held that artillery cannot be used against lawful military targets situated in populated areas'.[128] However, in light of the pattern of harm associated with the use of explosive weapons in these settings, the question is increasingly being raised whether further normative development may be required to prevent and reduce harm to civilians.[129] Notably, the use, in populated areas, of explosive weapons with wide-area effects is increasingly seen as a practice that should be avoided. Efforts to develop greater constraints on the use of explosive weapons would provide an opportunity to go beyond case-by-case analyses of individual attacks. A more categorical approach could build on existing legal commit-ments (such as the CCM), state policies, and operational restrictions already in place,

---

[127] Brian Rappert et al., 'The roles of civil society in the development of standards around new weapons and other technologies of warfare', *International Review of the Red Cross*, 94(886) (2012), p. 773.

[128] Huffmann, 'Margin of error: potential pitfalls of the ruling in *The Prosecutor v. Ante Gotovina*', p. 21.

[129] The UN Secretary-General observed in 2012 that 'while the use of certain explosive weapons in populated areas may, in some circumstances, fall within the confines of the law, the humanitarian impact, both short- and long-term, can be disastrous for civilians': UN doc. S/2012/376. ICRC President Peter Maurer questions in particular whether 'applicable IHL rules [are] sufficient to identify under which circumstances explosive force delivered by heavy weapons might be used in densely populated areas': 'ICRC President on the challenges of the evolving battlefield', *Intercross*, 4 April 2013, <http://intercrossblog .icrc.org/blog/icrc-president-challenges-evolving-battlefield>.

together with jurisprudence and scholarly writings, in order to build stronger standards for the protection of civilians from the effects of explosive weapons.[130]

Use of explosive weapons for purposes other than the conduct of hostilities appears a priori incompatible with the strict requirements of IHRL applicable to the use of lethal force. But these standards do not clearly exclude explosive weapons from law enforcement. An explicit recognition that the use of explosive weapons against or among people for purposes other than the conduct of hostilities is presumed unacceptable could, for instance, be formulated in relation to Principles 5(b) or 11(c) of the BPUFF.[131] In situations in which the use of explosive weapons is generally accepted—that is, in the conduct of hostilities—IHRL jurisprudence could increasingly be drawn upon to support the elaboration of practices and policies that would strengthen the protection of bystanders (respectively, civilians not participating in hostilities). The ECtHR, for instance, has developed a vigorous jurisprudence on the planning and execution of military operations in internal armed conflicts that could help to increase transparency about the decision-making processes involved, and provide more remedies to victims of explosive violence.[132]

---

[130] For suggestions along this line, see Richard Moyes and Brian Rappert, 'Looking inwards and looking outwards—specific challenges and strategic directions from the prohibition of cluster munition', *Austrian Review of International and European Law*, forthcoming.

[131] Explosive weapon use deemed legitimate (e.g. breaching charges, decoys, or flash-bang devices) could be justified in exceptional and well-defined circumstances.

[132] Abresch, 'A human rights law of internal armed conflict: the European Court of Human Rights in Chechnya', pp. 762–4.

2 Drone strikes in Pakistan in 2012

Stuart Casey-Maslen*

Introduction

On 31 January 2012, President Obama said, during an online discussion, that the drone strikes in Pakistan were a 'targeted, focused effort at the people who are on a list of active terrorists' and that the United States of America (USA) was not just 'sending in a whole bunch of strikes willy-nilly', but targeting '*al-Qaeda* suspects who are up in very tough terrain along the border between Afghanistan and Pakistan'.[1]

This chapter addresses some of the international legal issues engaged by drone strikes, focusing on strikes in Pakistan conducted by the US Central Intelligence Agency (CIA). (Unarmed) drones[2]—unmanned aerial vehicles (UAVs) or unmanned aircraft[3]—were first deployed on a significant scale for surveillance and reconnaissance in situations of armed conflict by the USA in Vietnam in the 1960s,[4] and in the 1990s first in Bosnia and Herzegovina and later in Kosovo.[5] Surveillance continues to be their primary role,[6] both

* Stuart Casey-Maslen is Head of Research at the Geneva Academy of International Humanitarian Law and Human Rights.

[1] See e.g. 'Obama discusses US use of drones in online Q&A—video', *The Guardian*, 31 January 2012, <http://www.guardian.co.uk/world/video/2012/jan/31/obama-us-drones-video>.

[2] The precise etymology of the word is disputed. One suggestion is that pilotless aircraft were used as air targets for training anti-aircraft gun crews. These targets were marked with black stripes along the tail part of the fuselage. These stripes looked like those of a drone (i.e. the insect). Another suggestion refers to the noise that the propeller aircraft versions made, akin to a bee. A third claims that the term 'drone' originated with a 1930s' pilotless version of the British *Fairey Queen* fighter, the 'Queen Bee'.

[3] According to US Federal legislation adopted in 2012, 'unmanned aircraft' means 'an aircraft that is operated without the possibility of direct human intervention from within or on the aircraft': section 331(8), FAA Modernization and Reform Act of 2012, signed into law by the US President on 14 February 2012.

[4] David Cenciotti, 'The dawn of the robot age: U.S. Air Force testing air-launched UCAVs capable to fire Maverick and Shrike missiles in 1972', *The Aviationist (weblog)*, 14 March 2012.

[5] 'Predator drones and unmanned aerial vehicles (UAVs)', *New York Times*, Updated 5 March 2012.

[6] One website (citing: *The Military Balance 2011*, IISS *Jane's Unmanned Aerial Vehicles and Targets 2011* 'US Unmanned Aerial Systems', Congressional Research Service, 2012; and various press reports) has listed 31 states with 'large' drones: Australia; Belgium; Canada; China; Ecuador; Egypt; Finland; France; Germany; Greece; India; Iran; Israel; Italy; Jordan; Malaysia; Mexico; Morocco; the Netherlands; Philippines; Singapore;

extraterritorially and, increasingly, domestically (by police and border/customs person-nel).[7] But although they retain this role (and some armed forces use them only for this), they are better known for firing missiles, in particular 100lb Hellfire missiles,[8] at suspected terrorists or members of non-state armed groups (NSAGs).

In a 'typical' cross-border drone operation, the aircraft is launched from a neighbour-ing state, then operated by someone—sometimes a civilian—who may be seated thou-sands of miles away watching a screen.[9] Aside from the USA, to date only Israel and the UK are known to have used armed drones to kill.[10] Other states are, though, either producing or procuring armed drones. In 2010, Iran announced its domestically devel-oped armed drone, referred to by Iranian President Mahmoud Ahmadinejad as the

South Africa; South Korea; Spain; Sri Lanka; Sweden; Switzerland; Thailand; Turkey; the United Kingdom (UK); and the USA. See Drone Wars UK, 'Large military drones in service', undated, <http://dronewars.net/6-who-has-drones/>. Other (unevidenced) estimates suggest that 50 or even 60 states possess drones.

[7] See e.g. 'Groups concerned over arming of domestic drones', *CBSDC*, Washington, DC, 23 May 2012; Vincent Kearney, 'Police in Northern Ireland consider using mini drones', *BBC*, 16 November 2011; 'Forces considering drone aircraft', *BBC*, 26 November 2009; Ted Thornhill, 'New work rotor: helicopter drones to be deployed by U.S. police forces for the first time (and it won't be long before the paparazzi use them, too)', *Daily Mail*, 23 March 2012. The US Federal Aviation Authority Modernization and Reform Act of 2012 grants increased powers to local police forces across the USA to use their own drones.

[8] The AGM-114 Hellfire is an air-to-surface missile developed primarily for anti-armour use, which can be launched from air, sea, or ground platforms. See e.g. Lockheed Martin, 'HELLFIRE II Missile', undated, <http://www.lockheedmartin.co.uk/us/products/HellfireII.html>. It is currently produced in three config-urations: anti-tank; blast/fragmentation; and thermobaric. The 'thermobaric' version of the missile, which uses a metal augmented explosive charge, is 'designed to inflict greater damage in multi-room structures, compared to the Hellfire's standard or blast-fragmentation warheads. The warhead contains a fluorinated aluminium powder that is layered between the warhead casing and the PBXN-112 explosive fill. When the explosive detonates, the aluminium mixture is dispersed and rapidly burns. The resultant sustained high pressure is extremely effective against enemy personnel'. The thermobaric version is said to be designed for deployment from UAVs such as Predator drones: 'Hellfire II missile system', *Defense Update*, 2007, <http://defense-update.com/products/h/hellfire.htm>. The name of the missile, whose first guided launch occurred in 1978, comes from its original intended use as a helicopter-launched 'fire-and-forget' weapon (HELicopter Launched FIRE-and-forget): Boeing, 'AGM-114A HELLFIRE missile', undated, <http://www.boeing.com/boeing/history/bna/hellfire.page>.

[9] See e.g. 'Drones: What are they and how do they work?', *BBC*, 31 January 2012. According to one media report, the two-second delay between a pilot moving a joystick in Nevada and an aircraft responding in Afghanistan is enough to cause a crash during take-off and landing. Crews in Afghanistan therefore control 'launch and recovery' through direct contact with antennae on the aircraft. Half an hour after take-off, control of the drone is handed to a crew in Nevada; half an hour before landing, it returns to the crews on the ground in Kandahar: Rob Blackhurst, 'The air force men who fly drones in Afghanistan by remote control', *Daily Telegraph*, 24 September 2012.

[10] In March 2013, it was suggested in the US media that Pakistan might have used armed drones on its own territory earlier in the year. See Declan Walsh, 'U.S. disavows 2 drone strikes over Pakistan', *New York Times*, 4 March 2013. According to the report: 'If American claims are correct, the United States has not conducted a drone strike in Pakistan since January 10, marking the longest pause of the campaign since November 2011, when the C.I.A. stopped strikes for 55 days after American warplanes killed 24 Pakistani soldiers in a disputed border clash . . . Some analysts believe the lull may be connected to Mr [John] Brennan's nomination [as CIA Director], pointing to a similar slowdown in Yemen, the other major theater of American drone operation. Others point to more prosaic explanations, like intelligence delays or bad weather.'

'Ambassador of Death', with a range of 620 miles.[11] In November 2012, China unveiled its Yi Long armed drone, equipped with under-wing missiles and an electro-optical sensor turret under the forward fuselage. Chinese sources have stated that the drone has 'already successfully entered the international market', but have provided no further details.[12] In February 2013, German Minister of Defence Thomas de Maizière declared that Germany would seek to procure armed drones.[13] In April 2012, Russia had announced that it would test-fly its first domestically produced armed drone in 2014.[14]

Indeed, over the last ten years, the use of drones for military and counterterrorism purposes has seen 'explosive growth', to use the words of the US Department of Defense.[15] In 2010, for example, President Obama's Administration is said to have authorized more than twice as many drone strikes in north-west Pakistan as it did in 2009—'itself a year in which there were more drone strikes than during George W. Bush's entire time in office'.[16] By early 2012, the Pentagon was said to have 7,500 drones under its control, representing about one-third of all US military aircraft.[17] The number of armed drones within this total is not known, and it does not include drones possessed by the CIA.[18] General N. A. Schwartz, the Air Force Chief of Staff, has reportedly deemed it 'conceivable' that drone pilots in the Air Force would outnumber those in cockpits in the foreseeable future, although he predicted that the Air Force would have traditional pilots for at least 30 more years.[19]

A. Drone strikes in Pakistan in 2012

The CIA has been carrying out drone strikes in Pakistan since, reportedly, 2004.[20] On 10 January 2012, according to the Bureau of Investigative Journalism (BIJ):

[11] Associated Press, 'Iran unveils "Ambassador of Death" unmanned drone bomber', *Fox News*, 22 August 2010.

[12] RIA Novosti, 'China unveils Yi Long UAV', *Military Aviation News and Media*, 14 November 2012.

[13] See e.g. Thomas Darnstaedt, 'Germany's drone conundrum: "new wars" demand new mindsets', Commentary, *Der Spiegel*, 8 February 2013.

[14] RIA Novosti, 'Russia to test fly first combat drone in 2014', *Military Aviation News and Media*, 24 April 2012.

[15] US Department of Defense, 'US unmanned systems integrated roadmap (fiscal years 2009–2034)', Washington, DC, 2009, p. 2, <http://www.acq.osd.mil/psa/docs/UMSIntegratedRoadmap2009.pdf>.

[16] Peter Bergen and Katherine Tiedemann, 'Hidden war, there were more drone strikes—and far fewer civilians killed', *New America Foundation*, 22 December 2010.

[17] W. J. Hennigan, 'New drone has no pilot anywhere, so who's accountable?', *Los Angeles Times*, 26 January 2012. A similar percentage of drones to piloted aircraft is expected within 20 years in the UK's Royal Air Force (RAF): Nick Hopkins, 'Afghan civilians killed by RAF drone', *The Guardian*, 5 July 2011.

[18] The increasing role of the CIA in drone attacks raises additional questions given the covert nature of that agency, including even greater lack of transparency and accountability than with the military, as well as whether the requisite consent of the territorial state has been secured.

[19] Elisabeth Bumiller, 'A day job waiting for a kill shot a world away', *New York Times*, 29 July 2012.

[20] According to one report, the first CIA drone assassination in Pakistan was of Tehrik-e-Taliban Pakistan (TTP) leader Nek Muhammad in 2004: Brian Glyn Williams, 'Private approval, public

[T]he longest pause of the Obama drone war in Pakistan (55 days) came to an abrupt end when in a late evening attack two missiles destroyed a mudbrick house just outside Miranshah. Up to four alleged militants were reported killed, with Reuters initially citing Pakistani officials as saying the victims were 'foreign fighters of Arab and possibly also Uzbek extraction'... Ten days after the strike *Reuters* reported that the attack killed Aslam Awan aka Abdullah Khorasani, who it described as a Pakistan-born senior external operations operative for al-Qaeda. Pakistan's *The News* reported that a Saudi national may also have died.[21]

The 10 January attack:

...led to a number of protests in Pakistan. On 22 February Reuters reported that US Vice President Joe Biden, Secretary of State Hillary Clinton, and General Martin Dempsey, chairman of the Joint Chiefs of Staff, all spoke with senior Pakistani officials just prior to the attack to let them know the campaign would be resuming. *The News* later claimed that according to its sources in the security establishment this strike—and one on 9 February 2012—'was carried out on a tip off provided by the Pakistani intelligence community'.[22]

The Bureau reported that up to 400 people had been killed in a total of 48 drone strikes during 2012. The final strike of 2012 is said to have taken place on 28 December, resulting in four or five deaths and two injured in the Shawal valley area on the border of North and South Waziristan. News International quoted official and tribal sources as saying this was the first drone strike to take place in cloudy weather. 'There was heavy snowfall in Shawal valley when the drone fired missiles and targeted a house', an unnamed official told the media outlet.[23]

B. **The applicable legal regime**

The legality of CIA drone strikes in Pakistan under the inter-state use of force is extremely contentious, but is generally beyond the scope of this chapter.[24] Previous Pakistani presidents seemingly gave their consent to the USA, but at least for 2012 no such consent

---

condemnation: drone warfare's implications for Pakistani sovereignty', *Terrorism Monitor*, 11(7) (4 April 2013), <http://www.jamestown.org/single/?no_cache=1&tx_ttnews%5Btt_news%5D=40697&tx_ttnews% 5BbackPid%5D=7&cHash=88db476b68cd2df314ccc081b0c319ea>.

[21] 'Obama 2012 Pakistan strikes', *Bureau of Investigative Journalism*, 11 January 2013, <http://www .thebureauinvestigates.com/2012/01/11/obama-2012-strikes/>.

[22] 'Obama 2012 Pakistan strikes', *Bureau of Investigative Journalism*, 11 January 2013.

[23] 'Obama 2012 Pakistan strikes', *Bureau of Investigative Journalism*, 11 January 2013.

[24] It is important not to conflate inter-state use of force issues with the parallel, but distinct, legal assessment of a drone strike under international human rights law (IHRL) and, where applicable, international humanitarian law (IHL). See e.g. R. P. Barnidge, Jr, 'A qualified defense of American drone attacks in Northwest Pakistan under international humanitarian law', *Boston University International Law Journal*, 30 (2012), p. 423.

is known to have been given and therefore at least some of the drone strikes by the USA on Pakistani territory in 2012 (the exact number is not known) were arguably conducted in violation of Pakistan's sovereignty.

Indeed, drone strikes were publically opposed by both Pakistan's government and its parliament in 2012, and could therefore be considered as acts falling within the scope of an international armed conflict (IAC) between the two states.[25] In April, for example, Pakistan's parliament demanded an immediate end to US drone attacks along with an unconditional apology for a North Atlantic Treaty Organization (NATO) airstrike on 26 November 2011 that killed 24 Pakistani soldiers.[26] Senator Raza Rabbani, chairman of the parliamentary committee on national security, said that, in order to protect the nation's sovereignty and territorial integrity, the US military must stop all incursions into Pakistan, including drone strikes.[27]

Opposition has included direct remonstrations to representatives of the USA. On 5 June 2012, US Chargé d'affaires Richard Hoagland was summoned to the Pakistani Ministry of Foreign Affairs, which conveyed the government's serious concern about drone strikes in the tribal regions. According to a statement released by the Ministry: 'He was informed that the drone strikes were unlawful, against international law and a violation of Pakistan's sovereignty. Parliament had emphatically stated that they were unacceptable. Drone strikes represented a clear red-line for Pakistan.'[28]

On 5 July, the Pakistan's Ministry of Foreign Affairs repeated the view that drone strikes were counterproductive and a violation of Pakistan's sovereignty. Ambassador Akbar Ahmed, Islamabad's former High Commissioner to London, told al Jazeera:

It can't go against the will of the people and Pakistan is quite unanimous in rejecting the drone strikes on its territory. All the political parties, parliament and military have categorically condemned the strikes. We know that in the past there were all kinds of backdoor dealings— we are told we don't know for sure—between Pakistan and the US which sort of winked and nudged and looked the other way while drone strikes would be conducted. Now those days have gone because the relationship between the two countries is so brittle and tense. And anything

---

[25] This is notwithstanding complicity in drone strikes that may exist within elements of the Pakistani state, such as its intelligence services. See e.g. Jack Serle and Chris Woods, 'Secret US documents show Brennan's "no civilian drone deaths" claim was false', *Bureau of Investigative Journalism*, 11 April 2013, <http://www.thebureauinvestigates.com/2013/04/11/secret-us-documents-show-brennans-no-civilian-drone-deaths-claim-was-false/>.

[26] See e.g. 'US admits mistakes over killings of Pakistan troops', *BBC*, 22 December 2011, <http://www.bbc.co.uk/news/world-asia-16302197>; Brian Padden, 'Pakistan's parliament demands an end to drone attacks', *Voice of America*, Updated 11 April 2012, <http://www.voanews.com/content/pakistans-parliament-demands-immediate-end-to-us-drone-strikes-147203445/181162.html>.

[27] 'US admits mistakes over killings of Pakistan troops', *BBC*, 22 December 2011.

[28] See e.g. 'Drone campaign: Pakistan summons US envoy, lodges protest', *Tribune*, 6 June 2012, <http://tribune.com.pk/story/389354/drone-campaign-pakistan-summons-us-envoy-lodges-protest/>.

smacking of backdoor dealings would really risk a reaction in the public against the government in Pakistan.[29]

The possibility of drone strikes also falling within the context of a global non-international armed conflict (NIAC) is equally contentious. Michael Schmitt, for example, notes that 'it is uncertain whether transnational terrorism without any nexus to an ongoing armed conflict constitutes an "armed conflict" as a matter of law'. He then asserts (citing as evidence the position of the USA) that 'the view that such activities are non-international armed conflict appears to increasingly be the preferred characterization'.[30] In fact, determining that any given drone strike is to be considered as an attack *in bello* (and therefore to be assessed by the law applicable in armed conflict) is to be judged on a case-by-case basis.

C. **Drone strikes and *jus in bello***

According to the United Nations (UN) Special Rapporteur on extrajudicial, summary, or arbitrary executions, although 'in most circumstances targeted killings violate the right to life, in the exceptional circumstance of armed conflict, they may be legal'.[31] If it is reliably established that the legality of a given drone strike is to be adjudged under *jus in bello*, the general rules of IHL will apply, arguably alongside applicable human rights law. The strike will thus have to comply with, at a minimum, the IHL rules applicable to the conduct of hostilities, in particular those relating to distinction, proportionality, and precautions in attacks, and the strike must not employ weapons whose use is unlawful under IHL.[32] These rules are discussed in turn.

THE RULE OF DISTINCTION IN ATTACKS

The rule on distinction—the duty to distinguish between lawful military objectives, on the one hand, and civilians and civilian objects, on the other—may be considered the most

---

[29] Cited in 'Many dead in triple Pakistan drone strike', *Al Jazeera*, 9 July 2012, <http://www.aljazeera.com/news/asia/2012/07/201277028968422.html>; see also 'Obama 2012 Pakistan strikes', *Bureau of Investigative Journalism*, 11 January 2013.

[30] M. N. Schmitt, 'Drone attacks under the jus ad bellum and jus in bello: clearing the "fog of law"' in M. N. Schmitt (ed.), *Yearbook of International Humanitarian Law 2010*, T. M. C. Asser Press, The Hague, 2011, p. 319.

[31] Philip Alston, 'Addendum, study on targeted killings', Report to the Human Rights Council, UN doc. A/HRC/14/24/Add.6, 28 May 2010 ('2010 Study on targeted killings'), §10.

[32] There is thus no difference in the content of the general IHL rules that govern the use of a means or method of warfare in armed conflict of a Cruise missile, an aerial bombardment, or an armed drone.

fundamental of all IHL rules. Only lawful military targets, including civilians 'participating directly in hostilities', may lawfully be targeted by attacks, in accordance with customary law (and, where applicable, Article 13(3) of the 1977 Additional Protocol II).

But continuing uncertainty enshrouds the notion of precisely who may be lawfully targeted by a state (aside from opposing state armed forces) under IHL. According to a general interpretation of the law, only a civilian who is 'actively participating in hostilities' or 'directly participating in hostilities' may be targeted.[33] The International Committee of the Red Cross (ICRC)'s *Interpretive Guidance on the Notion of Direct Participation in Hostilities under International Humanitarian Law* is highly controversial in this regard, particularly the assertion that (military) members of organized armed groups fulfil the criteria for being lawfully targeted on the basis of a claimed 'continuous combat function'.[34] Those who exercise such a continuous combat function may, in principle, be targeted by attacks at any time (although some, including the USA, argue that this general permissiveness is subject to a restrictive principle of military necessity). But as Alston observes:

[T]he creation of [the] CCF category is, *de facto*, a status determination that is questionable given the specific treaty language that limits direct participation to 'for such time' as opposed to 'all the time.'... Creation of the CCF category also raises the risk of erroneous targeting of someone who, for example, may have disengaged from his or her function.[35]

A further challenge is how to identify—legally and practically—who such members are. As the *Interpretive Guidance* published by the ICRC observes:

[U]nder IHL, the decisive criterion for individual membership in an organized armed group is whether a person assumes a continuous function for the group involving his or her direct participation in hostilities (hereafter: 'continuous combat function')....[This function]

---

[33] For a discussion of the International Criminal Court (ICC)'s unfortunate discussion of 'active' versus 'direct' participation in hostilities in the *Lubanga* case, see e.g. Nicole Urban, 'Direct and active participation in hostilities: the unintended consequences of the ICC's decision in *Lubanga*', *EJIL Talk*, 11 April 2012. Urban notes that:

In the ICRC's Interpretive Guidelines on the Notion of Direct Participation in Hostilities it was noted that although the Additional Protocols and the Geneva Conventions use different words, the phrase 'participent directement' is used consistently throughout French texts of each treaty...: a fact that strongly suggests a uniform meaning across IHL. Further, the ICRC found that the concept of participation in hostiles should be interpreted consistently across both international and non-international armed conflicts. Similarly, the Trial Chamber of the ICTR in the Akayesu Decision was called upon to interpret the meaning of the term 'active' in the concept of Common Article 3 and held that 'direct' and 'active' are so similar that, for the Chamber's purposes, they may be treated as synonymous.

[34] See N. Melzer, *Interpretive Guidance on the Notion of Direct Participation in Hostilities under International Humanitarian Law*, ICRC, Geneva, 2009, pp. 30–1. At p. 32: 'The term organized armed group...refers exclusively to the armed or military wing of a non-State party: its armed forces in a functional sense.'

[35] '2010 Study on Targeted Killings', §§65–6.

distinguishes members of the organized fighting forces of a non-State party from civilians who directly participate in hostilities on a merely spontaneous, sporadic, or unorganized basis, or who assume exclusively political, administrative or other non-combat functions.[36]

Those who directly participate in hostilities on a merely spontaneous, sporadic, or unorganized basis may only lawfully be targeted while they so participate (although at other times they may, of course, be arrested by a law enforcement operation and charged under domestic law for any offences allegedly committed). Those who assume exclusively political, administrative, or other non-combat functions may not be lawfully targeted unless and until they directly participate in hostilities, and only for such time as they undertake such acts.[37] In case of doubt as to his or her status, a person is to be considered a civilian *not* directly participating in hostilities.[38] Moreover, in situations that do not involve the conduct of hostilities, such as law enforcement operations conducted during an NIAC, human rights law would determine the lawful use of force.

On this basis, targeting with lethal force an al-Qaeda operative in Pakistan who is actively engaged in planning, directing, or carrying out an attack in Afghanistan against, for example, US forces would therefore be, a priori, lawful under the IHL rule of distinction. Targeting his son, his daughter, his wife, or wives would not be lawful unless

---

[36] Melzer, *Interpretive Guidance*, p. 33. According to Melzer, p. 35, continuous combat function 'may also be identified based on conclusive behaviour, for example where a person has repeatedly directly participated in hostilities in support of an organized armed group in circumstances indicating that such conduct constitutes a continuous function rather than a spontaneous, sporadic, or temporary role assumed for the duration of a particular operation'. See also N. Melzer, 'Keeping the balance between military necessity and humanity: a response to four critiques of the ICRC's Interpretive Guidance on the notion of direct participation in hostilities', *New York University Journal of International Law and Politics*, 42 (2010), p. 890.

[37] In contrast, Brigadier-General Kenneth Watkin proposes to significantly increase those who would fall within the definition, notably including persons assuming exclusively 'combat service support' functions, including cooks and administrative personnel: K. Watkin, 'Opportunity lost: organized armed groups and the ICRC "Direct Participation in the Hostilities" Interpretive Guidance', *New York University Journal of International Law and Politics*, 42 (2010), p. 692. See Melzer, 'Keeping the balance', pp. 848–9.

[38] According to Recommendation VIII of Melzer, *Interpretive Guidance*, pp. 75–6: 'All feasible precautions must be taken in determining whether a person is a civilian and, if so, whether that civilian is directly participating in hostilities. In case of doubt, the person must be presumed to be protected against direct attack.' See also Melzer, 'Keeping the balance', esp. pp. 874–7. Radsan asserts that, '[e]xcept in extraordinary circumstances, the agency may strike only if it is satisfied beyond a reasonable doubt that its target is a functional combatant of al Qaeda or a similar terrorist group. Drone strikes, in effect, are executions without any realistic chance for appeal to the courts through habeas corpus or other procedures': A. J. Radsan, 'Loftier standards for the CIA'S remote-control killing', Statement for the House Subcommittee on National Security & Foreign Affairs, Legal Studies Research Paper Series, Paper No. 2010–11, William Mitchell College of Law, St Paul, MN, May 2010, p. 3. Radsan later claims (at p. 5), however, that: 'There are, of course, exceptions to my general rule for CIA targeting. I summarize these exceptions under the label of extraordinary circumstances. The target, for example, may play an irreplaceable role in al Qaeda. A drone operator may see a person on the screen who is probably Bin Laden—but not Bin Laden beyond any doubt. Even so, the military advantage of killing Bin Laden, compared to a mid-level terrorist, may justify the additional risk of mistakenly harming a peaceful civilian.'

(and only for such time as) they were themselves directly participating in hostilities.[39] The legality of an attack against the operative that was also expected to kill or injure civilians incidentally would depend on a determination according to the rule of proportionality (*see section 'The rule of proportionality in attacks'*).

Failing to comply with the rule of distinction during attack would render that attack unlawful and constitute evidence of a war crime. In this regard, claims that numerous CIA drone strikes have targeted funerals or those rescuing the victims of drone strikes are extremely disquieting. According to a report by the Bureau of Investigative Journalism:

A three-month investigation including eye witness reports has found evidence that at least 50 civilians were killed in follow-up strikes when they had gone to help victims. More than 20 civilians have also been attacked in deliberate strikes on funerals and mourners.[40]

THE RULE OF PROPORTIONALITY IN ATTACKS

But even if a target is a lawful military objective under IHL, the question of proportionality arises either to affect the selection of the means and methods of warfare that may lawfully be used, or even effectively to prohibit an attack from being launched. Violating the rule of proportionality is an indiscriminate attack according to the 1977 Additional Protocol I.[41] The rule is not codified in either Common Article 3 to the 1949 Geneva Conventions or 1977 Additional Protocol II, but is deemed by the ICRC to be a customary rule of IHL applicable not only in IAC, but also in NIACs. According to Rule 14 of the ICRC's 2005 study of customary IHL:[42]

Launching an attack which may be expected to cause incidental loss of civilian life, injury to civilians, damage to civilian objects, or a combination thereof, which would be excessive in relation to the concrete and direct military advantage anticipated, is prohibited.

---

[39] In this regard, Melzer notes the USA's understanding, declared in the context of the Optional Protocol to the Convention on the Rights of the Child on the Involvement of Children in Armed Conflict, that: '[T]he phrase "direct part in hostilities": (i) means immediate and actual action on the battlefield likely to cause harm to the enemy because there is a direct causal relationship between the activity engaged in and the harm done to the enemy; and (ii) does not mean indirect participation in hostilities, such as gathering and transmitting military information, transporting weapons, munitions, or other supplies, or forward deployment.' See Melzer, 'Keeping the balance', p. 888, and n. 226.

[40] Chris Woods and Christina Lamb, 'Obama terror drones: CIA tactics in Pakistan include targeting rescuers and funerals', *Bureau of Investigative Journalism*, 4 February 2012.

[41] See Arts 51(5)(b) and 57(2)(a)(iii), 1977 Additional Protocol I.

[42] Jean-Marie Henckaerts and Louise Doswald-Beck (eds), *Customary International Humanitarian Law*, *vol. I: Rules*, ICRC and Cambridge University Press, Cambridge, 2005 (hereafter, Customary IHL Study).

The question, of course, is what is 'excessive'? In the commentary, published by the ICRC, to Article 51(5) of the 1977 Additional Protocol I, from where the text originates, it is stated that:

Of course, the disproportion between losses and damages caused and the military advantages anticipated raises a delicate problem; in some situations there will be no room for doubt, while in other situations there may be reason for hesitation. In such situations the interests of the civilian population should prevail...[43]

It is well known that different states have widely differing assessments of what is proportionate. Let us consider the example of the former Pakistani Taliban leader, Baitullah Mehsud. On 23 June 2009, the CIA killed Khwaz Wali Mehsud, a mid-ranking Pakistan Taliban commander. The CIA planned to use his body 'as bait' to target Baitullah Mehsud, who was expected to attend Khwaz Wali Mehsud's funeral. Up to 5,000 people attended the funeral, including not only Taliban fighters, but also many civilians. US drones struck again, killing up to 83 people. As many as 45 of the dead were reportedly civilians, among them ten children and four tribal leaders. Such an attack raises very serious questions about respect for the prohibition on indiscriminate attacks. Baitullah Mehsud himself escaped unharmed, reportedly dying six weeks later along with his wife in a fresh CIA drone strike while on a drip being treated for a kidney problem.[44]

THE RULE OF PRECAUTIONS IN ATTACKS

There are direct links between respect for the rules on precautions in attacks and respect for other customary rules applicable to the conduct of hostilities, notably distinction (also called 'discrimination' by some) and proportionality, as well as the prohibition on using means or methods of warfare that are of a nature to cause superfluous injury or unnecessary suffering. Most of the rules on precautions in attacks, which were codified in the 1977 Additional Protocol I, are of a customary nature and are applicable in NIACs as well as in IACs, according to the ICRC customary IHL study published in 2005. Central among them is the obligation to take 'constant care' in the conduct of military operations to 'spare the civilian population, civilians, and civilian objects'. In this regard, '[a]ll feasible precautions must be taken to avoid, and in any event to minimise, incidental loss

---

[43] Yves Sandoz, Christophe Swinarski, and Bruno Zimmermann (eds), *Commentary on the Additional Protocols*, ICRC, Geneva, 1987, §§1979–80.

[44] See e.g. Peter Finn and Joby Warrick, 'Under Panetta, a more aggressive CIA', *Washington Post*, 21 March 2010; see also Woods and Lamb, 'Obama terror drones: CIA tactics in Pakistan include targeting rescuers and funerals'. According to Meyer, the CIA conducted 16 missile strikes with the deaths of up to 321 people before they managed to kill Baitullah Mehsud: Meyer, 'The predator war', *New Yorker*, 26 October 2009, <http://www.newyorker.com/reporting/2009/10/26/091026fa_fact_mayer>.

of civilian life, injury to civilians, and damage to civilian objects'.[45] In so doing, under Article 57 of the Protocol (applicable in IACs), those who plan or decide upon an attack shall 'take all feasible precautions in the choice of means and methods of attack'.[46]

It can be argued that armed drones are capable of meeting the requirements for precautions in attacks. A video feed from the drone can give 'real-time' eyes on the target so that the absence of civilians close to the target can be monitored until the last few minutes or even seconds.[47] In addition, in certain cases (notably on Afghan soil), nearby military forces are also charged with monitoring the target.[48] Further, other than the thermobaric variant of the Hellfire missile,[49] most of the missiles fired from drones are believed to have a smaller blast radius than other conventional munitions that might typically be deployed from a fighter jet or bomber. These factors do not eliminate the risk of civilian casualties, but they certainly represent feasible precautions that *may* minimize incidental loss of civilian life.

Significant failings have undeniably occurred, however, with one drone strike in Afghanistan in 2010 alone said to have killed 23 Afghan civilians and wounded 12 others.[50] In May 2010, the US military released a report on the deaths, saying that 'inaccurate and unprofessional' reporting by Predator drone operators had led to the airstrike in February on the group of civilian men, women, and children.[51] The report

---

[45] ICRC Customary IHL Study, Rule 15.

[46] Art. 57(2)(a)(ii), 1977 Additional Protocol I. While, of course, Art. 57 of the 1977 Additional Protocol I applies only in an IAC, the norm it embodies also applies in NIAC. Cf. Rule 17 of the ICRC Customary IHL Study, which reads: 'Each party to the conflict must take all feasible precautions in the choice of means and methods of warfare with a view to avoiding, and in any event to minimizing, incidental loss of civilian life, injury to civilians and damage to civilian objects.'

[47] In contrast, an unnamed former White House counterterrorism official has reportedly asserted that '"there are so many drones" in the air over Pakistan that arguments have erupted over which remote operators can claim which targets, provoking "command-and-control issues"': Meyer, 'The predator war'.

[48] Although note the caution expressed in this regard by Alston: 'Drones' proponents argue that since drones have greater surveillance capability and afford greater precision than other weapons, they can better prevent collateral civilian casualties and injuries. This may well be true to an extent, but it presents an incomplete picture. The precision, accuracy and legality of a drone strike depend on the human intelligence upon which the targeting decision is based.' See '2010 Study on Targeted Killings', §81. Indeed, as Daniel Byman has argued: 'To reduce casualties, superb intelligence is necessary. Operators must know not only where the terrorists are, but also who is with them and who might be within the blast radius. This level of surveillance may often be lacking, and terrorists' deliberate use of children and other civilians as shields make civilian deaths even more likely.' See D. L. Byman, 'Do targeted killings work?', *Brookings Institution*, 14 July 2009.

[49] According to one US defence industry website, the AGM-114N thermobaric variant of the Hellfire can suck the air out of a cave, collapse a building, or produce 'an astoundingly large blast radius out in the open': 'US Hellfire missile orders, FY 2011–2014', *Defense Industry Daily*, 10 January 2012.

[50] 'First drone friendly fire deaths', *RT*, 12 April 2011. In October 2011, the US Department of Defense concluded that a number of miscommunication errors between military personnel had led to a drone strike the previous April that mistakenly killed two US troops in Afghanistan: 'Drone strike killed Americans', *RT*, 17 October 2011.

[51] Dexter Filkins, 'Operators of drones are faulted in Afghan deaths', *New York Times*, 29 May 2010. The report, signed by Major-General T. P. McHale, found that the Predator operators in Nevada and 'poorly functioning command posts' in the area failed to provide the ground commander with evidence that there

said that four American officers, including a brigade and battalion commander, had been reprimanded, and that two junior officers had also been disciplined. General Stanley A. McChrystal, who apologized to Afghan President Hamid Karzai after the attack, announced a series of training measures intended to reduce the chances of similar events. General McChrystal also asked Air Force commanders to open an investigation into the Predator operators.[52]

Concluding remarks

The issue of accountability is central to the question of drone strikes. The US Department of Justice has asserted that 'there exists no appropriate judicial forum'[53] to assess the constitutional considerations of targeted killings using armed drones:

It is well established that '[m]atters intimately related to foreign policy and national security are rarely proper subjects for judicial intervention,' *Haig v. Agee*, 453 US 280, 292 (1981), because such matters 'frequently turn on standards that defy judicial application,' or involve the exercise of a discretion demonstrably committed to the executive or legislature, *Baker v. Carr*, 369 US 186, 211 (1962). Were a court to intervene here, it might be required inappropriately to issue an ex ante command to the President and officials responsible for operations with respect to their specific tactical judgment to mount a potential lethal operation against a senior operational leader of al-Qa'ida or its associated forces. And judicial enforcement of such orders would require the Court to supervise inherently predictive judgments by the President and his national security advisors as to when and how to use force against a member of an enemy force against which Congress has authorized the use of force.[54]

This argument is not persuasive, in the present author's view. Domestic courts are capable of applying IHRL and IHL, whether from treaty or custom, and the lack of oversight of targeted killings using drones is a critical concern (in particular given that many US drone strikes are conducted by the CIA). On 24 January 2013, the UN Special Rapporteur on the promotion and protection of human rights and fundamental freedoms while countering terrorism issued a statement at a press conference in London, which included the following words:

---

were civilians in the trucks. According to military officials in Washington and Afghanistan, who spoke on the condition of anonymity, intelligence analysts who were monitoring the drone's video feed sent computer messages twice, warning the drone operators and ground command posts that children were visible.

[52] Filkins, 'Operators of drones are faulted in Afghan deaths'.

[53] US Department of Justice White Paper, 'Lawfulness of a lethal operation directed against a U.S. citizen who is a senior operational leader of al-Qaeda or an associated force', undated, but leaked in the press in February 2013, p. 9.

[54] US Department of Justice White Paper, 'Lawfulness of a lethal operation directed against a U.S. citizen who is a senior operational leader of al-Qaeda or an associated force', p. 10.

In June of last year, at the Human Rights Council in Geneva, a group of States, including two permanent members of the Security Council, as well as Pakistan and a number of other concerned States, made a joint statement asking me to carry out an investigation, within the framework of this mandate, into the use of drones in the context of counterterrorism operations.

I issued a statement shortly afterwards to the effect that those States using this technology, and those States on whose territory it is used, are under an international law obligation to establish effective independent and impartial investigations into any drone attack in which it is plausibly alleged that civilian casualties were sustained. I also indicated that if those States did not take steps to establish sufficiently robust and impartial investigations it may, in the final resort, be necessary for the UN to conduct investigations into individual drone strikes.

The Inquiry that I am launching today is a direct response to the requests made to me by States at the Human Rights Council last June, as well as to the increasing international concern surrounding the issue of remote targeted killing through the use of UAVs. The exponential rise in the use of drone technology in a variety of military and non-military contexts represents a real challenge to the framework of established international law and it is both right as a matter of principle, and inevitable as a matter of political reality, that the international community should now be focussing attention on the standards applicable to this technological development, particularly its deployment in counterterrorism and counter-insurgency initiatives, and attempt to reach a consensus on the legality of its use, and the standards and safeguards which should apply to it.[55]

In his February 2013 State of the Union Address, US President Obama made the following promise:

As we do, we must enlist our values in the fight. That is why my Administration has worked tirelessly to forge a durable legal and policy framework to guide our counterterrorism operations. Throughout, we have kept Congress fully informed of our efforts. I recognize that in our democracy, no one should just take my word that we're doing things the right way. So, in the months ahead, I will continue to engage with Congress to ensure not only that our targeting, detention, and prosecution of terrorists remains consistent with our laws and system of checks and balances, but that our efforts are even more transparent to the American people and to the world.[56]

Zeke Johnson, Director of Amnesty International USA's security and human rights campaign, stated that President Obama's State of the Union remarks fell short of what was required:

---

[55] 'Statement by Ben Emmerson, UN Special Rapporteur on counter-terrorism and human rights concerning the launch of an inquiry into the civilian impact, and human rights implications of the use of drones and other forms of targeted killing for the purpose of counter-terrorism and counter-insurgency', London, 24 January 2013, <http://www.ohchr.org/EN/NewsEvents/Pages/DisplayNews.aspx?NewsID=12943&LangID=E>.

[56] 'Obama's 2013 State of the Union Address', *New York Times*, 12 February 2013, <http://www.nytimes.com/2013/02/13/us/politics/obamas-2013-state-of-the-union-address.html?pagewanted=all&_r=0>.

What he should have done is made it clear that the U.S. government will follow its international human rights obligations when it comes to the use of lethal force, when it comes to detention, when it comes to the issue of torture. There are very clear obligations under law for the U.S. government and President Obama should recommit to meeting those obligations.[57]

A number of domestic legal cases have been initiated as a result of drone strikes. In the UK, the death in a CIA drone strike of Malik Daud Khan, a Pakistani tribal elder, and dozens of others at a tribal council meeting in North Waziristan in 2011 led to a claim that British officials have become 'secondary parties to murder' by passing intelligence to American officials that was later used in drone strikes. An appeal was lodged in January 2013 against an initial High Court decision not to hear the case, which has been brought by Mr Khan's son, Noor Khan.[58]

Indeed, in the words of a former CIA lawyer: 'The government's power to kill must be carefully controlled—or it could turn into a tyranny worse than terrorism.'[59] Moreover, it is only a matter of time before NSAGs widely develop or procure armed drone technology[60] (or hack into the operation of a state-controlled drone and assume control).[61] Will not such groups be seeking actively to 'level the killing field'? As a Senior Fellow with the Brookings Institute warned in 2011:

To believe that drones will remain the exclusive province of responsible nations is to disregard the long history of weapons technology. It is only a matter of time before rogue groups or nations hostile to the United States are able to build or acquire their own drones and to use them to launch attacks on our soil or on our soldiers abroad.[62]

[57] Dan Robinson, 'Critics continue to press Obama on targeted killing policy', *Voice of America*, 14 February 2013, <http://www.globalsecurity.org/security/library/news/2013/02/sec-130215-voa02.htm?_m= 3n%2e002a%2e732%2ezi0ao04fz6%2enzs>.

[58] See e.g. Ravi Somaiya, 'Drone strike prompts suit, raising fears for U.S. allies', *New York Times*, 30 January 2013.

[59] A. J. Radsan, 'Loftier standards for the CIA's remote-control killing', p. 8, <http://papers.ssrn.com/ sol3/papers.cfm?abstract_id=1604745>.

[60] In October 2012, the leader of Hezbollah claimed that his group was behind the launch of a drone shot down over Israel by the Israeli Defense Forces (IDF) on 6 October. Sheikh Hassan Nasrallah asserted that the drone was made in Iran and had flown over 'sensitive sites' in Israel: 'Hezbollah admits launching drone over Israel', *BBC*, 11 October 2012, <http://www.bbc.co.uk/news/world-middle-east-19914441>.

[61] In June 2012, US researchers took control of a flying drone by 'hacking' into its GPS system, acting on a US $1,000 dare from the US Department of Homeland Security (DHS). A University of Texas at Austin team used 'spoofing', a technique where by the drone mistakes the signal from hackers for the one sent from GPS satellites. The same method may have been used to bring down a US drone in Iran in 2011: 'Researchers use spoofing to "hack" into a flying drone', *BBC*, 29 June 2012, <http://www.bbc.co.uk/news/technology-18643134>.

[62] John Villasenor, 'Cyber-physical attacks and drone strikes: the next homeland security threat', *The Brookings Institution*, 5 July 2011, <http://www.brookings.edu/research/papers/2011/07/05-drones-villasenor>.

3 International norms on small arms control and the case of Libyan arms into Mali

Mireille Widmer*

Introduction

The Second Review Conference of the 2001 United Nations (UN) Programme of Action to Combat the Illicit Trade in Small Arms and Light Weapons in All its Aspects (the Programme of Action) was held in New York from 27 August to 7 September 2012. Eleven years after the adoption of the Programme of Action, a certain fatigue could be felt among diplomats and activists, who wonder whether their efforts have been worth it—whether the Programme of Action has made any difference to levels of armed conflict and gun violence. Ominously, the International Action Network on Small Arms, the coalition of non-governmental organizations (NGOs), closed down in early 2013. Meanwhile, the campaign for an arms trade treaty was in full swing and, after late setbacks at the diplomatic conferences in July 2012 and March 2013, the UN General Assembly finally adopted the treaty on 2 April 2013. Yet after the celebrations ended many were left to wonder, what now?

This is the context in which this chapter was written. It looks at Libya and Mali as a case study of how guns have ended up in the wrong hands, assessing the relevance and effectiveness of the Programme of Action and the measures it exhorts. The first section briefly outlines the sequence of events leading to the contagion of conflict from Libya to northern Mali, with a particular focus on small arms and light weapons. The second section details the diversion of weapons to insurgents and terrorists in Mali, comparing and contrasting the facts with the normative framework governing arms transfers, stockpile security, border controls, trafficking, and weapons collection, disarmament, and destruction.

* Mireille Widmer is an independent researcher with extensive experience in the UN process on small arms, as well as in armed violence reduction programming in Africa and the Caribbean. The author would like to thank Sarah Parker, Senior Researcher, Small Arms Survey, for her input into this chapter, as well as Nicolas Florquin and Cate Buchanan for their comments on an earlier draft.

The Programme of Action features prominently, although other relevant instruments are also cited, such as the 2001 Firearms Protocol,[1] the European Union (EU) Code of Conduct[2] (and 2008 EU Common Position),[3] the Wassenaar Arrangement,[4] and the Economic Community of West African States (ECOWAS) Convention on Small Arms and Light Weapons.[5] As we will see, the existing normative arsenal calls for most of the necessary measures. Accordingly, the final section discusses five proposals that could help to close the gap between the norms and reality, a suggested roadmap for 'what now?'.

A. Guns and the crisis in Mali (and Libya)

The visit on 7 and 8 February 2011 to northern Mali by Malian President Amanou Toumani Touré raised little interest in the international press. He had come to Kidal region to oversee a 'Flame of Peace' ceremony where a few hundred rifles, pistols, and sub-machine guns were destroyed in exchange for a development programme focusing on safety, hydraulics, and agriculture.[6] On 9 February 2011, local Tuareg leaders called the ceremony a 'provocation'—an attempt to weaken Tuareg groups to the benefit of al-Qaeda in the Islamic Maghreb (AQIM)—and threatened to take up arms again.[7] A year later, in January 2012, dispirited Malian troops were retreating before a much better armed alliance of Tuareg rebels of the Mouvement national pour la libération de l'Azawad (MNLA) and the Ansar Dine jihadist movement. On 21 March 2012, in the capital Bamako, Touré's government was toppled in an apparently spontaneous coup d'état. By the end of 2012, a jihadist coalition had established a proto-state in northern

---

[1] Protocol against the Illicit Manufacturing of and Trafficking in Firearms, their Parts and Components and Ammunition, supplementing the United Nations Convention against Transnational Organized Crime, adopted in New York on 31 May 2001.

[2] 1998 European Union Code of Conduct on Arms Exports.

[3] European Council Common Position 2008/944/CFSP of 8 December 2008 defining common rules governing control of exports of military technology and equipment, *Official Journal of the European Union*, L335, 8 December 2008.

[4] 1995 Wassenaar Arrangement on Export Controls for Conventional Arms and Dual-use Goods and Technologies. See <http://www.wassenaar.org>. Participating states include: Argentina; Australia; Austria; Belgium; Bulgaria; Canada; Croatia; Czech Republic; Denmark; Estonia; Finland; France; Germany; Greece; Hungary; Ireland; Italy; Japan; Latvia; Lithuania; Luxembourg; Malta; Mexico; Netherlands; New Zealand; Norway; Poland; Portugal; Republic of Korea; Romania; Russian Federation; Slovakia; Slovenia; South Africa; Spain; Sweden; Switzerland; Turkey; Ukraine; the United Kingdom (UK); and the United States of America (USA).

[5] ECOWAS Convention on Small Arms and Light Weapons, their Ammunition and Other Related Materials, adopted in Abuja on 14 June 2006.

[6] 'Mali destroys hundreds of weapons', *News24*, 8 February 2011, <http://www.news24.com/Africa/News/Mali-destroys-hundreds-of-weapons-20110208>.

[7] 'Mali: Les anciens rebelles touareg menacent de reprendre les armes', *Elwatan*, 9 February 2011, <http://www.city-dz.com/mali-les-anciens-rebelles-touareg-menacent-de-reprendre-les-armes/>.

Mali and its forces had advanced within striking distance of the capital. France was about to intervene militarily in the country.[8]

As of November 2012, the violence in Mali had led to the displacement of some 412,000 people.[9] The health system in the north of the country was completely disrupted.[10] In addition, Islamist groups who had taken control of the region reportedly committed serious human rights abuses, including summary and extrajudicial executions, sexual and gender-based violence, recruitment and use of children as soldiers, torture, and looting of hospitals.[11] According to the UN Secretary-General, the crisis stemmed 'from long-standing structural conditions such as weak State institutions; ineffective governance; fragile social cohesion; deep-seated feelings among communities in the north of being neglected, marginalized and unfairly treated by the central Government; a weak and externally dependent, albeit vibrant, civil society; and the effects of environmental degradation, climate change and economic shocks'.[12] But these conditions certainly already existed in early 2011. So what happened between February 2011 and January 2012 to explain the reigniting of armed violence?

An explanation can be found across the Sahara desert, in a country more than 1,000 km from Mali's borders: Libya. On 15 February 2011, just a week after Touré's visit to Kidal and at the height of the Arab Spring, the first peaceful demonstrations took place in Libya against Gaddafi's regime. Within weeks, the country was engulfed in a brutal conflict. The response of the international community included an arms embargo, the imposition of a no-fly zone, and North Atlantic Treaty Organization (NATO) air strikes to 'protect civilians'. When Gaddafi was killed and his regime toppled on 20 October 2011, the country had been in total chaos for weeks.

The problem was that Libya had a strong destabilizing potential for the region. Interdependence first rested on the movement of people and capital. Many countries in the Sahel region relied on Libya's relative economic success. The country hosted tens of thousands of immigrants from sub-Saharan countries, some of whom were integrated into Libyan security forces.[13] Economic migrants sent home remittances that constituted a substantial income for impoverished communities in northern Niger and Mali.

Weapons were also plentiful. Most were Soviet-era weaponry acquired in the 1970s and 1980s. After the UN and EU arms embargoes on the country were lifted in 2003 and 2004,

---

[8] For a detailed account of the Mali crisis, see e.g. International Crisis Group (ICG), 'Mali: avoiding escalation', Africa Report No. 189, July 2012; ICG, 'Mali: security, dialogue and meaningful reform', Africa Report No. 201, April 2013.

[9] 'Report of the Secretary-General on the situation in Mali', UN doc. S/2012/894, 29 November 2012, §18.

[10] 'Report of the Secretary-General on the situation in Mali', §19.

[11] 'Report of the Secretary-General on the situation in Mali', §§21–6.

[12] 'Report of the Secretary-General on the situation in Mali', §2.

[13] 'Final report of the Panel of Experts established pursuant to Security Council resolution 1973 (2011) concerning Libya', UN doc. S/2012/163, 20 March 2012, §61.

respectively, Gaddafi spent millions refurbishing a huge arsenal, importing weapons from China, France, Italy, the Russian Federation, Serbia, and the UK, among others.[14] Russia does not publish or share reports on arms exports, and so while there is evidence of Russian weapons in Libya, the scale of transfers is not known.[15] In terms of small arms, Libya's main declared suppliers included Belgium, Bulgaria, and Serbia, while in terms of ammunition, the largest exporters included Bulgaria, France, and the UK.[16] The majority of documented small-calibre ammunition circulating in Libya since early 2011, however, originates from Belgium, China, and former Eastern bloc countries.[17]

The weapons were stored in hundreds of arms caches around the country.[18] Civilian possession was not permitted.[19] But as the conflict spread, so did the weapons:

The conflict in Libya witnessed the loss of national control over military materiel and a complete redistribution of weapons ownership in the country. The distribution of weapons to civilians, the appropriation of the contents of depots by individuals and brigades, coupled with additional military materiel that entered Libya from elsewhere, resulted in the uncontrolled circulation of very large quantities of arms and ammunition during the conflict.[20]

NATO bombed more than 440 weapons storage sites during its campaign.[21] In September and October 2011, Human Rights Watch (HRW) visited several unguarded storage

---

[14] 'Final report of the Panel of Experts established pursuant to Security Council resolution 1973 (2011) concerning Libya', UN doc. S/2012/163, 20 March 2012, §§31–2; Conway Waddington, 'The arms proliferation threat of post-Gaddafi Libya', *Consultancy Africa Intelligence*, 19 December 2011; Vivienne Walt, 'Conflicting priorities imperil effort to gather up Gaddafi's discarded arms', *Time*, 15 November 2011; Gregg Carlstrom and Evan Hill, 'Tracing the Middle East weapons flow', *Al Jazeera*, 24 October 2011; Pieter D. Wezeman, 'Libya: Lessons in controlling the arms trade', *SIPRI*, March 2011.

[15] Amnesty International, *Arms Transfers to the Middle East and North Africa: Lessons for an Effective Arms Trade Treaty*, Amnesty International, London, 2011, p. 44.

[16] Amnesty International, *Arms Transfers to the Middle East and North Africa*, p. 9.

[17] N. R. Jenzen-Jones, *The Headstamp Trail: An Assessment of Small-Calibre Ammunition Found in Libya*, Working Paper 16, Small Arms Survey, Geneva, May 2013, p. 13.

[18] The Panel of Experts visited more than 120 weapons storage sites in its efforts to track man-portable air defence systems (MANPADS): 'Consolidated working document on the implementation of paragraph 5 of Security Council resolution 2017 (2011)', UN doc. S/2012/178, 16 March 2012, §9.

[19] Brian McQuinn, *After the Fall: Libya's Evolving Armed Groups*, Working Paper 12, Small Arms Survey, Geneva, October 2012, p. 43; Markus Symank, 'Libya's unchecked weapons trade: Gaddafi's gangster mentality lives on', *Qantara.de*, 14 November 2012, <http://en.qantara.de/Gaddafis-Gangster-Mentality-Lives-On/20156c21922i1p497/>. The 2010 Libya national report on Programme of Action implementation also states that 'Under the law, only the State may purchase, store, transfer or possess weapons' and that 'No person may carry or possess light weapons without authorization': Libya Arab Jamahiriya, 'Report of the Libyan Arab Jamahiriya on implementation of the United Nations Programme of Action to Prevent, Combat and Eradicate the Illicit Trade in Small Arms and Light Weapons in All Its Aspects submitted pursuant to General Assembly resolution 64/50', 2010, p. 2.

[20] 'Final report of the Panel of Experts established pursuant to Security Council resolution 1973 (2011) concerning Libya', UN doc. S/2012/163, 20 March 2012, p. 5; see also §§33–40. See also McQuinn, *After the Fall: Libya's Evolving Armed Groups*, pp. 43–8.

[21] 'Report of the Secretary-General on the United Nations Support Mission in Libya', UN doc. S/2011/727, 22 November 2011, §43.

facilities in and around Tripoli and Sirte.[22] Many were makeshift facilities located in farms or private companies of Gaddafi loyalists, close to military bases, but far enough to be protected from NATO strikes. HRW paid particular attention to mines and surface-to-air missiles, but in Sirte it reported that 'some weapons, such as AK-103 and FN-1 automatic rifles, had apparently been entirely removed from the site, based on the numerous empty crates there for those weapons'.[23]

Weapons typically fell under the control of hundreds of local brigades or *katibas*: light weapons were held collectively by the brigades, while individuals retained custody of their small arms.[24] The larger brigades attempted to introduce procedures for weapons registration, storage, and use, but accountability tended to decrease for small arms acquired privately by individual brigade members, as well as in smaller brigades with less sophisticated logistics.[25] The dramatic increase in weapons availability after the fall of Zlitan and Tripoli further defeated the brigades' efforts to retain oversight of their weapons.[26]

The weapons became the centre of a lucrative business, whether by arms traffickers[27] or by small contingents of foreign nationals who had fought alongside Gaddafi and had now decided to return home. Such illicit transfers of arms were, of course, not a new phenomenon in the region.[28] Arms traffickers in West Africa include security forces, former or current militants, mercenaries, and nomadic groups that possess the necessary knowledge of the desert terrain.[29] Neglected communities in border areas often derive significant profits from such illicit trafficking, which only lead them further from the reach of the state.[30] Almost all trafficking takes place on land, often through a

---

[22] HRW, 'Libya: secure unguarded arms depots', 9 September 2011, <http://www.hrw.org/news/2011/09/09/libya-secure-unguarded-arms-depots>; HRW, 'Libya: Transitional Council failing to secure weapons', 25 October 2011, <http://www.hrw.org/news/2011/10/25/libya-transitional-council-failing-secure-weapons>.

[23] HRW, 'Libya: Transitional Council failing to secure weapons'.

[24] For an excellent account of the formation and typology of armed groups during and after the Libyan revolution, as well as their procedures related to weapons, see McQuinn, *After the Fall: Libya's Evolving Armed Groups*. See also 'Final report of the Panel of Experts established pursuant to Security Council resolution 1973 (2011) concerning Libya', UN doc. S/2012/163, 20 March 2012, §36.

[25] McQuinn, *After the Fall: Libya's Evolving Armed Groups*, pp. 52–4.

[26] McQuinn, *After the Fall: Libya's Evolving Armed Groups*, p. 46.

[27] 'Final report of the Panel of Experts established pursuant to Security Council resolution 1973 (2011) concerning Libya', UN doc. S/2012/163, 20 March 2012, §§37 and 114.

[28] Arms have been the object of a lively trade in the Sahara since the 1930s. See N. Florquin and S. Pézard, 'Insurgency, disarmament, and insecurity in Northern Mali, 1990–2004' in Nicolas Florquin and Eric G. Berman (eds), *Armed and Aimless: Armed Groups, Guns, and Human Security in the ECOWAS Region*, Small Arms Survey, Geneva, 2005, p. 53.

[29] UN Office on Drugs and Crime (UNODC), *Transnational Organized Crime in West Africa: A Threat Assessment*, UNODC, Vienna, February 2013, p. 36.

[30] UNODC, *Transnational Organized Crime in West Africa*, p. 5. The clashes between Libyan minority and majority ethnic groups in border areas are often motivated by the control of smuggling routes. See 'Final Report of the Panel of Experts established pursuant to resolution 1973 (2011) concerning Libya', UN doc. S/2012/163, 20 March 2012, §30.

number of well-known trading hubs such as Agadez in Niger, Gao in Mali, or areas around the Aïr (Niger), Hoggar (Algeria), and Tibesti (Chad) mountain ranges.[31]

But what changed with the Libyan crisis is the scale of this trade. The 'ant trade' concerns neighbouring Algeria, Niger, and Tunisia from where fighters were streaming across the desert towards northern Mali.[32] It has been estimated that 1,500 to 2,000 Tuareg mercenaries returned to Mali from Libya, each carrying at least his own weapon.[33] Larger scale trafficking by organized criminal and terrorist networks occurred further away from official checkpoints. By way of illustration, in November 2011, the UN Panel of Experts appointed to monitor the arms embargo documented the case of an armed convoy of approximately ten vehicles intercepted by a Niger security patrol on its way from Libya to Mali. Six vehicles were seized containing small arms and light weapons, including 28 AK-type and nine FN FAL assault rifles, five light machine guns, and six heavy machine guns, as well as thousands of rounds of ammunition. The Panel was not able to identify the precise origin of the material.[34] The same month, however, an AQIM leader, Mokhtar Belmokhtar, claimed that AQIM had indeed acquired weapons from Libya.[35]

In January 2012, the imams in Libya forbade the sale of small arms and light weapons, driving the trade underground.[36] But weapons continued to follow these routes throughout 2012. In September 2012, for example, Algerian security forces intercepted a convoy carrying 32 weapons and 14,000 rounds of ammunition close to the Libyan border. The weapons were smuggled from the stockpiles of the Libyan army, and meant to be handed over in the Tazrouk district of Tamanrasset to smuggling gangs and drug dealers.[37] In

---

[31] UNODC, *Transnational Organized Crime in West Africa*, p. 35.

[32] 'Final report of the Panel of Experts established pursuant to Security Council resolution 1973 (2011) concerning Libya', UN doc. S/2013/99, 9 March 2013, §§118–47; see also 'Final report of the Panel of Experts established pursuant to Security Council resolution 1973 (2011) concerning Libya', UN doc. S/2012/163, 20 March 2012, §§116–37; 'Le Retour délicat au Mali d'ex-combattants libyens d'origine malienne', *RFI*, 12 October 2011.

[33] UNODC, *Transnational organized crime in West Africa*, p. 37. It should be noted that not all fighters who arrived from Libya sympathized with the rebellion dynamics in northern Mali: 'Consolidated working document on the implementation of paragraph 5 of Security Council resolution 2017 (2011)', UN doc. S/2012/178, 16 March 2012, §38.

[34] 'Final report of the Panel of Experts established pursuant to Security Council resolution 1973 (2011) concerning Libya', UN doc. S/2012/163, 20 March 2012, §§130–5.

[35] 'Final report of the Panel of Experts established pursuant to Security Council resolution 1973 (2011) concerning Libya', UN doc. S/2012/163, 20 March 2012, §144. The AQIM's financial resources allegedly came in part from the large ransoms paid by Western countries for the release of hostages: an estimated €50 million between 2003 and 2010. See ICG, 'Mali: Avoiding escalation', p. 6.

[36] McQuinn, *After the Fall: Libya's Evolving Armed Groups*, p. 50.

[37] Walid Ramzi, 'Algeria thwarts arms smuggling across Libya border', *Magharebia*, 21 September 2012, <http://magharebia.com/en_GB/articles/awi/features/2013/04/16/feature-01>.

January 2013, the President of Tunisia declared that his country was turning into a corridor for armaments between Libya and areas such as Mali.[38]

Other weapons flowed south towards Chad and Nigeria,[39] but increasingly also east towards Egypt and onwards towards the Gaza Strip.[40] In fact, the more complex weapons systems may have been smuggled to the Middle East rather than West Africa, 'because most West African groups lack the expertise to make optimal use of the latest technology'.[41] Some transfers were made by sea, including towards the Syrian Arab Republic, passing through either Turkey or Lebanon.[42] On 27 April 2012, for example, a shipment of arms and ammunition was seized aboard the *Letfallah II* in Tripoli, Lebanon. The shipment included three containers with MANPADS, anti-tank guided missiles, and various types of small arms, light and heavy weapons, and ammunition.[43]

What was being done to stem the tide? The brigades had little capacity to control the massive weapons stockpiles. In August 2011, shortly after Tripoli fell in the hands of National Transitional Council (NTC)-aligned forces, the US Department of State issued a factsheet outlining its efforts to stem the proliferation of nuclear material, chemical agents, ballistic missiles, and conventional weapons, primarily MANPADS.[44] The factsheet stated that the USA had provided US$3 million to two NGOs, MAG International and the Swiss Foundation for Mine Action (FSD), to 'recruit and train staff local explosive ordnance disposal teams'. The teams were said to have been in operation since May 2011 and to have destroyed 5.8 tons of munitions, including five MANPADS. A MANPADS task force also visited Libya's neighbours to discuss ways to counter weapons proliferation. On 2 September 2011, *The Guardian* reported that the USA and NATO were pressing Libya's NTC to address the problem, and that the USA had promised US$4.5 million to collect and destroy Libya's missiles and other light weapons.[45]

---

[38] *France 24* interview with Moncef Marzouki on 14 January 2013, cited in 'Final Report of the Panel of Experts established pursuant to resolution 1973 (2011) concerning Libya', UN doc. S/2013/99, 9 March 2013, §124.

[39] 'Final Report of the Panel of Experts established pursuant to resolution 1973 (2011) concerning Libya', UN doc. S/2013/99, 9 March 2013, §§148–54.

[40] 'Final Report of the Panel of Experts established pursuant to resolution 1973 (2011) concerning Libya', UN doc. S/2013/99, 9 March 2013, §§156–67. See also David D. Kirkpatrick, 'Egypt's arrests of smugglers show threat of Libya arms', *New York Times*, 13 October 2011, <http://www.nytimes.com/2011/10/14/world/middleeast/egypt-arrests-groups-smuggling-weapons-from-libya.html?_r=0>.

[41] UNODC, *Transnational Organized Crime in West Africa*, p. 33.

[42] 'Final report of the Panel of Experts established pursuant to Security Council resolution 1973 (2011) concerning Libya', UN doc. S/2013/99, 9 March 2013, §§114 and 168–88.

[43] 'Final report of the Panel of Experts established pursuant to Security Council resolution 1973 (2011) concerning Libya', UN doc. S/2013/99, 9 March 2013, §§171–82.

[44] US Department of State, 'Libya: securing stockpiles promotes security', Factsheet, 26 August 2011.

[45] Richard Norton-Taylor and Nick Hopkins, 'Libya warned smugglers are looting Gaddafi's guns', *The Guardian*, 2 September 2011, <http://www.guardian.co.uk/world/2011/sep/02/west-warns-smugglers-looting-libya-arms>.

The UN Support Mission in Libya (UNSMIL) was established through UN Security Council Resolution 2009, adopted on 16 September 2011. It was tasked, inter alia, with assisting and supporting national efforts to restore public security order and promote the rule of law. Concern at weapons proliferation was expressed by the Security Council on 31 October 2011 through Resolution 2017, which called on member states and international and regional organizations and entities, including relevant UN bodies, to provide the necessary assistance to the Libyan authorities and states in the region in order to 'prevent the proliferation of all arms and related materiel of all types, in particular man-portable surface-to-air missiles', in the region.[46]

By November, it was reported that the USA had contracted the private security company DynCorp to track MANPADS.[47] The UK sent a small military team to help find and dismantle missiles.[48] Germany also provided €750,000 to the FSD to secure and destroy small arms, including MANPADS.[49] More funds were pledged by Canada.[50] In Misrata, the UN supported the construction of two new storage facilities for ammunition and weapons depots, one funded by Libya and the other by Switzerland, while NGOs offered training on ammunition management, accounting, and firefighting.[51] But US concern extended mainly to surface-to-air missiles. It showed little to no interest in other weapons systems, such as assault rifles and landmines, and Western countries did not deploy their own personnel to this end.[52]

The international community's response was consistent with the 'light footprint' approach adopted by the international community, and supported by the NTC, when UN Security Council Resolution 1973 was adopted in 2011. The USA wanted to limit its involvement to airstrikes and a no-fly zone. The NTC rejected the deployment

---

[46] UN Security Council Resolution 2017 (2011), §§1 and 4.

[47] Vivienne Walt, 'Conflicting priorities imperil effort to gather up Gaddafi's discarded arms', *Time*, 15 November 2011. See also Mary Beth Sheridan, 'U.S. launches campaign to track down Libyan missiles', *Washington Post*, 14 October 2011; Eric Schmitt and Kareem Fahim, 'U.S. sending more contractors to secure Libya's weapons stockpile', *New York Times*, 14 October 2011. It should be noted that, in March 2012, the Panel of Experts reported that no MANPADS originating from Libya had been seized outside Libya: 'Consolidated working document on the implementation of paragraph 5 of Security Council resolution 2017 (2011)', UN doc. S/2012/178, 16 March 2012, §5.

[48] Mary Beth Sheridan, 'U.S. launches campaign to track down Libyan missiles'. *Washington Post*, 14 October 2011.

[49] German Federal Foreign Office, 'German Government provides EUR 750,000 for destruction of small arms in Libya', Press release, 16 October 2011, <http://www.auswaertiges-amt.de/EN/Infoservice/Presse/Meldungen/2011/111016_BuReg_Unterstuetzung_Kleinwaffenvernichtung_LBY.html>.

[50] HRW, 'Libya: Transitional Council failing to secure weapons'.

[51] UNSMIL, 'Stray weapons and ammunition: a threat to Libya and beyond', undated, <http://unsmil.unmissions.org/Default.aspx?tabid=3543&ctl=Details&mid=6187&ItemID=1142006&language=en-US>.

[52] Some voices in the region also opposed more direct intervention. Tunisia's Deputy Minister of Foreign Affairs was quoted saying that the proliferation of weapons was a Libyan national concern in which he could not interfere: Ahmed Ellali, 'Alarming UN Report highlights proliferation of weapons in Libya', *TunisiaLive*, 27 November 2011, <http://www.tunisia-live.net/2011/11/27/alarming-un-report-highlights-proliferation-of-weapons-in-libya/>.

of any kind of military force. The problem was, of course, that the NTC was in no position to secure stockpiles, and so the Council resolution effectively created a security vacuum. On 26 January 2012, South Africa declared at a Security Council meeting that 'Council resolution 1973 (2011) had been implemented in a way that would have dire consequences—such as the proliferation of arms—that could exacerbate terrorist activity'.[53]

B. **Relevance of the Programme of Action**

The flow of weapons from Libya to Mali and the Sahel since 2011 resembles a case of the 'destabilizing accumulation and transfer' of weapons that the UN process on small arms was meant to prevent.[54] The link between weapons transfers and the Malian insurgency was cautiously admitted by the Panel of Experts monitoring the implementation of the Libyan arms embargo.[55] In his report on the situation in Mali, the UN Secretary-General also states that 'the Tuareg rebellion was emboldened by the presence of well-equipped combatants returning from Libya in the wake of the fall of the regime there'.[56]

Of course, insurgents in northern Mali did not wait for the Gaddafi regime to collapse before acquiring weapons. Weapons sources abound in the region: from Eritrea and Sudan (Darfur), via Chad and Niger; from Sierra Leone and Liberia, via Guinea; from Mauritania and Algeria.[57] Mali's own armouries also provide a source of weapons for the illicit trade.[58] Yet the case of Libya is interesting because it is well documented

[53] 'Statement by Council President Baso Sangqu, speaking in his national capacity', UN doc. SC/10533, 26 January 2012.

[54] The Panel of Governmental Experts on Small Arms set up in 1995 to define the problem to be tackle was mandated to examine 'the ways and means to prevent and reduce the excessive and destabilizing accumulation and transfer of small arms and light weapons'. See UN General Assembly Resolution 50/70B, adopted on 12 December 1995, §1. In the Programme of Action, however, the expression was confined to the Preamble, mainly due to concerns expressed by Arab states. See Sarah Parker and Marcus Wilson, *A Diplomat's Guide to the UN Small Arms Process*, Small Arms Survey, Geneva, 2012, p. 30.

[55] 'Consolidated working document on the implementation of paragraph 5 of Security Council resolution 2017 (2011)', UN doc. S/2012/178, 16 March 2012, §38: '[W]hile some rebel dynamics were evident in northern Mali for some time, it is difficult to assess the influence of the fighters and the weapons that came out of Libya on current violent events . . . [T]he arrival of large quantities of weapons, light weapons in particular, including those mounted on vehicles, and armed fighters, some of whom may indeed be participating in the current armed violence, may have been an encouraging factor for predatory behaviour, often masked as a rebellion.'

[56] 'Report of the Secretary-General on the situation in Mali', UN doc. S/2012/894, 29 November 2012, §4.

[57] Laurent Touchard, 'Crise malienne: d'où viennent les armes des djihadistes?', *Jeune Afrique*, 8 November 2012, <http://www.jeuneafrique.com/Article/JA2703p010-013.xmll/>. For information on weapons purchases by armed groups in the 1990s, see Florquin and Pézard, 'Insurgency, disarmament, and insecurity in Northern Mali, 1990–2004', pp. 50–4.

[58] Commission nationale de lutte contre la prolifération des armes légères, *Rapport à la BMS-4*, Bamako, 2010.

by the Panel of Experts, monitoring groups, and independent media, and illustrates a wide array of issues. The crucial question is to determine why existing measures did not suffice to prevent such destabilizing accumulation and transfer. Is this a sign of failure for the UN process on small arms control? Could something more have been done to stem the flow of weapons to the Sahel?

TRANSFER CONTROLS

The first question is whether weapons should have been exported to Libya in the first place. Under the Programme of Action, states undertook to 'assess applications for export authorizations according to strict national regulations and procedures that cover all small arms and light weapons and are consistent with the existing responsibilities of States under relevant international law, taking into account in particular the risk of diversion of these weapons into the illegal trade'.[59]

Among other relevant international norms, the Wassenaar Arrangement commits participating states to maintain national export controls in accordance to a set of best practices, guidelines, and elements. Wassenaar includes the world's major arms producers (including the Russian Federation, the USA, and Ukraine) except for China. Participating states agree to report on transfers or denials to destinations outside of the Arrangement, and to exchange information on dual-use goods and technologies. Small arms and light weapons (including MANPADS and ammunition) are one of the categories of weapons covered by the Arrangement. Some of the elements to be taken into account for assessing transfer requests include existing tensions or armed conflict, record of compliance with humanitarian law, respect for human rights and fundamental freedoms, risk of diversion, existence of sanctions, risk of the weapons being used for repression, and facilitating organized crime, as well as criteria related to stockpile management and tracing.[60] But the decision to transfer weapons or not remains the sole prerogative of each participating state, and even when one states notifies a denial of a transfer request, other states do not have to deny similar transfers.[61] No state can be called to account for its decisions under the Wassenaar Arrangement.

The 2001 Firearms Protocol excludes state-to-state transfers from its scope of application.[62] It nevertheless mandates a system of export and import licensing or authorization, as well as measures on international transit.[63] The text does not, however, specify conditions for granting or not such licences, which of course reduces its effectiveness.

---

[59] Programme of Action, §11.
[60] Wassenaar Arrangement: Best practice guidelines for exports of small arms and light weapons.
[61] Wassenaar Arrangement: Initial Elements, §§II.3 and II.4.
[62] 2001 Firearms Protocol, Art. 4.   [63] 2001 Firearms Protocol, Art. 10.

At the regional level, the EU Common Position is considered one of the most advanced instruments on arms exports. Its eight criteria were first adopted in 1998 as a politically binding EU Code of Conduct, before being upgraded to this legally binding Common Position in 2008. The criteria include: respect for international obligations such as sanctions, arms embargoes, and non-proliferation treaties, including the Wassenaar Arrangement (criterion 1); respect for human rights and humanitarian law, including the risk of internal repression (criterion 2); existence of tensions or armed conflict in the recipient country (criterion 3); regional peace and security (criterion 4); national security of EU states and their allies (criterion 5); behaviour of the recipient states with regards to terrorism (criterion 6); risk of diversion (criterion 7); and proportionality of the arms purchase to the technical and economic capacity of the recipient country (criterion 8). However, despite the legally binding nature of the Common Position, states continue to maintain final control of all aspects of arms export licensing.[64]

Were these dispositions properly applied? The Arab Spring could hardly have been predicted before events unfolded in Tunisia in December 2010, and the possibility of weapons then seeping to neighbouring countries was only discussed once Libyan stockpiles were already dispersed. But Libya's human rights record, as well as its history of supplying weapons to armed groups in the region, was well documented. So while the arms embargoes (EU and UN) were lifted in 2003–04, questions should still have been raised about respect for human rights and the risks of diversion. The sales should also have been questioned on the basis that 'Tripoli attempted to import quantities of SALW [small arms and light weapons] far beyond the legitimate needs of its armed forces'.[65]

Indeed, during 2006–10, EU member states denied 54 applications to export military equipment (including, but not limited to, small arms and light weapons) to Libya.[66] But the application of the EU Common Position was uneven, and most export applications were granted. Two cases of small arms exports to Libya by European states in particular shed light on the weaknesses of these norms and commitments.

In October 2008, Libya signed a €11.5 million contract with Belgian arms producer FN Herstal for the supply of various small arms (2,000 semi-automatic riot guns, 417 pistols, 367 sub-machine guns, and 30 light machine guns, along with spare parts, accessories,

---

[64] Mark Bromley, 'The review of the EU Common Position on arms exports: prospects for strengthened controls', Non-Proliferation Papers No. 7, EU Non-Proliferation Consortium, January 2012, pp. 2 and 6. See also An Vranckx, Frank Slijper, and Roy Isbister (eds), *Lessons from MENA: Appraising EU Transfers of Military and Security Equipment to the Middle East and North Africa*, Academia Press, Gent, November 2011, p. 11.

[65] Vranckx, Slijper and Isbister (eds), *Lessons from MENA*, p. 40.

[66] Bromley, 'The review of the EU Common Position on arms exports: prospects for strengthened controls', p. 12. A few of the applications concerned small arms and light weapons. For example, in October 2008, the UK denied a brokering licence for the transfer of 130,000 Kalashnikov rifles from Ukraine to Libya, invoking the risk of diversion.

and ammunition).[67] The company sought five export licences from the Walloon regional government, incidentally its sole shareholder. In February 2009, an expert advisory commission concluded that, with the exception of the riot guns, the risk of proliferation was too high, and issued a negative advice. FN Herstal then submitted complementary information, which led the commission to reconsider the matter. This time, no conclusive advice was offered. Under pressure from the local trade union, the Walloon government signed the export authorization in June 2009. Civil society groups then complained, leading the Belgian government to put the licences on hold, arguing that the Walloon regional parliament had not reviewed the decision because it had, at that time, already resigned pending elections. So the Walloon government repeated the licensing procedure. The national government eventually cancelled the licences in April 2010, but by then the weapons seemed to have already been delivered to Libya.

In another case, somewhere between June and November 2009, Italy's Fabbrica d'Armi Pietro Beretta exported 7,500 revolvers and pistols, 1,900 semi-automatic carbines, and 1,800 shotguns to Libya's General People's Committee for Public Security, via Malta.[68] The items were marked as non-military, so that, under Italian law, the export permit would be granted by the Ministry of Interior's local authority in Brescia rather than the Ministry of Foreign Affairs in Rome.[69] As a result, Italy did not declare the export in the 2009 EU Annual Report. Malta, however, voluntarily reported the transit licence, which led to questions being asked. Italian officials first denied knowledge of the transaction. The Prefect of Brescia eventually admitted to having authorized the sale, but clearly the Ministry of Interior had not shared the information with the Ministries of Defence or Foreign Affairs. The arms that had been transferred were apt for military use, and were indeed received by the Libyan Ministry of Defence.

Outside the EU, the scale of small arms exports was also significant: for example 100,000 automatic rifles were imported from Ukraine in 2006–07 and a further 100,000 from Romania in 2008.[70] Both states participate in the Wassenaar Arrangement, but

---

[67] The story is detailed in Vranckx, Slijper, and Isbister (eds), *Lessons from MENA*, pp. 41–3. See also Bromley, 'The review of the EU Common Position on arms exports: prospects for strengthened controls', pp. 11–12; Damien Spleeters, 'Profit and proliferation: a special report on Belgian arms in the Arab Uprising, Part 1', *New York Times blog*, 5 April 2012, <http://atwar.blogs.nytimes.com/2012/04/05/profit-and-proliferation-a-special-report-on-belgian-arms-in-the-arab-uprising-part-i/>.

[68] Amnesty International, *Arms Transfers to the Middle East and North Africa*, p. 43. The shipment was initially declared with a value of €79.7 million. The Italian company later said it had made a mistake in declaring the value of the shipment to the Maltese authorities, which would have been instead €7.9 million. There are still doubts about the actual value and quantity shipped to Libya. See also Bromley, 'The review of the EU Common Position on arms exports: prospects for strengthened controls', p. 11; Vranckx, Slijper, and Isbister (eds), *Lessons from MENA*, pp. 43–4.

[69] Amnesty International, *Arms Transfers to the Middle East and North Africa*, p. 43.

[70] Vranckx, Slijper, and Isbister (eds), *Lessons from MENA*, p. 40. See also Wezeman, 'Libya: lessons in controlling the arms trade'.

neither seemingly saw grounds for denying export licences. By contrast, the USA restored diplomatic ties with Libya in 2006, but never gave military export clearance.[71]

Transfers to Mali could also be questioned, if not necessarily on human rights grounds, then at least for the risk of diversion and regional stability. As noted, tensions in the north were not new and the region has already experienced armed conflict.[72] ECOWAS states adopted in 2009 a Convention on Small Arms and Light Weapons, which bans the transfer of such weapons into, from, or through their territories, except when an exemption is granted 'to meet legitimate national defence and security needs'.[73] Such requests for exemptions are considered by the ECOWAS Executive Secretary and must be refused, inter alia, if the weapons will be used 'to worsen the internal situation in the country of final destination, in terms of provoking or prolonging armed conflicts, or aggravating existing tensions', or if they are 'likely to be diverted, within the transit or importing country or be re-exported, to unauthorized uses or users or into the illicit trade'.[74]

Press reports emerged of a shipment of undisclosed quantities of Bulgarian-made weapons acquired by Mali under President Touré, which arrived at the port in Conakry (Guinea) on 27 July 2012. Due to political instability in Mali following the March coup, the Guinean authorities decided to hold up the shipment pending a decision by ECO-WAS.[75] ECOWAS eventually allowed the weapons to be provided to Mali's new Unity government in October 2012.[76]

For exporting states, these examples are said to highlight the tension between economic considerations and peace and security.[77] In the view of Amnesty International: 'It is apparent that political and economic interests have often been prioritized in the decision-making process over human rights considerations.'[78] Are existing instruments still giving states too much latitude in deciding over export licences? And what about new instruments? While the new Arms Trade Treaty (ATT), adopted in April 2013, provides that states parties shall conduct export risk assessments in an 'objective and non-discriminatory manner',[79] ultimately a decision to export (unless

---

[71] Vranckx, Slijper, and Isbister (eds), *Lessons from MENA*, p. 36.

[72] ICG, 'Mali: Avoiding escalation', pp. 2–5; Florquin and Pézard, 'Insurgency, disarmament, and insecurity in Northern Mali, 1990–2004'.

[73] ECOWAS Convention on Small Arms and Light Weapons, Arts 3.1 and 4.1.

[74] ECOWAS Convention on Small Arms and Light Weapons, Arts 5 and 6.

[75] 'Mali: les armes bloquées sur le point d'être livrées à l'armée malienne', *Koaci.com*, 12 September 2012.

[76] 'Guinea frees blocked Mali arms shipment', *BBC*, 18 October 2012.

[77] Vranckx, Slijper, and Isbister (eds), *Lessons from MENA*, pp. 10 and 23: '[U]ntil a potential recipient reaches the point of being regarded as fundamentally unacceptable, it would seem that the potential for financial profit and political influence that arms sales provide may sometimes prove difficult for EU Member States to resist, especially where there is reason to think that trouble is not imminent'.

[78] Amnesty International, *Arms Transfers to the Middle East and North Africa*, p. 66.

[79] Arms Trade Treaty, Art. 7(1).

it is prohibited under the treaty or other applicable international law) is one of national prerogative. Even at the importing end, the example of Mali shows that, although strong regional arrangements can improve scrutiny, eventually weapons transfers may be permitted all the same.

ARMS EMBARGOES

Following the imposition of the UN and EU arms embargoes on the Libyan regime in 2011, many exporting states suspended or revoked export licences. Nevertheless, additional weapons were supplied to the rebels during the armed conflict with the Gaddafi regime, in contravention of the arms embargo.

Qatar was said to have organized many flights and deliveries of a range of arms and ammunition to the Libyan opposition.[80] In July 2011, for example, 'a news report broadcast by the Swiss channel SF1 showed that Swiss ammunition, Ball M80, 7.62×51 mm, made by the Swiss producer RUAG Ammotec was used by the revolutionaries. The box of ammunition clearly stated that the ammunition had been exported to the Qatar armed forces in 2009 by a Swiss company, FGS Frex'.[81] In this case, Qatar appears to have re-exported military material to Libyan rebels in contravention of a formal pledge not to re-export, and also in violation of the arms embargo. Qatar explained that this was an isolated 'misadventure'.[82] Yet other such cases have been documented, such as the transfer of Pakistani-made ammunition sold to Qatar in the 1980s,[83] or the transfer of a Belgian assault rifle that could have been exported to Qatar in 1980.[84]

The United Arab Emirates (UAE) was also found to have breached the arms embargo, notably in a complex operation whereby the UAE purchased surplus Albanian ammunition via a Ukrainian intermediary and an Armenian arms broker, which then organized the shipments to Libya via an Armenian air carrier.[85] According to media reports, these operations had likely received the blessing of the US administration, on condition

---

[80] 'Final Report of the Panel of Experts established pursuant to resolution 1973 (2011) concerning Libya' UN doc. S/2013/99, 9 March 2013, §62.

[81] 'Final report of the Panel of Experts established pursuant to Security Council resolution 1973 (2011) concerning Libya', UN doc. S/2012/163, 20 March 2012, §§97–102.

[82] 'Final report of the Panel of Experts established pursuant to Security Council resolution 1973 (2011) concerning Libya', UN doc. S/2012/163, 20 March 2012, §98.

[83] 'Final Report of the Panel of Experts established pursuant to resolution 1973 (2011) concerning Libya', UN doc. S/2013/99, 9 March 2013, §§67–70.

[84] 'Final Report of the Panel of Experts established pursuant to resolution 1973 (2011) concerning Libya', UN doc. S/2013/99, 9 March 2013, §73.

[85] 'Final Report of the Panel of Experts established pursuant to resolution 1973 (2011) concerning Libya', UN doc. S/2013/99, 9 March 2013, §§77–97.

that no US weapons would be shipped to Libya in this way.[86] Disturbingly, arms shipments from Qatar and the UAE had to be coordinated with NATO, so that its air and sea forces would not interdict the cargo planes and freighters.[87] The Panel of Experts indeed documented three cases in which flights received 'deconfliction' numbers from NATO.[88]

The media and monitoring groups widely reported airdrops or other shipments of armaments to rebel fighters by France, Italy, and the UK.[89] The Panel of Experts makes no mention of these, limiting its reports to the declared transfers of non-lethal materials by France, Italy, the UK, and the USA.[90] It does, however, note other suspected violations from Sudan, a Canadian private security company, and—after the end of the uprising—a Maltese national.[91]

In the Programme of Action, states undertook to 'take all appropriate measures, including all legal or administrative means, against any activity that violates a United Nations Security Council arms embargo in accordance with the Charter of the United Nations'.[92] Cooperation with the UN system to implement arms embargoes is also recommended at global level.[93] In addition, states undertook to 'make every effort, in accordance with national laws and practices, without prejudice to the right of States to re-export small arms and light weapons that they have previously imported, to notify the original exporting State in accordance with their bilateral agreements before the retransfer of those weapons'.[94] Both the Wassenaar Arrangement[95] and the EU Common Position[96] similarly mandate respect for UN sanctions and arms embargoes.

The transfer of weapons to Libyan opposition fighters despite the arms embargo illustrates a tension between political or strategic interests of states and their international obligations. In this instance, it could be asked whether certain states believe

---

[86] James Risen, Mark Mazzetti, and Michael S. Schmidt, 'U.S.-approved arms for Libya rebels fell into Jihadis' hands', *New York Times*, 5 December 2012, <http://www.nytimes.com/2012/12/06/world/africa/weapons-sent-to-libyan-rebels-with-us-approval-fell-into-islamist-hands.html?pagewanted=all>.

[87] Risen, Mazzetti, and Schmidt, 'U.S.-approved arms for Libya rebels fell into Jihadis' hands'.

[88] 'Final Report of the Panel of Experts established pursuant to resolution 1973 (2011) concerning Libya', UN doc. S/2013/99, 9 March 2013, §§94–7.

[89] Amnesty International, *Arms Transfers to the Middle East and North Africa*, pp. 48–9. See also Vranckx, Slijper, and Isbister (eds), *Lessons from MENA*, p. 47; Anirudh Sivaram and Theodore Karasik, 'An arms buyback for Libya?—Analysis', Institute for Near East and Gulf Military Analysis (INEGMA), 9 June 2012.

[90] 'Final report of the Panel of Experts established pursuant to Security Council resolution 1973 (2011) concerning Libya', UN doc. S/2012/163, 20 March 2012, §§76–85.

[91] 'Final Report of the Panel of Experts established pursuant to resolution 1973 (2011) concerning Libya', 'Final Report of the Panel of Experts established pursuant to resolution 1973 (2011) concerning Libya', UN doc. S/2013/99, 9 March 2013, §§101–3 and 109–11.

[92] Programme of Action, §15.   [93] Programme of Action, §32.

[94] Programme of Action, §13.

[95] Wassenaar Arrangement: Elements for objective analysis and advice concerning potentially destabilizing accumulations of conventional weapons, §2(f) and (g).

[96] 2008 European Council Common Position, Criterion 1a.

they have a moral right to violate arms embargoes when they view this as a necessary measure to correct a blatant imbalance between an 'oppressor' state's armed forces and a 'civilian' resistance movement.[97]

STOCKPILE SECURITY

While some weapons transferred to Libya after 2003–04 allegedly found their way to insurgent groups across the Sahel,[98] this is far from being systematically the case. When tracing has been possible, it generally points at weapons that had been in Libyan stockpiles for decades.[99] Clearly, the longevity of small arms and light weapons poses challenges that cannot be addressed by transfer controls alone: officials granting export licences can hardly be expected to anticipate events 30 or 40 years later. Furthermore, regional availability of weapons in West Africa is of such an extent today that it is no longer necessary to import weapons from outside the continent.[100] Preventing weapons from igniting or fuelling conflicts therefore calls for a discussion of measures able to control weapons that are *already* in the region. First in line is stockpile security of weapons and ammunition—both in Libya and Mali.

In the Programme of Action, states undertook to:

…ensure, subject to the respective constitutional and legal systems of States, that the armed forces, police or any other body authorized to hold small arms and light weapons establish adequate and detailed standards and procedures relating to the management and security of their stocks of these weapons. These standards and procedures should, inter alia, relate to: appropriate locations for stockpiles; physical security measures; control of access to stocks; inventory management and accounting control; staff training; security, accounting and control of small arms and light weapons held or transported by operational units or authorized personnel; and procedures and sanctions in the event of thefts or loss.[101]

[97] See e.g. Guy Desmond, 'NATO hits Libyan arms depot as West faces dilemma', *Reuters*, 9 May 2011. NATO states also sought to correct this imbalance by destroying weapons in the regime's hands through systematic bombardment of known weapons storage sites.

[98] Damien McElroy, 'Libya: Algeria closes borders as row rages over weapons smuggling', *Daily Telegraph*, 4 September 2011. See also Risen, Mazzetti, and Schmidt, 'US-approved arms for Libya rebels fell into Jihadi's hands'.

[99] On this issue, see C. J. Chivers, 'Looted Libyan arms in Mali may have shifted conflict's path', *New York Times*, 7 February 2013, <http://www.nytimes.com/2013/02/08/world/africa/looted-libyan-arms-in-mali-may-have-shifted-conflicts-path.html>. Of course, not all weapons used by Mali insurgents come from Libya. For more information on weapons and ammunition identified in Northern Mali, see Conflict Armament Research and Small Arms Survey, *Rebel Forces in Northern Mali: Documented Weapons, Ammunition and Related Materiel, April 2012–March 2013*, Conflict Armament Research/Small Arms Survey, London/Geneva, 2013.

[100] UNODC, *Transnational Organized Crime in West Africa*, p. 33.

[101] Programme of Action, §17. Paragraph 18 further mandates regular reviews of stocks, and destruction of surplus stocks.

At regional level also, the Programme of Action recommends to 'encourage States to promote safe, effective stockpile management and security, in particular physical security measures, for small arms and light weapons, and to implement, where appropriate, regional and subregional mechanisms in this regard'.[102]

Clearly, Libya, as probably many post-conflict states, does not have adequate stockpile security. For a long time, known weapons depots were not even guarded. According to Stohl, the threat 'wasn't taken that seriously until the looting began full-on'.[103] The challenges are enormous. Inventories need to be drawn up, weapons properly maintained and secured, and access and removal controlled. This requires action by the new Libyan authorities, but also the provision of technical expertise and resources by the international community.

Assistance was arguably slow in coming, particularly as the issues encountered in Libya echoed a scenario experienced in Iraq a few years earlier, and which could therefore be anticipated.[104] In November 2011, the UN reported that only one team had been deployed for the clearance of ammunition storage areas in Tobruk.[105] As already noted, priority was clearly given to surface-to-air missiles and mustard gas. While UNSMIL and international partners gradually moved in to help secure weapons storages, in March 2013 the Panel of Experts still regretted that 'these efforts are conducted only in certain parts of the country'.[106]

Revolutionary brigades have now come together under the National Shield, a self-proclaimed army-in-waiting reporting to the head of the National Army.[107] While they are willing and sometimes eager to transfer custody of conventional and light weapons to centralized facilities, brigade commanders complain of a lack of safe storage facilities that would enable the handover.[108] In parallel, a minority of unregulated brigades view their political weight as a function of military power, which makes them reluctant to coordinate efforts to secure stockpiles.[109] In March 2012, the Panel of Experts regretted the difficulty of accessing Libyan brigades' weapons stockpiles to map and secure them.[110]

[102] Programme of Action, §29.

[103] Rachel Stohl, quoted in Mary Beth Sheridan, 'U.S. launches campaign to track down Libyan missiles', *Washington Post*, 14 October 2011.

[104] C. J. Chivers, 'Reading the refuse: counting Qaddafi's heat-seeking missiles, and tracking them back to their sources', *New York Times blog*, 26 July 2011, <http://atwar.blogs.nytimes.com/2012/04/05/profit-and-proliferation-a-special-report-on-belgian-arms-in-the-arab-uprising-part-i/>.

[105] 'Report of the Secretary-General on the United Nations Support Mission in Libya', UN doc. S/2011/727, 22 November 2011, §43.

[106] 'Final Report of the Panel of Experts established pursuant to resolution 1973 (2011) concerning Libya', UN doc. S/2013/99, 9 March 2013, §43. Operations were likely constrained by the deterioration of security in parts of Libya.

[107] McQuinn, *After the Fall: Libya's Evolving Armed Groups*, pp. 12, 18, and 56.

[108] McQuinn, *After the Fall: Libya's Evolving Armed Groups*, pp. 21 and 50–4.

[109] 'Final report of the Panel of Experts established pursuant to Security Council resolution 1973 (2011) concerning Libya', UN doc. S/2012/163, 20 March 2012, §§26 and 35.

[110] 'Final report of the Panel of Experts established pursuant to Security Council resolution 1973 (2011) concerning Libya', UN doc. S/2012/163, 20 March 2012, §39. See also recommendation at §222 and

Twelve months later, the Panel of Experts remarked that 'most Libyan stockpiles remain under the control of non-State actors'.[111]

Stockpile management is also an issue in Mali. The 2009 ECOWAS Convention on Small Arms and Light Weapons sets up standards and procedures for stockpile management, storage and security. They include the following: '(a) appropriate site; (b) physical security measures of storage facilities; (c) inventory management and record keeping; (d) staff training; (e) security during manufacture and transportation; (f) sanctions in case of theft or loss.'[112] The Convention also provides that: 'Member States shall institute appropriate and effective measures for cooperation between administrative departments concerned and law enforcement agencies to curb corruption associated with the illicit manufacturing of, trafficking in, illicit possession and use of small arms and light weapons.'[113]

In a 2010 report, Mali's National Commission for Combatting Small Arms Proliferation noted that weapons and ammunition stockpiles need to be better secured: '[W]eapons and ammunition of all categories exist and circulate illicitly in all regions of the country. Some weapons stem from illicit trafficking, while others [come] from national weapons stockpiles due to inadequate storage and management.'[114] Mali reported at the time that it benefited from international support in this area, under the leadership of Switzerland, and that two missions were conducted focusing on weapons and ammunition stockpiles. In 2012, large quantities of weapons from Malian stockpiles nevertheless fell into insurgents' hands.[115]

Despite clear guidance from the Programme of Action and ECOWAS Convention, stockpile management and security remains a weak point in the arsenal of measures destined to control weapons. The issue is, of course, entangled with problems of security sector reform and corruption. Could more be done at the global level to ensure that standards are respected?

'Consolidated working document on the implementation of paragraph 5 of Security Council resolution 2017 (2011)', UN doc. S/2012/178, 16 March 2012, §13.

[111] 'Final Report of the Panel of Experts established pursuant to resolution 1973 (2011) concerning Libya', UN doc. S/2013/99, 9 March 2013, p. 5. It should be noted, however, that the distinction between 'state' and 'non-state' cannot be easily made in Libya at the moment, given that most 'non-state' revolutionary brigades actually perform government-mandated tasks, including securing elections. See McQuinn, *After the Fall: Libya's Evolving Armed Groups*, pp. 21–4.

[112] ECOWAS Convention on Small Arms and Light Weapons, Art. 16.

[113] ECOWAS Convention on Small Arms and Light Weapons, Art. 13.

[114] Commission nationale de lutte contre la prolifération des armes légères, *Rapport à la BMS-4*, Bamako, 2010 (free translation).

[115] 'Report of the Secretary-General on the situation in Mali', UN doc. S/2012/894, 29 November 2012, §10. See also Touchard, 'Crise malienne: d'où viennent les armes des djihadistes?'.

BORDER CONTROLS

Border controls are another line of defence in efforts to prevent the proliferation of weapons. In the Programme of Action, states undertook to 'establish, where appropriate, subregional or regional mechanisms, in particular trans-border customs cooperation and networks for information-sharing among law enforcement, border and customs control agencies, with a view to preventing, combating and eradicating the illicit trade in small arms and light weapons across borders'.[116] The 2001 Firearms Protocol also requires 'where appropriate, border controls and . . . police and customs transborder cooperation', and provides for the exchange of information on organized criminal groups' means of concealment of firearms, as well as 'methods and means, points of dispatch and destination and routes customarily used by organized criminal groups'.[117]

Land border management has been described by the Panel of Experts as Libya's 'greatest challenge'.[118] Libya has approximately 4,000 km of land borders, shared with six states, and 1,700 km of coastline. Even at the time of the 2011 arms embargo, the NATO operation covered the northern part of Libya only, and the southern borders of the country, in the Sahara desert, were not monitored.[119] Since the regime change, some border control activities are conducted by local brigades, but lack of resources—including logistics and communications—are a major challenge.[120] Tunisia, for example, reported difficulties collaborating with its Libyan counterparts at the Ra's Ajdir crossing point due to their limited experience of border control and management skills.[121] Niger and Chad only have limited cross-border security cooperation with Libya.[122] The Panel of Experts identifies a number of concrete measures to enhance cooperation between national security sectors in states neighbouring Libya and in the subregion, including legal and law enforcement measures, measures at entry and exit points, and measures for controlling open borders.[123] Border controls also raise the delicate issue of corruption. When discussing weapons shipped from Libya to Syria,

---

[116] Programme of Action, §27.   [117] 2001 Firearms Protocol, Art. 12.2.

[118] 'Final Report of the Panel of Experts established pursuant to resolution 1973 (2011) concerning Libya', UN doc. S/2013/99, 9 March 2013, §45.

[119] 'Final report of the Panel of Experts established pursuant to Security Council resolution 1973 (2011) concerning Libya', UN doc. S/2012/163, 20 March 2012, §45.

[120] 'Final report of the Panel of Experts established pursuant to Security Council resolution 1973 (2011) concerning Libya', UN doc. S/2012/163, 20 March 2012, §47.

[121] 'Final Report of the Panel of Experts established pursuant to resolution 1973 (2011) concerning Libya', UN doc. S/2013/99, 9 March 2013, §123.

[122] 'Final report of the Panel of Experts established pursuant to Security Council resolution 1973 (2011) concerning Libya', UN doc. S/2012/163, 20 March 2012, §§48–50.

[123] 'Consolidated working document on the implementation of paragraph 5 of Security Council resolution 2017 (2011)', UN doc. S/2012/178, 16 March 2012, §81. See also 'Final report of the Panel of Experts established pursuant to Security Council resolution 1973 (2011) concerning Libya', UN doc. S/2012/163, 20 March 2012, §221.

the Panel of Experts notes soberly that: 'The significant size of some shipments and the logistics involved suggest that representatives of the Libyan local authorities might have at least been aware of the transfers, if not actually directly involved.'[124]

In West Africa, the ECOWAS Convention provides that:

Member States, in collaboration with the ECOWAS Executive Secretary, shall:

(a) Strengthen sub-regional cooperation among defence and security forces, intelligence services, customs and border control officials in combating the illicit circulation of small arms and light weapons;

(b) Enhancing the capacity of national defence and security forces, law enforcement and security agencies, including appropriate training in investigative procedures, border control and law enforcement techniques, and upgrading of equipment and resources.[125]

Importantly, given the scale and nature of the terrain to be covered, simple border security initiatives, such as patrols, will not be enough. More effective intelligence on actors such as traffickers and clients is needed, as well as information sharing among the Sahel community of states.[126] Such measures are directed not so much at border control as at illicit trafficking.

COMBATING THE ILLICIT TRADE

In the Programme of Action, states undertook to 'adopt and implement, in the States that have not already done so, the necessary legislative or other measures to establish as criminal offences under their domestic law the illegal manufacture, possession, stockpiling and trade of small arms and light weapons within their areas of jurisdiction, in order to ensure that those engaged in such activities can be prosecuted under appropriate national penal codes'.[127] Once legislation is in place, they undertook to 'identify, where applicable, groups and individuals engaged in the illegal manufacture, trade, stockpiling, transfer, possession, as well as financing for acquisition, of illicit small arms and light weapons, and take action under appropriate national law against such groups and individuals'.[128] In addition, they undertook to 'submit, on a voluntary basis, to relevant regional and international organizations and in accordance with their national practices, information on, inter alia, . . . illicit trade routes and techniques of acquisition that can

---

[124] 'Final Report of the Panel of Experts established pursuant to resolution 1973 (2011) concerning Libya', UN doc. S/2013/99, 9 March 2013, §170.

[125] ECOWAS Convention on Small Arms and Light Weapons, Art. 22.

[126] Waddington, 'The arms proliferation threat of post-Gaddafi Libya'. See also Stewart M. Patrick and Isabella Bennet, 'Collateral damage: how Libyan weapons fueled Mali's violence', *The Internationalist*, Council on Foreign Relations, 29 January 2013.

[127] Programme of Action, §3.   [128] Programme of Action, §6.

contribute to the eradication of the illicit trade in small arms and light weapons'.[129] At the global level, they undertook to 'encourage States and the World Customs Organization, as well as other relevant organizations, to enhance cooperation with the International Criminal Police Organization (Interpol) to identify those groups and individuals engaged in the illicit trade in small arms and light weapons in all its aspects in order to allow national authorities to proceed against them in accordance with their national laws'.[130]

Broad measures are also provided by the 2001 Firearms Protocol, which requires the national criminalization of illicit trafficking.[131] The Convention on Transnational Organized Crime to which the Protocol is attached also calls for judicial cooperation to investigate such crimes.[132] What is often lacking is the capacity of law enforcement agencies to enforce the law. In the subregion, intercepting heavily armed convoys in mountainous or desert terrain resembles more a military than a policing operation—and the examples cited by the Panel of Experts of gun battles between armed forces and smugglers illustrate the scale of the problem. States are dealing with organized criminal networks, sometimes related to drug trafficking networks, sometimes supported by local tribes due to the profit generated, and sometimes associated with organizations labelled as terrorist groups. Such trade will not be easily rooted out.

However, regional states can count on a powerful ally in their efforts to curb the illicit trade. In 2005, the USA established the Trans-Sahara Counterterrorism Partnership (TSCTP) to coordinate activities by the Department of State, Department of Defense, and the US Agency for International Development (USAID).[133] It succeeded the earlier Pan Sahel Initiative, launched in 2002. Military efforts under the TSCTP fall under Operation Enduring Freedom-Trans-Sahara and are managed by US Africa Command. Involving ten states, including Algeria, Mali, and Niger, it supports 'efforts to increase regional and sub-regional cooperation and interoperability, in such areas as communication and intelligence sharing'.[134]

The USA is supporting regional security agencies seemingly with training and logistical means, including drones. In October 2011, strengthened USA–Algeria cooperation was announced to combat illicit trafficking in weapons from Libya.[135] In September

[129] Programme of Action, §23.   [130] Programme of Action, §37.

[131] 2001 Firearms Protocol, Art. 5.

[132] United Nations Convention against Transnational Organized Crime, adopted by General Assembly Resolution 55/25 of 15 November 2000; see particularly Art. 18.

[133] Andre LeSage, 'The evolving threat of al-Qaeda in the Islamic Maghreb', *Strategic Forum*, National Defense University, July 2011, pp. 1 and 9–10.

[134] Ambassador Daniel Benjamin, 'Examining U.S. Counterterrorism priorities, strategy across Africa's Sahel region', Testimony to the Senate Committee on Foreign Relations, Subcommittee on African Affairs, 17 November 2009.

[135] 'Washington veut coopérer avec Alger contre le trafic d'armes libyennes au Sahel, Le Nouvel Observateur', *Associated Press*, 24 October 2011.

2012, the media reported that the Algerian army had stepped up patrols along its southern border, its units equipped with 'powerful and sophisticated monitoring devices, allowing them to cover wider regions'.[136] In addition, 'a number of unmanned Algerian planes and jets equipped with thermal detection and night observation devices have been deployed along the border with Mali and Niger, as well as the eastern border with Libya'.[137] This apparatus, together with the work of intelligence services, was said to have thwarted a plan by AQIM to smuggle weapons from Libya to be buried in marked locations in the desert for later use by terrorists. Further measures were considered, including surveillance systems and electronic alarms along the border.

In March 2013, reports emerged of a new US drone base in Niger.[138] The drones were used to conduct surveillance over Mali and Niger, tracking broad patterns of human activity. This followed a report released by the White House on 22 February that 100 military personnel had been deployed to Niger on an 'intelligence collection' mission.[139] The supply and use of drones in the region of course raises a whole new set of issues, given the range of possible uses of such technology. Already in 2008 Austria had granted the export to Libya of four light rotor-driven drones on the understanding that these were to be used only for surveying migrants on Libyan territory and strengthening border control—an enticing proposal for European states.[140] Evidence later surfaced that the drones were used by the armed forces, not the authorities in charge of migration control.[141]

DISARMAMENT AND WEAPONS COLLECTION

Controlling borders and stockpiles will not be enough. In Libya and Mali, and areas in between, countless more weapons and ammunition are disseminated into the hands of former combatants and civilians, and continue to feed the illicit trade. In the Programme of Action, States undertook to:

...develop and implement, where possible, effective disarmament, demobilization and reintegration programmes, including the effective collection, control, storage and destruction of small arms and light weapons, particularly in post-conflict situations, unless another form of disposal or use has been duly authorized and such weapons have been marked and the alternate form of

---

[136] Walid Ramzi, 'Algeria thwarts arms smuggling across Libya border', *Magharebia*, 21 September 2012.

[137] Ramzi, 'Algeria thwarts arms smuggling across Libya border'. These likely refer to ten South African 'Seekers' delivered to Algeria in 1998/1999. Source: SIPRI Arms Trade Database.

[138] Craig Whitlock, 'Drone base in Niger gives U.S. a strategic foothold in West Africa', *Washington Post*, 22 March 2013.

[139] Whitlock, 'Drone base in Niger gives U.S. a strategic foothold in West Africa'.

[140] Vranckx, Slijper, and Isbister (eds), *Lessons from MENA*, pp. 37–8.

[141] Vranckx, Slijper, and Isbister (eds), *Lessons from MENA*, p. 38.

disposition or use has been recorded, and to include, where applicable, specific provisions for these programmes in peace agreements.[142]

Encouragement is also provided at a regional and global level.[143]

States also undertook to:

...develop and implement, including in conflict and post-conflict situations, public awareness and confidence-building programmes on the problems and consequences of the illicit trade in small arms and light weapons in all its aspects, including, where appropriate, the public destruction of surplus weapons and the voluntary surrender of small arms and light weapons, if possible, in cooperation with civil society and non-governmental organizations, with a view to eradicating the illicit trade in small arms and light weapons.[144]

In his November 2011 report on Libya, the UN Secretary-General stated: 'There is broad consensus that all heavy weaponry must be removed from city centres immediately; this would be followed by light arms collections, as well as decisions regarding the future of the revolutionary fighters.'[145] In addition, a working document by the Panel of Experts suggests that 'weapons proliferation, and the consequent increase in weapons possession by individuals and brigades outside the control of the central government, calls for the adoption of new legislation'.[146]

The adoption and implementation of gun laws regulating civilian possession and weapons (and ammunition) collection programmes obviously pose challenges. To be successful, they require a number of conditions, principally the return of a sense of security and rule of law.[147] This may take time. A *New York Times* article reported in December 2011 that: 'Guns, many Libyans say, set them free. And with the future uncertain and memories of persecution fresh, almost no one is yet sure how to give the guns up, even as they acknowledge that much of their former ruler's arsenal would be better not loose.'[148]

Some weapons collection initiatives nevertheless got under way in Libya. The first ones targeted combatants. On 24 October 2011, a day after the Libyan declaration of liberation, a ceremony was held in Misrata where brigades handed over 500 light arms to the Ministry of Interior.[149] The Misrata Union of Revolutionaries declared a ban on carrying

---

[142] Programme of Action, §21.   [143] Programme of Action, §§30, 34, 35.

[144] Programme of Action, §20 (emphasis added).

[145] 'Report of the Secretary-General on the United Nations Support Mission in Libya', UN doc. S/2011/727, 22 November 2011, §11.

[146] 'Consolidated working document on the implementation of paragraph 5 of Security Council resolution 2017 (2011)', UN doc. S/2012/178, 16 March 2012, §74.

[147] 'Consolidated working document on the implementation of paragraph 5 of Security Council resolution 2017 (2011)', UN doc. S/2012/178, 16 March 2012, §71.

[148] C. J. Chivers, 'Libyan civilians hold on to a deadly legacy', *New York Times*, 7 December 2011.

[149] 'Report of the Secretary-General on the United Nations Support Mission in Libya', UN doc. S/2011/727, 22 November 2011, §10.

assault rifles, and started registering small arms.[150] A commission was also created, one of whose tasks would be to develop plans for weapons collection. But the process was slow, prompting the UN to call for military councils to institute an arms registration process.[151] As the months went by, public pressure mounted against the continuing presence of armed brigades.

Weapons in civilian hands also came under scrutiny. Already in March 2012, the Panel of Experts reported that, in some places, population concerns of uncontrolled civilian arms ownership and circulation had led some community authorities, including religious entities, to organize basic registration activities.[152] A weapons collection programme was launched on 29 September 2012 in Tripoli and Benghazi.[153] Thousands of guns, mortars, rockets, and even tanks were reportedly handed in. People who handed in weapons could participate in a raffle, with prizes including four vehicles, air tickets, iPads, PCs, plasma TVs, and computer courses. But these small-scale initiatives were said to have mixed results. Ironically, rumours of impending government weapons buy-back programmes are complicating collection initiatives by encouraging individuals to hold on to their guns.[154]

In Mali also, weapons will need to be collected from civilians. The country is no stranger to such initiatives.[155] It is worth noting that the ECOWAS Convention to which Mali is party is unique in that it includes criteria to regulate civilian possession.[156] Unfortunately, the recent crisis seems to have inspired the Mali government instead to distribute weapons to self-defence militias.[157]

DESTRUCTION

Even more efficient than registration, collection, and secure storage of weapons is their physical destruction. As the Panel of Experts reminds us, 'generally it is far better to

---

[150] McQuinn, *After the Fall: Libya's Evolving Armed Groups*, pp. 21 and 50.

[151] 'Consolidated working document on the implementation of paragraph 5 of Security Council resolution 2017 (2011)', UN doc. S/2012/178, 16 March 2012, §§72–3.

[152] 'Consolidated working document on the implementation of paragraph 5 of Security Council resolution 2017 (2011)', UN doc. S/2012/178, 16 March 2012, §70.

[153] Asmaa Elourfi and Essam Mohamed, 'Libyans hand in thousands of weapons', *Magharebia*, 2 October 2012. See also 'Final Report of the Panel of Experts established pursuant to resolution 1973 (2011) concerning Libya', UN doc. S/2013/99, 9 March 2013, §44.

[154] McQuinn, *After the Fall: Libya's Evolving Armed Groups*, p. 55.

[155] Florquin and Pézard, 'Insurgency, disarmament, and insecurity in Northern Mali, 1990–2004', pp. 57–60.

[156] ECOWAS Convention on Small Arms and Light Weapons, Art. 14.

[157] 'Rapport de la Haut-Commissaire des Nations Unies aux droits de l'homme sur la situation des droits de l'homme au Mali', UN doc. A/HRC/22/33, 7 January 2012, §62.

destroy surplus and obsolete weapons than to store them'.[158] Furthermore, a UNODC report on transnational organized crime in West Africa notes that: '[M]ost official [weapons] stocks are out of proportion to local needs, so reducing their size would be advisable. When the ratio of security forces to firearms approaches parity, personnel will be more likely to be held accountable when weapons go missing.'[159]

In the Programme of Action, states undertook to 'ensure that all confiscated, seized or collected small arms and light weapons are destroyed, subject to any legal constraints associated with the preparation of criminal prosecutions, unless another form of disposition or use has been officially authorized and provided that such weapons have been duly marked and registered'.[160] They also undertook to:

> ... regularly review, as appropriate, subject to the respective constitutional and legal systems of States, the stocks of small arms and light weapons held by armed forces, police and other authorized bodies and to ensure that such stocks declared by competent national authorities to be surplus to requirements are clearly identified that programmes for the responsible disposal, preferably through destruction, of such stocks are established and implemented and that such stocks are adequately safeguarded until disposal.[161]

The 2001 Firearms Protocol also calls for measures to confiscate, seize, and destroy illicitly manufactured or trafficked firearms.[162] The ECOWAS Convention does not mandate destruction, although it provides that: 'Member States shall undertake to collect and/or destroy: (a) the arms which are surplus to the national needs or have become obsolete; (b) seized weapons; (c) unmarked weapons; (d) illicitly held weapons; (e) arms collected in the implementation of peace accords or programmes for the voluntary handing in of weapons.'[163]

In Libya, the destruction of weapons held in government stockpiles was a primary objective of the NATO operation.[164] Whether it still features on the agenda of the NTC is unclear. For its part, Mali has long been praised for the 'Flames of Peace' ceremonies whereby weapons collected in the country were publicly destroyed.[165] But reductions in government stockpiles have not been reported.

---

[158] 'Consolidated working document on the implementation of paragraph 5 of Security Council resolution 2017 (2011)', UN doc. S/2012/178, 16 March 2012, §60.

[159] UNODC, *Transnational Organized Crime in West Africa*, p. 37.

[160] Programme of Action, §16.

[161] Programme of Action, §18. Paragraph 19 further recommends taking into account the report of the UN Secretary-General on methods of destruction of small arms, light weapons, ammunition, and explosives: UN doc. S/2000/1092, 15 November 2000).

[162] Protocol against the Illicit Manufacturing of and Trafficking in Firearms, their Parts and Components and Ammunition, supplementing the United Nations Convention against Transnational Organized Crime, Art. 6.

[163] ECOWAS Convention on Small Arms and Light Weapons, Art. 17.

[164] See e.g. Desmond, 'NATO hits Libyan arms depot as West faces dilemma'.

[165] The first 'Flame of Peace' ceremony took in Timbuktu (Mali) in 1996 and saw the symbolic incineration of 3,000 small arms—but no ammunition. See Florquin and Pézard, 'Insurgency, disarmament, and insecurity in Northern Mali, 1990–2004', p. 47.

Perhaps weapons destruction should be given more prominence in international debates on small arms controls. For regions already saturated with guns, such as West Africa, it would seem the only measure capable of sustainably draining the pool of small arms and light weapons. However, governments could be reluctant to destroy serviceable weapons for both economic and security reasons (too often, only obsolete and unserviceable weapons are destroyed). In terms of security, governments may want to hold on to any weapons they can when they feel they are faced with well-armed insurgent or terrorist groups, even when their very stockpiles are found to feed the arsenals of such groups. Economically, weapons also constitute precious resources in resource-starved states. In addition, with no criteria provided to determine what would constitute 'surplus stocks', the notion is subject to very elastic interpretation. Could additional incentives or confidence-building measures be provided to encourage states to destroy weapons?

C. Five proposals to close the gaps between the normative framework and reality

A closer look at the diversion of Libyan weapons in the Sahel raises a number of issues, many of which are not of a legal nature and will therefore not be solved by norms alone. This last section does not pretend to offer solutions to all of them. Rather, it presents five ideas that might bring the international community closer to the aims set out in the Programme of Action.

AN INDEPENDENT RATING OF STATES' TRUSTWORTHINESS WITH WEAPONS IMPORTS

Much focus has been placed in recent years on improving transfer controls and the adoption in April 2013 of the ATT has been widely hailed as a historic success. Yet the treaty, as all other instruments with provisions on transfers of small arms and light weapons, suffers from one major weakness: ultimately, the decision to transfer weapons rests with individual states, and little can be done if they adopt dubious interpretations of export criteria.

Arms control advocates are well aware of this limitation and have suggested a number of measures to further constrain state practice. One interesting suggestion, addressed to the EU, has been to establish a list of 'countries of concern' and operate a policy of 'presumption of denial' in these cases.[166] Other voices call for governance to be adopted

---

[166] Vranckx, Slijper, and Isbister (eds), *Lessons from MENA*, p. 4.

as additional criteria when assessing export applications,[167] or to involve local delegations of the EU in monitoring weapons transfers for smaller states who may not have sufficient resources to do so. Among the most popular proposals figures the idea of a peer review of states' transfer decisions.[168] The suggested procedure would be similar to the process already existing in the ECOWAS region to vet states' decisions to import weapons. It would likely also suffer from similar weaknesses: it is simply very difficult to expect states to contradict a decision taken by one of their peers, particularly if the peer group consists of states in a regional organization likely enjoying very close diplomatic and economic relations.

Perhaps there is a role to be taken up by civil society when it comes to assessing export applications. A research institute or civil society coalition could create a composite index based on existing export criteria, such as human rights standards and risk of diversion. Several models come to mind: the UN Development Programme's (UNDP) Human Development Index; Transparency International's yearly rating of states' corruption levels; or the work of credit rating agencies such as Standard & Poor's or Moody's. For small arms transfers, the index could initially focus on two or three of the most important criteria, and gradually expand to include all the criteria of the ATT or Wassenaar Arrangements. A strong methodology would be needed to win the trust of exporting states. The index would then be calculated every year based on open-source information. While not politically binding, there would likely be strong political (and public) pressure to deny transfers of weapons to states that rank too low on the index. Relatedly, the index could also spur low-ranking states to improve their conditions, so that they would be again deemed worthy of importing weapons.

A CALL FOR TRANSPARENCY

Transparency and accountability will be improved if the licit flows of weapons become better documented. The 1998 EU Code of Conduct and its successor, the 2008 EU Common Position, have had positive effects on the transparency of European arms exports.[169] The problem is that, currently, governments, the UN, and the EU all use different methodologies when reporting arms data.[170] And many states still do not report transfers to the UN Register of Conventional Arms, with few consequences.

---

[167] Bromley, 'The review of the EU Common Position on arms exports: prospects for strengthened controls', p. 15.

[168] Bromley, 'The review of the EU Common Position on arms exports: prospects for strengthened controls', p. 14.

[169] Bromley, 'The review of the EU Common Position on arms exports: prospects for strengthened controls', pp. 6–7.

[170] Amnesty International, *Arms Transfers to the Middle East and North Africa*, p. 7.

The UN Office for Disarmament Affairs (UNODA) publishes a list of states that have reported on an annual basis, and the Small Arms Survey assesses the transparency of major small arms exporters through its annual Transparency Barometer; probably, though, more could be done to name states that do not report on arms transfers. Even within the EU, the three largest arms exporters—France, Germany, and the UK—failed to make submissions to the 12th and 13th EU annual reports,[171] and the reports were published late.

But other sources of information exist and must be encouraged. The reports of the Panel of Experts were one of the primary sources of information for this chapter. The Panel's authoritative fact-finding mission is so useful that states should consider extending their mandates beyond actual arms embargoes. In addition, Interpol plays an important role in tracing illicit small arms, a role recognized in the Programme of Action[172] and the International Tracing Instrument.[173] However, only states (and, since the Second Review Conference in 2012, peacekeeping missions) can initiate tracing requests and access information. It would be worth considering whether information could also be shared with the UN, civil society, and researchers, at least in an aggregate form.

CHALLENGING STATES' IMPLEMENTATION OF LEGALLY BINDING INSTRUMENTS

Many advocates of small arms control and some states were disappointed in 2001 when the Programme of Action could not be adopted as a legally binding instrument. Over the years, this perceived weakness came up time and again to explain insufficient implementation of its provisions. The degree of implementation of particular norms can, however, have little to do with their legally or politically binding nature—with one exception, though: states parties' respect for legally binding provisions can be formally challenged. Most instruments contain provisions on competent authorities and procedures to settle disputes. This distinction would seem largely rhetorical since no state has ever been challenged before an international court for lack of respect of a legally binding provision on small arms and light weapons. The question is: could they? If the UN Programme of Action were made legally binding—for example through a UN General Assembly resolution—would states be more inclined to implement their commitments and/or challenge others for failure to implement? And will the ATT live up to its promise

---

[171] Bromley, 'The review of the EU Common Position on arms exports: prospects for strengthened controls', p. 7.

[172] Programme of Action, §§7, 36, and 37.

[173] International Instrument to Enable States to Identify and Trace, in a Timely and Reliable Manner, Illicit Small Arms and Light Weapons, adopted by the UN General Assembly on 8 December 2005.

as a new legally binding instrument with the teeth to prevent irresponsible or illegal transfers in practice?

Four legally binding mechanisms/instruments have been mentioned in this chapter: UN arms embargoes; the UN Firearms Protocol; the EU Common Position; and the ECOWAS Convention. UN arms embargoes are normally imposed by the UN Security Council acting under Chapter VII of the UN Charter. In theory, when violations are noticed, they could be challenged before the International Court of Justice (ICJ). This is, however, unlikely to happen in the case of the Libyan arms embargo, given that neither Qatar nor the UAE, nor France, Italy, or the USA for that matter, have recognized the compulsory jurisdiction of the world Court (among the states cited in this chapter, only the UK has done so). Alternatively, the Security Council may decide to impose sanctions on offending states, but again this idea is largely theoretical when the embargo is being violated directly or indirectly by the same states that imposed it. The uncomfortable conclusion is that violations of UN arms embargoes effectively go unpunished. What remain are the Panel of Experts' efforts to at least disclose some state actions.

The Firearms Protocol provides that disputes must be resolved through negotiation and arbitration, although they can be referred to the ICJ as a last resort.[174] While Qatar and Niger have not yet adhered to the Protocol, Algeria, Libya, and Mali have. In theory, it would therefore be possible for Mali or Algeria to bring a case to the ICJ against Libya for failing to prevent illicit trafficking in firearms from its arms caches, once all other conciliation avenues have been exhausted. Whether this would be the best way to proceed on this issue is a different question.

The EU Common Position is also a legally binding document for EU member states. As such, it can be challenged before the European Court of Justice (ECJ) in Brussels. The European Commission or any member state can bring so-called 'proceedings for failure to fulfil an obligation' to the Court. In theory, therefore, the European Commission or any other member state would be able to challenge Italy's national laws for excepting from European legislation exports of civilian weapons (other than weapons used for hunting and sports shooting, which was clearly not the case in this particular instance). If it could be demonstrated that the weapons were then used to commit human rights violations, a case could perhaps even be brought to the European Court of Human Rights (ECtHR) against a state party to the 1950 European Convention on Human Rights (ECHR) that had produced and exported the weapons.

Finally, the ECOWAS Convention features an enforcement mechanism: the ECO-WAS Mediation and Security Council.[175] In fact, it is just such a legally binding provision that enabled Guinea to hold up a consignment of weapons destined for Mali.

---

[174] 2001 Firearms Protocol, Art. 16.
[175] ECOWAS Convention on Small Arms and Light Weapons, Art. 27.

Legally binding instruments have a muscle that needs to be exercised. In some cases, such as with Libya's stockpile management practices or border controls, it may be rather pointless to use the pressure of a court judgment to solve the problem. But in other cases it would be interesting to see if procedures could be initiated to formally challenge offending states. The deterring power of international norms could only be strengthened in the process.

A 'UNIVERSAL PERIODIC REVIEW' OF PROGRAMME OF ACTION IMPLEMENTATION

The Programme of Action remains the most comprehensive instrument on small arms control to date. It already covers every crossroads that have allowed weapons to end up in the hands of Malian insurgents. Since it was adopted in 2001, its provisions have been supplemented and elaborated through various regional and international instruments, such as the International Tracing Instrument, as well as processes including the Group of Governmental Experts on Brokering, the outcome documents of the Third and Fourth Biennial Meetings of States, the Chair's Summary of the Meeting of Governmental Experts in 2011, and the outcome document of the Second Review Conference in 2012.[176]

These meetings were designed to clarify some of the practical implications of giving effect to the Programme of Action and International Tracing Instrument in specific thematic areas and share experiences in meeting implementation challenges. However, while the meeting cycle and review process of the Programme of Action has been increasingly productive, it has yet to examine (real) progress made in implementation. Indeed, this is the formal mandate of the periodic review conferences, including the recent Second Review Conference.[177] And yet, to date, there has been no comprehensive assessment of the extent to which states, individually or collectively, are fulfilling their commitments under these instruments.[178]

Civil society has attempted to become more proactive in calling on states to comply with their responsibilities, not in general terms, but on specific issues of national implementation. A 'Red Book' was published by the Biting the Bullet consortium in 2003, 2005, and 2006, before being discontinued for lack of resources. Calls were made to set up an

---

[176] Sarah Parker, 'An arms trade treaty: will it support or supplant the PoA?', Small Arms Survey, Geneva, 2012, p. 1, <http://www.smallarmssurvey.org/fileadmin/docs/H-Research_Notes/SAS-Research-Note-15.pdf>.

[177] 'To review progress made in the implementation of the Programme of Action': UN General Assembly Resolution 63/72, adopted on 2 December 2008.

[178] Self-assessment has been conducted in the form of national reports, but these are neither comprehensive nor verified, and there is still no objective assessment of implementation. For a ten-year study of national reports, see Sarah Parker and Katherine Greene, *A Decade of Implementing the United Nations Programme of Action on Small Arms and Light Weapons: Analysis of National Reports*, UNIDIR, Geneva, 2012.

independent commission to review states' progress. A project got under way to review states' implementation.[179] But for the time being, we are still left with states' own national reports on implementation of the Programme of Action.

Perhaps there is something to be learned from the Universal Periodic Review process at the Human Rights Council. Several features of the procedure are interesting. First, it does not seek to review the records of all the states at every meeting; rather, each meeting focuses on a select number of states, while all states know they will come under scrutiny with in each three-year cycle. In addition, for each state review, civil society is invited to submit reports. In fact, the review of each state's record is based on its own national report, reports by UN treaty bodies (such as Special Rapporteurs), and civil society reports, each given equal weight. And during the debates, other states are invited to speak.

Adopting such a system for the Programme of Action will have cost implications. But the system has the potential to instil much-needed life in what remains a good document. After all, the Programme of Action does recommend that states cooperate with civil society 'in view of the important role that civil society plays in this area'.[180]

A TREATY AND VERIFICATION BODY TO DECREASE SMALL ARMS STOCKPILES

The adoption of the ATT in April 2013 has changed the normative landscape around small arms (and other conventional weapons). It is undoubtedly a very positive development. But the reality, as narrated in this chapter, is one of a region already saturated with weapons, where stricter transfer controls would likely come too late. What is needed now is a renewed focus on diminishing existing stockpiles, whether they are in the hands of armed groups, civilians, or governments.

Encouragingly, the chapter highlighted numerous norms that already exist, for example around stockpile management, disarmament, and weapons collection programmes, and the destruction of small arms and light weapons. One arguable gap is a standard to determine what are 'surplus stocks'. The International Small Arms Control Standards (ISACS) do provide a matrix to enable states to calculate surplus stocks, but leave it up to them to determine their preferred ratio of weapons per armed personnel.[181] In addition, their implementation will be subjected to states' goodwill.

---

[179] The Small Arms Survey Programme of Action Implementation Project was launched in March 2011.
[180] Programme of Action, §40.
[181] UN CASA, 'International Small Arms Control Standards', 2012. See in particular Module 05.20 Stockpile management: weapons, §12 and Annex 2, <http://www.smallarmsstandards.org/isacs/0520-en.pdf>.

In general, however, weaknesses of small arms control in West Africa derive not so much from lack of norms or commitments as from lack of technical capacity and resources to implement these norms and commitments. Perhaps lack of incentives and confidence could also be an obstacle to more thorough action by states to destroy surplus stocks.

International cooperation has been on states' agenda since the adoption of the Programme of Action in 2001. With most cooperation happening bilaterally, the focus has been placed on exchanging information on programmes and projects, matching needs and resources, developing best practice guides, and coordinating the multiple UN agencies active in this field. These efforts have been largely ad hoc and have still to demonstrate overall impact.

Perhaps something could be learned from other weapons systems. As a pragmatic measure to prevent the proliferation of nuclear weapons, the international community created the International Atomic Energy Agency in 1957. The idea was to offer states access to peaceful uses of atomic energy in exchange for international scrutiny of nuclear facilities. Similarly, the Organization for the Prohibition of Chemical Weapons was set up in 1997 to implement the Convention of the same name. Again, states parties agree to international scrutiny of chemical weapons storage sites in exchange for assistance in the destruction of stocks. After the Anti-Personnel Mine Ban Convention (APMBC) was adopted in 1997, states created the UN Mine Action Service (UNMAS). This agency is tasked with the coordination of UN activities to remove and destroy landmines, and benefits from much technical expertise in these areas.

Maybe it is time to consider a treaty and verification body to limit the risks of proliferation of small arms and light weapons? A legally binding treaty could be based on the ISACS, but could propose guidance on what would constitute a ceiling of acceptable weapons stockpiles for government (armed forces and law enforcement), private security companies, and civilians. A key commitment would be the destruction of surplus stocks. A verification body—akin to a technical UN agency on small arms—would be able to send inspectors to visit armouries and weapons storage sites to verify compliance in exchange for technical and financial assistance to improve the security and management procedures of facilities and to help with the destruction of such surplus stocks. Synergies could be found with existing UNMAS capacities; indeed, UNMAS has already expanded its scope of work to include ammunition and weapons safety management. Beyond government stockpiles, technical expertise would also be developed to design and implement large-scale weapons collection programmes and/or registration drives, and to update national weapons legislation. A fund for assistance to survivors of gun violence could also be included—as already exists for victims of chemical weapons and landmines.

Concluding remarks

For the last 10 to 15 years, much focus has been placed on addressing the problems posed by small arms and light weapons proliferation (and misuse). Norms have been developed or adopted to control them. Projects have been established in affected countries as small arms control has become recognized as a development concern. Some funding has followed. And yet there is doubt whether armed violence has been curbed by these efforts. The Libyan conflict resulted in an estimated 30,000 killed and 50,000 injured.[182] The exact toll in Mali will likely never be known.[183] Weapons continue to flow freely in West Africa, in such quantities that the problem seems to have no end. Has it all been for nothing?

There is value in asking the question. The international community should always challenge its assumptions, and search for new ways to improve human security. The new focus on armed violence reduction is a welcome reminder that people are at the heart of the problem, and a fertile terrain for experimenting with new approaches. But discarding the UN process on small arms as a whole appears too radical a proposition. Guns remain a large part of the problem, and should remain a focus.

The Programme of Action is a valuable document, which covers most issues that (still) permit weapons to wreak havoc, but has the international community made the best use of it? This chapter concludes it has not, and has ventured some ideas on how states could be supported, pushed, and prodded to fulfil their obligations. Its focus on the Libya–Mali connection limited the lessons that the chapter would draw. Other case studies, including in 'peaceful' settings, would almost certainly have highlighted other norms, gaps, and remedies. Yet it is hoped that these ideas will help provide new impetus to the global fight against the proliferation and misuse of small arms and light weapons.

---

[182] Sivaram and Karasik, 'An arms buyback for Libya?—Analysis'.

[183] In July 2012, the ICG spoke of several dozen military casualties in clashes, sieges, and the Aguelhoc massacre: ICG, 'Mali: avoiding escalation', p. 14.

4 Persons displaced internally by conflict and violence in 2012

Kate Halff*

Introduction

Worldwide, an estimated 28.8 million people were displaced internally by armed conflict, generalized violence, and human rights violations as of end 2012. This represents an increase of 2.4 million on the previous year, and is the highest figure recorded by the Internal Displacement Monitoring Centre (IDMC).[1] Some 6.5 million people were newly displaced during the year, almost twice the 3.5 million that were newly displaced during 2011.

This increase was the result of new large-scale population movements in several countries in Africa and the Middle East. The conflicts in Syria and the Democratic Republic of Congo (DRC) were responsible for around half of the new displacements, with 2.4 million and 1 million, respectively, while an estimated 500,000 people fled their homes in both Sudan and India.

The higher figures for both overall and new displacement are consistent with the rise in the number of violent conflicts around the world. The largest regional increase in the number of internally displaced people was in the Middle East and North Africa, where 2.5 million people were forced to flee their homes in 2012. There are now almost 6 million internally displaced persons (IDPs) in the region, a rise of 40 per cent on the 2011 total of 4.3 million. In the Middle East generally, and particularly in Syria, the sharp rise in the number of IDPs correlates closely with the rapid escalation of conflict. Since the beginning of the 'Arab Spring' uprisings in early 2011, displacement across the region has snowballed. Libya and Yemen were worst affected in 2011, but in 2012 Syria was the regional hotspot, with a fivefold increase in the number of IDPs. By the end of the year, Syria was the world's largest and

---

* Kate Halff was the Director of the Internal Displacement Monitoring Center of the Norwegian Refugee Council until 30 April 2013.

[1] This chapter is based on IDMC, 'Global overview: People Displaced by Conflict and Violence', Geneva, April 2013.

fastest evolving crisis in terms of new displacement. The country now has more than 3 million IDPs, of whom more than 80 per cent were newly displaced in 2012.

The region with the largest total number of IDPs was sub-Saharan Africa. As of end 2012, it was hosting 10.4 million, almost one-third of the world's internally displaced and an increase of 7.5 per cent compared with the year before, thereby reversing the downward trend recorded since 2004. Around 2.4 million people were newly displaced, of whom 1 million fled their homes as a result of escalating violence in DRC, the world's second largest crisis in terms of new displacement in 2012. The outbreak and escalation of violence in Mali in 2012, fuelled by an influx of weapons from Libya (*see Chapter 3*), led to the displacement of at least 227,000 people. Increased violence in Nigeria by the radical Islamist group Boko Haram also caused significant new displacements.

As was the case in 2011, the Americas region hosted the second largest number of IDPs in 2012, with a total of 5.8 million, an increase of 3 per cent. Colombia remains the state with the highest number of IDPs in the world, with a total of between 4.9 and 5.5 million. The continued non-international armed conflict (NIAC) in Colombia forced an estimated 230,000 people to flee their homes during the year. No figures were available for Mexico, but census information showed that violence had provoked significant displacement in the states most affected by drug cartel activity.

In Europe and Central Asia, the total number of IDPs remained stable at around 2.5 million, with the vast majority trapped in situations of protracted displacement, in many cases for 20 years or more.

Asia showed the second highest increase in new displacement after the Middle East and North Africa, with 1.4 million people forced to flee their homes during 2012, more than twice the number recorded in the previous 12 months. India saw a 10 per cent increase in new displacements in 2012 compared with the previous year, mainly the result of inter-communal violence in north-eastern Assam, which caused up to 500,000 people to flee their homes. Military operations against non-state armed groups (NSAGs) in Pakistan's Federally Administered Tribal Areas (FATA) caused more than 412,000 new displacements. Despite this, the total number of IDPs in Asia at the end of 2012 (4.1 million) remained reasonably stable compared with the previous year. Given that only 261,000 people were reported as having returned by the end of the year, this suggests that returns were either under-reported or not reported at all. This is also the case with many other states monitored.

Worldwide, only 2.1 million people were reported as having returned in 2012, a decrease of around 250,000 on the figure for 2011, although, again, overall figures suggest the number of IDPs who returned could be significantly higher. The identification of IDPs who do not live in camps is a key challenge to protecting, assisting, and monitoring them. Similarly, the assessment of whether IDPs have achieved durable solutions, whether through return to their places of origin, local integration, or settlement elsewhere in the country, is also highly challenging when data on those living outside camps is so scarce.

A. **Responding to large-scale displacement**

In 2012, international humanitarian actors had to respond to four concurrent large-scale complex displacement crises. In Syria, the social unrest that started in March 2011 and escalated into civil war had led to a fivefold increase in internal displacement, with at least 3 million IDPs reported at the end of 2012. Most IDPs have received very little or no assistance, in part because aid has become a deeply divisive issue, politicized by parties to the conflict as they compete for control of territory. The protracted crises in eastern DRC and Somalia continued to create new displacement.

At least 1 million people fled an upsurge in violence in DRC, bringing the total number of IDPs in the country to 2.7 million as of the end of the year. In Somalia, while famine affecting parts of the country came to an end, the number of IDPs at the end of the year was still estimated to be between 1.1 and 1.36 million. Violence in Mali, which began early in 2012, drove at least 227,000 people into internal displacement during the year, with IDPs' specific needs compounded by the impact of chronic food insecurity and years of underdevelopment.

Each of these crises has its roots in specific and complex national and subregional dynamics, but an examination of the humanitarian responses from an internal displacement perspective highlights the following common issues.

1. International humanitarian actors struggle to provide protection and assistance to IDPs because access to displaced populations is often limited. This may be because of risks to aid workers' physical security, poor transport infrastructure, or restrictive policies and practices imposed by governments or NSAGs.
2. The lack of comprehensive information about displaced people's needs and the risks they face, both in areas from which they have fled and those in which they have sought refuge, significantly hampers evidence-based responses.
3. Both of the above issues result in discrepancies in assistance, with a focus on location rather than need, undermining the humanitarian principles of humanity and impartiality.
4. Both protracted displacement and multiple displacements are striking features of the crises in DRC, Somalia, and Syria. Current methods for targeting and delivering assistance do not adequately take into account the specific needs of IDP or their hosts, nor have they systematically integrated the fact that IDPs' needs vary over time as the context within which they live evolves.

The persistence of such issues, seven years after the United Nations (UN)-initiated humanitarian reform—and as its transformative agenda is being rolled out with the aim of addressing continued weaknesses—raises the following questions: has the current international humanitarian response system retained enough focus and expertise in the assistance and protection of people affected by internal displacement, or has the issue been so 'mainstreamed' that their specific vulnerabilities and needs are no longer adequately identified or reflected in advocacy and response plans?

B. **Promoting IDP law and policy instruments**

Adequate law and policy instruments on internal displacement are important for states if they are to implement effective national responses and ensure that the rights of their displaced citizens are respected, protected, and fulfilled. In theory, constitutions, national legislation, and international law offer protection to IDPs, but they often struggle to access their basic rights in areas such as housing, health, and education as a result of their displacement. National legislation tends not to address the particularities of displacement, because it was often not drafted through such a lens. For example, national education laws that do not incorporate internally displaced children's needs for flexible enrolment systems impose unintentional obstacles to their access to schooling.

More than 25 states have adopted IDP law or policy instruments since the introduction of the Guiding Principles on Internal Displacement in 1998; some, such as Colombia and Georgia, had such laws in place before the Guiding Principles were published. The entry into force in December 2012 of the African Union Convention for the Protection and Assistance of Internally Displaced Persons in Africa (the Kampala Convention) was the most significant legal development of the year at regional level. By the end of 2012, 16 states were legally bound to adopt comprehensive legislation on the prevention of internal displacement, responses to it, and the achievement of durable solutions.

In 2012, national authorities of various states also took measures to implement their responsibility to provide protection and assistance to IDPs by developing or updating laws, policies, and strategy documents in support of their rights, as follows.

- In Afghanistan in early 2012, following a decision by President Hamid Karzai and the Cabinet, the Ministry of Refugees and Repatriation was tasked with developing a national IDP policy. The government held broad consultations and started the drafting process.
- In the Central African Republic (CAR), a multi-stakeholder workshop was held in August 2012 to review an existing draft of a law on IDPs, which was transferred to parliament for adoption.
- In Georgia, a revised Action Plan for the Implementation of the State Strategy for IDPs was adopted by Governmental Decree No. 1162 on 13 June 2012. An inter-agency working group was also set up to revise legislation on IDPs, with a view to shifting the legal basis for assistance from a status-based to a needs-based approach.

- The National Policy on the Prevention of Internal Displacement and the Protection and Assistance to Internally Displaced Persons in Kenya was adopted in October 2012. This comprehensive strategy was complemented by the Prevention, Protection and Assistance to Internally Displaced Persons and Affected Communities Act, signed into law by the President on 31 December 2012. It establishes an institutional framework for IDP protection and assistance.
- In Mexico, on 22 February 2012, the Chiapas state congress passed a bill on internal displacement based on the Guiding Principles (Ley para la Prevención y Atención del Desplazamiento Interno en el Estado de Chiapas).
- In the Philippines, Congress enacted the Rights of Internally Displaced Persons Act on 5 February 2013. The Act includes a prohibition on arbitrary displacement, the provision of monetary compensation for lost or damaged property or for the death of family members, and the designation of the Philippines Commission on Human Rights (PCHR) as the government's institutional focal point for IDPs. In May 2013, however, the Act was vetoed by the President.
- Somalia has no national legal or policy framework on internal displacement yet, but the authorities in Puntland adopted a policy on IDPs, and the authorities in Somaliland were in the process of developing one in 2012.

Such developments signal the need for coordinated, sustained, and consistent support to states to help them pursue robust processes that lead to national laws and policies, and their subsequent implementation. No single entity at either international or regional level can provide this. It will require concerted action from the international community to develop and resource a pool of technical experts to facilitate state-led consultation and the elaboration of laws and policies.

C. **Promoting durable solutions to internal displacement**

With IDPs living in protracted internal displacement in more than nine in ten of the states monitored by the IDMC, supporting durable solutions remains the biggest challenge for governments and their international partners as they struggle to put the 2007 Inter-Agency Steering Committee (IASC) Framework for Durable Solutions into practice.

While responsibility for finding durable solutions lies with governments, international actors need to improve their practice so as to:

- ensure that IDPs are consulted on, and participate in, decision-making that affects their lives;
- resource responses in a way that not only focuses on the IDPs themselves, but which also takes into account their broader environment, including host communities;

- develop comprehensive and durable solutions, strategies, and plans, regardless of whether IDPs' needs are framed as humanitarian or developmental; and
- establish multi-sectorial approaches of sufficient sophistication as to ensure that the specific vulnerabilities of each group of IDPs are addressed both in their own right and as part of broader social policy.

When understood as a dynamic concept rather than a 'final state', durable solutions require not only a humanitarian response at the height of a crisis, but also sustained engagement throughout displacement. This means the establishment of laws and policies, the strengthening of preparedness capacity, and the implementation of national prevention and development initiatives before, during, and after a humanitarian response. Such an approach requires the removal of the existing boundaries between humanitarian, development, human rights, and peace-building interventions to establish a truly integrated response.

Durable solutions will only be achieved when internal displacement is recognized as a developmental, as well as a humanitarian, challenge, and when addressing it is acknowledged as critical to the achievement of development goals. The 2011 UN Framework on Ending Displacement in the Aftermath of Conflict aims to support a more coherent, predictable, and effective UN response that leads to durable solutions for IDPs and returning refugees. The decision taken in 2012 to pilot it in three states—Afghanistan, Côte d'Ivoire, and Kyrgyzstan—represents an important opportunity to bring governments, communities, and international entities together to design and implement relevant plans for each of the three contexts, and so bridge the gap between humanitarian and development action.

D. **Persons displaced by conflict and violence by region in 2012**

AFRICA

There were more than 10.4 million IDPs in the 18 sub-Saharan countries that the IDMC monitored in 2012, almost one-third of the global total. The DRC, Sudan, and Somalia continued to have Africa's largest internally displaced populations, among the largest in the world. Displacement in Nigeria was also known to be significant, but no reliable figure was available. The sharp increase in the number of IDPs, up by 7.5 per cent from the 9.7 million at the end of 2011, reversed a steady downward trend in the region since 2004, and was linked to worsening conflict and violence throughout sub-Saharan Africa, with greater armed violence in Africa in 2012 than at any time since 1945.

Conflict in eastern DRC intensified dramatically during 2012, while new violence erupted in northern Mali at the beginning of the year. Violence by armed groups increased in Nigeria, and South Sudan experienced tensions, both internal over natural resources and with Sudan over contested border areas and the Heglig region. The causes of these and other conflicts, and more localized clashes, violence, and human rights violations that led to displacement, include struggles for political power, ideological domination, and natural resources, and inter-communal violence often linked to land disputes and criminality.

Sudden and slow-onset natural disasters also forced people to flee, in some cases affecting those already displaced by conflict and violence. Unprecedented floods caused massive displacement in Chad, Mali, Niger, Nigeria, Senegal, South Sudan, and Sudan. Drought and resource depletion caused the displacement of pastoralists in northern Kenya, and compounded the dynamics of violence throughout the region. The famine in the Horn of Africa was declared over in 2012, but extended drought in the Sahel caused food insecurity in eight states, coinciding with the spread of violence and instability across international borders.

New movements

The largest new displacement in the region took place in eastern DRC, where 1 million people fled worsening violence in the provinces of North and South Kivu, Orientale, and Katanga, bringing the total number of IDPs in the country to about 2.7 million. The March 23 Movement (M23), a new rebel group formed in April 2012, attacked the North Kivu capital of Goma in November. The conflict displaced 140,000 people in a week, many of them already IDPs living in a large camp on the outskirts of the city. Close to 230,000 people fled northern Mali throughout the year to escape the uprising by Tuareg rebels early in 2012 and widespread abuses by Islamist armed groups who took control of vast swathes of the country in June. Most IDPs fled to the south and the majority were unable to return or achieve other solutions to their displacement. In Nigeria, increased violence by the radical Islamist group Boko Haram, inter-communal violence between Christians and Muslims, and clashes between farmers and pastoralists led to burgeoning displacement. The government had still to compile reliable figures, but at least 63,000 people were documented as newly displaced by violence.

Fighting over natural resources and an ongoing uprising in South Sudan displaced more than 190,000, while in Kenya inter-communal violence and clashes over natural resources forced 118,000 to flee. The violence in Kenya was compounded by ethnic and political factors linked to the March 2013 elections. In CAR, as many as 106,000 people were displaced by various forms of violence, including tens of thousands who fled the march on the capital Bangui of Séléka, a coalition of armed groups, in December. In Sudan, inter-communal violence and fresh clashes between government forces and

NSAGs forced around 90,000 to flee their homes in Darfur. There were also considerable return movements, although a lack of reliable data, access restrictions, and in some cases the repeated displacement of those affected made figures hard to verify. An estimated 450,000 IDPs returned to their places of origin in DRC, at least 176,000 South Sudanese refugees went home from Sudan, and up to 91,000 IDPs returned in Darfur. Around 36,000 people reportedly returned in Chad and a similar number in CAR following a demobilization process in the north of the country. In Somalia, the number of returns was around 32,000.

Protection issues

IDPs continued to face threats to their physical security in 2012. In at least eight states, including DRC, Mali, South Sudan, and Sudan, where some of the worst violence and conflict took place, people fled armed attacks and clashes, forced recruitment, arbitrary killings, sexual violence, and abductions. IDPs faced similar threats in CAR, Chad, and Somalia, while in Chad and DRC people returning to their places of origin were also affected. In DRC, IDPs faced discrimination because they were seen as a source of further insecurity.

As in previous years, gender-based violence (GBV) was widespread in DRC. During the violence that erupted in North Kivu in November, both M23 and government forces were accused of perpetrating sexual violence, including against IDPs. In Mali, GBV was a significant cause of displacement, a threat during displacement, and an obstacle to return. In Côte d'Ivoire, there was a lack of assistance for women affected by GBV in previous years.

Prospects for durable solutions

Progress towards durable solutions in states where conflict had ended was limited in 2012. As of the end of the year, IDPs were living in protracted displacement in 15 states, evidence of the obstacles they face in their search for durable solutions, as well as their continued marginalization.

Uganda has been at the forefront of the region's response to internal displacement. It adopted a policy on IDPs in 2004 and was the first country to ratify the Kampala Convention. Its recovery and development efforts have, however, been insufficient. Returning IDPs continue to suffer inadequate basic services and receive only limited support to rebuild their livelihoods. Accusations of serious corruption at the highest levels of government led donors to withhold funding at the end of 2012, crippling further recovery efforts.

The international humanitarian community in Burundi wound down its operations in 2012, but it was unclear to what extent national authorities and both national and international development agencies would lead longer-term engagement in support of durable solutions.

In DRC, at least two-thirds of IDPs are thought to have suffered multiple displacements, either repeatedly from their places of origin, or onwards from places of refuge. Clearly, the prospects for durable solutions in such circumstances are remote. Côte d'Ivoire, meanwhile, was one of three states chosen globally to roll out the UN Secretary-General's landmark framework to end displacement in the two-year aftermath of conflict.

Responses

Several countries, and the African Union as a whole, reached important milestones in terms of framing cohesive responses to internal displacement. The Kampala Convention came into force on 6 December 2012, and by the end of the year 16 states had ratified it: Benin; Burkina Faso; CAR; Chad; Gabon; Gambia; Guinea Bissau; Lesotho; Mali; Niger; Nigeria; Sierra Leone; Swaziland; Togo; Uganda; and Zambia. By ratifying the world's first continental treaty on internal displacement, they have made a legal commitment to address all causes comprehensively. They have also committed to assisting and protecting IDPs and their human rights, including the creation of safe and sustainable conditions for voluntary return, local integration, or settlement elsewhere in the country. The Kampala Convention also requires states parties to adopt legislation and policies on internal displacement, to designate a coordinating body for all related issues, and to provide the necessary funds for protection and assistance.

Nigeria took steps to implement its obligations in 2012 by revising a draft policy on IDPs to bring it into line with the Convention, but the country's Cabinet was still to pass it as of the end of the year. Although it has not ratified the Convention, Kenya's government adopted a national policy on IDPs in October, and was in the final stages of adopting a new law governing their protection and assistance.

AMERICAS

As many as 5.8 million people were internally displaced in the Americas at the end of 2012, forced to flee their homes as a result of armed conflict, criminal violence, and human rights violations. Despite changing situations at national level, the overall figure for the region was the same as for the previous year. As of March 2013, the Colombian government had not published official figures either for new displacements during 2012 or for the total number of IDPs in the country, due to difficulties it encountered in updating its national registry. There were, however, reportedly 4.9 million people registered as IDPs as of December 2012. As the figure is cumulative, it does not account for the fact that some IDPs may have returned, integrated locally, or settled elsewhere in the country, nor does it include people displaced by armed groups that have emerged since the demobilization of paramilitary organizations between 2003 and 2006. The Consultancy for Human Rights and Displacement (*Consultoría para los Derechos Humanos y el Desplazamiento*, or CODHES), the main civil society organization monitoring displacement in Colombia and which also produces cumulative figures, has not published its totals for 2012 either.

In Mexico, the total of around 160,000 IDPs in the country included people who have been displaced by drug cartel violence since 2007 and others living in protracted displacement in the state of Chiapas since the late 1990s. In Guatemala and Peru, people were still internally displaced long after the end of the conflicts they fled. In Guatemala, little was known about the number or situation of people displaced during the country's internal conflict, which ended 16 years ago. In Peru, many people displaced during the early 1990s by the conflict between the government and the Shining Path and *Túpac Amaru* revolutionary NSAGs had still not found durable solutions to their situation.

New movements

As was the case in the previous year, people were newly displaced by conflict and violence in Colombia and Mexico in 2012, while others continued to live in protracted displacement. Colombia's internal armed conflict forced around 230,000 people to flee their homes during the year.[2] Additionally, people displaced by post-demobilization armed groups, which operate as criminal and drug-trafficking gangs with remnants of the extreme-right ideology of their paramilitary predecessors, are not counted or registered as IDPs. These groups were nevertheless responsible for a significant proportion of new displacement in Colombia, according to civil society sources.

No figures for new displacement in Mexico were made available in 2012, but census information correlated with data on homicides and violent crimes showed that criminal violence caused displacement in the states most affected by drug cartel activity in recent years—namely, Baja California, Chihuahua, Coahuila, Durango, Guerrero, Michoacán, Nuevo León, San Luis Potosí, Sinaloa, Sonora, Tamaulipas, and Veracruz. The link between drug cartel violence and displacement was even clearer at municipal level. Census data showed that, within the states most affected, the 100 municipalities with the highest levels of violence experienced the highest levels of population loss. When the effect of other causes of migration, including economic and demographic conditions and

---

[2] The figure is provisional, however, because the government faced significant challenges in updating its registry for IDPs, and it does not fully reflect the reality on the ground.

urbanization, were accounted for, people left violent municipalities at a rate four-and-a-half times higher than they left non-violent municipalities.[3]

In addition, sudden-onset natural hazards caused new displacement throughout the region. In Colombia, heavy seasonal rains attributed to the weather phenomenon known as La Niña caused major flooding across much of the country in April. More than 60,000 people were displaced, and the floods also increased the vulnerability of people already displaced by conflict. In Mexico, an earthquake in March in the state of Guerrero caused displacement, and a storm in August forced people to flee their homes in Guerrero, Oaxaca, Puebla, Quintana Roo, Tabasco, and Veracruz states. In Haiti, where more than 320,000 people are still living in displacement following the 2010 earthquake, around 80,000 more were displaced by floods and storms in 2012.

Protection issues

Threats to physical security were the main cause of displacement in Colombia and Mexico, the only two states in the region that experienced new displacements in 2012. People's physical security was affected in a number of ways, including: confrontations between different armed groups, and between armed groups and government forces, in both rural and urban areas; direct threats by armed groups against the civilian population; forced recruitment and the threat of it, which particularly affected younger people; and pressure on the civilian population to take part in the illegal activities of NSAGs.

The launch in October of a peace process between the government and the Revolutionary Armed Forces of Colombia (*Fuerzas Armadas Revolucionarias de Colombia*, or FARC) represent an important opportunity to reduce violence in the country. The talks have, however, taken place amid ongoing hostilities as both parties seemingly sought to use violence to consolidate their negotiating positions, actually making the security situation and its humanitarian consequences worse.

IDPs' access to the basic necessities of life is extremely limited in both Colombia and Mexico, despite their status as middle-income countries. Mexico is a member of the G20 and held the organization's presidency in 2012, while Colombia ranks as the world's 31st largest economy. Where data was available, it showed that IDPs' access to housing and income-generating opportunities remained extremely poor in Colombia, and that they had worse access to social services than the rest of the population. In Mexico, census data showed that people who move from violent to non-violent municipalities in search of safety had less access than the local population to livelihood opportunities, education, and housing. Data also showed that, in some cases, people displaced from cities had protection needs related to the property they left behind.

---

[3] The sketchy nature of the data strongly suggests that the Mexican government should make systematic efforts to gather more complete information.

As in previous years, displacement affected a disproportionate number of people from minority populations in the region. In Colombia, many Afro-Colombian and indigenous people live in rural areas where most of the confrontations between NSAGs and government forces take place, and which have the highest rates of displacement. In the Mexican state of Chiapas, indigenous people make up the majority of IDPs living in protracted displacement, which is also predominantly the case in Peru and Guatemala.

Prospects for durable solutions

In Colombia, the process of implementing the 2011 Victims' Law, which aims to provide redress for IDPs and other victims of violence, moved forward. It was hampered, however, by a number of obstacles, including a lack of financial resources and delays in the appointment of essential staff such as judges. The land restitution process faced violent resistance, and more than 700 leaders claiming their land rights received death threats.

In Peru, a reparations process has been in the pipeline for several years, but it was delayed again in 2012. Individual reparations are now due to start in 2013, but collective reparations have been postponed several times already. Of all the countries in the region, Colombia has made the most progress in integrating IDPs and their needs into structural long-term projects, including social protection programmes for vulnerable populations and development plans.

Responses

In Colombia, despite continuing improvements in the government's response, which was by far the most advanced in the region, programmes continued to fall short of meeting the scale of IDPs' needs. After declaring in 2004 that the government's inadequate response to internal displacement amounted to an 'unconstitutional state of affairs', the Constitutional Court continued its oversight of the response in 2012. In an important ruling in September, which strongly affirms the importance of the property restitution process for IDPs, it held that the killings of human rights activists and land restitution claimants were to be treated as crimes against humanity.

In Mexico, the state of Chiapas adopted a law on the protection of IDPs in February 2012. The law, the first of its kind in the country, was drafted with the support of various UN agencies and civil society organizations, and incorporates the Guiding Principles. In December, the same party that led the adoption of the Chiapas law introduced a bill in the Mexican senate to establish legislation on the prevention of internal displacement, the assistance of IDPs, and the facilitation of durable solutions. This was a welcome initiative in a country that still lacks a national framework on internal displacement.

EUROPE, THE CAUCASUS, AND CENTRAL ASIA

Around 2.5 million people were internally displaced in Europe as of the end of 2012. The vast majority fled armed conflict, generalized violence, and other human rights violations, and some have been living in displacement for up to 20 years. With more than 954,000 IDPs, Turkey had the largest number across the region. The count in Croatia was put at zero after government and UN assessments showed the nation's 2,000 remaining IDPs no longer had needs related to their displacement.

The only new displacement reported was in Turkey. Figures for Azerbaijan, Cyprus, and Georgia rose slightly as more displaced children were still eligible to register as IDPs, while the figure in Kyrgyzstan increased due to new information. In addition, sudden-onset disasters newly displaced more than 70,000 people in Russia and Azerbaijan.

The collection of data and information on IDPs is not consistent across the region, and does not always adhere to the criteria set out in the Guiding Principles. For example, in Russia, people who should qualify as IDPs are excluded, while in Georgia, people who should not are included. Meanwhile, the authorities in Turkmenistan and Uzbekistan do not acknowledge internal displacement in their countries, obstructing research and rendering information outdated. As displacement has become increasingly protracted in the region, government and donor attention has diminished. One result of this waning attention is that data and information on the situation of IDPs has become increasingly scarce.

Political developments

Several political developments in the region during 2012 may bode well for IDPs. Serbia gained European Union (EU) candidate status and the mandate for international supervision of Kosovo ended. The conflict between Serbia and Kosovo is not resolved, but EU-moderated talks resumed in October and had made progress by the end of the year, including on border issues. IDPs stand to benefit as key areas such as freedom of movement, civil registry, and property records are discussed. In Georgia, the new government initiated discussions on revising its law on IDPs and a shift towards needs-based assistance. The newly elected de facto authorities in the breakaway region of South Ossetia adopted a new law on housing intended to benefit families whose homes were destroyed or severely damaged during the hostilities in 2008.

Other political developments obstructed the resolution of displacement. Skirmishes continued between Azerbaijan and Armenia, and Russia and Turkey continued domestic counter-insurgency operations. Vladimir Putin once more became Russian President in March, and by the end of the year had asked the US Agency for International Development (USAID) to leave the country. He also signed new laws effectively limiting the activities and foreign funding of non-governmental organizations (NGOs). Whether the change of government in Georgia in October improves humanitarian access to break-away regions and the possibility of IDP returns remains to be seen. Progress in addressing the conflict in the former Yugoslav Republic of Macedonia (FYROM) was threatened by latent tensions and an upsurge of nationalism and inter-ethnic urban violence.

Protection issues

The majority of the region's IDPs live unseen with relatives or friends, or in housing that they rent, own, or occupy informally. Some are at risk of eviction. Their living conditions are largely unknown, but small-scale studies have shown their housing tends to be inadequate in terms of space, cost, tenure security, and general liveability. Some 310,000 IDPs still live in atrocious conditions in collective centres, the vast majority in Azerbaijan and Georgia.

Many IDPs in the Balkans are elderly, traumatized, mentally ill, or physically disabled. They are unable to provide for themselves, and their tenure security has become increasingly threatened in recent years as owners decide to sell their buildings or put them to other use. That said, there were fewer reports of evictions from collective centres in 2012. Eviction also continued to be an issue for IDPs living outside collective centres. In Kyrgyzstan, some had their reconstructed homes demolished as the city of Osh implemented its urban development plan. In Azerbaijan, the government is building housing for IDPs who have been squatting.

Limited income-generation opportunities are a leading concern for internally displaced families throughout the region. IDPs lose jobs, assets, resources, and networks when they flee, and a generally weak economic climate and high unemployment has made many of them more vulnerable in all states except Cyprus. There is no recent comprehensive data on unemployment rates among IDPs except in Serbia, where it was 32 per cent, compared with 19 per cent for the general population. Meagre pensions, social benefits, and allowances are often IDPs' main source of income, and many are unable to afford health care. Disrupted schooling means that many young IDPs do not enter the workforce fully educated, and in some cases children are taken out of school to work for the family. IDPs in Azerbaijan, Bosnia and Herzegovina, Kosovo, Russia, and Serbia continued to face difficulties in obtaining personal and other documents needed to access services and exercise their rights. The problem is most acute for displaced Roma and Ashkalis in Kosovo and Serbia, who continue to be one of the most vulnerable groups of IDPs in the region.

Discrimination in Bosnia and Herzegovina, Croatia, Kosovo, Russia, Serbia, and Turkey limits IDP access to housing, jobs, education, and health care. In Turkey, it has forced many Kurdish IDPs from rural areas to join the ranks of the urban poor, while in Bosnia and Herzegovina and Kosovo, hate crimes were a problem in areas where IDPs from minority groups had returned.

Prospects for durable solutions

While some governments in recent years have shifted their approach towards supporting IDPs who have opted to integrate locally or settle elsewhere in their countries, multiple obstacles to durable solutions remain. Some countries, such as Azerbaijan, continue to prioritize returns even if they are physically impossible or unsafe. This is often driven by a fear of losing territory as a result of border disputes or secession movements. In these cases, addressing internal displacement issues is tied to conflict resolution talks, and as such there are no mutually agreed mechanisms to restitute IDPs' property or compensate them in Azerbaijan, Cyprus, or Georgia. For many IDPs elsewhere, access to such mechanisms is restricted by language, cost, and distance either from their property or the relevant institutions, and the mechanisms have not always proven effective. The sustainability of returns is uncertain in Bosnia and Herzegovina, Croatia, Georgia, Kyrgyzstan, FYROM, and Russia, and it was particularly questionable in Kosovo in 2012 amid ongoing inter-ethnic tensions.

Despite continuing efforts to establish post-war justice in the region, reconciliation remains incomplete and reparations for IDPs inadequate. Impunity for perpetrators of human rights violations continues, and the fate of IDPs' missing relatives has not been clarified. As a result, the risk of further conflict and displacement remains.

Responses

Most governments in the region continued to assist IDPs during 2012. In Azerbaijan, Bosnia and Herzegovina, Georgia, Kosovo, and Serbia, authorities improved the housing conditions of some IDPs in collective centres. Bosnia and Herzegovina drafted long-overdue legislation as per the revised Annex VII of the Dayton Accords, which, after years of focusing on return, expands support to include areas outside of IDPs' places of origin. In Kyrgyzstan, consultations on a new four-year sustainable development plan and national unity concept provided opportunities to improve the rule of law and move towards reconciliation. Bosnia and Herzegovina, Croatia, Montenegro, and Serbia raised a total of some €261 million (US$342 million), almost half of the required funds for a regional housing programme for 74,000 refugees and IDPs under the Sarajevo Process. The Council of Europe Development Bank approved a €60 million ($78 million) loan for housing 7,200 IDPs in collective centres in Bosnia and Herzegovina. Overall, however, funding is in decline across the region, the result of waning donor interest.

Criticism of government responses to internal displacement during 2012 focused on a lack of transparency in assistance allocation, the exclusion of IDPs from decision-making processes (and, as a result, policies not being aligned with their needs, rights, and interests), and a lack of adequate resources. As of the end of the year, Serbia was still to develop an action plan to implement the strategy for IDPs and refugees it enacted in

2011, Turkey had still not finalized action plans for 13 south-eastern provinces, and most municipal authorities in Kosovo had not developed coherent policies to guide returns and reintegration. European institutions continued to express concern about internal displacement. The Council of Europe's new Human Rights Commissioner, Nils Muižnieks, visited Azerbaijan, FYROM, Russia, and Turkey. After meeting IDPs in Macedonia, he concluded that durable solutions were within reach and needed to be implemented urgently. Earlier in 2012, his predecessor, Thomas Hammerberg, called for 'wise vision and determined political leadership' to secure post-war justice and durable peace in the Balkans.

The Council of Europe also adopted a report and resolution on the situation of IDPs and returnees in the North Caucasus, calling on the Russian authorities to improve the humanitarian situation of IDPs. At the end of the year, Ukraine, as the incoming chair of the Organization for Security and Co-operation in Europe (OSCE), made resolution of the region's protracted conflicts a priority for 2013. The main donors in the region were the EU, Germany, Norway, Sweden, Switzerland, and the United States of America (USA). Turkey also received around US $20 million from both Saudi Arabia and the USA, and smaller amounts from other governments. The UN Human Rights Committee called on Armenia to improve IDPs' living conditions, and called on Bosnia and Herzegovina to provide adequate alternative housing to IDPs in collective centres and to ensure their sustainable integration. The UN Committee for the Rights of the Child noted that Azerbaijan had taken significant measures to improve the situation of its displaced population.

MIDDLE EAST AND NORTH AFRICA

The number of IDPs in the Middle East continued to rise in 2012, to stand at more than 6 million at the end of year, an increase of 40 per cent as compared to 2011, and the highest figure ever recorded. Over the last ten years, this regional upward trend has been constant, with two notable jumps and no dips—evidence that the vast majority of IDPs have not obtained durable solutions and are living in protracted displacement.

The first jump, between 2006 and 2008, was caused by the escalation of sectarian conflict in Iraq, which displaced as many as 2.8 million people. The number of IDPs in Yemen also started to rise significantly in 2008, when the figure jumped from 250,000 to more than 380,000. The second spike began in 2011 as social unrest associated with the Arab Spring degenerated into armed conflict in Libya, Syria, and Yemen.

Despite popular clamour for greater transparency and socio-economic justice, elections held in 2012 did not always herald a new era of democracy. Yemen's elections in February confirmed former President Ali Abdullah Saleh's deputy, Abd Rabbuh Mansur Hadi, as his Saudi-backed replacement. Parliamentary elections held in Syria in May led to the cosmetic loss of one seat by President Bashar al-Assad's Ba'ath party as the country descended into generalized armed conflict.

The Middle East was generally marked by instability in 2012, as new and inexperienced governments emerged following the downfall of decades-old repressive regimes. They sought legitimacy in political Islam rather than the secular Arab nationalism that had dominated the region since the end of the colonial period. From Tunisia to Iraq, this transition is reshaping both internal and regional dynamics and alliances. Some non-Arab Muslim minorities such as the Kurds, who have suffered discrimination and displacement in both Iraq and Syria, may come to benefit from the shift.

New movements

The most dramatic increase in the number of IDPs was in Syria, where the figure rose more than fivefold. With more than 3 million IDPs, Syria is one of the world's largest internal displacement crises. New displacements also took place in Yemen, where conflict forced another 132,000 people to flee their homes. In addition, 1,200 people were newly displaced by flood disaster in the Occupied Palestinian Territories (OPT). Libya was the only country where the number of IDPs dropped substantially. Only 50,000 people were still displaced as of the end of 2012, compared with 243,000 the year before. Most IDPs have managed to return since the fall of Muammar Gaddafi, but those alleged to have supported his regime are unable to go back for fear of retribution.

Where people from different ethnic and religious groups once coexisted, conflict and displacement have created more homogenous sectarian enclaves. This happened in Lebanon during the 1975–90 civil war, and the process is visible in Iraq and increasingly so in Syria. Non-Muslim minorities are finding less space to flee internally, and many have eventually sought refuge abroad. The UN-mandated Independent Commission of Inquiry on Syria released an update on 20 December 2012 that highlighted a deepening sectarian divide. The Commission found that, of 80,000 Christians in Homs, only a few hundred remained in the country. As in Iraq, Christians, Turkmen, and members of other minorities are increasingly the target of criminal activities in a lawless environment, with kidnapping for ransom on the rise. The Syrian conflict is taking place in urban centres, leading to massive displacement. Once displaced, minorities face continued insecurity, which renders return to their places of origin virtually impossible.

Protection issues

Most IDPs in the region, particularly those newly displaced, live in precarious conditions. Very few live in camp-like situations, with the vast majority preferring to stay with host communities, in rented accommodation, overcrowded housing, and makeshift shelters. Libya is a notable exception, where the majority of the remaining 50,000 IDPs live in 132 camps. In Syria, a few camps have been established and are hosting thousands of IDPs in opposition-controlled areas along the Turkish border. The region's IDPs have generally fled to urban centres, where they have better employment opportunities. This makes it harder to identify them, assess their needs, and determine the scale of displacement.

Palestinians have also borne the brunt of recent conflict in the Middle East, and the UN Relief and Works Agency (UNRWA), the UN agency mandated to assist Palestinian refugees in the OPT, Jordan, Lebanon, and Syria, has been underfunded in recent years. In Gaza, Israel's largest military operation in the territory for nearly four years displaced more than 12,000 people in November, of whom 3,000 remained so as of the end of 2012. Of the 27,000 Palestinians forced to flee the destruction of the Nahr el-Bared refugee camp in Lebanon in 2007, 23,000 remained in displacement. In Syria, UNRWA has assisted 400,000 out of an estimated 500,000 Palestinian refugees in the country. Government forces have attacked UNRWA camps in pursuit of Syrian IDPs who had sought refuge there.

Lack of humanitarian access has increased IDPs' vulnerabilities across the region, leaving many unable to benefit from assistance and protection, and jeopardizing prospects for durable solutions. In Libya, Yemen, and most of Iraq and Syria, lack of humanitarian access has been restricted by insecurity, leaving organizations struggling to reach 4 million people in need. In Syria, it has been further complicated by bureaucratic restrictions; in Iraq, the granting of visas for NGOs has also become ever more time-consuming. Finding interlocutors with whom to negotiate access to opposition-controlled areas also remains a major challenge, whether in northern Syria, disputed areas of Iraq, or some parts of Yemen. Lack of humanitarian access has become the greatest obstacle to IDPs' protection in the region, leading some organizations to consider cross-border activities.

Prospects for durable solutions

Although some returns have taken place, durable solutions remain a distant prospect for most IDPs in the region. In Yemen, more than 130,000 went back to their places or origin during 2012, and in Lebanon, around 4,000 Palestinians returned to Nahr el-Bared. Governments, however, have generally failed to respond to IDPs' needs in ways that would facilitate durable solutions, and the overwhelming majority find themselves living in protracted displacement. Significant numbers have expressed a desire to integrate locally, but authorities tend not to be supportive of this settlement option. Most governments would prefer IDPs to go back to their places of origin, but have done very little to create the right conditions for returns. On the political level, they have failed to address social and ethnic tensions caused by conflict, while on the logistical level, IDPs have struggled to obtain documentation and to access livelihood support and basic services. Many IDPs live in urban areas, placing a heavy burden on infrastructure and social services, and increasing competition for scarce employment.

Responses

National responses need to be improved if they are effectively to address both the scale and nature of internal displacement in the region, and the international response too has been hampered by political deadlock. That said, Qatar and other Gulf countries have become more responsive to humanitarian situations in the region. In October 2012, the Emir of Qatar, Sheikh Hamad bin Khalifa al-Thani, became the first Arab leader to visit Gaza since Hamas came to power, ending the group's isolation. The Emirate's pledge of US$400 million for housing projects dwarfed the contribution made through humanitarian aid, which continues to face security and political obstacles. The new involvement of regional states was all the more welcome given the destruction of around 300 homes during Israel's military operation in Gaza in November.

Of the eight states that the IDMC monitored in 2012, only Lebanon and Iraq have national institutions dedicated to internal displacement issues. Lebanon's Ministry of Displaced set up a fund for IDPs from the civil war, but political stalemate and a lack of national reconciliation has limited its effectiveness. Similarly, Iraq's Ministry of Migration and Displacement revised its national plan to end displacement in 2011, but the priorities of other ministries and local authorities have made it virtually impossible to implement. Governments in the region continue to face challenges related to the conflicts in Libya, Yemen, Syria, and to a lesser extent those in Iraq and the OPT. Ongoing insecurity and instability in these countries has obstructed efforts towards national reconciliation and the implementation of durable solutions. It has also threatened to spill over into neighbouring states, many of which face the same underlying tensions.

New donors in the region, such as Qatar and Kuwait, have provided welcome additional support, but the general capacity to respond to crises continues to be hampered by limited access, funding shortfalls, and a lack of political will. In the OPT, for example, the flouting of international humanitarian law (IHL) that has led to the repeated displacement of Palestinians can only be addressed once the Israeli government respects its legal obligations. The international response in Syria, which remains woefully inadequate given the scale of the crisis, has been severely curtailed by political deadlock. In Iraq, and to a certain extent in Libya, there are concerns that IDPs and their plight may fall off the agenda as the international response switches from the humanitarian to the development phase, with fewer funds available for projects targeting communities living in protracted displacement and in dire need of assistance.

SOUTH AND SOUTH-EAST ASIA

The decrease in the number of IDPs observed in 2011 in South and South-East Asia continued in 2012. Around 4.1 million people were internally displaced as of the end of the year as a result of internal armed conflict, violence, and human rights violations, down nearly 5.5 per cent from 4.3 million a year earlier. Pakistan, Afghanistan, and India had the highest number of reported IDPs, accounting for more than a third of the region's displaced population. In many states, counting and profiling of IDPs was complicated by their high level of mobility and lack of effective monitoring mechanisms. In addition, flawed registration systems also tend to exclude both IDPs outside official camps and those who do not fall within often narrow official definitions of what constitutes an IDP. Camp closures and premature deregistration also meant IDPs were often removed from official statistics and denied further assistance, despite not having achieved a durable solution.

Conflict between government forces and NSAGs was the main cause of conflict-induced displacement in India, Indonesia, Myanmar, Pakistan, the Philippines, Sri Lanka, and Thailand, and in the region as a whole. In some of these, as well as in Bangladesh, the violence was between ethnic and religious groups or clans competing for land, resources, and political power. Some states, notably Myanmar and the Philippines, made significant progress towards the peaceful settlement of long-standing conflicts, but it tended not to end displacement.

At least 1.4 million people were newly displaced in the region during 2012. Several waves of inter-communal violence displaced up to 500,000 people in India's north-eastern Assam state, while military operations against NSAGs in Pakistan's FATA forced about 412,000 people to flee. In the Philippines, at least 167,000 people fled clashes between government forces and NSAGs in Mindanao, and clan violence affecting mainly Muslim-majority areas. An estimated 166,000 people were newly displaced in Myanmar, most of them by inter-communal violence pitting Rakhine against Rohingya and other Muslim minorities in Rakhine state. In Afghanistan, an estimated 100,400 people were reportedly displaced, although the true figure is thought to be far higher. Most fled armed conflict between pro-government forces and the Taliban, and widespread conflict-related violence.

Patterns of displacement varied considerably, with the nature of the violence and the availability of protection and assistance influencing how far people fled and for how long. In most cases, IDPs aimed to find safety for their families while remaining as close as possible to their property to facilitate their return. Some sought refuge with friends and relatives or host communities and managed to return within a few days or weeks. In other cases, persistent insecurity and the loss of property and traditional livelihoods forced IDPs to remain in camps or to attempt, often unsuccessfully, to integrate with their host communities. Throughout the region, relative security, and better job prospects and basic services, encouraged some IDPs to seek refuge in cities, where most settled in informal settlements, often squatting on private or state-owned land. Protracted urban displacement was a particular concern in Afghanistan, where local authorities were reluctant to recognize urban IDPs. In contrast, relatively well-off IDPs from Nepal's Terai region and southern Thailand found it relatively easy to integrate in the major cities.

More than 14 million people were newly displaced by sudden-onset disasters in the same conflict-affected states. Disasters often increase the vulnerability of IDPs already displaced by conflict and violence, and in some cases it was hard to distinguish one clear cause of displacement.

Protection issues

Armed conflict, harassment, and intimidation by NSAGs and state forces alike, unexploded ordnance, and restricted freedom of movement put IDPs at risk of injury and death. In the Philippines, counter-insurgency operations against the New People's Army (NPA) were reportedly accompanied by human rights violations, including the extra-judicial killing of indigenous people suspected of supporting the rebels. In Assam, IDPs living in camps in the Bodoland Territorial Areas District were reportedly at risk of attacks. There were concerns of a severe humanitarian crisis in Rakhine, where tens of thousands of displaced Rohingya had no access to health care, clean water, proper shelter, or food. In Indonesia's Papua province, people displaced by military operations in Keerom district in July 2012 reportedly hid in the jungle for months, surviving on what little food they could collect. In Afghanistan, worrying numbers of IDPs were food insecure, with more than one half spending over 90 per cent of their income on food.

In Afghanistan, Pakistan, and the Philippines, displaced children were at risk of child labour, trafficking, and forced recruitment. Limited livelihood options, particularly in urban areas, left displaced women and girls at risk of forced and early marriage and other forms of GBV. Female-headed households were particularly vulnerable. In Pakistan, many women hold no national identity card, which is required for female-headed households to access most humanitarian assistance. The need to ensure *purdah*, or honour, also restricts women's access to food distribution points, information, and basic services.

Prospects for durable solutions

Some 261,000 people were reported to have returned to their homes during 2012. The true figure is, however, thought to be higher, as people often return in small groups or individually and such movements tend to go unreported. Most returns involved people displaced for just a few weeks or months, but in the Philippines a number of IDPs living in more protracted displacement went back to their homes in Central Mindanao thanks to improved security and a government-sponsored return and recovery programme. In Pakistan, the government declared a number of areas in FATA clear of armed groups, and voluntary repatriation programmes were undertaken. Nearly 60,000 people reportedly returned in 2012, but—as often also the case elsewhere—it was unclear whether the process was sustainable.

Persistent insecurity, damage, or destruction of housing, the slow restoration of basic services and infrastructure, unresolved land and property issues, and a lack of livelihood opportunities were all major obstacles to returns across the region, and in many cases prevented them outright. In Sri Lanka, the military's ongoing occupation of land in conflict-affected areas was a case in point. Throughout the region, governments largely continued to prioritize return over settlement or other options such as local integration or settlement elsewhere. In states such as Nepal or Afghanistan, where the majority of IDPs do not wish to return to their places of origin, there is an urgent need to support alternative settlement options to return, in particular, local integration.

Peace processes, which in recent years have enabled many IDPs to return, remained incomplete in many cases, and few states made progress in ensuring accountability for displacement-related human rights violations. Governments in Bangladesh, East Timor, Indonesia, and Nepal largely failed to follow up on their commitments to ensure truth, justice, and reparation for victims of conflict, including IDPs and their families.

Responses

Most governments made significant efforts, often with the support of the international community, to meet IDPs' immediate needs and so avert humanitarian crises. Responses, however, were often ad hoc and poorly coordinated, and based on a short-term humanitarian approach. Other obstacles included poor governance and a lack of state resources.

Effective humanitarian responses were hampered by access restrictions, whether imposed by governments—as in Indonesia (Papua)—or caused by insecurity, as in Afghanistan and Myanmar. The Indian government still refuses to acknowledge the existence of internal displacement as a result of conflict and violence. Many states have yet to develop comprehensive laws or policies to guarantee IDPs' rights. Progress was, however, made in the Philippines, where Congress enacted the Rights of Internally Displaced Persons Act in February 2013. In Afghanistan, the Ministry of Refugees and Repatriation initiated the development of a national policy on IDPs. Both the UN and civil society organizations criticized the Association of Southeast Asian Nations (ASEAN) Human Rights Declaration, which was adopted in November, for a lack of transparency and consultation during the drafting process, and the fact that it challenges the principle that human rights are universal by making respect for them subject to national laws.

The UN and the broader international community supported most governments of the region in their efforts to assist and protect IDPs. There is recognition that humanitarian relief alone will not address IDPs' needs, but a gap between humanitarian and development interventions remains. In Sri Lanka, where many UN agencies and NGOs are phasing out their humanitarian programmes, it is unclear whether the development sector will include people affected by displacement in development strategies.

A steep decline in humanitarian funding in some countries and a low level of support for early-recovery initiatives in others further undermined the overall response and were major obstacles to IDPs achieving durable solutions. In Afghanistan, humanitarian funding dropped by 50 per cent in 2012. In Pakistan, the government had still not adopted an early recovery assistance framework for FATA as of the end of 2012, so limiting funds for projects in many return areas.

Concluding remarks

Significant progress has been made since the Guiding Principles on Internal Displacement were first introduced more than ten years ago in 1998, in terms of awareness by states of the rights of IDPs and of their protection and assistance needs, and of states' own responsibility to protect IDPs, as well as in the capacity developed within the international humanitarian and human rights systems globally to support states in identifying and responding to the needs of IDPs.

Whilst the impetus for action in support of IDP rights initially came from the 'global level', with the appointment in 1992 of the first Representative of the UN Secretary-General for IDPs, increasingly change is taking place at the regional and national levels. This is where international efforts in support of IDP rights must focus to find solutions for IDPs trapped in situations of protracted displacement. International actors—whether humanitarian, development, or human rights—need to work together, and with a common agenda, in support of regional institutions, states, and national civil society organizations to identify and implement strategies for durable solutions for IDPs.

5 Sexual violence in armed conflict in 2012

Alice Priddy*

Twenty-five of us gathered together and said we should rape 10 women each, and we did it . . . I've raped 53 women. And children of five or six years old.

Congolese solder recounting crimes committed in December 2012 in Minova[1]

Introduction

Sexual violence continues to be a prominent feature of armed conflicts and post-conflict situations around the world. Sexual violence is not confined to conflicts in one region or dependent on the level of 'development'; it is truly a global problem. Afghanistan, the Central African Republic (CAR), Colombia, Côte d'Ivoire, the Democratic Republic of the Congo (DRC), Libya, Mali, Myanmar, Somalia, South Sudan, Sudan (Darfur region), Syria, Uganda, and Yemen were all the scene of large-scale sexual violence during 2012.[2] Of course, sexual violence in armed conflict is not a new phenomenon: entrenched discriminatory attitudes and practices, combined with lack of effective law enforcement, and internal instability, as well as a generalized culture of impunity, have allowed often systematic and large-scale sexual violence during armed conflicts to perpetuate.

It is a common misconception to think of sexual violence as a purely sexual act. Sexual violence is an act of aggression and one that is not always committed for sexual gratification. Indeed, a common form of sexual violence reported during 2012 was rape with objects and mutilation of genitalia of men as an interrogation technique. Sadly, as has been said of torture, the parameters of sexual violence are only limited by the perpetrator's

---

* Alice Priddy is a researcher at the Geneva Academy.

[1] Quotation from Pete Jones, 'Congo: we did whatever we wanted says soldier who raped 53', *The Guardian*, 11 April 2013, <http://www.guardian.co.uk/world/2013/apr/11/congo-rapes-g8-soldier>.

[2] See 'Report of the United Nations Secretary-General, sexual violence in conflict', UN General Assembly/UN Security Council, UN doc. A/67/792 and S/2013/149, 14 March 2013 ('UN Secretary-General's report on sexual violence in conflict').

imagination. Rape, genital mutilation, deliberate infection with HIV/AIDS, sexual slavery, forced marriage, forced sterilization, forced prostitution, and forced impregnation are all forms of sexual violence that commonly occur in situations of armed conflict and their aftermath. It should be remembered that sexual violence may not involve physical force or necessarily be confined to a party to the conflict, for example if a humanitarian aid worker offers food in exchange for a sexual act.[3]

The unfortunate truth is that sexual violence is an 'effective' weapon of terror in so far as it devastates victims, physically and psychologically, and it demoralizes the victims and their communities. Sexual violence is used to dominate and control the victims and their communities through ensuring compliance, or punishing them for lack of compliance. Sexual violence is used strategically in some conflicts to advance military objectives such as clearing a certain area of civilians. During 2012, sexual violence was used forcibly to displace civilians in Colombia, the DRC, Libya, Mali, and Syria.[4]

The perpetrators of sexual violence are wide-ranging in nature, including members of armed forces, civilians, government officials, armed non-state actors (ANSAs), and humanitarian personnel. The overwhelming majority of the perpetrators of sexual violence are male. Sexual violence occurs on the street, in homes, at checkpoints, in places of detention, and in places of refuge, such as refugee camps. Aside from the immediate pain, terror, and humiliation, survivors of sexual violence often face long-term physical health problems and psychological trauma. The physical consequences of sexual violence include fatal injuries, infertility, incontinence, chronic pain, debilitating injuries, infections, and unwanted pregnancies.[5] Owing to the insecurity that conflict inevitably brings, medical treatment for these deliberating injuries is all too often not available.

Sexual violence in armed conflict and in the immediate aftermath goes largely unreported; accordingly, accurate figures on its prevalence are not available. Underreporting may be due to a single factor or a combination of factors, including insecurity, social stigma, cultural taboos, fear of reprisals, geographic barriers (for example, where such violence occurs in remote villages, the nearest police station might be tens or even hundreds of miles away), economic barriers (in Côte d'Ivoire, an obligatory medical certificate is needed to bring a rape case to court, which costs US$100), apathy, and the perception that the exercise would be pointless due to lack of infrastructure and effective law enforcement. Cultural practices, such as where the burden of proof falls on the victim, may also deter reporting.

---

[3] Office of the UN High Commissioner for Refugees (UNHCR) and Save the Children, 'Sexual violence and exploitation: the experience of refugee children in Guinea, Liberia and Sierra Leone', February 2002.

[4] UN Secretary-General's report on sexual violence in conflict, §8.

[5] Anne G. Sadler et al., 'Health-related consequences of physical and sexual violence: women in the military', *Obstetrics and Gynaecology*, 96(3) (2000), pp. 473–80. Madina Haeri and Nadine Puechguirbal, 'From helplessness to agency: examining the plurality of women's experiences in armed conflict', *International Review of the Red Cross*, 92(887) (2010), pp. 103–22; Save the Children, *Unspeakable Crimes against Children: Sexual Violence in Conflict*, Save the Children, London, March 2013, p. 15, <http://www.savethechildren.org.uk/resources/online-library/unspeakable-crimes-against-children>.

This chapter will first look at the relationship between gender and age and sexual violence, then the international legal framework applicable to sexual violence in armed conflict, before providing an overview of selected situations of armed conflict during 2012. From the outset, the misconception that sexual violence is solely a side-effect of war must be dispelled. Sexual violence serves as a source of conflict and insecurity, and delays the onset of peace. As the United Nations (UN) Security Council has affirmed, 'sexual violence, when used or commissioned as a tactic or systematic attack against civilian populations, can significantly exacerbate situations of armed conflict and may impede the restoration of international peace and security'.[6]

A. **Gender and age and sexual violence**

WOMEN

The inequality between men and women in most societies, whereby women are viewed and treated as subordinate and inferior to men, means that, in all contexts, female victims of sexual violence outnumber the male victims. In armed conflict, however, the plight of women is exacerbated, since '[c]onflict creates a free-fire zone, a sort of "free-for-all" in which pre-existing ideas about women as inferior, and other discriminatory and misogynist ideas, may be given free expression by frequently all-male groups of soldiers and other combatants'.[7] These beliefs also mean that the consequences of sexual violence against women tend to be more severe, particularly where women are impregnated as a result of rape and denied access to termination services, and the violence is more likely to go unreported while the perpetrators enjoy impunity.

Women are all too often perceived as merely an extension of the opposition's male fighters, an object for fighters' pleasure, a 'warrior's reward', or a vessel for procreation. Women often do not have the capacity to flee the danger they face in conflict areas, due to lack of economic means, pregnancy, being responsible for young children, or sometimes encumbered by cultural or religious constraints that limit their ability to move freely without the presence or even permission of a male. Those women who can escape and find themselves displaced are also vulnerable. 'Survival sex', where desperate families agree to 'marriages' of girls to receive money for food and shelter and protection from further sexual violence against other members of the family, was widely reported in refugee camps in 2012.[8]

---

[6] UN Security Council Resolution 1960, 16 December 2010, §1.

[7] K. Bennounce, 'Do we need new international law to protect women in armed conflict?' *Case Western Reserve Journal of International Law*, 38 (2006), p. 370.

[8] Save the Children, *Unspeakable Crimes against Children: Sexual Violence in Conflict*, p. 11; Hamida Ghafour, 'Syria's refugee brides: "My daughter is willing to sacrifice herself for her family"', *The Star*, 22 March 2013.

The ability of women to access medical services and rehabilitation following acts of sexual violence during armed conflict is often limited, owing to security or resource constraints, as well as cultural and religious reasons. For a woman who has been raped, the ability to access medical treatment, including emergency contraception and termination services, is vital. Yet many women are denied these services, forcing them to undergo a dangerous and illegal abortion, expose themselves to severe penalties,[9] or carry on with an unwanted pregnancy.[10] The consequences of pregnancy are real for all women: maternal mortality is so grave a problem around the world that a woman dies of pregnancy-related complications every two minutes.[11] The consequences of pregnancy for a woman are even direr in certain countries, such as the DRC, particularly for girls whose underdeveloped bodies struggle to cope with pregnancy and childbirth aside from the internal injuries sustained during rape.[12] Over her lifetime, a Congolese woman faces a 1-in-24 chance of dying from complications arising from pregnancy or childbirth.[13] Yet, alarmingly, the United States of America (USA) currently does not allow its humanitarian aid to be used to provide terminations for women and girls that have been impregnated as a result of rape in an armed conflict.[14] I would argue

[9] In the DRC, for example, the penalty is a minimum of five years' imprisonment for attempting or seeking an illegal abortion.

[10] The Committee on Economic, Social and Cultural Rights (CESCR), in its General Comment on the right to health, highlights that women have specific needs relating to their reproductive and sexual health, and that 'the realization of women's right to health requires the removal of all barriers interfering with access to health services,... including in the area of sexual and reproductive health. It is also important to undertake preventive, promotive and remedial action to shield women from... norms that deny them [women] their full reproductive rights': CESCR, 'General Comment No. 14: Right to health', UN doc. E/C.12/2000/4, 11 August 2000, §21.

[11] The majority of deaths are in developing countries. The four most common causes of maternal death are severe bleeding during and after childbirth, infections, high blood pressure during pregnancy, and unsafe abortion: UN Population Fund, 'Maternal death halved in 20 years, but faster progress needed', Press release, 16 May 2012.

[12] In peacetime, girls aged 15 and under are five times more likely to die during pregnancy or childbirth compared to those aged over 20; this risk will be even higher during armed conflict when maternal health services are less likely to be available: Save the Children, *Unspeakable Crimes against Children: Sexual Violence in Conflict*, p. 16. See also Harvard Humanitarian Initiative and Oxfam International, 'Now the world is without me: an investigation of sexual violence in Eastern Democratic Republic of Congo', April 2010, p. 41, <http://www.oxfam.org/sites/www.oxfam.org/files/DRC-sexual-violence-2010-04.pdf>.

[13] 'Congo's maternal mortality rate exacerbated by poverty and ignorance', *The Guardian*, 11 May 2012.

[14] Under international humanitarian law (IHL), the basic requirement to give the necessary medical care to the wounded and sick reflects customary law, and the International Committee of the Red Cross (ICRC) Customary IHL Study, Rule 110, confirms that, in both international and non-international armed conflicts (IACs and NIACs, respectively): '[T]he wounded, sick and shipwrecked must receive, to the fullest extent practicable and with the least possible delay, the medical care and attention required by their condition. No distinction may be made among them founded on any grounds other than medical ones.' As Louise Doswald-Beck asserts, '[t]here can be no doubt that persons who are raped fall into the category of "wounded and sick," due to the severe mental, and often also physical, trauma suffered'. Therefore, '[e]xclusion of one medical service, abortion, from the comprehensive medical care provided to the "wounded and sick" in armed conflict, where such service is needed by only one gender, is not only a

that any policy that denies access to emergency contraception and termination services, thereby failing to take into account the often inevitable consequences of the rape of women, is both discriminatory on the grounds of gender (prohibited under international law)[15] and amounts to cruel, inhuman, or degrading treatment where this forces a female to either undergo a dangerous illegal termination or carry an unwanted pregnancy.[16]

The sociological impact of sexual violence on women is long-term and will stretch well beyond the end of a conflict. Sociological effects include the derogatory perception of victims as 'dishonoured' and 'disgraced', leaving them as outcasts,[17] ostracized by society and their families, and deemed 'unmarriable'.[18] It is not uncommon for female survivors of sexual violence to be shamed or even coerced into marrying the perpetrator or one of his family members, thereby further victimizing the survivor, allowing impunity for the perpetrators and sending the message that sexual violence is sociably acceptable.[19] Women may also face severe economic hardship as a result of being victims of sexual violence in armed conflict. Already marginalized, a female survivor of sexual violence may be unable to work as a result of her injuries and/or discriminatory attitudes towards

violation to their right to medical care, but also a violation of the prohibition on "adverse distinction" found in common Article 3, the Additional Protocols to the Geneva Conventions, and customary international law: Professor Doswald-Beck's open letter to President Obama, 10 April 2013, on file with the author.

[15] 1966 International Covenant on Civil and Political Rights (ICCPR), Art. 26; 1966 International Covenant on Economic, Social and Cultural Rights, Art. 2(2); 1950 European Convention on Human Rights (ECHR), Art. 14; 1969 American Convention on Human Rights (ACHR), Art. 1; 1981 African Charter on Human and Peoples' Rights (ACHPR), Art. 2; 2004 Arab Charter on Human Rights (ArCHR), Art. 3; 1979 Convention on the Elimination of All Forms of Discrimination against Women (CEDAW). A policy, even if neutral, will be discriminatory if it has a disproportionate impact on a protected group: European Court of Human Rights (ECtHR), *Hugh Jordan v. United Kingdom*, Judgment (App. No. 24746/94), 4 August 2001, §154. For further reading on discrimination and disproportionate impact, see O. M. Arnardóttir, 'Non-discrimination under Article 14 ECHR: the burden of proof', *Scandinavian Studies in Law*, 51 (2007), pp. 13–39.

[16] Torture or cruel, inhuman and degrading treatment is prohibited under various human rights instruments, including: the 1984 Convention against Torture and Other Cruel Inhuman or Degrading Treatment or Punishment (CAT); ICCPR, Art. 7; ACHR, Art 5; the 1985 Inter-American Convention to Prevent and Punish Torture and Inhuman or Degrading Treatment (IACPPT); ECHR, Art. 3; ACHPR, Art. 5; Common Art. 3 to the four 1949 Geneva Conventions. The prohibition on torture is a peremptory norm of international law.

[17] In discussing the causes and impact of sexual violence against women, the importance of 'honour' in some societies must not be underestimated. The concept of honour is one based around the notion of female virginity before marriage and sexual fidelity after it. 'Honour' prevents women reporting sexual violence and seeking or accessing medical help following it. Girls and women interviewed by the Independent Commission of Inquiry on Syria reported that it is worse for a girl to be raped than killed in Syrian society; therefore, many girls commit suicide after being raped: 'UN Secretary-General's report on sexual violence in conflict', §12. The survivors of sexual violence may not only fear reprisals from their attackers if they report the abuse, but also so-called 'honour killings' by their families or communities.

[18] 'UN Secretary-General's report on sexual violence in conflict', §12; 'Report of the UN High Commissioner for Human Rights on the situation of human rights in Mali', Human Rights Council, UN doc. A/HRC/22/33, 7 January 2012, §31.

[19] 'UN Secretary-General's report on sexual violence in conflict', §11.

her, leaving her in extreme poverty. Women who have children as a result of rape by members of the enemy often face particularly toxic discrimination, and the plight of children born as a result is all too often bleak.

Tackling impunity for acts of sexual violence committed during armed conflict or in its immediate aftermath is a major challenge, irrespective of the victim's gender. It has, though, been reported that sexual violence against women often increases after a period of insecurity if those who perpetrate such crimes are not held to account. Impunity for acts of sexual violence committed during a conflict may send the message that sexual violence is socially acceptable, or perpetuate a culture of tolerance of such abuse after the conflict. A further challenge to tackling sexual violence against women is the discourse that surrounds it: one that tends to be based around archaic notions of protecting women's honour and modesty.[20] This needs to be abandoned and emphasis placed instead on women as rights' holders, and on women's basic human rights to physical integrity, dignity, and protection from torture and other ill-treatment.

MEN

Although the majority of conflict-related sexual violence is committed against women, males are also the victims of such abuse.[21] The overwhelming majority of acts of sexual violence against men are committed by other men. The type of sexual violence used against men in armed conflict includes rape, forced sterilization, forced sexual acts with the victim's family members, and mutilation of the genitals. Sexual violence against men often takes a different form to that committed against women. The sexual violence will often form a tactic of the war and will be used as a method of interrogation to obtain information, elicit a confession, or secure compliance. During 2012, men in Afghanistan, Libya, Mali, and Syria were reported to have been victims of sexual violence during interrogation.[22]

Male victims of sexual violence are especially unlikely to seek medical help or rehabilitation services, leading to longer-term trauma, and the prevalence of the phenomenon is very likely to go unreported due to the unique sense of shame and trauma

---

[20] See Judith Gardham, 'Women and armed conflict: the response of international humanitarian law' in Helen Durham and Tracy Gurd (eds), *Listening to the Silences: Women and War*, Martinus Nijhoff, The Netherlands, 2005; Hilary Charlesworth and Christine Chinkin, *The Boundaries of International Law: A Feminist Analysis*, Manchester University Press, Manchester, 2000.

[21] See ad hoc International Criminal Tribunal for the former Yugoslavia (ICTY), *Prosecutor v. Brdanin*, Judgment (Trial Chamber) (Case No. IT-99-36), 1 September 2004; ICTY, *Prosecutor v. Zdravko Mucic*, Judgment (Trial Chamber) (Case No. IT-96-21-T), 16 November 1998. In both cases, male victims were forced to perform oral sex on each other, including between brothers.

[22] 'UN Secretary-General's report on sexual violence in conflict', §10.

experienced by men.[23] Men often feel that being a victim of sexual violence is 'incompatible with their masculinity...both at the level of the attack itself—a man should have been able to prevent himself from being attacked—and in dealing with the consequences of the attack—to be able to cope "like a man"'.[24]

CHILDREN

Girls and boys continue to be the targets of sexual violence during armed conflict and in its aftermath.[25] Save the Children reports that girls especially, but also boys, account for four-fifths of those who are victims of sexual violence in conflict and 'conflict-affected' situations.[26] Such violence might be motivated by sexual pleasure, to demoralize and terrorize the enemy, or in the pursuit of superstitions, such as the wholly incorrect belief that intercourse with a pre-pubescent child will make the perpetrator immune to HIV, or cure HIV, or protect the perpetrator from injury or death during combat.[27] Children are also forcibly recruited by armed groups to act as sex slaves, whereby they become the '"property" of one or more fighters, to who they provide sexual services, or act as "wives" to individual fighters'.[28] During periods of insecurity, children are also vulnerable to sexual violence committed by family members, other children, teachers, religious leaders, peacekeepers, and humanitarian staff.[29]

The short- and long-term effects of sexual violence on boys and girls are severe: physically, psychologically, and socially. Underdeveloped girls and boys are acutely vulnerable to internal injuries that may be fatal, or leave them infertile or with deliberating, life-long injuries. Underdeveloped girls who have been raped and who do not have access to termination services face heightened risk of maternal mortality. Girls who survive the birth of the child are often forced to drop out of education. Their chances of securing a job, further education, and marriage are severely diminished, leaving them facing a lifetime of poverty.[30] Children born as a result of rape, particularly by enemy

---

[23] Sandesh Sivakumaran, 'Male/male rape and the "trait" of homosexuality', *Human Rights Quarterly*, 27 (2005), pp. 1274–306; Pauline Oosterhoff, Prisca Zwanikken, and Evert Ketting, 'Sexual torture of men in war-time Croatia was common', *British Medical Journal*, 29 May 2004; P. Oosterhoff, 'Sexual torture of men in Croatia and other conflict situations: an open secret', *Reproductive Health Matters*, 12(23) (2004), pp. 68–77; S. Sivakumaran, 'Lost in translation: UN responses to sexual violence against men and boys in situations of armed conflict', *International Review of the Red Cross*, 92(877) (March 2010), pp. 259–77.

[24] S. Sivakumaran, 'Sexual violence against men in armed conflict', *European Journal of International Law*, 18 (2007), p. 255.

[25] Boys and girls are defined in this chapter as those less than 18 years of age.

[26] Save the Children, *Unspeakable Crimes against Children: Sexual Violence in Conflict*, p. v.

[27] Amnesty International, 'Democratic Republic of Congo: mass rape—time for remedies', October 2004, p. 14

[28] Save the Children, '*Unspeakable Crimes against Children: Sexual Violence in Conflict*', p. v.

[29] Save the Children, '*Unspeakable Crimes against Children: Sexual Violence in Conflict*', p. v.

[30] Save the Children, '*Unspeakable Crimes against Children: Sexual Violence in Conflict*', p. 15.

fighters, are also often stigmatized and may endure life-long discrimination, leaving them socially and economic isolated.

Girls and boys are unlikely to report sexual violence through fear of reprisals and social stigma, allowing a culture of impunity to flourish. Alarmingly, reports have emerged from some countries of children being prosecuted after reporting sexual violence. In Afghanistan, for example, a boy aged 13 was charged with 'moral crimes' after being raped.[31] The lack of age-appropriate reporting mechanisms and child-focused services is also credited with contributing to under-reporting of sexual violence against children.

B. Sexual violence under international law

THE 1949 GENEVA CONVENTIONS AND 1977 ADDITIONAL PROTOCOLS

IHL has long prohibited rape and sexual violence, albeit implicitly and conservatively. The 1863 Lieber Code prohibited, and made punishable by death, 'all wanton violence committed against persons in the invaded country...[including] all rape...of such inhabitants'.[32] The Code also provided that 'unarmed citizens were to be spared in person, property and honor',[33] and that 'persons of inhabitants, especially those of women; and the sacredness of domestic relations' require protection.[34]

The 1949 Geneva Conventions, the first treaties in modern history 'to achieve universal acceptance',[35] built upon the Lieber Code and largely codified customary international law. Of the four Conventions, only the 1949 Geneva Convention IV expressly refers to sexual violence. This reference concerns itself only with women, and is unfortunately framed in rather archaic and discriminatory language.[36] Thus Article 27 states: 'Women shall be especially protected against any attack on their honour, in particular against rape, enforced prostitution, or any form of indecent assault.' The provision thereby

---

[31] Human Rights Watch (HRW), 'Afghanistan: don't prosecute sexually assaulted children', 10 February 2013, <http://www.hrw.org/news/2013/02/09/afghanistan-don-t-prosecute-sexually-assaulted-children>.

[32] 1863 Lieber Code, General Orders No. 100, 24 April 1863, Art. 44.

[33] 1863 Lieber Code, General Orders No. 100, 24 April 1863, Art. 22.

[34] 1863 Lieber Code, General Orders No. 100, 24 April 1863, Art. 37.

[35] ICRC, 'A milestone for international humanitarian law', Press release, 22 September 2006.

[36] This archaic language, such as 'protected' and 'honour', feeds the stereotype of women as weaker than their male counterparts and perpetuates discriminatory attitudes. For an overview of IHL from a feminist perspective, see J. Gardam and M. J. Jarvis, *Women, Armed Conflict and International Law*, Kluwer Law International, The Hague, 2001. It has been suggested that a further instrument should be appended to the 1949 Geneva Conventions dedicated to the protection of women in times of armed conflict: J. Gardam, 'Women and the law of armed conflict: why the silence?', *International and Comparative Law Quarterly*, 46 (1997), p. 77.

places rape, enforced prostitution, and other forms of indecent assault within a protection framework rather than expressly prohibits the conduct. Furthermore, the protection afforded identifies these offences as attacks on women's 'honour' rather than as violent crimes. Despite the lack of an express mention in the 1949 Geneva Convention IV, males are undoubtedly protected from sexual violence under Common Article 3, which prohibits 'at any time and in any place whatsoever... outrages upon personal dignity, in particular humiliating and degrading treatment'.

The 1977 Additional Protocol I, which governs IAC, does not use the language of honour, but still treats women as persons in need of 'special respect' and protection. As with Article 27, 1949 Geneva Convention IV, however, rape, enforced prostitution, and other forms of sexual assault are still placed in a framework of protection rather than prohibition. Article 27 of the 1977 Additional Protocol I states: 'Women shall be the object of special respect and shall be protected in particular against rape, forced prostitution and any other form of indecent assault.' Although Article 27 does not apply to men, Article 75 lists fundamental guarantees that must be enjoyed 'without any adverse distinction' based upon, inter alia, 'sex', including the prohibition of 'outrages upon personal dignity, in particular humiliating and degrading treatment, enforced prostitution and any form of indecent assault', under which sexual violence clearly falls.

The 1977 Additional Protocol II, which governs non-international armed conflict (NIAC), takes a more gender-neutral approach, abandoning completely the language of protection. Article 4(2) contains fundamental guarantees that prohibit: 'violence to the life, health and physical or mental well-being of persons... [;] cruel treatment such as torture, mutilation'; and 'outrages upon personal dignity, in particular humiliating and degrading treatment, rape, enforced prostitution and any form of indecent assault'.[37]

Rape and other forms of sexual violence are also prohibited under customary international law in both IACs and NIACs, as reflected in Rule 93 of the ICRC study. The prohibition codified in Rule 93 is gender-neutral, applying equally to men as it does to women.

Controversially, rape, enforced prostitution, or any other forms of sexual violence are not explicitly included as grave breaches in the 1949 Geneva Conventions or the two 1977 Additional Protocols (and therefore war crimes). Instead, sexual violence falls under the umbrella of 'wilfully causing great suffering or serious bodily injury to body or health'.[38] In response to human rights activists calling for this to be corrected, and spurred by the atrocities that occurred during the conflict in Bosnia and Herzegovina in the early 1990s, the ICRC issued an *Aide-Mémoire* in 1992 to clarify that the grave breach regime 'obviously not only covers rape, but also any other attack on a women's dignity'.[39]

---

[37] 1977 Additional Protocol II, Art. 4(2)(a) and (e).
[38] 1949 Geneva Convention IV, Arts 146 and 147.
[39] ICRC, Update on *Aide-Memoire* of 3 December 1992; Theodor Meron, 'Rape as a crime under international humanitarian law', *American Journal of International Law*, 87 (1993), p. 427.

Furthermore, in the commentary on Rule 156, on the definition of war crimes, the ICRC reiterated that although rape was not 'explicitly listed as a grave breach... [it] would be considered a grave breach on the basis that it amounts to inhumane treatment or wilfully causing great suffering or serious injury to body or health'.

It is important to ascertain whether or not an offence is recognized as a grave breach since states are obligated to exercise universal jurisdiction over such breaches.[40] Universal jurisdiction is additional to other basis of jurisdiction that may be exercised over offences involving sexual violence, namely: territorial jurisdiction (based on the location of the crime);[41] the active personality principle of jurisdiction (based on the nationality of the perpetrator, under which a state may prosecute one of its nationals for acts committed abroad);[42] and the passive nationality principle of jurisdiction (based on the nationality of the victim, under which a state may prosecute a non-national for acts committed against a national abroad).[43] Under the principle of universal jurisdiction, any state can investigate and prosecute any individual in respect of international crimes committed abroad, regardless of the nationality of the perpetrator and victim, and even if the accused is not present in the state seeking to prosecute.[44] This form of jurisdiction is based on the principle that certain crimes are so heinous that every state should have the possibility, and responsibility, to hold to account those who perpetrate them.[45]

With regard to the sexual violence witnessed in 2012, the regimes of grave breaches and universal jurisdiction offer little help for victims because the regime only applies to IACs (although some diverging views exist)[46] and thus does not apply to the vast majority of contemporary conflicts: NIACs.[47] Therefore, although the United Kingdom (UK) should

---

[40] 1949 Geneva Convention I, Art. 49; 1949 Geneva Convention II, Art. 50; 1949 Geneva Convention III, Art. 129; 1949 Geneva Convention IV, Art. 146. States also have a *right* to exercise universal jurisdiction in their national courts over other war crimes. This is a norm of customary international law and applies to war crimes committed in both IACs and NIACs: ICRC Customary IHL Study, Rule 157. See e.g. Roger O'Keefe 'The grave breaches regime and universal jurisdiction', *Journal of International Criminal Justice*, 7(4) (2009), pp. 811–31.

[41] For further discussion of territorial jurisdiction, see e.g. Antonio Cassese, *International Criminal Law*, 3rd edn, Oxford University Press, Oxford, 2013, p. 271.

[42] Cassese, *International Criminal Law*, p. 276.

[43] Cassese, *International Criminal Law*.

[44] Unless the legal system of the state seeking to prosecute permits trials in absentia, national law may require the presence of the accused within its territory to initiate trial proceedings: Cassese, *International Criminal Law*, p. 278. For further discussion of universal jurisdiction, see R. O'Keefe, 'Universal jurisdiction: clarifying the basic concept', *Journal of International Criminal Justice*, 2 (2004) pp. 738–40 and 745–7.

[45] Indeed, a number of states have exercised universal jurisdiction to try suspected war criminals, including: Australia (see High Court of Australia, *Polyukhovich v. Australia and anor*, 172 CLR 501, 14 August 1991); Canada (see Supreme Court of Canada, *R. v. Finta*, File No. 23097, 24 March 1994); and the United Kingdom (UK) (see Court of Appeal, *R v. Sayoniuk*, 10 February 2000).

[46] Separate Opinion of Judge Georges Abi-Saab in ICTY, *Prosecutor v. Tadić*, Decision on Jurisdiction (Appeals Chamber) (Case No. IT-94-1), 15 July 1999.

[47] ICTY, *Prosecutor v. Tadić*, §§79–83. Furthermore the 1949 Geneva Conventions and 1977 Additional Protocol I limit the concept of grave breaches to acts 'against persons or property protected by the present

be congratulated on its recent enthusiasm to tackle impunity for acts of sexual violence in armed conflict, the Foreign Minister's statement declaring that the UK recognizes rape and sexual violence to amount to grave breaches of the Geneva Conventions,[48] and thus that the UK will prosecute such acts under universal jurisdiction, is of little additional value unless the UK is willing to accept that the regime applies to NIACs.[49]

THE AD HOC INTERNATIONAL CRIMINAL TRIBUNALS AND THE INTERNATIONAL CRIMINAL COURT

The ad hoc international criminal tribunals and the International Criminal Court (ICC) have clarified and expanded upon what constitutes sexual violence under international law. Rape, sexual slavery, enforced prostitution, forced pregnancy, enforced sterilization, 'or any other form of sexual violence of comparable gravity' are all included in the 1998 Rome Statute of the ICC (ICC Statute) as crimes against humanity as well as war crimes.[50] The contextual elements will determine whether the offence is a crime against humanity or a war crime. To constitute a crime against humanity, the acts must be 'committed as part of a widespread or systematic attack directed against a civilian population' with the perpetrator's knowledge that the conduct was part of such an attack.[51] To constitute a war crime, the offence must have taken place in the context of, and be associated with, either an IAC or an armed conflict 'not of an international character' with the perpetrator's awareness of the 'factual circumstances that established the existence of an armed conflict'.[52] It is worth noting that, of the states in which widespread sexual violence took place in 2012, Afghanistan, the CAR, Colombia, Côte d'Ivoire, the DRC, Mali, and Uganda are all states parties to the ICC Statute.[53]

Convention', and the term 'protected person' is, as far as civilians are concerned, limited to '[p]ersons ... who ... find themselves ... in the hands of a Party to the conflict ... of which they are not nationals'.

[48] The Secretary of State for Foreign and Commonwealth Affairs (Mr William Hague), Hansard col. 1141, 14 February 2013; Foreign and Commonwealth Office, 'Declaration on preventing sexual violence in conflict', 11 April 2013.

[49] Of course, the UK was already bound to prosecute such crimes committed in IAC because the UK is party to all four Geneva Conventions and to Additional Protocol I.

[50] ICC Statute, Arts 7(1)(g) (crimes against humanity), 8(2)(b)(xxii) (war crimes in an IAC), and 8(2)(e) (vi) (war crimes in an NIAC).

[51] 'Elements of Crimes', common elements in subparas 3 and 4, to Art. 7(1)(g) (rape, sexual slavery, enforced prostitution, enforced sterilization, and sexual violence) and subparas 2 and 3 to Art. 7(1)(g) (forced pregnancy).

[52] 'Elements of Crimes', common elements in subparas 3 and 4, to Art. 8(2)(b)(xxii) (rape, sexual slavery, enforced prostitution, forced pregnancy, enforced sterilization, and sexual violence, for IACs) and subparas 3 and 4 to Art. 8(2)(e)(vi) (sexual slavery, enforced prostitution, forced pregnancy, enforced sterilization, and sexual violence, for NIACs).

[53] For an updated list of states parties to the ICC Statute, see <http://www.icc-cpi.int/en_menus/asp/states %20parties/Pages/the%20states%20parties%20to%20the%20rome%20statute.aspx>.

Before we look at each specific offence of sexual violence, it should be borne in mind that, under international criminal law (ICL), not only can identified soldiers be prosecuted for their crimes, but also their commanders, under the doctrine of command responsibility.[54] At its essence, command responsibility imposes criminal responsibility on a commander for his to her 'failure to act when under a duty to do so'.[55] Thus a commander will be criminally responsible 'if he or she knows or has reasons to know that his or her subordinates are about to commit or have committed crimes, unless the superior prevents the subordinates' crimes or punishes the perpetrators after the crimes are committed'.[56] Therefore, it is not necessary that commanders order or encouraged crimes; if they have reason to know that soldiers under their command are about to commit, or have committed, an act of sexual violence and yet turn a blind eye, they can be prosecuted for the offence.[57]

Rape

A clear definition of rape did not exist in international law until 1998, when the International Criminal Tribunal for Rwanda (ICTR) defined rape as 'a physical invasion of a sexual nature, committed under circumstances which are coercive'.[58] Building upon this definition, and the jurisprudence of the ad hoc tribunals,[59] rape is defined in the ICC Elements of Crimes as having two elements. First, the perpetrator must have 'invaded the body of a person resulting in penetration however slight, of any part of the body of the victim or of the perpetrator with a sexual organ, or the anal or genital opening of the victim with any object or any part of the body'. A footnote to this element makes clear that such 'invasion' is to be regarded as gender-neutral. Secondly, the invasion must have been 'committed by force, or by threat of force or coercion, such as that caused by fear of violence, duress, detention, psychological oppression or abuse of power, against such a person on another person, or by taking advantage of a coercive environment, or the invasion was committed against a person incapable of giving genuine consent'. A

---

[54] The doctrine of command responsibility is contained in, among others: Arts 86 and 87 of 1977 Additional Protocol I; Art. 7(3), Statute of the ICTY; Art 6(3), Statute of the Special Court for Sierra Leone; and Art 28 of the ICC Statute.

[55] Judge Bakone Justice Moloto, 'Command responsibility in international criminal tribunals', *Berkeley Journal of International Law Publicist*, 3 (2009), p. 12.

[56] Moloto, 'Command responsibility in international criminal tribunals', p. 13.

[57] Indeed, the perpetrator need not even be identified; it is sufficient that the perpetrators are identified as belonging to a unit or group controlled by the superior: *Prosecutor v. Blaškić*, Judgment (Appeals Chamber) (Case No. IT-95-14-A), 29 July 2004, §217.

[58] ICTR, *Prosecutor v. Akayesu*, Judgment (Trial Chamber) (Case No. 96-4-T), 2 September 1998, §597.

[59] Shortly after *Akayesu*, the ICTY defined rape as 'the sexual penetration, however slight: of the vagina or anus of the victim by the penis of the perpetrator or any other object used by the perpetrator; or of the mouth of the victim by the penis of the perpetrator; by coercion or force or threat of force against a victim or third person': *Prosecutor v. Furundžija*, Judgment (Trial Chamber) (Case No. IT-95-17/1), 10 December 1998, §185.

footnote to this element states that 'it is understood that a person may be incapable of giving genuine consent if affected by natural, induced or age-related incapacity'.[60]

The ICTY has considered whether consent could ever be given in coercive circumstances. In *Kunarac*, victims were held in de facto military headquarters, detention centres, and apartments maintained as soldiers' residences. As the most egregious aspect of the conditions, the victims were considered the legitimate sexual prey of their captors and were repeatedly raped, often by several men and on a daily basis. Those who sought aid or resisted 'were treated to an extra level of brutality'. The Appeals Chamber of the ICTY held that 'such detentions amount to circumstances that were so coercive as to negate *any* possibility of consent'.[61]

Put simply, the use of force, threat of force, or coercion defeat the possibility of 'genuine consent' such that any person who engages in prohibited sexual violence in these circumstances is committing an act of rape, or another form of sexual violence.[62] Whether or not the victim of the violence put up a fight or resisted is irrelevant.[63] Coercive circumstances would include, for example, a soldier entering a home at night with arms.[64]

It is accepted under ICL that rape can constitute torture given that severe pain or suffering, an element of the definition of torture,[65] can 'be said to be established once rape has been proved, since the act of rape necessarily implies such pain or suffering'.[66] Furthermore, unlike under the 1984 CAT (*see section 'Torture and other forms of cruel, inhuman, or degrading treatment or punishment'*), ICL does not require the perpetrator of an act of torture to be a public official or a person acting with the acquiescence of a public official.[67]

---

[60] Elements 1 and 2 of the Elements of Crimes relating to Art. 7(1)(g), Art. 8(2)(b)(xxii), and Art. 8(2)(e) (vi). For discussion of sexual autonomy and the concept of consent, see e.g. Amnesty International, *Rape and Sexual Violence: Human Rights Law and Standards in the International Criminal Court*, AI Index: IOR 53/001/2011, Amnesty International, London, March 2011, p. 13.

[61] ICTY, *Prosecutor v. Kunarac, Kovać and Vuković*, Judgment (Appeals Chamber) (Case No. IT-96-23), 12 June 2002, §§131–2.

[62] Use or threat of force has been held to be 'clear evidence of non-consent': *Prosecutor v. Kunarac, Kovać and Vuković*, Judgment (Appeals Chamber), 12 June 2002, §99.

[63] *Prosecutor v. Kunarac, Kovać and Vuković*, Judgment (Appeals Chamber), 12 June 2002, §128. Rule 70 of the ICC Rules of Procedure and Evidence provides that '[c]onsent cannot be inferred by reason of the silence of, or lack of resistance by, a victim to the alleged sexual violence'.

[64] See comments of the Pre-Trial Chamber of the ICC in *Decision on the Confirmation of charges, Situation in the Central African Republic in the case of Jean-Pierre Bemba Gombo, Decision Pursuant to Article 61(7)(a)and (b) of the Rome Statute on the Charges of the Prosecutor against Jean-Pierre Bemba Gombo*, 15 June 2009, Case ICC-01/-5-01/08, §172.

[65] The ICC Statute defines torture as the 'intentional infliction of severe pain or suffering, whether physical or mental': Art. 7(2)(e).

[66] See *Decision on Jean-Pierre Bemba Gombo*, §151.

[67] See *Decision on Jean-Pierre Bemba Gombo; Prosecutor v. Kvocka and ors*, Judgment (Appeals Chamber) (Case No. IT-98-30/1-A), 28 February 2005, §284.

The ICTR has confirmed that rape and other forms of sexual violence can constitute genocide when committed with intent to destroy in whole or in part a national, ethical, racial, or religious group.[68] Sexual violence as a tool for genocide may be perpetrated through preventing births of a particular group by rape (where a women 'is deliberately impregnated by a man of another group, with the intent to have her give birth to a child who will consequently not belong to its mother's group'),[69] forced sterilization, sexual mutilation, or separation of the sexes.[70]

Sexual slavery and enforced prostitution

Sexual slavery is defined under the ICC Elements of Crimes as existing where the 'perpetrator exercised any or all of the powers attaching to the right of ownership over one or more person, such as by purchasing, selling, lending or bartering such a person or persons, or imposing on them a similar deprivation of liberty' and causing that person 'to engage in one or more acts of a sexual nature'.[71]

The ICC Elements of Crimes define enforced prostitution to be where the 'perpetrator caused one or more persons to engage in one or more acts of a sexual nature by force, or by threat of force or coercion, such as that caused by fear of violence, duress, detention, psychological oppression or abuse of power, against such person or persons or another person, or by taking advantage of a coercive environment or such person's or persons' incapacity to give genuine consent' and the perpetrator or another person obtained, or expected to obtain, pecuniary or other advantage in exchange for or in connection with the acts of a sexual nature.[72] It is the latter requirement that distinguishes the crime of enforced prostitution from that of slavery.

In practice, the distinction between enforced prostitution and sexual slavery is blurred. Indeed, a number of survivors, as well as commentators, advocate that enforced prostitution is better characterized as sexual slavery and should be prosecuted as such.[73] This is the position of the former Special Rapporteur on the issue of systematic rape, sexual slavery, and slavery-like practices in armed conflict, Gay McDougall, who argues that, in

---

[68] 1948 Convention on the Prevention and Punishment of the Crime of Genocide; ICTR, *Prosecutor v. Akayesu*, Judgment (Trial Chamber) (Case No. 96-4-T), 2 September 1998, §597; ICTR, *Prosecutor v. Musema*, Judgment (Trial Chamber) (Case No. ICTR-96-13-A), 27 January 2000.

[69] ICTR, *Prosecutor v. Akayesu*, Judgment (Trial Chamber), 2 September 1998, §507.

[70] Genocide Convention, Art. II(d); *Prosecutor v. Akayesu*, Judgment (Trial Chamber), 2 September 1998, §508.

[71] Art. 7(1)(g); Art. 8(2)(b)(xxii); and Art. 8(2)(e)(vi). For further reading on the ICC's approach to sexual slavery, see e.g. V. Oosterveld, 'Sexual slavery and the International Criminal Court: advancing international law', *Michigan Journal of International Law*, 25 (2004), p. 607.

[72] Art. 7(1)(g); Art. 8(2)(b)(xxii); and Art. 8(2)(e)(vi).

[73] Forced prostitution and forced servitude constitute a violation of the *jus cogens* norm prohibiting enslavement or slavery.

armed conflict, 'most factual scenarios that could be described as forced prostitution would also amount to sexual slavery and could more appropriately and more easily be characterized and prosecuted as slavery'.[74] Survivors have expressed concern 'that the term "forced prostitution" obscures the terrible gravity of the crime, suggests a level of voluntarism, and stigmatizes its victims as immoral or "used goods"'.[75] As one commentator has noted, the term forced prostitution:

... describes essentially the same conduct as 'sexual slavery', but it does not communicate the same level of egregiousness. 'Forced prostitution' tends to reflect the male view: that of the organizers, procurers, and those who take advantage of the system by raping the women. The term 'sexual slavery' reflects the victims' view. It focuses on the enslavement and the rape, and captures more accurately the enormity of subordination and suffering.[76]

However, by retaining enforced prostitution within the ICC Statute, sexual violence that does not meet the conditions required to meet the definition of sexual slavery will still fall within the jurisdiction of the ICC, thereby providing a further tool for future prosecutions of sexual violence in armed conflict situations.

Forced marriage

Forced marriage has been confirmed to be a crime against humanity by the Special Court for Sierra Leone.[77] The Appeals Chamber held that a separate crime of forced marriage existed in the context of Sierra Leone because a unique element was found in the 'bush marriages' that occurred in the region. The Court held that forced marriage involved a perpetrator compelling a person by force or threat of force, through words, or conduct of the perpetrator, or anyone associated with him, into a forced conjugal association. It concluded that this results in great suffering or serious physical or mental injury on the part of the victim.[78] The Court noted that the crime of forced marriage was

---

[74] 'Final report on systematic rape, sexual slavery and slavery-like practices during armed conflict: Gay J. McDougall, Special Rapporteur', UN doc. E/CN/.4/Sub.2/1998/13, 22 June 1998, §33.

[75] Carmen M. Argibay, 'Sexual slavery and the comfort women of World War II', *Berkeley Journal of International Law*, 21(375) (2003), p. 12.

[76] Argibay, 'Sexual slavery and the comfort women of World War II', p. 13.

[77] Special Court for Sierra Leone (SCSL), *Prosecutor v. Alex Tamba Brima*, Judgment (Appeals Chamber) (SCSL-2004-16-A), 22 February 2008. The ICTY had previously been referred to forced marriage as a possible form of sexual violence: see *Prosecutor v. Kvočka and ors*, Judgment (Trial Chamber) (Case No. IT-98-30/1), 2 November 2001, §180. For discussion of this case and the crime of forced marriage in general, see Neha Jain, 'Forced marriage as a crime against humanity: problems of definition and prosecution', *Journal of International Criminal Justice*, 6 (2008), pp. 1013–32; Augustine S. J. Park and Micaela Frulli, 'Advancing international criminal law: the Special Court for Sierra Leone recognizes forced marriage as a "new" crime against humanity', *Journal of International Criminal Justice*, 6 (2008), pp. 1033–42. Note also that forced marriage is prohibited under international human rights law (IHRL): see Art. 23(3), ICCPR, and Art. 16, CEDAW.

[78] *Prosecutor v. Alex Tamba Brima*, Judgment (Appeals Chamber), 22 February 2008, §183.

not exclusively, or predominantly, sexual, and as such was not fully encompassed by the crime of sexual slavery. The women who testified in the case described the marriages as having encompassed a series of abuses, including abduction, forced labour, deprivations of liberty, corporal punishment, assaults, and sexual violence. The Court concluded that forced marriage might also include one or more international crimes such as enslavement, imprisonment, rape, sexual slavery, or abduction.

Forced pregnancy

Forced pregnancy consists of two elements: forced impregnation and forced denial of access to a termination.[79] The ICC definition is, however, limited to circumstances in which there is 'intent of affecting the ethnic composition of any population'.[80] This is the only crime against humanity that requires an additional element of intent. Religious objections are surely the motivation for including this further element of intent. Indeed, the provision includes the rider that the definition 'shall not in any way be interpreted as affecting national laws regarding pregnancy'.[81] As Chinkin posits, forced pregnancy 'constitutes a very particular denial of a woman's autonomy and bodily integrity by forcing her to bear a child. Yet in this one instance the continuing insistence for control over women's reproductive capacity has subjugated gender identity, (that the crime was committed against her because she is a woman) to ethnic identity'.[82]

Enforced sterilization

The ICC Elements of Crimes describes enforced sterilization as taking place where the perpetrator 'deprived one or more persons of biological reproductive capacity' and the conduct was 'neither justified by the medical or hospital treatment of the person' nor 'carried out with their genuine consent'.[83] It is noted in the Elements of Crimes that deception is incompatible with genuine consent.

Sexual violence

Sexual violence is defined in the ICC Elements of Crimes to be where 'the perpetrator committed an act of sexual nature against one or more persons or caused such person or persons to engage in an act of sexual nature by force, threat of force or coercion, such as

---

[79] ICC Elements of Crimes: Art. 7(1)(g); Art. 8(2)(b)(xxii); and Art. 8(2)(e)(vi).
[80] ICC Statute, Art. 7(2)(f).   [81] ICC Statute, Art. 7(2)(f).
[82] C. Chinkin, 'Gender and armed conflict' in *Oxford Handbook of International Law in Armed Conflict*, Oxford University Press, Oxford, forthcoming (2013).
[83] ICC Elements of Crimes: Art. 7(1)(g); Art. 8(2)(vi); and Art. 8(2)(b)(xxii).

that caused by fear of violence, duress, detention, psychological oppression or abuse of power, against such person or persons or another person, or by taking advantage of a coercive environment such person's or persons' incapacity to give genuine consent'.[84]

The ICTR has broadly defined sexual violence to be 'any act of a sexual nature committed under circumstances that are coercive', explaining that: '[S]exual violence is not limited to a physical invasion of the human body and may include acts that do not involve penetration or physical contact. Sexual violence covers both physical and psychological attacks directed at a person's sexual characteristics.'[85] Similarly, the ICTY has held that sexual violence 'embraces all serious abuses of a sexual nature inflicted upon the integrity of a person by means of coercion, threat of force or intimidation in a way that is humiliating and degrading to the victim's dignity'.[86]

Effectiveness of the ICTY, ICTR, and the ICC

Despite progress in defining the various offences of sexual violence, the jurisprudence of the ad hoc tribunals, and in particular the ICC, is relatively scant. This is because charges are not being brought in cases in which there is sufficient evidence to warrant them. For example, in the only successful prosecution by the ICC to date, *Prosecutor v. Thomas Lubanga*, charges were limited to the recruitment of children despite there being ample evidence of sexual slavery and rape, much to the judges' disapproval.[87] In her dissenting opinion, Judge Odio Benito expressed frustration at this and affirmed that the exclusion of charges related to sexual violence restricts judges' ability to render justice for victims. Interestingly, despite charges of sexual violence not being bought against Lubanga, the judgment includes specific guidance on reparations for sexual violence and the Trial Chamber found that evidence of sexual violence should be taken into account when sentencing.[88]

INTERNATIONAL HUMAN RIGHTS LAW

Sexual violence is prohibited under IHRL primarily through the prohibition against torture, or other forms of cruel, inhuman, or degrading treatment or punishment, as well

---

[84] ICC Elements of Crimes: Art. 7(1)(g); Art. 8(2)(b)(xxii); and Art. 8(2)(e)(vi).

[85] *Prosecutor v. Akayesu*, Judgment (Trial Chamber), 2 September 1998, §§598 and 688. Similarly, Triffterer asserts: 'Sexual violence is a term broader than rape. The term is used to describe any kind of violence carried out through sexual means or by targeting sexuality'. See Otto Triffterer (ed.), *Commentary on the Rome Statute of the International Criminal Court*, 2nd edn, Hart Publishing, Oxford, 2008, p. 214.

[86] *Prosecutor v. Stakic*, Judgment (Trial Chamber) (Case No. IT-97-24), 31 July 2003, §757.

[87] ICC, *Prosecutor v. Thomas Lubanga*, Decision on Sentence (Trial Chamber) (Case No. ICC-01/04-01/06-2901), 10 July 2012, §60.

[88] *Prosecutor v. Thomas Lubanga*, Decision on Sentence (Trial Chamber), 10 July 2012, §69; however, because the evidence presented did not sufficiently link Mr Lubanga with the commission of sexual violence, the majority did not take into account evidence of sexual violence in sentencing in this particular case.

as the prohibition against slavery. States are bound by these prohibitions during armed conflict, and at least the prohibitions on torture and slavery are peremptory norms. Comparable prohibitions within international and regional human rights instruments may also apply, including in the situation in which the jurisdictional reach of those treaties is extended beyond the territorial borders of the state in question. The prohibitions against slavery, torture, and ill-treatment engage both positive and negative obligations upon the state.[89]

Torture and other forms of cruel, inhuman, or degrading treatment or punishment

The right to be free from torture or other forms of cruel, inhuman, or degrading treatment or punishment is a fundamental human right. The prohibition of torture has been enshrined as an absolute and non-derogable right in international treaties and regional instruments, and is widely accepted to be a norm of *jus cogens* under customary international law.[90] Any form of sexual violence committed during armed conflict that constitutes torture, or other forms of cruel, inhuman, or degrading treatment or punishment, would be a violation of international law.

Torture is defined under the 1984 CAT to be 'any act by which severe pain or suffering, whether physical or mental' is 'intentionally inflicted on a person' for the purposes of punishment, to obtain a confession or information, or to intimidate or coerce the victim or a third person 'for any reason based on discrimination of any kind' by the state or with the 'consent or acquiescence of a public official or other person acting in an official capacity'.[91] 'Severe pain or suffering', the element common to all treaty and case law definitions of torture,[92] is the ultimate test for determining whether an act

---

[89] For a discussion of the human rights obligations of non-state actors, see Ch. 9 of this volume.

[90] On the status of the prohibition of torture as *jus cogens*, see e.g. Nigel Rodley, *The Treatment of Prisoners under International Law*, 3rd edn, Oxford University Press, Oxford, pp. 64–81; Nigel Rodley, 'The prohibition of torture: absolute means absolute', *Denver Journal of International Law and Policy*, 34 (2006), p. 145; E. de Wet, 'The prohibition of torture as an international norm of *Jus Cogens* and its implications for national and customary law', *European Journal of International Law*, 15(1) (2004), p. 97.

[91] CAT, Art. 1. The Human Rights Committee has found that the prohibition of torture in the ICCPR applies regardless of whether the acts were committed by 'public officials or other persons acting on behalf of the State, or by private persons': Human Rights Committee, General Comment No. 20, 1992, §13.

[92] CAT, Art. 1; ICC Statute, Art. 7(2)(e); European Commission on Human Rights, *Greek case, Yearbook of the European Convention on Human Rights*, 12 (1969), p. 468; ECtHR, *Ireland v. United Kingdom*, Judgment (App. No. 18/91/1979), §96; ECtHR, *Selmouni v. France*, Judgment (App. No. 25803/94), 28 July 1999, §§96–7; ECtHR, *Kismir v. Turkey*, Judgment (App. No 27306/95), 31 May 2005, §129; ECtHR, *Tomasi v. France*, Judgment (App. No. 12850/87), 27 August 1992, §§108–15; ECtHR, *Ilhan v. Turkey*, Judgment (App. No. 22277/93), 27 June 2000, §84–7; ECtHR, *Romanov v. Russia*, Judgment (App. No, 41461/02), 24 July 2008, §§64–70; Committee against Torture, *Keremedchiev v. Bulgaria*, Decision (Comm. No. 257/2004), §9.2; Inter-American Court Human Rights (IACtHR), *Loayza-Tamayo v. Peru*, Series C, No. 33, (1997) §57; IACtHR, *Castillo-Petruzzi v. Peru*, Series C, No. 52 (1999), §196; IACtHR, *Caesar v. Trinidad and Tobago* Series C, No. 123 (2005), §69.

constitutes torture. In distinguishing an act of torture from one that constitutes cruel, inhuman, or degrading treatment or punishment, an assessment of the circumstances, including the purpose of the act, will have to be made.[93] This may ultimately be an intuitive decision.

Rape is accepted as constituting torture and therefore a violation of IHRL.[94] This has been affirmed by the ECtHR,[95] the Inter-American Commission on Human Rights (IACommHR),[96] the IACtHR,[97] the Committee on the Elimination of all Forms of Discrimination against Women (CEDAW),[98] and the Committee against Torture.[99] The ECtHR first held rape to constitute torture in *Aydin v. Turkey*, noting that 'rape leaves deep psychological scars on the victim which do not respond to the passage of time as quickly as other forms of physical and metal violence'. In that case, the Court noted that the applicant 'also experienced the acute physical pain of forced penetration, which must have left her feeling debased and violated both physically and emotionally'.[100]

Aside from rape as a form of torture, the ECtHR has also found the strip-search of a male prisoner in the presence of a female officer to be degrading treatment.[101] The Court concluded that, although strip-searches may be necessary on occasion: '[T]hey must

[93] Rodley argues that the 'purposive element' should be the 'sole or dominant element distinguishing torture from cruel or inhuman treatment': Rodley, *The Treatment of Prisoners under International Law*, p. 123. Manfred Nowak also takes this position: M. Nowak and Elizabeth McArthur, *United Nations Convention against Torture: A Commentary*, Oxford University Press, New York, 2008, p. 74. See also 'Report of the Special Rapporteur on torture and other cruel, inhuman or degrading treatment or punishment (Mr Manfred Nowak)', UN doc. E/CN.4/2006/6, §39.

[94] Pieter Kooijamans, the first Special Rapporteur on torture and other cruel, inhuman or degrading treatment or punishment, identified 'rape' and 'insertion of objects into the orifices of the body' as torture in 1986: UN doc. E/CN.4/1986/15, 19 February 1986, p. 29. His predecessor, Nigel Rodley, affirmed Pieter Kooijamans's analysis, confirming that '[s]ince it was clear that rape or other forms of sexual assault against women in detention was a particular ignominious violation of the inherent dignity and the right to physical integrity of the human being, they accordingly constituted an act of torture': UN doc. E/CN.4/1996/34, §§15–24.

[95] ECtHR, *Aydin v. Turkey*, Judgment (App. No. 23178/94), 25 September 1997, §86. For discussion of the impact of the case and the approach of the ECtHR to rape, see e.g. Clare McGlynn, 'Rape, torture and the European Convention on Human Rights', *International and Comparative Law Quarterly*, 58 (July 2009), pp. 565–95.

[96] *Raquel Martin de Mejia v. Peru*, Report No. 5/96, Annual Report of the IACommHR, 1995, OAS doc. OEA/Ser.L/V/II.9 Doc. 20 Rev. 7 (1996), pp. 186–7; *Gonzalez Pérez v. Mexico*, Report No. 53/01, Annual Report of the IACommHR, 2000, OAS doc. OEA/Ser.L/V/II.111 Doc.20 rev. (2000), §§45–52.

[97] *Miguel Castro-Castro Prison v. Peru*, IACtHR Series C No. 60, 25 November 2006. The IACtHR (§309) took the position that the notion of rape is not only 'non-consensual vaginal relationship, as traditionally considered', but also 'an act of vaginal or anal penetration without the victim's consent, through the use of other parts of the aggressor's body or objects, as well as oral penetration with the virile member'.

[98] CEDAW, General Recommendation No. 19 (1992).

[99] Committee against Torture, General Comment No. 2, UN doc. CAT/C/GC//2, 24 January 2008, §§18 and 22.

[100] *Aydin v. Turkey*, Judgment, 25 September 1997, §83. Also see ECtHR, *M. C. v. Bulgaria*, Judgment (App. No. 39272/98), 3 December 2003.

[101] ECtHR, *Valasinas v. Lithuania*, Judgment (App. No. 44558/98), 24 October 2001.

be conducted in an appropriate manner. Obliging the applicant to strip naked in the presence of a woman, and then touching his sexual organs and food with bare hands, showed a clear lack of respect for the applicant, and diminished in effect his human dignity. It must have left him with feelings of anguish and inferiority capable of humiliating and debasing him... therefore, [the ECtHR finds] that the search... amounted to degrading treatment within the meaning of Article 3 of the Convention.'[102] Furthermore, the Committee against Torture has held that domestic violence, female genital mutilation, and trafficking constitute acts of torture or ill-treatment.[103]

Given that rape has been confirmed to constitute torture, and that strip-searches with the effect of diminishing the victim's human dignity have been treated as amounting to degrading treatment, it seems certain that the acts of sexual violence that occurred in 2012 and addressed in this chapter—such as gang rape, sexual slavery, enforced sterilization, and genital mutilation—do amount to either torture or cruel, inhuman, or degrading treatment under IHRL.

Slavery

Slavery is prohibited under IHRL.[104] Adapted from the 1929 Slavery Convention, today slavery can be understood to mean 'the status or condition of a person over whom any or all of the powers attaching to the right of ownership are exercised, including sexual access through rape or other forms of sexual violence'.[105] Implicit within this definition is the limitation on the ability of the victim to exercise autonomy, freedom of movement, and 'power to decide matters relating to one's sexual activity'.[106] The ability of the victim to extract her or himself from the condition of slavery should not be interpreted as nullifying a claim of slavery. Rather: '[I]n all cases, a subjective, gender-conscious analysis must also be applied in interpreting an enslaved person's reasonable fear of harm or perception of coercion. This is particularly true when the victim is in a combat zone during an armed conflict, whether internal or international in character, and has been identified as a member of the opposing group or faction.'[107]

---

[102] *Valasinas v. Lithuania*, Judgment, 24 October 2001, §117.

[103] Committee against Torture, General Comment No. 2, 24 January 2008, §18.

[104] 1926 Slavery Convention, Art. 2; Supplementary Convention on the Abolition of Slavery, the Slave Trade, and Institutions and Practices similar to Slavery; ICCPR, Art. 8; ECHR, Art. 4(1); ACHR, Art. 6(1); ACHPR, Art. 5.

[105] 'Special Rapporteur on the situation of systematic rape, sexual slavery and slavery-like practices during wartime, Final report', UN doc. E/CN.4/sub.2/1998/13, 1998, §27.

[106] M. Cherif Bassiouni, 'Enslavement as an international crime', *New York University Journal of International Law and Politics*, 23 (1991), p. 458.

[107] 'Special Rapporteur on the situation of systematic rape, sexual slavery and slavery-like practices during wartime, Final report', E/CN.4/sub.2/1998/13, §29.

The definition of slavery is undoubtedly met in the case of the forced marriages (which are themselves expressly prohibited under IHRL)[108] and 'requisition' that took place in the CAR, the DRC, and Mali in 2012, as well as forced prostitution.[109] Like the prohibition of torture, the prohibition of slavery is a norm of *jus cogens*.[110] Any form of sexual slavery, including when committed during armed conflict, is therefore a violation of international law.

Application of human rights law prohibitions in armed conflict

Although it is clear that certain forms of sexual violence can constitute torture, cruel, inhuman, or degrading treatment, or slavery, further questions arise in the current discussion: what are states' obligations under these prohibitions and when can a state be held accountable for such acts? The starting point is that the norms in question are part of customary international law and apply in armed conflict as they do in times of peace.

On the question of what obligations these prohibitions entail, states are bound by the usual negative and positive obligations that exist under IHRL. They are clearly obligated *not* to participate in acts of slavery, torture, or cruel, inhuman, or degrading treatment. States also have a positive duty to protect those within their jurisdiction from these acts, including by criminalizing torture in national legislation and enforcing this legislation.[111] Under the ICCPR, this includes a duty to protect those within its jurisdiction from acts of slavery, torture, and ill-treatment committed by private individuals.[112] Since

---

[108] Supplementary Slavery Convention, Art. 1(D); ICCPR, Art. 23(2); CEDAW, Art. 16(1)(b); ACHR, Art. 17(2); 2003 Protocol to the ACHPR on the Rights of Women in Africa, Art. 6; see also 'Report of the Special Rapporteur on contemporary forms of slavery, including its causes and consequences', UN doc. A/HRC/21/41, 10 July 2012.

[109] 'Special Rapporteur on the situation of systematic rape, sexual slavery and slavery-like practices during wartime, Final report', UN doc. E/CN.4/sub.2/1998/13, §31.

[110] 'Special Rapporteur on the situation of systematic rape, sexual slavery and slavery-like practices during wartime, Final report', UN doc. E/CN.4/sub.2/1998/13, §28.

[111] CAT, Art. 1 (applies only to acts of torture); ICCPR, Art. 2(2); *M. C v. Bulgaria*, in which the ECtHR affirmed (§151) that 'states have a positive obligation inherent in Article 3 and 8 of the Convention [ECHR] to enact criminal-law provisions effectively punishing rape and to apply them in practice through effective investigation and prosecution'; ACHR, Arts 1 and 6.

[112] Human Rights Committee, General Comment No. 31, 'Nature of the general legal obligation imposed on states parties to the Covenant', UN doc. CCPR/C/21 Rev.1/Add.13, 26 May 2004, §8; IACPPT, Art. 3. The African Commission has held that 'if a state negates to ensure the rights in the African Charter, this can constitute a violation, even if the state or agent are not the immediate cause of the violation': *Commission Nationale des Droits de l' Homme et des Libertes v. Chad*, AfrCommHPR, Comm. No. 74/1992, 18th Session 2–11 October 1995; see also *Zimbabwe Human Rights NGO Forum v. Zimbabwe*, AfrCommHPR, Comm. No. 245/2002, 11–15 May 2006, §180, in which the African Court cited and followed the jurisprudence of the IACtHR on due diligence. Note also that the Protocol to the ACHPR on the Rights of Women in Africa requires states parties to protect women against all forms of violence, which includes 'all acts perpetrated against women which cause or could cause them physical, sexual, psychological, and economic harm, including the threat to take such acts; or to undertake the imposition of arbitrary restrictions on or deprivation of fundamental freedoms in private or public life': Art. 1(j).

the CAT recognizes torture and other cruel, inhuman, or degrading treatment only when committed at the instigation, or with the consent or acquiescence, of a public official or other person acting in official capacity, the acts of a private individual will not always fall within the scope of the treaty.[113] However, state failure to take steps to prevent torture or cruel, inhuman, or degrading treatment, or a failure to prosecute private individuals for acts of torture or ill-treatment, can constitute acquiescence and give rise to state responsibility under the CAT.[114] The Committee against Torture has affirmed that, where state authorities 'know or have reasonable grounds to believe that acts of torture or ill-treatment are being committed by non-state officials or private actors and they fail to exercise due diligence to prevent, investigate, prosecute or punish such non-State officials or private actors...the State bears responsibility...under the Convention'. The Committee has pointed out that this principle especially applied to gender-based violence including rape, female genital mutilation, and trafficking.[115]

The duty to investigate allegations of torture and cruel, inhuman, or degrading treatment[116] entails that the investigation must be prompt[117] and effective.[118] The Human Rights Committee has concluded that the duty to investigate extends to acts of a prior regime. This means that not only do the governments of today in states in which sexual violence was used in 2012 have a duty to investigate these acts, but so too do future

---

[113] CAT, Art. 1; Committee against Torture, *G.R.B. v. Sweden*, Decision (Comm. No. 83/1997), 15 May 1998, §6.5.

[114] Committee against Torture, *Dimitrijevic v. Serbia and Montenegro*, Decision (Comm. No. 207/2002), 24 November 2004, §5.4.

[115] CAT, General Comment No. 2, §18. Note that the ECtHR has found a similar obligation exists under Art. 3, ECHR, where the authorities 'had or ought to have had knowledge' of the torture, or cruel, inhuman, degrading, treatment: *Z and ors v. UK*, Judgment (App. No. 29392/95), 10 May 2001, §73. The IACtHR has also held that 'an illegal act which violates human rights and which is initially not directly imputable to a State (for example because it is the act of a private person or because the person responsible has not been identified) can lead to international responsibility of the State, not because of the act itself but because of the lack of due diligence to prevent the violation or to respond to it as required by the Convention': *Velasquez-Rodriguez v. Honduras*, Judgment, Series A, No. 4, 29 July 1982, §172.

[116] CAT, Art. 12; Human Rights Committee, General Comment No. 20, 1992, §14; ECtHR, *Ribitsch v. Austria*, Judgment (App. No. 18896/91), 4 December 1995, §§108–11. The ECtHR has held that states parties have a positive obligation under Art. 3 to 'enact criminal-law provisions effectively punishing rape and to apply them in practice through effective investigation and prosecution': *M. C. v. Bulgaria*, Judgment, 3 December 2003, §153. The IACtHR has affirmed that 'the duty to investigate is a compulsory obligation of the State embodies in international law, which cannot be mitigated by any domestic legislation whatsoever': *Vargas Areco v. Paraguay*, Series C, No. 155, 26 September 2006, §93.

[117] Committee against Torture, *Blanco Abad v. Spain*, Decision (Comm. No. 5971996), 14 May 1998, §8.2 (in which an 18-day delay in investigating the allegation was considered too long); ECtHR, *Colibaba v. Moldova*, Judgment (App. No. 29089/06), 23 October 2007, §53.

[118] Committee against Torture, *Ristoc v. Yugoslavia*, Decision (Comm. No. 113/1998), 11 May 2001, §9.5; Human Rights Committee, *Rodriguez v. Uruguay*, Decision (Comm. No. 32. 322/1988), 19 July 1994; ECtHR, *Assenov and ors v. Bulgaria*, Judgment (App. No. 24760/94), 28 October 1998.

governments.[119] Furthermore, states are obligated to grant redress and provide adequate compensation to victims of slavery, torture, or cruel, inhuman, or degrading treatment.[120]

In conclusion, it is clear that sexual violence is duly prohibited in IHRL and that the duty on states not to participate in sexual violence, as well as to protect those within its jurisdiction from such acts applies equally during armed conflict.

C. **Sexual violence in 2012**

Sexual abuse was widely reported in Afghanistan, the CAR, Colombia, Côte d'Ivoire, the DRC, Libya, Mali, Myanmar, Somalia, South Sudan, Sudan (Darfur), Syria, Uganda, and Yemen during 2012. It should be noted from the outset that statistics are used in this report to indicate a particular pattern and should not be taken as an accurate reflection of the scale of the violence, because sexual violence (for the reasons discussed above) is grossly under-reported.

MALI

Sexual violence in Mali increased in 2012, particularly between April and June when sexual violence 'was used to punish, intimidate and subjugate women and girls by the Mouvement National de Liberation de l'Azawad (MNLA)'.[121] There is also credible evidence to suggest that al-Qaeda in the Islamic Maghreb (AQIM), Ansar Dine, and the Movement for Oneness and Jihad in West Africa (*Mouvement pour l'Unicité et le Jihad en Afrique de l'Ouest*, or MOJWA) were also responsible for acts of sexual violence in Mali during 2012.[122] Since January 2012, at least 211 cases of sexual violence, including gang rape, rape, forced marriages, and sexual slavery, have been reported.[123]

---

[119] Human Rights Committee, General Comment No. 20, §5; *Rodriguez v. Uruguay*, Decision, 19 July 1994, §12.4.

[120] CAT, Art. 14; Committee against Torture, General Comment No. 3 (2012); Committee against Torture, *Agiza v. Sweden*, Decision (Comm. No. 23372003), 20 May 2005, §13.6 (only applies to torture); ICCPR, Art. 2(3); ECtHR, *Assanidez v. Georgia*, Judgment (App. No. 71503/01), 8 April 2008, §198; ACHR, Art. 3(1).

[121] 'UN Secretary-General's report on sexual violence in conflict', §50.

[122] 'UN Secretary-General's report on sexual violence in conflict', Annex VII.

[123] 'UN Secretary-General's report on sexual violence in conflict', §51. The Human Rights Council-mandated mission to Mali reports stigmatization of victims as a major hurdle to collecting accurate data on sexual violence in Mali, citing one victim who affirmed that, 'in Mali, if you say you have been raped your life is over': 'Report of the UN High Commissioner for Human Rights on the situation of human rights in Mali', Human Rights Council, UN doc. A/HRC/22/33, 7 January 2012, §31.

According to the UN Secretary-General's most recent report on conflict-related sexual violence, 'in rebel-controlled zones, rape was used as a tactic of war contributing to the mass displacement from the regions of Gao, Tombouctou and part of Mopti'. Those who were displaced reported a pattern of women and girls being abducted and raped, including gang-raped, by rebels in the city and 'requisition' taking place, a practice in which women and girls are abducted from a district to spend the night in camps. It is reported that, each night, a different district is required to provide a certain number of women and girls to the rebels.[124]

Forced marriage of women and girls by Islamist rebel groups—in particular Ansar Dine, AQIM, and MOJWA—were reported in all regions under the control of such groups. It was also reported that Islamic/Shari'a law was cited as a pretext to compel families to 'give' women and girls to armed groups (this phenomenon is also reported to be occurring in Somalia and Yemen).[125] Women and girls forced into these 'marriages' are often gang-raped, repeatedly, by other members of the armed group.[126] Reports have also emerged of these armed groups beating and flogging women for engaging in behaviour decreed as forbidden under their interpretation of Shari'a law.[127]

Men and boys were also the victims of sexual violence in Mali during 2012, where sexual violence was used as an interrogation technique.[128] Sexual violence has also been used in Mali to humiliate captured opponents or fighters. 'Red-berets' (Mali's parachutist regiment), for example, were allegedly forced to rape each other in Kati camp by elements of their enemy, the 'green-berets'.[129]

In October 2012, the Minister of Justice issued an administrative circular to the judicial authorities mandating them to prioritize the prosecution of crimes of sexual violence committed in the context of the conflict. A joint programme is being implemented by the Ministry of Defence with the support of the UN 'to build the capacity of the security forces and former combatants to prevent and protect women and girls from sexual violence'.[130] On 18 July 2012, the Malian government referred the situation in Mali since January 2012 to the ICC. The ICC Office of the Prosecutor's (OTP) report concluded there is a reasonable basis to believe that war crimes had been committed in Mali since January 2012, including rape under Article 8(2)(e)(vi). Accordingly, the Prosecutor decided to open an investigation into the situation in Mali since that date.[131]

---

[124] 'UN Secretary-General's report on sexual violence in conflict', §52.

[125] 'UN Secretary-General's report on sexual violence in conflict', §11.

[126] 'Report of the UN High Commissioner for Human Rights on the situation of human rights in Mali', 7 January 2012, §34.

[127] 'UN Secretary-General's report on sexual violence in conflict', §54.

[128] 'UN Secretary-General's report on sexual violence in conflict', §10.

[129] 'UN Secretary-General's report on sexual violence in conflict', §55.

[130] 'UN Secretary-General's report on sexual violence in conflict', §57.

[131] ICC OTP, 'Situation in Mali: Article 53(1) report', 16 January 2013.

DRC

The security situation in the DRC has been deteriorating further since early 2012 bringing with it increasing levels of sexual violence. Sexual violence in the DRC, alongside other human rights violations in the country, mainly occurs during attacks on villages by rebel groups or the Forces Armées de la République Démocratique du Congo (FARDC) and the Police Nationale Congolaise (PNC). Alarmingly, it is reported that instances have occurred in which improperly vetted ex-combatants have been redeployed to act within the security sector as part of reintegration programmes only to perpetrate acts of sexual violence.[132]

The UN Secretary-General's report documented 764 cases of sexual violence in the DRC between December 2011 and November 2012, although the actual number of cases is significantly higher.[133] Children were the victims of the sexual violence in 280 of the reported cases. Two cases involved sexual violence against men, one in which a man arrested by the PNC was raped by a FARDC sergeant while in custody.[134] Approximately half of all attacks were attributed to elements of FARDC and the PNC.[135]

In a well-documented incident on 22 November 2012, thousands of FARDC soldiers descended upon the town of Minova and raped hundreds of women and girls, following their defeat by the M23 in the city of Goma 30 miles from Minova.[136] The exact number of victims is not known, as victims are understandably terrified to come forward for fear of reprisals and/or rejection by their husbands and communities.[137] A 60-year-old survivor testified: 'They beat us and beat us, and then they started to rape. Three men raped me—two from the front and one from behind. My head is still not right. I thought I had Aids, and now my husband mocks me. He calls me the wife of a soldier, he has rejected me.'[138]

A correlation exists between incidences of sexual violence in the DRC and military activity linked to illegal extraction of natural resources. Rape has been used by armed

---

[132] 'UN Secretary-General's report on sexual violence in conflict', §7.

[133] 'UN Secretary-General's report on sexual violence in conflict', §39.

[134] 'UN Secretary-General's report on sexual violence in conflict', §45.

[135] Remaining cases were attributed to the Agence Nationale Renseignements (ANR), FDLR, (103 victims, including 20 children), Mayi-Mayi Lumumba (138 victims, including 42 children), Forces de Résistance Patriotiques de l'Ituri (FRPI) (20 victims, including ten children), Forces de Défense Congolaises (FDC) (16 victims), M23 (20 victims, including ten children), and other armed non-state actors (ANSAs) (846 victims, including 23 children): 'UN Secretary-General's report on sexual violence in conflict', §40.

[136] The UN reports at least 126 women, including 24 children, were raped in the attack: 'UN Secretary-General's report on sexual violence in conflict', §44.

[137] The director of the towns' hospital reported that the hospital dealt with more than 100 women with rape-related injuries after the rampage: 'Congo: we did whatever we wanted says soldier who raped 53', *The Guardian*, 11 April 2013.

[138] 'Congo: we did whatever we wanted says soldier who raped 53', *The Guardian*, 11 April 2013.

groups to punish civilians who attempt to prevent poaching and mineral trafficking.[139] During attacks on 24 and 25 June 2012, at least 28 women and 23 girls were sexually assaulted, including by rape, as part of a strategy by the Mayi-Mayi Lumumba and Mayi-Mayi Morgan to control resources in the gold-rich Okapi Reserve.[140]

A further pattern has emerged of sexual violence being used by armed groups and elements of the FARDC in retaliation against communities based on the real or perceived ethnicity of the survivors. On 6 August 2012, for instance, five women and four girls were reportedly raped in Masisi territory during an attack by Raïa Mutomboki combatants. These rapes were committed as part of a series of seemingly ethnically motivated attacks aimed at forcibly displacing civilians: '[W]itnesses reported that Raïa Mutomboki elements arrived in villages proclaiming that all Hutus should leave the village and not return.' Several witnesses also reported cases of sexual mutilation on corpses, including four cases in which fighters cut the foetuses out of pregnant women.[141]

On a positive note, rebel leader Bosco Ntaganda, who has been indicted by the ICC on several counts of war crimes including rape, as well as three counts of crimes against humanity, handed himself in to the US Embassy in Rwanda in March 2013. Zainab Hawa Hawa Bangura, UN Special Representative for Sexual Violence in Conflict, said Mr Ntaganda's compliance with the indictments 'should serve as a warning to all perpetrators of sexual violence in conflict that justice may be delayed, but it cannot be denied . . . Impunity for these crimes will not be accepted, and the International Criminal Court will ensure the survivors of Mr Ntaganda's reign of terror in Ituri will finally see justice served'.[142] It should be noted that the Congolese government has taken steps, albeit small ones, to arrest and prosecute perpetrators of sexual violence. During November and December 2012, at least 49 FARDC solders were prosecuted for acts of sexual violence, including rape.[143]

SYRIA

Owing to access restrictions and insecurity, little is known about the scale of sexual violence in Syria. What is known is that sexual violence has been committed by both government forces and members of the Free Syrian Army (FSA), and has occurred in places of detention, at checkpoints, during abductions, and during house searches.

---

[139] 'UN Secretary-General's report on sexual violence in conflict', §§9 and 39.
[140] 'UN Secretary-General's report on sexual violence in conflict', §41.
[141] 'UN Secretary-General's report on sexual violence in conflict', §43.
[142] UN News Centre, 'UN officials welcome surrender of wanted Congolese rebel leader Bosco Ntaganda', 19 March 2013.
[143] 'UN Secretary-General's report on sexual violence in conflict', §47.

In two reports,[144] the Independent International Commission of Inquiry on Syria notes two trends in the use of sexual violence in the country: first, its use against women during house searches and at checkpoints following the advance of government forces into towns and villages; and secondly, the increased use of sexual violence against men and women in detention as a means of extracting information during interrogations, as well as to humiliate and punish.[145] Sexual violence was also being used as a means to coerce male relatives fighting with anti-government armed groups to surrender themselves in return for the release of a detainee.[146] The main forms of sexual violence the Commission of Inquiry identified were rape, electrocution of the genitals by live wires, and the burning of the genitals with cigarettes, lighters, and melted plastic.[147] The Commission found, in the context of detention centres, that 'rape and other inhumane acts were perpetrated as part of a widespread attack directed against the civilian population, pursuant to or in furtherance of an organised policy'.[148]

The Commission of Inquiry identified government forces and government-controlled militia (*Shabbiha*) as the main perpetrators of this abuse.[149] The Commission recorded a number of incidents between February and June 2012 during which government soldiers and *Shabbiha* entered homes and raped women and girls in front of male family members, sometimes killing the victims afterwards.[150] The Commission found reasonable grounds to believe that these acts amounted to war crimes.[151] The Commission also concluded that the widespread rapes that occurred during military operations in Homs (during February and March) and in al-Haffe (in June 2012) could be prosecuted as crimes against humanity. Due to lack of access, the Commission was unable to reach a finding concerning crimes of sexual violence committed by anti-government ANSAs.[152]

OTHER STATES

Sexual violence in Afghanistan continued in 2012. A pattern emerged of women and girls in communities under the influence or control of anti-government elements being abducted and sexually assaulted, including raped.[153] There have also been reports of

---

[144] Dated 16 August 2012 (UN doc. A/HRC/21/50) and 5 February 2013 (UN doc. A/HRC/22/59).

[145] UN doc. A/HRC/22/59, 5 February 2013, §106.

[146] UN doc. A/HRC/22/59, 5 February 2013, Annex IX, §5.

[147] UN doc. A/HRC/22/59, 5 February 2013, §107.

[148] UN doc. A/HRC/22/59, 5 February 2013, §109.

[149] UN doc. A/HRC/22/59, 5 February 2013, Summary.

[150] UN doc. A/HRC/22/59, 5 February 2013, Annex IX, §§6–17.

[151] UN doc. A/HRC/22/59, 5 February 2013, Annex IX, §19.

[152] UN doc. A/HRC/22/59, 5 February 2013, §111.

[153] 'UN Secretary-General's report on sexual violence in conflict', §15.

armed groups and tribal militia (*arbakis*), some of whom have been employed as Afghan police, sexually assaulting women and girls. Boys and men are said to continue to be sexually assaulted or threatened with sexual violence by members of the National Directorate of Security and the Afghan National Police while in detention. The UN Secretary-General's report cites 'many instances', of children and women who report being victims of sexual violence themselves being subsequently accused of crimes, and publicly stoned or punished, and persons who offer help to survivors, including representatives of NGOs, facing reprisals.[154]

Sexual violence also continued to be widespread in the CAR, mainly in the form of rape and sexual slavery of women and girls. Most incidents took place in the north and east of the country, and were perpetrated by Convention des patriotes pour la justice et la paix en Centrafrique (CPJP), Union des forces démocratiques pour le rassemblement (UFDR), Front démocratique du people centrafricain (FDPC), Mouvement des libérateurs centrafricains pour la justice (MLCJ), Union des forces républicaines (UFR), and 'road bandits' known as 'Zaraguinas'. In June 2012, several girls were forced to marry CPJP members.[155] In the south-east, the abduction of women and girls by the Lord's Resistance Army (LRA) for use as sex slaves was reported by survivors, 'with a total of 85 abductions, including eight children, since January 2012'.[156]

In a positive step forward, on 11 January 2013 the rebel coalition, Séléka, composed of the Convention patriotique pour le salut du Kodro (CPSK), CPJP, UFDR, and FDPC, signed a cease-fire agreement and Declaration of Principles, which include provisions that require 'the immediate halt of sexual violence; [make] sexual violence a prohibited act in the definition of ceasefire, and [require] that sexual violence is addressed in a programme of urgent priority agreed to by the parties for the consolidation of peace'.[157]

In Colombia, sexual violence against women and girls has been used by armed groups to force civilians to flee rural areas where lucrative agricultural zones or mines exist, or where there are strategic paths for illegal narcotics trafficking. Sexual violence in the region is mainly targeted against young girls, who are abducted, raped, and kept as sex slaves, before having abortions performed on them by their kidnappers.[158] Sexual violence against women and boys has also been attributed to the military.[159]

High numbers of incidents of sexual violence were reported to have occurred in Somalia during 2012. In Mogadishu and surrounding areas, between January and

---

[154] 'UN Secretary-General's report on sexual violence in conflict', §17.
[155] 'UN Secretary-General's report on sexual violence in conflict', §21.
[156] 'UN Secretary-General's report on sexual violence in conflict', §21.
[157] 'UN Secretary-General's report on sexual violence in conflict', §20.
[158] 'UN Secretary-General's report on sexual violence in conflict', §24. Order #C-355 of 2006 by the Constitutional Court guarantees the right of survivors of rape access to terminations of unwanted pregnancies. However, the law is not well known and thus is underused.
[159] 'UN Secretary-General's report on sexual violence in conflict', §24.

November 2012, UN partners and service providers registered more than 1,700 cases of rape. Almost one-third of the recorded incidents were against children, a few of which involved boys. Analysis suggests a link between the spike in the number of incidents between April and July with the intensification of military operations against al-Shabaab in the Afgoye and Bala'd corridor near Mogadishu.[160] The trend of systematic sexual violence being committed against internally displaced women and girls in settlements in Mogadishu and surrounding areas continues. The perpetrators reportedly include members of armed groups, as well as Somali security forces. Survivors are often unable to affiliate the perpetrator to a specific armed group or security branch, or are afraid to do so for fear of retaliation.[161]

Radical armed groups, including Ansar al-Shari'a, operating in southern Yemen reportedly forcibly married up to 100 girls during 2012; in some instances, girls were 'offered as a token of appreciation by their brothers' who had been 'allowed' to join the armed groups.[162] Many of the girls have been impregnated as a result of the forced marriage. The girls and their families rarely report the abuse due to fear of reprisals.

Sexual abuse was also widespread in Darfur, where women and girls who are internally displaced are particularly vulnerable. During 2012, 121 cases of sexual violence were reported to the African Union–UN hybrid operation in Darfur (UNAMID), of which 72 cases, totalling 99 victims (52 children, including nine boys), were documented.[163] These cases involved: rape, including gang rape; abduction for sexual purposes; sexual slavery; injuries/assaults related to sexual violence attacks; and attempted rapes. Two cases of sexual slavery were recorded, in which two children were abducted and kept in captivity by Arab militia for three and eight years, respectively, in South Darfur, before escaping. In August, the killing of the commissioner of Alwaha locality in Kutum, North Darfur state, triggered retaliatory attacks on the Kassab internally displaced persons camp, resulting in more than 30 cases of rape, of which seven involved ten victims (including three children), all of which were verified by the UN.[164]

Concluding remarks

Sexual violence continued to be a prominent feature of armed conflict in 2012, in violation of IHL, ICL, and IHRL. While most survivors remain traumatized, stigmatized, and without redress, most perpetrators remain at large and enjoying impunity.

---

[160] 'UN Secretary-General's report on sexual violence in conflict', §61.
[161] 'UN Secretary-General's report on sexual violence in conflict', §62.
[162] 'UN Secretary-General's report on sexual violence in conflict', §91.
[163] 'UN Secretary-General's report on sexual violence in conflict', §73.
[164] 'UN Secretary-General's report on sexual violence in conflict', §73.

Positive steps have been taken to tackle impunity, including the promotion of domestic justice systems, referral of situations to the ICC, UN initiatives,[165] and the UK announcement, in May 2012, that it has compiled a team of experts devoted to combating and preventing sexual violence in conflict.[166] However, for any of these initiatives to work, the factors that serve as hurdles to survivors accessing justice (financial, practical, and rights' awareness) need to be overcome. Research needs to be conducted into the mind-set of those that carry out acts of sexual violence, particularly soldiers, and its findings used to correct behaviour. Furthermore, the stigma attached to sexual violence, and therefore the secrecy and silence that surrounds it, needs to be broken.

A significant proportion of sexual violence committed during 2012 was by ANSAs. As well as prosecuting members of such groups that participate in sexual violence, Geneva Call's Deed of Commitment for the Prohibition of Sexual Violence in Situations of Armed Conflict and Towards the Elimination of Gender Discrimination should be further promoted to increase its disappointingly few five signatories.[167]

With regard to women, the prevailing attitude in many societies that women are subordinate and inferior to men needs to be challenged. Women and men need to be educated on the rights of women. The archaic ideology that centres women's protection on honour and modesty needs to be challenged and abandoned. Not only is this ideology hindering women's protection, by distracting from the fundamental point that woman (and men) have a human right to be treated humanely, but also it implies that those who have been subjected to sexual violence have somehow become 'dishonoured', a very powerful and dangerous notion in some cultures.

Finally, sexual violence is a source of insecurity and conflict, rather than a by-product of it, and must be recognized as such. Unless those who participate in such acts are brought to justice and their victims given medical treatment, rehabilitation, and redress, the divisions and tensions that cause conflict will remain and long-term peace and security will not be realized.

[165] For example, the UN Security Council has issued a number of resolutions focused on sexual violence as part of its Women, Peace and Security agenda, most recently establishing a monitoring and reporting mechanism to enable the naming and shaming of state and non-state armed forces found to be using sexual violence as a tactic of conflict: UN Security Council Resolution 1960 (2010), §8.

[166] This team will be able to be deployed overseas at short notice to gather evidence and testimony that can be used to support investigations and prosecutions. The team is due to be deployed in Libya, South Sudan, eastern DRC, and Bosnia and Herzegovina (to help the address the backlog of war crimes cases that have still not been heard 20 years after the war): The Secretary of State for Foreign and Commonwealth Affairs (Mr William Hague), Hansard, col. 1141, 14 February 2013.

[167] The Democratic Party of Iranian Kurdistan, Komalah, the Kurdistan Organization of the Communist Party of Iran, the Komala Party of Iranian Kurdistan, the Kurdistan Democratic Party of Iran, and the Komala Party of Kurdistan are the Deed's signatories, as of May 2013. See <http://www.genevacall.org/resources/list-of-signatories/list-of-signatories.htm>.

6 Education as a 'battleground' in conflicts in 2012

Gilles Giacca and Takhmina Karimova*

Introduction

Schools as areas of combat are an all-too-common feature of contemporary armed conflicts. The prevalence of attacks by both state military forces and non-state armed groups (NSAGs) that impact on schools, students, and educational staff has been disturbingly high in Afghanistan, the Central African Republic (CAR), Chad, Colombia, the Democratic Republic of Congo (DRC), India, Iraq, Libya, Myanmar, Pakistan, Palestine, the Philippines, Somalia, South Sudan, Syria, Thailand, and Yemen. Indeed, evidence suggests that 'education' is not simply affected by 'collateral' damage, but has itself become a target of attacks.

Since the 2007 United Nations Educational Scientific and Cultural Organization (UNESCO) study on the problem of *Education under Attack*, the links between education and conflict have received growing attention from scholars, practitioners, civil society, and humanitarian organizations. One body of analysis focuses on the impact of armed conflict on education, and particularly the protection of education facilities, students, and staff from armed violence.[1] A second explores the links between education and conflict from humanitarian responses and development perspectives.[2] Another emerging topic is the involvement of education in counterterrorism and counter-insurgency strategies, and the associated risks of involving 'education' in security and

* Dr Gilles Giacca is Research Fellow at the Law Faculty of Oxford University, and Co-ordinator of the Human Rights for Future Generations Programme and Research Associate, Oxford Institute for Ethics, Law and Armed Conflict, and Dr Takhmina Karimova is Research Fellow at the Geneva Academy of International Humanitarian Law and Human Rights.

[1] Education Above All (EAA)/British Institute of International and Comparative Law (BIICL), *Protecting Education in Insecurity and Armed Conflict: An International Law Handbook*, 2012, <http://www.education aboveall.org>.

[2] See e.g. Christopher Talbot, 'Education in conflict emergencies in light of the post-2015 MDGs and EFA agendas', Paper for NORRAG, 2013.

political agendas.[3] A fourth theme concerns the positive effects of education in conflict resolution and peace-building.[4]

International bodies have expanded their monitoring of protection of civilians in times of armed conflict, and particularly children, to include reporting on attacks against educational facilities and related persons, with a view to ensuring the comprehensive protection of children. The United Nations (UN) Security Council affirmed that attacks on schools are also attacks on children. Indeed, the practice of the Security Council has led some in the protection of education community to assert that attacks on education are 'strictly forbidden under international law'.[5] This raises a question about the foundations of obligations related to the protection of education, which relates to two overlapping issues that lie at the heart of the debates: protection of civilians and/or civilian objects dedicated to education; and the right of individuals to education in times of armed conflict. These two formulations should not be confused. Moreover, the two bodies of law primarily involved—international humanitarian law (IHL) in the first case and international human rights law (IHRL) in the second—are not entirely consistent with each other on the protection of education.

A. **Attacks on education**

SCOPE AND SCALE OF THE PROBLEM

Attacks on education have become almost routine during armed conflict and other situations of armed violence. From available data on the incidence of attacks on schools, students, and teachers (*see Table 1*), it could be inferred that the number of targeted and incidental attacks from military operations has risen dramatically in recent years. However, despite an abundance of reports, there are still many gaps in the information, primarily as a result of the challenges of gathering data in armed conflicts.[6]

---

[3] Sonja C. Grover, *Schoolchildren as Propaganda Tools in the War on Terror: Violating the Rights of Afghani Children under International Law*, Springer, Berlin, 2011.

[4] The Special Rapporteur on the right to education specifies: 'Lastly, education provides the knowledge and skills to survive in a crisis through the dissemination of lifesaving information about landmine and cluster bomb safety, HIV/AIDS prevention, conflict resolution mechanisms and peacebuilding.' See 'Right to education in emergency situations: report of the Special Rapporteur on the right to education, Vernor Muñoz', UN doc. A/HRC/8/10, 20 May 2008, §35.

[5] According to the Global Education Cluster Unit, a body co-led by a UN agency and a non-governmental organization (NGO) that coordinates and guides education responses in situations of conflict and emergencies, '[a]ttacks on education and the occupation of schools are strictly forbidden under international law, including UN Security Council Resolutions 1612 and 1998': Global Education Cluster Unit, 'Occupation of schools by armed forces: South Sudan', Briefing note, 2012, p. 1.

[6] See e.g. Save the Children, *Childhood under Fire: The Impact of Two Years of Conflict in Syria*, Save the Children, London, March 2013.

Table 1 Data for calendar year 2012

	Attacks on protected persons (in relation to education)	Attacks on education facilities	Occupation, and forced closure and disruption of, schools	Total number of incidents involving attacks on education
Afghanistan	(IED and suicide attacks, acts of intimidation, threats against teachers and students, abduction and killing of education personnel)*	(burning of schools)*	32 (forced closure); 10 (military use)	167
CAR		1 (destruction of schools)	2 (military use)	3
Cote d'Ivoire			2 (military use)	7
Colombia	(targeting of education staff and schoolchildren)*	(attacks resulting in damage)*	(military use)*	n.a.**
DRC		6 (looting or attacks resulting in damage)	12 (military use)	18
India		3 (destruction of schools)		3
Iraq	20 (killing/injuring education staff, killing/injuring schoolchildren from IEDs)	15 (attacks resulting in damage, IEDs, shooting)		35
Israel/OPT	1 (children injured by tear gas)	285 (air strikes); 7 (rockets); (shooting, tear gas and stone-throwing by settlers)	17 (military use causing disruption/damage to schools)	n.a.**
Lebanon			(disruption of schooling)*	
Libya		(shooting, shelling, IEDs)*		c.6
Mali		(looted, damaged, bombed, contaminated with unexploded ordnance)*	(military use)*	115
Pakistan	1 (children injured by gunshots)	118 (damaged or destroyed)		119
Philippines		1 (burning of school); 4 (damaged by crossfire)	c.4 (military use)	9
Somalia				65
South Sudan			18 (military use); 15 (vacated)	n.a.**
Syria	167 (killing of education staff)	2,445 (damaged)	(military use, incl. as a weapon storage or as barracks, use as detention centres)*	n.a.**
Thailand	15 (killing/injuring education staff)	15 (attacks resulting in damage, IEDs, shooting); 1 (burning of school)		31
Yemen	61 (intimidations of/threats against education staff and schoolchildren)	11 (damaged, looted), 57 (shelling, aerial bombardment, IEDs)	36 (military use)	165

* The precise number of an incident is not known or unreported.

** The total number is either not known or remains distinct from reported number of specific incidents.

n.a. Not available

Source: 'Children and armed conflict: report of the Secretary-General', UN doc. A/67/845–S/2013/245, 15 May 2013.

The annual reports on children and armed conflict by the UN Secretary-General provide valuable information on country-specific situations. These reports represent essentially 'a monitoring and reporting' tool that forms the basis for action by the Security Council. The process of preparing this system-wide report is particularly demanding given that the country-specific information is shared with the states concerned prior to publication.[7] If the state concerned challenges the information is challenged, the SRSG-CIAC communicates with the country-level UN task force to verify it.[8]

Syria

In Syria, the Independent International Commission of Inquiry (Syrian Commission of Inquiry) has compiled a detailed list of incidents affecting schools in the bitter, ongoing non-international armed conflict (NIAC). According to the February 2013 report of the Commission, between 2,400 and 3,900 of the 20,000 schools in the country have been damaged by military operations[9] and approximately 2,000 are being used as shelters for internally displaced persons (IDPs).[10] Data provided by the Syrian Ministry of Education in December 2012 indicated that 1,468 schools were being used as collective centres 'hosting a large number of the two million people who have left their homes because of the current events'.[11] A further 2,362 public and private schools (more than 10 per cent of the total of 22,000) had been damaged or looted.[12] Displacement of affected students has put the existing education infrastructure under increasing pressure.[13] In certain areas, children have not been to school in more than 18 months.[14]

---

[7] Radhika Coomaraswamy, Special Representative of the UN Secretary-General for Children and Armed Conflict (SRSG-CIAC), 'The Security Council and children and armed conflict: an experiment in the making', Public lecture delivered at the Centre on Human Rights, University of East London School of Law, 12 April 2010.

[8] The information reflected in the UN Secretary-General's report, as specified by the UN SRSG-CIAC, includes statistics, 'but the main thrust of the reporting is incident-based reporting with an attempt to identify perpetrators where possible': Coomaraswamy, 'The Security Council and children and armed conflict: an experiment in the making'.

[9] 'Report of the Independent International Commission of Inquiry on the Syrian Arab Republic', UN doc. A/HRC/22/59, 5 February 2013, pp. 18, §116, and 82, §18.

[10] SRSG-CIAC, 'Security Council must ensure an end to the violence against children in Syria', Press release, New York, 18 April 2013, <http://childrenandarmedconflict.un.org/press-releases/sc-must-ensure-an-end-to-the-violence-against-children-in-syria/>.

[11] 'Report of the Independent International Commission of Inquiry on the Syrian Arab Republic', 5 February 2013, p. 43, §§7–8.

[12] 'Report of the Independent International Commission of Inquiry on the Syrian Arab Republic', 5 February 2013, p. 9, §33.

[13] According to the Commission of Inquiry, '[t]he movement of affected students in perceived "safe" areas has strained schools' capacity, both in terms of physical capacity and schools' ability to provide quality education': 'Report of the independent international Commission of inquiry on the Syrian Arab Republic', 5 February 2013, p. 43, §§7–8. See also pp. 82–3, §18.

[14] SRSG-CIAC, 'Security Council must ensure an end to the violence against children in Syria', 18 April 2013.

Schools in Syria are believed to have been used as shelters for displaced persons, barracks, offices, detention facilities, or used to conduct interrogations.[15] According to one fact-finding mission conducted in 2012, security agents, as well as teachers, interrogated students inside the school facilities about their political views, their participation in anti-government protests, and the activities of their parents and other family members.[16] Political interrogations have allegedly resulted in punishment, beatings, and other forms of corporal punishment for those giving answers deemed 'anti-government'.[17]

Anti-government armed groups routinely use schools for bases, accommodation, or meeting points, exposing civilians to the threat of attack.[18] On the one hand, occupation of schools is considered not to be 'justified by military necessity', while, on the other, such occupations have spread the belief that schools are not safe for children.[19] According to the Syrian Commission of Inquiry, these groups are 'violating their obligation under international humanitarian law to avoid locating military objectives within or near densely populated areas, to the extent feasible'.[20] For the period of inquiry, there was reliable information concerning attacks on 17 schools.[21] The Commission concluded, in relation to attacks on civilian objects, including schools, that 'a substantial number' were deliberate, indiscriminate[22] and, since civilian casualties were clearly in excess of the anticipated military advantage, disproportionate.[23]

Attacks on education also included threats on schoolchildren,[24] looting and destruction of three schools (with at least one school set on fire),[25] and the occupation

---

[15] 'Report of the Independent International Commission of Inquiry on the Syrian Arab Republic', 5 February 2013, pp. 16, §92, and 18, §116.

[16] Human Rights Watch (HRW), *Safe No More: Students and Schools under Attack in Syria*, HRW, New York, 2013, pp. 1–32. The findings are based on more than 70 interviews conducted between October and December 2012.

[17] HRW, *Safe No More: Students and Schools under Attack in Syria*, pp. 14–16.

[18] 'Report of the Independent International Commission of Inquiry on the Syrian Arab Republic', p. 20, §131.

[19] 'Report of the Independent International Commission of Inquiry on the Syrian Arab Republic', p. 18, §116.

[20] 'Report of the Independent International Commission of Inquiry on the Syrian Arab Republic', p. 103, §111.

[21] These attacks have been attributed to the government. In some instances, anti-government forces were present in the schools: 'Report of the Independent International Commission of Inquiry on the Syrian Arab Republic', p. 18, §114.

[22] 'One soldier from an army brigade stationed in Dara'a said that his commanding officer had verbally given an order to hit schools harshly "so that they don't go out on demonstrations." The soldier said that he had defected because the army was attacking children and schools without discrimination.' See 'Report of the Independent International Commission of Inquiry on the Syrian Arab Republic', pp. 82–3, §19.

[23] The report further states that: 'Fifty interviewees described the death and injury to children during shelling and aerial bombardments by Government forces. The use of artillery and air power against refugee camps, bakeries, schools, village houses and other everyday locales; and the use of excessive force against demonstrators by Government forces is well documented.' See 'Report of the Independent International Commission of Inquiry on the Syrian Arab Republic', p. 79, §4.

[24] In December 2012, government personnel later visited schools and told schoolgirls: 'Go home and tell your families that if the FSA shoot any bullets then we will kidnap you.' Girls stopped attending schools as a result: 'Report of the Independent International Commission of Inquiry on the Syrian Arab Republic', p. 80, §7.

[25] Annex IV, Section A, on Tremseh, 12 July 2012, in 'Report of the Independent International Commission of Inquiry on the Syrian Arab Republic', p. 46, §10.

of one school.[26] The Inquiry found violations of children's rights, including undermining of children's rights to education, 'putting...schools at the front line of the conflict and reversing painstaking gains in social services over many decades'.[27]

Afghanistan

In Afghanistan in 2012, according to the UN Country Task Force on Children and Armed Conflict, conflict-related violence continued to impact access to education in all regions of the country. The UN Assistance Mission in Afghanistan (UNAMA) reported 74 'verified' incidents, including burning of schools, intimidation and threats against teachers and staff, improvised explosive devices (IEDs) laid in the vicinity of schools, rocket attacks, raids, and ground engagements. During 2012, there were 14 reported incidents of occupation and use of schools for military purposes. According to UNAMA: 'Taliban public statements in 2012 repeatedly emphasized support for education, and denied responsibility for attacks against schools. The vast majority of documented incidents of attacks and interference with education, however, were attributed to Anti-Government Elements, including the Taliban.'[28]

Pakistan

The UN Committee on the Elimination of Discrimination against Women (CEDAW) issued its most recent concluding observations on Pakistan's report in March 2013, citing cases of 'on-going violent attacks and public threats on female students, teachers and professors by various non-State actors, as well as the escalating number of attacks on educational institutions, in particular a large number of girls' only schools, which has disproportionately affected girls and women's access to education'. These include attacks on school buses targeting children, including girls. The Committee referred to the attack on Malala Yousufzai, a girl student who was attacked in October 2012 for her advocacy of the right of girls to education.[29]

---

[26] F. al-Mastomah, 7 January 2012, in 'Report of the Independent International Commission of Inquiry on the Syrian Arab Republic'.

[27] 'Report of the Independent International Commission of Inquiry on the Syrian Arab Republic'; Annex X, p. 79, §2.

[28] UNAMA and the Office of the UN High Commissioner for Human Rights (OHCHR), 'Annual report 2012: protection of civilians in armed conflict', Kabul, February 2013, p. 12.

[29] The Committee recommended a number of measures for the state party, including to: 'c) Take the necessary measures to prevent the occurrence of attacks and threats against educational institutions which undermine women and girls' fundamental rights, in particular, the right to education, and to ensure that perpetrators of such acts of violence are promptly investigated, prosecuted and punished; and d) Consider the establishment of a rapid response system whenever there are attacks on educational institutions to promptly repair and rebuild them and replace educational materials so that women and girls can be reintegrated into school/universities as soon as possible.' CEDAW, 'Concluding observations: Pakistan', UN doc. CEDAW/C/PAK/CO/4, 1 March 2013, §§27–8.

POSSIBLE KEY DEFINITIONS

The protection of civilians in armed conflicts generally, as well as of women and children in particular, has been on the agenda of the UN Security Council since the end of the 1990s through a number of thematic resolutions. With respect to children, arguably the Council's most significant action was in adopting Resolution 1612 (2005), establishing a monitoring and reporting mechanism (MRM) at country level and a Security Council working group on children and armed conflict.[30] The mechanism addressed six 'grave violations' against children in situations of armed conflict, including attacks against schools.[31]

One of the main concerns of this mechanism was to address the trend towards greater victimization among the civilian population and to condemn the targeting of children or of objects that have many children in them, such as schools. This has led, among others, to formulations such as 'attacks on school or children' and 'threats to' or 'attacks on education' that have now entered the protection of civilians discourse. So far, however, there is no agreed definition of the concept of attacks on education. In 2012, the UN Secretary-General issued his regular report on children and armed conflict, which for the first time provided a definition of attacks for the purpose of 'listing':[32]

[A]ttacks on schools include direct attack against schools, indiscriminate attacks against schools, resulting in damage to or destruction of these facilities; or which have the effect of impeding the ability of a school to function and/or placing children at risk, acts of looting of these protected facilities; and *military use of schools*, although it does not constitute a trigger for listing.[33]

Furthermore:

An attack on a school or hospital that has retained its civilian character constitutes a violation of international humanitarian law. In addition, *even in cases where attacks on schools and/or*

---

[30] UN Security Council Resolution 1612, 26 July 2005, §3. See also Resolutions 1882 (2009) and 1998 (2011). The MRM is established when parties in a conflict-affected state are listed in the annexes of the UN Secretary-General's annual report on children and armed conflict.

[31] These grave violations against children are: killing or maiming children; recruitment or use of children as soldiers; rape and other grave sexual abuse of children; abduction of children; attacks against schools or hospitals; and denial of humanitarian access for children. See 'Children and armed conflict: report of the Secretary-General', UN doc. A/59/695–S/2005/72, 9 February 2005, §68; UN Security Council Resolution 1612, §2.

[32] In 2001, the Security Council passed Resolution 1379, which recommended that the Secretary-General list parties in his annual report who recruit and use children. Killing and maiming and sexual violence in conflict (Resolution 1882 in 2009), and attacks on schools and hospitals (Resolution 1998 in 2011), were later added as criteria for listing.

[33] 'Children and armed conflict: report of the Secretary-General', UN doc. A/66/782–S/2012/261, 26 April 2012, §227.

hospitals may not result in child casualties, they may affect children through the disruption of educational and/or medical service.[34]

Thus the UN Secretary-General's report, in line with IHL rules, recalls that attacks against schools that have not lost their status as a civilian object are prohibited. The latter passage that we have emphasized is interesting because it incorporates elements of human rights standards, given that access to education is a fundamental core of the right.

The definition of 'schools' provided by the Secretary-General's report is much broader in scope, as it includes not only 'schools' in the strict sense of the word, but also *all* educational facilities: 'The concepts of "school" and "hospital" include all educational and medical facilities, determined by the local context, including informal facilities of education and health care.'[35]

The report also attempts to define *threats* of attacks against protected persons in relation to schools, which would consist of, among others, a declared intention or determination to inflict harm, whether physical or moral, affecting the provision of education. For the purposes of listing, these threats need to be credible and the consequences plausible.[36]

Those protected in relation to schools include schoolchildren, teachers, and any civilian involved in education, unless and for such time as they participate directly in hostilities. Interestingly, the report clarifies that attacks 'need to have a link with the act of teaching'.[37]

Finally, another important definition provided by the Secretary-General's report is the concept of 'recurrent' attacks on schools, which are acts or threats of attacks that have been committed several times.[38] The concept is premised on the notion of a pattern and violations therefore need to be 'systematic, wilful and intentional'.[39]

---

[34] 'Children and armed conflict: report of the Secretary-General', UN doc. A/66/782–S/2012/261, 26 April 2012, §226. Emphasis added.

[35] It defers, however, the question of what is defined as 'schools' to the domestic order ('determined by the local context', as it states). The reference to 'children' seems, though, to situate the concept of 'schools' (no matter how broad) in primary and secondary levels of education, thus potentially excluding universities.

[36] 'Children and armed conflict: report of the Secretary-General', UN doc. A/66/782–S/2012/261, 26 April 2012, §228.

[37] 'Children and armed conflict: report of the Secretary-General', UN doc. A/66/782–S/2012/261, 26 April 2012, §229.

[38] 'Children and armed conflict: report of the Secretary-General', UN doc. A/66/782–S/2012/261, 26 April 2012, §230.

[39] Coomaraswamy, 'The Security Council and children and armed conflict: an experiment in the making'.

B. **Protection of education under international law**

INTERNATIONAL HUMANITARIAN LAW: THE BASIC FRAMEWORK

Protection of the civilian population in armed conflict

Fundamental rules of IHL demand that civilians shall neither be the object of attack nor the victims of disproportionate attacks. These rules apply in international armed conflicts (IACs) and in NIACs. In IACs, attacks against civilians are considered grave breaches (i.e. war crimes) under Article 85(3) of the 1977 Additional Protocol I to the Geneva Conventions, and Article 8(2)(b)(i) of the 1998 Rome Statute of the International Criminal Court (ICC Statute) qualifies an 'intentional' attack against civilian population or against individual civilians not taking direct part in hostilities as a war crime potentially falling under the ICC's jurisdiction. Article 8(2)(e)(i) of the ICC Statute makes intentional attacks in NIACs against the civilian population as such, or against individual civilians, a war crime. IHL also requires all feasible precautions to be taken to avoid civilian casualties.[40]

Protection of schools and other education institutions

The next relevant question to examine is the level of protection afforded to education buildings: whether IHL rules prohibit the military use of education facilities and whether the opposing party may attack education facilities that are used for military purposes. It is also useful to compare in this context the status afforded to hospitals, cultural property, and religious sites, to assess whether the legal protection of objects dedicated to education in times of armed conflict needs further strengthening.

IHL similarly prohibits direct or disproportionate attacks against civilian objects. Under the 1977 Additional Protocol I, school buildings are afforded general protection. IHL does not, though, grant 'direct', 'clear', and 'independent' privileged status to schools to the same extent as it does to hospitals and/or religious buildings.[41]

It is, however, possible, for a school or university to acquire additional protection on the basis of its cultural significance. To the extent that a school building qualifies as an object of 'great importance to the cultural heritage of every people', additional protection is provided by Article 1(a) of the 1954 Hague Convention for the Protection of Cultural Property in the Event of Armed Conflict, and the Second Protocol of 1999. According to Article 4 of the Convention, states parties must respect cultural property (in this case,

---

[40] See e.g. Art. 57, 1977 Additional Protocol I.

[41] Independent protection, similar to that afforded to hospitals, would require clear definition of such schools, maintenance of their status as a protected object (i.e. a prohibition of their use for military purposes), and their distinct identification.

'historic' schools) by refraining from any use and any act of hostility directed against such property. The problem, of course, is that the 1954 Hague Convention lacks clarity as to what can be defined as 'cultural property' and, besides, most of the schools will not fall under the scope of the protection. In contrast, the 1977 Additional Protocol I fails specifically to mention school buildings within the definition of cultural objects.[42]

The protection of schools is rather limited, concentrating on limiting the attackers' choice of lawful targets. IHL contains no prohibition against armed forces using educational buildings for military purposes. This is despite the fact that military use of schools makes students, teachers, and their school buildings vulnerable to attack from opposition forces.[43] Articles 51 and 58 of the 1977 Additional Protocol I require that parties to an international armed conflict 'to the maximum extent feasible' avoid locating military objects within or near civilians. Potentially, therefore, the presence of civilians rather than the nature of buildings makes the use of schools by the military unlawful. In accordance with IHL, the Syrian Commission of Inquiry's February 2013 report stated that: 'Anti-Government armed groups frequently use schools as barracks or offices. These occupations *are not always justified by military necessity*, and have spread the belief that schools are not safe.'[44]

INTERNATIONAL HUMAN RIGHTS LAW

The right to education

The basic premise of IHRL is to confer legal protection on all individuals in all types of situation, avoiding thereby the strict war/peace dichotomy. This is confirmed by abundant practice of various UN organs, human rights bodies, and jurisprudence.[45] Accordingly, two main legal issues are: (i) whether IHRL provides a clear and adequate set of rules effectively to protect students, teachers, and educational institutions; and (ii) whether this body of law prohibits the military use of education institutions.

---

[42] Art. 53, 1977 Additional Protocol I, stated, inter alia, that 'it is prohibited: (a) to commit any acts of hostility directed against the historic monuments, works of art or places of worship which constitute the cultural or spiritual heritage of peoples'. See also Art. 16, 1977 Additional Protocol II; International Committee of the Red Cross (ICRC), Customary IHL Study, Rules 38 and 40.

[43] Global Coalition to Protect Education from Attack (GCPEA), *Lessons in War: Military Use of Schools and Other Education Institutions during Conflict*, GCPEA, New York, November 2012, <http://www .humansecuritygateway.com/documents/GCPEA_LessonsinWar.pdf>.

[44] 'Report of the Independent International Commission of Inquiry on the Syrian Arab Republic', 5 February 2013, §116. Emphasis added.

[45] Most relevant case law and literature has focused on the ways *states* are bound by their human rights obligations while acting in situations of armed conflict. The existence of human rights obligations of armed non-state actors (ANSAs) within or outside NIACs remains controversial.

As far as attacks concern the life, liberty, and well-being of individuals (e.g. students, teachers, academics), identification of a violation of an individual's rights such as through extrajudicial killings, torture, or arbitrary detention is relatively straightforward. Similarly, failure to take measures to prevent third parties, such as NSAGs or paramilitaries, from depriving individuals of the enjoyment of their right to education will amount to a violation of an obligation to protect. States parties to human rights treaties have an obligation to provide security to students, teachers, education staff, and humanitarian workers engaged in providing education, and so on.

But what about damage and destruction to the education facilities, their occupation by the military, or their use as election polls in times of political instability? Do all these cases also amount to violations of the right to education? While answers to this question can be sought within the provisions of IHL and international criminal law (ICL), the human rights legal framework does not approach the use of force against civilian objects (as opposed to civilians) in the same way as IHL or ICL does. Protection under IHRL is granted first and foremost to an individual. Damage to 'infrastructural' determinants of human rights, vital for the enjoyment of socio-economic rights, does not (at least not always) automatically translate into a violation of a right to an individual. Conversely, certain essential elements of the right to education do require the existence, maintenance, and availability of physical structures.[46]

To date, the practice of human rights monitoring bodies on the issue is inconsistent and does not provide general guidance. In their practice, human rights treaty bodies do not always qualify acts that involve the use of force, such as attacks on educational facilities, or occupation of schools, as a violation of the right to education.[47] Ultimately, such a legal assessment depends on the circumstances of the case. Furthermore, ambiguities that sometimes surround the content of the economic, social, and cultural (ESC) rights make definition of their violation less straightforward. Hence, preference is given to terms such as 'impediments', 'obstacles', 'non-enjoyment', and so on to characterize situations of infringements upon the right to education. The determination of the existence of a violation is, of course, the function of 'qualified independent' bodies, which can be 'appropriately performed by the exercise of a right of individual petition'.[48]

---

[46] See generally the 'AAAQ' framework (availability, accessibility, acceptability, and quality of facilities, goods, services, and programmes) developed in the practice of the CESCR: 'UN Special Rapporteur on the right to education, K. Tomaševski, preliminary report', UN doc. E/CN.4/1999/49, 13 January 1999.

[47] See generally, *United Nations Human Rights Mechanisms and the Protection of Education in Armed Conflict and Insecurity*, Geneva Academy of International Humanitarian Law and Human Rights/Protect Education in Insecurity and Conflict, August 2013.

[48] Francoise Hampson, 'An overview of the reform of the UN human rights machinery', *Human Rights Law Review*, 7(1) (2007), pp. 7–27, at p. 11.

In the specific context of Israel and the Occupied Palestinian Territory (OPT), the Committee on Economic, Social, and Cultural Rights (CESCR) has enumerated the following as factors impeding children from enjoying their right to education: restrictions on movement of children; regular harassment by settlers of children and teachers on their way to and from school; attacks on educational facilities; and substandard school infrastructure.[49] The nuances of the right to education and ESC rights more generally make the elaboration of a universally applicable formula or list of possible ESC rights violations rather tentative, pending the clarification of this aspect of ESC rights under the Optional Protocol to the International Covenant on Economic, Social and Cultural Rights (OP-ICESCR) in the consideration of individual complaints.[50] The point here is how IHL can be used to identify cases of violations of the right to education in armed conflict.

The role of IHL in identifying the scope of international obligations and violations thereof

Most human rights monitoring bodies have taken the approach that human rights obligations in times of armed conflict may involve IHL components. Human rights bodies have recommended adherence to IHL treaties on many occasions.[51] States are regularly reminded/urged to 'comply with the fundamental principles of proportionality and distinction established in humanitarian law' in response to alleged attacks on civilians and civilian objects (including children and schools) and destruction of school infrastructure, which were qualified as resulting in 'denial of access to education'.[52] The CESCR's approach, similar to that of the Human Rights Committee, is that humanitarian law norms provide complementary guidance on how to respect and protect the relevant right in times of armed conflict.[53] Despite the comprehensive nature of the right to education, since elements of human rights are also found in humanitarian law and also because violations of IHL can affect human rights, the areas of potential overlap are

---

[49] CESCR, 'Concluding observations: Israel', UN doc. E/C.12/ISR/CO/3, 16 December 2011, §36.

[50] UN General Assembly Resolution 63/117, 10 December 2008. The Protocol entered into force on 5 May 2013, in accordance with its Art. 18(1).

[51] Committee on the Rights of the Child (CRC), 'Concluding observations: Turkey', UN doc. CRC/C/OPAC/TUR/CO/1, 29 October 2009, §16.

[52] CRC, 'Concluding observations: Israel', UN doc. CRC/C/OPAC/ISR/CO/1, 4 March 2010, §11. Similar recommendations have been made with regard to incidents of deliberate targeting of civilians or civilian infrastructure in the context of the rights of children. See CRC, 'Concluding observations: Sudan', UN doc. CRC/C/SDN/Co/3-4, 1 October 2010, §73; CRC, 'Concluding observations: Syria', UN doc. CRC/C/SYR/CO/3-4, 8 February 2012, §52.

[53] Gilles Giacca, 'Economic, social and cultural rights in armed conflict and other situations of armed violence', PhD thesis, Graduate Institute of International and Development Studies, Geneva, ch. IV.

rather important.[54] Important as they are, though, such references to IHL tend to remain general, without any detailed assessment of an individual humanitarian law provision.

General Comment No. 13 of the CESCR is not explicit as to the protection of school buildings. However, the CESCR has identified attacks on education facilities and students, barriers to access to education relating to restriction on movement, as well as non-attendance caused by a lack of registration, as a violation of the right to education.[55]

In contrast, the Convention on the Rights of the Child (CRC) specifically mentions the obligations of states in IHL terms by requiring them 'to respect and to ensure respect for rules of international humanitarian law applicable to them in armed conflicts which are relevant to the child'.[56] Equally, reporting in accordance with the obligations in the Optional Protocol to the CRC on the Involvement of Children in Armed Conflict requires states parties to report on 'measures taken to prevent attacks on civilian objects protected under international humanitarian law and other international instruments, including places that generally have a significant presence of children, such as *schools and hospitals*'.[57] In its general discussion on 'the right of the child to education in emergency situations', the Committee noted that the right to education in a situation of armed conflict is 'further protected' by the 1949 Geneva Convention IV and both 1977 Additional Protocols.[58] In this context, the CRC recommended that states parties ensure that schools are protected from military attacks or seizure and from use as centres for recruitment, and encouraged them to criminalize attacks on schools as war crimes in accordance with the 1998 ICC Statute.[59]

Regarding the report of Afghanistan, the CRC expressed its extreme concern over attacks by insurgent groups on school facilities and their use, in the prevailing conditions of conflict, as polling stations during elections, and occupation by international and national military forces.[60] This problem was dealt under the section 'Education' (Article 28 of the CRC) of the Concluding Observations. Thus the CRC recommended that the

---

[54] Walter Kälin, 'Universal human rights bodies and international humanitarian law' in Robert Kolb and Gloria Gaggioli (eds), *Research Handbook on Human Rights and Humanitarian Law*, Edward Elgar Publisher, Cheltenham, 2013, p. 445.

[55] CESCR, 'List of issues to be taken up in connection with the consideration of the third periodic reports of Israel', UN doc. E/C.12/ISR/Q/3, 9 December 2010, §36; CESCR, 'Concluding observations: Israel', UN doc. E/C.12/ISR/CO/3, 16 December 2011, §36.

[56] Under the CRC, children's human rights and humanitarian law protection are considered as interconnected and forming an integral part of the Convention. See Art. 38, CRC.

[57] 'Revised guidelines regarding initial reports to be submitted by states parties under Art. 8, para. 1, of the Optional Protocol to the Convention on the Rights of the Child on Involvement of Children in Armed Conflict', UN doc. CRC/C/OPAC/2, 19 October 2007, §16.

[58] CRC, Day of General Discussion on 'The rights of all children in the context of international migration', 28 September 2012, §3.

[59] Art. 8(2)(b)(ix).

[60] CRC, 'Concluding observations: Afghanistan', UN doc. CRC/C/AFG/CO/1, 8 April 2011, §60.

government '[u]se all means to protect schools, teachers and children from attacks, and include communities, in particular parents and children, in the development of measures to better protect schools against attacks and violence'.[61] Similarly, in its Concluding Observations for Nepal, the CRC expressed its concern at 'the large-scale bombing, destruction and closing of schools'.[62] While in the absence of a lawful military target and military necessity, destruction of education facilities clearly breaches IHL, the Committee did not frame such unlawful acts explicitly by reference to IHL, for instance by referring to Article 38 of the CRC that incorporates applicable IHL into the Convention. Instead, the CRC determined merely that such acts are 'in violation of the fundamental rights to education of children'.[63]

Generally, it is accepted that IHL rules may play the role of 'explanatory' variable, providing criteria to determine the way the content of certain human rights should be identified in situations of armed conflict. One could tentatively conclude that a violation of an IHL rule may lead to a human rights violation, although it would depend on the circumstances and whether both legal regimes deal with the subject matter or not.[64] This leaves open the question as to whether *unlawful attacks* on, or *military occupation* of, schools under IHL would constitute a violation in and of itself of the right to education.

In situations governed by the *conduct of hostilities*, involving the use of force or the military occupation of schools (and other education institutions) it seems that applicable IHL rules are to be taken into the assessment of the right to education. Arguably, human rights bodies tend to link the right to education to explicit IHL standards and seem to support the qualification of a violation. Such a standpoint could, however, be taken to mean that, should conduct be justified under IHL rules (e.g. military necessity), it would exclude violation of a right to education.

Somewhat surprisingly, disproportionate or excessive destruction and appropriation of protected property under IHL not justified by military exigencies can be a serious violation of IHL and may constitute a war crime in any armed conflict, but does not automatically qualify as a violation of socio-economic rights.[65] IHL rules may sometimes

---

[61] CRC, 'Concluding observations: Afghanistan', UN doc. CRC/C/AFG/CO/1, 8 April 2011, §61(i).

[62] CRC, 'Concluding observations: Nepal', UN doc. CRC/C/15/Add.261, 21 September 2005, §10.

[63] CRC, 'Concluding observations: Nepal', UN doc. CRC/C/15/Add.261, 21 September 2005, §10.

[64] As regards the interaction between IHL and human rights law, the Court noted in its *Wall* Advisory Opinion that some rights may be exclusively matters of IHL, others may be exclusively matters of human rights law, and others, matters of both: International Court of Justice (ICJ), *Legal Consequences of the Construction of a Wall in the Occupied Palestinian Territory*, Advisory Opinion, ICJ Reports 2004, §106.

[65] Art. 8(2)(b)(ix) of the ICC Statute provides specific protection to educational facilities and criminalizes acts of 'intentionally directing attacks against buildings dedicated to...education...provided they are not military objectives'. The crime of destruction of educational buildings as a war crime was considered by the International Criminal Tribunal for the former Yugoslavia (ICTY) as part of customary international law: *Kordić and Čerkez*, Appeals Judgment, 17 December 2004, §91; see also *Prosecutor v. Naletilić and Martinović* (Case No. IT-98-34), 31 March 2003, esp. §§604–5.

overlap with those rights, but they are not necessarily coterminous with one another. For instance, under IHL, the unlawful destruction or the arbitrary seizure of a private house does not necessarily amount to an interference with the right to housing of an individual if the object does not correspond to her or his formal residence.[66] Similarly, unlawfully directing attacks against an educational building may constitute a war crime, but may not concurrently qualify as a violation of the *right* to education. This raises the question of what would be the exact threshold, the attack per se or the damage caused? For instance, an unlawful attack on a school building, amounting to a war crime, may bring no destruction or only partial damage (e.g. destruction of the sport facility). As a result, it is reasonable to consider the right to education not to be violated in this context.

Caution is called for on the causal link between the acts and the victims, since IHRL does not protect civil infrastructure or 'objects' as such. In fact, human rights law treaties (as opposed to IHL instruments, which also generally protect civilian objects and property) aim to protect and promote individuals' rights. As such, their provisions do not confer any status on or directly protect objects or buildings (e.g. educational buildings). That said, certain essential elements of socio-economic rights do require the existence, maintenance, and availability of physical structures.[67] The element of availability requires the state to ensure that facilities, goods, or services/programmes developed and implemented are available to all in sufficient quantity.[68] For example, under the right to education, states parties have to make available 'functioning educational institutions and programmes', or under the right to health ensure the 'functioning public health and health-care facilities, goods and services as well as programmes ... in sufficient quantity'.[69] Since availability or access represents a main element in these rights, logically their physical protection may be implied or presumed.

[66] See e.g. the *Loizidou* case concerning the alleged violation of the rights of a Cypriot landowner who was prevented by Turkish troops from returning to and enjoying her land in northern Cyprus. While the lack of access of the applicant to her property amounted to a violation of the right to property under Art. 1 of Protocol No. 1 to the European Convention on Human Rights (ECHR), there was no violation of the right to home (Art. 8), since the applicant did not have a home on the land in question: European Court of Human Rights (ECtHR), *Loizidou v. Turkey*, Judgment (App. No. 15318/89), 18 December 1996, §§65–6.

[67] See generally the AAAQ framework (availability, accessibility, acceptability and quality of facilities, goods, services and programmes) developed in the practice of the CESCR: CESCR, General Comment No. 4: 'The right to adequate housing (Art. 11, para. 1, of the Covenant)', 1991, §8; 'UN Special Rapporteur on the right to education, K. Tomaševski, preliminary report', UN doc. E/CN.4/1999/49, 13 January 1999.

[68] CESCR, General Comment No. 14: 'The right to the highest attainable standard of health', 2000, §12 (a); similarly see General Comment No. 19: 'The right to social security', 2008, §11; General Comment No. 18: 'The right to work', 2005, §12(a); General Comment No. 15: 'The right to water (Arts 11 and 12 of the Covenant)', 2002, §12(a); General Comment No. 13: 'The right to education (Art. 13 of the Covenant)', 1999, §6(a).

[69] CESCR, General Comment No. 14, §12(a); General Comment No. 13, §6(a). Similarly, the Committee considers that the core content of the right to adequate food implies 'the availability of food in a quantity and quality sufficient to satisfy the dietary needs of individuals, free from adverse substances, and acceptable within a given culture': CESCR, General Comment No. 12: 'The right to adequate food (Art. 11 of the Covenant)', 1999, §8.

In sum, the final assessment on whether a violation of the right to education occurs would depend on the context and the individual victims. As Kälin explains:

One reason for this is the fact that, unlike in the case of the European Court of Human Rights, no individual communications have been brought yet to the UN treaty bodies of persons claiming to be victims of violations of their human rights during armed conflict. Such cases would provide the Human Rights Committee and other treaty bodies with an opportunity to explore the relationship between specific human rights and their equivalents in international humanitarian law.[70]

Thus, this process of interpretation is not a mechanical exercise with a preconceived outcome. Each situation should be analysed on a case-by-case basis, having in mind that it may not yet be possible to articulate a comprehensive theory concerning the interaction between IHL and the right to education.[71]

International practice

The evolving practice of international bodies points to several directions that may help interpret IHL rules and the interface between these rules and IHRL.

First, concern is growing about the need for enhanced legal protection of schools in light of increasing evidence of frequent attacks on schools, students, and teachers. As such, there is a growing *opinio juris* on the need to grant privileged status to schools. Such recognition is occurring through the inclusion of attacks on education in the list of six grave violations against children (as a means to protect 'education' in times of armed conflict). Schools, as well as hospitals, are referred to as 'zones of peace', 'safe zones', and 'conflict-free' zones. The UN Special Rapporteur on the right to education,[72] the UN Secretary-General, and the SRSG-CIAC have made recommendations on a number of occasions to designate schools as 'zones of peace'. It has been suggested, in particular, that parties to the conflict:

Refrain from engaging in combat and/or using heavy artillery in highly populated areas. In this context, the protection of schools and hospitals as 'zones of peace' should be paramount.[73]

Added to the concerns over protection of children, reference is increasingly being made to the special value and inherent qualities of education for the affected communities *as*

---

[70] Kälin, 'Universal human rights bodies and international humanitarian law', p. 448.

[71] Gilles Giacca, 'Economic, social and cultural rights and armed violence: challenges and prospects' in G. Giacca, C. Golay, and E. Riedel (eds), *Economic, Social and Cultural Rights: Contemporary Issues and Challenges*, Oxford University Press, Oxford, forthcoming (2014).

[72] 'Special Rapporteur on the right to education, report on mission to Colombia', UN doc. E/CN.4/2004/45/Add.2, 17 February 2004, §48.

[73] 'Annual report of the SRSG-CIAC', UN doc. A/66/256, 3 August 2011, Annex ('Suggested standard operating procedures for the protection of children in the conduct of military operations').

such. Education can help conflict-affected communities to cope with violence, as well as to recover from armed conflict. It is claimed that education can provide physical, psychological, and cognitive protection.[74] Education is an example of a vital socio-economic sector in which the consequences of armed conflict may be felt long after the conflict is over:

The function of education as an engine of positive change is lost, not only for promoting human dignity and fundamental rights but *even* in the most practical terms of providing technological and industrial competencies. Society becomes risk-averse, creation-averse, discovery-averse. It atrophies, making future development and recovery much more difficult.[75]

Secondly, there is some indication that military use of schools can be read into the notion of an *attack on schools*. As noted earlier, the UN Secretary-General's April 2012 report on children and armed conflict defines attacks against schools for the purposes of listing violators as including:

... direct attack against schools, indiscriminate attacks against schools, resulting in damage to or destruction of these facilities; or which have the effect of impeding the ability of a school to function and/or placing children at risk, acts of looting of these protected facilities; and *military use of schools, although it does not constitute a trigger for listing.*[76]

The implications of the latter phrase emphasized are not entirely clear. On one hand, military use is integrated into the definition of what is understood as an attack. On the other, it is specified that the fact of military use should not be the basis for listing.

The Syrian Commission of Inquiry stated that, based on its investigations between 15 July 2012 and 15 January 2013, schools were frequently used as barracks or offices by anti-government armed groups in situations in which this was not justified by military necessity. It also stated that: 'More than 2,400 of the 20,000 schools in the Syrian Arab Republic have been damaged by military operations. Thousands more have been converted into shelters for displaced persons, undermining access to education.'[77] Of course, military use of schools is only one parameter of a broader notion of military interaction with schools.[78]

---

[74] CRC, Day of General Discussion on 'The right of the child to education in emergency situations', Recommendations by the CRC, 49th Session, 3 October 2008, §§14–16.

[75] Robert Quinn, 'Attacks on higher education communities: a holistic, human rights approach to protection' in *Protecting Education from Attack: A State-of-the-Art Review*, UNESCO, Paris, 2010, p. 109.

[76] 'Children and armed conflict: report of the Secretary-General', UN doc. A/66/782–S/2012/261, 26 April 2012, §227 (emphasis added).

[77] 'Report of the Independent International Commission of Inquiry on the Syrian Arab Republic', 5 February 2013, §G.2, p. 18.

[78] Steven Haines, 'The protection of educational institutions during armed conflict', 12 February 2013, <http://www.history.ox.ac.uk/ccw/wp-content/uploads/2013/02/StevenHainesMP3.mp3>.

C. Other developments in 2012

ATTACKS ON EDUCATION AND THE QUESTION OF THE QUALIFICATION OF ARMED CONFLICT

The UN Secretary-General's 2012 report on children and armed conflict provided information on 'grave violations against children', including attacks on schools during 2011. In addition to the 16 states on the agenda of the UN Security Council, the report included a section 'on grave violations against children in situations *not* on the agenda of the Security Council or in *other situations*', reporting on the following seven states: Colombia; India; Pakistan; Philippines; Sri Lanka; Thailand; and Yemen.[79]

The Secretary-General's report resulted in strong objections from certain states listed. UN Security Council Resolution 2068 (2012) largely reproduces the content of previous resolutions on the topic. Yet, for the first time, four Security Council members, namely Azerbaijan, China, Pakistan, and the Russian Federation, did not support it. They claimed that the Secretary-General had gone outside the mandate authorized by the Security Council by including situations that did not meet the threshold of armed conflict or a threat to the maintenance of international peace and security.

Pakistan argued that the section of the report of the UN Secretary-General that addressed it did not concern armed conflict, but acts by terrorists and criminals.[80] It said that the section devoted to incidents in Pakistan was 'unwarranted and completely misleading', and that it 'not only misrepresents the context of Pakistan's law enforcement and counterterrorism measures, but also serves to accord undeserved respectability to terrorists and criminals'.[81] China supported Pakistan's position, noting that:

The resolution must not be wilfully interpreted to equate incidents of terrorist attack in Pakistan, for instance, to armed conflict, which would exceed the mandate of the Security Council. Pakistan is at the forefront of the international fight against terrorism and has made important contributions to cooperation in the international fight against terrorism. The international community should provide more support and help to Pakistan's efforts in counterterrorism rather than creating difficulties and obstacles.[82]

---

[79] Emphasis added.

[80] One needs to recall that the SRSG-CIAC's mandate involves reporting on situations of armed conflicts. UN Security Council Resolution 1882 (2009) links situations of concern under that resolution to §16 of Resolution 1379 (2001), which asks the Secretary-General to use the trigger mechanisms in the relevant resolutions to list parties in annexes to his reports in situations of armed conflict that are on the Security Council's agenda or that threaten the maintenance of international peace and security in light of Art. 99 of the UN Charter.

[81] UN Security Council, UN doc. S/PV.6838, 6838th meeting, 19 September 2012, 10 a.m., p. 25.

[82] UN Security Council, UN doc. S/PV.6838, 6838th meeting, 19 September 2012, 10 a.m., p. 3.

According to the (former) SRSG-CIAC, Radika Coomaraswamy, 'our determination was derived from a humanitarian angle with a pragmatic emphasis on children, what happens to them and how they can be protected'.[83] To avoid sensitive issues of legal determination of a situation, the formulation 'other situations of concern' has been invented.[84] Moreover, Resolution 2068 of 2012 reiterated the standard position that:

Having considered the report of the Secretary-General of 26 April 2012 (A/66/782-S/2012/261) and *stressing* that the present resolution does not seek to make any legal determination as to whether situations which are referred to in the Secretary-General's report are or are not armed conflicts within the context of the Geneva Conventions and the Additional Protocols thereto, nor does it prejudge the legal status of the non-State parties involved in these situations...

Thus, while there are legitimate and important questions to be asked about which body of law applies in the context of Pakistan, especially when the mandate clearly requests the Secretary-General to attach a *list* of parties to *armed conflict* that commit grave violations of relevant international norms, the politicization of the issue leading to the abstentions in the vote of member states is disappointing, since it is the first time this happened with a Security Council resolution devoted to the protection of children.

DEEDS OF COMMITMENTS BY ARMED NON-STATE ACTORS

Considerable experience has been gained over recent years through engagement with ANSAs on the protection of civilians in armed conflict.[85] How, and to what extent, international law formally binds these actors is still debated. While it is largely uncontested that IHL imposes certain obligations on ANSAs, application of other bodies of international law—particularly human rights law—is controversial. It therefore becomes crucial to engage with those non-state actors in view of the desire to enhance protection of persons caught in armed conflicts and other situations of violence.

In this regard, mention is merited of the work of the Swiss-based humanitarian organization Geneva Call, which is dedicated to promoting signature and compliance by ANSAs with a formal Deed of Commitment on humanitarian norms related to the anti-personnel mine ban, the protection of children, and the protection of women and

---

[83] Coomaraswamy, 'The Security Council and children and armed conflict: an experiment in the making'.

[84] UN Security Council Resolution 1882 (2009), 4 August 2009, §19(a), which requested the Secretary-General to include in its report '[a]nnexed lists of parties in situations of armed conflict on the agenda of the Security Council or in other situations of concern, in accordance with paragraph 3 of the present resolution'.

[85] Annyssa Bellal and Stuart Casey-Maslen, *Rules of Engagement: Protecting Civilians through Dialogue with Armed Non-State Actors*, Geneva Academy of International Humanitarian Law and Human Rights, Geneva, October 2011.

girls.[86] Upon signature, a system of reporting and monitoring on compliance with the Deed is implemented by the third-party organization and assistance is provided to supporting this. Experience of international organizations and NGOs shows that monitoring is a critical element in promoting effective compliance with norms and relevant agreements or declarations.[87]

More specifically on the protection of education in armed conflict, one approach to engage ANSAs is the 2010 Deed of Commitment for the Protection of Children from the Effects of Armed Conflict.[88] In 2012, the Karenni National Progressive Party/Karenni Army (KNPP/KA) and the New Mon State Party/Mon National Liberation Army (NMSP/MNLA) from Burma/Myanmar were the first to sign Geneva Call's Deed on the protection of children.[89] Five other non-state actors from Iran signed the Deed on 14 December 2012: the Democratic Party of Iranian Kurdistan; Komalah, the Kurdistan Organization of the Communist Party of Iran; the Komala Party of Iranian Kurdistan; the Kurdistan Democratic Party—Iran; and the Komala Party of Kurdistan.[90]

Among other commitments that include a prohibition on the recruitment of children under the age of 18 and their use in hostilities, the document includes the following provision:

To further endeavor to provide children in areas where we exercise authority with the aid and care they require, in cooperation with humanitarian or development organizations where appropriate. Towards these ends, and among other things, we will: . . . v) *avoid using for military purposes schools or premises primarily used by children.*[91]

---

[86] Geneva Call was created in 1998, one year after the 1997 Anti-Personnel Mine Ban Convention (APMBC) was adopted and signed, to begin engaging non-state actors on landmines through voluntary commitments. Based on its success in engaging ANSAs on landmines, Geneva Call has launched two new Deeds of Commitment: one concerns the 'Prohibition of Sexual Violence in Armed Conflict and towards the Elimination of Gender Discrimination'; and the other relates to the 'Protection of Children from the Effects of Armed Conflict'. Geneva Call defines itself as a 'neutral and impartial organization dedicated to engaging armed non-State actors (NSAs) towards compliance with the norms of international humanitarian law (IHL) and human right law (IHRL). The organization focuses on NSAs that operate outside effective State control'. For more information, see <http://www.genevacall.org>. See also Jonathan Somer, 'Engaging armed non-state actors to protect children from the effects of armed conflict: when the stick doesn't cut the mustard', *Journal of Human Rights Practice*, 4(1) (2012), pp. 106–27.

[87] Bellal and Casey-Maslen, *Rules of Engagement: Protecting Civilians through Dialogue with Armed Non-State Actors.*

[88] Geneva Call, Deed of Commitment under Geneva Call for the Protection of Children from the Effects of the Armed Conflict, 2010.

[89] Geneva Call, 'Burma/Myanmar: two armed groups undertake not to use child soldiers—the first to sign Geneva Call's Deed of Commitment on children', Press release, 6 August 2012, <http://www.genevacall.org/news/press-releases/f-press-releases/2001-2010/GC_2012_COMM_DoC_CANSA_JULY%20.pdf>.

[90] Geneva Call, 'Signatories to the Deed of Commitment on children and armed conflict', <http://www.genevacall.org/resources/list-of-signatories/list-of-signatories.htm>.

[91] Geneva Call, Deed of Commitment under Geneva Call for the Protection of Children from the Effects of the Armed Conflict, 2010, §7.V (emphasis added).

Direct engagement with ANSAs to encourage better respect for international norms can be a critical contribution to reducing the suffering of civilian populations in contemporary armed conflict, especially when relevant provisions of international law may not comprehensively create obligations for those entities. Moreover, in view of the fact that international standards may not always provide clear answers to regulate the behaviour of the parties to the conflict, this constructive dialogue with non-state actors and related deeds may go further than existing obligations under international law. As discussed previously, there is no IHL prohibition on armed forces using educational buildings for military purposes, and therefore voluntary commitments can usefully complement existing mechanisms.

INTERNATIONAL GUIDELINES REGULATING MILITARY USE OF SCHOOLS

The GCPEA has initiated the drafting of new international guidelines for protecting schools and universities from military use during armed conflict.[92] In May 2012, the idea of developing clear global standards to regulate the practice of military use of schools and other education institutions was discussed at an experts meeting in Geneva, which was further endorsed in a larger expert conference that was held in November 2012 in Switzerland. The result of the conference was general agreement on the need for guidelines to minimize military use of educational institutions, as well as input and suggestions on the draft guidelines that will be completed in 2013.[93]

Concluding remarks

Data for 2012 suggests that schools and other educational institutions as grounds of armed conflict add another dimension to the most distressing realities of war. Alarming statistics include the prevalence of attacks on—and targeting of—schools, students, and educational staff by both state military forces and NSAGs.

What would be the added value of choosing 'education as a framework' to structure matters already governed by various rules of IHL and IHRL? On one hand, as the Special Rapporteur on the right to education has observed, armed conflicts can 'impair or violate

---

[92] The Coalition's steering committee comprises three UN agencies—UNESCO, UNICEF, and UNHCR—and four international NGOs—the Council for Assisting Refugee Academics, Education above All, HRW, and Save the Children International.

[93] GCPEA, 'Draft Lucens guidelines for protecting schools and universities from military use during armed conflict', May 2013.

the right to education, impede its development and hold back its realisation' and 'put people's health and lives at risk and threaten or destroy public and private assets, limiting the capacity and resources to guarantee rights and uphold social responsibilities'.[94] On the other, as we have seen, an issue that urgently requires further normative development relates to the military occupation of schools and other education institutions, of which there is currently no general ban under IHL.

---

[94] 'Right to education in emergency situations: report of the Special Rapporteur on the right to education, Vernor Muñoz', UN doc. A/HRC/8/10, 20 May 2008, §5.

7 The protection of journalists in armed conflict

Nicole Urban*

Introduction

Reporting from armed conflict is inherently dangerous; journalists have always faced the risk of being killed or injured inadvertently. Increasingly, however, belligerents have targeted journalists, making them a particularly vulnerable group in contemporary armed conflicts.[1] Indeed, 2012 proved to be the deadliest year for journalists on record,[2] with reports indicating that up to 152 were killed in connection with their work.[3] Combat-related cross-fire accounted for one-third of the total deaths of journalists in armed conflict and armed violence in 2012,[4] but deliberate attacks (including murder)

* Nicole Urban is Research Fellow in International Humanitarian Law at the British Institute of International and Comparative Law. The author would like to thank Rebecca Francis and Ananda Reeves for their assistance in the preparation of this chapter.

[1] This report relies on annual statistics and analysis of several international media organizations (published on their websites) including: the Committee to Protect Journalists (CPJ); the International Federation of Journalists (IFJ); Reporters without Borders (RSF); the International News Safety Institute (INSI); the Press Emblem Campaign (PEC); the International Press Institute (IPI); and the United Nations Educational, Scientific and Cultural Organization (UNESCO).

[2] According to statistics on the deaths of journalists collected by: 'News providers decimated in 2012', *RSF*, 19 March 2013, <http://en.rsf.org/2012-journalists-netizens-decimated-19-12-2012,43806.html> (*RSF Report*); '2012 deadliest year for journalists', *IPI*, 31 December 2012, <http://www.freemedia.at/home/singleview/article/2012-deadliest-year-for-journalists.html?L=0&cHash=5fc6d8e576>; and 'Message from Ms Irina Bokova, Director-General of UNESCO on the occasion of the 2nd UN Inter-Agency on the Safety of Journalists and the Issue of Impunity', Vienna, 22 November 2012, <http://www.unesco.org/new/fileadmin/MULTIMEDIA/HQ/CI/CI/images/Themes/Freedom_of_expression/DGSpeech2ndUNInteragencySafety.pdf>.

[3] See assessments by and on the websites of: CPJ (70 deaths); RSF (89 deaths); UNESCO (at least 119 deaths); IFJ (121 violent deaths); IPI (133 deaths); PEC (139 deaths); INSI (152 deaths). The disparity between statistics is the result of a number of factors, including that some organizations do not include the deaths of 'media assistants' in this category: IPI and IFJ statistics include both 'journalists' and other 'media staff'; UNESCO statistics include 'citizen-journalists'; CPJ statistics separate 'journalists' and 'media workers'; and RSF statistics separate 'journalists' from 'netizens and citizen-journalists'. Further, in the case of the CPJ, investigations into 30 more deaths were being undertaken as of writing.

[4] See CPJ special report, 'Journalist deaths spike in 2012 due to Syria, Somalia', 18 December 2012, <http://www.cpj.org/reports/CPJ.Journalists.Killed.2012.pdf> (*CPJ Report*). These statistics are, however, only approximations as it is not clear that their classifications of conflict situations reflect those laid down under international humanitarian law (IHL).

accounted for as many as half.[5] Syria and Somalia were the most deadly in 2012,[6] followed by Pakistan[7] and Mexico.[8]

In its Resolution 1738 adopted on 23 December 2006, the United Nations (UN) Security Council expressed its deep concern about the frequency of acts of violence against journalists in armed conflict and 'in particular deliberate attacks in violation of international humanitarian law'. The Council called on parties to conflicts to adhere to their IHL obligation to refrain from attacking civilians, including journalists. In response to this escalation, the UN and UNESCO's International Programme for the Development of Communication announced their 2012 'UN Plan of Action on the Safety of Journalists and the Issue of Impunity'. The plan seeks to address attacks on journalists by, among other things, establishing a coordinated inter-agency mechanism to assist states to implement measures to protect journalists, including during armed conflict.[9]

THE DEADLIEST YEAR SO FAR . . .

Four international journalists were killed in 2012, all during the armed violence and subsequent non-international armed conflict (NIAC) in Syria. This includes the American Marie Colvin, an experienced journalist for the UK's *Sunday Times*, and Remi Ochlik, an award-winning French photojournalist, both of whom were killed during shelling of a media centre in Homs.[10] Also killed were *France 2* reporter Gilles Jacquier, who was killed by hostile fire in Homs,[11] and Japanese Press photojournalist Mika Yamamoto, who was shot by unknown persons in military uniform in northern Syria.[12]

The deaths of international journalists are, understandably, the focus of the international news media. These high-profile incidents are, however, only a fraction of the overall death toll for journalists in 2012. Most of those killed in 2012 were members of local media: the CPJ estimates they comprised 94 per cent of the total (conflict- and non-conflict-related) deaths.[13]

---

[5] *CPJ Report*.

[6] CPJ: 28 journalists killed in Syria, 12 in Somalia; RSF: Syria 18, Somalia 18; IFJ: Syria 33, Somalia 18; IPI: Syria 39, Somalia 16; UNESCO: Syria 42, Somalia 18; PEC: Syria 37, Somalia 19; INSI: Syria 28, Somalia 18.

[7] Journalists killed in Pakistan in 2012: CPJ, 7; RSF, 9; IFJ, 10; IPI, 8; PEC, 12; UNESCO, 10; INSI, 11.

[8] Journalists killed in Mexico in 2012: CPJ, 1 death (motive confirmed) and 5 others (motive unconfirmed); RSF, 6; IFJ, 10; IPI, 7; PEC, 2; UNESCO, 7; INSI, 11.

[9] UNESCO, 'UN Plan of Action on the Safety of Journalists and the Issue of Impunity', <http://www.unesco.org/new/en/communication-and-information/freedom-of-expression/safety-of-journalists/un-plan-of-action/>.

[10] See CPJ, <http://cpj.org/killed/2012/marie-colvin.php>.

[11] See CPJ, <http://www.cpj.org/killed/2012/gilles-jacquier.php>.

[12] See CPJ, <http://www.cpj.org/killed/2012/mika-yamamoto.php>.

[13] See *CPJ Report*; INSI, 'Killing the messenger: annual report', 2012, p. 7, concludes that 91 per cent (138 of 152 deaths) were of local journalists, <http://www.newssafety.org/KTM2012_Final%20%28May%

But while these statistics are horrifying, the broader picture is even more concerning. Recording the deaths of journalists is a good indication of the danger they face and their vulnerability, but in addition to attacks resulting in death, many other incidents during armed conflict, for which no comprehensive statistics exist, involve torture, sexual abuse, or kidnapping (hostage-taking). What we know pales in comparison to what we do not.

WHY JOURNALISTS?

Attacks on journalists are not random events. Journalists are targeted as a direct result of their work in conflict zones. Thus, a UN Human Rights Council panel noted in 2010 that 'journalists were deliberately targeted in areas of ongoing armed conflict as a result of their role in exposing human rights abuses and atrocities, corruption or unpopular opinions or situations'.[14]

The work of journalists in accessing and disseminating information is crucial to clearing 'the fog of war' and exposing its brutality to public scrutiny.[15] They also act as conduits for the rights of others and are key components of ensuring the right to freedom of expression during armed conflict.[16] Further, as witnesses to atrocities in wars, journalists can help to secure justice for the victims. The importance of this role was recognized by the ad hoc International Criminal Tribunal for the former Yugoslavia (ICTY) in the *Randal* case, which established the first, and so far only, qualified testimonial privilege for journalists in an international criminal court.[17]

Attacking journalists is a form of censorship;[18] not only does it have the effect of silencing the journalist who is attacked, but it also has a 'chilling effect' on all members of

---

202013%29.pdf>. See also IFJ, *In the Grip of Violence: Journalist and Media Staff Killed in 2012*, Beth Costa, Brussels, 2013, p. 4, <http://www.ifj.org/assets/banners/202/129/0b958ca-fc9fa81.pdf> (*IFJ Report*).

[14] 'Summary of the Human Rights Council panel discussion on the protection of journalists in armed conflict prepared by the Office of the United Nations Commissioner for Human Rights', Human Rights Council, UN doc. A/HRC/15/54, 2 August 2010 ('Summary of the Human Rights Council panel discussion'), p. 5; see also the concurring 'Report of the Special Rapporteur on the promotion and protection of freedom of opinion and expression, Mr Frank La Rue', UN doc. A/HRC/14/23, 20 April 2010, §16.

[15] See discussion in ICTY, *Prosecutor v. Brdjanin and Talić*, Decision on Interlocutory Appeal (Case No. IT-99-36-AR73.9), 11 December 2002 (the *Randal case*), §36.

[16] See *Randal case*, §37. See also UNESCO, *The Safety of Journalists and The Danger of Impunity: Report by the Director-General*, UNESCO, March 2012, §2; 'Report of the Special Rapporteur on the promotion and protection of freedom of opinion and expression, Mr Frank La Rue', UN doc. A/HRC/14/23, 20 April 2010, §3.

[17] *Randal case,* in particular §§35–7. See further Steven Powles, 'To testify or not to testify—privilege from testimony at the ad hoc tribunals: the *Randal* decision', *Leiden Journal of International Law*, 16(3) (2003).

[18] 'Summary of the Human Rights Council panel discussion', p. 5. See also 'Report of the Special Rapporteur on the promotion and protection of freedom of opinion and expression, Mr Frank La Rue', UN doc. A/HRC/14/23, 20 April 2010, p. 16.

the media operating in a conflict. The targeting of journalists must be seen as an attack on the rule of law in armed conflict and on human rights more generally.

A. The legal protection of journalists under international humanitarian law

Journalists reporting from international and non-international armed conflict alike have the status of civilians and are entitled to protection as such under IHL. To understand the scope of the protection afforded to journalists under the 1949 Geneva Conventions and the two 1977 Additional Protocols, one only needs to replace the word 'civilian' with 'journalist'.[19] Journalists do not generally benefit from special status or protection similar to medical, religious, or civil defence personnel, nor does IHL expressly recognize or protect the professional tasks of the media in armed conflict.[20] Aside from the general classification of journalists, IHL makes no specific mention of journalists or their work.

CLASSIFICATION OF JOURNALISTS IN ARMED CONFLICT

IHL recognizes two categories of journalists in armed conflict: independent journalists; and the subcategory of authorized war correspondents. Unless specifically noted, the term 'journalist' is used throughout to refer to both categories.

'Journalists' in international armed conflict

The term 'journalist' is used in Article 79 of the 1977 Additional Protocol I, which confirms the civilian status of journalists in international armed conflict (IAC). Journalists are also entitled to civilian protection independent of the operation of Article 79 as they meet the definition of 'civilian' contained in Article 50(1) of Additional Protocol I.[21]

---

[19] International Committee of the Red Cross (ICRC) interview with Robin Geiss, 'How does international humanitarian law protect journalists in armed-conflict situations?', *ICRC*, 2010, <http://www.icrc.org/eng/resources/documents/interview/protection-journalists-interview-270710.htm>; Knut Doermann, 'International humanitarian law and the protection of media professionals working in armed conflicts', *ICRC*, 2007, <http://www.icrc.org/eng/resources/documents/article/other/media-protection-article-.htm>.

[20] Hans-Peter Gasser, 'The journalist's right to information in time of war and on dangerous missions', *Yearbook of International Humanitarian Law*, 6 (2003), p. 366.

[21] Although the text of the article states that journalists are 'considered civilians', the ICRC Commentary makes it clear that journalist 'are' civilians: ICRC, 'Commentary on the Additional Protocols of 8 June 1977 to the Geneva Conventions of 12 August 1949', 1987 (*ICRC Commentary on the 1977 Additional Protocols*), §3259. See also Hans-Peter Gasser, 'The protection of journalists engaged in dangerous professional missions: law applicable in periods of armed conflict', *International Review of the Red Cross*, 232 (1983) p. 12.

'Journalist' is not defined in the text of Article 79. The ICRC commentary on the 1977 Additional Protocols states that 'journalist' is to be understood in a broad sense.[22] As such, it includes those working as 'correspondent, reporter, photographer, and their technical film, radio and television assistants who undertake such tasks as their "principal occupation"'.[23] This definition is broader than the one used by many media organizations to collect statistics on the vulnerability of journalists.[24]

Article 79 applies to journalists 'engaged in dangerous professional missions in areas of armed conflict'. 'Professional mission' is wide enough to cover 'all activities which normally form part of the journalist's profession in a broad sense'.[25] This includes conducting interviews and taking notes, photographs, or film, and transmitting them to a broadcaster or publisher.[26] The provision also calls for states to issue journalists with an identification card, which attests to, but is not a condition of, their civilian status.

'War correspondents' under the 1949 Geneva Convention III

The term 'war correspondent' is used in Article 4(A)A of the 1949 Geneva Convention III, applicable in IAC. War correspondents are a subset of the more general category of 'journalist' and form part of those civilians who 'accompany the armed forces without actually being members thereof'.[27] In order to qualify as a war correspondent, a journalist must have 'authorization, from the armed forces which they accompany'[28] and be provided with an identity card demonstrating such authorization. Those journalists who are so authorized are afforded prisoner of war (POW) status upon capture. The operation of Article 79 of the 1977 Additional Protocol I does not affect the status of war correspondents under the Geneva Conventions.[29]

The significance of 'war correspondent' status is limited to treatment in detention (as a POW) and at all other times authorized war correspondents are entitled to the same civilian protection as independent journalists.

Embedded journalists

Embedded journalists are not specifically referred to in any IHL treaty. The practice of embedding a reporter with a military unit has a long history, commencing in the

---

[22] *ICRC Commentary on the 1977 Additional Protocols*, §3261.

[23] *ICRC Commentary on the 1977 Additional Protocols*, §3260. UN Security Council Resolution 1738 (2006) supports this interpretation as it applies to 'journalists, media professionals and associated personnel'.

[24] See analysis of this in n. 4.

[25] *ICRC Commentary on the 1977 Additional Protocols*, §3264.

[26] *ICRC Commentary on the 1977 Additional Protocols*, §3264.

[27] Art. 4(A)A, 1949 Geneva Convention III.   [28] Art. 4(A)A, 1949 Geneva Convention III.

[29] Art. 79(2), 1977 Additional Protocol I.

1939–45 War; however, it was during the 2003 Gulf War that the practice 'culminated in the first broad implementation of the modern embedded press system'.[30] Although it is tempting to argue that all embedded journalists are war correspondents,[31] war correspondent status is dependent only upon authorization by a state's armed forces and not the physical proximity of a journalist to a military unit.[32] The practice of embedding does not affect the civilian status of journalists under the Geneva Conventions or Additional Protocol I.[33]

The classification of journalists in non-international armed conflict

Most of the conflicts in 2012 are classified in this book as NIACs.[34] Article 79 of the Additional Protocol I applies to IACs and the question of whether the provision applies to NIACs as customary international law is not finally settled.[35] There is, however, no doubt that journalists are nevertheless entitled to protection as civilians in NIACs regardless of the application of Article 79.[36] Under customary law applicable to IAC and NIAC alike, journalists who do not directly participate in hostilities are protected from intentional attack by the principle of distinction. Similarly, while there is no specific reference to 'journalists' in treaty law governing NIACs, the broad notion of 'journalist' is 'applicable as much to NIACs as it is to IACs.'[37]

The law of NIAC does not recognize POW status,[38] and accordingly 'war correspondents' benefit from the same protection as journalists except for their POW status

---

[30] Major Douglas W. Moore, 'Twenty-first century embedded journalists: lawful targets?', *The Army Lawyer*, July 2009, p. 10.

[31] Moore, 'Twenty-first century embedded journalists: lawful targets?', p. 14.

[32] Yoram Dinstein, 'The international status, rights and duties of journalists in times of armed conflict', 11th Commission, Institut de Droit International, 2009, §18, <http://www.idi-iil.org/idiE/annuaireE/2009/Dinstein.pdf>.

[33] Dinstein, 'The international status, rights and duties of journalists in times of armed conflict', §18.

[34] See Part I of this volume.

[35] Jean-Marie Henckaerts and Louise Doswald-Beck, *Customary International Humanitarian Law, Vol. I: Rules* and *Vol. II: Practice*, Cambridge University Press, Cambridge, 2005. ICRC Customary IHL Study in Rule 34 concludes that it does. Some, however, question the methodology and practice used to support this conclusion: see Susan C. Breau, 'Protected persons and objects' in Elizabeth Wilmshurst and Susan Breau (eds), *Perspectives on the ICRC Study on Customary International Humanitarian Law*, Chatham House/BIICL, London, 2007, p. 185.

[36] See Dinstein, *The International Status, Rights and Duties of Journalists in Times of Armed Conflict*, §64; Gasser, 'The protection of journalists engaged in dangerous professional missions: law applicable in periods of armed conflict', p. 14; Ben Saul, 'The international protection of journalists in armed conflict and other violent situations', *Australian Journal of Human Rights*, 14(1) (2008), pp. 119 and 123.

[37] See e.g. Sandesh Sivakumaran *The Law of Non-International Armed Conflict*, Oxford University Press, Oxford, 2012, p. 311.

[38] Dieter Fleck, 'The law of non-international armed conflicts' in D. Fleck (ed.), *The Handbook of Humanitarian Law in Armed Conflicts*, 2nd edn, Oxford University Press, Oxford, 2009, §§1213–15.

upon capture. As in IACs, the civilian status of journalists in a NIAC is unaffected by the process of embedding.

Members of the armed forces

Sometimes, members of the armed forces undertake media-related duties, including reporting on hostilities for military publications or broadcasts, briefing journalists, and giving interviews or assisting journalists with their tasks. As members of the armed forces, these persons are not entitled to civilian status and they do not fall within the categories of 'journalist' or 'war correspondent'.[39]

Other members of the media

The definition of 'journalist' set out in the ICRC Commentary on the 1977 Additional Protocols limits the scope of the term to those who work in the media as their 'principal occupation'.[40] However, since the drafting of the Protocols in the 1970s, the news media industry has changed significantly. In particular, foreign news desks increasingly rely on part-time or freelance media workers to support or replace the work of full-time journalists.[41] Modern news reporting from conflicts is increasingly dependent on local stringers 'recruited on the spot on part-time contacts'[42] and freelance personnel 'who are not currently employed by any specific news agency, but have a certain record of publication and can expect to sell their stories or pictures at a later stage'.[43] Freelance journalists are increasingly vulnerable, and in 2012 the CPJ reports that they represented more than one in four journalists killed.[44]

Another emerging trend in journalism, not captured by the IHL definition of 'journalists', is the rise of citizen journalists (ordinary people who use technology to transmit news and images via the Internet) and bloggers (who are often not trained media professionals),[45] who operate as a parallel news source to mainstream

---

[39] *ICRC Commentary on the 1977 Additional Protocols*, §3262.

[40] *ICRC Commentary on the 1977 Additional Protocols*, §3260.

[41] For a more detailed account of the changing nature of foreign news reporting, including the reliance on stringers and fixers by foreign news services, see e.g. Mel Bunce, *The New Foreign Correspondent at Work: Local-National 'Stringers' and the Global News Coverage of the Conflict in Darfur*, Reuters Institute for the Study of Journalism, University of Oxford, 2011; Richard Sambrook, *Challenges: The Changing Face of International News*, Reuters Institute for the Study of Journalism, University of Oxford, 2010.

[42] Dinstein, *The International Status, Rights and Duties of Journalists in Times of Armed Conflict*, §32.

[43] Dinstein, *The International Status, Rights and Duties of Journalists in Times of Armed Conflict*, §32.

[44] *CPJ Report*.

[45] For example, university lecturer Lina Ben Mhenni, who reported events relating to the Tunisian revolution in 2011 and was nominated for a Nobel Peace Prize in 2012. Her blog is available at <http://atunisiangirl .blogspot.co.uk/>.

media,[46] providing news and information directly to the public, including from conflicts.[47] The events of the so-called 'Arab Spring' brought this group to the forefront of international attention, while the Syrian conflict in 2012 highlighted the increasing importance of their work. International media access has been significantly restricted throughout that conflict[48] and mainstream media organizations have been forced to rely on activists rather than traditional fixers for assistance, as well as uploaded images and material from locals.[49] Without such alternative news sources, 'the Syrian regime would be able to impose a complete news blackout on certain regions'.[50]

The rising importance of this group of non-traditional journalists correlates with their increasing vulnerability in conflict. In 2012, 47 citizen journalists were killed compared with five in 2011. RSF attributes most of these deaths to the Syrian conflict.[51] But many of the people falling into this important group of freelance media workers and alternative media workers do not receive their principal income, if any, from this work.[52] This raises serious doubts that these increasingly significant groups fall into the IHL definition of 'journalist'.

DELIBERATE AND DIRECT ATTACKS AGAINST JOURNALISTS

The deliberate targeting of journalists is fast becoming a fixture of modern armed conflict. The leading cause of death for journalists generally in 2012 was deliberate killing, which, according to the CPJ, accounted for approximately half of the overall death toll.[53] It is not, though, certain from available statistics how many deaths occurred during or in relation to armed conflict.

In Syria, the IFJ reports that while some of the 34 deaths of journalists during the violence in 2012 were the result of getting 'caught in the cross-fire', there is 'strong evidence that

---

[46] John Kelly, *Red Kayaks and Hidden Gold: The Rise, Challenges and Value of Citizen Journalism*, Reuters Institute for the Study of Journalism, University of Oxford, 2009, p. 4.

[47] For example, Christopher Allbritton, a freelance American journalist who sought private funding from his readers to cover the recent Iraqi conflict for his own news blog. His blog is available at <http://www.back-to-iraq.com/>.

[48] See RSF, 'Country report: Syria', September 2011, <http://en.rsf.org/report-syrie,163.html>. See generally Salama Abdelaziz, 'Syrian opposition strive to get world's attention in year of carnage', *CNN*, 16 March 2012, <http://edition.cnn.com/2012/03/15/opinion/syria-anniversary-outreach>; Hugh Macleod, 'Syria's young cyber activists heel protests in view', *The Guardian*, 15 April 2011, <http://www.guardian.co.uk/world/2011/apr/15/syria-activists-protests-in-view?INTCMP=SRCH>.

[49] *CPJ Report.*   [50] *RSF Report.*   [51] *RSF Report.*

[52] William Horsley, 'Interview with Frank La Rue UN Special Rapporteur for freedom of opinion and expression', The Initiative on Impunity and the Rule of Law, Centre for Freedom of the Media, 12 February 2011, <http://www.cfom.org.uk/un-special-rapporteur-on-freedom-of-opinion-and-expression/>.

[53] *CPJ Report.*

warring sides involved in the civil war have deliberately targeted journalists'.[54] For example, the death of Japanese photojournalist Mika Yamamoto occurred in what appears to be a deliberate shooting by belligerents during hostilities in the city of Aleppo.[55] Similarly, the deaths of two cameramen, Mahmoud al-Kumi and Hussam Salama, cameramen on 20 November 2012 in Gaza were reportedly caused by a missile strike against them by the Israeli Defense Forces (IDF) while they were in their car marked with the letters 'TV'.[56]

The conflict in Somalia has been characterized by total impunity in relation to the deliberate killing of journalists. All 12 reported deaths of journalists[57] in Somalia in 2012 were attributed to deliberate attacks, none of which has led to a prosecution.[58] al-Shabaab militants have claimed responsibility for at least four of these killings.[59] It is not clear whether these deaths are connected to hostilities directly, although several were reportedly retaliation for coverage of the conflict.[60]

The legal context

Journalists in armed conflict are not lawful targets for attack: direct and deliberate targeting of them is prohibited by both the IHL rule of distinction in the conduct of hostilities, and elsewhere, by the prohibition of murder. Other conduct also prohibited by IHL includes torture, sexual violence, and hostage taking. These types of offence are also increasingly carried out against journalists in armed conflict.

As civilians, the fundamental protection afforded to journalists by IHL is through the operation of the rule of distinction. Accordingly, parties to a conflict must distinguish between civilians not taking a direct part in hostilities, on the one hand, and combatants or civilians taking a direct part in hostilities, on the other. Parties are, inter alia, prohibited from deliberately attacking civilians and the civilian population.[61] Deliberate and direct attacks against journalists not directly participating in hostilities are a violation of IHL in both IAC and NIAC; attacks against civilians constitute a war crime in both types of conflict.[62]

---

[54] *IFJ Report*, p. 28.   [55] See CPJ, <http://cpj.org/killed/2012/mika-yamamoto.php>.

[56] See David Carr, 'Using war as cover to target journalists', *New York Times*, 25 November 2012, <http://www.nytimes.com/2012/11/26/business/media/using-war-as-cover-to-target-journalists.html?_r=0>. See also CPJ, <http://cpj.org/killed/2012/hussam-salama.php>; Human Rights Watch (HRW), 'Israel/Gaza: Unlawful attacks on Palestinian media', 20 December 2012 ('HRW Report on Gaza'), <http://www .hrw.org/news/2012/12/20/israelgaza-unlawful-israeli-attacks-palestinian-media>.

[57] *CPJ Report*. The IFJ reports 18 deaths including 'media workers': *IFJ Report*, p. 9.

[58] No attacks against journalists have been prosecuted in the last decade in Somalia: *CPJ Report*.

[59] *CPJ Report*.   [60] *IFJ Report*, pp. 10–12.

[61] 1977 Additional Protocol I, Arts 48 and 51; 1977 Additional Protocol II, Art. 13; Common Art. 3 to the 1949 Geneva Conventions.

[62] 1998 Rome Statute of the International Criminal Court (ICC Statute), Arts 8(2)(b)(i) (in IAC) and 8(2)(e)(i) (in NIAC).

In addition to prohibiting belligerents from deliberately targeting journalists during hostilities, IHL prohibits 'wilful killing' (including murder and manslaughter) in armed conflict.[63] This prohibition includes the killing of a journalist, for example, putting someone to death as a reprisal,[64] or executing a hostage.[65] The unlawful killing of persons during armed conflict is also a war crime.[66]

OTHER PROHIBITED FORMS OF ATTACK

There is some evidence to suggest that many journalists' deaths in 2012 involved torture.[67] For example, Hisham Moussali, editor of the Syrian General Organization of Radio and TV, is reported to have died while being tortured during detention by Syrian security services.[68] Similarly, prominent editor Murtaza Razvi was found dead after having been tortured by unknown assailants in Pakistan.[69] IHL expressly prohibits torture, regardless of whether it occurs in an IAC or NIAC.[70] This prohibition forms part of customary international law[71] and is also prohibited by core human rights instruments,[72] including the 1984 Convention against Torture (CAT). Torture during an armed conflict is also a war crime.[73]

It is not only deliberate attacks resulting in death that affect journalists in armed conflict. During 2012, sexual violence was reportedly used to intimidate and threaten female journalists into silence.[74] Although few statistics are available on the incidence

---

[63] 1977 Additional Protocol I, Art. 75(2)(a)(i); 1977 Additional Protocol II, Art. 4; Common Art. 3(1)(a); Rules 89–90, ICRC Customary IHL Study.

[64] Reprisals against protected persons are also prohibited by IHL: 1949 Geneva Convention I, Art. 46; 1949 Geneva Convention II, Art. 47; 1949 Geneva Convention III, Art. 13; 1949 Geneva Convention IV, Art. 33.

[65] See Jean Pictet (ed.), *Commentary on the Geneva Conventions of 12 August 1949*, ICRC, 1952–60, Vol. 4 (*ICRC Commentary on Geneva Convention IV*), p. 597.

[66] See 1949 Geneva Convention IV, Art. 147. See ICC Statute, Arts 8(2)(a)(i) (IAC) and 8(2)(c)(i) (NIAC).

[67] See generally *IFJ Report*.   [68] *IFJ Report*, p. 31.

[69] 'Pakistani journalist tortured, killed in Karachi', *CPJ*, 19 April 2012, <http://cpj.org/2012/04/pakistani-journalist-tortured-killed-in-karachi.php>.

[70] 1977 Additional Protocol I, Art. 75; 1977 Additional Protocol II, Art. 4; Common Art. 3; Rule 90, ICRC Customary IHL Study.

[71] It is part of the *jus cogens* of international law: ICTY, *Prosecutor v. Delalic, Mucic, Delic and Lando* (*'Celebici Camp' case*), Judgment (Case No. IT-69-21-T), 16 November 1998. See also Rule 90, ICRC Customary IHL Study; 1984 CAT, adopted on 10 December 1984.

[72] International Covenant on Civil and Political Rights (ICCPR), Art. 7; Convention on the Rights of the Child (CRC), Art. 37(a); European Convention on Human Rights (ECHR), Art. 3; Inter-American Convention on Human Rights (IACHR), Art. 5; African Charter on Human and Peoples' Rights (ACHPR), Art. 5.

[73] See 1998 Rome Statute, Art. 8(2)(a)(ii) (AIC) and 8(2)(c)(i) (IAC).

[74] *IFJ Report*, p. 4.

of sexually based violence against journalists, the IFJ reports, anecdotally, that sexual violence against female journalists greatly increased in 2012, including during armed conflict.[75]

Rape and other forms of sexual violence are strictly prohibited by IHL in all circumstances and must never be committed against journalists. Sexual violence is prohibited by numerous provisions of IHL that apply in both IAC[76] and NIAC;[77] the prohibition forms part of customary international law.[78] Women and children benefit from special protection against sexual and indecent assault,[79] although sexual violence against men and boys in armed conflict is also strictly prohibited. Sexual violence linked to armed conflict, including rape, is a war crime.[80]

Hostage-taking is an increasingly common form of attack against journalists in armed conflict.[81] IHL prohibits the taking of hostages in both IAC and NIAC.[82] This prohibition forms part of customary international law.[83] International law defines hostage-taking as seizing, detaining, or threatening with violence a person (hostage) in order to compel a third party to do or abstain from doing something, as a condition for the release of the hostage.[84] This would include, for example, demands for money or to prevent particular information being published or broadcast. Hostage-taking is a serious threat to the freedom of the press and their ability to report from conflict zones. During 2012, kidnapping and hostage-taking had 'become part of the landscape' of the conflict in Syria.[85] This includes the kidnapping of NBC correspondent Richard Engel[86] and Ukrainian journalist Anhar Kochneva,[87] both of whom survived their ordeal.

---

[75] *IFJ Report*, p. 4.

[76] 1949 Geneva Convention IV, Art. 27(2); 1977 Additional Protocol I, Arts 75(2)(b), 76(1), and 77(1).

[77] Common Art. 3(1); 1977 Additional Protocol I, Art. 4(2)(e).

[78] See further Rule 93, ICRC Customary IHL Study.

[79] Children: 1977 Additional Protocol I, Art. 77; women: 1977 Additional Protocol I, Art. 27. See also Rule 134, ICRC Customary IHL Study.

[80] Art. 8(2)(b)(xxii) and 8(2)(e)(vi), ICC Statute; *ICRC Commentary on the 1977 Additional Protocols*, § 3049.

[81] 'Abduction of journalists becoming increasingly common', *RSF*, 29 January 2013, <http://en.rsf.org/syria-abduction-of-journalists-becoming-29-01-2013,43965.html>.

[82] 1949 Geneva Convention IV, Arts 34 and 147; 1977 Additional Protocol I, Art. 75(2)(c); Common Art. 3; Rule 96, ICRC Customary IHL Study.

[83] Rule 96, ICRC Customary IHL Study.

[84] 1979 International Convention against the Taking of Hostages, adopted on 17 December 1979, Art. 1.

[85] Jon Lee Anderson, 'Richard Engel's return and the risks of reporting in Syria', *The New Yorker*, 18 December 2012, <http://www.newyorker.com/online/blogs/newsdesk/2012/12/richard-engels-return-and-the-risks-of-reporting-in-syria.html>.

[86] Anderson, 'Richard Engel's return and the risks of reporting in Syria'.

[87] See Ellen Barry, 'Ukrainian blogger escapes her Syrian captors', *New York Times*, 11 March 2013, <http://www.nytimes.com/2013/03/12/world/middleeast/anhar-kochneva-ukrainian-blogger-escapes-her-syrian-captors.html>; 'Fears grow for Ukrainian reporter held hostage in Syria', *BBC*, 13 December 2012, <http://www.bbc.co.uk/news/world-europe-20709427>.

LOSS OF PROTECTION

Journalists are protected from direct and deliberate attack 'provided they take no action adversely affecting their status as civilians'.[88] This means that, like all civilians, journalists are protected unless and for such time as they take a direct or active part in hostilities.[89] This rule of IHL forms a central part of the protection afforded by the principle of distinction, and applies in both IAC and NIAC through treaty and customary international law.[90] It is a war crime to attack a civilian who is not taking a direct part in hostilities.[91]

During 2012, a number of journalists were deliberately attacked and killed by belligerents in armed conflict who claimed that these attacks were lawful under IHL (or for grounds that could constitute lawful reasons under IHL). These include the missile attack on two al-Aqsa cameramen in Gaza (cited earlier), reportedly for their affiliation with Hamas, and the purported detention of Anhar Kochneva in Syria on the grounds that she was a spy. These two incidents highlight a number of issues relating to the loss of protection of journalists under IHL that will be considered here.

The legal context

Journalists lose their protection from deliberate attack if they directly participate in hostilities. While the 1949 Geneva Conventions and 1977 Additional Protocols do not define this concept, it is clear that it includes 'acts of war which by their nature or purpose are likely to cause actual harm to the personnel and equipment of the enemy armed forces'.[92] The ICRC's *Interpretive Guidance on the Notion of Direct Participation in Hostilities*[93] further elucidates this concept by providing that, for an act to constitute a direct participation in hostilities, it must meet three cumulative criteria: the threshold of

---

[88] 1977 Additional Protocol I, Art. 79.

[89] Note that 'direct' and 'active', as used throughout the 1949 Geneva Conventions and 1977 Additional Protocols, are considered to have the same meaning: N. Melzer, *Interpretive Guidance on the Notion of Direct Participation in Hostilities under International Humanitarian Law*, ICRC, Geneva, 2009, <http:// www.icrc .org/eng/resources/documents/publication/p0990.htm>, pp. 43–4; ICTR, *Prosecutor v. Jean Paul Akayesu*, Judgment (Trial Chamber) (Case No ICTR-96-4-T), 2 September 1998, p. 629.

[90] 1977 Additional Protocol I, Art. 51(3); 1977 Additional Protocol II, Art. 13(3). This principle was held to be customary international law by Supreme Court of Israel, *Public Committee against Torture in Israel v. Government of Israel*, Judgment, HCJ 769/02, 13 December 2006 ('*Targeted Killings case*'), §30.

[91] ICC Statute, Art. 8(2)(b)(i) (in IAC) and Art. 8(2)(e)(i) (NIAC).

[92] *ICRC Commentary on the 1977 Additional Protocols*, §1944. This was confirmed by the ICTY in *Prosecutor v. Strugar*, Judgment (Appeals Chamber) (Case No. IT-01-42-A), 17 July 2008.

[93] Melzer, *Interpretive Guidance on the Notion of Direct Participation in Hostilities under International Humanitarian Law*.

harm;[94] direct causation;[95] and belligerent nexus.[96] These criteria will be used to assess when a journalist might lose civilian immunity from attack.[97]

The ordinary professional tasks of journalists

Numerous abductions and killings of journalists in conflict zones have been reported in 2012 where the motive for such attacks was retaliation or punishment for coverage of the conflict. An example is the death of Abukar Hassan Mohamoud, who is reported to have been shot for his attempts to relaunch the radio station Somaliweyn in Somalia after it was raided by al-Shabaab in 2010.[98] Similarly, death by gunfire of Farhan Jeemis Abdulle in Somalia was reported to have been the work of al-Shabaab fighters in retaliation for the radio reporter's coverage of the conflict between that group and the Somali government.[99]

The ordinary professional tasks of the media in armed conflict do not constitute direct participation in hostilities. The tasks of journalists, as identified in the commentary on Article 79 of the 1977 Additional Protocol I, include 'doing interviews, taking notes, taking photographs or films, sound recording etc. and transmitting them to his newspaper or agency'.[100] By recognizing journalists as civilians, states are implicitly recognizing the civilian nature of their work.[101]

Similarly, the usual activities of the media do not meet the ICRC Guidance's criteria for direct participation in hostilities: such activities do not usually result in the type of

---

[94] In summary, harm that is of a military nature or inflicts death and serious injury on those protected from attack: Melzer, *Interpretive Guidance on the Notion of Direct Participation in Hostilities under International Humanitarian Law*, p. 46.

[95] In summary, this requires a direct causal link between the act and the harm likely to result: Melzer, *Interpretive Guidance on the Notion of Direct Participation in Hostilities under International Humanitarian Law*, p. 46.

[96] In summary, this requires a connection to hostilities, in particular that the harm caused was in support of a party to the conflict and to the detriment of another: Melzer, *Interpretive Guidance on the Notion of Direct Participation in Hostilities under International Humanitarian Law*, p. 46.

[97] This chapter will not use the more expansive approach to direct participation in hostilities embraced by the United States of America (USA), among others: see further Colonel W. Hays Parks, 'Memorandum of law: Executive Order 12333 and assassination', *The Army Lawyer*, 12 (1989), p. 4. For a more recent discussion of US government policy, see Gabriella Blum and Phillip Heymann, 'Law and policy of targeted killing', *Harvard National Security Journal*, 1 (2010) p. 145. This approach does not contain a strict causation requirement, and includes those acts of significant value to the war effort and 'conduct that functionally corresponds to that of governmental armed forces, including not only the actual conduct of hostilities but also activities such as planning, organising, recruiting and assuming logistical functions': Nils Melzer, *Targeted Killing in International Law*, Oxford University Press, Oxford, 2008, p. 338. Consideration of this approach is beyond the scope of this chapter.

[98] *IFJ Report*, p. 10.   [99] *IFJ Report*, p. 10.

[100] *ICRC Commentary on the 1977 Additional Protocols*, §3264.

[101] Gasser, 'The protection of journalists engaged in dangerous professional missions: law applicable in periods of armed conflict', p. 14. Some states, including the United Kingdom (UK), expressly recognize the civilian nature of such activities: see Ministry of Defence, *Green Book*, Vol. 8, January 2013, p. 4.

harm to a party to a conflict or protected persons necessary to constitute the 'threshold of harm'. Further, even if parties use the information published by the media to assist them in their military operations, the collection and reporting of this information is, at best, indirectly assisting a party and cannot, therefore, meet the 'direct causation' requirement. Similarly, activities such as collecting news and information about a conflict and communicating this to the public are not usually designed to support one party to the detriment of another.[102]

Attacks against journalists for their work in armed conflict are a violation of IHL and may also constitute a war crime.[103]

Accusations of espionage

The situation is, though, not always as straightforward in practice as this analysis suggests. The professional tasks of journalists, including collecting information and communicating it to others, can often appear to be very similar to that of spies. Indeed, journalists are increasingly accused of espionage during armed conflict.[104]

Espionage is defined in IHL as 'gathering or attempting to gather information in territory controlled by an adverse party through an act undertaken on false pretences or deliberately in a clandestine manner' on behalf of another party to the conflict.[105] The act of espionage is not, itself, a violation of IHL,[106] but collection and transmission of military and tactical information to a party to a conflict may be direct participation in hostilities,[107] and any journalist who engages in it risks lawful attack. Significantly, however, the ordinary work of journalist does not involve the transmission of information on behalf of a party to a conflict to another; crucially, journalists collect information (sometimes undercover and in a clandestine manner) with the intention of transmitting such information to the public.

Parties to a conflict are entitled to detain a person on security grounds for suspicion of espionage.[108] However, should a party wish to punish a journalist under domestic laws

---

[102] When they are designed to assist in this way, see the discussion below on participation in the war effort through news reporting and the issue of propaganda.

[103] See discussion above of the issue of direct and deliberate targeting.

[104] 'Summary of the Human Rights Council panel discussion', p. 5.

[105] See Rule 107, ICRC Customary IHL Study; Lieber Code, Art. 88; Brussels Declaration, Art. 19; 1907 Hague Regulations, Art. 29. This definition is now codified in 1977 Additional Protocol I, Art. 46.

[106] See Richard Baxter, 'So-called unprivileged belligerency: spies, guerrillas, and saboteurs', *British Yearbook of International Law*, 28 (1951), p. 323; Knut Ipsen 'Combatant and non-combatants' in Fleck (ed.), *The Handbook of Humanitarian Law in Armed Conflicts*, §§322–5.

[107] The ICRC Guidance lists the following conduct as direct participation in hostilities: identification and marking of targets; and analysis and transmission of tactical information to attacking forces. See Melzer, *Interpretive Guidance on the Notion of Direct Participation in Hostilities under International Humanitarian Law*, p. 55.

[108] See Baxter, 'So-called unprivileged belligerency: spies, guerrillas, and saboteurs'.

for spying in either IAC or NIAC, they must first be subject to criminal proceedings and a fair trial according to international law.[109] Article 5 of 1949 Geneva Convention IV, applicable in IAC, allows the detaining power to also deny a person detained for espionage certain rights that, if exercised, would be prejudicial to the security of the state. In particular, this includes the right to communication and correspondence.[110] It is likely that similar restrictions apply under IHL to those detained for espionage in NIACs.[111] Journalists cannot be lawfully attacked or detained under IHL as spies for undertaking their ordinary professional tasks.

Often, accusations of espionage against journalists are illegitimate and made in bad faith by belligerents. The case of Anhar Kochneva, who was kidnapped and detained in Syria in 2012, highlights this increasingly common phenomenon. Ms Kochneva was detained supposedly on suspicion of engaging in espionage and held against the payment of a ransom. The request for a ransom strongly suggests that the espionage accusations against her were not legitimate and her detention likely amounts to the unlawful act of hostage-taking.

Expressing support for a party to a conflict

In the case of the fatal missile attack against Mahmoud al-Kumi and Hussam Salama in Gaza, the IDF claimed that these journalists were lawful targets because, inter alia,[112] they were cameramen for al-Aqsam which had, on numerous occasions, broadcast news and other material that expressed support of Hamas and their operations.[113] Implicit in this justification is the claim that engaging in broadcasts or publications that support one side to a conflict (i.e. political propaganda) amounts to direct participation in hostilities.

Leaving aside complex questions relating to membership of a non-state armed group (NSAG),[114] such conduct does not meet the ICRC Guidance test for direct participation

---

[109] 1907 Hague Regulations, Art. 30; 1949 Geneva Conventions, Art. 5; 1977 Additional Protocol I, Art. 75(3), which, inter alia, set out the right to be presumed innocent until proven guilty. See also the right to a fair trial: 1907 Hague Regulations, Art. 30; 1949 Geneva Conventions, Art. 5. See also Common Art. 3 and 1977 Additional Protocol II, Arts 4–6.

[110] Art. 5 identifies this in relation to occupation, but it undoubtedly applies in other situations of IAC too. See also *ICRC Commentary on Geneva Convention IV*, p. 56.

[111] The right for detainees to receive letters and cards is subject to limitation if deemed necessary by a competent authority: 1977 Additional Protocol II, Art. 5. It is highly likely that suspicion of espionage qualifies as a legitimate reason to limit the right to correspondence of a detained media professional.

[112] The other issue was that these cameramen were accused by the IDF of being Hamas operatives. However, HRW found no evidence that these accusations could be substantiated: 'HRW Report on Gaza'. Consideration of this ground of DPH is beyond the scope of this chapter.

[113] 'HRW Report on Gaza'.

[114] The ICRC's approach to this question, and issues with it, are discussed in detail in Dapo Akande, 'Clearing the fog of war? The ICRC's *Interpretive Guidance on Direct Participation in Hostilities*', *International Comparative Law Quarterly*, 59(I) (2010), p. 180 at pp. 183–7.

in hostilities (DPH). The ICRC Guidance on DPH distinguishes between the actual conduct of hostilities and other activities that form part of the 'general war effort',[115] including media activities amounting to political propaganda.[116] Mere involvement in broadcasts or publications that express support for a party to a conflict may result in harm that meets the 'threshold of harm' requirement; it may also form an indispensable part of military operations and sustaining a war in general, meeting the 'belligerent nexus' test. Crucially, however, openly and publically expressing support of a party to a conflict is too indirect to amount to 'direct participation in hostilities' and fails to meet the 'direct causation' requirement set out in the ICRC Guidance.[117] IHL does not, therefore, permit the targeting of journalists, including Mahmoud al-Kumi and Hussam Salama, merely for engaging in political propaganda in support of a party to a conflict, no matter how vital such propaganda might be to sustaining a conflict.

This should be compared to radio broadcasts by Radio Rwanda and Radio Mille Collines (RTLM), which took place during the conflict and genocide in Rwanda in 1994, transcripts of which were submitted before the ICTR in the *Media case*.[118] Similarly, the prosecution and conviction of Julius Streicher in the International Military Tribunal (IMT)[119] for the dissemination of anti-semitic propaganda calling for the death of Jewish people in his newspaper, *Der Stürmer*, during the Second World War is also relevant. Although the *Media case* and the *Streicher case* did not address the issue of direct participation in hostilities, they are illustrative of the type of conduct that might expose a journalist to lawful attack for such participation.[120]

The broadcasts set out in transcripts before the ad hoc International Criminal Tribunal for Rwanda (ICTR) included the transmission of specific information about the location of Tutsis (and misinformation to encourage Tutsis to collect in areas where they were said to be safe from attacks) in order to facilitate the Hutu population attacking them as part of the genocide.[121] This specific facilitation and coordination of attacks is much more likely to meet the criteria for direct participation in hostilities than

---

[115] This is defined as 'all activities objectively contributing to the military defeat of an adversary': Melzer, *Interpretive Guidance on the Notion of Direct Participation in Hostilities under International Humanitarian Law*, pp. 51–2.

[116] Melzer, *Interpretive Guidance on the Notion of Direct Participation in Hostilities under International Humanitarian Law*, p. 51. The *Targeted Killings case* takes the same approach to the issue of propaganda: see §§34–7, in particular §35.

[117] See Melzer, *Interpretive Guidance on the Notion of Direct Participation in Hostilities under International Humanitarian Law*, pp. 51–2.

[118] ICTR, *Prosecutor v. Nahimana, Barayagwize and Ngeze*, Judgment (Case No. ICTR 99-52-T), 3 December 2003 (the '*Media case*').

[119] *Streicher Judgment*, in *Trial of German Major War Criminals*, Vol. 22 (1946), p. 501.

[120] However, many of the transcripts relevant to this analysis were not cited in the judgments of the trial or appeal chamber. See analysis of these transcripts in Alison Des Forges, 'Call to genocide: Radio Rwanda, 1994' in Allan Thompson (ed.), *The Media and the Rwanda Genocide*, Pluto Press, London, 2007.

[121] Des Forges, 'Call to genocide: Radio Rwanda, 1994', pp. 47–9.

the transmission of political propaganda alone, as it results in harm to protected persons of the nature envisaged by the 'threshold of harm' requirement,[122] is clearly 'directly causative' of that harm (as it facilitated and coordinated it), and is specifically designed to cause harm to one side of the conflict (in this case, a particular ethnic group), meeting the 'belligerent nexus' requirement.

In contrast, other broadcasts by RTLM in Rwanda and the publications by Streicher before the IMT called for the expulsion and alienation of a particular race (genocide), but they did not involve specific coordination of hostile activities. Such public statements are undoubtedly a crime under international law,[123] but are likely too indirect to meet the 'direct causation' requirement of direct participation in hostilities.

Differentiating between broadcasts and publications that constitute direct participation in hostilities and those that do not is not an easy task. The lack of clarity on this issue makes journalists even more vulnerable to allegedly lawful deliberate and direct attacks.

INCIDENTAL VICTIMS OF HOSTILITIES

According to the CPJ, 36 per cent of journalists killed in 2012 died as the result of 'getting caught in the crossfire of combat'.[124] In other words, they suffered death as an incidental effect of a purportedly legal attack on a military objective. The overwhelming majority of these deaths occurred in Syria (22), followed by Israel and the Occupied Palestinian Territories (OPT) (two), and Lebanon (one).[125] Assessing whether or not a journalist died as the result of an incidental or deliberate attack is not always possible, as there are very few official investigations into the deaths of journalists in armed conflict. Similarly, in Syria, deliberate attacks against journalists have reportedly been disguised as incidental deaths, making assessment almost impossible.[126]

The legal context

Incidental loss of life in armed conflict is regrettable, but not always a violation of IHL, which permits belligerents to attack lawful military objectives during armed conflict in

---

[122] The *Targeted Killings case* also concluded that causing harm to civilians is considered a hostile act: §33.

[123] In the case of RTLM, the broadcasts amounted to 'incitement to genocide', and in the case of Streicher, the publications constituted 'crimes against humanity'. However, if Streicher's publications were prosecuted today, they would also likely amount to 'incitement to genocide' under the ICC Statute.

[124] See CPJ, <http://www.cpj.org/2013/02/attacks-on-the-press-in-2012.php>.

[125] See CPJ, <http://www.cpj.org/killed/2012/in-combat.php>.

[126] See Martin Chulov and Angelique Chrisafis, 'Marie Colvin's killing piles pressure on Assad as civilian death toll grows', *The Guardian*, 21 February 2012, <http://www.guardian.co.uk/world/2012/feb/22/marie-colvin-killing-pressure-assad>.

accordance with the rule of proportionality.[127] Proportionality requires belligerents to make a calculation as to whether the expected loss of civilian life or injury to civilians from such attacks outweighs the concrete and direct military advantage anticipated from the attack.[128] Attacks where the expected loss of civilian life is greater than the military advantage of an attack are disproportionate and therefore illegal. If it becomes clear during the course of an attack that it can no longer be considered proportionate, the attack must be stopped or postponed.[129] Knowingly engaging in disproportionate attacks is a war crime.[130]

Belligerents may attempt to exploit the principle of proportionality by placing a military target (such as a sniper or weapon) in a civilian area, for example on the roof of a hotel where media professionals might be staying. This is done with the hope that the opposing side will not attack the target because to do so would result in a disproportionate number of civilian casualties. This practice is called using 'human shields' and it is strictly prohibited by IHL.[131]

Indiscriminate attacks

IHL prohibits means and methods of warfare that are indiscriminate.[132] This means parties may not launch attacks or use weapons that do not or cannot differentiate between the civilian population and civilian objects and lawful military targets. For example, it is prohibited to fire blindly without verifying a target. Engaging in indiscriminate attacks is a war crime.[133]

Some rules of IHL are designed to minimize indiscriminate attacks and also the opportunities for disguised unlawful attacks. In particular, IHL places obligations on parties launching an attack to verify the lawful nature of the target and to take steps to minimize civilian casualties.

[127] See 1977 Additional Protocol I, Arts 51(5)(b) and 57(2)(a)(iii). This forms part of customary international law: see Rule 14, ICRC Customary IHL Study.

[128] 1977 Additional Protocol I, Art. 57(2)(a)(iii).

[129] 1977 Additional Protocol I, Art. 57(2)(b).

[130] ICC Statute, Art. 8(2)(b)(iv). Although the ICC Statute only lists this crime in relation to IAC, the principle of proportionality (that this crime embodies) is so fundamental to IHL that it also forms part of customary international criminal law (ICL) applicable to NIAC. See discussion in R. Cryer et al., *An Introduction to International Criminal Law and Procedure*, 2nd edn, Cambridge University Press, Cambridge, 2010, p. 298.

[131] 1949 Geneva Convention IV, Art. 28; 1977 Additional Protocol I, Art. 51(7); Rule 97, ICRC Customary IHL Study.

[132] 1977 Additional Protocol I, Art. 51(4). This also forms part of customary international law: Rule 11, ICRC Customary IHL Study. In relation to use of indiscriminate weapons, see International Court of Justice (ICJ), *Nuclear Weapons Advisory Opinion*, 1986.

[133] Although not listed in the ICC Statute, this offence is the same as that of 'attacking a civilian' outlined above. See ICJ, *Nuclear Weapons Advisory Opinion, 1996*; ICTY, *Galić case*, Judgment and Opinion (Case No. IT-98-29-T), 5 December 2003, §57. See also Rule 156, ICRC Customary IHL Study.

Parties must exercise constant care to spare civilians during an attack[134] and they are obliged to verify that the intended objects of the attack are not civilian.[135] An attack must be cancelled or suspended if it becomes clear that the attack is indiscriminate.[136] Parties are also obliged to issue an advance warning of attacks that may affect the civilian population where circumstances permit.[137]

It is not clear from the statistics how many of the deaths of journalists recorded in 2012 resulted from indiscriminate or disproportionate attacks by belligerents.

Media objects

Journalists may be more likely to suffer incidental damage from attacks when belligerents target media objects such as media centres, broadcasters, and newspaper offices. A number of deaths of journalists resulted from such attacks in 2012. This includes the death of seven journalists and media technicians in Syria when the pro-government al-Ikhbariya TV station was bombed. The al-Nusra Front claimed responsibility.[138]

Commercial media objects are typically civilian in nature (where they are not part of a military base or military communication equipment). However, parties to a conflict may target media objects when they constitute a lawful military objective under IHL. Military objectives are those objects that, by their nature, location, purpose or use, make an effective contribution to military action, and whose total or partial destruction, capture, or neutralization, in the circumstances ruling at the time, offers a concrete and direct military advantage.[139] This definition of military objective is customary international law,[140] binding on all parties to both IACs and NIACs.

Commercial media outlets used, for example, to broadcast military communications, either permanently or intermittently are therefore potential military objectives under IHL. It is also possible that civilian broadcast facilities that are used to coordinate and facilitate specific attacks on protected civilians—as, for example, were those of Radio Rwanda and RTLM during the Rwandan conflict in 1994[141]—might constitute

---

[134] 1977 Additional Protocol I, Art. 57(1); Rule 19, ICRC Customary IHL Study.

[135] 1977 Additional Protocol I, Art. 57(2)(a)(i); Rule 16, ICRC Customary IHL Study.

[136] 1977 Additional Protocol I, Art. 57(2)(b); Rule 19, ICRC Customary IHL Study.

[137] 1977 Additional Protocol I, Art. 57(2)(c); Rule 20, ICRC Customary IHL Study.

[138] *IFJ Report*, p. 30.

[139] 1977 Additional Protocol I, Art. 52(2); Rule 8, ICRC Customary IHL Study.

[140] Eritrea–Ethiopia Claims Commission, *Partial Award on Western Front, Aerial Bombardment and Related Claims*, 19 December 2005, §113; Rule 8, ICRC Customary IHL Study.

[141] See transcripts of broadcasts by Radio Rwanda and RTLM as submitted before the ICTR in the *Media case* (but not all were relied on in the judgment), as analysed in Des Forges, 'Call to genocide: Radio Rwanda, 1994'. Many of these broadcasts involved specific coordination of attacks against the Tutsi (as opposed to race hate and incitement to genocide generally). The *Media case* assessed individual criminal responsibility for genocide and related offences, and did not consider the potential lawfulness of any direct targeting of media facilities or media staff under IHL.

legitimate military targets. However, in its report to the Prosecutor of the ICTY, the Committee Established to Review the NATO Bombing Campaign against the Federal Republic of Yugoslavia considered that the transmission of propaganda alone was an insufficient justification for the bombing of RTS, a Serbian radio and television station in Belgrade in 1999.[142] This strongly suggests that the transmission or broadcast of propaganda or other statements in support of a party to a conflict (or critical of another) by a civilian broadcasting facility (or other media object) does not render it a legitimate military objective: without more, any attack against such a facility is a violation of IHL.

B. The legal protection of journalists under international human rights law

The statistics of 2012 highlight the vulnerability of journalists to often fatal attacks during armed conflict. Journalists in conflict zones are entitled to protection from physical attacks under international human rights law (IHRL), in addition to their protection under IHL.[143] However, unlike the rules of IHL, human rights law recognizes both the physical protection of journalists under various rights including the right to life, as well as protection of the professional activities of journalists through the right to freedom of opinion and expression.

Killing a journalist is the most severe form of censorship[144] and has far-reaching consequences, not only for individual victims of attack, but also on the freedom of the press in general. Particular human rights protect the person of journalists from unlawful and arbitrary violence. These include the right to life and the prohibition on torture and other forms of ill-treatment, among other rights. However, not all human rights law bodies have recognized the relationship between the physical protection of journalists and freedom of expression, preferring to address the two issues as unconnected.

---

[142] *Final Report to the Prosecutor by the Committee Established to Review the NATO Bombing Campaign against the Federal Republic of Yugoslavia*, 2000, §§75–6.

[143] IHRL applies concurrently with IHL to situations of IAC and NIAC: *Nuclear Weapons Advisory Opinion*, §25; *Legal Consequences of the Construction of a Wall in the Occupied Palestinian Territory*, Advisory Opinion, 2004; *Armed Activities on the Territory of the Congo (Democratic Republic of the Congo v. Uganda)*, Judgment, 19 December 2005. See also UN General Assembly Resolution 2675 (XXV) on 'Basic principles for the protection of civilian populations in armed conflict', 9 December 1970; Human Rights Committee, General Comment No. 31, 'The nature of the general legal obligations imposed on state parties to the Covenant', UN doc. CCPR/C/21/Rev.1/Add.13, 26 May 2004.

[144] 'Report of the Special Rapporteur on extrajudicial, summary or arbitrary executions, Christof Heyns', Human Rights Council, UN doc. A/HRC/20/22, 10 April 2012, §21.

THE RIGHT TO LIFE OF JOURNALISTS

Journalists are entitled to protection from arbitrary deprivation of life under human rights law. This right is generally non-derogable and applies at all times, including during armed conflict. In situations of armed conflict, what constitutes an 'arbitrary' deprivation of life may require consideration of the rules of IHL in accordance with the *lex specialis* principle of interpretation.[145]

Attacks on journalists by state forces

The deliberate targeting of journalists by state forces, including during armed conflict, can constitute a violation of the right to life if the use of such force was arbitrary. For example, the Inter-American Court of Human Rights (IACtHR) in *Bustíos Saaverda v. Peru*[146] found that, inter alia, the extrajudicial killing of newspaper journalist Hugo Bustíos Saavedra by Peruvian armed forces during the NIAC occurring at that time was a violation of his right to life.[147] Mr Saaverda published numerous articles critical of human rights violations committed by Peruvian armed forces during that conflict.

The European Court of Human Rights (ECtHR) reached a similar conclusion in the case *Trévalec v. Belgium*.[148] In that case, Yves Trévalec, an unarmed cameraman, embedded within an anti-gang police unit with prior state permission, was shot seven times at close range by Belgian police. The Court found that the shooting of Mr Trévalec, who survived, constituted a violation of his right to life under Article 2 of the 1950 European Convention on Human Rights (ECHR) resulting from the carelessness of the police in ensuring the protection of Mr Trévalec.[149]

Attacks on journalists by non-state actors

Positive obligation on states to protect journalists from attacks by non-state actors. In addition to requiring states to refrain from conduct in violation of the right to life, human rights law also imposes a positive obligation on states to protect the right to life against the conduct of others, including non-state actors.[150] This comprises the

---

[145] See *Nuclear Weapons Advisory Opinion*, §25. For a further discussion of the right to life in armed conflict, see Louise Doswald-Beck, *Human Rights in Times of Conflict and Terrorism*, Oxford University Press, Oxford, 2011, pp. 188–93.

[146] IACtHR, *Bustios-Saavedra v. Peru*, Judgment, 5 June 1990.

[147] IACtHR, *Bustios-Saavedra v. Peru*, Judgment, 5 June 1990, §77.

[148] ECtHR, *Trévalec v. Belgium*, Judgment (App. No. 30812/07), 28 November 2011.

[149] ECtHR, *Trévalec v. Belgium*, Judgment, 28 November 2011, §§86–7.

[150] See Human Rights Committee, General Comment No. 31, 'The nature of the general legal obligations imposed on state parties to the Covenant', UN doc. CCPR/C/21/Rev.1/Add.13, 26 May 2004; see also General Comment no. 6 (Right to Life), 30 April 1982.

obligation to implement legal measures (such as national criminal legislation) and to take protective measures in cases in which they know, or ought to know, that there is a real and immediate risk to the life of an individual from criminal acts.[151] The failure of state authorities to respond to complaints about threats, intimidation, or harassment of a journalist by non-state actors, including during armed conflict, can constitute a violation of the right to life.

In the case of *Kiliç v. Turkey*, the ECtHR found that Turkish authorities knew of real and immediate threats to the life of Kemal Kiliç, a journalist working for *Özgür Gündem*, a Kurdish separatist newspaper that had been subject to a campaign of violence and harassment by non-state actors.[152] Mr Kiliç was shot and killed after he had informed Turkish authorities of threats against his life. Turkey argued that Mr Kiliç was in no more danger than any other person located in the territory of the NIAC occurring at the time;[153] however, the Court found that the failure of Turkey to take protective measures in this case, even during a conflict, constituted a violation of Mr Kiliç's right to life.

Similarly, in the case of *Dink v. Turkey*,[154] the ECtHR found that Turkey had a positive obligation to protect Mr Firat Dink, a journalist who published articles critical of Turkey's failure to recognize the suffering of Armenians, from attacks by non-state extremist groups that led to his death. The ECtHR reached a similar finding in the case of *Gongadze v. Ukraine*, in which a political journalist requested assistance and protection from the state prosecutor in relation to threats to his life by unknown assailants. The prosecutor refused to provide such measures and Mr Gongadze disappeared shortly afterwards. His body was discovered several weeks later. The Court found that the refusal to assist was negligent and that Ukraine had violated its positive obligations to protect the right to life.[155] The Court also held that authorities should have been aware of the vulnerability of journalists who covered political topics in the region.[156]

Positive obligation on states to investigate attacks against journalists. The right to life also creates a positive duty on states to establish procedures and facilities for undertaking

---

[151] See ECtHR, *Kiliç v. Turkey*, Judgment (App. No. 22492/93), 28 March 2000; ECtHR, *Gongadze v. Ukraine*, Judgment, 8 November 2005; IACtHR, *Velásquez v. Rodriguez v. Honduras*, Judgment, 29 July 1988; *Riofrio massacre v. Colombia* (Inter-American Commission on Human Rights (IACommHR) Report No. 62/01, Case 11.654), 6 April 2001; African Commission on Human and Peoples' Rights (ACommHPR), *Commission Nationale des Droits de l'Homme et des Libertés v. Chad*, Decision (ACommHPR 74/92), 11 October 1995.

[152] For further details of the harassment, including the death of seven people, see ECtHR, *Özgür Gündem v. Turkey*, Judgment (App. No. 23144/93), 16 March 2000.

[153] ECtHR, *Kiliç v. Turkey*, Judgment, 28 March 2000, §66.

[154] ECtHR, *Dink v. Turkey*, Judgment (App. Nos 2668/07, 6102/08, 30079/08, 7072/09, 7124/09), 14 September 2010.

[155] ECtHR, *Gongadze v. Ukraine*, Judgment, 8 November 2005, §§167–71.

[156] ECtHR, *Gongadze v. Ukraine*, Judgment, 8 November 2005, §168.

investigations of criminal acts that may constitute a separate violation of the right to life, including during conflict situations.[157] This positive duty of investigation under the right to life is of particular relevance to journalists, as attacks against them are often subject to impunity.

The failure to adequately investigate a death of a journalist caused by the actions of state or non-state actors is a violation of this positive duty arising out of the right to life. In two cases resulting from the campaign of harassment and violence against the Kurdish separatist newspaper *Özgür Gündem* in Turkey, the ECtHR found that Turkey had violated its positive obligations arising from the right to life by failing to adequately investigate the deaths of two members of the media. In *Yasa v. Turkey*,[158] a distributor of *Özgür Gündem* was assassinated. Turkey failed adequately to investigate the cause and perpetrators of this crime, arguing that the surrounding conflict and terrorist activity made such investigations challenging. The Court held that the difficulty in undertaking investigations in such circumstances did not relieve Turkey of its obligations under Article 2, ECHR.[159] In *Tepe v. Turkey*[160] the ECtHR found that Turkey's investigation into the assassination of a reporter employed by *Özgür Gündem* contained 'striking omissions'[161] and failed to meet the requirements for such an investigation set by human rights law. Consequently, Turkey had violated the right to life under Article 2, ECHR.[162]

THE FREEDOM OF EXPRESSION OF JOURNALISTS

It is clear that physical attacks against journalists constitute more than a violation of the individual journalist's right to life: they are censorship attacks designed to silence specific journalists and the media more generally. The vulnerability of journalists to attacks during the conflicts of 2012, and the concerns raised in relation to the exclusion of international journalists from the conflict in Syria, highlights the devastating effect that physical attacks and threats to journalists can have on the ability of the wider public to exercise the right to freedom of expression.

---

[157] See Human Rights Committee, General Comment No. 6 (Right to Life), 30 April 1982. See also e.g. Human Rights Committee, *Hernandez v. Philippines*, Decision (Comm. 1559/2007), 26 July 2010; ACommHPR, *Amnesty International and ors v. Sudan*, Decision (Comms. 48/90, 50/91, 52/91, 89/93), 15 November 1999; ECtHR, *Isayeva, Yusopova and Bazayeva v. Russia*, Judgment, 24 February 2005; IACtHR, *Myrna Mack Chang v. Guatemala*, Judgment, 25 November 2003.

[158] ECtHR, *Yasa v. Turkey*, Judgment (App. No. 22495/93), 2 September 1998.

[159] ECtHR, *Yasa v. Turkey*, Judgment, 2 September 1998, §104.

[160] ECtHR, *Tepe v. Turkey*, Judgment (App. No. 27244/95), 9 May 2003.

[161] ECtHR, *Tepe v. Turkey*, Judgment, 9 May 2003, §178.

[162] ECtHR, *Tepe v. Turkey*, Judgment, 9 May 2003, §182.

The right to freedom of expression is found in each of the major international and regional human rights treaties.[163] It includes the right to both receive and impart information. The right to freedom of expression is a collective right, held both by individuals and by society in general. Human rights bodies frequently consider restrictive measures taken by states against the media and journalists as acts affecting freedom of expression. For example, seizure of a journalist's work or material,[164] closure of a newspaper or broadcaster or prohibition on publications that are critical of a government,[165] and the searching of journalists' homes[166] have all been considered to be violations of this right.

However, not all interferences with this right are prohibited: restrictions of freedom of expression are permissible under the conditions listed in Article 19(3) of the ICCPR,[167] which include where it is necessary (and in accordance with the law) in cases of respect for the rights of others and for the protection of national security or public order and morals. Restrictions on grounds of national security include grounds relating to defence. However, this limitation does not allow a state to restrict a publication or broadcast that is part of a public discourse on human rights or to suppress information that the military finds embarrassing, but which otherwise does not endanger national security.[168] Further lawful restrictions are set out in Article 20 of the ICCPR, including the prohibition of speech that constitutes propaganda for war or advocacy of national, racial, or religious hatred that constitutes incitement to discrimination, hostility, or violence. The limitation on 'propaganda for war' is distinct from the IHL consideration of whether propaganda (for war or otherwise) might constitute direct participation in hostilities or expose a media object to lawful attack.

---

[163] See Art. 19, ICCPR; Art. 9, ACHPR; Art. 13, ACHR; Art. 10, ECHR; Art. 32, Arab Charter. States are permitted under the ICCPR, ECHR, ACHR, and the Arab Charter to derogate from this right in times of emergency, which can include armed conflict.

[164] See IACommHR, *Alejandra Marcela Matus Acuña and ors v. Chile*, Decision (No. 12.142), 2 October 2000; ACommHPR, *Zimbabwe Lawyers for Human Rights & Associated Newspapers of Zimbabwe/Zimbabwe* (Case No. 284/03), 3 April 2009; ECtHR, *Özgür Gündem v. Turkey*, Judgment, 16 March 2000.

[165] See e.g. ACommHPR, *Constitutional Rights Project, Civil Liberties Organisation and Media Rights Agenda v. Nigeria*, Decision (App. Nos 140/94. 141/94 and 145/95), 5 November 1999; ECtHR, *Ürper and ors v. Turkey*, Judgment, 20 October 2009.

[166] See ECtHR, *Roemen and Schmit v. Luxembourg*, Judgment (App. No. 51772/99), 25 February 2003; *Ernst and ors v. Belgium*, Judgment (App. No. 33400/96), 15 July 2003.

[167] This is similar in content to restrictions permitted under Art. 13, ACHR. The ECHR sets out in Art. 10 a list of grounds for possible limitations. Art. 32 of the Arab Charter also contains prohibitions on propaganda for war and hate speech that incites violence. Art. 9 of the ACHPR specifies only that the right to freedom of speech and expression must be exercised 'within the law', which has been interpreted by the African Commission as referring to 'international law': see *Article 19 v. Eritrea* (AComHR 275/2003), 30 May 2007, §104.

[168] See e.g. IACtHR, *Usón Ramírez v. Venezuela*, Judgment, 20 November 2009, §88–90.

Physical attacks against journalists by state forces

It is not only restrictive measures taken against the press that constitute a violation of the right to freedom of expression. International human rights bodies have recognized, to varying degrees, that the inextricable relationship between the media and the right to freedom of expression means that physical attacks against journalists are 'an assault on the foundations of the human rights project ... [and constitute] not only an attack on one particular victim, but on all members of the society'.[169] The Human Rights Committee and IACtHR's jurisprudence on freedom of expression strongly emphasizes the relationship between the physical safety of journalists and a free press. In contrast, however, the ECtHR has failed to take advantage of the opportunity to adopt a similar approach in cases before it[170] relating both to attacks on journalists by state forces and to attacks by non-state actors (discussed in further detail below).

The Human Rights Committee and the IACtHR both recognize the freedom of expression implications of physical attacks against journalists by states, including during armed conflict. In *Njaru v. Cameroon*,[171] the Human Rights Committee concluded that harassment, persecution, and serious physical attacks against Mr Njaru, a journalist and human rights advocate, perpetrated by state agents, constituted, among other violations, a breach of Article 19 of the ICCPR. In finding that the attacks constituted an illegitimate restriction on Mr Njaru's right to freedom of expression, the Committee emphasizes the relationship between the violence and his work as a journalist.[172]

The IACtHR also recognizes the fact that state-sponsored violence against journalists is an illegitimate restriction on an individual journalist's freedom of expression, and further that the chilling effect of such attacks on the media more generally constitutes a violation of the collective right of society to receive information through the press.[173] In its 2012 decision, *Luis Gonzalo 'Richard' Vélez Restrepo and Family v. Colombia*,[174] the Court considered non-fatal attacks by Colombian soldiers against a Colombian journalist filming at a demonstration. The Court found that the soldiers attacked Mr Restrepo in an attempt to obtain his cassette tape footage of the demonstrations. These attacks were

---

[169] 'Report of the Special Rapporteur on extrajudicial, summary or arbitrary executions, Christof Heyns', UN doc. A/HRC/20/22, 10 April 2012, §24. Similarly, the mandate of the UN Special Rapporteur on the promotion and protection of the right to freedom of opinion and expression includes maintenance and collection of information about physical attacks on journalists: see Human Rights Council Resolution 7/36, 'Mandate of the Special Rapporteur on the promotion and protection of the right to freedom of opinion and expression', 28 March 2008.

[170] Carmen Draghici and Lorna Woods, 'Individual torts and collective victims: the societal impact of crimes against journalists in international law', Paper given at the conference on *Obstacles to Free Speech and the Safety of Journalists*, City University London, 3 May 2013.

[171] Human Rights Committee, *Njaru v. Cameroon*, Decision (Comm. No. 1353/200), 3 April 2007.

[172] Human Rights Committee, *Njaru v. Cameroon*, Decision, 3 April 2007, §6.4.

[173] IACtHR, *Bustios-Saavedra v. Peru*, Judgment, 5 June 1990, §77.

[174] IACtHR, *Restrepo v. Colombia*, Judgement, 3 September 2012.

intended to silence Mr Restrepo, and consequently violated both his individual right and had an 'intimidating effect' on other journalists, which also violated the collective right of society to exercise its right to freedom of expression.[175]

In contrast, the ECtHR case of *Tekin v. Turkey*[176] considered the argument that the torture and detention of a journalist working for the *Özgür Gündem* newspaper by state forces constituted a violation of both Article 3 of the ECHR (the prohibition of torture and inhuman or degrading treatment or punishment) and Article 10 (the right to freedom of expression). Despite the references to Mr Tekin's employment at the paper during the torture, the Court found insufficient evidence to link it to his employment. It was, therefore, unnecessary for the Court to address the issue of an Article 10 violation.

Physical attacks on journalists by non-state actors

States also have positive obligations arising from the right to freedom of expression to promote and protect the physical safety and work of journalists.[177] This means that they ought to enact procedures and laws that prohibit criminal activity intended to silence the media, and also to take measures to investigate and punish such violations. A failure to do so may amount to a separate and further violation of the right to freedom of expression.[178] The ECtHR has emphasized the obligation of states to create an environment that is conducive to participation in public debate (including by the media) without fear of reprisals.[179] Further, the IACtHR has held that 'journalism can only be exercised freely when those who carry out this work are not victims of threats or physical, mental or moral attacks or other acts of harassment'.[180] The Court has found that there is a special obligation on states to protect journalists who are at risk, in particular during armed conflict.[181]

Despite similar recognition of these positive obligations, there is a contrast between the jurisprudence of the IACtHR and the ECtHR regarding the extent to which physical attacks against individual journalists are considered to violate the right to freedom of

---

[175] IACtHR, *Restrepo v. Colombia*, Judgement, 4 September 2012, §§137–46.

[176] ECtHR, *Tekin v. Turkey*, Judgment (App. No. 22496/93), 9 June 1998.

[177] General Comment No. 34; Human Rights Council Resolution 12/16, 'Freedom of opinion and expression', 12 October 2009; ECtHR, *Özgür Gündem v. Turkey*, Judgment, 16 March 2000; ECtHR, *Appleby and ors v. United Kingdom*, Judgment (App. No. 44306/98), 6 May 2003, §§42–3 and 47–9; IACtHR, *Perozo and ors v. Venezuela*, Judgment, 28 January 2009; IACtHR, *Restrepo v. Colombia*, Judgement, 4 September 2012.

[178] General Comment No. 34, §23. See also discussion of case law below.

[179] ECtHR, *Dink v. Turkey*, Judgment, 14 September 2010, §137.

[180] IACtHR, *Restrepo v. Colombia*, §209; IACommHR, Office of the Special Rapporteur for freedom of expression, 'Impunity, self-censorship and armed internal conflict: an analysis of the state of freedom of expression in Colombia', OEA/Ser.L/V/II Doc. 51 of 31 August 2005, §102.

[181] IACtHR, *Restrepo v. Colombia*, §§186–205; IACtHR, *Bustios-Saavedra v. Peru*, Judgment, 5 June 1990, §75.

expression.[182] The IACtHR expressly recognizes the chilling effect on the media more generally of the failure of a state to investigate individual attacks and that impunity is a separate violation of the right to freedom of expression. The ECtHR, however, in situations in which there is not a campaign of harassment of violence (i.e. cases of attacks against individual journalists), has demonstrated reluctance to address broader freedom of expression issues, preferring to consider the issue as a discrete right to life violation.

The IACtHR held in both *Perozo v. Venezuela*[183] and *Restrepo v. Colombia* that the failure of the state to prevent harassment of journalists and to investigate and prosecute attacks on them constituted a violation of freedom of expression. In *Restrepo*, the Court found that, by failing in its positive duties, the state was effectively silencing journalists and violating Mr Restrepo's individual right. The Court also found that Colombia's failure to protect and investigate was tantamount to permitting impunity for attacks against journalists, which encouraged self-censorship among the media in Colombia and violated the social dimension of freedom of expression.[184]

The case of *Özgür Gündem v. Turkey* involved a campaign of violence and harassment against members of the media associated with the Kurdish newspaper and damage to the paper's offices. In the context of such extreme and targeted violence, the ECtHR held that, inter alia,[185] the failure of Turkey to take action after requests for assistance by the paper's employees and the failure to investigate the harassment amounted to a violation of freedom of expression under Article 10 of the ECHR. The fact that the newspaper was affiliated with the Kurdish Worker's Party (PKK), classified by Turkey as a terrorist group, was not considered by the Court justification for Turkey's inaction in response to unlawful violence in this case.[186] Similarly, in *Dink v. Turkey*, the ECtHR concluded that an illegitimate criminal prosecution of a journalist by the state was in itself, or in conjunction with Turkey's failure to protect a journalist from a lethal attack by a non-state actor, a violation of both his right to life and freedom of expression.[187] The Court did not clarify whether the attack alone would have constituted a violation of freedom of expression.

This is to be compared to the ECtHR's jurisprudence addressing cases of violence that constitutes only physical attacks against individual journalists, and does not involve other forms of harassment or a 'campaign of violence'. In several cases before the Court

---

[182] Draghici and Woods, 'Individual torts and collective victims: the societal impact of crimes against journalists in international law'.

[183] IACtHR, *Perozo and ors v. Venezuela*, Judgment, 28 January 2009.

[184] IACtHR, *Restrepo v. Colombia*, Judgement, 4 September 2012, §§206–12.

[185] The case also involved harassment in the form of illegitimate criminal prosecutions of journalists and searches of the paper's offices by state authorities, for which Turkey was also held to have violated Art. 10 directly: ECtHR, *Özgür Gündem v. Turkey*, Judgment, 16 March 2000, §46.

[186] ECtHR, *Özgür Gündem v. Turkey*, Judgment, 16 March 2000, §45.

[187] The judgment is not available in English. The relevant French text, at §108, states that the prosecution 'prise isolément ou combinée avec l'absence de mesures protégeant celui-ci contre l'attaque'.

involving attacks by non-state actors on journalists, the applicants had sought to argue that such attacks constituted violations of, among other rights, their right to freedom of expression. However, in each case, the Court addressed the issue of physical violence under another right, such as the right to life, and considered it unnecessary to address the Article 10 freedom of expression violation.[188] In *Kelic v. Turkey*,[189] the applicant argued that his brother, a journalist, was killed as a result of his work and, that therefore, the killing was of a dual character and ought to give rise to both right to life and freedom of expression violations. The Court, however, did not consider it necessary to address the application of Article 10, as any violation of it arose from the same set of facts.[190]

Concluding remarks

Assessing the specific vulnerability of journalist in armed conflict is difficult: descriptions of the circumstances of attacks are often vague, despite the tireless work of international media organizations such as the CPJ, INSI, IFJ, and RSF. The lack of clarity about exactly how and why journalists are vulnerable exists for the same reason that the overall death toll of journalists is so high: impunity.

There are very few official investigations (criminal or otherwise) into the deaths of journalists and impunity for targeting them is rife.[191] Reports of prosecutions and convictions for attacks against journalists, in armed conflict or otherwise, are few. An exception in 2012 was the prosecution in Pakistan relating to the kidnapping and subsequent murder of Daniel Pearlman in 2002. This represents a step forward for Pakistan, which in 2010 and 2011 was the deadliest place for journalists and suffered from what was said by one media organization to be 'near-perfect impunity'.[192] In 2013, the CPJ released its 'Impunity Index',[193] which Iraq topped, followed by Somalia. States identified in this *War Report* as being involved in an armed conflict in 2012 represented five of the top 12 states on the Impunity Index.[194]

---

[188] See ECtHR, *Yasa v. Turkey*, Judgment, 2 September 1998, §§118 and 119; ECtHR, *Kelic v. Turkey*, Judgment (App. No. 22492/93), 28 March 2000, §87; ECtHR, *Tepe v. Turkey*, Judgment, 9 May 2003, §191.

[189] ECtHR, *Kelic v. Turkey*, Judgment, 28 March 2000.

[190] ECtHR, *Kelic v. Turkey*, Judgment, 28 March 2000, §87.

[191] See further UNESCO, 'Director-General's report on impunity'. See also Carmen Draghici and Lorna Woods, 'The initiative on impunity and the rule of law: legal instruments study', Centre for Freedom of the Media, 2011, <http://www.cfom.org.uk/impunity/research/>.

[192] See *CPJ Report*; also <http://cpj.org/blog/2011/11/a-call-to-continue-the-struggle-against-impunity.php>.

[193] This index includes figures for 2012. See CPJ, 'Getting away with murder: CPJ's 2013 Impunity Index', 2013, <http://www.cpj.org/reports/2013/05/impunity-index-getting-away-with-murder.php>.

[194] Somalia, the Philippines, Colombia, Afghanistan, and Mexico.

The alarming death toll for journalists in conflict during 2012 is, unfortunately, neither a recent nor isolated phenomenon. Rather, it is the culmination of a steady increase in attacks against journalists over the last several years. The conflict in Iraq still remains the single deadliest conflict for journalists in history[195] despite having relatively few recorded journalist deaths in 2012.[196] The issue of vulnerability of journalists in conflict, and impunity for their deaths, needs urgent international attention. Initiatives such as the 2012 UN Plan of Action are just the start of what will hopefully be a coordinated and dedicated international response to this problem.

[195] Dahr Jamail, 'Iraq, the deadliest war for journalist', *Al Jazeera*, 11 April 2013, <http://www.aljazeera .com/humanrights/2013/04/2013481202781452.html>.

[196] Compared to Syria and Somalia. For Iraq, the CPJ reports three (motive unconfirmed) deaths for 2012, compared with five in 2011 and 2010; the IFI reports four deaths in 2012, compared with nine in 2011 and six in 2010; the IFJ reports four deaths in 2012, compared with 11 in 2011 and six in 2010.

8 A legal 'black hole'? A decade of detention at Guantánamo, 2002–12

Silvia Suteu*

Introduction

Ever since Lord Steyn called Guantánamo a legal 'black hole' in a speech at the British Institute of International and Comparative Law in London in 2003,[1] the phrase has become ubiquitous in writings about the legal regime governing detentions in the military centre. Lord Steyn had warned against of the dangers of democracies misusing counterterrorism measures, including 'executive' detention—that is, detention without criminal charge or trial.[2]

When it came to Guantánamo, however, his counsel of restraint went unheeded. Following the 11 September 2001 attacks, the United States of America (USA) launched what it termed a 'global war on terror' and, on 7 October 2001, invaded Afghanistan in pursuit of al-Qaeda members and the Taliban regime, which it said was harbouring them. A total of almost 800 detainees from some 40 states are said to have been incarcerated at the naval base since then.[3] Some were captured on the battlefield, others not; some were members of al-Qaeda or the Taliban, others not; and finally, most were foreign nationals but some were US citizens. All of these aspects—the nature of the conflict, the applicable law, the status of the detainees, and the protections to which they were legally entitled—

---

* Silvia Suteu is a doctoral research student in law at the University of Edinburgh, UK. She holds a Master's degree in international law from the Graduate Institute of International and Development Studies in Geneva, having previously studied at the Central European University in Budapest, Hungary, and at Harvard University in Cambridge, MA, USA. She has been a researcher for the Rule of Law in Armed Conflicts Project since July 2009. Previously, she worked at the Program on Humanitarian Policy and Conflict Research (HPCR) and the Radcliffe Institute for Advanced Study, both at Harvard University.

[1] Lord Johan Steyn, 'Guantánamo Bay: the legal black hole', Twenty-Seventh F.A. Mann Lecture, organized by the British Institute of International and Comparative Law and Herbert Smith, Lincoln's Inn Old Hall, 25 November 2003, reproduced in the *International and Comparative Law Quarterly*, 53 (January 2004), pp. 1–15.

[2] Lord Steyn, 'Guantánamo Bay: the legal black hole', p. 1.

[3] Amnesty International, 'Guantánamo: 11 years in numbers', 8 January 2013.

raised complex legal issues. Indeed, it seemed that the legal complexities surrounding Guantánamo were being exploited with a view to placing suspected terrorists 'outside the realm of the law'.[4] A review and critical appraisal of the US response to these difficult questions in the decade of detention at Guantánamo are the object of this chapter.

I first unpack the legal problems posed by Guantánamo, beginning with the arrival of the first detainees in the 'war on terror' in January 2002. This necessitates an assessment of the nature of the conflicts and the bodies of law (domestic and international) applicable to them. I then explore the related issue of the status of the detainees and the rights to which they were (and are) entitled, according to their status.[5] I present the US arguments as they were put forth by the government in official statements, legal memoranda, and legal enactments, but also as they took shape following years of judicial proceedings. There is a note of irony in the fact that US government attempts to avoid virtually any law governing the treatment of prisoners in Guantánamo ultimately ushered in 'a resurgence of attention and fidelity to international law principles and normative concepts of universal human rights—two legal systems that had been roundly dismissed as irrelevant to U.S. jurisprudence during the past two decades'.[6]

In looking beyond the US legal system to international human rights bodies' reactions to detainee treatment in Guantánamo, I must inevitably address the notion of extraterritorial application of human rights obligations, which the USA sought to manoeuvre around by imprisoning detainees at Guantánamo. The latter part of this chapter examines the evolution of the official stance towards Guantánamo once a change in administration occurred. US President Barack Obama's promise to close the detention facility and relocate detainees encountered obstacles from the beginning, and has still, as of writing, to become reality. Accordingly, I also examine the issues, legal and other, around the closure of Guantánamo. Set against the backdrop of the hunger strike—and force-feeding—of hundreds of detainees that started in April 2013, writing about Guantánamo remains as morally imperative today as it has been legally relevant ever since it first opened its doors to suspected terrorists more than a decade ago.

A. **The 'war on terror' begins**

On 20 September 2001, US President George W. Bush spoke to the US Congress of war. First, he spoke of the war on America: 'On September 11th, enemies of freedom

---

[4] Editorial, *International Review of the Red Cross*, 857 (March 2005).

[5] I argue that three bodies of law are relevant to their incarceration: US domestic law; international humanitarian law (IHL); and international human rights law (IHRL).

[6] Joshua L. Dratel, 'Repeating history: rights and security in the war on terror' in Karen J. Greenberg and J. L. Dratel, *The Enemy Combatant Papers*, Cambridge University Press, Cambridge, 2008, p. xiv.

committed an act of war against our country.'[7] He then proceeded to announce that: 'Our war on terror begins with Al Qaida, but it does not end there. It will not end until every terrorist group of global reach has been found, stopped, and defeated.'[8] This declaration came in the aftermath of Congress passing a joint resolution titled 'Authorization for Use of Military Force', which sanctioned the use of US Armed Forces against those responsible for the attacks:

[T]he President is authorized to use all necessary and appropriate force against those nations, organizations, or persons he determines planned, authorized, committed, or aided the terrorist attacks that occurred on September 11, 2001, or harbored such organizations or persons, in order to prevent any future acts of international terrorism against the United States by such nations, organizations or persons.[9]

It also followed United Nations (UN) Security Council Resolution 1368, adopted the day after the attacks, which not only condemned the acts, but also stated that the Security Council 'regards such acts, like any act of international terrorism, as a threat to international peace and security'.[10] The attackers too saw themselves as engaged in a war with the USA.[11] Why, then, all the legal hoopla?

First, the problem with declaring a war on terrorism is that it targets a technique, not an identifiable enemy. Although al-Qaeda and the Taliban regime in Afghanistan were the immediate targets of this 'war', as the presidential speech quoted above made clear, 'it did not end there'. Initial defenders of such rhetoric explained the war-based approach as a necessity in the face of an unprecedented threat:

These two sources of power—from Congress, and from the Constitution—allow war not against terrorism-the-technique, but rather against specific people, groups, and nations that commit terrorist attacks on the United States or that imminently threaten to do so. It is harder in this war than in past wars to identify the uniformless and ever-changing enemy with precision.[12]

Such reasoning links to the second problem posed by this language, namely, the absence of a clear end to the conflict. Fighting a global, 'uniformless' enemy that employs

---

[7] George W. Bush, Address to the Joint Session of the 107th Congress, 20 September 2001, in 'Selected speeches of President George W. Bush, 2001–2008', p. 66, <http://georgewbush-whitehouse.archives.gov/infocus/bushrecord/documents/Selected_Speeches_George_W_Bush.pdf>.

[8] 'Selected speeches of President George W. Bush, 2001–2008', p. 68.

[9] Joint Resolution to authorize the use of United States Armed Forces against those responsible for the recent attacks launched against the United States, Public Law 107–40, 107th Congress, 14 September 2001 (hereafter 'AUMF'), <http://www.gpo.gov/fdsys/pkg/PLAW-107publ40/pdf/PLAW-107publ40.pdf>.

[10] UN Security Council Resolution 1368, 'Threats to international peace and security caused by terrorist acts', 12 September 2001.

[11] Toni Pfanner, 'Asymmetrical warfare from the perspective of humanitarian law and humanitarian action', *International Review of the Red Cross*, 87(857) (March 2005), p. 155.

[12] Jack Goldsmith, *The Terror Presidency: Law and Judgment Inside the Bush Administration*, W. W. Norton, New York, 2007, p. 104.

terrorism as its method of attack may require prolonged effort, the end of which could not be foreseen, or indeed easily identified. Defenders of the 'war' language have also come to see its pitfalls as outweighing any benefits and have called for renouncing the rhetoric:

In 2007 and beyond, it may be a good idea to stop using the rhetoric of a 'war on terror,' either because the phrase misleads the public to think we are fighting a tactic; or because, as Donald Rumsfeld noted in 2006, it 'creates a level of expectation of victory and an ending within 30 or 60 minutes [like] a soap opera'; or because, as the British Foreign Office concluded at about the same time, the very use of 'war' rhetoric strengthens terrorists and invites attacks; or for some other reason.[13]

The third and most important issue raised by the 'war on terror' label is the conflict's status with regard to *jus in bello*—the law applicable in armed conflict. The conflict in Afghanistan was initially of an international character, although it became non-international at least once a new government was elected in June 2002. As will be made clearer in the following section, the Bush administration invoked the 1949 Geneva Conventions in an unclear and often misguided way, while effectively disavowing any import from IHL when it came to protections to afford detainees. In a nutshell, the US position at this time was that, because it was engaged in an armed conflict with a non-state actor, al-Qaeda, which was not a party to the 1949 Geneva Conventions, it did not need to afford captured members of this group the protections listed in the Conventions.[14] This position not only ignored the customary nature of the Conventions' protections, the non-derogable guarantee of humane treatment included in Common Article 3 to the Conventions, but also the fact that al-Qaeda members were also nationals of states that had ratified the Conventions.[15]

Moreover, the Bush administration's stance implied no differentiation between detainees based on either nationality, conduct, or place of apprehension, whereas an approach consistent with the laws of armed conflict would have meant that: 'Each component of the "war on terrorism"—and every situation in which persons held in Guantánamo were arrested—ha[d] to be classified separately.'[16] Such an evaluation would have had to first establish that such action under the banner of the 'war on

---

[13] Goldsmith, *The Terror Presidency*, p. 105.

[14] Patrick F. Philbin and John C. Yoo, 'Possible habeas jurisdiction over aliens held in Guantánamo Bay, Cuba', Memorandum for William J. Haynes, II, General Counsel, Department of Defense, US Department of Justice, Office of Legal Counsel, 28 December 2001, reprinted in K. J. Greenberg and J. L. Dratel (eds), *The Torture Papers: The Road to Abu Ghraib*, New York, Cambridge University Press, 2005, pp. 29–37.

[15] Jordan J. Paust, 'Antiterrorism military commissions: courting illegality', *Michigan Journal of International Law*, 23 (2003), n. 15.

[16] Marco Sassòli, 'The status of persons held in Guantánamo under international humanitarian law', *Journal of International Criminal Justice*, 2 (2004), p. 99.

terrorism' constituted an armed conflict.[17] This is not an obvious fact,[18] particularly after the international armed conflict (IAC) with Afghanistan ended, and would have had to be assessed in each instance of capture of a detainee. Finally, an evaluation would have needed a qualification of the type of armed conflict engaged in. The problem of ending the conflict thus resurfaces, since:

If IHL applies, each conflict has its own beginning and its own end. At the end of active hostilities in a given international armed conflict, prisoners of war (not accused of or sentenced for a crime) must be repatriated. The detention, e.g. of Taliban fighters arrested in Afghanistan, cannot be prolonged simply because, in the Philippines or in Iraq, the 'war on terrorism' goes on.[19]

Indeed, the 'war on terror' would soon spread to Iraq, with then-President Bush declaring it 'the latest battlefield in this war'.[20] With it, the same practices that had come under severe criticism in Guantánamo also migrated to Iraq, with even less 'adequate safeguard'.[21]

A final point on the consequences of terming the fight against terrorism a 'war' relates to its (attempted) limiting effect on judicial involvement. As one commentator has noted, 'if the armed struggle with al-Qaeda involves war rather than crime, then it is for the military and political branches of government alone, not for the courts'.[22] The National Defense Strategy of 2005 went even further, declaring that: 'Our strength as a nation state will continue to be challenged by those who employ a strategy of the weak using international fora, *judicial processes*, and terrorism.'[23] Furthermore, the vast array of executive actions intended to deny the applicability of international law has been described as a particularly disturbing 'attempt to mislead and misuse the judiciary to further the denial of required rights and protections'.[24] To these issues of applicable law and the involvement of the judicial branch in curtailing, or not, the excesses at Guantánamo, I now turn.

---

[17] Sassòli, 'The status of persons held in Guantánamo under international humanitarian law', p. 99.

[18] See Alain Pellet, '"No, this is not war!" The attack on the World Trade Center: legal responses', *European Journal of International Law*, 3 October 2001; Frederic Megret, '"War"? Legal semantics and the move to violence', *European Journal of International Law*, 13(2) (2002), pp. 361–99; Helen Duffy, *The 'War on Terror' and the Framework of International Law*, Cambridge University Press, Cambridge, 2005, pp. 249–55.

[19] Sassòli, 'The status of persons held in Guantánamo under international humanitarian law', p. 100.

[20] George W. Bush, 'Iraq and the Global War on Terror, Address to the Nation', 28 June 2005, <http://2001-2009.state.gov/p/nea/rls/rm/48716.htm>.

[21] 'Final Report of the Independent Panel to Review DoD Detention', August 2004, p. 9, <http://www.defense.gov/news/aug2004/d20040824finalreport.pdf>.

[22] K. J. Greenberg, 'Caught in the War on Terror: redefining prisoners in the post-9/11 era' in Greenberg and Dratel, *The Enemy Combatant Papers*, p. xi.

[23] US Department of Defense, 'National Defense Strategy of the United States of America', March 2005, p. 6, <http://www.defense.gov/news/Apr2005/d20050408strategy.pdf> (emphasis added).

[24] J. J. Paust, *Beyond the Law: The Bush Administration's Unlawful Responses in the 'War' on Terror*, Cambridge University Press, New York, 2007, p. 19.

B. **The status of detainees: 'enemy combatants' enter the legal 'black hole'**

Three bodies of law are potentially relevant to the situation of detainees in the 'war on terror': IHL, IHRL, and domestic US law.[25] From the beginning of its Guantánamo detention policy, the Bush administration denied the applicability of any of these laws, a position that changed only slightly with time. The conditions of applicability and protections afforded under all three bodies are explored below, as are the arguments presented by the US government in denying their relevance to Guantánamo. An assessment of the legal force of the arguments is then offered, with an exploration of the practical implications for prisoners of the denial of their rights under each body of law.

DOMESTIC LAW

Laying out the complex legal machinery surrounding Guantánamo is no easy feat. President Bush acted swiftly following the invasion of Afghanistan and took steps to regulate both the treatment and procedural rights available to individuals in military detention. On the procedural front, in November 2001, he signed the Military Order on the Detention, Treatment, and Trial of Certain Non-Citizens in the War against Terrorism.[26] The order applied to non-US citizens whom the President determined were engaged in acts of terror and constituted a threat to American security; it placed them under the authority of the Department of Defense and required their trials to take place before military commissions. Military Commission Order No. 1 would be adopted in March 2002 and would establish the procedures for trials before such commissions.[27] The Supreme Court accepted that the government had the power to detain both aliens (*Rasul v. Bush*[28]) and US citizens (*Hamdi v. Rumsfeld*[29]) at Guantánamo, but ruled that they must have the ability to challenge their enemy combatant status before an

---

[25] For a perspective on the international criminal law implications of Guantánamo that goes beyond the scope of this chapter, see James G. Stewart, 'Rethinking Guantánamo: unlawful confinement as applied in international criminal law', *Journal of International Criminal Justice*, 4 (2006), pp. 12–30.

[26] 'President issues military order: detention, treatment, and trial of certain non-citizens in the War against Terrorism', White House Office of the Press Secretary, 13 November 2001, <http://georgewbush-whitehouse.archives.gov/news/releases/2001/11/20011113-27.html>.

[27] Military Commission Order No. 1, Department of Defense, 21 March 2002, <http://www.defense.gov/news/mar2002/d20020321ord.pdf>. The order, as amended on 31 August 2005, is available at <http://www.defense.gov/news/Sep2005/d20050902order.pdf>.

[28] US Supreme Court, *Rasul v. Bush*, 542 US 466 (2004).

[29] US Supreme Court, *Hamdi v. Rumsfeld*, 542 US 507 (2004).

impartial authority.[30] A 2004 order followed, establishing the Combatant Status Review Tribunals whose task it was to review the 'enemy combatant' status of detainees.[31]

A Supreme Court challenge in *Hamdan v. Rumsfeld*[32] resulted in the Court finding that the structure and procedures of the Combatant Status Review Tribunals violated both the US Uniform Code of Military Justice and the four 1949 Geneva Conventions. In response to this outcome, the Military Commissions Act was passed in 2006.[33] The Act defined the categories of unlawful and lawful enemy combatants, and explicitly prohibited the invocation of the Geneva Conventions in *habeas corpus* and civil challenges of detainee status.[34] It would itself be found unconstitutional in *Boumediene v. Bush*,[35] wherein the US Supreme Court found the Act to be an unconstitutional restriction on the writ of *habeas corpus* and access to federal courts.

The legal apparatus set in place to regulate the treatment of Guantánamo prisoners was equally troubling. A Department of Justice legal memorandum from December 2001 (one of the now infamous 'torture memos') indicated, erroneously, that 'the great weight of legal authority' indicated that a federal court would not have jurisdiction over writs of *habeas corpus* filed by alien detainees at Guantánamo.[36] The memorandum was, despite opposition from within his administration,[37] endorsed by the President. A presidential memorandum from February 2002 further argued that: (1) 'none of the provisions of Geneva apply to our conflict with al-Qaeda in Afghanistan or elsewhere throughout the world because, among other reasons, al-Qaeda is not a High Contracting Party to [the] Geneva [Conventions]'; (2) the President had 'the authority under the Constitution to suspend Geneva as between the United States and Afghanistan' (although he did not choose to exercise it at that time); (3) the conflicts with al-Qaeda and the Taliban were international

---

[30] US Supreme Court, *Hamdi v. Rumsfeld*, 542 US 507 (2004). For critical appraisals of the military commissions established, see also Harold Hongju Koh, 'The case against military commissions', *American Journal of International Law*, 96 (2002), pp. 337–44, and J. J. Paust, 'Antiterrorism military commissions: courting illegality'.

[31] Deputy Secretary of Defense, Memorandum for the Secretary of the Navy, Subject: Order Establishing Combatant Status Review Tribunal, 7 July 2004, <http://www.defense.gov/news/jul2004/d20040707review.pdf>.

[32] US Supreme Court, *Hamdan v. Rumsfeld*, 548 US 557 (2006).

[33] Military Commissions Act of 2006, 17 October 2006, <http://www.gpo.gov/fdsys/pkg/BILLS-109s3930es/pdf/BILLS-109s3930es.pdf>.

[34] See Gregory E. Maggs, *Terrorism and the Law: Cases and Materials*, 2nd edn, Thomson Reuters, New York, 2010, ch. 12, 'Classifications of detainees', pp. 271–39; Anthony Gregory, *The Power of Habeas Corpus in America: From the King's Prerogative to the War on Terror*, Cambridge University Press, New York, 2013, pp. 183–270.

[35] US Supreme Court, *Boumediene v. Bush*, 553 US 723 (2008).

[36] Philbin and Yoo, 'Possible habeas jurisdiction over aliens held in Guantánamo Bay, Cuba'.

[37] See William H. Taft, IV, 'Comments on your paper on the Geneva Convention', Memorandum to Counsel to the President, 2 February 2002, reprinted in Greenberg and Dratel, *The Torture Papers: The Road to Abu Ghraib*, pp. 129–33; Colin L. Powell, 'Draft decision memorandum for the President on the applicability of the Geneva Convention to the conflict in Afghanistan', 26 January 2002, <http://www.gwu.edu/~nsarchiv/NSAEBB/NSAEBB127/02.01.26.pdf>.

in character and thus Article 3 common to the Geneva Conventions did not apply to either of them because, among other reasons, it only applied in NIACs; and (4) neither al-Qaeda nor the Taliban was entitled to prisoner of war (POW) status, but were 'unlawful combatants' instead.[38] A Department of Justice memorandum later that same year muddled the definition of torture when endorsing the use of 'enhanced interrogation techniques' against terrorism suspects in detention.[39] Another memorandum, approved by Secretary of Defense Donald Rumsfeld in December 2002, included among these techniques waterboarding, the use of stress positions, sleep deprivation, isolation, and other methods elsewhere deemed to amount to torture.[40] The blanket approval was later partially rescinded, although the option still existed to have repealed practices approved on an individual basis.[41] As already noted, these same interrogation practices migrated to military detention centres in Afghanistan and Iraq, where they were implemented with even more resource and leadership shortfalls.[42] The 2005 Detainee Treatment Act purported to address the criticism by, among others, prohibiting the cruel, inhuman, or degrading treatment or punishment of any person in US custody or under its control, and referring to the US Army's Field Manual on interrogation for guidelines on interrogations and providing for the Combatant Status Review Tribunals to function at Guantánamo.[43] It also sought to protect government personnel from civil or criminal prosecution for engaging in actions 'determined to be lawful at the time that they were conducted'.[44] The Act came under fire for its vague language and legal loopholes that would continue to allow reliance on evidence obtained through torture.[45] In a report released in April 2013, an independent panel tasked with reviewing the treatment of detainees, including at

---

[38] 'Humane treatment of al-Qaeda and Taliban detainees', Memorandum for the Vice President et al., The White House, 7 February 2002, reprinted in Greenberg and Dratel, *The Torture Papers: The Road to Abu Ghraib*, pp. 134–5.

[39] Jay S. Bybee, Assistant Attorney-General, 'Memorandum for Alberto R. Gonzales Counsel to the President RE: Standards of conduct for interrogation under 18 U.S.C. §§2340–2340A', US Department of Justice, Office of Legal Counsel, 1 August 2002, reprinted in Greenberg and Dratel, *The Torture Papers: The Road to Abu Ghraib*, pp. 172–217.

[40] William J. Haynes II, General Counsel, 'Counter-resistance techniques', Action Memorandum for Secretary of Defense, 27 November 2002 (approved on 2 December 2002), <http://www.gwu.edu/~nsarchiv/NSAEBB/NSAEBB127/02.12.02.pdf>.

[41] Donald Rumsfeld, 'Counter-resistance techniques, memorandum for Commander of USSOUTHCOM', 15 January 2003, reprinted in Greenberg and Dratel, *The Torture Papers: The Road to Abu Ghraib*, p. 239.

[42] See 'Final Report of the Independent Panel to Review DoD Detention'.

[43] 2005 Detainee Treatment Act, Title X of the National Defense Authorization Act for Fiscal Year 2006, 30 December 2005, <http://www.dni.gov/index.php/about/organization/ic-legal-reference-book-2012/ref-book-detainee-treatment-act-of-2005>.

[44] 2005 Detainee Treatment Act, Title X of the National Defense Authorization Act for Fiscal Year 2006, 30 December 2005.

[45] Alfred McCoy, 'Invisible in plain sight: CIA torture techniques go mainstream', *Amnesty International USA Magazine* (Spring 2006); Arsalan M. Suleman, 'Detainee Treatment Act of 2005', *Harvard Human Rights Journal*, 19 (Spring 2006), pp. 257–65.

Guantánamo, would conclude that the US government had engaged in torture while pursuing its counterterrorism detention practices.[46]

The curtailment of domestic law remedies to Guantánamo detainees was thus quite extensive. This move was particularly relevant given the Bush administration's reasoning that 'none of the [international human rights] treaties in question, such as the 1984 Convention against Torture, can impose any additional legal obligations beyond those already found in American law. So if it is consistent with American law, then it must be consistent with international law'.[47] As will be seen shortly, however, it was not the case that international law could simply be legislated out of the equation.

INTERNATIONAL HUMANITARIAN LAW

IHL covers the treatment of detainees in armed conflicts via the 1949 Geneva Conventions, notably the Convention relative to the Treatment of Prisoners of War the (1949 Geneva Convention III) and the Convention relative to the Protection of Civilian Persons in Time of War (the 1949 Geneva Convention IV). Article 4 of the 1949 Geneva Convention III stipulates the conditions for an individual to be afforded POW status, while Article 5 indicates that, in case of doubt as to the status of the person, 'such persons shall enjoy the protection of the present Convention until such time as their status has been determined by a competent tribunal'. Article 4 of the 1949 Geneva Convention IV indicates the requirements for the status of protected person, while its Article 5 lists the cases in which this status may not be afforded. This possibility is nevertheless not to be understood as curtailing all of the detainee's rights and:

. . . such persons shall nevertheless be treated with humanity and, in case of trial, shall not be deprived of the rights of fair and regular trial prescribed by the present Convention. They shall also be granted the full rights and privileges of a protected person under the present Convention at the earliest date consistent with the security of the State or Occupying Power, as the case may be.

Article 75 of the 1977 Additional Protocol I to the Geneva Conventions provides further minimum guarantees to detainees 'who do not benefit from more favourable treatment

---

[46] 'Report of the Constitution Project's Task Force on Detainee Treatment', 16 April 2013, <http://www.nytimes.com/2013/04/16/world/us-practiced-torture-after-9-11-nonpartisan-review-concludes.html?_r%20=%200>. See also Scott Shane, 'U.S. engaged in torture after 9/11, review concludes', *The New York Times*, 16 April 2013, <http://www.nytimes.com/2013/04/16/world/us-practiced-torture-after-9-11-nonpartisan-review-concludes.html>.

[47] Philippe Sands, *Lawless World: America and the Making and Breaking of Global Rules*, Allen Lane, London, 2005, pp. 145–6.

under the Conventions or under this Protocol'. It has attained customary status, a fact also recognized by the USA (which is not party to the Protocol).[48] While a comprehensive analysis of the protections afforded detainees under the laws of armed conflict goes beyond the scope of this chapter,[49] it is worth noting that, contrary to the US government's arguments, IHL was not silent on either the type of conflict the US was engaged in or the potential status of detainees.

The Bush administration claimed that Guantánamo detainees would be treated 'in a manner consistent with the principles of the Geneva Conventions of 1949', but only 'to the extent appropriate and consistent with military necessity'.[50] They were then classified as 'unlawful combatants' in a move that essentially ensured that they benefited from no IHL protection. Since al-Qaeda was not a state, the argument went, its fighters could not be part of regular armed forces and entitled to POW status, while Taliban fighters had failed to effectively distinguish themselves on the battlefield and had been allied with a terrorist group.[51] The traditional combatant/civilian distinction at the heart of IHL was thus subverted with the creation of the third category of 'unlawful', later renamed 'enemy', combatants, who seemed to benefit from no legal protections whatsoever.[52] Moreover, the executive believed it had the authority to 'suspend' the applicability of the Geneva Conventions to the conflict and detainees.

While it is true that POW status is only required in international armed conflicts, detainees in NIACs are entitled to the protection of Common Article 3, which calls for the humane treatment of such prisoners. Numerous international instruments prohibit the murder, torture, mutilation, and corporal punishment of prisoners.[53] The same

---

[48] See Paust, *Beyond the Law*, p. 10; Duffy, *The 'War on Terror' and the Framework of International Law*, pp. 391–2.

[49] Such analyses have been amply provided elsewhere: see e.g. Duffy, *The 'War on Terror' and the Framework of International Law*; Sibylle Scheipers, *Prisoners in War*, Oxford University Press, Oxford, 2010.

[50] George W. Bush, 'Address to the Joint Session of the 107th Congress'.

[51] See Sands, *Lawless World*, p. 145; Duffy, *The 'War on Terror' and the Framework of International Law*, pp. 399–400.

[52] For a more in-depth discussion of the 'unlawful combatant' status than is possible here, see e.g. George H. Aldrich, 'The Taliban, al-Qaeda, and the determination of illegal combatants', *American Journal of International Law*, 96(4) (October 2002), pp. 891–8; Thomas M. Franck, 'Criminals, combatants, or what? An examination of the role of law in responding to the threat of terror', *American Journal of International Law*, 98(4) (October 2004), pp. 686–8; Knut Doermann, 'The legal situation of "unlawful/unprivileged combatants"', *International Review of the Red Cross*, 85(849) (March 2003), pp. 45–73; Luisa Vierucci, 'Prisoners of war or protected persons qua unlawful combatants? The judicial safeguards to which Guantánamo Bay detainees are entitled', *Journal of International Criminal Justice*, 1(2) (2003), pp. 284–314; Mark David Maxwell and Sean M. Watts, '"Unlawful enemy combatant": status, theory of culpability, or neither?', *Journal of International Criminal Justice*, 5(1) (2007), pp. 19–25.

[53] 1949 Geneva Convention III, Art. 87; Geneva Convention IV, Art. 32; 1977 Additional Protocol I, Art. 75(2) 1977 Additional Protocol II, Art. 4(2).

prohibition exists in customary international law.[54] Critics of the Bush administration thus rejected its arguments and explained that the provisions of the laws of armed conflict left no gap in the protection of individuals.[55] Even where the applicable legal regime is uncertain, the dilemma may indeed be a false one, or at least overstated.[56] As one scholar has noted, there is 'convergence between the protections and guarantees afforded combatants and prisoners of war in both international and non-international armed conflicts',[57] and whatever gaps still exist under international humanitarian law may be filled by human rights law.[58] Moreover, '[a]s a matter of international law, this "enemy combatant" classification does not, however, denote the legal status of prisoners'; this status is determined by the rules of IHL, not government action.[59]

The US government's stance also came under fire domestically. In the cases of *Hamdan v. Rumsfeld* and *Boumediene v. Bush*, the US Supreme Court rejected the government's attempt to deny detainees the protection of the Geneva Conventions and access to writs of *habeas corpus*. The Court affirmed the universality of Common Article 3 and its function 'as the minimum legal standard applicable to all detainees captured in non-international armed conflicts', such as the one with al-Qaeda in Afghanistan.[60] By 2009, the Obama administration had retired the 'enemy combatant' categorization,[61] although human rights advocates warned, and subsequent developments proved, that this did not mean the discontinuing of the practice of seemingly indefinite detention without charge.

---

[54] See Jean-Marie Henckaerts and Louise Doswald-Beck, *Customary International Humanitarian Law*, International Committee of the Red Cross/Cambridge University Press, Cambridge, 2005, Section V on the 'Treatment of civilians and persons hors de combat', in particular ch. 32 'Fundamental guarantees' (Rules 87 on humane treatment, 89 on violence to life, 90 on torture, cruel, inhuman or degrading treatment', and 91 on corporal punishment), ch. 33 'Combatants and prisoner of war status', and ch. 37 'Persons deprived of their liberty'.

[55] 'No one should fall outside the law and, in particular, not outside the carefully built protective system offered by the Geneva Conventions': Sassòli, 'The status of persons held in Guantánamo under international humanitarian law', p. 102. 'Thus for the purposes of the law on the conduct of hostilities, there is no gap. Either a person is a combatant or a civilian': Doermann, 'The legal situation of "unlawful/unprivileged combatants"', pp. 72–3.

[56] See also discussion in John B. Bellinger III and Vijay M. Padmanabhan, 'Detention operation in contemporary conflicts: four challenges for the Geneva Conventions and other existing law', *American Journal of International Law*, 105(2) (April 2011), pp. 201–43, on the gaps in the protection of persons in detention in NIACs.

[57] Emily Crawford, *The Treatment of Combatants and Insurgents under the Law of Armed Conflict*, Oxford University Press, Oxford, 2010, p. 152.

[58] Crawford, *The Treatment of Combatants and Insurgents under the Law of Armed Conflict*, p. 117.

[59] Duffy, *The 'War on Terror' and the Framework of International Law*, p. 397.

[60] Crawford, *The Treatment of Combatants and Insurgents under the Law of Armed Conflict*, p. 59.

[61] Del Quentin Wilber and Peter Finn, 'U.S. retires "enemy combatant," keeps broad right to detain', *Washington Post*, 14 March 2009, <http://www.washingtonpost.com/wp-dyn/content/article/2009/03/13/AR2009031302371.html>.

INTERNATIONAL HUMAN RIGHTS LAW

Another body of law relevant to Guantánamo detainees and the 'war on terror' more generally is IHRL.[62] As noted above, recourse to its provisions may fill whatever gaps IHL might leave in the protection of individuals detained in counterterrorism operations. The international framework for their protection is rich and includes the 1966 International Covenant on Civil and Political Rights (ICCPR), which prohibits torture and cruel, inhuman or degrading treatment or punishment (Article 7) and calls for the treatment 'with humanity and with respect for the inherent dignity of the human person of "all persons deprived of their liberty"' (Article 10). The UN Standard Minimum Rules for the Treatment of Prisoners provide guidance in interpreting these rules, and the Human Rights Committee and the UN Special Rapporteur on torture and other cruel, inhuman and degrading treatment have further elucidated the norms that states must apply in their treatment of prisoners, including those in military detention centres.[63] The various regional human rights regimes echo this approach. While the USA is only a signatory, not a party, to the 1969 American Convention on Human Rights (ACHR), it has signed the Declaration on the Rights and Duties of Man and may be seen as having expressed 'its willingness to act consistently with [the Convention's] provisions'.[64] Specifically in the case of detainees at Guantánamo, their claims of abuses would be addressable via international human rights treaty and customary law, whereas cases of torture would also constitute violations of peremptory norms.

The US government denied the application of its human rights law obligations to Guantánamo detainees, however, by refusing to acknowledge the military base as US sovereign territory. In the words of the Solicitor General in *Rasul v. Bush*, 'the ICCPR is inapplicable to conduct by the USA outside its "sovereign" territory',[65] which Guantánamo supposedly was. The Bush administration made these claims relying on the 1903 lease agreement with Cuba according to which the USA would have 'complete jurisdiction and control' over the island, while Cuba would retain 'ultimate jurisdiction'.[66] The paradoxical argument was put forth that the naval base was outside American jurisdiction, despite the fact that assertions to the contrary had previously abounded, including

---

[62] Richard Ashby Wilson (ed.), *Human Rights in the 'War on Terror'*, Cambridge University Press, New York, 2005; Fiona de Londras, *Detention in the 'War on Terror': Can Human Rights Fight Back?*, Cambridge University Press, Cambridge, 2011.

[63] For a more thorough account of the international human rights framework for the protection of detainees, see Silvia Suteu, 'The use of weapons in custodial centres' in Stuart Casey-Maslen (ed.), *Weapons under International Human Rights Law*, Cambridge University Press, Cambridge, forthcoming (2014).

[64] Duffy, *The 'War on Terror' and the Framework of International Law*, pp. 392–3.

[65] Brief for the Respondents in Opposition, *Rasul v. Bush*, 542 US 466 (2004).

[66] Art. III, Agreement between the United States and Cuba for the Lease of Lands for Coaling and Naval Stations, 16–23 February 1903.

'for the purposes of excluding the application of the Torture Victim Protection Act which gives US courts jurisdiction over torture committed in foreign jurisdictions'.[67]

The extraterritorial application of human rights obligations has been amply established.[68] A state's jurisdiction over a territory is established based on the doctrine of 'effective control', which has been recognized by the European Court of Human Rights (ECtHR)[69] and by the International Court of Justice (ICJ),[70] as well as by the Human Rights Committee. The latter has stated that ICCPR human rights protection extends to 'anyone within the power or effective control of that State Party, even if not situated within the territory of the State Party'.[71] The Human Rights Committee has also found it 'unconscionable to so interpret the responsibility under article 2 of the Covenant as to permit a State party to perpetrate violations of the Covenant on the territory of another State, which violations it could not perpetrate on its own territory'.[72]

Human rights bodies assumed US jurisdiction over Guantánamo and proceeded to evaluate the situation of detainees as against the panoply of international human rights protections. The Inter-American Commission on Human Rights (IACommHR) addressed it early on by issuing preventive measures and explicitly rejecting the US government's jurisdictional claims. It thus stated that:

[W]here persons find themselves within the authority and control of a state and where a circumstance of armed conflict may be involved, their fundamental rights may be determined in part by reference to international humanitarian law as well as international human rights law. Where it may be considered that the protections of international humanitarian law do not apply, however, such persons remain the beneficiaries at least of the non-derogable protections under international human rights law. In short, no person under the authority and control of a state, regardless of his or her circumstances, is devoid of legal protection for his or her fundamental and non-derogable human rights.[73]

---

[67] Duffy, *The 'War on Terror' and the Framework of International Law*, pp. 381–2.

[68] See Duffy, *The 'War on Terror' and the Framework of International Law*, pp. 282–9; Hugh King, 'The extraterritorial human rights obligations of states', *Human Rights Law Review*, 9(4) (2009), pp. 521–56; Oona Hathaway et al., 'Human rights abroad: when do human rights treaty obligations apply extraterritorially?', *Arizona State Law Journal*, 43 (2011), pp. 389–426; Marko Milanovic, *Extraterritorial Application of Human Rights Treaties: Law, Principles, and Policy*, Oxford University Press, Oxford, 2011.

[69] ECtHR, *Loizidou v. Turkey*, Judgment (App. No. 15318/89), 18 December 1996, §62; *Ilascu and ors v. Moldova and Russia*, Judgment (App. No. 48787/99), 8 July 2004, §§384, 393; *Issa and ors v. Turkey*, Judgment (App. No. 31821/96), 16 November 2004, §71; *Öcalan v. Turkey*, Judgment (App. No. 46221/99), 12 May 2005, §91. See also ECtHR, *Al-Saadoon and Mufdhi v. United Kingdom*, Judgment (App. No. 61498/08), 2 March 2010; *Al-Skeini v. United Kingdom*, Judgment (App. No. 55721/07), 7 July 2011.

[70] ICJ, *Legal Consequences of the Construction of a Wall in the Occupied Palestinian Territory*, Advisory Opinion, 9 July 2004, and *Armed Activities on the Territory of the Congo (Democratic Republic of Congo (DRC) v. Uganda)*, Judgment, 19 December 2005.

[71] Human Rights Committee, General Comment No. 31, 'Nature of the general legal obligation on states parties to the Covenant', UN doc. CCPR/C/21/Rev.1/Add.13, May 2004, §10.

[72] Human Rights Committee, *Sergio Euben Lopez Burgos v. Uruguay*, Decision (Comm. No. R.12/52), UN doc. Supp. No. 40 (A/36/40) at 176 (1981), §12.3.

[73] IACommHR, 'Precautionary measures in Guantánamo Bay, Cuba', PM 259/02, 13 March 2002.

The US response was to dispute the Commission's findings on both jurisdictional and substantive grounds, asking instead that they be rescinded.[74] The UN Committee against Torture had also called on the US government to cease detention in Guantánamo and to close the facilities there.[75] More recently, the Inter-American Court of Human Rights (IACtHR) has agreed to hear the case of Djamel Ameziane,[76] an Algerian national held in Guantánamo without charge since 2002, who challenged his indefinite detention by US authorities, the conditions of this detention, and the failure of the state to relocate him.[77]

In sum, this analysis of the legal rules applicable to Guantánamo detainees has shown that the legal 'black hole' terminology was sadly fitting to their plight. By labelling them 'unlawful combatants', the USA 'had attempted to create a category of persons without rights under law, either those rights afforded to criminal suspects, or those rights given to POWs or other detainees captured in any armed conflict'.[78] Through convoluted, often secret, and also erroneous legal argumentation, 'the lawyers for the Bush Administration have, in effect, constructed a scheme which takes the United States beyond the constraints of international law'.[79] The next section examines whether things changed in the following administration, as the President (and Commander-in-Chief of the US Armed Forces) had promised it would.

C. **The Obama years**

A sense of hope surrounded the inauguration of President Barack Obama in January 2009. Throughout his nomination and presidential campaigns, he had stated his opposition to the Bush-era practices in the treatment of Guantánamo detainees and had made the closing of the detention centre a campaign point. In the aftermath of the *Boumediene* decision in 2008, for instance, he called the decision 'a rejection of the Bush Administration's attempt to create a legal black hole at Guantánamo'.[80] He criticized the *Hamdan*

---

[74] IACommHR, 'US additional response to the request for precautionary measures—detention of enemy combatants at Guantánamo Bay, Cuba', 15 July 2002.

[75] UN Committee against Torture, 'Conclusions and recommendations of the Committee against Torture: United States of America', UN doc. CAT/C/USA/CO/2, 25 July 2006, §22.

[76] *Djamel Ameziane v. USA*, Petition and Request for Precautionary Measures, submitted by the Center for Constitutional Rights (CCR) and the Center for Justice and International Law (CEJIL) to the IACommHR, 6 August 2008.

[77] 'Human rights court agrees to hear Guantánamo detainee case', *Jurist*, 31 March 2012, <http://jurist.org/paperchase/2012/03/human-rights-court-agrees-to-hear-guantanamo-detainee-case.php>. See also J. Wells Dixon, 'IACHR Guantánamo case a hallmark for human rights', *Jurist*, 27 April 2012, <http://jurist.org/hotline/2012/04/wells-dixon-iachr-guantanamo.php>.

[78] Crawford, *The Treatment of Combatants and Insurgents under the Law of Armed Conflict*, pp. 59–60.

[79] Sands, *Lawless World*, p. 146.

[80] Gregory, *The Power of Habeas Corpus in America*, p. 248.

trial for its length, which 'underscores the dangerous flaws in the Administration's legal framework', and called for 'swift and sure justice to terrorists through our courts and our Uniform Code of Military Justice'.[81]

Sure enough, on his second full day in office, he signed an executive order calling for a review of the status of all Guantánamo detainees, suspending military commission trials and affirming the need to conform to Common Article 3 to the 1949 Geneva Conventions in the treatment of prisoners.[82] He also ordered that a 'Special Interagency Task Force on Detainee Disposition' be set up with a view to developing 'policies for the detention, trial, transfer, release, or other disposition of individuals captured or apprehended in connection with armed conflicts and counterterrorism operations'.[83] Obama indicated that the closure of Guantánamo was to take place no later than one year from the date of the order.

Those who had seen in the order more than a 'symbolic gesture'[84] were in for a rude awakening. Numerous obstacles remained before the closure could come into effect, not least due to the extensive review process set in motion by Obama's executive order. Five types of hurdle were soon identified.[85] The first was the incompleteness of detainee case files, with information often scattered across agencies; this delayed their review process. The second included problems of prosecution in US courts related to the need to use classified evidence and the dubious nature of some interrogations, which would make confessions obtained therefrom inadmissible. The third obstacle was the opposition by Congress to the detention and trial of terrorist suspects in the USA, for fear of the security risk they would pose. The fourth problem related to the detainees' release, repatriation, or relocation. Releasing former suspects in the USA had been opposed by the US government and courts, while relocation to third countries was met with calls for the release of complete information on the individuals in question or with outright refusal. Repatriation was also occasionally problematic, with some suspects refusing to be repatriated and later, in the case of Yemeni nationals, with the US government's refusal to repatriate them on account of the security environment in the country. Finally, a fifth obstacle to release was the evidence of continued terrorist activity by some of the former detainees.

---

[81] Gregory, *The Power of Habeas Corpus in America*, p. 249.

[82] Executive Order 13492—Review and Disposition of Individuals Detained at the Guantánamo Bay Naval Base and Closure of Detention Facilities, 22 January 2009, <http://www.gpo.gov/fdsys/pkg/FR-2009-01-27/pdf/E9-1893.pdf>. See also Executive Order 13491—Ensuring Lawful Interrogations, 22 January 2009, <http://www.gpo.gov/fdsys/pkg/CFR-2010-title3-vol1/pdf/CFR-2010-title3-vol1-eo13491.pdf>.

[83] Executive Order 13493—Review of Detention Policy Options, 22 January 2009.

[84] Gregory, *The Power of Habeas Corpus in America*, p. 244.

[85] The following is based on John R. Cook, 'Contemporary practice of the United States relating to international law', *American Journal of International Law*, 103(2) (April 2009), pp. 328–30.

The report of the Guantánamo Review Task Force was completed in January 2010 and made public in May of that year.[86] Its evaluation of the 240 detainees still held yielded the following results.

- A total of 126 detainees were approved for transfer. To date, 44 of these detainees have been transferred from Guantánamo to nations outside the USA.
- The 44 detainees, over the course of the review, were referred for prosecution either in federal court or a military commission, and 36 remain the subject of active cases or investigations. The US Attorney General has announced that the government will pursue prosecutions against six of these detainees in federal court and will pursue prosecutions against six others in military commissions.
- A total of 48 detainees were determined to be too dangerous to transfer, but not feasible for prosecution. They will remain in detention pursuant to the government's authority under the AUMF. Detainees may challenge the legality of their detention in federal court and will periodically receive further review within the executive branch.
- Thirty detainees from Yemen were designated for 'conditional' detention based on the current security environment in that country. They are not approved for repatriation to Yemen at this time, but may be transferred to third countries, or repatriated to Yemen in the future if the current moratorium on transfers to Yemen is lifted and other security conditions are met.

Notwithstanding the results of this review, the Obama administration's actions have been seen as moving away from the stated aim of promptly closing Guantánamo. For one thing, the government 'has continued to vigorously defend all *habeas corpus* petitions in federal courts', arguing against the courts' power to order the release of detainees, 'even where the detainees are deemed to be of insufficient risk to justify detention'.[87] Furthermore, following the judicial finding in *Boumediene* that *habeas corpus* claims were available to Guantánamo detainees, the administration sought to use military bases abroad in order to detain suspected terrorists, notably Bagram Air Force Base in Afghanistan.[88] In the wake of a district court ruling in favour of several Bagram detainees' writ of *habeas corpus*, the government announced that it would appeal the decision.[89] Faced with such actions, critics have faulted the Obama administration for creating its own legal 'black hole'.[90]

---

[86] 'Final Report of the Guantánamo Review Task Force', 22 January 2010.

[87] Londres, *Detention in the 'War on Terror'*, pp. 78–9, citing *Kiyemba v. Obama*, 555 F3d 1022 (DC Circuit, 2009) and Government Brief in Opposition to Petition for Certiorari in *Kiyemba v. Obama*, 29 May 2009.

[88] Faiza Patel, 'The writ stops here: no habeas for prisoners held by U.S. forces in Afghanistan', *ASIL Insight*, 14(13) (3 June 2010), <http://www.asil.org/files/insight100603pdf.pdf>. See also Gregory, *The Power of Habeas Corpus in America*, pp. 257–9.

[89] Gregory, *The Power of Habeas Corpus in America*, pp. 250–1.

[90] Gregory, *The Power of Habeas Corpus in America*, p. 251.

Further actions taken by the Obama presidency underscore the move away from the commitment to closing Guantánamo.[91] In October 2009, the President signed the Military Commissions Act of 2009,[92] designed to amend the 2006 Act and to address the legal issues raised by the Supreme Court in the *Boumediene* case. The 2009 Act was followed by the US Manual for Military Commissions in April 2010,[93] which contained detailed rules of procedure and evidence, as well as a list of prosecutable offences. Critics of the Act saw it as a case of '[t]inkering with the discredited military commissions system', which, while making some 'important improvements on the Bush administration's system', ultimately left in place 'a substandard system of justice'.[94] The Manual's publication hours before the trial of Canadian citizen Omar Khadr was due to begin was met with suspicion.[95] Amnesty International saw it as confirmation that the Obama administration was continuing the line set by its predecessor in embracing indefinite detention at Guantánamo. A former lead defence counsel with the Office of Military Commissions pointed to the 'absurdity' in the Manual's language, which still allowed for the possibility of a conviction for murder in violation of the law of war without a requirement first to prove an actual law of war violation—the very crime of which Khadr was being accused.[96]

Things got worse when the President signed the 2011 National Defense Authorization Act.[97] Two sections of the Act referred to Guantánamo: section 1032 prohibited the use of federal funds to relocate detainees to the USA; while section 1033 barred the use of funds to transfer detainees to the custody or effective control of foreign nations unless specified conditions were met. The President criticized the two sections, but on account of the restrictions they placed on executive powers to direct counterterrorism efforts rather than because of the serious dent they made on plans to close Guantánamo.[98] Later that year, he lifted the suspension on military commission trials and these resumed.[99] The simultaneous

---

[91] For a more in depth account, see Gregory, *The Power of Habeas Corpus in America*, pp. 251–70.

[92] Title XVIII of the National Defense Authorization Act for Fiscal Year 2010 ('Military Commissions Act of 2009'), 28 October 2009, <http://www.defense.gov/news/2009%20MCA%20Pub%20Law%20111-84.pdf>.

[93] USA, 'Manual for Military Commissions', 2010 edn, <http://www.defense.gov/news/d2010manual.pdf>.

[94] Human Rights Watch (HRW), 'US: new legislation on military commissions doesn't fix fundamental flaws: proceedings to try detainees at Guantánamo remain substandard', 8 October 2009.

[95] Omar Khadr is a Canadian citizen who was detained at the age of 15 after he allegedly threw a grenade that killed a US marine in Afghanistan. He was charged with murder in violation of the law of war and with providing material support for terrorism.

[96] David Frakt, 'New Manual for Military Commissions disregards the Commander-in-Chief, Congressional intent and the laws of war', *Huffington Post*, 29 April 2010, <http://www.huffingtonpost.com/david-frakt/new-manual-for-military-c_b_557720.html>.

[97] National Defense Authorization Act for the Fiscal Year 2011, 7 January 2011, <http://www.gpo.gov/fdsys/pkg/CRPT-111hrpt491/pdf/CRPT-111hrpt491.pdf>.

[98] 'Statement by the President on H.R. 6523', White House, Office of the Press Secretary, 7 January 2011, <http://www.whitehouse.gov/the-press-office/2011/01/07/statement-president-hr-6523>.

[99] Ed Pilkington, 'Obama lifts suspension on military terror trials at Guantánamo Bay', *The Guardian*, 7 March 2011, <http://www.guardian.co.uk/world/2011/mar/07/guantanamo-military-terrorism-trials-resume>.

issuing of an executive order disposing for the periodic review of detainees did little to assuage the fears of those who had hoped to see Guantánamo closed, not perpetuated.[100] Praise for the order as confirmation of the previous administration's policies ('it affirms the Bush Administration policy that our government has the right to detain dangerous terrorists until the cessation of hostilities')[101] further underscores the point.

The 2012 National Defense Authorization Act again worsened the situation of Guantánamo detainees.[102] Section 1021 authorized the military detention of terrorism suspects 'under the law of war without trial until the end of the hostilities' (thus arguably indefinitely). Section 1022 made such military detention obligatory for most terrorism suspects. The dispositions meant to prevent the transfer of prisoners to either US soil or to foreign nations not meeting certain conditions were maintained. The Act was criticized by two retired army generals as allowing for the transfer of suspects captured on American soil to Guantánamo, as well as for making counterterrorism the business of the armed forces to an unprecedented extent.[103] They saw such measures as moving towards extending, not closing, Guantánamo. All of these legal moves, in fact, have been pointed to as evidence of the Obama administration not merely continuing the policies of its predecessor, but even expanding them.[104]

Another notable development during Obama's presidency has been the trial of alleged September 11 mastermind Khalid Sheikh Mohammed. Pre-trial hearings for him and four co-accused began in December 2008 and January 2009 before a military commission. Charges against them include 169 overt acts and 2,973 individual counts of murder, one for each person killed in the September 11 attacks.[105] In November 2009, it was announced that the trial was to be moved to a civilian court in New York.[106] In 2011, however, following the passing of legislation by Congress that prevented the use of federal funds to house or transfer detainees to the metropolitan territory of the USA (*see earlier*), Attorney General Eric Holder announced that the trial would again move to a

---

[100] Executive Order 13567—Periodic Review of Individuals Detained at Guantánamo Bay Naval Station Pursuant to the Authorization for Use of Military Force, 7 March 2011, <http://www.gpo.gov/fdsys/pkg/FR-2011-03-10/pdf/2011-5728.pdf>.

[101] 'Statement made by Republican Representative and Chairman of the House Homeland Security Committee, Peter T. King', cited in Peter Finn and Anne E. Kornblut, 'Obama creates indefinite detention system for prisoners at Guantánamo Bay', *Washington Post*, 8 March 2011, <http://www.washingtonpost.com/wp-dyn/content/article/2011/03/07/AR2011030704871.html>.

[102] National Defense Authorization Act for the Fiscal Year 2012, 31 December 2011, <http://www.gpo.gov/fdsys/pkg/BILLS-112hr1540enr/pdf/BILLS-112hr1540enr.pdf>.

[103] Charles C. Krulak and Joseph P. Hoar, 'Guantánamo forever?', *New York Times*, 12 December 2011, <http://www.nytimes.com/2011/12/13/opinion/guantanamo-forever.html>.

[104] Gregory, *The Power of Habeas Corpus in America*, p. 244.

[105] See Charge Sheet, January 2007, <http://news.findlaw.com/wsj\docs\terrorism\usksmetal20808chrgs.pdf.

[106] 'Accused 9/11 plotter Khalid Sheikh Mohammed faces New York trial', *CNN*, 13 November 2009, <http://edition.cnn.com/2009/CRIME/11/13/khalid.sheikh.mohammed/index.html>.

military commission in Guantánamo.[107] This occurred despite his determination 'that the best venue for prosecution was in federal court'.[108] A second round of hearings was concluded in January 2013. The proceedings raised new controversies when they were disrupted following the discovery of a government censor when courtroom sound (the trial was being screened for journalists on closed-circuit television) was cut during a discussion about Central Intelligence Agency (CIA) prisons.[109] The combination of legal disruptions by the defendants themselves and their credible allegations that torture was used against them have led to the trial's start being labelled 'chaotic'.[110]

Khalid Sheikh Mohamed's trial is indicative of the wider problems still remaining at Guantánamo. The prospect of moving detainees to civilian courts was hampered by congressional bars on federal spending. The legitimacy of the military commission trying the suspects remains in question. Most damagingly, they have verified evidence of unlawful interrogation practices used against them, including waterboarding, which have long been criticized as amounting to torture. The secrecy still surrounding much of what goes on at Guantánamo and in the trials of detainees there further ensures a loss of credibility in the Obama administration's ability and commitment to close down the prison.

Concluding remarks

In November 2012, the Pentagon's outgoing General Counsel Jeh Johnson for the first time raised the issue of the 'war on terror' needing to end after more than a decade:

But, now that efforts by the U.S. military against al-Qaeda are in their 12th year, we must also ask ourselves: how will this conflict end? It is an unconventional conflict, against an unconventional enemy, and will not end in conventional terms . . . We cannot and should not expect al-Qaeda and its associated forces to all surrender, all lay down their weapons in an open field, or to sign a peace treaty with us. They are terrorist organizations. Nor can we capture or kill every last terrorist who claims an affiliation with al-Qaeda.[111]

---

[107] Alan Silverleib, 'Accused 9/11 terror suspects to face military trials', *CNN*, 5 April 2011, <http://edition.cnn.com/2011/US/04/04/guantanamo.tribunals/index.html>.

[108] Silverleib, 'Accused 9/11 terror suspects to face military trials'.

[109] Jane Sutton, 'Who's silencing Guantánamo court audio feed, judge asks', *Reuters*, 28 January 2013, <http://www.reuters.com/article/2013/01/29/us-usa-guantanamo-idUSBRE90R07I20130129>.

[110] 'Khalid Sheikh Mohammed Guantánamo hearing gets chaotic start', *BBC*, 6 May 2012, <http://www.bbc.co.uk/news/world-us-canada-17966362>.

[111] Jeh Charles Johnson, 'The conflict against al-Qaeda and its affiliates: how will it end?', Speech at the Oxford Union, Oxford University, 30 November 2012, <http://www.lawfareblog.com/2012/11/jeh-johnson-speech-at-the-oxford-union/>.

Despite such difficulties, Johnson still expressed belief in the possibility of a 'tipping point':

...a tipping point at which so many of the leaders and operatives of al-Qaeda and its affiliates have been killed or captured, and the group is no longer able to attempt or launch a strategic attack against the United States, such that al-Qaeda as we know it, the organization that our Congress authorized the military to pursue in 2001, has been effectively destroyed.[112]

After that point, he noted, the categorization of the fight against al-Qaeda as an armed conflict needs to cease and the methods used in that fight must change towards the targeting of individuals, relying on law enforcement and intelligence resources rather than the military. The question of the situation of prisoners held in military detention without criminal conviction and sentence would also need to be addressed, with 'conventional legal principles to supply the answer'.[113]

Despite such statements, the closing of Guantánamo remains an elusive goal. 2013 brought renewed criticism at home and abroad on account of an escalating prisoner hunger strike. Of the 166 inmates remaining, more than 100 went on hunger strike in protest of their indefinite detention without charge, 21 of whom were being force-fed.[114] Clashes were reported between prisoners and guards.[115] Letters from current[116] and former detainees[117] transformed the hunger strike into a public relations disaster for the Obama administration. Even the Yemeni President criticized the prolonged detention practices at Guantánamo as 'clear-cut tyranny'.[118]

President Obama's reaction was to reaffirm the need to close the 'no-man's land' that is Guantánamo:

Guantánamo is not necessary to keep America safe. It is expensive. It is inefficient. It hurts us in terms of our international standing. It lessens cooperation with our allies on counterterrorism efforts. It is a recruitment tool for extremists. It needs to be closed.[119]

---

[112] Johnson, 'The conflict against al-Qaeda and its affiliates: how will it end?'.

[113] Johnson, 'The conflict against al-Qaeda and its affiliates: how will it end?'.

[114] 'Q&A: Guantánamo detentions', *BBC*, 30 April 2013, <http://www.bbc.co.uk/news/world-us-canada-12966676>.

[115] 'Clashes at Guantánamo over hunger strike prisoners', *BBC*, 13 April 2013, <http://www.bbc.co.uk/news/world-us-canada-22140663>.

[116] Samir Naji al Hasan Moqbel, 'Gitmo is killing me', *New York Times*, 14 April 2013, <http://www.nytimes.com/2013/04/15/opinion/hunger-striking-at-guantanamo-bay.html>.

[117] 'Open letter from former Guantánamo prisoners', *The Observer*, 4 May 2013, <http://www.guardian.co.uk/world/2013/may/04/open-letter-former-guantanamo-prisoners>.

[118] Cited in Glenn Greenwald, 'Obama, Guantánamo, and the enduring national shame', *The Guardian*, 15 April 2013, <http://www.guardian.co.uk/commentisfree/2013/apr/15/obama-guantanamo-hunger-strike-moqbel>.

[119] 'News Conference by the President', The White House, Office of the Press Secretary, 30 April 2013, <http://www.whitehouse.gov/the-press-office/2013/04/30/news-conference-president>.

What continues to be missing from these official statements is a concrete plan about how to achieve this goal. While the Obama administration continued to blame Congress for tying its hands financially with concern to action on Guantánamo, outsiders feared this merely showed a lack of political will to ensure respect for the USA's international human rights obligations. Some concluded there was little difference between the Obama administration and its predecessor in this area, with the former having, despite protestations to the contrary, adopted a 'unilateral and flawed "global war" paradigm and accepted indefinite detentions under this framework'.[120]

In May 2013, the IACommHR, together with multiple UN human rights monitoring bodies, issued a joint statement urgently calling on the US government to adopt 'concrete measures to end the indefinite detention of persons', and to ensure their trials and respect for their due process and human rights, as well as to close the detention centre at Guantánamo.[121] Concrete recommendations on how to achieve these objectives had already been put forth.[122] What remains missing is the type of leadership and commitment to see these goals become a long overdue reality.

---

[120] Amnesty International, 'Guantánamo: in his second term Obama must correct human rights failure', 8 January 2013.

[121] Office of the UN High Commissioner for Human Rights (OHCHR), 'IACHR, UN Working Group on arbitrary detention, UN Rapporteur on torture, UN Rapporteur on human rights and counter-terrorism, and UN Rapporteur on health reiterate need to end the indefinite detention of individuals at Guantánamo Naval Base in light of current human rights crisis', Press release, 1 May 2013, <http://www.ohchr.org/EN/NewsEvents/Pages/DisplayNews.aspx?NewsID%20=%2013278&LangID=E>.

[122] See, inter alia, Human Rights First, 'How to close Guantánamo: blueprint for the next administration', December 2012, <http://www.humanrightsfirst.org/wp-content/uploads/pdf/blueprints2012/HRF_Guantánamo_blueprint.pdf>.

9 Armed non-state actors and international law in the Democratic Republic of Congo, Libya, Mali, and Syria in 2012

Marina Mattirolo*

Introduction

With most of today's armed conflicts qualified under international humanitarian law (IHL) as being of a non-international character,[1] as Marco Sassòli has noted, 'by definition, at least half the belligerents...are non-State armed groups'.[2] In fact, such 'organized armed groups' significantly outnumber the number of state armed forces, posing major challenges to ensuring respect for the applicable rules of international law.[3] For while it is 'well settled' that non-state parties to an armed conflict are bound by IHL, determining their formal obligations under international human rights law (IHRL) remains a controversial issue.

To look at this issue, I will focus on four states affected by conflict, three of which saw a non-international armed conflict (NIAC) break out in 2012: the Democratic Republic of Congo (DRC); Mali; and Syria. The decision was taken also to review Libya, even though the armed conflict formally ended in October 2011, because the country is struggling in its transition to stability, with armed groups and militia continuing to play an important role, and because accountability of former Libyan rebel forces for war crimes and crimes against humanity committed during the conflict has still to be

* Marina Mattirolo is a researcher at the Geneva Academy specializing in armed non-state actors (ANSAs) and international norms.

[1] Marco Sassòli, 'Taking armed groups seriously: ways to improve their compliance with international humanitarian law', International Humanitarian Legal Studies, No. 1 (2010), p. 5, <http://www.cdp-hrc.uottawa.ca/uploads/TakingArmedGroupsSeriously.pdf>.

[2] Sassòli, 'Taking armed groups seriously', p. 6.

[3] Jean-Daniel Vigny and Cecilia Thomson, 'Fundamental standards of humanity: what future?', Netherlands Quarterly of Human Rights, 20(2) (2002), p. 185.

achieved. In looking at the international legal treatment of armed non-state actors (ANSAs) in the four selected countries, and the disparate nature of the groups and the conflicts notwithstanding, I will seek to identify trends with respect to compliance (or non-compliance) with international norms.

A. Armed non-state actors and armed violence in 2012

This opening section provides a brief overview of the type of armed violence prevalent in the four selected states, in addition to a description of the characteristics of the various ANSAs involved in hostilities in the DRC, Libya, Mali, and Syria.

THE DRC: A NEVER-ENDING CYCLE OF VIOLENCE?

The DRC is host to one of the world's worst ongoing humanitarian crises. After two successive national conflicts, which tore apart the country between 1996 and 2003, the DRC government has failed to assert its authority across the vast territory, the size of Western Europe, confronted by a proliferation of foreign and local armed groups, particularly in the east. These groups have fought each other and the Congolese army (FARDC) for power and control of natural resources.

In April 2012, the M23 rebel group launched an offensive against the government forces in the Rutshuru region, north of Goma. The M23 was formed after some 300 soldiers, former members of the Congrès National pour la Défense du Peuple (CNDP), participated in a mutiny from the FARDC to protest against the government's failure to implement fully the 23 March 2009 peace agreement which, inter alia, had integrated them into the Congolese army.[4] Clashes continued through the summer, and on 20 November 2012 M23 wrested control of Goma from the national army and threatened Kinshasa. After months of terrorizing the civilian population, at the end of the year M23 withdrew from Goma, agreed to a cease-fire, and opened peace negotiations with the government and regional powers.[5] Throughout hostilities in 2012, M23 was responsible for gross violations of human rights and serious violations of IHL against the civilian population, including killings, rape, forced labour, recruitment and use of children, cruel, inhuman, or degrading treatment, and looting of property in North Kivu.[6]

---

[4] Amnesty International, '10 facts you should know about the crisis in the Democratic Republic of the Congo', 20 March 2013, <http://www.amnesty.org/en/library/asset/AFR62/004/2013/en/23e9c4f2-8282-4570-b532-e5f72670b2a2/afr620042013en.pdf>.

[5] Gashegu Muramira, 'Congo-Kinshasa: M23 rebels declare ceasefire', *All Africa*, 9 January 2013, <http://allafrica.com/stories/201301090018.html>.

[6] 'Report of the United Nations Joint Human Rights Office on human rights violations perpetrated by soldiers of the Congolese armed forces and combatants of the M23 in Goma and Sake, North Kivu Province,

LIBYA: A CHAOTIC TRANSITION AND A LACK OF ACCOUNTABILITY

More than a year since Gaddafi's regime was ousted, a functioning court system was still missing in several regions of the country, leaving armed groups to run prisons and enforce their own forms of justice.[7] Some of these groups, not trusting newly established state institutions to 'enforce' justice as they would wish, are said to detain arbitrarily, torture, or even execute presumed Gaddafi loyalists.[8] In parallel, other groups, taking advantage of widespread disorder, engage in acts of violence for political or purely criminal aims.[9] These include local Islamist armed groups, some operating within the official state structure and others, such as Ansar al-Shari, that function independently.[10] As the International Crisis Group (ICG) noted in its April 2013 report on Libya:

The situation evoke[d] a vicious cycle: the proliferation of armed groups undermined people's trust in the central authority; this lack of trust in turn vindicated the armed groups' claim that it was their duty to take matters in their own hands; and the actions of the groups further undermined State institutions' ability to function.[11]

Many ordinary Libyans have a longing for justice—indeed it was one of the central themes behind the 2011 uprising[12]—and look to the new state to hold accountable not only former regime loyalists, but also rebels guilty of war crimes.[13] Efforts have begun to reverse the politicization and corruption of the justice system during the Gaddafi regime, combined with extrajudicial targeting of political opponents, but serious deficiencies are hampering its effectiveness.[14] Structural problems concern, inter alia, continued politicization, lack of independence of the Supreme Court, and widespread disagreement on the remedies needed to resolve these problems. Moreover, judicial authority has been

---

and in and around Minova, South Kivu Province, from 15 November to 2 December 2012', May 2013, §17, <http://www.ohchr.org/Documents/Countries/ZR/UNJHROMay2013_en.pdf>. See also Human Rights Watch (HRW), 'DR Congo: M23 rebels committing war crimes', 11 September 2012, <http://www.hrw.org/news/2012/09/11/dr-congo-m23-rebels-committing-war-crimes>.

[7] The Libyan civil war formally ended on 23 October 2011, three days after former leader Colonel Gaddafi was captured and killed by rebels outside Sirte.

[8] ICG, 'Trial by error: justice in post-Qadhafi Libya', Middle East/North Africa Report No. 140, 17 April 2013, <http://www.crisisgroup.org/~/media/Files/Middle%20East%20North%20Africa/North%20Africa/libya/140-trial-by-error-justice-in-post-qadhafi-libya.pdf>, p. i.

[9] ICG, 'Trial by error: justice in post-Qadhafi Libya', p. i.

[10] 'Islamist militant groups in post-Qadhafi Libya', *CTC Sentinel*, 6(2) (20 February 2013), p. 3, <http://www.ctc.usma.edu/posts/islamist-militant-groups-in-post-qadhafi-libya>.

[11] ICG, 'Trial by error: justice in post-Qadhafi Libya', p. 21.

[12] Paul Brennan, 'Libya justice system stagnant despite funding', *Al Jazeera*, 1 July 2012, <http://www.aljazeera.com/news/middleeast/2012/07/20127171647345975.html>.

[13] ICG, 'Trial by error: justice in post-Qadhafi Libya', p. 39.

[14] ICG, 'Trial by error: justice in post-Qadhafi Libya', p. 3.

undermined by the constant lack of security in the country. The absence of an effective national police force, the easy availability of weapons, and frequent assassination of security officials have all gravely prejudiced the state's capacity to investigate alleged crimes and ensure justice.[15] As a consequence, certain armed groups, dissatisfied with the state's apparent 'lack of prosecutorial capability', operate beyond the law, assuming the role of police, prosecutor, judge, and jailer.[16] State authorities have been incapable, or reluctant, to prevent those groups from applying 'victor's justice', which is carried out arbitrarily and in disregard of all due process.[17]

There has been no apparent progress in investigating the killing of Gaddafi—one clear example of a generalized lack of accountability for alleged crimes committed by rebel fighters during and after the conflict.[18] Instead of being investigated and, when necessary, prosecuted, those suspected of such unlawful acts are considered national heroes.[19]

SYRIA: FROM PEACEFUL DEMONSTRATIONS TO CIVIL WAR

Peaceful anti-government demonstrations started in Syria in March 2011, with protesters gatherings across the country, calling for social reform and, subsequently, an end to President Assad's regime. From the beginning, the Syrian government responded violently, with its security forces and militia, known as *shabbiha*, engaging in grossly excessive use of force and other human rights violations that the Independent International Commission of Inquiry on the Syrian Arab Republic considered, in its first report in November 2011, amounted to crimes against humanity.[20] As a consequence, localized violent episodes started to spread to the nation's major cities and the level of violence between government and opposition increased quickly. Initially, at least, the vast majority of anti-government armed opposition was gathered under the Free Syrian Army (FSA) banner, and efforts were made to improve their organization and ability to fight.[21]

---

[15] Amnesty International, 'Libya: rule of law or rule of militias?', 5 July 2012, <http://www.amnesty.org/en/library/info/MDE19/012/2012/en>. See also Amnesty International, '10 steps for human rights: Amnesty International's human rights manifesto for Libya', 25 September 2012, <http://www.amnesty.org/en/library/info/MDE19/017/2012/en>.

[16] ICG, 'Trial by error: justice in post-Qadhafi Libya', p. i.

[17] ICG, 'Trial by error: justice in post-Qadhafi Libya', p. 4.

[18] HRW, 'Death of a dictator: bloody vengeance in Sirte', 17 October 2012, pp. 41–50, <http://www.hrw.org/reports/2012/10/16/death-dictator-0>.

[19] ICG, 'Trial by error: justice in post-Qadhafi Libya', p. 28.

[20] 'Report of the Independent International Commission of Inquiry on the Syrian Arab Republic', UN doc. A/HRC/S-17/2/Add.1, 23 November 2011, §1.

[21] Prior to September 2012, the FSA operated its command and headquarters from Turkey's southern Hatay province close to the Syrian border, with field commanders operating inside Syria. In September 2012, the FSA announced that it had moved its headquarters to Idlib Governorate inside Syria. See e.g. Ruth Sherlock, 'Syria rebel army shifts from Turkey', *Daily Telegraph*, 23 September 2012, <http://www.telegraph.co.uk/news/worldnews/middleeast/syria/9560925/Syria-rebel-army-shifts-from-Turkey.html>.

By July 2012, the situation in Syria had clearly reached the threshold of intensity of an NIAC. The violence had escalated into an increasingly sectarian conflict, with a fragmented armed opposition becoming significantly more radicalized and militarized.[22] Armed clashes between government forces and anti-government armed groups intensified, with opposition gains in the centre and north of the country forcing the government to cede control of several areas. Government forces no longer tried to win back control over those areas, preferring instead to inflict extensive destruction through heavy artillery shelling and aerial bombardment.[23] The humanitarian situation of the Syrian population dramatically deteriorated, with massacres of civilians occurring on a daily basis.[24] As the February 2013 report of the Independent Commission of Inquiry (the Syrian Commission of Inquiry) affirmed:

The destructive dynamics of the civil war not only have an impact on the civilian population but are also tearing apart the country's complex social fabric, jeopardizing future generations and undermining peace and security in the entire region.[25]

The majority of the Syrian rebels come from civilian life, but defectors from the Syrian army have also constituted an important part of the force and have improved the FSA's level of organization. According to one journalist: 'The Free Syrian Army is much more organized than the rebel fighters in Libya. Because of the growing number of defectors, there's a stock of able, trained soldiers and officers mounting in Syria.'[26] The FSA leadership resided in Turkey until September 2012, making its control over the different FSA groups inside the country extremely weak.[27] Indeed, opposition fighters tend to answer to local commanders and operate independently on tribal and geographic bases. As the Syrian Commission of Inquiry has suggested, 'the lines of separation between the Salafi, FSA and other armed groups are ambiguous with fighters shifting from one group to another based on the availability of funds and weapons'.[28] However, Syrian opposition

---

[22] 'Report of the Independent International Commission of Inquiry on the Syrian Arab Republic', UN Human Rights Council, UN doc. A/HRC/22/59, 5 February 2013, p. 1. For a detailed analysis of Syrian armed opposition, see e.g. ICG, 'Tentative jihad: Syria's fundamentalist opposition', Middle East Report No. 131, 12 October 2012, <http://www.crisisgroup.org/~/media/Files/Middle%20East%20North%20Africa/Iraq%20Syria%20Lebanon/Syria/131-tentative-jihad-syrias-fundamentalist-opposition.pdf>.

[23] 'Report of the Independent International Commission of Inquiry on the Syrian Arab Republic', 5 February 2013, §2.

[24] 'Report of the Independent International Commission of Inquiry on the Syrian Arab Republic', 5 February 2013, §§1–3.

[25] 'Report of the Independent International Commission of Inquiry on the Syrian Arab Republic', 5 February 2013, §1.

[26] Tyler Hicks, 'Bearing witness in Syria: a correspondent's last days', *New York Times*, 3 March 2012, <http://www.nytimes.com/2012/03/04/world/middleeast/bearing-witness-in-syria-a-war-reporters-last-days.html?pagewanted=all&_r=0>.

[27] Sherlock, 'Syria rebel army shifts from Turkey'.

[28] 'Report of the Independent International Commission of Inquiry on the Syrian Arab Republic', 5 February 2013, Annex II, §§12–15.

fragmentation did not prevent it from becoming a fighting force increasingly able to challenge the state's control of the country.

At its core, the rebel movement is said to be 'inspired' by Islam, but not based on it.[29] However, as Assad's regime increased the ferocity of its attacks on both civilians and opposition armed groups, many rebels have turned overtly religious in their rhetoric.[30] Such radicalization is said to have favoured Salafist armed groups receiving financial support and weapons transfers from certain Gulf countries, reportedly Qatar and Saudi Arabia.[31]

MALI: THE NORTH AS A 'SAFE HAVEN' FOR SALAFIST-JIHADI GROUPS

On 17 January 2012, a Tuareg armed group known as the Mouvement national pour la libération de l'Azawad (MNLA), along with several Islamic groups including Ansar Dine, al-Qaeda in the Islamic Maghreb (AQIM) and the Movement for Oneness and Jihad in West Africa (MOJWA), initiated a series of attacks against government forces in the north of the country. The Tuareg rebellion was emboldened by the presence of well-equipped combatants, as well as great quantities of weapons coming from Libya after the regime collapsed. On 22 March, disgruntled Malian soldiers from the units defeated by the armed groups in the north, upset by the lack of support from the government, staged a *coup d'état* overthrowing President Touré.[32] The *coup* precipitated the collapse of the state structures in the north, allowing the MNLA to seize control of the regions of Gao, Kidal, and Timbuktu, and, on 6 April, to proclaim the independence of the 'State of Azawad'.[33]

By July 2012, however, the allied forces of Ansar Dine, AQIM, and MOJWA, and the MNLA turned to fighting themselves, in part due to widely contrasting ideological approaches. The MNLA were defeated and forced to withdraw from all northern Mali cities.[34] This resulted in the Islamist armed groups controlling two-thirds of the country,

---

[29] Institute for the Study of War (ISW), 'Syria's armed opposition', Middle East Security Report No. 3, March 2012, p. 14, <http://www.understandingwar.org/sites/default/files/Syrias_Armed_Opposition.pdf>.
[30] 'A fight for the spoils: the future role of Syria's armed groups', CTC Sentinel, 5(8) (23 August 2012), p. 2, <http://www.ctc .usma.edu/posts/a-fight-for-the-spoils-the-future-role-of-syrias-armed-groups>.
[31] ICG, 'Tentative jihad: Syria's fundamentalist opposition', p. i.
[32] 'Between Islamization and secession: the contest for northern Mali', CTC Sentinel, 5(7) (24 July 2012), p. 1, <http://www.ctc.usma.edu/posts/between-islamization-and-secession-the-contest-for-northern-mali>.
[33] 'Report of the Secretary-General on the situation in Mali', UN doc. S/2012/894, 29 November 2012, §§4–10.
[34] From the beginning of the rebellion, MNLA's goal was the 'swift formal political partition of Mali', while Ansar Dine had as its only goal the implementation of Shari'a law throughout Mali. For further details, see 'Between Islamization and secession: the contest for northern Mali', CTC Sentinel, 5(7) (24 July 2012), p. 2, <http://www.ctc.usma.edu/posts/between-islamization-and-secession-the-contest-for-northern-mali>.

with the opportunity to achieve their declared goal of implementing Shari'a law.[35] It has been reported that the armed groups can count on some 3,000 core fighters, that they are recruiting more, and that they are well armed, with relatively sophisticated equipment obtained from Libya and weapons captured from the Malian armed forces. The region has become a 'safe haven' for drug traffickers and other criminal elements who have built cooperative relationships with the Islamist groups.[36]

AQIM controlled Timbuktu and Tessile, and admitted destroying several holy and cultural sites in Timbuktu.[37] MOJWA, largely comprising foreign fighters from the Sahel region and North Africa,[38] controlled the main city of Gao and other smaller towns, while Kidal is controlled by Ansar Dine.[39] With the aim of implementing Shari'a law, these groups created a context in which most cultural and recreational activities are prohibited, rejecting and combating the cultural identities of the communities of the north, and committing grave human rights violations.

Immediately after the *coup* in March 2012, the Heads of State and Government of the Economic Community of West African States (ECOWAS) appointed the President of Burkina Faso, Blaise Compaoré, to mediate in the crisis.[40] On 11 January 2013, after the failure of several attempts to find a negotiated solution to the crisis, and with the government of Mali calling for foreign military help to retake the north, fearing the Islamists' advance towards Bamako, France launched a military intervention in northern Mali.[41] A few weeks later, forces from ECOWAS were also activated. As of writing, hostilities were ongoing.

B. **Acts of armed non-state actors under international law**

The set of international norms addressed, directly or indirectly, to ANSAs is an uncertain, but evolving, area of the law. Given the number of internal crises we witnessed during 2012, there is an evident need for clarification of their international legal obligations.

---

[35] 'Report of the Secretary-General on the situation in Mali', 29 November 2012, §9.
[36] 'Report of the Secretary-General on the situation in Mali', 29 November 2012, §10.
[37] Some were listed as 'world heritage' sites by the UN Educational, Scientific and Cultural Organization.
[38] MOJWA and Ansar Dine are said to be supported by fighters from the terrorist group Boko Haram, which is active in Nigeria.
[39] 'Report of the Secretary-General on the situation in Mali', 29 November 2012, §10.
[40] 'Report of the Secretary-General on the situation in Mali', 29 November 2012, §§5–9.
[41] 'France launches Mali military intervention', *Al Jazeera*, 11 January 2013, <http://www.aljazeera.com/news/africa/2013/01/2013111135659836345.html>.

APPLICABILITY OF INTERNATIONAL HUMAN RIGHTS AND HUMANITARIAN LAW TO ANSAS

In IHL, the provisions governing NIACs, as contained in Common Article 3 to the four 1949 Geneva Conventions, are fewer, less detailed, and, in certain instances, less protective than those regulating international armed conflicts (IACs). More detailed treaty rules are provided by 1977 Additional Protocol II to the four Geneva Conventions, but this instrument applies only when an armed group that is party to the conflict controls part of the territory of a state party.[42] Customary IHL, however, as identified by the International Committee of the Red Cross (ICRC) study, has found that the rules of distinction, proportionality, and precautions in attacks all apply in NIACs.[43] Furthermore, it is generally uncontested today that war crimes may be committed in an NIAC.[44]

Nowadays, it is generally accepted that IHL binds an ANSA where it is adjudged to be a party to an armed conflict.[45] In order for an ANSA to be considered a party to an armed conflict, two criteria have to be fulfilled: the group must be sufficiently organized; and the fighting it is involved in must have reached a certain intensity.[46]

Certain other IHL treaties, in contrast to the 1949 Geneva Conventions and 1977 Additional Protocol II, still only address states. This is the case of the 1997 Anti-Personnel Mine Ban Convention (APMBC). In these situations, it is important to underline the important role played by, inter alia, Geneva Call, a non-governmental organization (NGO) that engages with non-state actors to enhance their compliance

---

[42] Art. 1, 1977 Additional Protocol II to the Geneva Conventions.

[43] Jean-Marie Henckaerts and Louise Doswald-Beck (eds), *Customary International Humanitarian Law*, International Committee of the Red Cross/Cambridge University Press, Cambridge, 2005.

[44] See Statute of the International Criminal Tribunal for Rwanda (ICTR), Art. 4; Rome Statute of the International Criminal Court (ICC Statute), Art. 8(2)(c); International Criminal Tribunal for the former Yugoslavia (ICTY), *Prosecutor v. Dusko Tadić*, Judgment (Case No. IT-94-1-A-R77 4), 15 July 1999, §137.

[45] As noted above, the Appeals Chamber of the Sierra Leone Special Court (SCSL) declared in 2004 that 'it is well settled that all parties to an armed conflict, whether states or non-state actors, are bound by international humanitarian law, even though only states may become parties to international treaties': SCSL, *Prosecutor v. Sam Hinga Norman*, Decision on Preliminary Motion Based on Lack of Jurisdiction (Child Recruitment), (Case No. SCSL-2004-14-AR72(E)), May 2004, §22. See further e.g. Sassòli, 'Taking armed groups seriously', p. 14; Jann K. Kleffner, 'The applicability of international humanitarian law to organized armed groups', *International Review of the Red Cross*, 93(882) (June 2011), p. 444; Andrew Clapham, 'Weapons and armed non-state actors' in S. Casey-Maslen, *Weapons under International Human Rights Law*, Cambridge University Press, Cambridge, forthcoming (2013).

[46] See ICTY, *Prosecutor v. Dusko Tadić*, Judgment (Case No. IT-94-1-A-R77 4), 15 July 1995, §70. On the 'organizational' criterion, see e.g. ICTY, *Prosecutor v. Ljube Boskoski and Johan Tarulovski*, Judgment (Case No. IT-04-82-T), 10 July 2008, §§194–203. In this judgment, a number of relevant factors and indicators were identified, including: (1) the existence of a command structure; (2) the military (operational) capacity of the armed group; (3) the logistical capacity of the armed group; (4) the existence of an internal disciplinary system and the ability to implement IHL; and (5) the armed group's ability to speak with one voice.

with international humanitarian norms through the signature of thematic Deeds of Commitment.[47] The Deed of Commitment for Adherence to a Total Ban on Anti-Personnel Mines and for Cooperation in Mine Action, signed by 42 ANSAs as of May 2013, is a good example of how it is possible in some cases to overcome the relative lack of international legal regulation of ANSAs.[48]

In contrast to IHL, IHRL applies generally at all times, including during situations of armed conflict. This has been affirmed on several occasions by the International Court of Justice (ICJ), as well as other international courts and tribunals.[49] In situations of armed conflict, IHRL and IHL are considered to be complementary and mutually reinforcing. However, within and outside armed conflict, the application of human rights law to ANSAs is still highly divisive.[50] The main arguments used to refute legal application are threefold. The first relies on the fact that human rights law is considered, doctrinally, to apply exclusively to states. Secondly, it is often noted that human rights treaties rarely explicitly address ANSAs. Thirdly, there is a fear, especially among certain states, that recognizing that ANSAs have human rights obligations could give them recognition and therefore legitimacy.[51] However, a wider conception of human rights law has been suggested by Andrew Clapham:

[T]he most promising theoretical basis for human rights obligations for non-State actors is first, to remind ourselves the foundational basis of human rights is best explained as rights which belong to the individual in recognition of each person's dignity. The implication is that these natural rights should be respected by everyone and every entity.[52]

---

[47] Geneva Call was launched in March 2000 as a neutral and impartial humanitarian organization dedicated to engaging ANSAs in compliance with IHL and IHRL norms, consistent with Common Art. 3 of the Geneva Conventions. Geneva Call engages ANSAs in 'a constructive dialogue' aimed at persuading them to change behaviour and to respect specific humanitarian norms, starting with a total ban on anti-personnel mines. For further details about Geneva Call's action, visit <http://www.genevacall.org/>.

[48] The text of the Deed of Commitment banning anti-personnel mines is available at <http://www.genevacall .org/resources/deed-of-commitment/f-deed-of-commitment/doc.pdf>. See also Sassòli, 'Taking armed groups seriously', p. 12.

[49] See ICJ, *Legality of the Threat or Use of Nuclear Weapons,* Advisory Opinion, 1996, §25; *Legal Consequences of the Construction of a Wall in the Occupied Palestinian Territory,* Advisory Opinion, 2004, §106; *Armed Activities on the Territory of the Congo (Democratic Republic of the Congo v. Uganda),* Judgment, 2005, §216. See also African Commission on Human and Peoples' Rights (ACommHPR), *Commission Nationale des Droits de l'Homme et des Libertés v. Chad,* No. 74/92, 9th Annual Activity Report 1995–96, §21; Human Rights Committee, General Comment No. 31, UN doc. HRI/GEN/1/Rev. 9 (Vol. I), 27 May 2008, p. 243, §11.

[50] Sandesh Sivakumaran, 'Re-envisaging the international law of internal armed conflict', *European Journal of International Law,* 22(1) (2011), p. 251.

[51] A. Clapham, *Human Rights Obligations of Non-State Actors,* Oxford University Press, Oxford, 2006, pp. 46–53.

[52] A. Clapham, 'The rights and responsibilities of armed non-state actors: the legal landscape and issues surrounding engagement', Geneva Academy of International Humanitarian Law and Human Rights, 1 February 2010.

Several theoretical bases have been suggested to explain how and why ANSAs may be bound by IHRL.[53] First, the equality of obligation theory asserts that if one party is bound by an obligation,[54] that same obligation should bind the other side as well. Secondly, obligations can be a correlative of rights,[55] relying on the fact that if ANSAs benefit from human rights, they must also be subject to obligations. The third, more predominant approach is based on the notion of effective control over territory.[56] This means that when ANSAs exercise effective control over certain territory, they are considered to have human rights obligations. In such a situation, the need to regulate the relationship between those who govern and those who are governed, representing the very essence of human rights law, would be reproduced.[57]

Another, arguably more persuasive approach to the application to ANSAs of IHRL (and IHL) is through customary law. In order for rules of customary international law to emerge, two criteria have generally to be fulfilled: the existence of a persistent and coherent state practice in a particular field and the fact that such practice is perceived and accepted as legally binding (*opinio juris*).[58] Customary law is often used to hold non-state actors accountable under international law; this is because the international legal order perceives rights and obligations derived from custom as 'generally applicable and binding on every entity that has the capacity to bear them'.[59] Referring to customary law has been crucial in the context of fact-finding missions and commissions of inquiry that aim to determine and report on violations of international law by armed groups.

UN PRACTICE: INCREASING ACCEPTANCE OF ANSAS' HUMAN RIGHTS OBLIGATIONS

Although the applicability of international human rights law to ANSAs remains controversial, UN practice is evolving rapidly in a more positive direction. UN-mandated bodies such as the commissions of inquiry, Special Rapporteur reports to the Human

---

[53] Sivakumaran, 'Re-envisaging the international law of internal armed conflict', pp. 251–2.

[54] Christian Tomuschat, 'The applicability of human rights law to insurgent movements' in Horst Fischer et al. (eds), *Krisensicherung und Humanitärer Schutz—Crisis Management and Humanitarian Protection: Festschrift für Dieter Fleck*, Berliner Wissenschafts-Verlag, Berlin, 2004, pp. 573 and 576.

[55] D. Fleck, 'Humanitarian protection against non-state actors' in Jochen A. Frowein et al. (eds), *Verhandeln für den Frieden—Negotiating for Peace: Liber Amicorum Tono Eitel*, Springer, Berlin, 2003, pp. 69 and 79.

[56] 'Report of the Special Rapporteur on extrajudicial, summary or arbitrary executions', UN doc. E/CN.4/2005/7, 22 December 2004, §76.

[57] 'Rules of engagement: protecting civilians through dialogue with armed non-state actors', Geneva Academy of International Humanitarian and Human Rights, October 2011, p. 25.

[58] Clapham, *Human Rights Obligations of Non-State Actors*, pp. 85–6.

[59] Clapham, *Human Rights Obligations of Non-State Actors*, p. 87.

Rights Council, and UN Security Council resolutions have expressed the above-mentioned view on several occasions. The UN Assistance Mission in Afghanistan (UNAMA) and the Office of the UN High Commissioner for Human Rights (OHCHR), in their annual report on the protection of civilians in armed conflict in 2012, again expressly refer to the human rights obligations of armed groups, using the 'effective control over territory' argument:

While non-State actors in Afghanistan, including non-State armed groups, cannot formally become parties to international human rights treaties, international human rights law increasingly recognizes that where non-State actors, such as the Taliban, exercise *de facto* control over territory, they are bound by international human rights obligations.[60]

The Commission of Inquiry on Libya uses the same argument of de facto control to affirm that it is increasingly accepted that armed groups exercising effective control over territory are obligated to respect at least the fundamental human rights of those within that territory:

Non-state actors in Libya, in particular the authorities and forces of the National Transitional Council [NTC], cannot formally become parties to the international human rights treaties and are thus not formally given obligations under the treaties. Although the extent to which international human rights law binds non-state actors remains contested as a matter of international law, ... it is increasingly accepted that, where non-state groups exercise *de facto* control over territory, they must respect fundamental human rights of persons in that territory ... The Commission has taken the approach that since the NTC has been exercising *de facto* control over territory akin to that of a Governmental authority, it will examine also allegations of human rights violations committed by its forces. The Commission notes that the NTC has made a public undertaking in which it committed to 'build a constitutional democratic civil state based on the rule of law, respect for human rights and the guarantee of equal rights and opportunities for all its citizens including full political participations by all citizens and equal opportunities between men and women and the promotion of women empowerment.'[61]

Interestingly, the Syrian Commission of Inquiry, in its second report of February 2012, makes no reference to the 'territorial control' condition, affirming that FSA groups are bound by human right obligations that are considered *jus cogens:*

The commission carefully reviewed the information gathered on the operations and activities to date of FSA groups. In this regard, the commission notes that, at a minimum, human rights obligations constituting peremptory international law (*ius cogens*) bind States, individuals and

---

[60] UNAMA and OHCHR, 'Afghanistan, annual report on protection of civilians in armed conflict 2012', Kabul, February 2013.

[61] 'Report of the International Commission of Inquiry to investigate all alleged violations of international human rights law in the Libyan Arab Jamahiriya', UN Human Rights Council, UN doc. A/HRC/17/44, 1 June 2011, §72.

non-State collective entities, including armed groups. Acts violating *ius cogens* – for instance, torture or enforced disappearances – can never be justified.[62]

The Commission of Inquiry seems to use the sliding-scale approach in the paragraph above when mentioning that 'at minimum' peremptory international law binds armed groups. This could be explained by the fact that, at the time, the Commission had not yet concluded that the violence in Syria (or the level of organization of the armed groups) had reached the threshold of an NIAC. Since the Commission did not determine that these groups exercised effective control over Syrian territory, the Commission chose to affirm that they nonetheless had to respect *jus cogens* rules. Indeed, in the Commission's third report (August 2012), after acknowledging the existence of an NIAC in Syria, it returned to the 'territorial control' condition:

Non-state actors cannot formally become parties to international human rights treaties. They must nevertheless respect the fundamental human rights of persons forming customary international law (CIL), in areas where such actors exercise *de facto* control. The commission therefore examined allegations of human rights violations committed by the Syrian Government as well as abuses of customary international human rights norms perpetrated by the anti-Government armed groups.[63]

In this paragraph, the Syrian Commission of Inquiry refers to 'fundamental human rights . . . forming customary international law', a specification that was missing in the above-mentioned Libyan Commission's report, where the notion of 'fundamental human rights' stood alone. This does not help to clarify which rights are included and which are not.

Finally, in its fourth report (February 2013), the Commission found also that the FSA groups had violated the Optional Protocol to the UN Convention on the Rights of the Child on the Involvement of Children in Armed Conflict (CRC-OPAC):

Anti-Government armed groups are also responsible for using children under the age of 18 in hostilities in violation of the CRC-OPAC, which by its terms applies to non-State actors.[64]

This finding is controversial to say the least. Although Article 4(1) of CRC-OPAC addresses the acts of ANSAs, arguably it does so in terms that do not directly address ANSAs.[65] Some commentators argue that the text of Article 4(1) does not necessarily

---

[62] 'Report of the Independent International Commission of Inquiry on the Syrian Arab Republic', UN doc. A/HRC/19/69, 22 February 2012, §106.

[63] 'Report of the Independent International Commission of Inquiry on the Syrian Arab Republic', UN doc. A/HRC/21/50, 16 August 2012, §10.

[64] 'Report of the Independent International Commission of Inquiry on the Syrian Arab Republic', 5 February 2013, §§43–4.

[65] Art. 4(1) of the Protocol states: 'Armed groups, distinct from the armed forces of a State, should not, under any circumstances, recruit or use in hostilities persons under the age of 18 years.' The Protocol was adopted in June 2000.

create direct legal obligations on ANSAs, mostly because the drafters of the Protocol used the wording 'should not', as opposed to 'shall not', when referring to the prohibition of recruiting child soldiers. This wording seems to impose a moral obligation rather than a legal obligation under international law.[66] However, other authorities note that both 'should' and 'shall' can set out an obligation. This argument is reinforced by the wording 'under any circumstances' after 'should not', which suggests a legally binding obligation. More generally, General Comment No. 5 issued by the Committee on the Rights of the Child acknowledges that the Convention on the Rights of the Child does bind, even though indirectly, non-state actors:

The Committee emphasizes that States parties to the Convention have a legal obligation to respect and ensure the rights of children as stipulated in the Convention, which includes the obligation to ensure that non-State service providers operate in accordance with its provisions, thus creating indirect obligations on such actors.[67]

Notwithstanding the absence, to date, of a Commission of Inquiry on the situation in Mali, it is still interesting, for the purpose of this chapter, to analyse relevant resolutions by the Human Rights Council and the UN Security Council. In July 2012, the Human Rights Council adopted a resolution by consensus in which it:

Condemns the human rights violations and acts of violence committed in northern Mali, in particular by rebels, terrorist groups and other organized transnational crime network, including the violence perpetrated against women and children, the killings, hostage-takings, pillaging, theft and destruction of religious and cultural sites, as well as the recruitment of child soldiers, and calls for the perpetrators of these acts to be brought to justice.[68]

By explicitly condemning human rights *violations* (as opposed to 'abuses') committed by armed groups, the Council indirectly affirmed that armed groups are bound by human rights law; in this resolution, neither the territorial effective control argument nor the restriction to violations of *jus cogens* rules are mentioned. It is, though, noteworthy that all previous and subsequent resolutions by the Security Council on the situation in Mali substitute the wording 'human rights violations' with 'abuses of human rights and violations of international humanitarian law'.[69] The same practice is followed in the

---

[66] Daniel Helle, 'Optional Protocol on the Involvement of Children in Armed Conflict to the Convention on the Rights of the Child', *International Review of the Red Cross*, 82(839) (30 August 2000), pp. 797–809; Jonathan Somer, 'Engaging armed non-state actors to protect children from the effects of armed conflict: when the stick doesn't cut the mustard', *Journal of Human Rights Practice*, 4(1) (2012), p. 5.

[67] Committee on the Rights of the Child, General Comment No. 5, 'General measures of implementation of the Convention on the Rights of the Child', UN doc. CRC/GC/2003/5, 3 October 2003, §§42–3.

[68] Human Rights Council Resolution 17/20, 17 July 2012, §2.

[69] UN Security Council Resolutions: 2056 (2012), 5 July 2012, §13; 2071 (2012), 12 October 2012, §14; and 2085 (2012), 20 December 2012, §6.

UN Secretary-General's report on the situation in Mali that was released in November 2012.[70]

In January 2013, the Office of the Prosecutor (OTP) of the International Criminal Court (ICC) opened an investigation into alleged crimes committed in Mali, with a focus on the north of the country. In its report, the Court concludes that, based on the information available, there is a reasonable basis to believe that war crimes were committed in the context of an NIAC in Mali since around 17 January 2012.[71] The ICC report also states that 'the information available does not provide a reasonable basis to believe that crimes against humanity under Article 7 have been committed'.[72]

C. Patterns of compliance with international norms

Of course, ANSAs are not homogenous or 'monolithic entities'.[73] The term 'armed group' includes a great variety of actors, differing widely in the degree of organization and control over their members, territory, or people, aims, and willingness to abide by international norms. Some groups engage in guerrilla tactics, while others have air and sea capabilities; many are divided into military wings and political wings, with political representatives often based abroad. Recognizing the great diversity among NSAGs helps us to understand the reasons for them to comply with, or, in the contrary, to violate international norms.

WAYS IN WHICH ANSAS CAN EXPRESS THEIR CONSENT TO BE BOUND BY INTERNATIONAL NORMS

There are many different reasons for ANSAs to decide whether or not to recognize and respect international law. Among factors supporting respect of the law, also known as 'positive incentives', are the self-image of the group, the need to win popular support, the group's own internal beliefs, and perceived military advantage. Self-image is said to be one of the most powerful reasons for compliance with international norms.[74] Furthermore, many armed groups wish to be seen as respectable and legitimate by the

---

[70] The UN Secretary-General refers to 'gross human rights abuses': see 'Report of the Secretary-General on the situation in Mali', UN Security Council, UN doc. S/2012/894, 29 November 2012, §§21 and 75.

[71] ICC OTP, 'Situation in Mali—Article 53(1) report', 16 January 2013, §133.

[72] ICC OTP, 'Situation in Mali—Article 53(1) report', 16 January 2013, §128.

[73] Sivakumaran, *Re-envisaging the International Law*, p. 256.

[74] O. Bangerter, 'Reasons why armed groups choose to respect international humanitarian law or not', *International Review of the Red Cross*, 93(882) (June 2011), p. 358.

international community; avoiding violations can contribute to this goal and convey a positive image to the outside world.[75] Lastly, from a legal point of view, complying with international norms could prevent the imposition of international criminal sanctions or other coercive measures, such as travel bans, asset freezes, and embargoes.[76]

Reasons for lack of compliance by ANSAs are also various and diverse.[77] It is often said by armed groups themselves that, for instance, the asymmetrical nature of most NIACs may constrain them to resort to unlawful conduct of hostilities, such as carrying out attacks in populated areas, as a matter of survival and to prevent the risk of annihilation of the group.[78] Another factor is the likelihood of prosecution under domestic legislation for having taken up arms against the state. In an NIAC, a fighter in an armed group, once captured by the adversary (the armed forces of the state or states he is fighting), is not entitled to prisoner of war status. Thus, he faces the risk of prosecution under domestic law for the mere fact of having taken up arms, irrespective of his conduct during the conflict.[79]

Other factors leading to violations by ANSAs include the lack of knowledge and understanding of international norms,[80] allegiance to other beliefs that may be in contrast with international norms, and the lack of ownership of international norms. Indeed, ANSAs are required to respect certain international norms without having had the chance to be part of the making of such norms.[81]

ANSAs can decide to express their consent to be bound by international norms in many ways. They may sign political documents such as special agreements, memoranda of understanding, and action plans, or issue internal regulations such as unilateral declarations, codes of conduct, standing orders, and deeds of commitment. These political measures, together with policy decisions on doctrine, education, training, and sanctions, may have a significant impact, as they can make violations more or less likely. By issuing a unilateral declaration, an NSAG confirms its willingness to comply with certain international norms that are already binding on it or other norms that are not. Unilateral declarations can be issued *proprio motu* by ANSAs or encouraged by other

---

[75] Some armed groups have found that the way in which they treat the adversary's captured soldiers may influence the way the adversary will treat their combatants: Bangerter, 'Reasons why armed groups choose to respect international humanitarian law or not', p. 366.

[76] 'Rules of engagement', p. 23.

[77] Cedric Ryngaert and Anneleen Van de Meulebroucke, 'Enhancing and enforcing compliance with international humanitarian law by non-state armed groups: an inquiry into some mechanisms', *Journal of Conflict & Security Law*, 16(3) (2012), pp. 443–72, 444.

[78] Bangerter, 'Reasons why armed groups choose to respect international humanitarian law or not', pp. 371–2.

[79] Sassòli, 'Taking armed groups seriously', p. 26. See also 'Rules of engagement', p. 6.

[80] Bangerter, 'Reasons why armed groups choose to respect international humanitarian law or not', pp. 369–70.

[81] Ryngaert and Van de Meulebroucke, 'Enhancing and enforcing compliance with international humanitarian law by non-state armed groups', p. 443.

humanitarian actors and their content varies considerably.[82] A well-known form of unilateral declaration are the Deeds of Commitment issued by Geneva Call.[83] The Deed of Commitment on the ban of anti-personal landmines, for instance, was signed by 42 NSAGs, which demonstrates its great dissemination.[84] Those kinds of endorsement are extremely relevant not only for the sense of ownership that they can originate, but also because it may be said that such a declaration can be considered to bind the armed group under international law.[85]

Codes of conduct are a logical 'next step' after an armed group has issued a general unilateral declaration committing to IHL and IHRL norms.[86] Codes of conducts are defined as 'the set of rules an organization expects its members to respect under all circumstances' and, as such, they lay down the group's minimum standards.[87] As Bangerter has suggested, codes of conduct have to be short for pedagogical reasons: 'If the organization intends all its members—regardless of rank—to apply the rules, they must be understandable by the least educated members and must be learned by heart.'[88] In order to enhance respect by fighters, codes of conduct should provide standing operational procedures for military operations, and implementation and monitoring mechanisms, as well as possible punishments for violations.[89]

Special agreements are usually bilateral agreements that reflect the understanding of the parties to the conflict of applicable law and the agreed interpretation of such norms. The Commitments are reciprocal, meaning that the parties have the same obligations.[90] Special agreements may be very general, or specific and detailed, but they all usually include some enforcement and monitoring measures.[91] As it has been shown, ANSAs

[82] Ryngaert and Van de Meulebroucke, 'Enhancing and enforcing compliance with international humanitarian law by non-state armed groups', p. 445.

[83] Geneva Call has issued three deeds of commitment so far: the Deed of Commitment for Adherence to a Total Ban on Anti-Personnel Mines and for Cooperation in Mine Action (42 signatories); the Deed of Commitment under Geneva Call for the Protection of Children from the Effects of the Armed Conflict (7 signatories); and the Deed of Commitment under Geneva Call for the Prohibition of Sexual Violence in Situations of Armed Conflict and towards the Elimination of Gender Discrimination (five signatories). For further information, visit <http://www.genevacall.org/home.htm>.

[84] Geneva Call, 'Anti-personnel mines and armed non-state actors', 3 May 2012, <http://www.genevacall. org/Themes/Landmines/landmines.htm>.

[85] Clapham, *Human Rights Obligations*, pp. 291–4.

[86] ICRC, *Increasing Respect for International Humanitarian Law in Non-International Armed Conflicts*, ICRC, Geneva, 2008, p. 22.

[87] O. Bangerter, 'Internal control—codes of conduct within insurgent armed groups', Occasional Paper No. 31, Small Arms Survey, November 2012, p. 12.

[88] Bangerter, 'Internal control—codes of conduct within insurgent armed groups', p. 14. See also, M. Sassòli, 'The implementation of international humanitarian law: current and inherent challenges', *Yearbook of International Humanitarian Law*, 10 (2007), p. 64.

[89] 'Rules of engagement', p. 35.

[90] Ryngaert and Van de Meulebroucke, 'Enhancing and enforcing compliance with international humanitarian law by non-state armed groups: an inquiry into some mechanisms', pp. 453–5.

[91] 'Rules of engagement', p. 34.

have numerous ways to express their consent to be bound by international norms. I will now assess how this may have influenced, in 2012, the conduct of the main armed groups in the four countries this chapter focuses on.

HOW ANSAS' COMMITMENT TO COMPLY WITH IHL AND IHRL INFLUENCES THEIR CONDUCT

We will see that even if the leadership of a group takes the 'right' decisions, this will not necessarily bring violations to an end. Indeed, many factors can prevent a group that has officially declared its intention to abide by international law from implementing that commitment.

In Libya,[92] the National Transitional Council (NTC) released, in May 2011, the 'Frontline guidelines on the fundamental rules which must be adhered to in times of conflict'.[93] As the NTC declared, these guidelines were produced 'to help instruct those civilians who have taken up arms in support of the NTC'.[94] The five-page document contains an explicit commitment to both Common Article 3 to the four 1949 Geneva Conventions and to the 1977 Additional Protocol II. Furthermore, NTC leadership, during and after the conflict, reaffirmed on several occasions its willingness to respect international norms.[95] Nevertheless, as has been reported by NGOs and by the International Commission of Inquiry on Libya (Libyan Commission of Inquiry), many anti-Gaddafi fighters have been accused of war crimes and human rights abuses during and after the Libyan civil war.[96] In May 2012, however, the NTC published Law 38 (2012) granting

---

[92] See Section A of the present chapter for background on the situation in Libya.

[93] NTC, 'Frontline guidelines on the fundamental rules which must be adhered to in times of conflict plus introduction to guidelines', 17 May 2011, <http://www.ejiltalk.org/wp-content/uploads/2011/08/Final-Libyan-LOAC-Guidelines-17-May-2011.ppt>.

[94] NTC, 'NTC launches frontline manual', Press Statement No. 21, 20 May 2011, <http://feb17.info/news/national-council-launches-frontline-manual/>.

[95] NTC, Press statement, June 2011, <http://ntclibyaus.files.wordpress.com/2011/08/ntc-ps-laws2.pdf>; NTC, Press statement, 10 May 2011, <http://pdfcast.org/pdf/the-ntc-condemns-the-use-of-child-soldiers>; NTC, 'Communiqué by the Libyan National Transitional Council regarding landmines', 30 April 2011, <http://www.hrw.org/sites/default/files/related_material/Communique.pdf>; NTC, 'The treatment of detainees and prisoners', Press statement, 25 March 2011, <http://www.ntclibya.org/english/prisoners/>.

[96] See generally 'Report of the International Commission of Inquiry on Libya', Human Rights Council, UN doc. A/HRC/19/68, 8 March 2012, p. 1. See also Sarah Leah Whitson, 'Libya's human rights problem', *Foreign Policy*, 15 May 2012, <http://mideast.foreignpolicy.com/posts/2012/05/15/libyas_human_rights_problem>. In March 2012, the Libyan Commission of Inquiry reaffirmed that rebel forces had committed war crimes and crimes against humanity during the uprising, and stressed the fact that no investigation has been carried out: 'Report of the International Commission of Inquiry on Libya', 8 March 2012, §§95–110. Likewise, HRW blamed former opposition's armed groups for the extrajudicial execution of Muammar Gaddafi and his son Muatasim, together with 66 other prisoners captured outside Sirte: HRW, 'Death of a dictator: bloody vengeance in Sirte'.

immunity from prosecution to 'revolutionaries', for 'military, security and civilian acts required by the 17 February Revolution' committed with the 'purpose of leading the revolution to victory'.[97] The same law also gives legal weight to interrogation reports and other information gathered by 'revolutionaries', legitimizing the seizure, detention, and interrogation of detainees outside a legal framework.[98] Libya is currently in a dispute with the ICC over the question of jurisdiction for the trials of Saif al-Islam, one of Gaddafi's sons held in custody by a Zintani armed group since his capture in November 2011, and Abdullah Senussi, a former intelligence chief who was extradited to Libya from Mauritania in September 2012.[99] Both the Libyan government and the armed groups want to hold the trial of the two men in a domestic court.[100]

As we have already stated, the Syrian resistance is characterized by a multitude of armed groups the majority of which are affiliated to the FSA.[101] Despite numerous efforts by FSA leadership to unify and structure the undefined number of anti-government groups, the armed opposition remains largely fragmented. This is mostly due to the fact that the FSA has proven unable to logistically sustain its supporters and, as the Syrian Commission of Inquiry highlighted in its last report, it has become more and more common to see 'fighters shifting from one group to another based on the availability of funds and weapons'.[102]

In August 2012, the FSA issued a two-page Code of Conduct containing, in 11 articles, all basic principles of IHL and IHRL. The Code was published and opened for signature shortly afterwards.[103] Following its release, the FSA called for respect of

---

[97] Those are extracted from Law 38/2012 on Special Procedures during the Transitional Period, 2 May 2012.

[98] ICG, 'Trial by error: justice in post-Qadhafi Libya', p. 28.

[99] HRW, 'Libya: Q&A on the ICC and Saif al-Islam Gaddafi', 23 January 2012, <http://www.hrw.org/news/2012/01/23/libya-qa-icc-and-saif-al-islam-gaddafi>.

[100] In order to do so in compliance with international law, Libya would need to prove to the ICC judges that it has the willingness and ability to guarantee a fair trial. For further detail, see 'Application on the behalf of the Government of Libya pursuant to article 19 of the ICC statute', ICC doc. ICC-01/11-01/11-130Red, 1 May 2012. In April 2013, Libya filed a separate admissibility challenge pertaining to Abdullah Senussi. See 'Application on behalf of the Government of Libya relating to Abdullah al-Sanusi pursuant to Article 19 of the ICC Statute' (Case No. ICC-01/11-01/11-307-Red2), 2 April 2013. The ICC still has to issue a final decision on both cases. See also HRW, 'UN Security Council: Press Libya on ICC cooperation, impunity', 6 November 2012, <http://www.hrw.org/news/2012/11/06/un-security-council-press-libya-icc-cooperation-impunity>.

[101] See 'Report of the Independent International Commission of Inquiry on the Syrian Arab Republic', 5 February 2013, §§24–6.

[102] 'Report of the Independent International Commission of Inquiry on the Syrian Arab Republic', 5 February 2013, §12.

[103] Razan Ghazzawi, 'Battalions sign Free Syrian Army's Code of Conduct', *North Star*, 15 October 2012, <http://www.thenorthstar.info/?p=2781>.

international norms by its affiliates.[104] However, numerous reports, notably those of the Syrian Commission of Inquiry, have condemned the opposition's serious violations of both IHL and IHRL.[105] The most important reason seems to be the inability of the FSA leadership to exercise effective control over the group's activities and conduct.[106]

Fragmentation brings confusion even to those groups that are, in theory, willing to respect international norms, but who often find themselves in situations in which they have to respond to contradictory orders coming from the same authorities.[107] In December 2012, for instance, the National Coalition of Syrian Revolution issued a statement condemning declarations from other FSA sources that called for any Russian civilian in Syria to be considered a legitimate target by the Syrian revolution because of Russia's support to the Assad's regime. The National Coalition of Syrian Revolution and Opposition Forces explained that 'the Russian government alone bears full responsibility of their actions without any blame to Russian civilians', and further added that 'such statements do not represent the opinions, positions, or policies of the Coalition and are completely rejected based on the principles of the Syrian revolution, its ethical standards, interests and policies'.[108] Another possible reason for lack of compliance by opposition fighters with FSA commitments could be the increased ferocity of the conduct of regime forces. As Assad's regime has increased the brutality of its attacks against both civilians and opposition armed groups, the rebels have become more radicalized.

In Mali, contrary to the position of the MNLA, which explicitly committed to respect IHL and IHRL through several declarations and statements,[109] the Islamist groups occupying northern Mali have shown no interest in recognizing and complying with international norms. The groups seem to justify their conduct in the name of religious beliefs. Indeed, Ansar Dine, AQIM, and MOJWA openly affirmed their intent to implement an extremely strict interpretation of Shari'a law. Some of the rules derived from Shari'a clearly contradict international norms. AQIM and Ansar Dine, for instance,

---

[104] 'Free Syrian Army slams executions of regime loyalists', *Daily Star*, 4 August 2012, <http://www.dailystar.com.lb/News/Middle-East/2012/Aug-04/183383-free-syrian-army-slams-executions-of-regime-loyalists.ashx#axzz22maDYGO5>.

[105] Such violations include extrajudicial executions, torture, and inhuman or degrading treatment, targeting civilians, and recruiting child soldiers. See 'Report of the Independent International Commission of Inquiry on the Syrian Arab Republic', 5 February 2013, §§105–20.

[106] Jonathan Spyer, 'Defying a dictator: meet the Free Syrian Army', *World Affairs*, May/June 2012, <http://www.worldaffairsjournal.org/article/defying-dictator-meet-free-syrian-army>.

[107] Indeed, opposition fighters tend to answer to local commanders and operate independently on tribal and geographic bases. See 'Report of the Independent International Commission of Inquiry on the Syrian Arab Republic', 22 February 2012, §§106–10.

[108] National Coalition of Syrian Revolution and Opposition Forces, 'National Coalition's position on Russian civilians in Syria', Press release, December 2012, <http://us6.campaign-archive1.com/?u=91f7a2c8b39d32e7ac9968d75&id=5e88b334b3&e=61b90484c1>.

[109] MNLA, 'Le MNLA respecte la personne humaine', 15 February 2012, <http://www.mnlamov.net/component/content/article/124-le-mnla-respecte-la-personne-humaine.html>.

are responsible for destroying holy, historic, and cultural sites in Timbuktu, including some listed as world heritage sites by UNESCO. The head of Ansar Dine, Abou Dardar, in an interview with Agence France-Presse, declared 'Not a single mausoleum will remain in Timbuktu, Allah doesn't like it', and 'We are in the process of smashing all the hidden mausoleums in the area'.[110] The smashing of holy sites seems to be part of what the fighters call 'defending the purity of their faith against idol worship'. As the UN Secretary-General concluded in his November 2012 report:

These groups have created a context in which most cultural and recreational activities are prohibited, thus rejecting and combating the cultural identities and undermining the social fabric of the communities of the north . . . The human rights situation in Mali, especially in the north, has continued to deteriorate since January. Extremist Islamist groups have reportedly committed gross human rights abuses, including summary and extrajudicial executions, sexual and gender-based violence, recruitment and use of child soldiers, torture and looting of hospitals. It appears that there have been changes in the pattern, character and prevalence of the abuses since the beginning of the crisis . . . Since the extremist Islamist groups of Ansar Dine, MUJAO and AQIM have taken control, other types of abuses are being witnessed, mostly relating to the implementation of an extremely strict interpretation of sharia law. Executions, floggings and stonings, among other cruel and inhuman punishments, have been reported. Freedom of speech and assembly and the rights of women and children are also being curtailed.[111]

The Secretary-General also reported serious abuses against children:

Grave violations against children in northern Mali have been a salient characteristic of the crisis since it began. All armed groups in the north, including MNLA, Ansar Dine, MUJAO and AQIM, are reported to have targeted children, resulting in the recruitment of hundreds of minors into their ranks. Particularly alarming are reports of training camps in Gao run by armed groups, in addition to reports of cross-border recruitment of children in refugee camps in Burkina Faso, Mauritania and the Niger.[112]

In relation to the DRC, in June 2012, the UN High Commissioner for Human Rights, Navi Pillay, identified five of the M23's leaders as 'among the worst perpetrators of human rights violations in the DRC, or in the world. They include General Bosco Ntaganda, who is wanted on two arrest warrants by the International Criminal Court (ICC) for war crimes and crimes against humanity in Ituri district, and Col. Sultani Makenga, who is implicated in the recruitment of children and several massacres in eastern Congo'.[113]

---

[110] 'Mali fighters destroy more Timbuktu tombs', *Al Jazeera*, 23 December 2012, <http://www.aljazeera.com/news/africa/2012/12/2012122317115353560.html>.

[111] 'Report of the Secretary-General on the situation in Mali', 29 November 2012, §21.

[112] 'Report of the Secretary-General on the situation in Mali', 29 November 2012, §26.

[113] 'UN rights chief concerned over civilian safety as fighting continues in Democratic Republic Congo's east', *UN News Service*, 19 June 2012, <http://www.refworld.org/docid/4fe42d4b2.html>.

The conduct of M23 could look somehow paradoxical since rebels attack the very people on whose behalf they claim to be fighting. However, this paradox could also be part of a military strategy consisting of the use of terror as a way to control people.[114] HRW has reported finding evidence of forced recruitment by M23 rebels of at least 137 young men and boys in Rutshuru territory, eastern Congo, since July 2012. The reports adds that: 'Most were abducted from their homes, in the market, or while walking to their farms. At least seven were under age 15. Witnesses told Human Rights Watch that at least 33 new recruits and other M23 fighters were summarily executed when they attempted to flee. Some were tied up and shot in front of other recruits as an example of the punishment they could receive.'[115] This last sentence clearly shows the use of fear and threat as a way of securing obedience to the groups' orders. It also can happen that armed group leaders condone violations as an explicit means of rewarding or paying fighters; this may be the case with looting.[116] Many cases of looting in North Kivu have been reported by HRW.[117]

Although M23 has not released any public declaration expressing its will to respect IHL or IHRL, and despite openly committing serious human rights violations, in an interview with HRW on 8 August 2012, Colonel Makenga, one of M23's leaders, said 'We recruit our brothers, not by force, but because they want to help their big brothers ... That's their decision', adding also: 'They are our little brothers, so we can't kill them.'[118] Colonel Makenga also affirmed that numerous reports denouncing child recruitment by his forces were part of Congolese government propaganda.[119]

Concluding remarks

The present chapter highlights two major trends related to ANSAs and international law in 2012. From a legal framework perspective, it is important to stress the role of UN practice, especially through the reports of commissions of inquiry; UN Security Council and Human Rights Council resolutions are moving increasingly towards an acceptance that ANSAs have obligations under IHRL. Practice is not yet consistent, however.

From a practical perspective, after analysing patterns of compliance with international norms by ANSAs in Libya, Syria, Mali, and the DRC, the overall outlook is not reassuring.

---

[114] O. Bangerter, 'Talking to armed groups', *Forced Migration Review*, 16 March 2011, p. 7, <http://www.fmreview.org/non-state/Bangerter.html>.

[115] HRW, 'DR Congo: M23 rebels committing war crimes', 11 September 2012, <http://www.hrw.org/print/news/2012/09/11/dr-congo-m23-rebels-committing-war-crimes>.

[116] Bangerter, 'Talking to armed groups', p. 7.

[117] HRW, 'DR Congo: M23 rebels committing war crimes'.

[118] HRW, 'DR Congo: M23 rebels committing war crimes'.

[119] HRW, 'DR Congo: M23 rebels committing war crimes'.

Keeping in mind the unique situation in each of the selected states, it does seem that commitments to respect international norms by armed groups in Syria and in Libya have not been widely respected. In contrast, in Mali and the DRC, no public commitment to international norms was even made.

Finally, this chapter's findings emphasize the need for a systematic and consistent engagement with NSAGs given that, as the Secretary-General stated in 2010, 'experience shows that lives can be saved by engaging armed groups in order to seek compliance with international humanitarian law in their combat operations and general conduct, gain safe access for humanitarian purposes and dissuade them from using certain types of weapons'.[120]

---

[120] 'Report of the UN Secretary-General on the protection of civilians in armed conflict', UN Security Council, UN doc. S/2010/579, 11 November 2010, §52.

10 Investigation of torture claims in Israel: analysis of the 2012 High Court of Justice ruling and the Türkel Commission Report

Sharon Weill and Irit Ballas*

If we want things to stay as they are, things will have to change.[1]

Introduction

In its landmark 1999 ruling on the use of torture, the Israeli High Court of Justice (HCJ) outlawed certain inhuman and degrading methods of interrogation. Nonetheless, the practice of torture continues. Since the ruling, more than 700 complaints of torture have been submitted to human rights organizations. Yet, not only has none led to a prosecution, none has even resulted in a criminal investigation. Every single complaint was closed at the *examination* stage, either due to 'lack of evidence' or due to the 'necessity' defence.

In August 2012, the HCJ rendered a decision on a petition claiming that the internal examination mechanism provided de facto immunity for the General Security Services' (GSS) interrogation personnel. The petitioners had claimed that a criminal investigation should be opened following every allegation of torture. A few months later, in February 2013, the long-awaited state commission report on whether Israel's domestic investigation mechanism conforms to international law, the Türkel Commission Report,[2] was released. The report specifically addresses the issue of investigations of torture allegations.

* Dr Sharon Weill is a researcher and lecturer at Geneva Academy/CERAH and Science Po, Paris. She specialized in the application of international law by domestic courts (*The Application of IHL by National Courts*, Oxford University Press, forthcoming, 2014). Irit Ballas is a human rights lawyer who drafted several of the key reports and petitions of the Public Committee against Torture in Israel, including the petition discussed in this chapter, together with att. Samah al-Khatib Ayub.
[1] Giuseppe Tomasi di Lampedusa, *The Leopard*, Feltrinelli, Milan, 1958, p. 40.
[2] Resolution No. 1796 of the 32nd Government, Appointment of an Independent Public Commission, Chaired by Supreme Court Justice (ret.) Jacob Türkel, to Examine the Maritime Incident of 31 May 2010 (6 June 2010).

This chapter examines domestic Israeli investigations (or, more precisely, their absence) following torture allegations in light of the 2012 HCJ decision and the Türkel Commission Report, within the broader context of Israeli willingness to investigate and prosecute international crimes. In the wake of the General Assembly recognition of Palestine as a non-member observer state at the United Nations (UN) in November 2012, and its potential to join the 1998 Rome Statute of the International Criminal Court (ICC Statute), the question of domestic investigations of war crimes has become a matter of international concern.

Section A of this chapter provides general background concerning Israeli domestic investigations and potential ICC jurisdiction. Section B outlines the sources of the obligation to investigate torture allegations and the fundamental requirements of such investigations. Section C describes the torture allegations in Israel. Sections D, E, and F analyse the functioning of the immunity mechanism that shields perpetrators from being criminally investigated and prosecuted. This mechanism is based on three foundations: (1) the policy guidelines drafted by Israel's Attorney General, which exempt interrogators from investigations in cases in which their activities were purportedly grounded in 'necessity'; (2) lack of evidence, a lack that is a direct result of legislation and practice, such as exempting Israel Security Agency (ISA) interrogation from being video recorded; and (3) the internal examination mechanism, which effectively prevents alleged crimes from being subjected to criminal investigation. A final section discusses the relevant recommendations of the Türkel Commission Report and analyses disparities with HCJ rulings.

A. **From Goldstone to Türkel**

Israeli domestic investigations of war crime allegations were subjected to the review of the UN Fact Finding Mission on the Gaza Conflict. The report released in September 2009 (known as the 'Goldstone Report'), presented prima facie evidence of the commission of international crimes, including torture, and was the first international report to address the issue of domestic investigation of war crimes. The report found that Israeli military investigation did not comply with international standards.[3] The two follow-up reports of the UN Committee of Independent Experts, established by the

---

[3] 'Human rights in Palestine and other occupied Arab territories, report of the United Nations Fact–Finding Mission on the Gaza conflict', Human Rights Council, UN doc. A/HRC/12/48, 25 September 2009, §§1773–835. See e.g. at §1832: 'The Mission concludes that there are serious doubts about the willingness of Israel to carry out genuine investigations in an impartial, independent, prompt and effective way as required by international law. The Mission is also of the view that the Israeli system presents inherently discriminatory features that have proven to make the pursuit of justice for Palestinian victims very difficult.' See also the recommendations made to Israel by the Committee against Torture to 'conduct an independent inquiry to ensure a prompt, independent and full investigation' into the responsibility of the state during the war: Committee against Torture, 'Concluding observations: Israel', UN doc. CAT/C/ISR/CO/4, 14 May 2009, §29.

Human Rights Council and mandated to report on domestic investigations and prosecutions and their conformity with international standards, found that the Israeli system lacked the structural and institutional independence required for a proper investigation of alleged international crimes and that the investigations carried out were neither sufficiently transparent nor prompt, inherently flawing their effectiveness. Furthermore, the reports criticized Israel for not investigating those who had designed, planned, ordered, or overseen the alleged crimes.[4]

A few months before, on 21 January 2009, immediately after the Israeli military Operation 'Cast Lead' in Gaza, the Palestinian Minister of Justice submitted a declaration to the ICC under Article 12(3) of the ICC Statute in an attempt to activate the Court's jurisdiction over allegations of war crimes and crimes against humanity committed during Israel's operation. At the time that the Goldstone Report and the two follow-up reports were released, the ICC Prosecutor's decision on whether the Palestinian Authority (PA) was competent to submit such a declaration was still pending.[5] This is why the effectiveness of the Israeli domestic investigations of allegation of war crimes, in light of the complementary principle, became so significant: if jurisdiction were established, the ICC would need to decide whether the case was admissible, namely whether Israel was 'unwilling' or 'unable' genuinely to undertake investigations and prosecutions of allegations of international crimes.[6] Therefore, it was not mere coincidence that the Türkel Commission—the Israeli state commission established in June 2010 by the government in the aftermath of the Flotilla incident—was also mandated to examine 'whether the investigation and inquiry mechanism that is practiced in Israel in general . . . is consistent with the duties of the State of Israel pursuant to the rules of international law'.[7]

---

[4] 'Report of the Committee of Independent Experts in international humanitarian and human rights laws to monitor and assess any domestic, legal or other proceedings undertaken by both the Government of Israel and the Palestinian side, in the light of General Assembly resolution 64/254, including the independence, effectiveness, genuineness of these investigations and their conformity with international standards', UN doc. A/HRC/15/50, 23 September 2010, §§91–5; 'Report of the Committee of Independent Experts in international humanitarian and human rights law established pursuant to Council Resolution 13/9', UN doc. A/HRC/16/24, 18 March 2011, §§40–6 and 79–83.

[5] The PA declaration is available at <http://www.icc-cpi.int/NR/rdonlyres/74EEE201-0FED-4481-95D4-C8071087102C/279777/20090122PalestinianDeclaration2.pdf>.

[6] The complementarity principle is defined in Art. 17 of the ICC Statute. For analysis of Israeli domestic investigations in light of the complementarity principle after Operation Cast Lead in Gaza, see Sharon Weill and Valentina Azarov, 'Shielded from accountability: Israel's unwillingness to investigate and prosecute international crimes', FIDH No. 572a, Paris, September 2011; V. Azarov and S. Weill, 'Israel's unwillingness? The follow-up investigations to the UN Gaza conflict report and international criminal justice', *International Criminal Law Review*, 12 (2012), pp. 905–35.

[7] See the explicit reference that appears in the introduction of the Committee's report (second part): 'This particular mandate required the Commission to determine whether Israel is complying with its obligations to examine and investigate such complaints and claims, *inter alia*, in view of the criticisms levelled in Israel and internationally with regard to the manner in which Israel investigates complaints and claims of violations of international humanitarian law.'

The Türkel Commission heard testimony from the military and from political echelons, Israeli law professors, and leading non-governmental organizations (NGOs), including the Public Committee against Torture, which presented in detail the various deficiencies of the state mechanisms in charge of investigating allegations of torture.[8]

On 3 April 2012, in parallel with the work of the Türkel Commission, the Office of the Prosecutor (OTP) of the ICC issued an 'Update on the situation in Palestine' in which it held that it was unable to proceed with the preliminary examination under Article 12(3) of the ICC Statute at this stage due to its incompetence to determine the question concerning Palestine's status as a 'state'. Instead, it deferred this determination to the UN General Assembly and Security Council, and to the ICC's Assembly of States Parties. A few months later, in November 2012, the UN General Assembly upgraded Palestine's status in the Assembly to that of 'non-member observer state'[9]. Since that resolution, at least legally, Palestine can join the ICC Statute (or request the ICC Prosecutor to reopen the examination of the ad hoc declaration, thereby potentially triggering the activation of the jurisdiction of the ICC retroactively as of July 2002).[10]

On February 2013, three months after the General Assembly vote, the Türkel Commission rendered its long-awaited report. In the preface, it states:

The subject matter of the Commission's work is of fundamental importance, not only for Israel but also for other States desirous of complying with international legal obligations and for the International Criminal Court itself given the complementarity formula in Article 17 of the Rome Statute [ICC Statute].[11]

Article 17(2) of the ICC Statute cites the following three principal factors to assess a state's unwillingness genuinely to carry out investigations and prosecutions: (1) lack of independence and impartiality; (2) unjustified delays in investigation; and (3) shielding the higher military and political echelons from criminal liability.[12] It is in light of these

---

[8] The testimony of the Public Committee against Torture in Israel to the Türkel Committee of 12 April 2011 is available in Hebrew at <http://www.turkel-committee.gov.il/content-147-b.html>.

[9] On 29 November 2012, by 138 votes to nine (Canada, the Czech Republic, Israel, the Marshall Islands, Micronesia, Nauru, Panama, Palau, and the United States of America (USA)), with 41 abstentions, the UN General Assembly accorded Palestine the status of non-member observer state in the UN. See Resolution 67/19, 29 November 2012.

[10] See further, in this regard, Part II of this book.

[11] Public Commission to Examine the Maritime Incident of 31 May 2010, 'Second report: Israeli's mechanisms for examining and investigating complaints and claims of violations of the laws of armed conflict according to international law', February 2013 (the Türkel Commission Report), <http://www .turkelcommittee.gov.il/files/newDoc3/The%20Turkel%20Report%20for%20website.pdf>. See also the only legal opinion, which appears on the Committee's website: Claus Kreß, 'The principle of complementarity under the Rome Statute of the International Criminal Court', <http://www.turkel-committee.gov.il/files/ wordocs/Manuskript.pdf>.

[12] For an interpretation of Art. 17(2) of the ICC Statute, see e.g. Azarov and Weill, 'Israel's unwillingness? The follow-up investigations to the UN Gaza conflict report and international criminal justice', p. 911.

that the following sections dealing with Israeli domestic investigations of torture claims should be understood.

B. **The international obligation to investigate alleged torture and the principles of effective investigations**

The right to be free from torture is among the rare legal principles holding the status of *jus cogens*: peremptory norms binding upon all nations without exception.[13] The prohibition on torture under any circumstances is codified in the 1984 UN Convention against Torture and Other Cruel, Inhuman or Degrading Treatment or Punishment (CAT), as well as the 1966 International Covenant on Civil and Political Rights (ICCPR), which emphasizes the duty to treat suspects and detainees humanely and with dignity.[14] International humanitarian law (IHL) similarly establishes an absolute prohibition on torture in situations of armed conflict.[15] Moreover, a violation of the absolute prohibition entails not only state responsibility, but also individual criminal responsibility,[16] while international human rights law (IHRL) and IHL impose a duty upon states to investigate allegations of torture and, where torture is identified, to prosecute those responsible.[17] According to international law, investigations have to be independent, impartial, effective, prompt, and transparent.[18] More specifically in the context of

---

[13] Manfred Nowak and Elizabeth McArthur, *The United Nations Convention against Torture—A Commentary*, Oxford University Press, Oxford, 2008, pp. 117–18; International Criminal Tribunal for the former Yugoslavia (ICTY), *Prosecutor v. Furundžija*, Judgment (Trial Chamber) (Case No. IT–95–17/1-T), 10 December 1998, §§137–8, 153.

[14] ICCPR, Arts 7 and 4.2, and Art 2(2) of CAT set the absolute character of the prohibition.

[15] Common Art. 3 to all four 1949 Geneva Conventions anchors the prohibition of torture and cruel treatment and of mutilation. This Article applies explicitly to people being held in detention. The 1949 Geneva Convention Relative to the Protection of Civilian Persons in Time of War (1949 Geneva Convention IV) lays down the absolute prohibition on torture and other inhumane treatment of protected persons. Art. 27 of the 1949 Geneva Convention IV anchors the right of protected persons to humane treatment, and to protection from any act or threat of violence. Art. 31 of the Convention prohibits any physical or moral coercion with the intention of obtaining information. In addition, Art. 32 lays down a broad prohibition of torture and all brutal measures.

[16] Torture is defined as a war crime under Art. 8(2)(a)(ii) and (b)(xxi) of the ICC Statute, as well as Art. 147 of the 1949 Geneva Convention III and Art. 129 of the 1949 Geneva Convention III. Art. 4, CAT, imposes on states the obligation to ensure that acts of torture are offences under their criminal law.

[17] IHL imposes an obligation upon states to investigate and prosecute grave breaches of the Geneva Conventions, including torture and ill-treatment. See Art. 129, 1949 Geneva Convention III; Art. 146, 1949 Geneva Convention IV; Rule 158, International Committee of the Red Cross (ICRC) Customary IHL Study.

[18] Michael N. Schmitt, 'Investigating violations of international law in armed conflict', *Harvard National Security Journal*, 2(1) (2011), pp. 35–48; 2010 UN follow-up report to the Fact Finding Mission to Gaza, fn. 5, §§18–34; Türkel Commission Report, pp. 137–8. See also 'Principles on the effective investigation and documentation of torture and other cruel, inhuman or degrading treatment or punishment', Annex to

torture, CAT requires in Article 12 prompt and impartial investigations by competent authorities. The UN Committee against Torture has noted on several occasions that the relevant authorities must initiate a prompt and impartial investigation whenever the suspicion arises that torture has been practised, followed, when relevant, by prosecution and penal sanction, as well as accountability of senior military and civilian officials.[19]

C. **Torture allegations in Israel**

In 1987, the use by Israeli GSS agents of 'a moderate measure of physical pressure' in a wide range of circumstances was officially institutionalized, based on the 'necessity' defence clause in the Israeli Penal Code.[20] The clause stipulates that a person will be exempt from criminal liability for an act required in an immediate manner in order to save his or someone else's life, liberty, or property, when no alternative course of action is available. The state-appointed Landau Commission interpreted this clause as conferring general, *ex ante* permission to use 'moderate physical pressure' in interrogations, and its recommendations were adopted in their entirety by the Israeli government at the time.[21] This legal construction remained intact for more than a decade and resulted, according to the Israeli NGO B'tselem, in the use of physical methods that constituted torture against 850 persons a year.[22]

General Assembly Resolution 55/89, 'Torture and other cruel, inhuman or degrading treatment or punishment', 22 February 2001.

[19] The Human Rights Committee, which monitors the implementation of the ICCPR, has consistently stated that criminal investigations and the trying of perpetrators are necessary remedies, and that the decision not to initiate a criminal investigation amounts to a denial of justice and a violation of the Covenant. See e.g. *Umetaliev and ors v. Kyrgyzstan*, Decision (Comm. No. 1275/2004), 30 October 2008, §9.2; *Amirov v. Russian Federation*, Decision (Comm. No. 1447/2006), 2 April 2009, §§11.2–11.4; 'General Comment No. 31 on the nature of the legal obligation on states parties to the Covenant', 2004, §§15, 18; *Sathasivam v. Sri Lanka*, Decision (Comm. No. 1436/2005), 8 July 2008, §6.4; *Mohammed Alzery v. Sweden*, UN doc. CCPR/C/88/D/1416/2005, 10 November 2006, §11.7. See also Committee against Torture, 'Concluding observations: Burundi', UN doc. CAT/C/BDI/CO/1, 2007, §§21–2; Committee against Torture, 'Concluding observations: France', UN doc. CAT/C/FRA/CO/3, 2006, §21; Committee against Torture, 'Concluding observations: United States of America', UN doc. CAT/C/USA/CO/2, 2006, §19.

[20] 'Report of the Commission of Inquiry concerning the methods of investigation of the Israel Security Agency regarding hostile terrorist activity', Jerusalem, October 1987 (the Landau Commission).

[21] The Landau Commission also found that, for many years, GSS staff had systematically lied to the courts and sought to change this situation. The Commission's report noted 'the feeling on the part of the interrogators that their actions not only enjoyed the backing of their superiors but were also known to elements outside the service who gave their tacit consent. It was claimed that these elements include the prosecution system—both civilian and the military, the courts, and the political echelon': Landau Commission, pp. 28–9.

[22] B'Tselem, 'Routine torture: interrogation methods of the General Security Service', February 1998, pp. 5 and 16, <http://www.btselem.org/publications/summaries/199802_routine_torture>.

In 1999, the HCJ rendered its famous landmark ruling on torture.[23] In that ruling, President Aharon Barak recognized the absolute prohibition of torture and inhuman treatment under international law, stating that: 'They have no exceptions and no balances.'[24] The HCJ further rejected the state's position that the Penal Code's necessity defence provides an *ex ante* authorization of the use of otherwise illegal methods, explicitly noting that 'the government or the heads of the General Security Service do not have the authority to establish guidelines, rules, and permissions concerning the use of physical force during interrogation of persons suspected of terrorist activities'.[25] While the Court left open the possibility of legislation specifically allowing torture, the judgment made it clear that any such law could be constitutionally reviewed by the HCJ in light of Israeli constitutional law.[26]

Nonetheless, the HCJ went one step further in allowing an important deferral to the discretion of the executive, which would result in allowing, to some extent, existing practices to persist over the following decade. The HCJ ruled that the Attorney General 'can establish guidelines regarding circumstances in which investigators shall not stand trial, if they claim to have acted from "necessity"'.[27] Thus, on the one hand, the HCJ affirmed that the 'necessity defence' could not serve as a legal authorization to use torture,[28] while on the other, it allowed the Attorney General, who stands at the head of the state prosecutorial system and serves as the state's legal adviser, to define the circumstances in which interrogators should not be prosecuted, when they claimed to have used a prohibited method of torture due to 'necessity'.

As a result, complaints and allegations of torture by Palestinian detainees continued. Since the HCJ ruling in 1999, more than 700 allegations of torture in detailed affidavits have been submitted by human rights organizations.[29] Among the many allegations of torture and abuse, sleep deprivation and prolonged interrogations are commonplace, as are acts such as being bound to a chair in painful positions, beatings, slapping, kicking, threats, verbal abuse, and degradation. Special methods include bending the body into painful positions, manacling from behind for long periods of time, intentional tightening of handcuffs, exposure to extreme heat and cold, permanent exposure to artificial light,

---

[23] HCJ, *Public Committee against Torture in Israel v. Government of Israel*, Judgment (5100/94), 1999 (the *Torture case* (1999)).

[24] *Torture case* (1999), §27.   [25] *Torture case* (1999), §§23, 35.

[26] See *Torture case* (1999), §§23 and 39: '[The authorizing] legislation may be passed, provided, of course, that the law "befit[s] the values of the State of Israel, is enacted for a proper purpose, and [infringes the suspect's liberty] to an extent no greater than required."' This corresponds to derogation as set out in Art. 8 of the Israeli Basic Law: Human Dignity and Liberty. Because Israeli constitutional legislation includes a derogation clause, it does not correspond to the absolute international prohibition to torture, which reflects a *jus cogens* norm allowing for no exceptions.

[27] *Torture case* (1999), §38.

[28] *Torture case* (1999), §37: 'The principle of "necessity" cannot serve as a basis of authority.'

[29] Türkel Commission Report, p. 354.

and detention in substandard conditions contrary to the basic standards set down by the UN. Various forms of psychological torture, such as threats and exploitation of family members, are also commonly used.[30] Allegations include being denied the right to contact attorneys and family members, often for extended periods of time.[31] These allegations have not gone unnoticed by the international bodies in charge of promoting the implementation of CAT.[32]

Yet none of these hundreds of complaints has led to a criminal investigation, let alone a prosecution. An analysis of correspondence between complainants and the Attorney General's office shows that the grounds given for shelving complaints of torture and ill-treatment fall into one of two main categories: justification under the necessity defence, or denial. The following sections provide an analysis of the investigation mechanism and policy, which shield those responsible for torture from criminal accountability.

D. **Immunity in cases of necessity**

> *[The UN Committee against Torture] remains concerned that the necessity defence exception may still arise...*[33]

On the basis of the HCJ's ruling, the Attorney General in office in 1999, Mr Elyakim Rubinstein, swiftly published guidelines effectively granting a priori permission to use physical force against detainees in so-called 'ticking bomb' cases.[34] The guidelines describe in detail the considerations to take into account when deciding whether or not the necessity defence applies to a particular case, and recommend that senior officials should be involved in this decision. They explicitly provide that where an interrogator has employed a means of interrogation in order to secure vital information to prevent

---

[30] See Irit Ballas, 'Family matters', Public Committee against Torture, 2012; Maya Rosenfeld, 'When the exception becomes the rule', Public Committee against Torture, 2012; Elkhatib Samakh, 'Shackling as a form of torture and ill treatment', Public Committee against Torture, 2009.

[31] Under Israeli military law, in the West Bank a suspect can be detained for up to eight days before being brought before a judge, and can be prevented from meeting a lawyer for up to 90 days.

[32] In its concluding observations of May 2009, the Committee against Torture expressed its concern about the continuing use of such methods: 'The Committee is concerned that there are numerous, ongoing and consistent allegations of the use of methods by Israeli security officials that were prohibited by the September 1999 ruling of the Israeli Supreme Court.' See Committee against Torture, 'Concluding observations: Israel', UN doc. CAT/C/ISR/CO/4, 14 May 2009, §19.

[33] Committee against Torture, 'Concluding observations: Israel', UN doc. CAT/C/ISR/CO/4, 14 May 2009, §14.

[34] The Attorney General's guidelines are reproduced in English in the Annex of the Report of the Public Committee against Torture in Israel, 'Accountability denied: the absence of investigation and punishment of torture in Israel', 2009, <http://www.stoptorture.org.il/files/Accountability_Denied_Eng.pdf>.

tangible danger of grave threat to state security or to human life, liberty, and integrity, and when, under the circumstances, no other reasonable means to prevent this injury exist, the Attorney General will consider refraining from initiating criminal proceedings. Although the Attorney General mentioned that these guidelines 'shall not apply to means of interrogation the use of which constitutes "torture" as defined in' the CAT,[35] as President Barak did in the 1999 torture ruling, the Attorney General does not specify which acts amount to torture. Perhaps this explains why the guidelines have not prevented him—or his successors—from applying the necessity defence to what appear to be overt instances of torture.[36]

As a result of this policy, in more than one in six of the complaints the Attorney General does not deny the factual basis of the complaint, but alludes to a 'ticking bomb' scenario. In such cases, which imply a tacit admission of the allegations, the complaint does not lead to a criminal investigation since the interrogation was conducted in accordance with regulations, presumably, under the necessity defence doctrine. In doing so, the Attorney General is in fact condoning the interrogation methods used by the GSS, because of the seriousness of the allegations against the complainant.

THE CONTEMPT OF COURT CASE (2009)

In 2008, three major human rights organizations filed a contempt of court motion to the HCJ against the Israeli government and the GSS for their policy of granting a priori permission to use torture in interrogations, in violation of the 1999 ruling.[37] The motion states that the 1999 judgment categorically declared that past GSS actions upon a large number of suspects are illegal, and yet these practices continued. The petitioners point out that the perpetrators of these acts incur criminal liability and can be held accountable for these serious crimes in Israel or in a foreign jurisdiction, according to domestic law and international law.

The motion provides evidence for the routine granting of a priori authorization by the interrogator's supervisors, and even by the head of the GSS himself, to use physical interrogation methods in accordance with established procedures known to interrogators, prosecutors and judges as 'the necessity interrogation procedure'. This evidence includes testimonies by GSS interrogators from court proceedings, as well as testimony from victims, and public responses by the GSS and the Prime Minister's Office.

---

[35] 1999 Guidelines of the Attorney General, Section G(1).

[36] See e.g. Noam Hoffstadter, 'Ticking bombs—testimonies of torture victims in Israel', Public Committee against Torture, 2007.

[37] HCJ, *Public Committee against Torture in Israel v. Government of Israel*, Contempt of Court (Case No. 5100/94), 2009.

For example, in a GSS response to an item published in the *Ha'aretz* newspaper, it states that 'authorization to use force in an interrogation is always given by an agent with at least the rank of interrogation team head, and at times it is even granted by the head of the Service himself'. And in another instance: 'It should be made clear that the authorization to use special procedures in an interrogation can be given by the head of the GSS alone.'[38]

In July 2009, the motion was rejected on the grounds that the Court does not address general policies in contempt procedures, with the recommendation to submit individual cases. Since then, the Public Committee against Torture has submitted a dozen of such individual cases, none of which has resulted, until now, in a substantive ruling.

E. **Immunity as a result of lack of evidence**

In most cases, torture allegations are dismissed because of a lack of corroborating evidence. The Attorney General's office simply denies the facts, using formulations such as: 'There is no basis for your complaint.' This shifts the burden of proof onto the victim, whose version of events is deemed inconsistent with those of the GSS and therefore labelled false. In the absence of video or audio recordings of interrogations, from which GSS interrogations are exempted, GSS accounts cannot be independently verified. A legal limbo is thus created given that, wherever inconsistencies arise, the Attorney General invariably decides in favour of the GSS. Its shelving of complaints implies a de facto requirement for evidence that will corroborate the facts as presented by the complainant. However, in light of the special status of the complainants, a range of legal and circumstantial obstacles prevents them from establishing the evidentiary basis without which the respondent refuses to open a criminal investigation.

Among these obstacles are: the presumption of administrative propriety in favour of the authorities; the complainants' detention and subjection to the authority of the same interrogators suspected of perpetrating the violations; their isolation from the outside world, including access to an attorney, which prevents them from describing their ordeal in real time, from receiving legal advice, and from acquiring potential witnesses; the problem of poor medical documentation from the period of the interrogation;[39] and the system of nicknames customary among GSS interrogators, which obscure the identity of the alleged perpetrators. In addition, victims' classification as suspects of security violations exempts the authorities from the compulsory visual and audio documentation of their

---

[38] Nir Hasson, 'ISA interrogators sodomize interrogatees and pluck off their beards', *Ha'aretz*, 8 November 2006, <http://www.haaretz.co.il/misc/1.1152146> (in Hebrew).

[39] Doctors who see interrogatees in detention facilities are employees of the Israel Prison Authority, and therefore do not have the professional independence required. For more information, see Public Committee against Torture in Israel, 'Doctoring the evidence, abandoning the victim', November 2011, <http://stoptorture.org.il/files/Doctoring%20the%20Evidence%20Abandoning%20the%20Victim_November2011.pdf>.

interrogation, as required under the Criminal Procedure Law. In that context, it should be noted that the UN Special Rapporteur on torture stated that placing the burden of proof on the victim while he lacks the means for collecting evidence to corroborate his complaint—and thus preventing him from meeting the required evidentiary threshold for taking criminal steps against the perpetrators—foils any effective investigation.[40]

THE VIDEO CASE (2013)

Since 2002, the Israeli parliament has continuously extended the temporary order that grants the exemption to the police and the GSS from the duty to make audio and video recordings of their interrogations of individuals suspected of security offences, and the state has not committed itself to making any fundamental modifications to it. Following the latest extension in 2012, the exempting legislation is valid until July 2015. On 7 February 2013, the Israeli Supreme Court dismissed a petition by human rights organizations that requested the Court to cancel a sweeping exemption granted to the police and the GSS allowing them not to make audio or video recordings of their interrogations of suspected security offenders.[41]

Both the GSS and the police claim that the interrogations of individuals suspected of committing security offences should not be recorded in order to avoid exposing the techniques and methods that are employed in such interrogations. According to the petitioners, however, such an aim does not justify the violation of the constitutional rights of detainees that results from the lack of recording, including the rights to due process, equality, and dignity, as well as the freedom from torture and other forms of ill-treatment. Moreover, the exemption entails discrimination on the basis of national identity, since the overwhelming majority of individuals suspected of committing security offences are Palestinians, and it is therefore Palestinians who will suffer its consequences.

The petitioners argued that the methods of interrogation used by the police and GSS should be subject to judicial review and standards of transparency. In addition, the duty to record interrogations is aimed not only at protecting the rights of detainees, but also at ascertaining the truth and preventing extraction of false confessions. Recording is a potentially

[40] Manfred Nowak, 'Report of the Special Rapporteur on torture and other cruel, inhuman or degrading treatment or punishment: study on the phenomena of torture, cruel, inhuman or degrading treatment or punishment in the world, including an assessment of conditions of detention', Human Rights Council, UN doc. A/HRC/13/39/Add.5, 5 February 2010, p. 36.

[41] HCJ, *Adalah and ors v. Ministry of Public Security* (Case No. 9416/2010), 2013. An unofficial English translation is available at <http://adalah.org/Public/files/English/Legal_Advocacy/Petitions/2010/HCJ-9416-10-Judgement-English.pdf>. For more background on the case, see e.g. <http://www.adalah.org/eng/Articles/704/Cancel-Exemption-for-Israeli-Police-and-GSS-from-of>.

effective means of supervision that can deter attempts by interrogators to exceed the authorities granted them by law, in particular by employing illegitimate methods of investigation, including those that amount to torture or cruel, inhuman, or degrading treatment or punishment. The petitioners further argued that the exemption violates Israel's obligation under Article 2(a) of the CAT to take measures to prevent acts of torture. By exempting the police and GSS from the duty to record these investigations, they alleged that Israel also violates Article 11 of the same Convention, according to which each state party 'shall keep under systematic review interrogation rules, instructions, methods and practices as well as arrangements for the custody and treatment of persons subjected to any form of arrest, detention or imprisonment in any territory under its jurisdiction, with a view to preventing any cases of torture'.

Chief Justice Asher Gronis justified the Court's decision on the grounds that the Ministry of Justice is currently examining alternatives to the exemption and is due to report its findings by 2015.

F. Immunity as a result of the investigation mechanism: preliminary internal examination as a shield against criminal investigation

The examination procedure of complaints of torture or ill-treatment by the GSS was established by the state in 1992 in the form of ministerial guidelines.[42] Since then, practice has shown that the wholesale dismissal of all complaints has actually created a mechanism that grants full impunity to GSS interrogators. How does it work?

Complaints are first subjected to a preliminary examination, which is conducted by a GSS agent with a rank equivalent to the rank of brigadier general, whose identity remains secret (the 'Interrogatee Complaints Comptroller', known in Hebrew as the *Mavtan*). While the preliminary inquiry includes a meeting with the GSS official and the complainant, it is often far more akin to an interrogation than a proceeding intended to give the victim the feeling that justice is being done: the interview is conducted in prison, by a person whose identity remains obscure, and without the victim enjoying legal representation. The findings of the preliminary inquiry are not transparent and almost impossible to challenge.[43] When the preliminary examination is over, the GSS transfers its

---

[42] Decision No. IS/16 of the Ministerial Committee for Israel Security Agency Matters of the 24th Government, 'Procedure for examining interrogatees' complaints', 20 May 1992. The procedure currently applicable was last revised on 1 February 2006 (quoted in the Türkel Commission Report, p. 305, at n. 150).

[43] See also the Türkel Commission Report at p. 415. The Mavtan 'is very limited in his skills as an investigator' and his questions are 'laconic'. The conclusions of the State Attorney's examination also found that the investigation process of the Mavtan takes too much time. An additional flaw that the examination

findings to a senior prosecutor from the State Attorney's Office ('the Mavtan superior'). While the State Attorney is competent to adopt the recommendation of the GSS official and to close the file, only the Attorney General is competent to instruct an opening of a criminal investigation.[44] The Attorney General's decision can be appealed before the HCJ.

Thus the mere decision to open a criminal investigation is a daunting process: it has to pass through a GSS internal examination, a recommendation of an attorney at the Ministry of Justice, a decision by the Attorney General, and an optional appeal to the HCJ (as a judicial review procedure of any administrative decision). Moreover, in practice, complaints of torture are met with foot-dragging and bureaucratic doublespeak, and complaints often remain unanswered for months or even years. As data shows, none of the preliminary examinations has ever recommended that a criminal investigation be initiated on the basis of a complaint, and the Attorney General has never instructed that such a criminal investigation be opened.[45] All of the hundreds of complaints submitted over the last decade were closed due to lack of evidence or the necessity defence.

In 2007, the State Attorney's Office conducted an examination of this investigation mechanism, and in 2010 the Attorney General decided that the examination process would no longer be conducted by a GSS agent, but by an employee of the Ministry of Justice. Three years later, the decision has yet to be implemented.

THE TORTURE INVESTIGATION SYSTEM CASE (2012)

In order to address the flawed mechanism of investigation, which effectively grants impunity to GSS interrogators, a petition was submitted to the HCJ in February 2011 by the Public Committee against Torture along with other NGOs. The petitioners argued that it was inconceivable that in more than, 600 complaints of torture or ill-treatment that had been filed during 2001–10, not one ever led to even a criminal

---

identified was that ISA interrogations are not sufficiently documented, and that this lack of documentation creates a difficulty for the Mavtan's investigations.

[44] Police Ordinance in Art. 49(I)a: 'An offense that an employee of the Israel Security Agency is suspected of committing, within the framework of carrying out his duties or with regard to his duties, shall be investigated by the department [PIID], if the Attorney General so decides.' See also the Türkel Commission Report, pp. 305–6, quoting the Deputy State Attorney: 'The discretion to initiate an investigation is limited to the Attorney General because of the unique nature of the ISA's work, the ISA's mission and the great sensitivity surrounding its work as the authority responsible for frustrating and preventing illegal operations whose purpose is to harm the security of the State, the democratic system of government or its institutions, in view of its fight, *inter alia*, against terrorist organizations.

[45] Türkel Commission Report, p. 414. According to Israel's statements to various international bodies, in the past decade four disciplinary actions took place following complaints of torture and ill-treatment. See also HCJ, *Harizat and ors v. Attorney-General and ors*, State–s response (Case No. 2150/96).

investigation. It was claimed that the mechanism put in place by the Attorney General creates an intolerable situation in which these serious offences are treated more leniently than minor felonies. Indeed, the whole complaint-examination mechanism is tainted by 'extreme unreasonableness': the comprehensive policy of closing all of the hundreds of such complaints cannot be deemed reasonable by any means. The petitioners asked the court to grant an order nisi requiring the Attorney General to initiate criminal investigations in all cases of complaints of torture or ill-treatment filed by Palestinian security detainees interrogated by the GSS.[46]

The decision rendered in August 2012 was delivered by Justice Rubinstein, who was the State Attorney General in 1999 and in charge of the implementation of the HCJ torture ruling, which included the drafting of the immunity guidelines.[47] Justice Rubinstein started by ruling that a preliminary inquiry, and not a criminal investigation, is not only permissible, but even necessary. Regardless of whether complaints are investigated in the framework of a preliminary examination or by way of criminal investigation, they must be independent, impartial, effective, prompt, and transparent. These are fundamental principles for the conduct of any effective inquiry. Nonetheless, the HCJ was prepared to balance them against the special needs of the GSS. According to the HCJ, a preliminary internal investigation provides the right balance between the need to scrutinize GSS actions and the need to avoid disrupting its routines. The methods of GSS investigations must remain secret, as dictated by the very nature of such interrogations, and the fact that the scrutiny of GSS methods is in the hands of one body—the preliminary inquiry body—ensures that this secrecy is maintained. Hence, according to Justice Rubinstein, the GSS Interrogatee Complaints Comptroller continues to be:

The person with the relevant expertise to examine the complains, who can both guarantee an overall preliminary examination while keeping the secrecy required to protect the work of the GSS and to prevent an interruption of its routine work which may occur in case of the opening of an inquiry by a body external to the 'Service' [GSS] for each complaint.[48]

After legitimizing GSS examination practice in force since 1992, conducted in secrecy, as a result of the need to strike a balance between the demands of impartiality and the demands dictated by nature of the GSS work, the HCJ ruled that there was no obligation automatically to open a criminal investigation for each complaint, only in cases in which the examination phase leads to the disclosure of sufficient evidence.[49] In so ruling, the HCJ allowed the narrative of lack of evidence to prevail, a lack that it identified as being

---

[46] HCJ, *Public Committee against Torture in Israel and ors v. Attorney General* (Case No. 1265/11), 2012 (the *Torture Investigation System case* (2012)).

[47] Justice Rubinstein mentions this in the ruling itself, but does not see this as a conflict of interest that should lead to his recusing himself: *Torture Investigation System case* (2012), §17.

[48] *Torture Investigation System case* (2012), §21.

[49] *Torture Investigation System case* (2012), §31.

the result of false complaints, and not as a result of a structure that precluded the possession of such evidence, in order to justify the preliminary examination system (as well as the fact that no complaint had ever generated a criminal investigation). With this portrayal of the *facts* (or absence of facts), the HCJ was more concerned with false complaints—mentioned a few times in the ruling[50]—and less with the possibility of true allegations, an option that was never cited.

Having provided a general legitimization for the internal examination procedure, yet still uncomfortable with the fact that none of the complaints had ever triggered a criminal investigation, the HCJ *proposed* that the state move to implement the Attorney General's guidelines for structural change, issued in 2010 (in which he decided that the GSS Interrogatee Complaints Comptroller would henceforth operate under the auspices of the Ministry of Justice, instead of the GSS), and also that measures be taken to increase the transparency of the procedure:[51]

It seems that it can be assumed that the GSS have learned the lessons from their problematic 'organization culture' that was practiced in the past. Indeed, no body is immune from mistakes and slips.[52]

Thus, 12 years of torture allegations and the absence of criminal investigation or prosecution of more than 600 complaints of alleged war crimes are portrayed by the HCJ as the result of a 'culture of organization', a bureaucratic problem, which can be solved by the transfer of the GSS Interrogatee Complaints Comptroller from the GSS to the Ministry of Justice. At several junctures, Justice Rubinstein mentions the 'maturing' of the 'security and human rights' issue in Israeli jurisprudence, interpreting the current situation as only a stage in a series of 'evolutionary steps'.[53] One of the evolutionary steps mentioned in the ruling is the fact that preliminary inquiries are in the process of being transferred to the Ministry of Justice. The 'maturing' narrative enables Justice Rubinstein to avoid demanding that the state comply with its international obligations in relation to past allegations. Instead, the state receives licence to be tolerant of human rights abuses that are related to security issues, in the hope that in the future the system will improve. Yet the importance attached to this structural change—the transfer of the preliminary inquiry to the Ministry of Justice—puts the spotlight on procedure rather than substance: the fact that all complaints are shelved because of a policy of unwillingness of the state to prosecute torture allegations, which is the official policy chosen at the highest level of decision-making.

Moreover, the fact that the GSS Interrogatee Complaints Comptroller will still be a former GSS agent does not appear to pose a problem of impartiality:

---

[50] For examples, see *Torture Investigation System case* (2012), §§19, 21, and 34.
[51] *Torture Investigation System case* (2012), §21.
[52] *Torture Investigation System case* (2012), §35.
[53] *Torture Investigation System case* (2012), §21.

The decision to transfer the GSS Interrogatee Complaints Comptroller to the Ministry of Justice is significant both on a substantive level – for even if the comptroller is going to be a former GSS worker, he will know his task, and the framework in which it is situated – and also in terms of appearance – to the extent that the review is not performed by a party who owes an 'institutional duty of loyalty' to the GSS.[54]

A guarantee of independence and impartiality, as asserted by the HCJ, is the possibility of appeal. The ruling suggests that complainants' appeals relating to the shelving of their complaints should be submitted on an individual basis to a higher instance in the Attorney General's office, thereby ignoring the fact that this avenue for appeal is problematic: the appeals are addressed to the same body that decided to shelve the complaints and the inquiry materials remain out of reach. Also, even though the Court extended the deadline for the submission of appeals for the complainants, it did not do so for the hundreds of complainants whose complaints were dismissed before this new mechanism for appeal was created.

The ruling left the petitioners with only one option: petitioning for a remedy in individual cases rather than addressing the systemic nature of the complaint mechanism. This not only fragments the picture, but, as experience has shown, it also exhausts numerous resources and rarely brings about the desired results. The ruling perpetuates the decade-long adherence to the principle of 'balancing' as a means of indirectly legalizing the use of torture and ill-treatment, and, since it is now sanctioned by the HCJ, leaves the impunity mechanism in full force.

G. **The recommendations of the Türkel Commission**

On the surface, the report provides a shield for past events, finding that 'on the whole' the investigation policy of war crimes allegations is consistent with Israel's international legal obligations.[55] At the same time, the report presented 18 recommendations to the state for improvement of the examination and investigation mechanisms and for changes to the accepted policy, some of them challenging their basic structure and function. As noted by one of the jurists who worked with the Commission:

The more open-eyed approach would interpret the general conclusion that Israel complies with international law as no more than politics at work and an attempt to soften and make more palatable critical recommendations.[56]

---

[54] *Torture Investigation System case* (2012), §21.   [55] Türkel Commission Report, p. 377.
[56] Michelle Lesh, 'The nature of investigations under international law: reflection on the Türkel Report and beyond', Draft paper presented at the International Law Forum of the Law Faculty of Hebrew University, Jerusalem, March 2013, p. 3.

TORTURE LEGISLATION

Because Israel does not have comprehensive legislation dealing with war crimes, the first recommendation by the Commission was to incorporate international norms into Israeli domestic law. It emphasized the normative and educational values of explicitly incorporating legislation concerning war crimes into Israeli law.[57] In addition, the Commission recommended legislating 'provisions that impose direct criminal liability on commanders and civilian superiors for offences committed by their subordinates'.[58]

Despite signing and ratifying the CAT in 1991 and adhering to the four 1949 Geneva Conventions, Israel has never recognized the absolute nature of the prohibition on torture in its domestic law. Moreover, torture legislation within Israeli legal and political discourse has usually been understood as referring to the need for direct legislation that authorizes the use of certain interrogation methods, rather than to prohibit them.[59] This is why the Commission's direct reference to the need to domestically implement the absolute prohibition of torture and inhuman and degrading treatment is particularly significant:

The Ministry [of Justice] should ensure that there is legislation to transpose clearly into law and practice the absolute prohibition in international law of torture and inhuman and degrading treatment. This is in order to enable 'effective penal sanction' for those committing war crimes, as required by international law.[60]

FROM THE OBLIGATION TO INVESTIGATE AND PROSECUTE, TO THE OBLIGATION TO EXAMINE AND INVESTIGATE

Generally, the Türkel Commission distinguishes between the duty to examine and the duty to investigate. It states that there is a general duty to broadly *examine* all suspected violations of IHL. And there is an additional duty to *investigate* certain 'war crimes'.[61] The scope of the term 'war crimes' is defined by the Commission in broader terms than the grave breaches of the Geneva Conventions. It encompasses 'serious violations' of IHL, as well as the acts listed in the ICC Statute and the 1977 Additional Protocol I, to which

---

[57] 'The Commission sees importance in the explicit adoption of the international norms relating to war crimes into Israeli domestic legislation. This is because such legislation goes beyond the *practical* needs (i.e., to charge and punish violators of international humanitarian law), and also serves a *normative* purpose (i.e., to promote deterrence and education)': Türkel Commission Report, pp. 365–6.

[58] Türkel Commission Report, p. 369.

[59] See the *Torture case* (1999), §§23 and 39, and *Torture Investigation System case* (2012), §19.

[60] Türkel Commission Report, p. 365.   [61] Türkel Commission Report, pp. 73–4.

Israel is not a party.[62] As with the HCJ, the Commission takes the view that not every war crime allegation merits a criminal investigation, but only those for which there is sufficient evidence:

In determining the grounds for carrying out the obligation to examine and investigate we will distinguish between the general duty to examine every violation of the rules of international humanitarian law and the specific duty to conduct an investigation. The Commission's approach is that the threshold required for an investigation is where a credible accusation is made or a reasonable suspicion arises that a war crime has been committed...Whether a reasonable suspicion of a war crime exists depends on the facts of the concrete event and its particular context. In certain cases, the facts of the matter are sufficient to indicate that the act allegedly committed is ostensibly of a criminal nature and, consequently, an investigation should be commenced immediately. Examples of cases of this kind include alleged violations of absolute prohibitions of international law...therefore *credible information* suggesting their occurrence in itself gives rise to a reasonable suspicion that a war crime has been committed.[63]

Had the Commission ended here, it would be merely a reiteration of the HCJ ruling as far as it concerns torture examinations and investigations. Yet the Commission's recommendation was far more comprehensive. It recommended a full visual documentation of the interrogations,[64] in contrast to extant Israeli legislation and the HCJ ruling[65] that was delivered just a few days after the Türkel Commission Report was issued.

EFFECTIVE INQUIRIES

Like the HCJ, the Commission notes that not all violations of IHL and HRL necessarily give rise to the obligation to conduct a criminal investigation. Yet unlike the HCJ, the Commission emphasizes that inquiries, whatever form they take, need to adhere to the principles of an 'effective investigation', namely independence, impartiality, thoroughness, effectiveness, promptness, and transparency.[66] In the context of examination of torture claims, while citing the Attorney General, the Commission finds that the Interrogatee Complaints Comptroller does not comply with the requirement of an effective investigation:

The *first reason* concerns a *problem of performance*, i.e., the inherent difficulty of the Mavtan to fulfil his role, by virtue of the fact that he is a worker of the Israel Security Agency, who is

---

[62] Türkel Commission Report, pp. 94–9. Particularly interesting is the fact that the Commission recognized the criminality of 'the transfer by the Occupying Power of parts of its own civilian population into the territory it occupies' provided by Art. 85(4)(a) of the 1977 Additional Protocol I and Art. 8(2)(b)(viii) of the ICC Statute.

[63] Türkel Commission Report, pp. 99–100.   [64] Türkel Commission Report, p. 417.

[65] See the HCJ *Video case* (2013).   [66] Türkel Commission Report, p. 413.

inspecting the activities of his colleagues. *The second reason* primarily concerns the *problem of perception*, i.e., the difficulty to justify a situation where an individual who is perceived to be internal to the Israel Security Agency examines complaints—ostensibly criminal—against his colleagues in the service.[67]

Having found that the current mechanism does not comply with the requirement of an effective investigation and criticizing the fact that, to date, the Attorney General's decision to transfer that investigation body to the Ministry of Justice remained a dead letter and had not been implemented,[68] the Commission is now adopting a position that departs from the position of the HCJ, which, as noted above, described the function and structure of the Interrogatee Complaints Comptroller as a necessary balancing of need, and which looked forward to the maturating of the system. Thus the Commission now points out, much more explicitly than the HCJ, that the GSS Interrogatee Complaints Comptroller does not have the impartiality and independence required for the conduct of an effective investigation, and it also notes that 'there are serious failures in the effectiveness and thoroughness and also in the promptness of the investigation process'.[69]

Concluding remarks

Hundreds of torture claims have been submitted in Israel over the last decade. The question of whether these claims are effectively investigated by Israeli authorities, and in appropriate cases, prosecuted, should be examined in light of the complementarity principle, given that the possibility of the ICC exercising jurisdiction over Israel's acts is no longer purely an academic matter. As shown above, the Türkel Commission Report recommended more effective investigation, which, in certain aspects, goes further than the proposition made by the HCJ in its rulings on the matter. Whether or not the state actually intends to implement the Türkel Commission recommendations is unclear at this point in time. Yet, in dealing with the responsibility of the command level, including the political echelons, the possibility of their being held accountable seems remote, because of lack of political will (and probably also inability) to do so, irrespective of any other structural improvements that may be introduced.

---

[67] Türkel Commission Report, pp. 415–16.

[68] Türkel Commission Report, p. 416: 'The said 2010 decision of the Attorney General emphasized the lack of independence in the Mavtan's investigation process, as well as a perception of a lack of independence, because "he is a worker of the Israel Security Agency who is inspecting the activity of his colleagues". The fact that no criminal investigations were ever opened only exacerbates these concerns.' In a footnote to this sentence (n. 176), it is mentioned that: 'It should be noted that meanwhile the Supreme Court handed down a decision on the legality of the special investigative mechanism to examine complaints by ISA interrogatees against their interrogators.'

[69] Türkel Commission Report, p. 416.

Postscript

On 5 June 2013, a new Interrogatee Complaints Comptroller was appointed, who is now an employee of the Ministry of Justice. He is an ex-army officer, whose identity is known to the public for the first time. The effects of the new appointment on the investigation mechanism remain to be seen. Yet this structural change is unlikely to have any significant effect on the ongoing policy of providing immunity for high-level personnel responsible in the chain of command responsible for torture acts committed since 1999.

11 Complementarity and universal jurisdiction: South Africa's ICC Act and the domestic investigation of extraterritorial international crimes

Manuel J. Ventura*

Introduction

On 4 August 2012, a spokeswoman for the National Prosecuting Authority of South Africa (NPA) publicly confirmed that it was undertaking the country's first ever investigation into alleged crimes against humanity relating to events in Madagascar during its political crisis that began in January 2009. In particular, the investigation would focus on the individual criminal responsibility of the ousted former President Marc Ravalomanana, who had by then been exiled from Madagascar and was residing in South Africa.[1] The investigation was initiated on the basis of South Africa's Implementation of the Rome Statute of the International Criminal Court Act (ICC Act),[2] which incorporated the Rome Statute's international crimes, cooperation, and related provisions into South African domestic law. In making this announcement, the NPA was making clear that it would be investigating the acts and conduct of a foreign citizen for events wholly

* BA/LLB (University of Western Sydney); BEcSocSc (Hons) (University of Sydney). Manuel Ventura is Director of The Peace and Justice Initiative, a non-governmental organization (NGO) of international criminal law professionals that assist states in the domestic implementation of the 1998 Rome Statute of the International Criminal Court (ICC). See <http://www.peaceandjusticeinitiative.org>.

[1] 'NPA investigating Ravalomanana for crimes against humanity', *Times Live*, 5 August 2012, <http://www.timeslive.co.za/local/2012/08/05/npa-investigating-ravalomanana-for-crimes-against-humanity>. Online documents cited in this chapter were last accessed on 18 May 2013 unless otherwise stated.

[2] Implementation of the Rome Statute of the International Criminal Court Act, No. 27 of 2002. For a more thorough review of this law, see Max du Plessis, 'South Africa's implementation of the ICC Statute: an African example', *Journal of International Criminal Justice*, 5(2) (2007), p. 460.

removed from South Africa, with no obvious territorial or personal link to the state, other than Ravalomanana's presence on her soil. This situation reveals one of the most interesting jurisdictional aspects of the ICC Act:

In order to secure the jurisdiction of a South African court for [the] purposes of this Chapter, any person who commits a[n International Criminal Court (ICC)] crime contemplated in subsection (1) outside the territory of the Republic, is deemed to have committed that crime in the territory of the Republic if... (c) that person, after the commission of the crime, is present in the territory of the Republic[.][3]

In other words, this is an express grant of universal jurisdiction to South African authorities (and their courts) for international crimes that occur anywhere in the world, to the extent that the relevant person is present on South Africa's territory.[4]

In February 2013, it was reported that the NPA and the South African Police Service (SAPS) had opened a second investigation using the same jurisdictional provision, this time concerning allegations of widespread rape as crimes against humanity allegedly committed in Zimbabwe in the lead-up to its 2008 presidential elections.[5] While no specific suspects were named and South African authorities were hesitant even to confirm the existence of the investigation,[6] it would in all likelihood probe the acts and conduct of Zimbabwean nationals in Zimbabwe. Unlike Madagascar, Zimbabwe is not a state party to the ICC, an issue discussed below.

Arguably, the opening of these investigations was the indirect result of a landmark ruling by the North Gauteng High Court in *Southern African Litigation Centre and anor v. National Director of Public Prosecution and ors*[7] ('the *Zimbabwe Torture Judgment*'), a case that concerned allegations of torture as crimes against humanity by Zimbabweans against detained opposition members in Zimbabwe. This case held—for the first time

---

[3] Section 4(3)(c), ICC Act. That South Africa relied upon this provision for its Madagascar investigation was later confirmed in incidental proceedings: *Rakoto and ors v. Head: Directorate for Priority Crimes Investigation and ors* [2012] ZAGPPHC 281, 19 November 2012, §§47, 50.

[4] This is to be distinguished from universal jurisdiction 'in absentia' or without the presence of the accused on the relevant state's territory, as was at issue in the International Court of Justice's (ICJ) *Case Concerning the Arrest Warrant of 11 April 2000 (Democratic Republic of the Congo v. Belgium)*, Judgment, 14 February 2002, ICJ Reports 2002, p. 3. See, in particular: the Separate Opinions of Judges Guillaume and Rezek; the Joint Separate Opinion of Judges Higgins, Kooijmans, and Buergenthal; the Declaration of Judge Ranjeva; and the Dissenting Opinion of Judge Van Den Wyngaert.

[5] AIDS-Free World, 'For Mugabe's rape gangs, time has run out: South Africa to investigate Zimbabwe's politically motivated rape', 25 February 2013, Press release, <http://www.aidsfreeworld.org/Newsroom/Press-Releases/2013/Zimbabwe-Investigation.aspx>.

[6] Khulekani Magubane and Franny Rabkin, 'Advocacy group hails NPA's decision to probe allegations of mass rape in Zimbabwe', *Business Day Live*, 27 February 2013, <http://www.bdlive.co.za/national/2013/02/27/advocacy-group-hails-npas-decision-to-probe-allegations-of-mass-rape-in-zimbabwe>. As such, it remains unclear as of writing whether or not an investigation has been formally initiated.

[7] *Southern African Litigation Centre and anor v. National Director of Public Prosecution and ors* [2012] ZAGPPHC 61, 8 May 2012 (the *Zimbabwe Torture Judgment*).

anywhere in world—that a state was legally obliged to initiate an investigation of alleged international crimes pursuant to universal jurisdiction as enacted in its domestic ICC incorporation law *and* as a result of its international obligations as a state party to the ICC, based, in particular, on the principle of complementarity.[8]

Other than the flagging of the *Zimbabwe Torture Judgment* case on various law blogs,[9] these developments have not yet attracted the attention of the larger academic community. This is unfortunate, as they raise novel issues about the interaction and compatibility of complementarity and universal jurisdiction, particularly in an era in which the ICC's consistent reach into Africa has been criticized by a number of African states. This chapter explores some of these issues, and considers the practical and legal implications of the ruling, as well as the South African investigations that have resulted from it.

A. **The *Zimbabwe Torture Judgment***

The facts of the case are fairly straightforward. On 27 March 2007, the Harare head-quarters of the Movement for Democratic Change, the main opposition political party in Zimbabwe, were raided by police, who proceeded to arrest and detain more than 100 people. It was alleged that, during several days of police detention, a number of these persons were tortured.

Since these acts did not lead to any prosecution or accountability in Zimbabwe and it was deemed unlikely that the situation would change in the future, the Southern Africa Litigation Centre (SALC) began collecting evidence from the victims and from medical and non-governmental organization (NGO) records, and sought other corroborating information of the allegations. On 14 March 2008, a dossier of the collated material was submitted to the NPA's Priority Crimes Litigation Unit, the unit specifically empowered to undertake ICC Act investigations. It was claimed that the acts of torture described in the dossier had been carried out by the state as part of a widespread or

---

[8] Contrary to the belief of some international lawyers, the term 'complementarity' has been in use for many years, at least among physicists. It was originally coined by Professor Niels Bohr in his Como lecture of 1927 when interpreting the inherent contradictions observed in the realm of quantum mechanics. See generally Arkady Plotnitsky, *Niels Bohr and Complementarity: An Introduction*, Springer, New York, 2013.

[9] See Christopher Gevers, 'The application of universal jurisdiction in South African law', *EJIL: Talk! blog*, 24 April 2012, <http://www.ejiltalk.org/universal-jurisdiction-in-south-africa>; Christopher Gevers, 'The "landmark" Zimbabwe Torture Docket decision', *War and Law blog*, 9 May 2012, <http://warandlaw. blogspot.ch/2012/05/landmark-zimbabwe-torture-docket.html>; Diane Marie Amann, 'Complementarity in action: applying South Africa's ICC Act, national court orders South African prosecutors to investigate torture in Zimbabwe', *IntLawGrrls blog*, 11 May 2012, <http://www.intlawgrrls.com/2012/05/complementarity-in-action-south-african.html>; Rosalind English, 'South Africa shrinks from investigating Zimbabwe torture allegations', *UK Human Rights blog*, 14 May 2012, <http://ukhumanrightsblog.com/2012/05/14/south-africa-shrinks-from-investigating-zimbabwe-torture-allegations>.

systematic attack against the political opposition to the ruling party, the Zimbabwe African National Union—Patriotic Front (ZANU-PF), and therefore constituted a crime against humanity as defined in the ICC Act and international criminal law. The dossier named six incumbent ministers and heads of department, along with members of a police task force, as bearing responsibility for the crimes and noted that they had been present in South Africa during different intervals. Citing the above jurisdictional provision of the ICC Act and South Africa's international obligations as a state party to the ICC, the SALC requested that the NPA open an investigation.[10]

After some delay, the NPA refused to do so, but would later concede that the ICC Act had not been considered in making its decision. It cited a number of reasons for its refusal, including: (i) that the dossier's contents were inadequate for prosecution purposes; (ii) the difficulty in conducting investigations and obtaining evidence of extraterritorial crimes without the consent of Zimbabwe; and (iii) the negative impact of such an investigation on South Africa's international relations and diplomatic activities with Zimbabwe. In response, the SALC, together with an organization of Zimbabwean exiles (the Zimbabwe Exiles Forum), initiated proceedings in the North Gauteng High Court challenging the NPA's refusal.

On 8 May 2012, Judge Fabricius rendered his judgment. Important for our purposes was the holding that South Africa was legally obliged to investigate alleged international crimes falling under the ICC Act. In assuming otherwise, he concluded that the national investigation and prosecutorial authorities had erred. Judge Fabricius grounded this duty upon the strength of domestic law coupled with international law. With respect to the former, he pointed to the ICC Act's Preamble and declared objective, which was, inter alia, to enshrine the principle of complementarity in domestic law so as to enable South African authorities and courts to prosecute and adjudicate cases involving the commission of international crimes as far as possible.[11] This objective was reinforced by the expansive nature of the universal jurisdiction provision in section 4(3)(c) of the ICC Act. Running in parallel with domestic law were South Africa's international obligations as state party to the 1998 Rome Statute of the ICC (ICC Statute), in particular, the principle

---

[10] While the conduct in question in Zimbabwe would also likely meet the definition of torture as an autonomous international crime as per the 1984 United Nations (UN) Convention against Torture (CAT), South Africa has not yet incorporated the Convention into its domestic law. A bill is, however, before the National Assembly (South African parliament) that seeks to do just that: Prevention and Combating of Torture of Persons Bill (B 21–2012). Interestingly, s. 6(1)(c) of the bill, in language very similar to s. 4(3)(c) of the ICC Act, also grants universal jurisdiction to South African authorities and her courts over acts of torture.

[11] *Zimbabwe Torture Judgment*, §§1.15.1.8.1 and 1.15.1.8.3. The relevant provision of the ICC Act (s. 3(d)) reads as follows: 'The object of this Act are ... (d) to enable, as far as possible and in accordance with the principle of complementarity as referred to in Article 1 of the [ICC] Statute, the national prosecuting authority of the Republic to prosecute and the High Courts of the Republic to adjudicate in cases brought against any person accused of having committed a[n international] crime in the Republic and beyond the Republic in certain circumstances ...'

of complementarity referred to in Article 1, together with its Preamble, which states that 'it is the duty of every State to exercise its criminal jurisdiction over those responsible for international crimes'.[12] Judge Fabricius concluded that:

Seen holistically therefore, all the mentioned provisions place an obligation on South Africa to comply with its obligations to investigate and prosecute, crimes against humanity within the ambit of the provisions of s. 4(3) of the ICC Act, and it is in the public interest that they do so.[13]

Since South African authorities conceded that they had not considered the ICC Act in making their decision not to initiate an investigation, it was not difficult for Judge Fabricius to hold that:

[South African authorities] had the power and the duty to investigate ICC crimes committed inside or outside of South Africa...Respondents did not discharge their obligations in accordance with South Africa's international obligations, nor with an appreciation and sound understanding of international customary and criminal law, nor in accordance with the ICC Act [and other relevant domestic statutes].[14]

Further, he held that there was 'an international consensus on the normative desirability of prosecuting such [international] criminals and, by necessary implication, a proper investigation had to be done in all such instances'.[15]

In light of this, Judge Fabricius proceeded to analyse the reasons provided for the refusal to commence an investigation. In this context, emphasis was placed on the obligation of South African police and investigative authorities to act independently and objectively,[16] together with their concession during the litigation that the information provided by the SALC was sufficient for the existence of a reasonable basis—the same standard used by the ICC[17]—that the crimes alleged had in fact taken place.[18]

Each of the main proffered reasons was addressed in turn. First, with respect to the inadequacies of the evidence in the dossier, Judge Fabricius held that South African authorities 'asked the wrong question and gave the wrong answer. The question ought to have been: is there enough information to warrant an investigation in terms of the

---

[12] ICC Statute, Preamble, para. 6. One should also note para. 10: '[T]he International Criminal Court established under this Statute shall be complementary to national criminal jurisdictions'. See *Zimbabwe Torture Judgment*, §13.4.

[13] *Zimbabwe Torture Judgment*, §13.4. It should be pointed out that although this holding was rendered in the context of determining the applicants' standing, this fact that does not diminish its effect in any way.

[14] *Zimbabwe Torture Judgment*, §26.

[15] *Zimbabwe Torture Judgment*, §27.

[16] *Zimbabwe Torture Judgment*, §§28–9.

[17] ICC Statute, Art. 53(1) (concerning the initiation of a *proprio motu* investigation by the ICC Prosecutor). For an analysis—in an ICC context—of what is required for this threshold to be met, see M. J. Ventura, 'The "reasonable basis to proceed" threshold in the Kenya and Côte d'Ivoire *Proprio Motu* investigations decisions: the International Criminal Court's lowest evidentiary standard?', *The Law and Practice of International Courts and Tribunals*, 12(1) (2013), p. 49.

[18] *Zimbabwe Torture Judgment*, §§28, 31.

applicable law?',[19] Instead, the content of the dossier had been reviewed with a view to *prosecution* rather than the commencement of an investigation. Secondly, if Zimbabwean consent to investigative action was required, the result would be that 'no prosecution could ever succeed or even be instituted, let alone investigated if the relevant government was complicit in the commission of such crimes, as it would obviously protect itself and the particular perpetrators'.[20] This was described as an irrelevant political consideration based on a preconceived refusal to commence an investigation.

Similar comments were made of the diplomatic and international relations concerns raised by South African authorities. The Court stipulated that these were, having regard to the purpose ICC Act, 'not relevant' at the point of determining whether to initiate an investigation, but conceded that they might be relevant in deciding whether to commence a prosecution.[21] In any event, Judge Fabricius pointed out that the head of the NPA had an independent mandate, 'which he must exercise impartially without fear or favour[;] it is not for him to blindly follow political views or policies, let alone anticipate as such'.[22]

Last of all, an argument that the relevant person(s) had to be present in South Africa if an investigation (as opposed to a prosecution) were to commence was quickly dismissed. Judge Fabricius held that this interpretation of South Africa's jurisdiction pursuant to section 4(3)(c) would lead to an absurdity: as soon as the suspect stepped out of South Africa, even for a short period, any investigation would cease and could be reinitiated only upon his or her return. Instead, he held that the suspect's presence in South Africa was only a prerequisite for the commencement of a criminal trial, but not for an investigation.[23]

As a result, South African authorities were held to have acted unlawfully by reason of errors of law in their decision-making. They were ordered to initiate an investigation of the allegations of torture committed in Zimbabwe, as crimes against humanity, based on the material contained in the SALC dossier, 'in so far as it is practicable and lawful, and with regard to the domestic laws of the Republic of South Africa and the principles of international law'.[24]

B. Complementarity and universal jurisdiction 'South Africa-style': a match made in heaven or incompatible concepts?

Undoubtedly, at the core of the ICC is its complementarity regime. The institution was envisioned and created so as to complement the work of national authorities and judiciaries of states parties; only where a state party is unwilling or unable, or where

---

[19] *Zimbabwe Torture Judgment*, §28.
[20] *Zimbabwe Torture Judgment*, §28.
[21] *Zimbabwe Torture Judgment*, §31.
[22] *Zimbabwe Torture Judgment*, §31.
[23] *Zimbabwe Torture Judgment*, §31.
[24] *Zimbabwe Torture Judgment*, §33.

there is inaction[25] with respect to international crimes, is there any potential for the ICC to step in. It is a court of last—not first—resort. However, the ability of states to investigate and/or prosecute such crimes is obviously dependent on their domestic jurisdiction over such offences. Thus, the relevant provisions of the ICC Statute concerning the principle of complementarity all refer to a state's 'jurisdiction' over such offences.[26] Only where they do not exercise this *jurisdiction* can complementarity be potentially triggered.

In this respect, the jurisdictional bases most commonly used by states in a criminal context are: (i) territorial jurisdiction (for offences committed on a state's territory); and (ii) active personality jurisdiction (for offences committed by a state's nationals). In both of these circumstances, the complementarity principle works well, since the ICC's jurisdiction *ratione personae* and *ratione loci* aligns exactly with national jurisdiction; that is, it covers crimes committed on the territory of states parties or crimes committed by their nationals.[27] In such instances, where a state party does not investigate/prosecute international crimes, the ICC would be able to 'complement' national authorities, as it too would have jurisdiction over such offences.

But territorial and active personality jurisdiction are hardly the only manifestations of a state's potential jurisdiction over criminal offences; other avenues exist. These include the passive personality principle (jurisdiction over offences committed against a state's nationals, regardless of who committed them or where they were committed), the protective principle (jurisdiction by reference to the national interest injured by the offence), and universal jurisdiction. While these are not the most popular bases for grounding domestic jurisdiction over crimes, they are nonetheless used by a number of states. In South Africa's case, its legislature, through the ICC Act, opted for the last of these jurisdictional bases, universal jurisdiction.

In light of the facts, a central issue that the *Zimbabwe Torture Judgment* should have raised, but to which Judge Fabricius did not speak or to which he was oblivious, was this: how can complementarity work when an ICC state party's jurisdiction over international crimes *exceeds* that provided for under the ICC Statute? The present case concerned international crimes allegedly committed in Zimbabwe, by Zimbabwean nationals against Zimbabwean citizens. The ICC does not have any jurisdiction over such events, as Zimbabwe is not a state party. But South Africa *is* a state party, and the ICC Act granted its authorities and courts with jurisdiction over such offences. Yet the

---

[25] This additional ground of 'inaction' has been recognized in ICC jurisprudence. See ICC, *Prosecutor v. Katanga and Ngudjolo*, Judgment on the Appeal of Mr Germain Katanga against the Oral Decision of Trial Chamber II of 12 June 2009 on the Admissibility of the Case (Case No. ICC-01-/04-01/07-1497), 25 September 2009, §78.

[26] ICC Statute, Preamble, paras 6 and 10, and Arts and 17(1)(a) and (1)(b).

[27] ICC Statute, Art. 12(2)(a)–(b). A state party referral (Arts 13(a) and 14), UN Security Council referral (Art. 13(b)), or an ad hoc declaration (Art. 12(3)) do not apply to our present inquiry.

complementarity regime, as expressed in the ICC Statute, refers not to international crimes committed in South Africa's territory or by its nationals, but to where they fall within its national criminal *jurisdiction*, as the events in Zimbabwe clearly did. In such circumstances, could Judge Fabricius have relied on the relevant provisions of the ICC Statute where the ICC would have been powerless to act if South Africa had been unwilling or unable, or had been inactive, in investigating the torture allegations in Zimbabwe? In other words, was South Africa really under an international obligation, as an ICC state party, to investigate/prosecute events that fall outside of the ICC's jurisdiction but within its own question?

If the answer to this is 'yes', as Judge Fabricius' judgment clearly implies, there are profound and completely unforeseen consequences for the complementarity regime as a whole, at least with respect to states that possess domestic jurisdiction over international crimes beyond the territorial and active personality principles. To submit that an international obligation exists to prosecute *all* international crimes under a state's domestic criminal jurisdiction—even where the ICC cannot complement such action (for lack of jurisdiction)—redefines the traditional understanding of complementarity. This is because it removes and renders irrelevant one of the principal 'enforcement' components of complementarity: the ICC Prosecutor's independent ability to investigate/prosecute, *proprio motu* and upon approval by the ICC Pre-Trial Chamber, situations in which the relevant state is unwilling or unable to exercise its domestic jurisdiction over international crimes, or is inactive in doing so.[28] If the ICC has no jurisdiction, then any such case would be thrown out and the Prosecutor would not be able to 'enforce' the complementarity regime envisaged by the ICC Statute's drafters. Without this model of enforcement as an ingredient in the complementarity soup, the ICC is reduced to being a 'toothless tiger', unable to fulfil one of the central tenets of its existence.[29] It is very

---

[28] ICC Statute, Art. 15(1)–(6). The Prosecutor has so far exercised this power in two situations: Côte d'Ivoire and Kenya. See ICC, *Decision Pursuant to Article 15 of the Rome Statute on the Authorization of an Investigation into the Situation in the Republic of Kenya* (Case No. ICC-01/09-19-Corr), 31 March 2010; ICC, *Corrigendum to 'Decision Pursuant to Article 15 of the Rome Statute on the Authorisation of an Investigation into the Situation in the Republic of Côte d'Ivoire'* (Case No. ICC-02/11-14-Corr), 15 November 2011.

[29] Of course, this is not to say that the ICC Statute is the perfect model for the enforcement of treaty provisions. One need only look at the number of times states parties have refused to arrest Sudanese President Omar al-Bashir when he was present on their territory, despite the existence of an ICC arrest warrant against him and the obligation of states parties to execute it. In response, the ICC has issued a number of decisions and referred states to the UN Security Council, all to no avail. See ICC, *Prosecutor v. Al Bashir*, Corrigendum to the Decision Pursuant to Article 87(7) of the Rome Statute on the Failure by the Republic of Malawi to Comply with the Cooperation Requests Issued by the Court with Respect to the Arrest and Surrender of Omar Hassan Ahmad al-Bashir (Case No. ICC-02/05-01/09-139-Corr), 13 December 2011; ICC, *Prosecutor v. Al Bashir*, Decision Pursuant to Article 87(7) of the Rome Statute on the Refusal of the Republic of Chad to Comply with the Cooperation Requests Issued by the Court with Respect to the Arrest and Surrender of Omar Hassan Ahmad al-Bashir (Case No. ICC-02/05-01/09-140-tENG), 13 December 2011; ICC, *Prosecutor v. Al Bashir*, Decision on the Non-compliance of the Republic of

doubtful that the drafters of the ICC Statute had this in mind when negotiating and finalizing complementarity. It leads to an unreasonable, if not absurd, result.

This situation has other implications as well. Suppose that instead of crimes against humanity in Zimbabwe, the crime had been aggression. Here, the ICC would also not have jurisdiction over the crime, this time on jurisdiction *ratione materiae* grounds.[30] Had the ICC Act included provisions on aggression, would South Africa have been under a similar international obligation to investigate/prosecute? One would instinctively answer 'no'. But consider this: if there is an international obligation on ICC states parties to prosecute crimes that fall outside of the ICC's jurisdiction *ratione personae* and *ratione loci*, why is jurisdiction *ratione materiae* all of a sudden excluded? Consider other international crimes that are not within the ICC's current jurisdiction *ratione materiae*, such as terrorism[31] and piracy. Since both offences exist under South African criminal law,[32] would South Africa also be internationally obliged under the principle of complementarity to investigate/prosecute such crimes when they occur within its domestic criminal jurisdiction?

The same could be said of crimes that took place outside of the ICC's jurisdiction *ratione temporis*, that is to say before 1 July 2002. In South Africa's case, if the ICC Act had had retroactive temporal scope[33] and given that its statute of limitations do not

Chad with the Cooperation Requests Issued by the Court Regarding the Arrest and Surrender of Omar Hassan Ahmad al-Bashir (Case No. ICC-02/05-01/09-151), 26 March 2013.

[30] For the 2010 Kampala Review Conference amendments relating to the crime of aggression to enter into force, a decision is required by the ICC Assembly of States Parties to activate the Court's jurisdiction over the crime at the earliest on 1 January 2017, but only if one year has elapsed after 30 states parties have ratified the amendments: ICC Res. RC/Res.6, Annex I, Arts 15*bis* (2)–(3) and 15*ter* (2)–(3) (2011). As of May 2013, only five states—Estonia, Liechtenstein, Luxembourg, Samoa, and Trinidad and Tobago—have ratified the relevant Kampala amendments.

[31] The Appeals Chamber of the Special Tribunal for Lebanon (STL) has held that such an international crime exists at customary law and has proceeded to define it: STL, *Interlocutory Decision on the Applicable Law: Terrorism, Conspiracy, Homicide, Perpetration, Cumulative Convictions* (Case No. STL-11-01/I/AC/R176*bis*), 16 February 2011, §§83–112. For academic debate surrounding the STL's holding, see Ben Saul, 'Legislating from a radical Hague: the United Nations Special Tribunal for Lebanon invents an international crime of transnational terrorism', *Leiden Journal of International Law*, 24(3) (2011), p. 677; M. J. Ventura, 'Terrorism according to the STL's interlocutory decision on the applicable law: a defining moment or a moment of defining?', *Journal of International Criminal Justice*, 9(5) (2011), p. 1021. The Court of Appeal of England and Wales has also agreed with the STL: *R v. Gul* [2012] EWCA Crim 280, 22 February 2012, §§32–5 (currently on appeal before the United Kingdom Supreme Court). For a discussion of this decision, see Antonio Coco, 'The mark of Cain: the crime of terrorism in times of armed conflict as interpreted by the Court of Appeal of England and Wales in *R v. Mohammed Gul*', *Journal of International Criminal Justice*, 11(2) (2013), p. 425.

[32] With respect to terrorism, see s. 1(xxv), Protection of Constitutional Democracy against Terrorist and Related Activities Act, No. 33 of 2004. With respect to piracy, see s. 24, Defence Act, No. 42 of 2002.

[33] International human rights law (IHRL) permits the retroactive domestic prosecution of international crimes: Art. 15(2), 1966 International Covenant on Civil and Political Rights (ICCPR). This is reflected in s. 3(l) of the South African Constitution. Jurisprudence confirms this understanding: *Polyukhovich v. Commonwealth* (1991) 172 CLR 501, pp. 572–6 (High Court of Australia); European Court of Human

apply to ICC crimes,[34] would it now be internationally obliged under the principle of complementarity to investigate and prosecute its historical apartheid[35] and other related crimes as crimes against humanity, notwithstanding the granting of numerous amnesties by its Truth and Reconciliation Commission in 1995–98 and the endorsement of this practice by the Constitutional Court of South Africa in 1996?[36] If complementarity is as fluid as the *Zimbabwe Torture Judgment* suggests, there is no logical reason why South Africa's international obligations should be confined to some jurisdictional bases that go beyond that of the ICC, but not others.

However, it is true that, as relied upon by Judge Fabricius,[37] the ICC Statute explicitly recalls 'that it is the duty of every State to exercise its criminal jurisdiction over those responsible for international crimes'.[38] Hall and others have opined that states parties merely recognized that states have customary or treaty law obligations—outside of the ICC Statute—to exercise jurisdiction with respect to international crimes:

They recognize that every state—not just a state party—has a pre-existing duty, not merely to exercise all jurisdiction permitted or required under national law (for example, under the legality principle), but also to exercise all jurisdiction permitted or required under international law (for example, under an *aut dedere aut judicare* obligation), at least, where feasible.[39]

This is because, in his view:

The teleological interpretation reflected in Article 21(1)(a) and (b) of the Rome Statute, Article 31 of the Vienna Convention on the Law of Treaties and the normative and constitutive nature of the Statute favours an interpretation providing the broadest possible protection of victims of crimes under international law over alternative interpretations which would restrict the scope of the obligations recognized by states. An interpretation limiting 'its criminal jurisdiction' to jurisdiction as defined under national, as opposed to international, law would lead to the

---

Rights (ECtHR), *Kolk and Kislyiy v. Estonia*, Decision on Admissibility (App. Nos 23052/04 and 24018/04), 17 January 2006, and ECtHR, *Šimšić v. Bosnia and Herzegovina*, Decision on Admissibility (App. No. 51552/10), 10 April 2012, §§23–5, (both interpreting Art. 7(2) of the 1950 European Convention on Human Rights (ECHR) which provides for the same exception as Art. 15(2) of the ICCPR; *R v. Finta* [1994] 1 SCR 701, 24 March 1994, §343 (Supreme Court of Canada) (interpreting s. 11(g) of the Canadian Constitution, which provides for the same exception as Art. 15(2) of the ICCPR).

[34] See s. 18(g), Criminal Procedure Act, No. 51 of 1977 (as amended by the ICC Act).

[35] ICC Statute, Art. 7(1)(j).

[36] See *Azanian Peoples Organization (AZAPO) and ors v. President of the Republic of South Africa and ors* [1996] ZACC 16, 25 July 1996.

[37] *Zimbabwe Torture Judgment*, §13.4.

[38] ICC Statute, Preamble, para. 6.

[39] Christopher K. Hall, 'The role of universal jurisdiction in the International Criminal Court complementarity system' in Morten Bergsmo (ed.), *Complementarity and the Exercise of Universal Jurisdiction for Core International Crimes*, Torkel Opsahl Academic EPublisher, Oslo, 2010, p. 211. To the same effect, see William A. Schabas, *The International Criminal Court: A Commentary on the Rome Statute*, Oxford University Press, Oxford, 2010, p. 45. See also Louise Arbour, 'Will the ICC have an impact on universal jurisdiction?', *Journal of International Criminal Justice*, 1(3) (2003), pp. 587–8.

absurd result that each state could define its duty independently of international law and change it at will. A similarly absurd result would arise if each state could determine the scope of its duty by picking and choosing only certain forms of geographic jurisdiction.[40]

In other words, a state's obligation to exercise its jurisdiction over international crimes as stipulated in the ICC Statute's Preamble (paragraph 6) was intended to refer to duties that existed at international law at the time of the Statute's conclusion (1998), not necessarily duties that *arose* from the Statute.[41] Unfortunately, Judge Fabricius relied heavily upon the ICC Statute—and no other international treaty—to ground South Africa's international obligation to investigate/prosecute international crimes pursuant to its universal jurisdiction. Outside the treaty context, Judge Fabricius did nonetheless stipulate that there was 'an international consensus on the normative desirability of prosecuting such [international] criminals', which necessarily meant that 'a proper investigation had to be done in all such instances'.[42] This is, however, not at all the same as holding that customary international law obliges all states to investigate/prosecute all international crimes pursuant to domestic universal jurisdiction. Indeed, such an international obligation was not at all readily apparent to the ICC Statute's drafters. As Professor Triffterer has noted, 'the only dispute' with respect to paragraph 6 of the Preamble was 'whether there is an obligation to proceed on the basis of universal jurisdiction or on a territorial or national basis. The paragraph was deliberately left ambiguous'.[43]

In short, it appears that Judge Fabricius did not fully appreciate the ICC Statute's complementarity principle or the logical conclusions of his holdings. The myriad of questions and implications that the *Zimbabwe Torture Judgment* raise suggests strongly that, under international law, a state's obligation to investigate/prosecute international crimes under the principle of complementarity extends only to those cases in which the ICC would have concurrent jurisdiction to that of the relevant state—where they are committed by a state's nationals or on their territory.[44]

This conclusion, however, is not the end of the matter, nor would it necessarily leave victims out in the cold. In this case, it may simply be that South Africa, on the strength of domestic and constitutional law, still has a duty to investigate international crimes under

---

[40] Hall, 'The role of universal jurisdiction in the International Criminal Court complementarity system', pp. 211–12.

[41] And even if it did, as concluded below, a state's international obligation arising from the principle of complementarity under the ICC Statute to prosecute/investigate must be limited to international crimes committed by its nationals or on its territory.

[42] *Zimbabwe Torture Judgment*, §27.

[43] Otto Triffterer, 'Preamble, paragraph 6: recalling to states their duties' in O. Triffterer (ed.), *Commentary on the Rome Statute of the International Criminal Court: Observers' Notes, Article by Article*, 2nd edn, Verlag C. H. Beck, Hart Publishing/Nomos, Munich/Oxford/Baden-Baden, 2008, p. 11.

[44] See also Britta Lisa Krings, 'The principles of "complementarity" and universal jurisdiction in international criminal law: antagonists or perfect match?', *Goettingen Journal of International Law*, 4(3) (2012), pp. 752–3.

the ICC Act. But this would be a *domestic* obligation only; South Africa's *international* ICC obligations would exist only when the ICC can potentially step in—that is, when international crimes are allegedly committed in South Africa or by South African nationals. This is not to say that there cannot be an international obligation at all on South Africa to investigate/prosecute events in Zimbabwe. There may very well be, but the point that this chapter has attempted to make is that it cannot be grounded on the ICC Statute or the principle of complementarity. It must be found elsewhere at international law.

Lastly, it should also be remembered that the ICC Statute does not impede domestic universal jurisdiction. South Africa is perfectly entitled to exercise such jurisdiction as an ICC state party. As Judge Van Den Wyngaert rightly asserted:

The Rome Statute does not prohibit universal jurisdiction. It would be absurd to read the Rome Statute in such a way that it limits the jurisdiction for core crimes to either the national State or the territorial State or the International Criminal Court ... The Rome Statute does not establish a *new* legal basis for third States to introduce universal jurisdiction. It does not prohibit it but does not authorize it either.[45]

C. **Subsequent South African criminal investigations pursuant to the ICC Act**

The opening of subsequent investigations in the wake of the *Zimbabwe Torture Judgment* raises other issues. As mentioned above, pursuant to the ICC Act, South Africa opened an investigation into allegations of crimes against humanity committed in Madagascar by Malagasy against other Malagasy, with the target of their investigations being former President Ravalomanana, residing in South Africa. In that case, Madagascar was an ICC state party during the commission of the alleged crimes.[46] This is exactly the situation that Pocar and Maystre recently foresaw:

---

[45] ICJ, *Case Concerning the Arrest Warrant of 11 April 2000 (Democratic Republic of the Congo v. Belgium)*, Judgment, 14 February 2002, Dissenting Opinion of Judge Van Den Wyngaert, ICJ Reports 2002, p. 176.

[46] Madagascar became a state party to the ICC Statute on 14 March 2008. It should be noted that Madagascar passed two amnesty laws with respect to the events surrounding its 2009 political crisis. Interestingly, they specifically exclude the granting of amnesty for war crimes, crimes against humanity, and genocide: Loi No. 2012-007, Portant amnistie pour la réconciliation nationale; Loi No. 2012-006, Portant amnistie pour la réconciliation nationale, Art. 5. This appears consistent with a recent observation by the ECtHR that '[g]ranting amnesty in respect of "international crimes"—which include crimes against humanity, war crimes and genocide—is increasingly considered to be prohibited by international law': ECtHR, *Marguš v. Croatia*, Judgment (App. No. 4455/10), 13 November 2012, §74.

A more interesting scenario is where the territorial state, or the national state, of the commission of the crimes (state A [Madagascar]) is unwilling or unable genuinely to carry out the investigation or prosecution and the state on which the alleged perpetrator is found (state B [South Africa]) has jurisdiction over the crimes under the principle of universality. Would state B in this case be under any incentive to investigate or prosecute the case?[47]

Contrary to Pocar and Maystre, South Africa is not 'incentivized' to investigate/prosecute (although, granted, they were not terribly enthusiastic about it in the *Zimbabwe* case), but according to the *Zimbabwe Torture Judgment* it is under a *legal obligation* to do so. But the even more interesting question is: what is the effect of such action by South Africa on Madagascar's international obligations vis-à-vis complementarity and the ICC? If South Africa has decided to horizontally 'complement' Madagascar's unwillingness, inability, or inaction, are Madagascar's complementarity obligations under the ICC Statute now satisfied? Is the ICC Prosecutor precluded from initiating a *proprio motu* investigation because South Africa, rather than Madagascar, has taken it upon itself to investigate/prosecute?

These are not easy questions to answer, but on the publicly available facts one would have to answer 'no', since the South African investigation targets only one (former) high-ranking individual's individual criminal responsibility. While it is true that the ICC Office of the Prosecutor (OTP) has an explicit policy in place whereby it will generally only investigate a small number of persons in leadership positions in states or in organizations responsible for ICC crimes,[48] this is not a legal impediment to the ICC's jurisdiction *ratione personae*, but simply an exercise of prosecutorial discretion. Thus, in the Madagascar case, it is likely that other senior or middle-tier individuals from the former Ravalomanana government also bear responsibility for the international crimes allegedly committed. The fact that South Africa's investigative efforts focus on only one person would therefore not negate Madagascar's general obligation to investigate and/or prosecute others who may also share in the responsibility for the crimes committed.

Given the fact that South Africa has initiated an investigation, one could be excused for instinctively believing that there has been action on the part of the ICC. After all, if South African authorities believed there was enough information to warrant the commencement of an investigation, surely the ICC OTP would have also made some inroads?

---

[47] Fausto Pocar and Magali Maystre, 'The principle of complementarity: a means towards a more pragmatic enforcement of the goal pursued by universal jurisdiction?' in Bergsmo (ed.), *Complementarity and the Exercise of Universal Jurisdiction for Core International Crimes*, p. 297.

[48] See ICC OTP, 'Paper on some policy issues before the Office of the Prosecutor', September 2003, p. 7, <http://icc-cpi.int/NR/rdonlyres/1FA7C4C6-DE5F-42B7-8B25-60AA962ED8B6/143594/030905_Policy_Paper.pdf>; ICC OTP, 'Report on prosecutorial strategy', 14 September 2006, §2(b), <http://icc-cpi.int/NR/rdonlyres/D673DD8C-D427-4547-BC69-2D363E07274B/143708/ProsecutorialStrategy20060914_English.pdf>; ICC OTP, 'Prosecutorial strategy 2009–2012', 1 February 2010, §19, <http://icc-cpi.int/NR/rdonlyres/66A8DCDC-3650-4514-AA62-D229D1128F65/281506/OTPProsecutorialStrategy20092013.pdf>.

However, despite being requested to look into the matter—by Ravalomanana himself—more than a year before South African authorities confirmed their investigation,[49] the ICC OTP has, to this day, not even opened a preliminary examination into the events in Madagascar.[50] Yet South African authorities, under their domestic law, determined that the available information was enough for a reasonable basis to believe that crimes against humanity occurred,[51] meriting not just the opening of the South African equivalent of a preliminary examination, but even a fully fledged criminal investigation.

What are we to make of this vis-à-vis the ICC Prosecutor, who is obliged to open an investigation upon exactly the same standard being satisfied?[52] It is submitted that what we could be possibly witnessing is the first instance in which an ICC state party pursuant to its universal jurisdiction has 'complemented' the ICC Prosecutor. Of course, much remains unknown; there could very well be good reasons for the lack of ICC engagement in Madagascar. But on the face of it, without any explanation on the part of the Prosecutor, it appears that this may be a case of inaction on the part of the ICC.

On the other hand, if confirmed, the second putative South African investigation into alleged international crimes in Zimbabwe initiated on the basis of the ICC Act (this time for rapes as crimes against humanity) would come as a great surprise. This is because South African authorities have actively opposed the *Zimbabwe Torture Judgment*. Initially, they requested leave to appeal from Judge Fabricius directly, which he denied.[53] The Supreme Court of Appeal was then approached and oral arguments on whether leave to appeal should be granted or not were expected to take place during the first quarter of 2013,[54]

---

[49] Rivonala Razafison, 'Madagascar: ICC accepts Ravalomanana's massacre probe request', *Africafrique.com*, 7 June 2011, <http://www.africafrique.com/index.php/home/2471-madagascar-icc-accepts-ravalomananas-massacre-probe-request>.

[50] This is to be contrasted with the opening of a preliminary examination, investigation, and subsequent prosecutions for post-election violence in Kenya in late 2007 to early 2008. Exactly what is required—in a legal sense—to open a preliminary examination (rather than an investigation) by the ICC OTP remains unclear. A recent draft policy paper on preliminary examinations states the following: 'The preliminary examination of a situation may be initiated on the basis of: (a) a decision of the Prosecutor, taking into consideration any information on crimes under the jurisdiction of the Court, including information sent by individuals or groups, States, intergovernmental or non-governmental organisations[.]' See ICC OTP, 'Draft policy paper on preliminary examinations', 4 October 2010, §25, <http://icc-cpi.int/NR/rdonlyres/E278F5A2-A4F9-43D7-83D2-6A2C9CF5D7D7/282515/OTP_Draftpolicypaperonpreliminaryexamin ations04101.pdf>.

[51] *Rakoto and ors v. Head: Directorate for Priority Crimes Investigation and ors* [2012] ZAGPPHC 281, 19 November 2012, §50.

[52] 'The Prosecutor *shall*, having evaluated the information made available to him or her, initiate an investigation unless he or she determines that there is no *reasonable basis to proceed* under this Statute. In deciding whether to initiate an investigation, the Prosecutor shall consider whether:...(a) The information available to the Prosecutor provides *a reasonable basis to believe* that a crime within the jurisdiction of the Court has been or is being committed[.]' ICC Statute, Art. 53(1)(a) (emphasis added).

[53] *Southern African Litigation Centre and anor v. National Director of Public Prosecution and ors*, Case No. 77150/09, 7 June 2012.

[54] SALC, 'Zimbabwe: challenging the NPA's refusal to act in terms of the Rome Statute Act', <http://www.southernafricalitigationcentre.org/cases/ongoing-cases/challenging-the-npas-refusal-to-act-in-terms-of-the-rome-statute-act/>.

but as of time of writing this had still to occur. This would, however, all be rendered moot if it were confirmed that a second Zimbabwe investigation had been initiated, since it is difficult to conceive how the two Zimbabwean cases could be readily distinguished. It would be inherently inconsistent for South African authorities to continue to deny investigating one case while investigating the other. But until more details are released and the appeal process eventually plays out, it is difficult to give definitive answers at the present time on this issue.

Concluding remarks

The *Zimbabwe Torture Judgment* marks the first time that the relationship between complementarity and universal jurisdiction has been considered by a domestic court, resulting in the ordering of the commencement of an investigation for international crimes committed extraterritorially. Its importance should not be downplayed. A recent study of universal jurisdiction from around the world concluded that more than three-quarters of states (147) provide for universal jurisdiction over one or more international crimes, as such.[55] A large majority of these are ICC states parties and their international complementarity obligations are, in principle, no different from those of South Africa.

Further, the implications of the *Zimbabwe Torture Judgment* as outlined in this chapter are not purely hypothetical or abstract. In Australia, for example, which also has universal jurisdiction over international crimes,[56] federal authorities were presented with a brief of evidence in October 2011 containing information and testimony from victims of and eyewitnesses to the final stages of the Sri Lankan civil war in 2009. Citing Australia's universal jurisdiction over international crimes, the opening of an investigation for alleged war crimes committed by Sri Lankan forces was requested.[57] Like Zimbabwe, Sri Lanka is not a party to the ICC Statute. The similarities with the *Zimbabwe Torture Judgment* are striking and the holdings of Judge Fabricius support the proposition that Australia would be internationally obliged to investigate such allegations pursuant to its ICC obligations, even though such a case could not be brought before the ICC for lack of jurisdiction.[58]

---

[55] Amnesty International, *Universal Jurisdiction: A Preliminary Survey of Legislation around the World—2012 Update*, Amnesty International, London, October 2012, p. 2, <http://www.amnesty.org/en/library/asset/IOR53/019/2012/en/2769ce03-16b7-4dd7-8ea3-95f4c64a522a/ior530192012en.pdf>.

[56] Sections 268.117, 15.4, and 16.1, Criminal Code (Cth), requiring the consent of the federal Attorney General for prosecution (as opposed to investigation).

[57] International Commission of Jurists—Australian Section, 'Investigation of Sri Lankan war crimes', <http://www.icj-aust.org.au/media/latest-news/investigation-sri-lankan-war-crimes>; 'Allegations of Sri Lankan war crimes in the spotlight', *Australian Broadcasting Corporation*, 18 October 2011, <http://www.abc.net.au/7.30/content/2011/s3342849.htm>.

[58] Given the war crimes context, one could perhaps rely on customary international law alone to ground such an international obligation. As the International Committee of the Red Cross (ICRC) has concluded:

Meanwhile, South African investigations continue. For his part, Ravalomanana was ordered by the North Gauteng High Court to surrender his passport to South African authorities for the duration of the investigation and has had strict conditions placed upon him for leaving the country.[59] Leave to appeal these orders to the Constitutional Court of South Africa was denied.[60] Reactions have been mixed, ranging from outright praise, to some commentators going as far as saying that 'it may have been a politically motivated attempt to prevent [Ravalomanana] from being free to campaign abroad against Rajoelina [his political rival]'.[61] With respect to the Zimbabwe investigation, the government's response has been predictable, with the Zimbabwean Minister of Justice commenting that the judgment 'is a wish by the South African judge [Fabricius] pushing an agenda of former Rhodesians who want to effect regime change in Zimbabwe'.[62] This bears the distinctive hallmarks of similar criticisms levelled against the ICC: that it is a 'Western' or neo-colonial[63] tool to advance political agendas. Nevertheless, its force is distinctively weaker when it is levelled against *Africans* pursuing other Africans for international crimes.

Whatever the merits of the *Zimbabwe Torture Judgment*, it has undoubtedly opened an entirely new chapter in the story of international criminal law, one in which complementarity has a distinctive effect on how domestic jurisdictions deal with allegations of international crimes. As more and more states implement the ICC Statute domestically, situations like those explored in this chapter are likely to increase. What remains to be seen is how states will respond to the tangible effects of their creation. Will they experience buyer's remorse or embrace complementarity's reflection in the mirror? Chances are, given the rapid pace of international criminal justice, we will not have to wait too long to find out.

'There is . . . sufficient practice . . . to establish the obligation under customary international law to investigate war crimes allegedly committed in non-international armed conflicts and to prosecute the suspects if appropriate.' See Jean-Marie Henckaerts and Louise Doswald-Beck, *ICRC Customary International Humanitarian Law, Vol. I: Rules*, Cambridge University Press, Cambridge, 2009, pp. 609–10. It is unclear, however, whether this conclusion also applies to states wholly unconnected to the conflict, such as Australia, pursuant to domestic universal jurisdiction.

[59] *Rakoto and ors v. Head: Directorate for Priority Crimes Investigation and ors* [2012] ZAGPPHC 281, 19 November 2012.

[60] *Ravalomanana v. Rakoto and ors*, Order (Case No. CCT 127/12), 4 February 2013.

[61] Bob Dewar, Simon Massey, and Bruce Baker, *Madagascar: Time to Make a Fresh Start*, Chatham House, London, January 2013, p. 5, <http://www.chathamhouse.org/sites/default/files/public/Research/Africa/0113pp_madagascar.pdf>.

[62] 'Chinamsa blasts South African court ruling', *The Zimbabwe Mail*, 8 May 2012, <http://www.thezimbabwemail.com/zimbabwe/11654-chinamsa-blasts-south-africa-court-ruling.html>.

[63] One (ad hoc) ICJ judge made similar comments in light of the exercise of universal jurisdiction *in absentia* by Belgium over international crimes allegedly committed in the Democratic Republic of the Congo: ICJ, *Case Concerning the Arrest Warrant of 11 April 2000 (Democratic Republic of the Congo v. Belgium)*, Judgment, 14 February 2002, Separate Opinion of Judge Bula-Bula, ICJ Reports 2002, p. 100.

12 Jurisprudence in the ad hoc international criminal tribunals in 2012: contributions and controversy

Damien Scalia*

Introduction

This chapter presents and analyses the main substantive contributions to international criminal law made by the International Criminal Tribunal for former Yugoslavia (ICTY) and the International Criminal Tribunal for Rwanda (ICTR) in 2012. During the year, many judgments were issued by the two tribunals. The ICTR issued judgments by the Trial Chamber or the Appeals Chamber in seven cases (*Nizeyimana*,[1] *Nzabonimana*,[2] *Ntabakuze*,[3] *Gatete*,[4] *Ngirabatware*,[5] *Hategekimana*,[6] and *Kanyarukiga*),[7] while the ICTY issued judgments in four cases (*Lukić and Lukić*,[8] *Tolimir*,[9] *Haradinaj*,[10] and *Gotovina*

---

* Damien Scalia holds a PhD in international criminal law from the Universities of Geneva and Paris-Ouest Nanterre La Défense. He is a researcher at the Université Saint-Louis—Bruxelles and a lecturer in international humanitarian law and international criminal law.

[1] ICTR, *Prosecutor v. Nizeyimana*, Judgment and Sentence (Trial Chamber) (Case No. ICTR-2000-55C-T), 19 June 2012.

[2] ICTR, *Prosecutor v. Nzabonimana*, Judgment and Sentence (Trial Chamber) (Case No. ICTR-98-44D-T), 31 May 2012.

[3] ICTR, *Prosecutor v. Ntabakuze*, Judgment (Appeals Chamber) (Case No. ICTR-98-41A-A), 8 May 2012.

[4] ICTR, *Prosecutor v. Gatete*, Judgment (Appeals Chamber) (Case No. ICTR-00-61-A), 9 October 2012.

[5] ICTR, *Prosecutor v. Ngirabatware*, Judgment (Trial Chamber) (Case No. ICTR-99-55-T), 20 December 2012.

[6] ICTR, *Prosecutor v. Hategekimana*, Judgment (Appeals Chamber) (Case No. ICTR -00-55B-A), 8 May 2012.

[7] ICTR, *Prosecutor v. Kanyarukiga*, Judgment (Appeals Chamber) (Case No. ICTR-02-78-A, 8 May 2012.

[8] ICTY, *Prosecutor v. Lukić and Lukić*, Judgment (Appeals Chamber) (Case No. IT-98-32/1-A), 4 December 2012.

[9] ICTY, *Prosecutor v. Tolimir*, Judgment (Trial Chamber) (Case No. IT-05-88/2), 12 December 2012.

[10] ICTY, *Prosecutor v. Haradinaj, Balaj and Brahimal*, Public Judgment with Confidential Annex (Trial Chamber) (Case No. IT-04-84bis-T), 29 November 2012.

and Markač).[11] This chapter will focus on points from these cases that I consider to be the most important.

After initially presenting some specific interpretations of the different elements of definitions of crimes (Section A) and forms of responsibility (Section B), I will outline some of the issues relating to sentencing (Section C). The chapter concludes by focusing on the well-known *Gotovina and Markač* case. This case was (and is still) 'the talk of the town' not only in Croatia and Serbia, but also in Western nations, and raises questions about the role of the ad hoc international criminal tribunals (ICTs) (Section D).

A. **Elements of crimes**

Contributions on elements of crimes in the 2012 jurisprudence of the ICTs principally affect the crime of genocide and crimes committed in relation with genocide. The main elements of the crime are long established in the jurisprudence of the ICTs, but some of the criteria of the definition were made more precise or were further interpreted or clarified in 2012. These points will now be discussed.

In the *Ntabakuze* case, the ICTR rendered an important appeal judgment linked to the definition of genocide. Aloys Ntabakuze was the commander of the Para-Commando Battalion of the Rwandan Army from 1988 to July 1994. The ICTR Trial Chamber found Mr Ntabakuze guilty of genocide, crimes against humanity (murder, extermination, persecution, and other inhuman acts), and serious violations of Article 3 common to the 1949 Geneva Conventions and of the 1977 Additional Protocol II (violence to life), pursuant to Article 6(3) (command responsibility) of the Statute of the ICTR. Mr Ntabakuze was responsible for his subordinates' killing of Tutsi civilians in the Kabeza area of Kigali on 7 and 8 April 1994, at Nyanza Hill on 11 April 1994, and at the Institut Africain et Mauricien de Statistiques et d'Économie in the Remra area of Kigali around 15 April 1994. The Trial Chamber also found him responsible for his subordinates' preventing the refugees who were killed at Nyanza Hill from seeking sanctuary. The Trial Chamber sentenced Ntabakuze to life imprisonment.

Mr Ntabakuze appealed his conviction, arguing that the Trial Chamber 'reached its finding concerning the crime of genocide despite evidence that among the victims... were persons of Hutu ethnicity', and alleged a lack of proof of the perpetrators' intent to destroy the Tutsi group 'as such'.[12] In other words, if the perpetrators killed Hutus at the same time as Tutsis, no genocide had been committed. The Appeals Chamber dismissed

---

[11] ICTY, *Prosecutor v. Gotovina and Markač*, Judgment (Appeals Chamber) (Case No. IT-06-90-A), 16 November 2012.

[12] ICTR, *Prosecutor v. Ntabakuze*, Judgment (Appeals Chamber), 8 May 2012, §235.

this ground of appeal, rejecting the proposition that 'the fact that there may have been some Hutu victims among the large group of Tutsi victims suffices' to undermine a finding of genocidal intent.[13] This approach should be read in conjunction with the position generally established by the ICTs that the victims' group should be defined positively[14] in a case of genocide and not negatively (i.e. other individuals than perpetrators). The *Ntabakuze* appeal judgment clarifies this element of the definition of genocide: when individuals who do not belong to the targeted group are present in the group that is attacked, genocide may nevertheless have been committed.

In connection with the crime of direct and public incitement to commit genocide, in *Nzabonimana*, the Trial Chamber helped to clarify the definition of the term 'public'. Mr Nzabonimana was the Rwandan Minister of Youth and Associative Movements during the relevant period. He was convicted of genocide, conspiracy to commit genocide, and direct and public incitement to commit genocide, particularly for speeches he made inciting the killing of civilian Tutsis. Nzabonimana was sentenced to life imprisonment. According to long-established jurisprudence, 'all convictions before the Tribunal for direct and public incitement to commit genocide involve speeches made to large, fully public assemblies, messages disseminated by the media, and communications made through a public address system over a broad public area'.[15] As summarized by the Appeals Chamber, incitement is 'public' when conducted through speeches, shouting, or threats uttered in public places or at public gatherings.[16] In the present case, the Trial Chamber stated that:

Nzabonimana made the speech in a public location near the Nyabikenke *commune* office. The witnesses did not indicate the specific audience to whom the speech was addressed; however, Witness CNAX described a crowd of approximately 30 people. The fact that Witness CNAI was summoned over, and that Evariste Munyagatare, a Tutsi, was also present, established beyond reasonable doubt that the words were intended to be heard by anyone in the area, rather than by than an exclusive and limited group.

The Chamber therefore concluded that Nzabonimana's conduct satisfied the 'public' element of the crime.[17] The Trial Chamber added that the fact that a journalist from

---

[13] ICTR, *Prosecutor v. Ntabakuze*, Judgment (Appeals Chamber), 8 May 2012, §237.

[14] ICTY, *Prosecutor v. Stakić*, Judgment (Appeals Chamber) (Case No. IT-97-24), 22 March 2006, §§16–28; ICJ, *Case Concerning Application of the Convention on the Prevention and Punishment of the Crime of Genocide (Bosnia and Herzegovina v. Serbia and Montenegro)*, Judgment, 26 February 2007, §193.

[15] ICTR, *Prosecutor v. Nzabonimana*, Judgment and Sentence (Trial Chamber), 31 May 2012, §1754; ICTR, *Prosecutor v. Kalimanzira*, Judgment (Appeals Chamber) (Case No. ICTR-05-88-A), 20 October 2010, §§155–6, citing especially, inter alia, ICTR, *Prosecutor v. Bikindi*, Judgment (Appeals Chamber) (Case No. CTR-01-72-A), 18 March 2010, §§50, 86; ICTR, *Prosecutor v. Nahimana and ors*, Judgment (Appeals Chamber) (Case No. ICTR-99-52-A), 28 November 2007, §§758, 775, 862; ICTR, *Prosecutor v. Kajelijeli*, Judgment (Appeals Chamber) (Case No. ICTR-98-44A-A), 23 May 2005, §§105, 133.

[16] ICTR, *Prosecutor v. Muvunyi II*, Judgment (Appeals Chamber) (Case No. ICTR-2000-55A-A), 1 April 2011, §27.

[17] ICTR, *Prosecutor v. Nzabonimana*, Judgment and Sentence (Trial Chamber), 31 May 2012, §1766.

Radio Rwanda was present during the meeting 'was a factor suggesting that the message of the meeting was intended to be broadcast to the public at large'.[18] Nzabonimana thus had the requisite *mens rea* to incite genocide publicly.

The *Gatete* case produced an interesting decision in terms of cumulative convictions for both genocide and conspiracy to commit genocide. As observed by the Appeals Chamber, 'this [was] the first time that it ha[d] been called upon to adjudicate the issue of whether an accused can be convicted both of genocide and conspiracy to commit genocide'.[19] First, the judges recalled 'that convictions entered under different statutory provisions but based on the same conduct are permissible only if each statutory provision involved has a materially distinct element not contained in the other'.[20] In affirming this, the judges reiterated long-established jurisprudence on this point.[21] The judgment stated that genocide and conspiracy to commit genocide are different crimes (Article 2(3)(a) and Article 2(3)(b), respectively, of the Statute of the ICTR), because each crime has a different *actus reus* and is based on different underlying conduct. Indeed, the crime of genocide requires the commission of one of the acts enumerated in Article 2(2) of the Statute,[22] while the crime of conspiracy to commit genocide requires the act of entering into an agreement to commit genocide.[23] Following this interpretation, the Appeals Chamber concluded that 'by convicting Gatete only of genocide while he was also found criminally responsible for conspiracy to commit genocide, the Trial Chamber failed to hold him responsible for the totality of his criminal conduct, which included entering into the unlawful agreement to commit genocide'.[24] It is important to highlight, though, that Judges Pocar and Agius dissented from this judgment.[25]

---

[18] Patrick Hayden and Katerina. I. Kappos, 'Current developments at the ad hoc international criminal tribunals', *Journal of International Criminal Justice*, 11 (2013), p. 249; ICTR, *Prosecutor v. Nzabonimana*, Judgment and Sentence (Trial Chamber), 31 May 2012, §1772.

[19] ICTR, *Prosecutor v. Gatete*, Judgment (Appeals Chamber) (Case No. ICTR-00-61-A), 9 October 2012, §259.

[20] ICTR, *Prosecutor v. Gatete*, Judgment (Appeals Chamber), 9 October 2012, §259.

[21] ICTY, *Prosecutor v. Delalić and ors*, Judgment (Appeals Chamber) (Case No. T-96-21-A), 20 February 2001, §412. See also ICTR, *Prosecutor v. Ntabakuze*, Judgment (Appeals Chamber), 8 May 2012, §260; ICTR, *Prosecutor v. Bagosora and Nsengiyumva*, Judgment (Appeals Chamber) (Case No. ICTR-98-41-A), 14 December 2011, §413; ICTR, *Prosecutor v. Nahimana and ors*, Judgment (Appeals Chamber), 28 November 2007, §1019; ICTR, *Prosecutor v. Ntakirutimana*, Judgment (Appeals Chamber) (Case Nos ICTR-96-10-A and ICTR-96-17-A), 13 December 2004, §542.

[22] ICTR, *Nahimana and ors*, Judgment (Appeals Chamber), 28 November 2007, §492.

[23] ICTR, *Prosecutor v. Seromba*, Judgment (Appeals Chamber) (Case No. ICTR-2001-66-A), 12 March 2008, §218; ICTR, *Prosecutor v. Nahimana and ors*, Judgment (Appeals Chamber), 28 November 2007, §894; ICTR, *Prosecutor v. Ntagerura and ors*, Judgment (Appeals Chamber) (Case No. ICTR-99-46-A), 7 July 2006, §92.

[24] ICTR, *Prosecutor v. Gatete*, Judgment (Appeals Chamber) (Case No. ICTR-00-61-A), 9 October 2012, §261.

[25] ICTR, *Prosecutor v. Gatete*, Judgment (Appeals Chamber), 9 October 2012, Partially Dissenting Opinion of Judge Pocar and Dissenting Opinion of Judge Agius.

B. **Elements of responsibility**

The elements of responsibility enumerated by the ICTs in 2012 were principally related to command responsibility. Nevertheless, certain other forms of responsibility were also concerned by the year's jurisprudence.

COMMAND RESPONSIBILITY

In the *Ntabakuze* case (as cited earlier), details were provided about command responsibility. The Appeals Chamber upheld the Trial Chamber's finding that Ntabakuze's subordinates had the requisite specific intent for the crime of genocide, and that he knew that his subordinates had such intent. This suggests that knowledge of a subordinate's intent is necessary to establish an accused's superior responsibility for genocide pursuant to Article 6(3) of the ICTR Statute.[26] Nevertheless, in a joint dissenting opinion, despite agreeing with the conclusion of the Appeal judgment, Judges Pocar and Liu highlighted that '[f]or the purpose of criminal responsibility for genocide pursuant to Article 6(3) of the Statute, it is not necessary to establish that a superior knew of the specific intent of his subordinates'. In their view, and as reflected in long-established jurisprudence, 'it is sufficient for a superior to know or have reason to know that his subordinates are about to commit *a crime* but it is not necessary that he be aware of their specific *mens rea*'.[27]

In the same decision, the Appeals Chamber recalled (still in relation to command responsibility) that, in respect of failure to prevent or punish: '[I]n many cases it will be sufficient to plead that the accused did not take any necessary and reasonable measures to prevent or punish the commission of criminal acts. This stems from the fact that the accused's failure to prevent or punish may often be inferred from the continuing or widespread nature of the violations committed by his subordinates as alleged in the indictment.'[28] However, the Appeals Chamber observed that the indictment 'pleads that the crimes alleged in the Indictment were carried out on his orders and directives. This, in the Appeals Chamber's opinion, gave notice to Ntabakuze that he was alleged to have failed to take the necessary measures to prevent or punish the crimes'.[29]

---

[26] Patrick Hayden and Katerina I. Kappos, 'Current developments at the ad hoc international criminal tribunals', p. 250.

[27] ICTY, *Prosecutor v. Delalić and ors*, Judgment (Appeals Chamber) (Case No. T-96-21-A), 20 February 2001, §238; ICTR, *Prosecutor v. Bagosora and Nsengiyumva*, Judgement (Appeals Chamber), 14 December 2011, §384; ICTR, *Prosecutor v. Nahimana and ors*, Judgment (Appeals Chamber), 28 November 2007, §865; ICTR, *Prosecutor v. Ntabakuze*, Judgment (Appeals Chamber), 8 May 2012, Declaration of Judges Pocar and Liu, §1.

[28] ICTR, *Prosecutor v. Ntabakuze*, Judgment (Appeals Chamber), 8 May 2012, §123.

[29] ICTR, *Prosecutor v. Ntabakuze*, Judgment (Appeals Chamber), 8 May 2012, §125.

When considering command responsibility, the judgment in the *Nizeyimana* case should also be analysed. Nizeyimana was a captain at the military training school in Butare town called the École des Sous-Officiers (ESO). He was responsible for mobilizing ESO soldiers who committed crimes in the Butare area, and was condemned for genocide and extermination and murder as crimes against humanity, as well as murder as a war crime pursuant to Article 6(1) of the ICTR Statute. He was sentenced to life imprisonment.

Even though he was condemned pursuant to Article 6(1), a question was raised in connection with the fact that there were two commanders in relation to the superior criteria defining command responsibility. The judges stated that 'the reasonable possibility that ESO Commander Lieutenant Colonel Tharcisse Muvunyi, Nizeyimana's *de jure* superior, may have also ordered and authorised killings at this roadblock ... does not reasonably eliminate Nizeyimana's effective control over the perpetrators of these crimes'.[30] In this case, Nizeyimana was directly ordering the ESO soldiers to commit killings. They were also threatened with death if they did not comply with his order. 'Nizeyimana's actions, which were a necessary condition to the ensuing attack, fully reflect his material ability to prevent and punish this criminal conduct of these ESO soldiers at that moment.'[31]

OTHER RESPONSIBILITIES

In relation to the act of murder, the Appeals Chamber has applied a consistent jurisprudence when it concerns the commission of genocide.[32] This judgment states that 'a person who did not personally physically commit a crime—in the present case, personally shooting each victim—can nonetheless be liable for committing the crime of murder, if there is evidence that the perpetrator's acts were as much an integral part of the murder as the killings which the crime enabled'.[33]

Even though, in the *Lukić and Lukić* case, the crimes alleged were not genocide, the reasoning was applicable to the crime of murder, as the Trial Chamber observed.[34] The Appeals Chamber added a reference to the *Limaj* case, in which the Appeals Chamber

---

[30] ICTR, *Prosecutor v. Nizeyimana*, Judgment and Sentence (Trial Chamber) (Case No. ICTR-2000-55C-T), 19 June 2012, §1528.

[31] ICTR, *Prosecutor v. Nizeyimana*, Judgment and Sentence (Trial Chamber), 19 June 2012, §1526.

[32] ICTR, *Prosecutor v. Seromba*, Judgment (Appeals Chamber) (Case No. ICTR-2001-66-A), 12 March 2008,§161; ICTR, *Prosecutor v. Gacumbitsi*, Judgment (Appeals Chamber) (Case No. ICTR-2001-64-A), 7 July 2006, §60.

[33] ICTY, *Prosecutor v. Lukić and Lukić*, Judgment (Appeals Chamber) (Case No. IT-98-32/1-A), 4 December 2012, §157.

[34] ICTY, *Prosecutor v. Lukić and Lukić*, Judgment (Trial Chamber) (Case No. IT-98-32/1-T), 20 July 2009, §908.

convicted an accused, 'in the absence of a JCE [joint criminal enterprise], for committing murder by executing nine prisoners, on the basis that he "participated physically in the material elements of the crime of murder, jointly with Murrizi, and perhaps with a third KLA soldier" and without a need to show whose bullet killed each victim'.[35] Similarly, the Appeals Chamber was satisfied that the Trial Chamber did not err in finding that Milan Lukić, jointly with others, participated in the material elements of the crime of murder, and was therefore responsible for the death of all five victims, regardless of whether or not he personally fired the fatal bullet in each case.[36] The difference between this form of responsibility for committing crimes and the third type of JCE thus becomes very narrow.

C. **Sentencing**

In terms of sentencing, from the jurisprudence of the ICTs, we know that criteria are identified in the decisions, which are then taken into account to determine the sentence 'tariff'.[37] The judgments issued in 2012 follow this approach. In the *Ntabakuze* case, the Appeals Chamber judgment states that 'grounds for denying mitigation do not, per se, constitute aggravating circumstances, and there is nothing in the Trial Judgement which suggests that the Trial Chamber considered them as such'.[38] This means that the mitigating and aggravating circumstances are evaluated separately, and an overall assessment is not required. Moreover, the Appeals Chamber specifies that:

[T]he form of liability is not an individual circumstance of the accused but the objective definition of his participation in the criminal conduct. Further, failure to prevent or punish subordinates' crimes constitutes the culpable conduct under Article 6(3) of the Statute and the absence of conviction under Article 6(1) of the Statute does not reduce that culpability...The Appeals Chamber finds that the Trial Chamber was therefore correct in not considering in mitigation the fact that Ntabakuze was not convicted pursuant to Article 6(1) of the Statute and, accordingly, rejects Ntabakuze's argument in this respect.[39]

In the same case, however, the Appeals Chamber stated that the Trial Chamber took into consideration mitigating circumstances on a discretionary basis (to evaluate what constitutes a mitigating circumstance and the weight to be accorded). The Appeals Chamber considered 'the existence of mitigating circumstances does not automatically imply a

---

[35] ICTY, *Prosecutor v. Limaj and ors*, Judgment (Trial Chamber) (Case No. IT-03-66), 27 September 2007, §§47–50.

[36] ICTY, *Prosecutor v. Lukić and Lukić*, Judgment (Appeals Chamber), 4 December 2012, §162.

[37] Damien Scalia, *Du principe de légalité des peines en droit international pénal*, Bruylant, Brussels, 2011.

[38] ICTR, *Prosecutor v. Ntabakuze*, Judgment (Appeals Chamber), 8 May 2012, §271.

[39] ICTR, *Prosecutor v. Ntabakuze*, Judgment (Appeals Chamber), 8 May 2012, §282.

reduction of sentence[40] or preclude the imposition of a sentence of life imprisonment where the gravity of the offence so requires'.[41] I have elsewhere expressed my lack of understanding of such an affirmation;[42] for how can mitigating circumstances be such if they do not mitigate the sentence?

In the same vein, the Appeals Chamber noted, in determining the sentence that:

[T]he Trial Chamber expressly took into account Ntabakuze's family situation and his lengthy public service to his country as a military officer, as well as his social, educational, and professional background. The Trial Chamber, however, concluded that the gravity of the crimes and the aggravating factors greatly outweighed these mitigating factors. The Appeals Chamber recalls that in general only little weight is afforded to the family situation of the convicted person in the absence of exceptional family circumstances. Similarly, the lack of a previous criminal record and a purported likelihood of successful rehabilitation are common characteristics among many convicted persons which are accorded little weight, if any, in mitigation in the absence of exceptional circumstances. As for Ntabakuze's 'exemplary' military career, the Appeals Chamber also considers that it was in the Trial Chamber's discretion not to accord this factor any mitigating value in the absence of particular reasons for doing so. Ntabakuze does not submit that exceptional circumstances obliged the Trial Chamber to accord special value to any of the factors listed above.[43]

What kind of mitigating circumstances have to be present to mitigate a sentence? The Appeals Chamber judgment gave the same explanation about another mitigating circumstance: regret. It stated that Ntabakuze's expression of regret should have been considered as a mitigating factor in sentencing (the Trial Chamber erred in failing to consider it as such). However, the Appeals Chamber stated that this error did not invalidate the sentence imposed by the Trial Chamber, as it considered that the gravity of the crimes for which Ntabakuze was convicted and the aggravating factors identified by the Trial Chamber greatly outweighed this mitigating factor.[44] The Appeals Chamber made the same decision in the *Lukić and Lukić* case.[45] Since the ICTs began to act, the case law on penalties has been regrettably consistent in this regard.

Moreover, it is important to highlight that Mr Ntabakuze was the first individual before the ICTR to be sentenced to life imprisonment solely based on superior responsibility. In doing so, the Appeals Chamber recalled that 'superior responsibility under Article 6(3) of the Statute is not to be seen as less grave than criminal responsibility

---

[40] ICTR, *Prosecutor v. Nahimana and ors*, Judgment (Appeals Chamber), 28 November 2007, §1038; *Prosecutor v. Kajelijeli*, Judgment (Appeals Chamber) (Case No. ICTR-98-44A-A), 23 May 2005, §299.

[41] ICTR, *Prosecutor v. Ntabakuze*, Judgment (Appeals Chamber), 8 May 2012, §280.

[42] Scalia, *Du principe de légalité des peines en droit international pénal*.

[43] ICTR, *Prosecutor v. Ntabakuze*, Judgment (Appeals Chamber), 8 May 2012, §284.

[44] ICTR, *Prosecutor v. Ntabakuze*, Judgment (Appeals Chamber), 8 May 2012, §294.

[45] ICTR, *Prosecutor v. Ntabakuze*, Judgment (Appeals Chamber), 8 May 2012, §662.

under Article 6(1) of the Statute'[46] and that 'the seriousness of a superior's conduct in failing to prevent or punish crimes must be measured to some degree by the nature of the crimes to which this failure relates, *i.e.* the gravity of the crimes committed by the direct perpetrators'.[47]

In addition, in the *Nizeyimana* judgment, the Trial Chamber rejected the accused's submission that he should be given a lower sentence than his *de jure* commander. The Chamber considered that the gravity of the Nizeyimana's offences should be the primary consideration in sentencing: the most serious of Nizeyimana's convictions was based on a single incident of incitement, which stands in stark contrast to the extensive proven criminal conduct in the present case.[48]

Finally, in connection to sentencing, it is important to highlight the case of *Jelena Rašić*, the case manager of Milan Lukić. Ms Rašić was convicted for interfering with witnesses (in bribing witnesses to provide false testimony and inciting others to bribe potential witnesses) and sentenced to 12 months' imprisonment. She was released after three months' imprisonment when the Trial Chamber suspended the sentence. The prosecution appealed against the judgment. First, the Appeals Chamber found that: '[T]he power to suspend a sentence must be distinguished from the power to issue a pardon, commutation of sentence, or early release. Such suspension of a sentence, either in full or in part, does not infringe the authority of the enforcing State to execute the sentence in accordance with the applicable law of that State.' Similarly, it does not 'effectively remove the power from the President of the Tribunal to make the final determination regarding the [execution of the] sentence' imposed by the Trial Chamber.[49] Rather, the decision to suspend the last eight months of Rašić's sentence of 12 months' imprisonment 'forms an integral part of the Trial Chamber's judicial discretion in the determination of the sentence'.[50]

The Trial Chamber decided to suspend the remainder of the accused's sentence 'because she was the only female prisoner detained at the United Nations Detention Unit and therefore in quasi-solitary confinement'.[51] The Trial Chamber based its decision to impose a suspended sentence on Rašić's '*perception* of her detention and the practical impact upon her well-being', and on her 'comparably young age and that

---

[46] ICTR, *Prosecutor v. Ntabakuze*, Judgment (Appeals Chamber), 8 May 2012, §299.

[47] ICTR, *Prosecutor v. Ntabakuze*, Judgment (Appeals Chamber), 8 May 2012, §302.

[48] Hayden and Kappos, 'Current developments at the ad hoc international criminal tribunals', p. 253; ICTR, *Prosecutor v. Nizeyimana*, Judgment and Sentence (Trial Chamber) (Case No. ICTR-2000-55C-T), 19 June 2012, §§1596–7.

[49] ICTY, *Prosecutor v. Stakić*, Judgement (Appeals Chamber), 22 March 2006, §392.

[50] ICTY, *Prosecutor v. Jelena Rašić*, Judgment (Appeals Chamber) (Case No. IT-98-32/1-R77.2-A), 16 November 2012, §18.

[51] Hayden and Kappos, 'Current developments at the ad hoc international criminal tribunals', pp. 252–3; ICTY, *Prosecutor v. Jelena Rašić*, Judgment (Appeals Chamber), 16 November 2012, §§29–31.

this is the first time she is sentenced to a prison sentence'.[52] It would perhaps be interesting to apply the same criteria to other persons convicted by the ICTY.

Alongside this overview of some of the jurisprudential contributions made by the ICTs in 2012, I will now focus on the judgment that provoked by far the greatest controversy.

D. **The *Gotovina and Markač* judgment on appeal**

In June 1991, Croatia declared independence from Yugoslavia, which triggered the conflict between Croat forces and the Serb minority, who represented approximately 12 per cent of the population. The Serb minority was supported by Belgrade and the Yugoslav National Army, the JNA. In 1992, after a cease-fire was agreed, Goran Hadžić proclaimed a new state: the Republika Srpska Krajina (RSK). The situation remained unchanged until 1995, when Croatian forces launched Operation Storm. The indictment of Gotovina, Markač, and Černmak stated that Operation Storm was a military operation to retake control of territory in the Krajina region of Croatia.[53]

The indictment alleged that, before, during, and after Operation Storm, there was an orchestrated campaign to drive the Serbs from the Krajina region, which involved 'during the Indictment period, forcible transfers;...the shelling of civilians and cruel treatment; unlawful attacks on civilians and civilian objects'.[54] In this context, the Trial Chamber concluded that Mr Gotovina shared the objective of and significantly contributed to a JCE, the common purpose of which was to remove the Serb civilian population by ordering unlawful artillery attacks on Benkovac, Gračac, Knin, and Obrovac (the so-called 'Four Towns'). It found Mr Gotovina and Mr Markač guilty pursuant to both the first and third types of JCE[55] of crimes against humanity and violations of the laws or customs of war. The first form of JCE is characterized as 'all co-defendants, acting pursuant to a common design, possess[ing] the same criminal intention',[56] while the third form of JCE is characterized by 'a common criminal design to pursue a course of conduct where one or more of the co-perpetrator[s] commit an act which, while outside

---

[52] ICTY, *Prosecutor v. Jelena Rašić*, Judgment (Appeals Chamber), 16 November 2012, §31.

[53] ICTY, *Prosecutor v. Gotovina, Černmak and Markač*, Judgment (Trial Chamber) (Case No. IT-06-90-A), 15 April 2011, §2.

[54] ICTY, *Prosecutor v. Gotovina and Markač*, Judgment (Appeals Chamber) (Case No. IT-06-90-A), 16 November 2012, §2.

[55] Antonio Cassese, *International Criminal Law*, 2nd edn, Oxford University Press, Oxford, 2008; Olivier de Frouville (ed.), *Punir les crimes de masses: entreprise criminelle commune ou co-action?*, Anthémis, Brussels, 2012.

[56] ICTY, *Prosecutor v. Gotovina, Černmak and Markač*, Judgment (Trial Chamber), 15 April 2011, §1950.

the common design, is a natural and foreseeable consequence of the implementation of that design'.[57]

On 15 April 2011, the Trial Chamber pronounced guilty verdicts against two Croatian generals who played a leading role in Operation Storm: Ante Gotovina and Mladen Markač. Mr Gotovina was the commander of the Split military district of the Croatian army and the overall operational commander of the southern Krajina region during Operation Storm.[58] He was sentenced to 24 years' imprisonment. Mr Markač was commander of the special police of Croatia and Assistant Minister of the Interior.[59] He was sentenced to 18 years' imprisonment. A third accused—Ivan Černmak, former commander of the Knin garrison—was tried and acquitted.

After their 2011 conviction, both defendants appealed. The Appeals Chamber issued its judgment on 16 November 2012, reversing the trial judgment and acquitting both accused. Not surprisingly, the judgment was received differently in Croatia than in Serbia. While Croatia rejoiced, in Serbia the Deputy Prime Minister stated that the verdict was the 'proof of selective justice which is worse than any injustice'.[60] As explained by James McDonald a few months later:

[T]his verdict, in particular, has damaged relations with Serbia and dismayed Croatia's Serb minority . . . The political scientist Roland Kostić has demonstrated the way in which transitional justice in the former Yugoslavia has often impeded reconciliation and empowered local nationalist leaders: as a result, national public opinion in each republic has tended to view the ICTY verdict [as having] widened divisions between Serbian and Croatian interpretations of the war not only because it absolved Gotovina and Markač [of] individual involvement in a joint criminal enterprise to expel Serbs from Croatia, but also because in finding that there was no joint criminal enterprise at all, it exonerated the very Croatian state which had facilitated that expulsion too. The ICTY verdict judged that even preparations for deportations discussed in the Brioni transcripts was not evidence of a joint criminal enterprise to forcibly deport Serbs, but a legitimate action to help civilians leave an area of conflict and reduce civilian casualties.[61]

Controversy was not limited to Serbia and Croatia: '[I]n the European press, the verdict was widely interpreted not as an exoneration of defendants but as an injustice to victims.'[62] However, it is not the purpose of this chapter to discuss the political issues of the *Gotovina* judgment.[63]

---

[57] ICTY, *Prosecutor v. Gotovina, Černmak and Markač*, Judgment (Trial Chamber), 15 April 2011, §1952.

[58] ICTY, *Prosecutor v. Gotovina and Markač*, Judgment (Appeals Chamber), 16 November 2012, §3.

[59] ICTY, *Prosecutor v. Gotovina and Markač*, Judgment (Appeals Chamber), 16 November 2012, §4.

[60] Bethany Bell, 'Hague war court acquits Croat Generals Gotovina and Markač', *BBC*, 17 November 2012, <http://www.bbc.co.uk/news/world-europe-20352187>.

[61] James McDonald, 'When the war is over: the *Gotovina* verdict and confronting the past—analysis', *Eurasia Review*, 11 April 2013, <http://www.eurasiareview.com/11042013-when-the-war-is-over-the-gotovina-verdict-and-confronting-the-past-analysis/>.

[62] McDonald, 'When the war is over: the *Gotovina* verdict and confronting the past—analysis'.

[63] See Janine Natalya Clark, 'Courting controversy: the ICTY's acquittal of Croatian Generals Gotovina and Markač', *Journal of International Criminal Justice*, 1 (2013), pp. 20–5; see also e.g. '"Bombshell" at the

It is, however, important to note that this judgment (and some others) have resulted in an unprecedented crisis within the Tribunal. A few months after the Gotovina appeals judgment, Judge Harhoff (reportedly!) wrote a letter to his colleagues on the bench, which was leaked to a newspaper.[64] In the letter, it is suggested that the US tribunal president has exercised 'persistent' and 'intense' pressure on his fellow judges to allow top-ranking officers to go free.[65] Judge Harhoff asked: 'Has an Israeli or American official influenced the American President of the tribunal to effect a change of course?'[66]

The fall-out continues from this affair (and, as of writing, Judge Harhoff had not publicly confirmed his authorship of the letter). Leaving the controversy aside, I will present here only the legal elements that have been assessed as problematic both by the dissenting opinion and by the majority of authors. I then analyse the issues raised by this decision.

CONTROVERSY ON LEGAL ELEMENTS

According to dissenting opinions of two of the five judges (Judge Pocar and Judge Agius) and the limited doctrine that has emerged after the judgment, three main elements are problematic: the 200-metre standard set for the denotation of an indiscriminate attack; the other elements related to the crime of unlawful attacks; and liability.

Regarding the 200-metre standard, in the Trial Judgment, the Trial Chamber heard three witnesses as to 'the accuracy of the weaponry . . . that the Croatian army was using during Operation Storm'.[67] Taking these testimonies into account,[68] the Trial Chamber held that 'those artillery projectiles which impacted within a distance of 200 metres of an identified target were deliberately fired at the artillery target'.[69] The Trial Chamber's finding that the artillery attacks on the Four Towns were unlawful was heavily premised on its analysis of individual impact sites within the Four Towns. It found that the shelling of towns was an indiscriminate attack, and was therefore an unlawful attack on civilians

---

Tribunal', The Hague, 13 June 2013, <http://www.sense-agency.com/icty/%E2%80%9Cbombshell-at-the-tribunal.29.html?cat_id=1&news_id=15053>.

[64] Simon Andersen, 'Murderers are being allowed to go free', *BT*, Copenhagen, 13 June 2013, <http://www.bt.dk/udland/english-version-murderers-are-being-allowed-to-go-free>.

[65] Andersen, 'Murderers are being allowed to go free'.

[66] Andersen, 'Murderers are being allowed to go free'.

[67] Clark, 'Courting controversy: the ICTY's acquittal of Croatian Generals Gotovina and Markač', pp. 11–12; ICTY, *Gotovina, Černmak and Markač*, Judgement (Trial Chamber), 15 April 2011, §§1164 and 1898.

[68] As explained by Clark, 'A careful reading [of the Trial Judgment], however, makes clear that the Trial Chamber did not apply the very black and white metric approach that the Appeal Judgment suggests': Clark, 'Courting controversy: the ICTY's acquittal of Croatian Generals Gotovina and Markač', pp. 11–12.

[69] ICTY, *Prosecutor v. Gotovina, Černmak and Markač*, Judgment (Trial Chamber), 15 April 2011, §1898.

and civilian objects within those towns.[70] The shelling was against the Krajina Serbs and constituted a crime against humanity.[71] Moreover, the shelling 'amounted to the forcible displacement of persons from Benkovac, Gračac, Knin and Obrovac'.[72] The Trial Chamber also concluded that a crime of deportation was committed by the same shelling.

The Appeals Chamber focused on this element in order to invalidate the Trial Judgment. Linked to this point, Clark states that the summary of the Trial Chamber's judgment makes no reference to the 200-metre standard. For her, this absence suggests that, from the trial judges' point of view, this was not a fundamental part of the full judgment, but merely one element of it.[73] Despite this, all of the Appeals Chamber judgment was founded on overturning this standard. Moreover, as explained by Judge Agius in his dissenting opinion:

[T]he Majority erroneously regards the 200 Metre Standard as the critical piece underpinning all of the Trial Chamber's finding regarding the unlawfulness of the attacks on the Four Towns. On this basis, it concludes that the Trial Chamber's error in respect to the 200 Metre Standard, together with its error in relation to targets of opportunity in Knin, ... undermines the Trial Chamber's relevant finding with regard to the Impact Analysis, and in turn undermines the Trial Chamber's broader findings that the attacks on the Four Towns were unlawful. In this way, the 200 Metre Standard becomes fatal to the whole Trial Judgment.[74]

Thus, the Appeals Chamber observed that: '[T]he Trial Chamber adopted a margin of error that was not linked to any evidence it received; this constituted an error on the part of the Trial Chamber. The Trial Chamber also provided no explanation as to the basis for the margin of error it adopted; this amounted to a failure to provide a reasoned opinion, another error.'[75]

In addition, as explained by Judge Pocar:

[I]n its analysis, the Majority seems to identify two distinct errors. One of them is the adoption of a margin of error of artillery weapons, which according to the Majority is 'not linked to any evidence' ... However, the Majority falls short of identifying what type of error it is. The second error identified by the Majority is the failure to provide a reasoned opinion as to the basis for the margin of error of artillery weapons, which it correctly characterizes as an error of law. Having found that the Trial Chamber committed an error of law by failing to provide a reasoned opinion

---

[70] ICTY, *Prosecutor v. Gotovina, Černmak and Markač*, Judgment (Trial Chamber), 15 April 2011, §§1911, 1923, 1935, 1943.

[71] ICTY, *Prosecutor v. Gotovina, Černmak and Markač*, Judgment (Trial Chamber), 15 April 2011, §1840.

[72] ICTY, *Prosecutor v. Gotovina, Černmak and Markač*, Judgment (Trial Chamber), 15 April 2011, §1744.

[73] Clark, 'Courting controversy: the ICTY's acquittal of Croatian Generals Gotovina and Markač', pp. 6–7.

[74] ICTY, *Prosecutor v. Gotovina and Markač*, Judgment (Appeals Chamber), 16 November 2012, Dissenting Opinion of Judge Carmel Agius, §4.

[75] ICTY, *Prosecutor v. Gotovina and Markač*, Judgment (Appeals Chamber), 16 November 2012, §58.

as to the basis for the margin of error of artillery weapons, and that the Trial Chamber's findings do not support the Trial Chamber's conclusion to adopt the 200 Metre Standard, the Majority states that, '[i]n view of this legal error, [it] will consider *de novo* the remaining evidence on the record to determine whether the conclusions of the Impact Analysis are still valid.' However, the Majority's subsequent analysis is erroneous, fails to do what it enounces, and is in violation of our standard of review appeal.[76]

Having found the 200-metre standard to be erroneous, the Appeals Chamber had two obligations: first, to identify and articulate the correct legal standard; and secondly, to apply this standard to the evidence contained in the trial record. However, the Appeals Chamber fulfilled neither of these requirements.[77] Moreover, according to Judge Pocar, the Appeals Chamber '[did] not consider the *evidence in the trial record* to determine whether the conclusion of the Trial Chamber is still valid, but limit[ed] its assessment to the *Trial Chamber's analysis and findings*'.[78]

It is important to highlight the problem raised by dissenting opinions of Judges Agius and Pocar in relation to the error of law made by the Trial Chamber in using the 200-metre standard. For Judge Agius, the majority 'simply identified an error of law in the Trial Chamber's failing to provide a reasoned opinion, and such a failure is clearly not an error of law arising from the application of an incorrect legal standard'.[79] For Judge Pocar, the Appeals Chamber failed in its mission to clarify the correct legal standard, finding errors without providing the necessary guidance to other trial chambers:

By failing [to] articulate a legal standard, the Majority further omits to assess whether the shelling of the Four Towns was done in respect of IHL [international humanitarian law] principles and, therefore, whether the attacks on the Four Towns was lawful or not. In that sense, the Majority's approach does not leave a good legacy in terms of respecting IHL principles when assessing the legality of an attack on towns where civilians and civilian objects are present. The Majority imputes to the Trial Chamber the failure to provide a reasoned opinion regarding the standard adopted and reverses its conclusions while simultaneously failing to articulate the standard that should have been applied.[80]

[76] ICTY, *Prosecutor v. Gotovina and Markač*, Judgment (Appeals Chamber), 16 November 2012, Dissenting Opinion of Judge Fausto Pocar, §6.
[77] ICTY, *Prosecutor v. Gotovina and Markač*, Judgment (Appeals Chamber), 16 November 2012, Dissenting Opinion of Judge Fausto Pocar, §11.
[78] ICTY, *Prosecutor v. Gotovina and Markač*, Judgment (Appeals Chamber), 16 November 2012, Dissenting Opinion of Judge Fausto Pocar, §12.
[79] ICTY, *Prosecutor v. Gotovina and Markač*, Judgment (Appeals Chamber), 16 November 2012, Dissenting Opinion of Judge Carmel Agius, §9.
[80] ICTY, *Prosecutor v. Gotovina and Markač*, Judgment (Appeals Chamber), 16 November 2012, Dissenting Opinion of Judge Pocar, §14.

Both judges concluded that the majority failed to apply the correct legal standard to the evidence.[81] On this point, the Appeals Chamber noted that: 'Absent an established range of error, the Appeals Chamber, Judge Agius and Judge Pocar dissenting, cannot exclude the possibility that all of the impact sites considered in the Trial Judgment were the result of shelling aimed at targets that the Trial Chamber considered to be legitimate. The fact a relatively large number of shells fell more than 200 metres from fixed artillery targets could be consistent with a much broader range of error.'[82] Therefore, as stated by Judge Pocar, 'the Majority pretends to review the evidence in the trial record without having first determined the correct legal standard. It therefore starts on a wrong premise'.[83]

Even if all five judges had agreed that the Trial Chamber's reliance on the 200-metre standard was flawed,[84] the problem with the Appeals Chamber judgment lies in the significance and impact of this error. As mentioned, Judge Agius stated that the use of the standard did not undermine the Trial Chamber's finding that the artillery attacks were unlawful because it was only one element in all elements. As Judge Pocar noted, 'unfortunately, the paucity of the legal analysis in the Majority's reasoning opens more questions than it provides answers'.[85]

The second element to consider is the other evidence about the unlawfulness of attacks. The Trial Chamber consulted 'a rich and substantial body of evidence'.[86] As explained by Clark:

[T]he Trial Chamber reached the conclusion that the artillery attacks on the Four Towns were unlawful based on the following: an order that Gotovina had issued on 2 August 1995, instructing the Croatian army to shell the Four Towns; evidence relating to the implementation of that order; the transcript of the Brioni meeting in July 1995, which provided important insights into the intentions of the Croatian leadership; evidence from witnesses in Knin; and evidence regarding the proportionality of artillery attacks aimed at the home of the leader of Krajina Serbs, Milan Martić [and the 200-metre standard].[87]

However, as mentioned above, the Appeals Chamber only took into account the standard to invalidate the Trial Chamber's decision. As Judge Pocar also stated:

---

[81] ICTY, *Prosecutor v. Gotovina and Markač*, Judgment (Appeals Chamber), 16 November 2012, §11, and Dissenting Opinion of Judge Agius, §11.

[82] ICTY, *Prosecutor v. Gotovina and Markač*, Judgment (Appeals Chamber), 16 November 2012, §65.

[83] ICTY, *Prosecutor v. Gotovina and Markač*, Judgment (Appeals Chamber), 16 November 2012, Dissenting Opinion of Judge Pocar, §11.

[84] ICTY, *Prosecutor v. Gotovina and Markač*, Judgment (Appeals Chamber), 16 November 2012, Dissenting Opinion of Judge Agius, §5, and Dissenting Opinion of Judge Pocar, §5.

[85] ICTY, *Prosecutor v. Gotovina and Markač*, Judgment (Appeals Chamber), 16 November 2012, Dissenting Opinion of Judge Pocar, §14.

[86] Clark, 'Courting controversy: the ICTY's acquittal of Croatian Generals Gotovina and Markač', p. 11.

[87] Clark, 'Courting controversy: the ICTY's acquittal of Croatian Generals Gotovina and Markač', p. 13.

If the Majority wishes to reverse Gotovina's and Markač's convictions for one of the underlying acts of persecutions as crime against humanity, namely unlawful attacks on civilians and civilian objects, it needs to demonstrate that *all* the other remaining findings of the Trial Chamber establishing the unlawfulness of the attacks *cannot stand* in the face of the quashing of the Trial Chamber's application of the 200 Metre standard.[88]

Indeed, the Appeals Chamber very briefly invalidates all of other arguments in relation to the 200-metre standard. For example, concerning the common purpose of the JCE ('the permanent removal of the Serb civilian population from the Krajina by force of threat of force'[89]), it was invalidated with these words:

Having reversed the Trial Chamber's findings related to unlawful artillery attacks, the Appeals Chamber, Judge Agius and Judge Pocar dissenting, cannot affirm the Trial Chamber's conclusion that the only reasonable interpretation of the circumstantial evidence on the record was that a JCE aiming to permanently remove the Serb civilian population from the Krajina by force or threat of force existed.[90]

Finally, the question of liability is also highlighted, particularly by the two dissenting opinions of Judges Agius and Pocar. They disagreed with the conclusion in relation to the existence of a JCE (JCE is not accepted in connection with the demonstration of the 200-metre standard).[91] They also disagreed with the Appeals Chambers' decision to not condemn the accused persons pursuant to other forms of liability. In fact, after having reversed the convictions for committing crimes (by participation in a JCE), the majority engaged in an assessment 'on the possibility of entering convictions under alternate modes of liability'.[92] Without going into detail (which would lead us back to the detail of the facts of the case), the two judges considered the option of the Trial Chamber to be wrong in both form and substance.[93]

Concluding remarks

I do not wish to enter into a discussion of the correctness of the decision of the Appeals Chamber—everything has already been said in the dissenting opinions and in the doctrine. Moreover, such a decision falls within the sovereignty of the Appeals Chamber.

---

[88] ICTY, *Prosecutor v. Gotovina and Markač*, Judgment (Appeals Chamber), 16 November 2012, Dissenting Opinion of Judge Pocar, §17.

[89] ICTY, *Prosecutor v. Gotovina, Černmak and Markač*, Judgment (Trial Chamber), 15 April 2011, §2314.

[90] ICTY, *Prosecutor v. Gotovina and Markač*, Judgment (Appeals Chamber), 16 November 2012, §31.

[91] ICTY, *Prosecutor v. Gotovina and Markač*, Judgment (Appeals Chamber), 16 November 2012, Dissenting Opinion of Judge Agius, §§47–50, and Dissenting Opinion of Judge Pocar, §§19–30.

[92] ICTY, *Prosecutor v. Gotovina and Markač*, Judgment (Appeals Chamber), 16 November 2012, §99.

[93] ICTY, *Prosecutor v. Gotovina and Markač*, Judgment (Appeals Chamber), 16 November 2012, Dissenting Opinion of Judge Agius, §§51–90, and Dissenting Opinion of Judge Pocar, §§31–8.

Nevertheless, the trial process of the *Gotovina* case seems to demonstrate some difficulties, which I will now briefly address.

First, the Appeal judgment demonstrates the difficulties with proving violations of the principles of proportionality or distinction, which are the criteria of unlawful attack.[94] The principle of distinction outlaws the direct targeting of civilians or civilian objects.[95] The principle of proportionality outlaws the launching of attacks against legitimate military targets that will cause civilian damage that is disproportionate to the 'concrete and direct' military advantage expected to result from destroying such a target.[96] The difficulty with proving crimes usually stems from a lack of clarity in the definition of the crime, particularly when elements of the definition do not refer to facts, but rather to principles. This explains the small number of criminal cases related to violations of the laws on the conduct of hostilities. In the *Gotovina* case, denying the 200-metre standard seems logical. Moreover, in this case, 'there would have been no need to set such a precise quantitative standard'.[97]

Secondly, the present case raises an ironic issue, as explained by Ohlin:

When a court applies the law to the facts, they are obligated to state *reasons* for their decisions (although juries do not). In announcing that decision, they justifiably feel compelled to articulate standards that explain the basis for that decision. But when they do so, they often get reversed if the standard or legal theory is ill-advised. This creates a law of perverse incentives. Trial Chambers (and courts generally) should be as terse as possible with their explanations if they want to be successful. Although this renders their decision-making process comparatively opaque, it might immunize them from eventual reversal on appeal.[98]

Thirdly, the *Gotovina* case seems to fail to attempt to fulfil the purpose of the ICTY: to contribute to the restoration and maintenance of peace.[99] As explained by Clark, 'the verdict has inevitably triggered strong and diametrically opposed reactions in Serbia and Croatia which are not conducive to any reconciliation process'.[100] That is right, but it is not surprising. It is not the first judgment to create 'strong and diametrically opposed reactions'. Other such cases include the *Plavsić* case, the *Haradinaj* case, or the *Orić* case, for example. Thus the question should be about the link between international criminal law and reconciliation. In arguing that reconciliation needs criminal justice, perhaps the

---

[94] ICTY, *Prosecutor v. Galić*, Judgment (Trial Chamber) (Case No. IT-98-29-T), 5 December 2003, §§57–61.

[95] Jens D. Ohlin, 'Why the *Gotovina* appeals judgment matters', *EJIL Talk*, 21 December 2012, <http://www.ejiltalk.org/why-the-gotovina-appeals-judgment-matters/>.

[96] Ohlin, 'Why the *Gotovina* appeals judgment matters'.

[97] Rosemary Byrne and Gregor Noll, *International Criminal Justice: The Gotovina Judgment and the Making of Refugees*, Lund University Faculty of Law, <http://works.bepress.com/gregor_noll/>.

[98] Ohlin, 'Why the *Gotovina* appeals judgment matters'.

[99] See e.g. UN Security Council Resolution 827 (1993), Preamble.

[100] Clark, 'Courting controversy: the ICTY's acquittal of Croatian Generals Gotovina and Markač', p. 25.

'international community' asked too much of simple and unique tools, these tools being criminal law. International criminal law cannot be an answer to every question, and problems often appear after international crimes. Reconciliation is not an objective that can be simply resolved by criminal law.

In the same vein, the legitimacy of the dissenting opinions raises problems here. How can we understand a decision that was criticized at the time it was issued—indeed, by the judges themselves? How can we conclude that this decision is legitimate? In the *Gotovina* case, the process can sustain critical views born in Serbia. In other cases (when a person is convicted), the consequences are also important: the condemned individual can explain that he was wrongly convicted 'as even some judges did not agree with the decision'. Both in terms of establishing the truth and in terms of reconciliation, such questions necessarily arise.

13 Two controversies in the *Lubanga* trial judgment of the ICC: the nature of co-perpetration's common plan and the classification of the armed conflict

Manuel J. Ventura*

Introduction

On 14 March 2012, in the *Lubanga* case, the International Criminal Court (ICC) (Trial Chamber I) issued its first ever judgment pursuant to Article 74 of the 1998 Rome Statute of the ICC (the ICC Statute).[1] Like any first judgment of an international tribunal, the opinion brought to light and offered its views on a diverse number of legal issues relevant to the case to a degree of detail not seen before. This chapter, however, concentrates on two of these: the nature of the common plan in co-perpetration as a mode of liability; and the classification of the armed conflict. A number of other issues could have been highlighted from the judgment, but these two are particularly prominent, and both have, as of writing, attracted a sparse amount of in-depth attention from expert commentators.

* BA/LLB (University of Western Sydney); BEcSocSc (Hons) (University of Sydney). Manuel Ventura is Director of The Peace and Justice Initiative, a non-governmental organization (NGO) of international criminal law professionals that assist states in the domestic implementation of the 1998 Rome Statute of the International Criminal Court (ICC). (See <http://www.peaceandjusticeinitiative.org>.)

[1] ICC, *Prosecutor v. Thomas Lubanga Dyilo*, Judgment pursuant to Article 74 of the Statute (Case No. ICC-01/04-01/06), 14 March 2012 (*Lubanga* Trial Judgment).

First, the nature of the common plan in co-perpetration as a mode of liability (Section A) is explored. This issue arises from the Trial Chamber's holding that the common plan element of (direct) co-perpetration under Article 25(3)(a) of the ICC Statute[2] does not need to be inherently criminal in nature (that is, the objective of the common plan need not be a crime at all) nor even need necessarily involve the commission of crimes. This surprising finding, particularly in light of prior ICC jurisprudence, has so far managed to fly largely below the academic radar.[3]

Secondly, in Section B, the classification of armed conflict is discussed, especially with respect to the question of whether it is overall or effective control by a foreign state over an armed non-state actor (ANSA) that determines (or should determine) whether its actions are attributable to that state so as to identify whether an international armed conflict (IAC) is in progress (or not). This issue, unfortunately, received next to no attention from the Trial Chamber, despite the controversy and debate on the matter at public international law.

A. The nature of the common plan element in co-perpetration as a mode of liability

It has been well accepted from the beginning of the ICC's jurisprudence that co-perpetration requires, inter alia, the existence of a common plan. What has been less clear is the nature of such a plan—does it have to be a *criminal* plan or not? In the *Lubanga* case, Trial Chamber I, by majority, gave its answer. It held that the requisite common plan in co-perpetration as a mode of liability requires only 'a critical element of criminality' (agreeing with what Pre-Trial Chamber I had previously found in the *Lubanga* Confirmation of Charges Decision):[4]

In the view of the Majority of the Chamber, the prosecution is not required to prove that the [common] plan was specifically directed at committing the crime in question (the conscription, enlistment or use of children), nor does the plan need to have been intrinsically criminal as suggested by the defence. However, it is necessary, as a minimum, for the prosecution to establish

---

[2] Art. 25(3)(a), ICC Statute reads: 'In accordance with this Statute, a person shall be criminally responsible and liable for punishment for a crime within the jurisdiction of the Court if that person: (a) Commits such a crime, whether as an individual, jointly with another or through another person, regardless of whether that other person is criminally responsible.'

[3] For one (very brief) exception, see Kai Ambos, 'The first judgment of the International Criminal Court (*Prosecutor v. Lubanga*): a comprehensive analysis of the legal issues', *International Criminal Law Review*, 12(2) (2012), pp. 139–40.

[4] ICC, *Prosecutor v. Lubanga*, Decision on the Confirmation of Charges (Case No. ICC-01/04-01/06-803-tENG), 29 January 2007, §344 (*Lubanga* Confirmation of Charges Decision). See also *Prosecutor v. Ntaganda*, Decision on the Prosecutor's Application under Article 58 (Case No. ICC-01/04-02/06-36-Red), 13 July 2012, §69.

[that] the common plan included a critical element of criminality, namely that, its implementation embodied a sufficient risk that, if events followed the ordinary course, a crime will be committed.[5]

This holding was based on the majority's reading of Article 25(3)(a) in light of the ICC Statute's overarching mental element contained in Article 30.[6] Particular emphasis was placed on the fact that both intent and knowledge in Article 30 were framed around the idea that the crime 'will occur in the ordinary course of events'.[7] In the Chamber's majority view, 'the mental requirement that the common plan included the commission of a crime will be satisfied if the co-perpetrators knew that, in the ordinary course of events, implementing the plan will lead to that result'.[8] This necessarily meant that the perpetrators were aware of a *risk* of an ICC crime being committed. The majority of the Chamber concluded that 'this means that the agreement on a common plan leads to co-perpetration if its implementation embodies a sufficient risk that, in the ordinary course of events, a crime will be committed'.[9]

In the end, the Trial Chamber was satisfied that a common plan existed, but not one that was criminal or which necessarily involved the commission of crimes per se (at least not under international law):

The accused and his co-perpetrators agreed to, and participated in, a common plan to build an army for the purpose of establishing and maintaining political and military control over Ituri.

---

[5] *Lubanga* Trial Judgment, §984.

[6] Art. 30, ICC Statute, reads:

1. Unless otherwise provided, a person shall be criminally responsible and liable for punishment for a crime within the jurisdiction of the Court only if the material elements are committed with intent and knowledge.
2. For the purposes of this article, a person has intent where:
   (a) In relation to conduct, that person means to engage in the conduct;
   (b) In relation to a consequence, that person means to cause that consequence or is aware that it will occur in the ordinary course of events.
3. For the purposes of this article, 'knowledge' means awareness that a circumstance exists or a consequence will occur in the ordinary course of events. 'Know' and 'knowingly' shall be construed accordingly.

[7] As Trial Chamber I put it: 'Under Article 30(2)(b), intent is established if the person is aware that a consequence will occur in the ordinary course of events. Similarly, Article 30(3) provides that "knowledge" of a consequence means awareness that it (the consequence) "will occur in the ordinary course of events".' See *Lubanga* Trial Judgment, §986.

[8] *Lubanga* Trial Judgment, §986.

[9] *Lubanga* Trial Judgment, §987. Wirth, however, reads the judgment a little differently: 'Co-perpetration requires a common plan which includes "an element of criminality, meaning that it must involve the commission of a crime with which the suspect is charged". The Trial Chamber, in addition, required that, "once implemented, [the common plan must] result in the commission of the relevant crime in the ordinary course of events".' See Steffen Wirth, 'Co-perpetration in the Lubanga Trial Judgment', *Journal of International Criminal Justice*, 10(4) (2012), p. 986 (references omitted). This reading, however, glosses over the discrepancies alluded to in this section.

This resulted, in the ordinary course of events, in the conscription and enlistment of boys and girls under the age of 15, and their use to participate actively in hostilities.[10]

In his separate opinion, Judge Fulford criticized the application of co-perpetration through control over the crime, and especially the two main reasons proffered for its invocation: the need to distinguish between principals and accessories, and the need to ensure the extension of principal liability beyond those who are physically present at the scene of the crime(s).[11] Although, after outlining his understanding of Article 25(3)(a), he refused to apply it to the facts on fair trial grounds,[12] in doing so Judge Fulford offered his own thoughts as to the nature of the common plan element:

Although the text of the Statute does not provide that the agreement, common plan or joint understanding must have an overarching criminal goal, the mental element of Article 30 of the Statute must be satisfied, and unless the Court's legal framework has 'otherwise provided', the joint perpetrators must, at a minimum, be aware that executing the agreement or plan will lead to the commission of a crime within the jurisdiction of the Court 'in the ordinary course of events'.[13]

Unlike the majority's opinion, Judge Fulford is not exactly clear as to whether the common plan must be criminal per se. Nonetheless, it is evident that, under his understanding, the common plan element departs from the majority and is a stricter approach.

These holdings in the *Lubanga* Trial Judgment, the majority in particular, must be contrasted with other interpretations of the common plan element in ICC jurisprudence, none of which were addressed in any detail. For example, in the *Katanga and Ngudjolo* Confirmation of Charges Decision,[14] it was held that 'the common plan *must* include the commission of a crime'.[15] Consistent with this pronouncement, the Chamber concluded that there were substantial grounds to believe that the common criminal plan was 'to "wipe out" Bogoro village by directing the attack against the civilian population, killing and murdering the predominantly Hema population and destroying their properties'.[16] In turn, this finding aligned with the charges against the accused, which were, inter alia,

---

[10] *Lubanga* Trial Judgment, §1351.

[11] *Lubanga* Trial Judgment—Separate Opinion of Judge Fulford, §§5–12.

[12] *Lubanga* Trial Judgment—Separate Opinion of Judge Fulford, §§19–21.

[13] *Lubanga* Trial Judgment—Separate Opinion of Judge Fulford, §15 (references omitted).

[14] While the *Katanga and Ngudjolo* case involved indirect co-perpetration liability (as did the *Ruto and ors* and *Muthaura and ors* cases), this mode also contains the same common plan element as direct co-perpetration as applied in the *Lubanga* case.

[15] ICC, *Prosecutor v. Katanga and Ngudjolo*, Decision on the Confirmation of Charges (Case No. ICC-01/04-01/07-717), 30 September 2008, §523 (emphasis added) (*Katanga and Ngudjolo* Confirmation of Charges Decision). Inexplicably, Pre-Trial Chamber I relied on the *Lubanga* Confirmation of Charges Decision, which, as we have seen, did not per se require the commission of a crime, but merely a sufficient risk that the relevant crime would occur.

[16] *Katanga and Ngudjolo* Confirmation of Charges Decision, §549.

directing attacks against a civilian population, wilful killings and destruction of property as war crimes, and murder and other inhumane acts (inflicting serious injury upon civilians) as crimes against humanity.[17]

Similarly, the *Ruto and ors* Confirmation of Charges Decision repeated this understanding: '[The common plan] *must* involve the commission of the crime with which the accused is charged.'[18] The Chamber concluded that there were substantial grounds to believe that the common criminal plan was to 'evict members of the Kikuyu, Kisii, and Kamba communities in particular because they were perceived as PNU supporters'.[19] This was consistent with the charges, which included, inter alia, deportations and forcible transfers as crimes against humanity.[20] The same formula was replicated in the *Muthaura and ors* Confirmation of Charges Decision, in which it was held that there must be 'the existence of a common plan to commit the crimes charged ... [I]t must involve the commission of a crime with which the suspect is charged'.[21] On the evidence, it concluded that 'a common plan *to commit the crimes* in Nakuru and Naivasha was agreed upon between Mr Muthaura, Mr Kenyatta and Maina Njenga'.[22]

In short, there is a distinct split in ICC jurisprudence with respect to the nature of the common plan requirement of co-perpetration (whether direct or indirect). The *Lubanga* Trial Judgment should have addressed this situation (or at least acknowledged its existence). Instead, it seemed fixated with the holdings of the *Lubanga* Confirmation of Charges Decision and Article 30 of the ICC Statute, and not much else.

---

[17] ICC, *Prosecutor v. Katanga and Ngudjolo*, Amended Document Containing the Charges Pursuant to Article 61(3)(a) of the Statute (Case No. ICC-01/04-01/07-649-Anx1A), 26 June 2008. These particular charges remained unchanged up to the trial, with the exception of other inhumane acts (inflicting serious injury upon civilians) as a crime against humanity, which was not confirmed in the *Katanga and Ngudjolo* Confirmation of Charges Decision (§465).

[18] ICC, *Prosecutor v. Ruto and ors*, Decision on the Confirmation of Charges Pursuant to Article 61(7)(a) and (b) of the Rome Statute (Case No. ICC-01/09-01/11-373), 23 January 2012, §301 (emphasis added) (*Ruto and ors* Confirmation of Charges Decision). Reliance was also placed on the *Lubanga* Confirmation of Charges Decision, which clearly does not align with this holding.

[19] *Ruto and ors* Confirmation of Charges Decision, §302.

[20] ICC, *Prosecutor v. Ruto and ors*, Document Containing the Charges (Case No. ICC-01/09-01/11-261-AnxA), 15 August 2011. The charges have since been amended, but they maintain forcible transfers and deportations as crimes against humanity: ICC, *Prosecutor v. Ruto and ors*, Updated Document Containing the Charges Pursuant to the Decision on the Content of the Updated Document Containing the Charges (ICC-01/09-01/11-522) (Case No. ICC-01/09-01/11-533-AnxA), 7 January 2013.

[21] ICC, *Prosecutor v. Muthaura and ors*, Decision on the Confirmation of Charges Pursuant to Article 61(7)(a) and (b) of the Rome Statute (Case No. ICC-01/09-02/11-382-Red), 23 January 2012, §399 (*Muthaura and ors* Confirmation of Charges Decision). Reliance was also placed on the *Lubanga* Confirmation of Charges decision, which clearly does not align with this holding.

[22] *Muthaura and ors* Confirmation of Charges Decision, §400 (emphasis added). The charges for events in and around Nakuru and Naivasha (later confirmed) included murder, deportation or forcible transfers, rape, other inhumane acts (infliction of severe physical injury and serious mental suffering), and persecution as crimes against humanity: ICC, *Prosecutor v. Muthaura and ors*, Document Containing the Charges (Case No. ICC-01/09-02/11-280-AnxA), 2 September 2011.

Nevertheless, while Article 30 may have been useful in interpreting Article 25(3)(a), the *Lubanga* Trial Judgment could have considered another relevant provision. Article 25(3)(d) reads:

3. In accordance with this Statute, a person shall be criminally responsible and liable for punishment for a crime within the jurisdiction of the Court if that person: ...

    (d) In any other way contributes to the commission or attempted commission of such a crime by a group of persons acting with a common purpose. Such contribution shall be intentional and shall either:

        (i) Be made with the aim of furthering the *criminal activity* or *criminal purpose* of the group, where such activity or purpose *involves the commission of a crime within the jurisdiction of the Court*; or

        (ii) Be made in the knowledge of the intention of the group *to commit the crime*[.][23]

While Judge Fulford is entirely correct in pointing out that nothing in Article 25(3)(a) requires the common plan to have an overarching criminal goal/purpose, the *Mbarushimana* Confirmation of Charges Decision stressed that there is a link between Article 25(3)(a) and the common plan element contained in Article 25(3)(d): 'Though it appears in a discussion of co-perpetration liability, the *Lubanga* Confirmation Decision's concept of a "common plan" in functionally identical to the statutory requirement of article 25(3)(d) of the Statute that there be a "group of persons acting with a common purpose".'[24] Indeed, Article 25(3)(a) has already been previously read in light of Article 25(3)(d).[25]

Based on the plain text of Article 25(3)(d), we gain an insight into the nature of the common purpose/plan, since the contributions must be either aimed at furthering the *criminal activity* or *criminal purpose* of the group (where such activity or purpose *involves the commission of a crime* within the jurisdiction of the Court) or be made in the knowledge of the intention of the group *to commit the crime*. When read together with the *travaux préparatoires*, in this context, the common plan *itself* must be criminal or alternatively *must* involve the commission of a crime (as understood and applied in the *Katanga and Ngudjolo*, *Ruto and ors* and the *Muthaura and ors* Confirmation of Charges Decisions).[26] It is not enough, as the *Lubanga* Trial Chamber asserted, that the

---

[23] Art. 25(3)(d), ICC Statute (emphasis added).

[24] ICC, *Prosecutor v. Mbarushimana*, Decision on the Confirmation of Charges (Case No. ICC-01/04-01/10-465-Red), 16 December 2011, §271 (*Mbarushimana* Confirmation of Charges Decision).

[25] *Lubanga* Confirmation of Charges Decision, §334 (finding that Art. 25(3)(a), read in light of Art. 25(3)(d), did not take into account subjective criteria for distinguishing between principals and accessories).

[26] 'Although only subpara. (3)(d)(i) explicitly refers to "the *criminal* activity or *criminal* purpose of the group, where such activity or purpose involves the commission of a crime within the jurisdiction of the Court" (emphasis added), it is clear from the *travaux préparatoires* that the common purpose referred to in the chapeau of subpara. (3)(d) must involve the commission of a crime': Gideon Boas, James L. Bischoff, and Natalie L. Reid, *International Criminal Law Practitioner Library, Vol. I: Forms of Responsibility in International Criminal Law*, Cambridge University Press, Cambridge, 2007, p. 126, n. 727 (references omitted). See also

implementation of a non-criminal plan simply 'embodied a sufficient risk that, if events followed the ordinary course, a crime [would] be committed'.[27] In other words, under Article 25(3)(d), where the drafters *explicitly* referred to a common plan/purpose element and described it in far more detail than in paragraph (3)(a), the common plan element differs in nature from that contained in Article 25(3)(a) despite it being *exactly* the same functional element in both provisions.

This reveals an interesting outcome: it is easier to convict an accused, as far as the common plan element is concerned, as a principal under Article 25(3)(a) than it is to do so as an accessory under Article 25(3)(d),[28] since in practice it is more difficult to prove a common *criminal* plan than it is to demonstrate the existence of a common plan per se. This is an odd outcome that begs the question whether it was really the intent of the ICC Statute's drafters to ensure that principals are held to a lower standard than accessories for potentially the same criminal offences.

One could perhaps attribute this result to the language of Article 25(3)(d), which displaces the overarching *mens rea* standard of Article 30[29] (relied upon by the *Lubanga* Trial Judgment to inform its understanding of the common plan element). But this would assume that the *mens rea* of Article 30 is lower than that in Article 25(3)(d). The reasoning of the *Lubanga* Confirmation of Charges Decision certainly pointed in that direction with its holding that Article 30 encompasses instances in which there is awareness of the risk that a crime may result from the accused's conduct, and that the accused accepted that result (*dolus eventualis*).[30] If one accepts this and uses it to inform the nature of the common plan element in Article 25(3)(a), then it is much easier to conclude that it does not have to be a crime per se or inherently criminal, but need

Elies van Sliedregt, *Individual Criminal Responsibility in International Law*, Oxford University Press, Oxford, 2012, pp. 145–6; Héctor Olásolo, *The Criminal Responsibility of Senior Political and Military Leaders as Principals to International Crimes*, Hart Publishing, Oxford and Portland, OR 2009, p. 270 (referring to the 'common *criminal* purpose' in Art. 25(3)(d)).

[27] *Lubanga* Trial Judgment, §984. Yet, despite the clear language of Art. 25(3)(d) and the strength of scholarly opinion, the *Mbarushimana* Confirmation of Charges Decision held that '[a] common purpose [under Art. 25(3)(d)] must include an element of criminality, but does not need to be specifically directed at the commission of a crime' magreeing with (and referencing) the formulation of this element in the *Lubanga* Confirmation of Charges Decision (*Lubanga*, of course, was an Art. 25(3)(a) case, not one based on Art. 25(3)(d)) without any sophisticated reasoning justifying this conclusion *Mbarushimana* Confirmation of Charges Decision, §271.

[28] The jurisprudence of the ICC has held that its modes of liability are divided between principals and accessories, with the former contained in Art. 25(3)(a) and the latter in Art. 25(3)(b)–(d). See *Lubanga* Confirmation of Charges Decision, §320. This principal/accessory distinction has been subsequently followed by numerous other Chambers. Yet some judges have voiced criticisms of such a distinction: *Lubanga* Trial Judgment—Separate Opinion of Judge Fulford, §§6–11; ICC, *Prosecutor v. Ngudjolo*, Judgment Pursuant to Article 74 of the Statute—Concurring Opinion of Judge van den Wyngaert (Case No. ICC-01/04-02/12-4), 18 December 2012, §§22–9.

[29] *Mbarushimana* Confirmation of Charges Decision, §288.

[30] *Lubanga* Confirmation of Charges Decision, §352.

only carry a sufficient risk of a crime being committed in the ordinary course of events. However, the *Lubanga* Trial Judgment expressly rejected the notion that Article 30 includes *dolus eventualis* and instead followed the *Bemba* Confirmation of Charges Decision, which did likewise.[31] Yet, despite this clear rejection, the nature of the common plan as outlined in the *Lubanga* Confirmation of Charges Decision[32] remained virtually the same in the *Lubanga* Trial Judgment, despite the latter being informed by a *different* understanding of Article 30, one devoid of *dolus eventualis*.[33]

This discussion has a potentially significant impact on ICC proceedings, as the entire issue of the nature of the common plan element is now squarely before the ICC Appeals Chamber, having been raised by Mr Lubanga's defence team in its appeal of the *Lubanga* Trial Judgment.[34] Consider also the *Katanga and Ngudjolo* case (originally an Article 25(3)(a) liability case), supposing that the Confirmation of Charges Decision (and Prosecution) had followed the *Lubanga* Confirmation of Charges Decision and accepted (and found) a *non-criminal* common plan. When the Trial Chamber (by majority) subsequently invoked Regulation 55 and changed the legal characterization of the facts so as to invoke Article 25(3)(d) criminal responsibility instead (but for Katanga only, since the case against Ngudjolo was severed),[35] the Chamber would find itself in a situation in which the evidence led during the trial was tailored to support the existence of a *non-criminal* common plan. That would somehow have to be reconciled (if at all possible) with the fact that it was now operating within a mode of liability where the common plan must be inherently criminal or involve the commission of a crime.[36]

---

[31] *Lubanga* Trial Judgment, §§1011–12. See ICC, *Prosecutor v. Bemba*, Decision Pursuant to Article 61(7) (a) and (b) of the Rome Statute on the Charges of the Prosecutor against Jean-Pierre Bemba Gombo (Case No. ICC-01/05-01/08-424), 15 June 2009, §§364–9.

[32] The *Lubanga* Confirmation of Charges Decision described the relevant common plan element as follows (at §344): 'The common plan must include an element of criminality, although it does not need to be specifically directed at the commission of a crime. It suffices: . . . (ii) that the co-perpetrators (a) are aware of the risk that implementing the common plan (which is specifically directed at the achievement of a non-criminal goal) will result in the commission of the crime, and (b) accept such an outcome.'

[33] Whether or not Art. 30 includes *dolus eventualis* remains unsettled. See *Katanga and Ngudjolo* Confirmation of Charges Decision, §251, n. 329 (siding with the inclusion of *dolus eventualis* in Art. 30, but also noting that it need not resolve the question at §531); *Ruto and ors* Confirmation of Charges Decision, §336 (siding with the rejection of *dolus eventualis* in Art. 30).

[34] ICC, *Prosecutor v. Lubanga*, Mémoire de la Défense de M. Thomas Lubanga relatif à l'appel à l'encontre du *'Jugement rendu en application de l'Article 74 du Statut'* rendu le 14 mars 2012 (Case No. ICC-01/04-01/06-2948-Red), 3 December 2012, §§327–31.

[35] ICC, *Prosecutor v. Katanga and Ngudjolo*, Decision on the Implementation of Regulation 55 of the Regulations of the Court and Severing the Charges against the Accused Persons (Case No. ICC-01/04-01/07-3319-tENG/FRA), 21 November 2012. This move was subsequently upheld by the Appeals Chamber: ICC, *Prosecutor v. Katanga*, Judgment on the Appeal of Mr Germain Katanga against the Decision of Trial Chamber II of 21 November 2012 entitled 'Decision on the Implementation of Regulation 55 of the Regulations of the Court and Severing the Charges against the Accused Persons' (Case No. ICC-01/04-01/ 07-3363), 27 March 2013.

[36] This issue was flagged by Judge Van Den Wyngaert (in dissent), albeit in different terms: ICC, *Prosecutor v. Katanga and Ngudjolo*, Decision on the Implementation of Regulation 55 of the Regulations

One final matter merits attention. At the ad hoc tribunals, co-perpetration's 'competitor', joint criminal enterprise (JCE), also includes a common plan/purpose element. As the *Lubanga* Confirmation of Charges Decision commented, Article 25(3)(d) 'is closely akin to the concept of joint criminal enterprise or the common purpose doctrine adopted by the jurisprudence of the ICTY'.[37] And as we have seen, the *Mbarushimana* Confirmation of Charges Decision held that the common plan element in Article 25(3)(d) is functionally identical to that in Article 25(3)(a). So how have the ad hoc tribunals considered their common plan element pursuant to JCE?[38] Here, the jurisprudence, from *Tadić* onwards, has been relatively clear: the common plan must amount to (that is, it must be inherently criminal) or involve the commission of a crime under the relevant statute[39] (in line with the *Katanga and Ngudjolo*, *Ruto and ors*, and the *Muthaura and ors* Confirmation of Charges Decisions). Therefore, as one commentator has rightly pointed out:

[T]he fact that the common plan [in the *Lubanga* case] to further the UPC/RP and FPLC war effort did not specifically target children under the age of fifteen, would have prevented the application of the notion of joint criminal enterprise or the common purpose doctrine as elaborated by the case law of the *ad hoc* tribunals... [JCE] requires that the [co-perpetrators] all agree on a common plan, which is specifically directed at the commission of one or more crimes, and that they all act with the aim to have the crimes encompassed by the common plan committed (*dolus directus in the first degree*).[40]

However, this line of jurisprudence is to be contrasted with that applied at the Special Court for Sierra Leone (SCSL). There, a very particular understanding of the common plan element emerged, arguably arising from the manner in which its indictments had

---

of the Court and Severing the Charges against the Accused Persons—Dissenting Opinion of Judge Van Den Wyngaert (Case No. ICC-01/04-01/07-3319), 21 November 2012, §43.

[37] *Lubanga* Confirmation of Charges Decision, §335 (but noting that, unlike joint criminal enterprise, co-perpetration takes an objective approach in distinguishing between principals and accessories).

[38] This is not to equate JCE with co-perpetration. They are obviously different, but do share at least the same common plan/purpose element.

[39] See, inter alia, ICTY, *Prosecutor v. Tadić*, Judgment (Appeals Chamber) (Case No. IT-94-1-A), 15 July 1999, §227(ii) (*Tadić* Appeal Judgment); ICTY, *Prosecutor v. Vasiljević*, Judgment (Appeals Chamber) (Case No. IT-98-32-A), 25 February 2004, §100; ICTR, *Prosecutor v. Ntakirutimana and Ntakirutimana*, Judgment (Appeals Chamber) (Case Nos ICTR-96-10-A and ICTR-96-17-A), 13 December 2004, §463; ICTY, *Prosecutor v. Kvočka*, Judgment (Appeals Chamber) (Case No. IT-98-30/1-A), 28 February 2005, §81; ICTY, *Prosecutor v. Brđanin*, Judgment (Appeals Chamber) (Case No. IT-99-36-A), 3 April 2007, §§418, 430; ICTY, *Prosecutor v. Krajišnik*, Judgment (Appeals Chamber) (Case No. IT-00-39-A), 17 March 2009, §§184, 662; ICTY, *Prosecutor v. Gotovina and Markač*, Judgment (Appeals Chamber) (Case No. IT-06-90-A), 16 November 2012, §89.

[40] Héctor Olásolo, 'Developments in the distinction between principal and accessorial liability in light of the first case law of the International Criminal Court' in Carsten Stahn and Göran Sluiter (eds), *The Emerging Practice of the International Criminal Court*, Martinus Nijhoff, Leiden, 2009, p. 357 (references omitted). See also Wirth, 'Co-perpetration in the *Lubanga* Trial Judgment', p. 976.

been (badly) drafted, which, although alleging the existence of a JCE, did not identify an inherently criminal JCE or a JCE to commit certain crimes.[41] This carried through to the Appeals Chamber, which held that the common plan need not be criminal at all, as long as 'the actions contemplated as a means to achieve [the common plan's] objective are crimes within the Statute'.[42] In other words, the SCSL, like the *Lubanga* Trial Judgment, has accepted a common non-criminal plan.

The reaction to this development was overwhelmingly negative: Jordash and van Tuyl opined that this version of JCE was based on 'profound doctrinal confusion and overreaching';[43] Easterday called it 'unsound jurisprudence';[44] da Silva asserted that the Appeals Chamber had 'stretched the JCE theory of liability even further';[45] while Jordash and Martin considered convictions based on it (and other troubling SCSL holdings) as constituting 'collective punishment'.[46] We must contrast such reactions to the silence that has accompanied a rather similar holding in the *Lubanga* Trial Judgment at the ICC in its interpretation of the common plan element. True, JCE relies far more on the *mens rea* of the accused than co-perpetration under the ICC Statute, but at the end of the day under either mode there is still either (a) joint control over the crime pursuant to a *common plan* (co-perpetration), or (b) joint intent to carry out the crime pursuant to a *common plan* (JCE). Thus both theories have at the core of their existence a common plan element; it is therefore equally relevant whether it must be criminal in nature or not. When coupled with the misgivings expressed against the SCSL, one would have expected

---

[41] For a more thorough discussion of the problematic SCSL indictments, see Cecily Rose, 'Troubled indictments at the Special Court for Sierra Leone: the pleading of joint criminal enterprise and sex-based crimes', *Journal of International Criminal Justice*, 7(2) (2009), p. 353; Boas, Bischoff, and Reid, *International Criminal Law Practitioner Library, Vol. I: Forms of Responsibility in International Criminal Law*, pp. 129–33; William A. Schabas, *The UN International Criminal Tribunals: The Former Yugoslavia, Rwanda and Sierra Leone*, Cambridge University Press, Cambridge, 2006, p. 312.

[42] SCSL, *Prosecutor v. Brima and ors*, Judgment (Appeals Chamber) (Case No. SCSL-2004-16-A), 22 February 2008, §84 (reversing the Trial Judgment's finding that JCE liability had not been adequately pleaded because of the lack of a criminal purpose/goal). See also SCSL, *Prosecutor v. Sesay and ors*, Judgment (Appeals Chamber) (Case No. SCSL-04-15-A), 26 October 2009, §§294–5.

[43] Wayne Jordash and Penelope Van Tuyl, 'Failure to carry the burden of proof: how joint criminal enterprise lost its way at the Special Court for Sierra Leone', *Journal of International Criminal Justice*, 8(2) (2010), p. 609. The authors also opined that mere criminal '[c]ontemplation is, at best, synonymous with foreseeability'.

[44] Jennifer Easterday, 'Obscuring joint criminal enterprise liability: the conviction of Augustine Gbao by the Special Court of Sierra Leone', *Berkeley Journal of International Law Publicist*, 3 (2009), p. 42.

[45] Clare da Silva, 'The hybrid experience of the Special Court for Sierra Leone' in Bartram S. Brown (ed.), *Research Handbook on International Criminal Law*, Edward Elgar Publishing, Cheltenham, 2011, p. 248.

[46] Wayne Jordash and Scott Martin, 'Due process and fair trial rights at the Special Court: how the desire for accountability outweighed the demands of justice at the Special Court for Sierra Leone', *Leiden Journal of International Law*, 23(3) (2010), p. 608.

a certain level of consistency in criticism when the ICC chose to go down a fairly similar route. With one exception, we have not (yet) seen this.[47] It is not at all clear why this is so.

B. **Classification of armed conflict and the overall/effective control debate**

The war crimes provisions of the ICC Statute are divided between those committed in IAC (Article 8(2)(a)–(b)) and those in non-international armed conflict (NIAC) (Article 8(2)(c) and 8(2)(e)). Therefore, in any ICC war crimes prosecution, the classification of the conflict is a critical element that must be proved so as to attribute individual criminal responsibility pursuant to the aforementioned provisions. While such a proposition sounds perfectly reasonable at first glance, in practice it can cause all sorts of headaches, particularly in mixed conflicts in which state and non-state armed groups support each other and fight together, among themselves, and each other.

The conflict in the Ituri region during the relevant period is a textbook example of such practical difficulties. The *Lubanga* Trial Judgment's classification analysis names no fewer than six non-state actors and three states as having some involvement either with the armed groups or in direct hostilities in and around Ituri: Union des Patriotes Congolais (UPC) (and its military wing, the Force Patriotique pour la Libération du Congo (FPLC)), Rassemblement Congolais pour la Démocratie—Kisangani/Mouvement de Libération (RCD-ML) (and its military wing, the Armée Populaire Congolaise (APC)), Front des Nationalistes Intégrationnistes (FNI), Force de Résistance Patriotique en Ituri (FRPI), Parti pour l'Unité et la Sauvegarde de l'Intégrité du Congo (PUSIC), and the Forces Armées du Peuple Congolais (FAPC), together with Uganda, Rwanda, and the Democratic Republic of Congo (DRC). Such a factual scenario was destined to cause classification difficulties, and this was indeed a source of ongoing dispute in the *Lubanga* case. Of course, it need not have been this way. Had the ICC Statute's drafters simply mirrored and adapted the ICTY Statute's Article 3 war crimes provision[48]—which does

---

[47] The one exception being Professor Ambos, who has commented: 'I am not even convinced that a mere "critical element of criminality" suffices for a plan of co-perpetrators. After all, we are not dealing here with any plan (for example to pay a visit to London next weekend) but with a plan which forms the basis of a joint commission of a crime and, as a consequence, of the mutual attribution of the respective contributions of the co-perpetrators. Such a plan cannot be predominantly non-criminal but must at least—that would be my "minimum"—contain a more or less concrete crime to be committed, otherwise there is nothing (agreed) what could be mutually attributed.' See Ambos, 'The first judgment of the International Criminal Court (*Prosecutor v. Lubanga*): a comprehensive analysis of the legal issues', p. 140 (references omitted).

[48] Art. 3 of the ICTY Statute reads:

The International Tribunal shall have the power to prosecute persons violating the laws or customs of war. Such violations shall include, but not be limited to:

  (a) employment of poisonous weapons or other weapons calculated to cause unnecessary suffering;
  (b) wanton destruction of cities, towns or villages, or devastation not justified by military necessity;

not require conflicts to be classified—almost all of these difficulties would have instantly disappeared. Alas, the drafters chose a different option, one that preserves the distinction between IACs and NIACs as opposed to their gradual unification, and as the *Lubanga* Trial Judgment rightly put it: '[ICC] Chamber[s do] not have the power to reformulate the Court's statutory framework.'[49]

Originally, the Prosecutor had charged Lubanga with the conscription, enlistment, and use of child soldiers in an NIAC (Article 8(2)(e)(vii)).[50] However, the *Lubanga* Confirmation of Charges Decision invoked Article 8(2)(b)(xxvi) (the IAC cousin of Article 8(2)(e)(vii)), as it found that the conflict was international in nature from July 2002 until 2 June 2003, owing to the Ituri region being occupied by Uganda (relying, in part, on jurisprudence from the International Court of Justice (ICJ)),[51] and only after its withdrawal on 2 June 2003 until December 2003 was the conflict classified as non-international.[52] This appeared to assume, although without directly spelling it out, that the existence of an NIAC is negated when the relevant territory falls under the occupation of a foreign state.

There is a certain logical sense with this proposition: how can a state be said to exercise 'effective control' (in the Article 42, 1907 Hague Regulations, sense) over foreign territory if there is an NIAC occurring within it? Yet, at the same time, the aforementioned non-state armed groups (NSAGs) did not disappear during Uganda's occupation only to spontaneously reappear immediately upon its withdrawal on 2 June 2003. The point here is that the existence of an NIAC need not mean the loss of effective control by an occupying power over territory. Territorial control is only required in an NIAC as defined in Article 1(1) of the 1977 Additional Protocol II to the Geneva Conventions (which in any event only applies within the territory of the relevant state);[53] it is not

---

(c) attack, or bombardment, by whatever means, of undefended towns, villages, dwellings, or buildings;
(d) seizure of, destruction or willful damage done to institutions dedicated to religion, charity and education, the arts and sciences, historic monuments and works of art and science;
(e) plunder of public or private property.

[49] *Lubanga* Trial Judgment, §539.
[50] ICC, *Prosecutor v. Lubanga*, Document Containing the Charges, Article 61(3)(a) (Case No. ICC-01/04-01/06-356-Anx2), 28 August 2006.
[51] Namely, ICJ, *Case Concerning Armed Activities on the Territory of the Congo (Democratic Republic of the Congo v. Uganda)*, Judgment (Merits), 19 December 2005, ICJ Reports 2005, p. 168.
[52] *Lubanga* Confirmation of Charges Decision, §§220, 236–7. It should be pointed out that this was done without following the procedure outlined in Art. 61(7)(c)(ii), despite the Chamber recognizing its duties pursuant to this provision (at §§202–4).
[53] Art. 1(1) of the 1977 Additional Protocol II to the Geneva Conventions of 1949 reads (emphasis added):

This Protocol, which develops and supplements Article 3 common to the Geneva Conventions of 12 August 1949 without modifying its existing conditions of application, shall apply to all armed conflicts which are not covered by Article 1 of the Protocol Additional to the Geneva Conventions of 12 August 1949, and relating to the Protection of Victims of International Armed Conflicts (Protocol I) and which take place in the territory of a High Contracting Party between its armed forces and dissident armed forces or other organized

required for NIACs pursuant to Common Article 3 of the 1949 Geneva Conventions.[54] Likewise, Article 8(2)(f) of the ICC Statute, which elaborates on the meaning of NIACs in the context of Article 8(2)(e) crimes, also does not refer to any territorial control requirement by NSAGs.

Despite highlighting this territorial control element,[55] the *Lubanga* Trial Chamber, after agreeing with ICTY (*Tadić*) and ICJ (*Nicaragua*) jurisprudence that IACs and NIACs can coexist,[56] chose to concentrate its analysis on the specific armed groups relevant to the case that were engaged in armed conflict. In other words, it focused solely on the hostilities in which the UPC/FPLC (with Lubanga at its head) participated. Since this only involved fighting with other armed groups (namely, the RCD-ML/APC and FPRI), it necessarily meant that the conflict did not directly involve any states, negating the existence of an IAC notwithstanding the fact that certain areas were under Ugandan military occupation.[57]

This still left open the question whether the conflict could have *indirectly* involved states through their active support for one or more of the various NSAGs so as to internationalize an otherwise non-international armed conflict. Here, the *Lubanga* Trial Judgment, like the *Lubanga* Confirmation of Charges Decision,[58] invoked and applied the ICTY's *Tadić* test of 'overall control'.[59] On the facts, it found that, despite evidence of support by Rwanda, the DRC, and Uganda to various armed groups (mostly through the provision of training and weapons, other evidence being found to be unconvincing),[60] the required threshold of support was not met, namely neither country had had 'a role in *organizing, coordinating or planning the military actions of the military group*, in addition to financing, training and equipping or providing operational support to [them]'.[61] This result is undoubtedly correct. If only training and the provision of military aid were

---

armed groups which, under responsible command, *exercise such control over a part of its territory as to enable them to carry out sustained and concerted military operations and to implement this Protocol.*

For the view that this provision does not apply extraterritorially, see Elizabeth Wilmshurst, *International Law and the Classification of Conflicts*, Oxford University Press, Oxford, 2012, p. 55; Dieter Fleck, 'The law of non-international armed conflicts' in Dieter Fleck (ed.), *The Handbook of International Humanitarian Law*, 2nd edn, Oxford University Press, Oxford, 2009, pp. 610 and 622.

[54] The relevant part of Common Art. 3 of the 1949 Geneva Conventions reads: 'In the case of armed conflict not of an international character occurring in the territory of one of the High Contracting Parties, each Party to the conflict shall be bound to apply, as a minimum, the following provisions[.]'

[55] *Lubanga* Trial Judgment, §536.

[56] *Lubanga* Trial Judgment, §540, nn. 1643, 1644.

[57] *Lubanga* Trial Judgment, §§564–7.

[58] *Lubanga* Confirmation of Charges Decision, §§210–11. Interestingly, in the *Katanga and Ngudjolo* Confirmation of Charges Decision (Katanga and Ngudjolo were leaders of armed groups that directly engaged Lubanga's UPC/FPLC), overall control was not invoked or explored at all in its classification analysis: *Katanga and Ngudjolo* Confirmation of Charges Decision, §§238–41.

[59] *Lubanga* Trial Judgment, §541.   [60] *Lubanga* Trial Judgment, §§552–61.

[61] *Lubanga* Trial Judgment, §541 (emphasis added) (citing *Tadić* Appeal Judgment, §137).

enough, then the actions of many NSAGs could easily be imputed to states, and the territory under their control could even be viewed as being 'occupied' by their sponsoring state.[62] We need only consider the current conflict in Syria and the military, economic, and political support being given to the Free Syrian Army by numerous states to imagine the sort of issues that could potentially arise.[63] However, the *Lubanga* Trial Judgment's analysis cleverly masked what is perhaps the quintessential example of fragmentation at international law: the ICTY's *Tadić* 'overall control' test versus the ICJ's *Nicaragua* test of 'effective control'.

As is well known, this split arose when the ICTY Appeals Chamber felt that it had to address the same issue as the ICJ did in *Nicaragua*, albeit from a different perspective.[64] In *Nicaragua*, the ICJ had to pronounce on the requisite level of control by the United States of America (USA) over two entities that were neither its formal (*de jure*) agents nor its organs—the *Contras* (a non-state paramilitary group) and 'Unilaterally Controlled Latino Assets' (individuals acting at the behest of the USA)—to determine whether their actions in Nicaragua could be attributed to the USA for state responsibility purposes.[65] In *Tadić*, the Appeals Chamber was faced with the question of whether the armed conflict with which it was seized was international or non-international in nature after 19 May 1992, when the Yugoslav People's Army (JNA) formally withdrew from Bosnia and Herzegovina.[66] This was determinative as to whether the grave breaches provisions of the 1949 Geneva Conventions applied or not (as required for war crimes

---

[62] This theory of 'proxy occupation' has been applied by the ICTY: ICTY, *Prosecutor v. Blaškić*, Judgment (Trial Chamber) (Case No. IT-95-14-T), 3 March 2000, §§148–50. On the other hand, this was rejected by another Trial Chamber: ICTY, *Prosecutor v. Naletilić and Martinović*, Judgment (Trial Chamber) (Case No. IT-98-34-T), 31 March 2003, §214. The ICTY Appeals Chamber has not yet resolved this conflicting line of jurisprudence.

[63] It is important to remember that the Grand Chamber of the European Court of Human Rights (ECtHR) has held that the provision of substantial military, economic, and political support for an insurgent movement, where such support ensures its survival, is enough to bring its human rights violations within the extraterritorial jurisdiction of the relevant state: ECtHR, *Ilaşcu and ors v. Moldova and Russia*, Judgment (App. No. 48787/99), 8 July 2004, §§379–94. While it is difficult to reconcile this with *Tadić* (and even less with *Nicaragua*), it does bring up an interesting prospect: European states could potentially be held liable (in a human rights sense) for any war crimes committed by the Free Syrian Army (FSA) due to their provision of substantial support that ensures the FSA's survival. In any event, an argument can be made that continuing to support the FSA in light of numerous reports of serious international humanitarian law (IHL) violations on its part can itself constitute a violation of the customary norm of ensuring respect for IHL by those states that actively support the FSA. See Olivier Corten and Vaios Koutroulis, 'The illegality of military support to rebels in the Libyan war: aspects of *jus contra bellum* and *jus in bello*', *Journal of Conflict and Security Law*, 18(1) (2013), pp. 78–91 (making this argument in the context of the Libyan civil war, but which is equally applicable to the current situation in Syria).

[64] *Tadić* Appeal Judgment, §104.

[65] ICJ, *Case Concerning Military and Paramilitary Activities in and against Nicaragua (Nicaragua v. United States of America)*, Judgment (Merits), 27 June 1986, ICJ Reports 1986, p. 45 (*Nicaragua*).

[66] *Tadić* Appeal Judgment, §87.

under Article 2 of the ICTY Statute, with which Tadić was charged).[67] In order to do so, it had to determine whether an NSAG (the Bosnian Serbs and the Republika Srpska Army, or VRS) fighting in Bosnia-Herzegovina 'belong[ed] to a Party to the conflict' pursuant to Article 4A(2) of the 1949 Geneva Convention III, in that case Yugoslavia.[68] If the Bosnian Serbs/VRS 'belonged' to Yugoslavia, then the conflict was no longer between the Bosnian Serbs/VRS and Bosnia and Herzegovina (an NIAC), but rather between Yugoslavia (through the Bosnian Serbs/VRS) and Bosnia-Herzegovina (an IAC).

It was in the context of inquiring into the test for determining whether an NSAG 'belonged' to a state that the Appeals Chamber looked to *Nicaragua*. It opined that Article 4A(2) 'implicitly refers to a test of control',[69] but since IHL did not speak to the requisite degree of control nor the criteria that needed to be satisfied, public international law was required to supplement it. It found this in the rules on attribution for the purposes of state responsibility.[70] It was here that the ICTY Appeals Chamber split with *Nicaragua*. While it agreed that 'effective control' was required to attribute the actions of *individuals* without *de jure* status to a state (that is, the state must have issued specific directions or instructions, which were followed),[71] it disagreed that the same level of control was required to attribute the actions of an organized non-state hierarchical group like the Bosnian Serbs/VRS (comparable to the Contras in *Nicaragua*) to Yugoslavia. Instead, a state only needed to wield 'overall control' 'not only by equipping and financing [them] but also by coordinating or helping in the general planning of [their] military activity'.[72] Only then could the Bosnians Serbs/VRS 'belong' to Yugoslavia pursuant to Article 4A(2) of the 1949 Geneva Convention III and thus render the conflict international in nature.

It was obvious to all that these two holdings did not sit well with each other, if at all. However, in the years that followed, a popular idea began to take hold that the two could

---

[67] Tadić was also charged under Art. 3 (violations of the laws or customs of war) and Art. 5 (crimes against humanity) of the ICTY Statute. See ICTY, *Prosecutor v. Tadić*, Judgment (Trial Chamber) (Case No. IT-94-1-T), 7 May 1997, §9. But note the (minority) view of Judge Abi-Saab in *Tadić* that the grave breaches provisions can also apply in non-international armed conflicts: ICTY, *Prosecutor v. Tadić*, Separate Opinion of Judge Abi-Saab on the Defence Motion for Interlocutory Appeal on Jurisdiction (Case No. IT-94-1-AR72), 2 October 1995. This view has been recently resurrected by Judge Antonetti in ICTY, *Prosecutor v. Prlić and ors*, Opinion individuelle séparée et partiellement dissidente du juge Jean-Claude Antonetti Président de la chambre (Case No. IT-04-74-T), 29 May 2013, pp. 233–8.

[68] *Tadić* Appeal Judgment, §§92–4.

[69] *Tadić* Appeal Judgment, §95.

[70] *Tadić* Appeal Judgment, §98.

[71] *Tadić* Appeal Judgment, §§118–19. But note Milanović, who points out that the ICJ employed *two* tests for attribution, one that he termed 'complete control' and a 'subsidiary' test of 'effective control': Marko Milanović, 'State responsibility for genocide', *European Journal of International Law*, 17(3) (2006), pp. 576–8.

[72] *Tadić* Appeal Judgment, §§120, 131. For a critical view of the sources discussed by the ICTY Appeals Chamber in reaching this conclusion, see Milanović, 'State responsibility for genocide', pp. 585–7.

be distinguished from one another on the basis that *Tadić* concerned the classification of armed conflicts for IHL purposes, whereas *Nicaragua* was concerned with attribution and state responsibility for general pubic international law purposes. This was accorded particular academic weight when it found its way into the commentary to Article 8 of the International Law Commission (ILC) Draft Articles on State Responsibility.[73] Further, when the ICJ was called upon to revisit the issue in the *Genocide Case*, it placed its judicial stamp upon this theory by pointing out that the ICTY in *Tadić* 'was not called upon... to rule on questions of State responsibility',[74] but rather 'to determine whether or not an armed conflict [wa]s international [in nature]'.[75] In other words, the ICJ, in contrast to the ICTY, was adjudicating a dispute between two states, in particular assessing whether the actions of the Bosnian Serbs/VRS in Bosnia and Herzegovina were attributable to Serbia and Montenegro to determine the latter's state responsibility at international law.

Nevertheless, it openly acknowledged that 'the [ICTY Appeals] Chamber did not follow the jurisprudence of the [ICJ] in the [*Nicaragua*] case',[76] but only because it 'presented the "overall control" test as equally applicable under the law of State responsibility'.[77] In doing so, the ICJ insisted, the ICTY adopted a position to an issue that did 'not lie within the specific purview of its jurisdiction'.[78] It was only in so far as it had stepped beyond its judicial boundaries that the ICJ 'f[ound] itself unable to subscribe to the [ICTY Appeals Chamber]'s view'.[79] Instead, it upheld its *Nicaragua* formulation of 'effective control', which it claimed was reflective of customary international law as set out in Article 8 of the ILC Draft Articles on State Responsibility.[80]

On the face of it, it is attractive to suggest that different tests should apply to different contexts: one for the classification of an armed conflict and the other for state responsibility. The most attractive feature is that it serves to play down and/or hide the defining example of the fragmentation of international law; *Tadić* and *Nicaragua* have become synonymous with the term. The problem is that, as *Tadić* rightly pointed out, it is simply a case of the same rule of international law (but on which the ICTY and the ICJ disagreed) being applied in *different* factual contexts, but to achieve the *same* end result[81]—that is, to impute the acts of a non-state actor to a state. For the ICJ, however, context is where the conversation ended, rather than where it should have begun. The

---

[73] 'Draft Articles on Responsibility of States for Internationally Wrongful Acts, with Commentary—Report of the International Law Commissions on the Work of its Fifty-Third Session', *Yearbook of the International Law Commission*, 2001, Vol. II, Pt 2, p. 48.

[74] ICJ, *Case Concerning Application of the Convention on the Prevention and Punishment of the Crime of Genocide (Bosnia and Herzegovina v. Serbia and Montenegro)*, Judgment (Merits), 26 February 2007, ICJ Reports 2007, p. 209 (*Genocide Case*).

[75] *Genocide Case*, p. 210.   [76] *Genocide Case*, p. 209.

[77] *Genocide Case*, p. 210.   [78] *Genocide Case*, pp. 209–10.

[79] *Genocide Case*, p. 209.   [80] *Genocide Case*, pp. 210–11.   [81] *Tadić* Appeal Judgment, §104.

question it did not ask, but should have, is whether there is anything inherent in the respective contexts that serves to modify or negate the relevant rule of international law; we must thus look deeper than simply pointing to context. Therefore, as Professor Cassese correctly asserted, the debate:

...should not be confined to the flimsy argument that *Tadić* was about the nature of armed conflicts whereas *Nicaragua* revolved around state responsibility and [that] therefore two different tests *may* coexist in that they relate to different subject-matters.[82]

In the present instance, there is little that suggests that context alone should modify the rules of attribution. However, this is not at all the impression one gets from the framing of the issue in the *Genocide Case*:

[L]ogic does not require the same test to be adopted in resolving the two issues, which are very different in nature: the degree and nature of a State's involvement in an armed conflict on another State's territory which is required for the conflict to be characterized as international, can very well, and without logical inconsistency, differ from the degree and nature of involvement required to give rise to that State's responsibility for a specific act committed in the course of the conflict.[83]

This is only correct if one narrowly defines the issue in *Tadić* as purely about the classification of the conflict rather than the underlying aim of that exercise, which was to attribute (or not) the acts of non-state actors to a state, which has the *secondary result* of classifying the conflict as either international or non-international. This is exactly the same in *Nicaragua* and the *Genocide Case*: the attribution (or not) of the acts of non-state actors to a state, which has the *secondary result* of making the relevant state responsible or not responsible for those acts. When one scratches below the surface, it becomes rather clear that we are not in fact dealing with two inherently different things, despite the ICJ's insistence to the contrary.

As such, the further question is whether we should be bending over backwards in order to simply maintain a facade of coherence. This is, in effect, what many academics do,[84] clothed in the (usually implicit) policy argument that we should strive to avoid

---

[82] Antonio Cassese, 'The *Nicaragua* and *Tadić* tests revisited in light of the ICJ judgment on genocide in Bosnia', *European Journal of International Law*, 18(4) (2007), p. 663 (emphasis in original).

[83] *Genocide Case*, p. 210.

[84] See e.g. Rosanne van Alebeek, 'The judicial dialogue between the ICJ and the International Criminal Courts on the question of immunity' in Larissa J. van den Herik and Carsten Stahn (eds), *The Diversification and Fragmentation of International Criminal Law*, Martinus Nijhoff, Leiden/Boston, 2012, pp. 93–4 (who insists that the ICJ's *Genocide Case* 'undid' the controversy between *Tadić* and *Nicaragua* by holding that overall control could apply to the classification of armed conflicts as distinct from state responsibility). See also Mario Prost, *The Concept of Unity in Public International Law*, Hart Publishing, Oxford/Portland, OR, 2012, pp. 194–201 (where the author explores different interpretations—some conflicting, some consistent—of the *Tadić/Nicaragua* controversy).

international law conflicts—fragmentation—at all costs. Instead of directly confronting the issue and leaving it to the marketplace of ideas to determine which standard should prevail based on their respective legal merits,[85] it is becoming accepted canon that simply because of the different contexts of *Nicaragua* and *Tadić* alone (and without any further legal explanation) different standards should apply.[86]

In the end, this is what the *Lubanga* Trial Judgment serves to perpetuate, because the above discussions or the relevant ICJ jurisprudence are not found or flagged anywhere in its classification analysis (or, for that matter, in classification analysis of the *Lubanga* Confirmation of Charges Decision);[87] they were entirely dodged. It was enough to point out that they were simply classifying the conflict in order to avoid these larger and more difficult questions. Yet the *Lubanga* Trial Judgment's analysis includes telling phrases such as 'the necessary degree of control of another State over an armed group acting on its behalf',[88] and 'whether...the UPC/FPLC, the APC and the FRPI were used as agents or "proxies" for fighting between two or more states'.[89] As such, how can it be seriously asserted that this is *not* about the attribution of the acts of non-state actors to a state (which has the *secondary result* of classifying the conflict)?

Of course, a different attitude prevailed in the *Lubanga* Trial Judgment when it came to espousing the uncontroversial view that an NIAC can coexist with an IAC. There, the jurisprudence of the ICJ (*Nicaragua*) was looked upon and cited with authority.[90] Yet, in the classification analysis, there is not a single reference to, or mention of, the ICJ's *Genocide Case* (or *Nicaragua*). A distinct impression is left that, in not alluding to the controversy, the Chamber hoped that the reader might just overlook it entirely. Nevertheless, at the end of the day, the ICC will have to tackle this issue sooner or later. Because of the strict delineation between the IAC and NIAC war crimes provisions in the ICC Statute, and thus the need to classify every armed conflict, there will almost certainly be future litigation that will attempt to raise this issue.

---

[85] See e.g. the ILC Study Group's report on fragmentation in international law, which, while directly (and rightly) pointing out the conflict between *Tadić* and *Nicaragua*, expressly declined to take a position one way or the other: 'Fragmentation of international law: difficulties arising from the diversification and expansion of international law: report of the Study Group of the International Law Commission', UN doc. A/CN.4/L.682, 13 April 2006, §§49–51.

[86] On a more practical level, accepting that different standards apply for the classification of an armed conflict and for state responsibility results in absurdities. To see this in action, consider the end result of the *Genocide Case*: although the ICTY held that it was seized of an IAC in *Tadić* because the Bosnian Serbs/VRS 'belonged' to Yugoslavia (later Serbia and Montenegro), Serbia and Montenegro could not be held liable for any of the Bosnian Serbs/VRS' genocidal actions at Srebrenica because it did not exercise 'effective control' over them as per *Nicaragua* (*Genocide Case*, pp. 214–15).

[87] The *Lubanga* Confirmation of Charges Decision, rendered on 29 January 2007, could not refer to the ICJ's *Genocide Case*, because this was rendered on 26 February 2007.

[88] *Lubanga* Trial Judgment, §541.   [89] *Lubanga* Trial Judgment, §552.

[90] *Lubanga* Trial Judgment, §540, n. 1644. *Tadić* was also cited in the same footnote to support the same point, notwithstanding the *Nicaragua/Tadić* friction discussed here.

Concluding remarks

While there is much that can be written about the *Lubanga* Trial Judgment, there is also much more that could have been written by the *Lubanga* Trial Judgment itself. Yet, where vague or conflicting lines of case law exist, the ICC as an institution, and international law as a subject, benefits greatly from clarity and sound jurisprudence. It is in the judicial interest to achieve this result. Ducking issues and avoiding (legal) confrontation today only serves to leave questions fermenting, perhaps to arise tomorrow with unexpected[91] and/or unwelcome[92] results. As the *Lubanga* Trial Judgment undergoes the scrutiny of the ICC Appeals Chamber, and as other cases at trial near their conclusion, it would be wise for the ICC's internal actors to keep this in mind.

[91] See e.g. M. J. Ventura and M. Gillett, 'The fog of war: prosecuting illegal uses of force as crimes against humanity', *Washington University Global Studies Law Review*, 12(3) (2013), forthcoming, <http://ssrn.com/abstract=2206660> (where the authors use the non-criminal nature of the common plan element in co-perpetration as per the *Lubanga* Trial Judgment to formulate a legal strategy that would see the ICC adjudicate the crime of aggression without the need for the 2010 Kampala aggression amendments to enter into force).

[92] See e.g. ICC, *Prosecutor v. Ruto and ors*, Decision on the Appeals of Mr William Samoei Ruto and Mr Joshua Arap Sang against the Decision of Pre-Trial Chamber II of 23 January 2012 entitled 'Decision on the Confirmation of Charges Pursuant to Article 61(7)(a) and (b) of the Rome Statute' (Case No. ICC-01/09-01/11-414), 24 May 2012; ICC, *Prosecutor v. Muthaura and ors*, Decision on the Appeal of Mr Francis Kirimi Muthaura and Mr Uhuru Muigai Kenyatta against the Decision of Pre-Trial Chamber II of 23 January 2012 entitled 'Decision on the Confirmation of Charges Pursuant to Article 61(7)(a) and (b) of the Rome Statute' (Case No. ICC-01/09-02/11-425), 24 May 2012 (in which the ICC Appeals Chamber refused to permit the parties to address the controversy surrounding Pre-Trial Chamber II's interpretation of what an 'organization' means in the context of the state or organizational policy element of crimes against humanity, which, if found in the end to be erroneous, could result in the negation of the entire trial (and pre-trial) process).

INDEX